ANTHONY BURGESS

GARLAND REFERENCE LIBRARY
OF THE HUMANITIES
(VOL. 406)

"The forum was a sea of faces. . . ." Anthony Burgess before an audience at Bucknell University in April 1973.

ANTHONY BURGESS
*An Annotated Bibliography
and Reference Guide*

Paul Boytinck

GARLAND PUBLISHING, INC. • NEW YORK & LONDON
1985

Library of Congress Cataloging in Publication Data

Boytinck, Paul W.
  Anthony Burgess : an annotated bibliography and
reference guide.

  (Garland reference library of the humanities ; vol.
406)
  Includes index.
  1. Burgess, Anthony, 1917–   —Bibliography.
I. Title. II. Series: Garland reference library of the
humanities ; v. 406.
Z8132.2.B693 1985   016.823′914   82-49268
[PR6052.U638]
ISBN 0-8240-9135-3 (alk. paper)

Printed on acid-free, 250-year-life paper
Manufactured in the United States of America

TABLE OF CONTENTS

Works by Burgess: Fiction and Non-Fiction

i

Other Works:

Works About Burgess:

Chronology

1917 Born February 25, 1917 in Manchester. Son of Joseph Wilson, a piano player and pub landlord, and "Beautiful Belle Burgess," a musical comedy actress. Baptised John Burgess Wilson. "Anthony," his confirmation name, came later.

1918 Mother and only sister died of 'Spanish' influenza.

1940 Graduated, Manchester University, B.A., English literature.

1940 British Army (1940-1946). Musical director, 54th Division Entertainment Section (1940-1943). Education sergeant and warrant officer, Gibraltar (1943-1946).

1942 Married Llewela Isherwood Jones (January 28, 1942).

1943 Wife attacked and assaulted by G.I. deserters in war-time London.

1946 Discharged from army with rank of sergeant-major.

1946 Chief Instructor, Western Command College (1946-1948).

1948 Lecturer in Speech and Drama, Ministry of Education (1948-1950).

1949 Wrote **Vision of Battlements** during Easter vacation.

1950 Master, Banbury Grammar School (1950-1954). Taught English literature, phonetics, Spanish and music.

1954 Education Officer, Malaya and Borneo (1954-1959).

1956 **Time for a Tiger** (a novel). Adopted pseud. "Anthony Burgess."

1958 **Enemy in the Blanket** (a novel). **English Literature; A Survey for Students** (literary criticism).

1959 **Beds in the East** (a novel). Diagnosis (false) of brain tumor. Invalided home from Borneo. Began career as full-time novelist (November 1959 — to present).

1960 **The Doctor Is Sick** (a novel). **The Right to an Answer** (a novel).

1961 **Devil of a State** (a novel; Book Society selection). **One Hand Clapping** (a novel; published under pseud. "Joseph Kell" at Heinemann's request). **The Worm and the Ring** (a novel; publication suppressed on threat of libel action, later reissued with revisions). Vacation trip to Leningrad. Began to publish essays and reviews in **Yorkshire Post, Listener, Country Life, Spectator, Times Literary Supplement, Manchester Guardian, Encounter, New York Times Book Review**, etc. etc.

1962 **The Wanting Seed** (a novel). **A Clockwork Orange** (a novel).

1963 **Honey for the Bears** (a novel). **Inside Mr. Enderby** (a novel; published under pseud. "Joseph Kell.") **The Novel Today** (criticism). Regular television critic, **Listener** (May 23, 1963 — July 4, 1968).

1964 **The Eve of Saint Venus** (a novel). **Language Made Plain** (philology and linguistics). **Malayan Trilogy** (novel; includes **Time for a Tiger, Enemy in the Blanket, Beds in the East**). **Nothing Like the Sun** (a novel). Son Andrew (Andrea) born August 1964.

1965 **Here Comes Everybody** (literary criticism). **The Long Day Wanes** (a novel; American title of **Malayan Trilogy**.) Drama critic for **Listener** (March 12, 1965 — May 21, 1965). **Vision of Battlements** (a novel).

1966 **Tremor of Intent** (a novel).

1967 **The Novel Now** (literary criticism).

1968 Wife Llewela Burgess died (March 20, 1968) of cirrhosis of the liver, possible complications 1943 assault. Married (December 1968) Liliana Macellari, Countess Pasi. **Enderby Outside** (a novel). **Enderby** (a novel; American title which includes **Inside Mr. Enderby** and **Enderby Outside**). **Urgent Copy** (literary criticism). Noisy, defiant exile from Britain to avoid confiscatory taxation; moved to Malta.

1969 Writer-in-residence, University of North Carolina.

1970 **Shakespeare** (biography). Taught creative writing in the Princeton Creative Arts Program (1970-71).

1971 **MF** (a novel). Kubrick's film version of **A Clockwork Orange**. Moved to Rome.

1972 Visiting distinguished Professor of English at City College, New York City (1972-1973).

1973 **Joysprick** (literary criticism). **Cyrano!** (musical comedy). **Obscenity and the Arts** (lecture to Malta Library Association). "The Lawgiver," (play for television). "Lots of Fun at **Finnegans Wake**," (radio drama).

1974 **Clockwork Testament; Or, Enderby's End** (a novel). **Napoleon Symphony** (a novel).

1975 "Michelangelo" (play for television). "Symphony in C," (musical composition; performed in Iowa City).

1976 **Beard's Roman Women** (a novel). **A Long Trip to Teatime** (juvenile). **Moses: A Narrative** (narrative poem). **New York** (travel book). **Puma** (unpublished novel). Moved to Monaco.

1977 **Abba Abba** (a novel). "Jesus of Nazareth," (television drama). **A Christmas Recipe** (recipe in verse; expensive ltd. ed.) **Will and Testament** (story about Shakespeare; very expensive ltd. ed.) **Jesus of Nazareth** (novel by William Barclay; based on Burgess' screenplay for "Jesus of Nazareth"). Fiction reviewer for Dublin **Irish Press** (January 13 — September 15, 1977?).

1978 **Ernest Hemingway and His World** (biography). **1985** (a novel). "The Brides of Enderby," (musical composition).

1979 **Man of Nazareth** (a novel; based on Burgess' screenplay for "Jesus of Nazareth"). "Mr. WS," (musical composition).

1980 **Earthly Powers** (a novel; Book-of-the-Month Club selection).

1982 **On Going to Bed** (essay on beds and sleeping customs). **The End of the World News** (a novel).

Foreword

Fame, said Rilke, is the sum of all the misunderstandings that cluster about a name. In the case of Burgess the misunderstanding can be put in three words: **A Clockwork Orange**. Soon dubbed *'poeta della violenza'* Burgess fought back with *'jeu de spleen,'* a kinetic work flawed by its own didacticism, a little thing written very rapidly to make some money. Italian students learned he was the author of innumerable bland novellas about love. In this deadpan catalog 'innumerable' is not quite right; 'bland' will not do in that astringent quarter; and the meaning of 'novella' has to be expanded to include some thick tomes. This book is for those who want to know the other Anthony Burgess, to survey the output and take the measure of the man.

Burgess has written many novels, countless reviews (although a bibliographer should beware of such loose formulations) and many incidental pieces designed to bring down the Common Sawbuck. He has written both for love and for money. He has given interviews by the dozen, if not by the hundred. He has composed musical works, collaborated in the production of teledramas, plays and at least one musical. His works, or sections of his works, have been committed to phonodisc and videotape.

This bibliography is intended to be a preliminary guide to his work. However, as the previous paragraph implies, it is not only a bibliography but a discography and a videography as well. The first duty of an author, as Burgess reminds us, is to feed himself and his dependents. To hell with the Shavian notion that the true artist lets his wife and children starve. To survive, the poor author must collaborate with the film and television industry. It is high time, in the last few decades of the 20th century, for the term bibliography to expand its narrow etymological boundaries to take in phonodiscs and vidskeins.

In the course of working on this *bibliovideodiscography,* it occurred to me that many autobiographical shards and fragments are buried in Burgess' occasional journalistic pieces. This fact prompted the notion of compiling a biographical sketch based on Burgess' own writings. The final result, "Anthony Burgess: Biographical Background," must be read with more than the usual *caveats.* It is by no means a critical biographical sketch written with the help and affidavits of Burgess' contemporaries, friends and enemies alike. The account is based on Burgess' published writings; it is therefore very much an account of how he sees himself — a harried individual struggling, in an indifferent if not hostile universe, to find some small grounds on which to rejoice. We have to wait for the full-dress biography, assuming the material for such a work exists, to confirm or dispel this impression.

The bibliography which follows is intended to answer the following questions: what was the reception of Burgess' works by the journalists who, valiantly in the face of all the odds, pass for critics in the present day? what articles did Burgess write in the course of his free-lance career and what did he have to say in them? and finally, what have the academic critics, those leisurely Walter Bagehots of criticism, written about his serious fiction?

In a time when so many books are unread, it is presumptuous to hope that a mere bibliography will be read. Anyway, those of his readers who care to persevere will find, in these pages, many examples of authentic Burgess. He is here in all his manifestations: magnanimous, learned and light, furiously apolitical and giving the politicians hell, playful, scabrous and beset by the ills of the body, sometimes absurd, eager to put down nonsense with spear and club and sneer, often querulous about the paltry financial rewards of the literary life, but always fundamentally a literary man through all the tedious and painful flux of existence; or, to convey his aim in the better words of Joyce "Loud, heap miseries upon us yet entwine our arts with laughters low."

Paul Boytinck
Lewisburg, Pa.

Anthony Burgess: Biographical Background

The man's achievement is brilliant enough to elicit periodic announcements that his one enduring masterpiece is surely at hand. So Martin Seymour-Smith, in an early appraisal, memorably remarked that "Burgess is unquestionably the most gifted English novelist of his generation; but he has not yet produced the major novel of which he is so clearly capable . . . . No writer of our time is more obviously highly intelligent — and aware of the essentially subversive function of the writer. No contemporary novelist more clearly displays genius. And yet no single book has yet contained all this genius and sensibility [but] we are grateful for Burgess' prodigious output, for the fecundity for which he has unfairly been blamed."[1]

The generous conviction that Burgess can produce a vast and witty masterpiece, a reasonable supposition given his past achievement, gives rise to a tortured tergiversation when the indisputable masterpiece is not at hand. If Burgess pours his energies into slight, scabrous novels and a flood of journalism, then surely he is guilty of a culpable prodigality? reprehensible conduct reminiscent of the minor Elizabethans? And soon the names of Greene, Nashe and Deloney are heard in the land. Chiefly young men who died young; their promise unfulfilled; their works the impulse of high spirits and low incomes (editors hammering on the front door with creditors clamoring at the back; they serve as useful reproaches to dilatory Burgess obstinately delaying his one enduring masterpiece for perverse reasons known to himself alone.

Burgess has gladly aided and abetted the process. Humility is often hammered a little too roughly into young Catholic skulls as Wilfred Sheed has rightly observed. Burgess, a lapsed Catholic, is in many ways a good son of the pre-Johannine Church. He is also a genuinely humble man. So in **Clockwork Testament** Enderby, afflicted with aphasia following a heart attack, invents a minor Elizabethan with the unlikely name of Gervase Whitelady. 'Forget him,' Enderby/Burgess brutally tells his willing students, 'he was nothing.' Burgess who, in real life, has delivered a similar lecture or mini-lecture on one fictitious Grasmere Tadsworth knows what he is doing. Modesty is the screen behind which the work can proceed.

Modesty is not the whole of it. His life betrays, at key moments, an indiscipline verging on suicidal recklessness. He is less the statesman of letters than a kind of street brawler — and, of course, all the more approachable and likeable on that account. Those who assess his personality as coarse and unattractive, as Geoffrey Grigson and Jonathan Raban have done in their different ways, tend to be the sons of Protestant ministers: the coolness of the rectory their single standard of decorum. It may well be that Americans are more receptive to his work than the English for precisely this reason. The typical Burgess openness endears itself to them; the standard English coolness would estrange and alienate them, and lead them to consult their God.

Restraint is not typical of Burgess as man or writer. Educated at the University of Manchester (B.A., honors in English) he was quite naturally condemned to a life of pedagogy. (He is a born teacher, willing to jaw away the hours.) What he disliked about it was not the pedagogy but the penury. Life on 500 pounds ($1,400) a year did not permit an exploration of the rich bawdy variety of life. So Burgess typically solved his problem by getting drunk and, plastered, wrote an application for a teaching job on the Isle of Sark; discovered, on his sober visit to the Colonial Office on Great Smith Street (smiles evident, mouths open to take in the improbable epic contours of the story — pub material here, lads) that he had applied for a post in Malaya. So off to Malaya after some minimal debate. In the tropical heat, the words came, and **The Malayan Trilogy** deservedly came out to more than minimal applause.

The legend was beginning to take shape. An improbable series of events, calculated to subdue lesser men, would be met with resilience. In Borneo, where he was transferred after Malaya, events conspired with a careless vengeance. He lived in the same house with some revolutionaries. The colonial police fixed on him with cold and curious eyes. His wife Llewela Burgess, meeting Prince Philip at a garden party, told the Patrician Presence that everything was bloody well not all right in little Borneo. Burgess, facing the young intellectuals of Borneo *en masse* one day, fell on the classroom floor in a fit of utter frustration and, in his own words, let the world take over.

The world acted with summary speed. Burgess and wife, *persona non grata*, were soon out of Borneo and flown back to London. There at the National Neurological Hospital spinal taps tentatively confirmed the presence of a brain tumor. Burgess ruled out an operation "lest they hit my talent, not the tumor." No mere Elizabethan quibble there. The quacks gave him a year to live. He then set up shop, in sheer desperation and with great delight, as the British Balzac in his so-called terminal year.

The words came again in a great flood, and the works were published. Between November 1959 and the same month in the following year, he wrote five novels: **The Doctor Is Sick, Inside Mr. Enderby, One Hand Clapping, The Wanting Seed,** and **The Worm and the Ring** (the last a revision of an earlier draft). A miraculous year, a year of marvels. Burgess unwisely set himself a standard he would never again be able to match. At the end of the year the tumor was gone, the talent triumphant.

Talent yes; talents no. Risible royalties of 800 pounds were his only tangible reward. Heinemann, his publishers, willfully issued two of these novels under the pseudonym of Joseph Kell. Both novels, good and excellent novels, **Inside Mr. Enderby** and **One Hand Clapping**, promptly sank without a trace. Burgess, surveying his publisher's wisdom in choosing so perversely to starve him to death, quickly renamed the firm Hangman & Co.

So the British Balzac turned in 1961 to journalism for the sake of some ready cash. Somewhere in the background lives or lived his beloved and exasperating wife Llewela, sleeping with Dylan Thomas and others, drinking gin, dispensing advice, making margin plays on the London Stock Exchange, and otherwise making herself useful in the way of all wives. It was, after all, for the sake of this divinity that Burgess produced the five sterling novels.

An estate was steadily eluding him, but the legend acquired new riches. Early in 1963 he was asked to review a book by one Joseph Kell for the provincial **Yorkshire Post. KILLER WORMS THREATEN SPRING LAMBS** the *Post* fearlessly told its readers. **WHY THE BRIDE WORE RED,** *Post* staffers zealously reported. Burgess, who was then a paid reviewer of this high organ, darkly suspected newspaper waggery at work. He rose to the occasion, and, on May 16, 1963, his review of his own pseudonymously issued **Inside Mr. Enderby** was published in **Post** pages. Part of the text, full of some small wheezes, is included here for the curious:

> "This is, in many ways, a dirty book. It is full of bowel-blasts and flatulent borborygms, emetic meals ('thin but over-savory stews' Enderby calls them) and halitosis. It may well make some people sick, and those of my readers with tender stomachs are advised to let it alone. It turns sex, religion, the State into a series of laughing-stocks. The book itself is a laughing stock."

By 1968, five years later, Burgess had published his most interesting and immediately accessible novels. There was **The Malayan Trilogy**, composed of three novels, with a gorgeous garlicky cast of characters and colonial grotesques. There was **The Doctor Is Sick**, suggested by his hospital experiences, with poor Edwin Spindrift, cuckold and wordmonger but no shaftsman, as his central character. It was followed by **The Right to an Answer**, a savage account of an ex-colonial returning to England and finding the country sunk into a lethargy of triviality, adultery and drunkenness. There was **Devil of a State**, a Waughsian account of a colonial discovering that hell is women scorned. **One Hand Clapping**, a cunning female monologue, explored the psyche of one woman, the opportunism of poets, and the death-wish of one atypical Englishman who longs for the blood and guts and high buccaneering seriousness of Elizabethan England. **The Worm and the Ring**, suggested by Wagner's **Ring,** depicts the struggle for control of a school; the opportunist bests the idealist. There was **The Wanting Seed**, a hair-raising but hilarious dystopia which describes the wanton consequences of overpopulation: cannibalism, fertility rites, State encouragement of homosexuality to keep the population down.

There was **A Clockwork Orange** with a ratty young hero who sings his song of violence and redemption with a serpent's cunning, and permits his author to insert a cunning sermon of his own. There was **Honey for the Bears**: a study of a cozy marriage disintegrating in Leningrad as wife turns lesbian and husband, as they say, gay. It sounds dismal. Yet, in accordance with the fine Joycean dictum "Loud, heap miseries upon us yet entwine our arts with laughters low," it is actually hilarious. There was **Inside Mr. Enderby** which proves, beyond any doubt, that if you take everything away from a poet, he still has words and possessing words, can still find his way to some kind of redemption. There was the lazy and logorrheic **Eve of Saint Venus**, the only one of his works which extols simple, uncomplicated physical love as a *summum bonum*. **Nothing Like the Sun** made a serious attempt to get inside that fiddle-shaped dome to let us know how the young Shakespeare thought and felt. If it is not perfect, as certain critics have delicately hinted here and there, the assignment is an impossible one, and Burgess' failure is better than the successes of lesser men. There was **Tremor of Intent** with villains villainous, ladies lecherous, valets treacherous.

The minor Elizabethan had done his work well and the paying public could now show its gratitude by buying the books and supporting the author in a certain (if far from baronial) style, and freeing him from want, garret, patron and the jail; and permitting him, should that be required, his lordly choice of publishers.

At first the obstinate public refused. Then, in some mysterious fashion, a minimal boom began. **A Clockwork Orange**, dismissed in England ("a viscous verbiage . . . which is the swag-bellied offspring of decay . . . English is being slowly killed by her practitioners" in the words of an anonymous *savant* at the **Times Literary Supplement**), began to sell in the U.S. and sell well. **Nothing Like the Sun** brought Burgess to the attention of the theatrical world. Terry Southern, novelist and scriptwriter in this same world **(Dr. Strangelove)**, read Clockwork and like many readers, mysteriously charmed, passed the book along to maestro Stanley Kubrick.

Kubrick, bearded, sardonic, skeptical of any notions of progress anchored in premises about the natural goodness of man, reader of Robert Ardrey, was charmed in turn. "It seemed to me to be a unique and marvelous work of imagination and perhaps even genius." (Pity he did not write for the TLS but you cannot have everything.) Then began a clamor for the rights or, as the cry is raised in **Clockwork Testament** 'Who is he, where is he, who do I see about the rights?' All, of course, very good questions.

The author is indisputably Burgess. His wife Llewela was assaulted by thugs in the war-time London blackout and so gave her husband, in the regrettable fashion of real life, the idea for the story. Nauseated by the content of his tale, he wrote it with the help of gin and dexedrine. The assault not only induced a miscarriage but caused long-term gynecological problems which left its strains on both husband and wife.

As to 'where is he?' the answer is clear. He is either in London in a modest house or in Etchingham, Sussex, in an equally modest house, probably working on the daily journalism to pay the bills.

The crucial question is the third: 'who do I see about the rights?' A very good question indeed. Not Burgess. *Not Burgess? You really mean that?* Indisputably and regrettably I do mean: not Burgess. What in the name of God happened, and what happened to the sacred rights?

The truth may be galling, but the answer is simple. Burgess' agent, a commercial genius presently anonymous, sold the rights to a lawyer, Si Litvinoff, for the sum of $500.00. Kubrick and Warner Brothers then approached the holder of the rights. Behold, at the end of the bargaining process, a small miracle. For, after the lawyers had ended their cautious sparring, and the civilized process had come to its happy culmination, the present holder of the rights, the lucky or prescient Litvinoff, was rewarded with the sum of about $500,000.00. The transaction deserves to stand as a shining example of the wise exhortation to buy low and sell high. *Well, I'm buggered.* You might well say that.

It can be argued that Burgess was reckless and unwise; that he should have sold the *option* with a cheerful heart, but not the rights. And in fact I have made precisely that observation to Burgess himself. His reasonable response was that life is short and contracts long. Did I have any idea of the obscene length of these documents? I did not, and held my peace thereafter, preferring now to believe, as Burgess does, that the real mischief was done by the agent.

The filmed version of **Clockwork** premiered in late 1971 just in time for the Christmas season. Observe then a grotesque juxtaposition from real life: the emergence of a small but cheerful and priapic prince of darkness and the Prince of Peace. Wonders never cease. It was, as they like to say in the industry, a fantastic success at the box-office, earning the distributor $15,000,000 or more in rental income, and transforming Kubrick into a multi-millionaire overnight if he was not one already. There ensued cries of 'author' as the controversial content of the film was viewed and hotly debated from every conceivable angle. These cries came mainly from newshounds and and other such philosophers who wanted the author to defend the film from its detractors. Burgess was not grateful for the belated attention. His answer to all the hullaballoo can be read in that sad and hilarious book, **Clockwork Testament**.

The comedy now turned to fiscal melodrama. The first new player was Her Britannic Majesty's Department of Inland Revenue where "Inland" includes everything that moves, breathes and promises to deliver, with whatever grace, revenues to the Exchequer. For, if Burgess did not greatly and commensurately profit from the filmed version of **A Clockwork Orange**, Hollywood was fluttering its fat lashes. Money was coming his way at last. There was a grandiose proposal, suitably ballyhooed at the time in newspaper articles now consigned to the morgue, to make a film based on the life of Shakespeare. Burgess prepared a shooting script and was reportedly paid the sum of $25,000. He also sold the film rights to **Enderby** for a reasonable sum. (Neither film was ever produced; the Bitch Goddess, fattened by real profits, continues in her necessary profligate style, feeding manuscripts into that great crowned maw.)

Burgess, now modestly well off if not actually rich, and alarmed at the singular rapacity of Her Majesty's Commissioners as early as 1966 when they demanded a thousand pounds he did not readily have, made it his business to study the tax laws of the land. He was startled and alarmed by the revelations that came his way. A writer friend earned $192,000 in one miraculous year; the Exchequer prepared to confiscate, for the sake of the country's good, his own good, the good of his children, his wife, mistresses if any, $180,000 of this sum. *Are you on the level?* So it hath been related to me on the word of one Burgess if not burgesses. I am merely the conduit of this wordly wisdom. *Well I'm buggered.* You might well say that.

The other player, not new at all, was Llewela Burgess. This once lovely and always intimate companion, now quarrelsome, gin-loving wife, entered the hospital at Hastings for the last time. The truth-loving nurses from the colonies reproached her: "You have drunk too much," they said, "you have damaged your liver" moving Burgess to wonder "Well, who hasn't?" Did she attempt to be what, in that other sad little book, **Beard's Roman Women**, is called a drink-for-drink companion? If so, it was a fatal error. Burgess tried, but failed, to stop her boozing and Llewela Isherwood Jones Burgess died in March 1968 of cirrhosis of the liver.

The third player was a ravishing newcomer by the name of Liliana Macellari, countess Pasi. It appears that Burgess first met her some years before the death of his first wife and began an affair. "It was not a regular affair," Burgess has been quoted as saying, "it was very very clandestine." The words are a little puzzling. Most such affairs are very very clandestine indeed, but Burgess' words can probably be glossed by reference to certain facts. First, he was brought up as a Roman Catholic, and he has all the old Catholic horror of divorce. Second, it can be presumed that Llewela Burgess, had she learned of the liaison and the existence of her charming and lovely rival, would not have taken the news lightly. Third, it is entirely possible that Burgess knew she was a dying woman and did everything possible to keep the news from her. Finally, we have the son of Burgess and Liliana Macellari, Paolo Andrea (Andrew in English), who will sometimes gladden his father's heart. (See, for example, no. 1350 in the bibliography that follows.)

Now, with all the actors in place, the drama and denouement can begin. Burgess determined that, for his own sake, and the sake of his wife and child, he had to leave England and go into exile or, to use his own inimitable words: "Fill up to a spumous overflow with death duties and tax on the living. Drink it all down and, drunk, convince yourself that the world needs your writing. Then scuttle or sneak or run." In an obstreperous farewell to his native land, Burgess denounced the British attitude to writers ("all poor Evelyn Waugh ever wanted was a knighthood; of course he never got it"); prophesied that his future books would be more experimental, difficult and unsaleable; and then departed, accompanied by his wife and son, for the island of Malta.

In Malta he discovered the rich culture, gentle toleration, feverish intellectual life and overall kindliness so absurdly typical of your priest-ridden island. The postal censorship was not only intolerable but ignorant, based on superficial distinctions and therefore wildly inconsistent. His French translation of **Tremor of Intent** was held up by the smuthounds; the Danish version under the title of **Martyr's Blood** sailed through with a virtual archepiescopal blessing. It was a maddening state of affairs, and Burgess soon left Malta for Rome about 1971.

He lived in the noisy Plaza Santa Cecilia, wrote some more books, but eventually learned from a friendly mafiosi that his son was next on the terrorist's ransom hit list. After that, he moved to Monaco in 1975 and continued to write and publish in the usual unobtrusive way of authors who lead outwardly dull lives. This is the essence of the story stripped of its details, and those who want to know more must read on. For it is time to get this prodigy born, baptised, and put in his proper social milieux of sinners, publicans and tellers of tall tales.

* * * * * * * *

He was born Feburary 25, 1917, in a small rented house on Carisbrook Street in the Harpurhey district of Manchester. His father was Joseph Wilson, a piano player, pubman, later a tobacconist (retail and wholesale), still later a pub landlord. His mother was known, in the feverish words of an anonymous press-agent, as 'Beautiful Belle Burgess,' a Gaiety Girl, singer and dancer in pubs and parlors. The family history on both sides was respectable but utterly undistinguished: small shopkeepers, tradesmen, lower middle-class or working class — hard-working, rough-spoken Teutonic Celts.

> The family begins mistily for me with my great-grandfather, a professional non-commissioned soldier and later the keeper of a herb-shop which sold healthful drinks like dandelion-and-burdock and sarsparilla. He spoke in old age of having seen the Duke of Wellington and always referred to the Prussians as the Prooshians. His son, John or Jack Wilson, kept a public house in Manchester called the Derby Inn. He married an Irishwoman, like so many Lancashire Catholics — a Mary Ann Finnegan from Tipperary. He begot four sons — John, James, William and Joseph, my father.[2]

The youngest son Joseph, Burgess' father, was a gifted piano player who moved easily from ragtime to Chopin but refused to call himself a pianist, modestly reserving that honor for the grim virtuosos of the concert hall. Very little is known of the mother, except that she was the descendent of small tradesmen.

> My mother, born Elizabeth Burgess, I never knew, and I can see no propriety in searching among the shadowy figures behind her blessed shade. She was, it seems, the daughter of a respectable small tradesman and became a singer and dancer, chiefly in such Manchester music halls as the Gentlemen's Concert Rooms (popularly known as the Snotty Parlour). She was professionally, and pleonastically, called the Beautiful Belle Burgess, and a surviving photograph shows a comely smiling woman with a mass of fair hair. She then became a convert to Catholicism, a wife and a mother and, not long after my birth, died.[3]

She was a victim of the 'Spanish' influenza, that post-war pandemic which, between August 1918 (some accounts mention June) and March 1919, spread throughout the world and claimed 25 million victims. They were not less mourned than the battle deaths; they were simply less commemorated. Perhaps the human imagination finds it difficult to absorb two bloody butcheries in succession. Still, in total casualties, the lowly virus claimed more deaths than all the bayonets, machine-guns and howitzers of World War I.

Early childhood is a time of great poetry and abject fear in arguably equal proportions, and the young Burgess was no exception to this rule. If anything, his imagination contrived fearful horrors unknown to most of us. Hell was evidently bred into his bones.

> When I was a child I would always cry when I was told it was time to go to bed. It was not just a matter of having to abandon the lively fireplace and go out into the cold after dark. It was like being sentenced to death and a sure hell after it. In those days bedrooms were never heated, and to take off one's little shirt was like inviting the slash of metal on one's body. The shadows were full of executioners' axes. The quick night prayer, one knew, would yield no comfort. 'If I die before I wake, I pray the Lord my soul to take.' What could this mean except that the causes of premature death lay somehow in sleep itself. If sleep was an imitation of death, the impersonation could all too easily transform itself into an identity. But when I got into the cold lumpy bed I did not die: I was all too horribly alive in a world of monsters.

> On the wall, opposite my bed, was a painting of a gipsy woman telling the cards. Attached to the frame was the title **Beware!** This picture was the last thing I saw before putting out the light, but with the putting out of the light and the closing of

my eyes it expanded and became a huge door. The door would open to mocking tinny music and disclose a landscape of bones and horse-droppings brilliantly illuminated by a sort of hellfire. Little men with the faces of dogs would caper and leap and call my name: they wanted me there with them, presumably to kill and bury among the bones and ordure. I would scream and scream and wake to the dark, except for dim lamplight from the street glowing on the gipsy with her cards (had she turned up the nine of spades? I knew nothing then of cartomancy) and the words I had been told spelt out **Beware!** . . . .Who can talk of the blessing of sleep, especially for lonely and imaginative children, when sleep unlocks so many horrors?[4]

Nursery rhymes, with their blood-and-thunder content, terrified and tantalized him. This one, for example, haunted him for years:

> There was a man of double deed
> Who sowed his garden full of seed,
> And when the seed began to grow
> 'Twas like a garden full of snow.
> And when the snow began to fall
> Like birds it was upon the wall,
> And when the birds began to fly
> 'Twas like a shipwreck in the sky.
> And when the sky began to crack
> 'Twas like a stick upon my back,
> And when my back began to smart
> 'Twas like a pen-knife in my heart,
> And when my heart began to bleed
> Then I was dead and dead indeed.[5]

He entertained fears that the crucifix above his head would come crashing down, a fear perhaps not uncommon among guilty little Catholic boys — and what Catholic boy is not guilty?

The father of this young aesthete, Joseph Wilson the music hall pianist, cinema pianist, pub pianist and later cashier and chief cashier in Swift's Beef Market, now decided on a marriage with a woman who kept a large public house, 'The Golden Eagle,' in Manchester. (One gets the impression that the lives of Lancashire publicans are as inbred and rigidly exclusive as that of policemen.)

The true nature and character of this step-mother are hard to assess. Burgess claims that he was forced to sleep in cold and cheerless attics. She was conceivably the hard-hearted, hypocritical stepmother of legend. On the other hand, she might have proved a passable siren with a reasonably good heart to a man of robust tastes: a cheerful Letty to some scrofulous Johnson.

To the young Burgess she was a monster of sluttishness incarnate; he was scornful of her intellect, revolted by her habits, and provided the world with a short view of the woman in his **Inside Mr. Enderby**. It is an unforgettable passage. Its origin may lie in Burton — Burgess determined to outdo Burton in calculated misogyny — but it is for all that — perhaps because of that — one of the great unaphrodisiac evocations of woman in all literature. It makes you want, in Mencken's phrase, to burn every bed in the world.

> Oh, she had been graceless and coarse, that one. A hundred-weight of ringed and brooched blubber, smelling to high heaven of female smells, rank as long-hung hare or blown beef, her bedroom strewn with soiled bloomers, crumby combinations, malodorous bust-bodices. She had swollen finger-joints, puffy palms, wrists girdled with fat, slug-white upper arms that, when naked, showed indecent as thighs. She was corned, bunioned, calloused, varicose-veined. Healthy as a sow, she moaned of pains in all her joints, a perpetual migraine, a bad back, toothache. 'The pains in me legs,' she would say, 'is killin' me.' Her wind was loud, even in public places. 'The doctor says to let it come up. You can always say excuse me.' Her habits were loathsome. She picked her teeth with old tram-tickets, cleaned out her ears with hair-clips in whose U-bend earwax was trapped to darken and harden, scratched her private parts through her clothes with a matchbox-rasping noise audible two rooms away, made gross sandwiches of all her meals or cut her meat with scissors, spat chewed

bacon-rind or pork-crackling back on her plate, excavated beef-fibres from her cavernous molars and held them up for all the world to see, hooked out larger chunks with a soiled sausage finger, belched like a ship in the fog, was sick on stout on Saturday nights, tromboned vigorously in the lavatory, ranted without aitches or grammar, scoffed at all books except **Old Moore's Almanac,** whose apocalyptic pictures she could follow. Literally illiterate all her life, she would sign cheques by copying her name from a prototype on a greasy piece of paper, drawing it carefully as a Chinese draws an ideogram. She provided fried meals mostly, ensuring first that the fat was tepid. But she brewed good tea, potent with tannin, and taught young Enderby the technique, that he might bring her a cup in the morning: three for each person and two for the pot, condensed milk rather than fresh, be lavish with the sugar. Enderby, sixth-form boy, would stand over her while she drank it in bed — tousled, wrinkled, puffed, ill-smelling, a wreck — though she did not really drink it: the tea seemed to soak into her, as into parched earth. One day he would put rat-poison in her cup. But he never did, even though there was rat-poison in the kitchen. *Hate?* You've just no idea.[6]

To which account one can only add, apart from God help us all, and God pity the young Burgess, that it is a bravura passage (the novelist Paul Theroux learned it by heart), and the furious energy of the piece makes one recall every desirable feature of every desirable woman one has ever known. For the small comfort that's in it.

Later he took a weary pride in his youthful self-sufficiency.

I was brought up by an Irish stepmother and had very little love, very little affection, not that I wanted this very much [from her], and I went purely to the local schools in Manchester. I had no intellectual companionship, no intellectual stimulants at all.

Everything I did, I did on my own. I read on my own. I taught myself music on my own. I owe nothing. I'm not saying that I have achieved anything [Catholic humility up to the front], but if I have achieved anything I owe nothing at all to family, nothing at all to environment. I can't praise or dispraise environment. Nothing was against me, I was just totally alone and I learned to live without family, without affection.[7]

This appraisal seems fair enough. His father, Joseph Wilson, was not interested in books ("he would read the library novels by Pett Ridge, Hall Caine, Marie Corelli, and other literary giants of his youth") and showed little interest in the son by his first marriage. He was a piano player in pubs; he drank draught Bass in impressive quantities, and his professional career, such as it was, sometimes appeared to hang by a thread. Banging on the piano one night to accompany a scene of evident merriment above him on the silent screen, he promptly played "For He's a Jolly Good Fellow." A fine sentiment but a dull tune: and not the best possible accompaniment to The Last Supper.

The Wilson line shows little trace of the solid Burgher virtues. Its members strut in the old burlesque show fashion. Their escapades beg to be recited in a pub, preferably Irish. This may well be one reason why Burgess, who appreciates the family art in this line, but disapproves of it as a steady matter of daily routine, returned to the Victorian stereotype of the solid Burgher Shakespeare in his biography of the poet. And I have heard him say to an assembled group of students that he, Burgess, entirely approves of Shakespeare's decision to return to Stratford and, weary of the player's art, set up as a small gentleman.

One of Burgess' uncles, a certain uncle Billy, reached virtuoso standards in the course of his short but bibulous life. He died an early death in a drunken fall from a ladder while working as a bricklayer's assistant. Before his death, however, Uncle Billy was good for a few good stories, pub material of a high order. Burgess tells the yarn in his ferocious-facetious mode:

Two stories relate to his [Uncle Billy's] brief career as assistant to a local undertaker. Told to put the finishing touches to an alderman's corpse arrayed for the leavetaking, he had difficulty in affixing its toupee. He called: "Mr. Henshaw, have you got a bit of glue?" And then: "Never mind, I've found a nail." One evening he entered his local public house flashing a sovereign, calling for drinks all round in a lordly manner. When asked where he had obtained the coin, for it was not yet payday, he said he had found it in the mouth of a Jewish male cadaver. "That," someone said, "is to pay his fare across the river Jordan." My uncle Billy said, pocketing his change, "T'booger'll have to swim."[8]

It is a story virtually guaranteed to make Messrs. Raban and Grigson wince and to make unfinnicky pubmates roar. We must face the fact that Burgess was brought up in a large pub and roared as a sergeant-major in the British army; he is not necessarily, first and foremost, a gentleman.

His ancestors, down through the generations, held tenaciously to the one true faith, but they had little talent, perhaps even inclination, to get on in the world. The young Burgess, unlike them all, showed early evidence of an artistic bent. He began to draw at the age of four, and at the precocious age of eleven had a drawing of his father published in the **Manchester Guardian** ("I got five guineas for it, a lot of money in those days"). The pictorial talent burned out early, and he turned to music. His father, ex-piano player himself, refused to teach his son how to play the instrument. He argued the case on narrow grounds of utility. Had he himself not seen the source of his livelihood threatened by the radio, then threatened once again by the introduction of the talkies? His son would have to learn to play the instrument himself. Besides, he was drunk much of the time. The young Burgess picked out middle C and soon progressed to the point where he not only played with ease, but wanted to be a composer.

At the Manchester Free Trade Hall, in an atmosphere of gamy mustiness, he heard great bloody gobbets of Wagner's **Ring.** Bloody, of course, because they were torn from context in that provincial house. Wagner's music is more reminiscent of a sea of brass, but bloody Wagner it would be from now on, one of his tenacious private associations. There he heard **The Valkyrie,** the **Forest Murmurs,** or **Siegfried's Journey** or the closing scene of the **Gotterdammerung,** the budget on a shoe-string, the tenors decayed. But he felt the power of Wagner, and it was enough to stoke the artistic fires in earnest, and between the ages of fourteen and thirty-five Burgess was convinced that he was a composer and not a writer at all. His father gave him, if nothing else, a love of music.

Agonbite of Jacobite

Roman-Catholicism, the no-nonsense pre-Johannine version with hell no empty phrase, was the ancestral religion of the Wilsons. They never deviated from the faith — and their devotion to the House of Stuart — through the centuries. (On his deathbed, Joseph Wilson reminded his son of sacred truths. The Hanoverians were usurpers and heretics. He owed his true allegiance to the House of Stuart. The scene is surely one of breath-taking intransigence. Burgess, incidentally, honored his father's dying wish. He has praised the basic decency of the Hanoverians, but the curious will find, here and there, unregenerate calls for the restoration of the Stuart monarchy.)[9] Given this background, the young Burgess was uneasy, to put it mildly, in Anglican England. On Guy Fawkes Day he went through abysmal agonies; finally convinced himself that Fawkes deserved to be burned in effigy for *failing* to blow up the House of Commons. The first of the Wilson line to lose the faith, he found the process agonizing. He did not float into latitudarianism; he landed in hell feet first.

> I have a portrait of an ancestor who lost his land to the Crown because he was a Catholic; there is a tradition of an earlier ancestor who lost his life. The family suffered, apparently, so that I could achieve apostasy; an ironical end to the fight for freedom of worship. I am far from happy about this situation, but nobody can actively *will* loss of faith."[10]

It was no easy process for the young Burgess in part because the idea of hell ("a very Nordic notion") had such a powerful hold over his mind, and partly because, as the first apostate in the family, there were recriminations, arguments, evasions.

> The God my religious upbringing forced upon me was a God wholly dedicated to doing me harm. You know, like the 'young man' invoked by Magwitch in **Great Expectations,** to terrorize Pip, God had a secret way *pecooliar* to Himself of getting at a boy, and at his heart and liver . . . . That's pretty much what my elders said — priests and nuns and relatives, as well as the penny catechism. A big vindictive invisibility.[11]

He stopped going to Mass at the age of sixteen. The family accused him of laziness, rank unwillingness to get out of bed. A more subtle disputant suggested that sleep meant a longing for death, Winston's Smith's "black velvet." The old woman in Samuel Butler's **The Way of All Flesh** was quoted at him: "I can do without heaven, sir, but I can't with hell." A no-nonsense family, the Wilsons.

In this period of his life, full of the wrath of God, ignorant of His mercy, fearing hellfire and eternal damnation, Burgess searched for kindred spirits, old campaigners in the theological wars. He providentially discovered the works of James Joyce and the discovery of this fastidious artist, gay aesthete of gray Dublin, a cheerful renegade who survived the fearful apostasy, led to a life-long devotion.

> When I first read Joyce's **Ulysses**, it was in a copy smuggled in from Paris: Paris, not Dublin. I was drawn to a great Irish Catholic when he had ceased to be either truly Irish or truly Catholic. He was a renegade. I myself at the age of sixteen was a renegade. He had made his world out of the materials of the world he had rejected. I wanted confirmation that the agonies and elation I knew as a renegade had some sort of artistic significance, meant something. I should imagine that when an Anglican loses his faith it is a smooth, sweet process, rather like the shedding of a skin. His Church has as good as told him not to take its doctrines too seriously. But for a cradle Catholic to leave his Church is like the wrenching of palpable bone and muscle — it is like the draining of the very content of the skull. To me, at an age when I could neither accept nor answer the arguments of the Jesuits, it was unavoidable agony because it seemed to be happening totally against my will. What caused it? Too much reading of the wrong books, too much half-baked philosophizing, or was it just the failure of some small, nameless organ of the brain? Anyway, it seemed to me that what I called reason was tugging one way, and emotion, instinct, loyalty, and fear were tugging the other. James Joyce summed it all up for me in **A Portrait of the Artist as a Young Man . . . .**[12]

He read the hell scene in **Portrait of the Artist as a Young Man** and was so terrified that he very nearly recanted his apostasy. A helpful friend or acquaintance, hoping to cement the foundations of unbelief, made a suggestion. Read, he observed, Grant Allen's **The Evolution of the Idea of God.** Burgess did so; but the work, intended as a prod to cheerful unbelief, to snuff out his inherited Christianity, had quite the opposite effect. The faith of his fathers died hard.[13]

Burgess' present position is relatively simple but final. "I find that I have no quarrel with any aspect of the whole corpus of Catholic doctrine; granted the ignition spark of faith, all the tenets of the Church would hold for me. Indeed, I tend to be puristic about these, even uneasy about what I consider to be dangerous tendencies to slackness, cheapness, ecumenical dilutions."[14] Or, as a waggish writer once suggested, Burgess is a lapsed Catholic, and the Church he does not worship in is pre-*aggiornamento*.

Reason, such as it is, tells him that the anthropomorphic God of the Old Testament, with its sheep and eating fit to burst and getting drunk and the tribal God on your side and a sneer at your enemies and your hair dripping with oil, is a very strange sort of God, guilty of bloody-minded boorishness one would not tolerate in a neighbour. As for Christianity, Burgess knows very well that, if God had intended to create a religion that incorporates every known element of paganism, He could not have done better than to create Christianity in exactly its present form. Burgess may brood about religion in this fashion (and the words found in this paragraph are chiefly his own), but he continues to think, and possibly to feel, in the terms of his old faith.

Education

Little is known of his early education, but the little there is suggests deprivation, not privilege. He attended Bishop Bilsborough Memorial School until the age of eleven where some of the nuns were apparently sadistic. (They exist; but many are unduly kind, and some love your small successes as if they were their own; Burgess was unlucky.) He then won two scholarships which enabled him to attend Xaverian College in Manchester, where he was taught by the Xaverian Brothers. Less sadism here, but more damnable reflection. One of the Brothers who taught history encouraged discussions of unbelief, and it may well be that the nascent Burgess apostasy was fomented or reinforced by a man himself troubled by Doubts. Early friends, early little love affairs, have left no trace. Sex, of course, is intimately associated with schooldays, and the schoolboy experienced the occasional feverish "dreams of [his] moaning adolescence — the harem houri, plump, pouting, perfumed from a spout not a stopper, her embracing fingers sticky with Turkish delight."[15] The young devise harems the Church denounces — from now until the end of time.

He was the recipient of the Higher School Certificate (English literature, history, Latin) from Xaverian College at the age of seventeen with such distinction that he was encouraged to repeat the year for the purpose of gaining a scholarship. Burgess' passionate musical interests came to the fore and, to the astonishment of his teachers, he decided to switch his energies to the study of music. He won a 'distinction' in music, but no scholarship. He was just eighteen. What next?

The past history of the Wilson clan suggested that work was the only honorable thing, the only decent thing. "A Wilson left the elementary school as soon as it was legally permissible and started to look for a job." He was composing music in his spare time; convinced himself that he wanted to study music at the University of Manchester. He had the talent but no ready cash. He was perhaps the first of the Wilsons in generations to propose the impiety of a college education. There were probably wrangles with his parents about the doubtful utility and probable folly of higher education. For two years after his graduation, he worked at various odd jobs to pay his way. Then at the age of twenty, Burgess entered the University of Manchester, a lively place ("My own university was set among slums, brothels, public bars"), began his studies and, one presumes, observed or participated in the ambient debauchery.

He had failed a physics course, the demanding science of acoustics, and was debarred from the study of music. He studied English literature instead (as one would have expected in any case) and did moderately well: contributed poems and papers to the local school journal. In his first year, he organized a public reading of T.S. Eliot's **The Wasteland** accompanied by a gallimaufry of music: ragtime, Wagner, plain chant, a setting of the Thames Daughters' Song made out of Wagner's *weilala* wailings in **Das Rheingold**.

At the University he discovered, or rediscovered, Christopher Marlowe. Did not Marlowe place the negatives very softly in his **Doctor Faustus**? *"Ugly hell gape not; come not Lucifer,"* is not the strongest possible repudiation of Satan and all his works. Was it possible that Marlowe, another renegade, with a blasphemous death and a dagger through the frontal lobes, was imperfectly emancipated from his cradle Catholicism?

> I was a renegade Catholic who mocked at hell but was still secretly scared of it, especially as it might come any night now. I felt, despite all the biographical evidence, that Marlowe himself might be such a man, his blasphemies and beery jags the true voice of imperfect emancipation.[16]

Burgess wrote his thesis about Christopher Marlowe and graduated with a B.A. in English literature in 1940. Some years later, a witness to the student shamanism of the sixties, he felt moved to comment on his own hard-won university degree.

> It is, I know, useless to throw at them lessons from one's own student past, but memories of what it was like to be a student in a British provincial university, while the 1939-45 war was beginning, are bound to suffuse my own attitude to them and make sympathy difficult. Like many others of my class, I believed that to go to a university was an honor and that one must pay for the honor with hard work. Entrance to the university was no right, even with the possession of high scholastic qualifications. There were few scholarships: my own city of Manchester offered three annually. Fees were subsidized, but they still had to be paid. I had to work for two years between leaving school and going to the university — as a pub pianist, a private tutor and a deliverer of tobacco orders. This enabled me to save enough money to enter the School of English Language and Literature. I wanted my money's worth, although I fear I did not always get it.
>
> There was too much bad lecturing — paper phonetics, the droning of Old Norse, dogmatic evaluations, the transmutation of golden poetry into prose dross. We should have protested, but we didn't — not many of us anyway. If you didn't like the course, it was implied by the hierarchy, you could get out: there were plenty of youngsters trying to get in. But learning, even if not well purveyed, was respected in those days

for its own sake. We were still in the Middle Ages. We tried to climb out of them
in our own little protest sessions, which usually ended with collections of money —
there was not much of it around — for orphans of the Spanish Civil War or, a little
later, Jewish refugees from Germany.

I remember taking my finals while bombs were dropping on Manchester. We were
in the huge glass-roofed gymnasium and we translated **Beowulf** while the air war went
irrelevantly on outside. Strangely, it was the Anglo-Saxon that seemed real, not the
war. It still seems to me that it would have been better to be blown up while wrestling
with ancient syntax than while raising fretful and ineffectual fists at the bombers.[17]

Some time in the course of his undergraduate years Burgess met Llewela Isherwood Jones, his future
wife. She is a woman who arouses much unsatisfied curiosity, since her presence plainly gives much
interest to the early fiction. She is the woman in the background, by turns amused, amusing, promiscuous,
irascible, but always seemingly alive, always a kind of companion even if not necessarily a kind companion. She studied economics at the same University and later put her talents and industry to work
improving the family finances by margin plays on the London stock exchange with such success that
Burgess was put in the unenviable position of paying taxes on the proceeds and on the residue of her
estate. She will be heard from later.

Battles of Northumberland and Gibraltar

In 1940 Burgess received a tactful invitation to join the British Army and followed the tradition
established by his great-grandfather and father to become an enlisted man. He remained in the army
from 1940 to 1946, chiefly as a musical director of the 54th Division entertainments section, and as
education sergeant and warrant officer in Gibraltar. He was in the army when he first heard of the
death of James Joyce on January 13, 1941, after an operation for a perforated duodenal ulcer. The
story is told in **Re Joyce**.

In January, 1941, when the news of Joyce's death filtered through from Zurich, the
world was distracted by other preoccupations, other deaths. Few of his admirers could
take time off for a wake. I myself, a private soldier in snow-bound Northumberland,
learned the news when I was polishing the windows of the Sergeants' Mess with a
week-old copy of the **Daily Mail.** There it was, on the front page, rightly dwarfed
by the bombing of Plymouth.
'Good God, James Joyce is dead.'
'Who the hell's he?' asked a sergeant.
'A writer. Irish. The author of **Ulysses.**'
'Aaaah, a **dirty** book that is. Get on with the job.' So Joyce's quizzical photograph
polished away, looking out at the snow ('faintly falling, like the descent of their last
end, upon all the living and the dead.' A great writer modifies everything.)[18]

Enderby the poet, quizzed about his army career by an elderly, hard-eyed ex-army officer, tells his
tormentor that he was a lieutenant in the last war. The assertion, strenuously disbelieved, is made in
a spoken exchange of artful equivocation.

'Now,' said the major-general, as Enderby sat down again with a new whisky, 'what
did you say your rank was?'
'Lieutenant-general,' said Enderby. In speech a comma is as good as a hyphen.
'I don't believe you.'
'Look it up.' . . . .
The major-general said, 'I don't believe you, sir.'
'You must please yourself, General,' said Ex-lieutenant Enderby. And, with a general
salute, he left.[19]

Burgess never made it to either rank. He was never a lieutenant, much less a lieutenant-general. He
was, from the beginning to the end of his army service, a mere other rank. The reason, or reasons,
for this fact are not clear; but, if Burgess has interpreted the witholding of a commission as a deprivation, there is no indication of the fact in his fiction or non-fiction. There is, in fact, a good deal of

evidence to suggest that Burgess identified with the rank and file, distrusted the officer class, and resolved not to forget the common soldier in his fiction. The proof can be found in **Napoleon Symphony**.

Whatever the reason for Burgess' failure to rise in the ranks, in 1943 he was posted to the Rock of Gibraltar, to guard that British outpost of Jurassic limestone against the Germans or the Spaniards, or possibly a combination of the two. This attack, known in the planning phase under the code name 'Ferdinand and Isabella' did not, of course, materialize. So, in the course of preventing an attack that never came, Burgess toiled and tunneled on the Rock. He filled up the larders with the dubious luxuries of army cuisine: tins of corned beef and baked beans. He oiled, or helped to oil, the guns. He took part in the interminable drill. He grew to hate it all, to consider it a kind of barracks incarceration, a sentence within a sentence.

As a result of this extended service in the ranks, Burgess never forgot his proper world: the world of common soldiers, of tommies and ercs. He knew this world from the inside: the monotonous obscenities (Enderby the poet is ready with his 'for coughs' at moments of insolence and stress), the ludic tropes of the common soldier ("Roll on death and let's have a go at the angels," "Put another pea in the pot and hang the expense," "Never mind, lads, it'll soon be Christmas," — some cheerful laughter, all fondly remembered, there) and the damnable deprivations of army life. "The Army was rather like the Church, conditioning one to sweat with wholly irrational fears."[20] If his presence on the Rock during the war sounds like an enviable posting, here is a voluptuous vignette to banish all such notions. It might be called "The Pleasures of Army Life, Chapter 939."

> If the lover's bed should be air or roseleaves or swansdown, the bed of the soldier
> should be hard and usually is. When I joined the British Army in 1940, my winter
> Scottish barrack-room had neither bedsteads nor palliasses. I slept on the floor
> wrapped in seven blankets — far too few — and was glad when reveille sounded.
> I would have got up long before reveille sounded, but that would have been inter-
> preted under Army Law as being up after lights out. When I became a sergeant I
> was allotted the bottom bunk of a two-tier structure in a three-stripers' dorter. The
> bunk above me belonged to a wizened pioneer sergeant who drank and was inconti-
> nent: he dripped aromatically on me all night long. His blankets were moist and had
> to be dried daily, but he would not exchange them for new: to him they were a sort
> of diary, or noctuary, of pleasurable potation. When I was posted to Gibraltar I
> became acquainted with fleas, lice and bedbugs, especially bedbugs. Putting down
> my head at night in the dark, I would sense that my own personal squad was mar-
> shalling for the attack; switching on the light suddenly, I would see them timorously
> but temporarily retreating. They would march along the floors and up the walls and
> over the ceiling, only to return, with the restoration of darkness, to their bloody but-
> chery of the bed. The feet of the bedstead would be placed in cigarette-tins filled
> with paraffin. The bedstead itself, solid iron, would be burnt every Sunday in the
> yard, a Magritte-like apparition. But the bugs could not be put down. They were
> a nocturnal terror, all too solid despite their squashiness. They helped to put me off
> beds.[21]

Off army beds, perhaps, but not the marriage bed, an entity not much celebrated in **On Going to Bed** (or elsewhere in Burgess' fiction for that matter).

"Hobby: Wife"

On January 28, 1942, Burgess married Llewela Isherwood Jones, a distant relation of Christopher Isherwood. (The fact helps to explain the inordinately cheerful tone of Burgess' review of Isherwood's **A Meeting by the River** which is signed, unusually for Burgess, with a hearty "Love from Burgy.") Llewela Jones — Burgess has talked with his usual candor — was cheerfully promiscuous. She argued that her casual affairs did not change her feelings for him; hence, his jealousy was ridiculous. *"Ca vous donne tant de plaisir et moi si peu de peine"* (It gives you no less pleasure, and me so little pain) was her customary line, a gaunt defense fit for Huxley's Viveash. She slept with Dylan Thomas and cheerfully reported to her husband that Dylan was not the great lover of later American legend. To all this promiscuity Burgess did not object on principle, but he strenuously objected to witnessing her extra-marital sexual acts. "We may talk as rationally as we please, but when we *see* — I think this is true of all of us — it's very hard not to bring out a knife. And I think it's just because of this irrational element that a danger lies in too much promiscuity. We've got to accept the irrational in us, that we can become as mad as any Sicilian on such occasions."[22]

It is hard to describe a marriage when one of the partners is dead and the documents (letters, photographs, mementoes) are not filed and indexed. It is certain that this particular marriage received an early blow or, more literally, a series of blows. It occurred in war-time London at the height of the blackout. Burgess has speculated that three American G.I. deserters drank what they presumed to be weak British beer, and got violently drunk. They roamed the streets looking for trouble.

> My wife was one of their unlucky victims. It wasn't a sexual assault, it was an attempted robbery, and they tried to take her wedding ring off and she screamed and then they hit her; she was pregnant at the time and lost the child. Involuntary abortion. This was followed by a disease that was very hard for the gynecologists to explain. It brought on perpetual loss of blood, perpetual menstruation, so there had to be a corresponding intake of fluid. She was not able to have any children or even to have intercourse for a long time. The gynecological complex begot its own psychological aura. Things never got really right again.[23]

He received the news while on active duty in Gibraltar; felt the usual rage and, raging, expressed the usual sentiments. "Let me get back there, let me get back to England. Bloody Yanks. I want to do something about it."[24] He was unable, of course, to do anything at all: the fate of most victims. The unhappy episode helped to form **A Clockwork Orange**. The writer in the happy place called **HOME** who is assaulted by Alex and his fellow hoods is depicted working, in a curious Chinese box-like scene, on a tract called **A Clockwork Orange**. The scene was added by design to indicate that the story was no mere invention.

She was, but for the excessive promiscuity which sometimes made Burgess as mad as any Sicilian, a marvellous mate for Burgess — if not necessarily the best woman for him. It is reasonable to assume common literary interests. The companionship of this somewhat fiery, argumentative, but still compatible spirit, led Burgess, plausibly and insistently, to describe marriage as a civilization in miniature which is broken up at the peril of one's soul.

The point can be demonstrated in some detail. Burgess, brought up in pubs, has a taste for levity, broad humor, the kind of story that has the bibulous company in a roar. He was also, at least in his salad days, saddled with an incurable facetiousness.

> I remember an old film about Alcatraz or Sing Sing or somewhere in which Wallace Beery, having organized the killing of several warders, broken up the prison hospital, and kicked the deputy governor in the guts, said in his defense: "I was only kiddin'." I've never gone so far, but I fear that my own kind of kidding may be the death of me. Like giving a college lecture on a purely fictitious Elizabethan dramatist called Grasmere Tadsworth (1578-1621). Like writing a pseudonymous review of one of my own books. Like, when asked by the editors of **Who's Who** to give the names of my clubs, answering with Toby's Gym, the Nudorama Strip Club, the Naked City and so on. This is not really funny. When the same editors asked me for hobbies, I gave wife as one of them, and they let that go through. There it is now, perpetuated from edition to edition [i.e. from 1965 to 1968/69], waiting for **Who Was Who,** and sooner or later I was bound to be asked what the hell I meant, mean.
>
> It's tempting to retreat into that high-school thicket of evasiveness, the dictionary. Thus, my wife is a small species of falcon, *jalco subboteo*. My wife is a horse of middle size, a pacing horse, a stick of a horse on which boys ride. My wife is (Old French *hobin*) a stupid fellow. All right, all right, stop fooling about: try the definition "favorite pursuit" and don't for God's sake, say: "Ha, ha, I stopped pursuing her a long time ago."[25]

The sense in which his wife is his hobby, he goes on, along with music composition, piano-playing, painting, language-learning and broadcasting, is that "The vital element in any civilized community is language, and without language there can be no marriage.'' He has shared, with his wife, sounds, noises, grunts, idioms, jokes, bits of silliness and even inconsequential stupidities.

> I think I have a vocation for gaining the maximal social fulfillment which means communicative fulfillment, which means even a kind of spiritual fulfillment, out of living with a particular woman. But, frightened of the big words, and also incurably facetious, I have to talk of my wife as a hobby. . . .[26]

Did he entertain the party to excess by banging out tunes on the piano? his wife had only to say Mary! to bring the whole performance to an end. The reference is, of course, to **Pride and Prejudice** where Mary Bennett is told, after another mildly agonizing performance, ''Mary, you have delighted us long enough.'' It all sounds delightful. Yet this celebration of marriage as communication is uncommonly labored, and we have hints in **Beard's Roman Women** and elsewhere that the bliss was not unconfined.

To Banbury Then He Came

The town of Banbury, 22 miles north of Oxford, has not had a favorable press. The town is infamous for the more repellent puritannical virtues. Richard Brathwaite (1588-1673) author of **Drunken Barnaby's Four Journeys**, summed it all up in this trenchant verse.

> To Banbury came I, o profane one,
> Where I saw a Puritane One
> Hanging of his cat on Monday
> For killing of a mouse on Sunday.[27]

Burgess' life in Banbury was one long, joyless Sabbath. He arrived there in 1950 and took up the post of English Master at Banbury Grammar School (and, in his judgment, an excellent school of its kind); enjoyed his job but not his pay. The name, God knows, is not propitious, and he suffered many maddening deprivations which finally goaded him to action.

He was, like most of the teachers at this time, grossly underpaid. The yearly salary of 500 English pounds (about $1,400 in American currency), low enough by itself, seemed even lower compared to the relative affluence of his students. Burgess, who does not generally think in terms of abstractions when he can help it, paints a Hogarthian picture of penny-pinching penury. At Banbury, his luxuries included a mere two pints of draught cider and a derisory limit of five Woodbines a day. For a man who loves to drink, and unfortunately loves to smoke (his father was, after all, a tobacconist) the situation was bleak. It was made even worse by the comparative affluence of his students, who were able to buy books outside his reach.

He is, in his own words, the son of a small shopkeeper who has reacted powerfully against the shop-keeping element. He takes a certain small pride in his carelessness about money matters. (This misplaced pride will be the source of misfortune later in his life.) But there are times when, goaded by desperation, he is forced to act. There will be two times in his life when he is forced to talk, tediously and at length, about money matters. This is the first time. Banishment from Banbury, and avoidance of odious comparisons between the affluence of small schoolboys and the penury of schoolteachers seem infinitely desirable. He is driven by a wild desperation.

One night he made out an application for a teaching position on the channel island of Sark. His logic is impeccable; he will try to find the nearest equivalent to the rich bawdy variety of life. To hell with the cenobitic virtues. The drinks will be cheaper there; the coffin nails more plentiful; his big border collie can roam the island at will. The cavalier gesture was soon forgotten. Shortly afterwards, asked to report to the Colonial Office, he thought it strange that the Colonial Office would have charge of one of the channel islands but dismissed the thought by the reflection ''that one of the great glories of the British Way of Life was its cultivation of anomalies that worked.''[28]

He made his appearance soon afterwards at Great Smith Street and heard the Colonial Officer ask him: ''Now why do you want to work in Malaya, Mr. Burgess?'' The time was January 1954. Malaya, in that first, startled moment, must have seemed enticing. He replied firmly that he had not applied to Malaya; that he was interested in a job on the isle of Sark. The Colonial Officer — mouths were beginning to gape — one man was watching the proceedings intently to get the epic contours of the story right — showed Burgess the application. Malaya it was, not the isle of Sark. At the sight of the letter, Burgess remembered and reconstructed the event. He had filled out the application, despairing of his lot, while drunk; typed it out in a rage of penury with chill accuracy and controlled eloquence, and then forgot the event. He replied, smiling, that he had not specifically made himself available for a job at Tahi Panas. (The name is fictitious. It means, roughly, prickly heat and probably involves an additional bawdy joke.) The Colonial Office, sensing an element of creative wildness in the applicant, put him on the payroll and offered him a job as a permanent pensionable civil servant in Malaya.

Preparations for the departure got under way. The mortgaged cottage was put on the market. The border collie bitch was given away to friends. Books, most of them second-hand, were winnowed and all the useless things were burned or given away. Regret soon set in because "now we began to realize that it is the useless things that are the least dispensable: a home is made out of useless things . . . .torn schoolboy annuals, home-framed Holman Hunts, a chipped China pig that cost fourpence." But there was a sense of exhilaration, freedom. Now there was no need to hide dislike of people any more. Tell X and Y to go to hell in a final show-down. (There was, of course, no final show-down and the dislike was hidden.) But the exhilaration was real:

> It was exhilarating to be able to say: Look, we don't just sit and grumble about middle-class poverty and the decadence of teddy-boy England; we've actually done something about it. The replies: (a) rats, leaving sinking national ship; (b) good for you, pioneering spirit.[29]

In the final days before departure, the English papers included accounts of communist terrorism. A Scottish estate manager was garrotted two miles from the town in which they were to be posted (presumably Khata Baru). A man on leave from Malaya had been bitten on the foot by a ginger centipede. He reported that the money went nowhere. So, at the time of the Malayan insurgency, the cutlery sold, the double bed and the two armchairs disposed of, they boarded the Dutch ship **Willem Ruys** of the Rotterdam-Lloyd line and departed for Malaya.

It was all very leisurely. The cruise ship took five weeks to get close to its destination, finally threaded its way through the Indonesian islands, and then arrived at the hot dish-rag air of Singapore. He soon found he had more money and, vastly more important, increased leisure. In the long sweaty afternoons, while other colleagues slept, he worked. Miraculously, the words came.

> We had, without doubt, changed for the financially better. We had a cook, a car, an amah. This did not mean there was more time for lazing than there had been in England; it meant there was more time for work, learning languages and customs, and — for me — writing . . . . The impact of a mixed culture opened up my imagination and dissolved a creative block that had persisted since the end of the war. I began to write and publish.[30]

Expatriation improved his finances, but that was trivial and petty compared to the central issue. He grew to love the country, a process that started "I think, on the day of the local police sports, when a fat Sikh sergeant lost his turban in the three-legged race. Ordinary things can inexplicably conspire to induce a conviction of love: the sun on your neck, bottled beer in a tub of melted ice, the aftertaste of red pepppers, the breath of musk from a Malay body, the crispness of somebody's white shirt, the sudden laughter of a crowd of fantastically diverse races."[31] Note, in this eclectic catalog, the very concreteness of the things itemized. What we have here is the beginning of the Burgess aesthetic: beauty lies in things and the function of the novelist is, above all, to be concrete. "The minutiae that make real novels are the taste of eggs and bacon, the bad tooth, and the pang of heartburn."[32] But these minutes of life's sorrows must not be chronicled in a pared-down, dryasdust style. His temperament rebels at that; he does not take easily to the plain style.

> The beauties of the plain style are often urged on me, the duty of excising rather than adding. But the Elizabethan spirit doesn't take kindly to the Hemingwayesque, the spare and laconic, nor does my own spirit. I don't think that **Nothing Like the Sun** has too many words; I think perhaps it has too few. One has to be true to one's own temperament, and mine is closer to that of the baroque writers than that of the stark toughies. To hell with cheeseparing and verbal meanness: it all reeks of Banbury puritanism.[33]

Time for a Tiger (1956), that "marvellous early book" as Warren Miller rightly called it, and his first work with an Eastern setting, was published under the pseudonym 'Anthony Burgess,' for a number of reasons. It was strenuously urged on him that a colonial officer did not publish anything as frivolous as fiction under his own name. Besides, there were too many writing Wilsons around, and so Burgess headed and tailed the total onomastic shrimp to leave only the edible essence behind. The book, pseudonym and all, had a Burgessian origin: a Balzacian brooding about many foreign debts.

> I was living in Malaya in 1955, working for the Government and, in my spare time, carrying on with what I thought was my true artistic vocation — the composing of music. One morning I woke to hear the muezzin calling — 'There is no God but Allah' — and, as often happens when one first wakes, to find the names of my creditors parading through my mind, together with what I owed them. Something like this:
>
> *La ilaha illa'lah*
> Lim Kean Swee $395
> Chee Sin Hye $120
> Tan Meng Kwang $250
> *La ilaha illa'lah*
>
> And so on. Here obviously was the beginning of a novel: a man lying in bed in the Malayan dawn, listening to the muezzin calling, worrying about his debts. So, out of this little *collage,* I began to write, with suspicious ease, my first published work of fiction.[34]

It makes for a charming story and it is probably the literal truth — like most of Burgess' disclosures. Another little-known fact about this novel deserves to be better known. It will be recalled that Nabby Adams lusts after Tiger beer as other men lust after tigresses of another kind. Yet Nabby, delirious winner of $350,000 in the State lottery, abandons Tiger beer with these immortal (but improbable) words: "No, make it Carlsberg." Is it reasonable for a toper to abandon a favorite brew in this festive moment? The short answer is, of course: never, given the major magic of hops.

Invited to show their gratitude for the title of his first book, **Time for a Tiger**, the brewers of Tiger cautiously declined, observing the book, if obscene or seditious, might damage sales. "I was very hurt [he only wanted a wooden Tiger-advertising clock found in the *kedais,* Malayan pubs], and showed this in an emendation I at once made in the text. My hero wins the Federation Lottery first prize of $350,000, and it is suggested that a celebratory case of Tiger be sent out for. 'No,' he says, 'make it Carlsberg. It costs a bit more but it's a better beer'." The makers of Carlsberg, connoisseurs of literature and the plug that cheers, promptly rewarded Burgess with a celebratory case of their brew. Literature, as Burgess likes to observe, is an epiphenomenon of the life of the flesh.[35]

In Malaya and Borneo, Burgess wrote the three novels that collectively make up **The Malayan Trilogy** (British title) or **The Long Day Wanes** (American title): **Time for a Tiger** (1956), **Enemy in the Blanket** (1958) and **Beds in the East** (1959). They were all written in direct response to an exotic stimulus, and they proved to be, for a long time, the most popular and profitable of his early novels.

It is easy enough to see why. They are not only concerned with an exotic setting, the chaotic and violent Malaya prior to independence, with its resident Malays, busy Chinese and priapic sultans, but loving studies of relatively amiable characters. It supplies proof, if proof is needed, of the humanity of Burgess in his early forties. The predominant attitude is one of loving indulgence for his characters — particularly if they step out of character. His policemen drink on duty, his martial Sikhs try to set up shop as businessmen, the teetotaling sons of Islam fail in their duty, prostitutes give away their one worldy good. Even the resident Malays, who observe the doings of the white man and mutter their murderous imprecations, seem a kindly lot of grumbling malcontents. It is only when the novel abandons the world of Malaya for the smaller world of the local school administration that the mood becomes shrill and unpleasant.

The final volume of the trilogy, **Beds in the East**, was published while Burgess was in Borneo. There, two events ensured Burgess' recall to London by the Colonial Office. The first was political; the second medical or pseudo-medical. The full story is not known, and the following account is wholly derived from Burgess himself. It may well be, although he is a man dedicated to telling the truth on a heroic scale, somewhat brief and non-committal.

Burgess somehow found himself involved in revolutionary politics against his will. The Borneo house was occupied by a revolutionary leader (not identified) who was lying low at the time. Burgess was, by his own account, friendly with some of the men. He was asked, such was the general esteem in which he was held, to become the head of the Freedom Party. It was clear to him that government spies were observing his activities. In the middle of this very atypical behavior, for the later Burgess comes as close as any man now living to the true Bellocian disdain —

> Here richly, with ridiculous display,
> The Politician's corpse was laid away.
> While all of his acquaintance sneered and slanged
> I wept; for I had hoped to see him hanged.

— his wife Llewela ingratiated herself in her fashion. They were not, as a couple, considered quite suitable in any case. Burgess showed a disquieting interest in native languages and customs; avoided club-life; ran the danger of going native. In colonial circles, the man who shows these traits is commonly regarded with great suspicion which does nothing to help his career. The case of Sir Richard Burton in India, who occasionally dove into the native netherworld and plummeted in the estimation of his fellow officers, is an instructive example. An imperial power casts seeming ambivalence out into the darkmans where there is weeping and gnashing of teeth.

Outright defiance was soon added to ambivalence. Prince Philip paid a visit to Borneo. At a garden party, the Patrician Presence mingled with the expatriates to inquire 'if everything was all right?' The correct answer to the question was, of course, that everything is definitely all right, if not now then in the near and foreseeable future. Llewela Burgess failed every conceivable test of diplomatic tact by protesting that everything was bloody well not all right. The details of her dissent are regrettably not available but it can well be imagined that the story, furiously heightened and suitably embroidered, made the rounds of the British community. The Burgesses cemented their claims, already perhaps substantial enough, to the appellation of 'bolshy.' (A curious charge. Burgess has no discernable politics in his fiction by deliberate, blessed choice. Outside of fiction, he has damned the party in power on the spur of the moment. He has denounced the ideology of Labour, the timocracy of America, and the theocracy of Malta. His contention is, or was, that politics should be unobtrusive as a sewer. Burgess has, like Byron before him, "simplified" his "politics into an utter detestation of all existing governments.")

The next event gave the authorities the necessary pretext to pack the two undesirables out of the country under the guise of solicitude. Burgess, in the course of teaching some young Malays, "lay on the floor in utter frustration [exhausted by the agony of trying to instil Western ideas into Eastern minds] and let the world take over. The world found too much protein in the spinal fluid and sent me home to die, if that could be arranged. Actually I was fit but FRUSTRATED."[36]

The world took over with great efficiency and the 'permanent pensionable civil servant' along with his pleasant wife Llewela were bundled out of the country and put on a plane bound for London. Burgess has always wondered ('Can they do that?') if the celerity of official action was designed to eliminate troublesome elements from politically volatile Borneo.

In the National Neurological Hospital he went through the usual diagnostic procedures, and after the luxury of several spinal taps, learned that he had only a year to live on this, on the whole, tolerable planet which tends, after such a prognosis, to become more than ever intolerably bearable and even lovely. There are those who love the treatment and almost hate the recovery, and there are those who love the recovery and hate the treatment. Burgess falls in the latter category. The experience provided the material for the madcap adventures of Edwin Spindrift in **The Devil Is Sick**. His real-life memories are more subdued.

> The link between life and death is illness, and the bed of sickness, as opposed to convalescence, is the wheel of fire that Shakespeare mentions in **King Lear.** Its terrors can be mitigated only by making it a bed in a hospital ward, when it becomes highly functional, unassociable with sexual pleasure, and indeed set around with so much banal discomfort that illness has no chance to be exalted to noble agony and classical terror. Sheets and coverlet are very plain and are so tucked in as to evoke ancestral memories of chains and straps and other stabilizers premonitory of torture. The

processes of bodily excretion have to be fulfilled in impossible vessels. One is awakened at an unreasonable hour, in order that the hospital routine, which never consults the superficial welfare of the patients, may function like the heartless machine it is. At dawn, or foredawn even, the interests of health may be subverted. I remember once being made to get up in black London December and go out to a news-agent not yet open, there to wait shivering so that I could buy the ward's copies of the **Daily Mirror.** The following day I was due to be investigated for a possible cerebral tumour.

The only thing that can be said for being dangerously ill in a hospital is that it is not conducive to dying quietly: it raises the pulse rate with anger and resentment, fires the system with combative adrenalin, and makes one determined to outlive one's white-clad oppressors.[37]

Many a true word spoken in that final paragraph. So Burgess got out of his hospital bed, if not fit, then in full fighting spirit. He was told a) that he had a year to live, but b) if, after the end of a year he found himself still alive, to distrust the initial prognosis. A provisional guillotine of the Johnsonian kind that reputedly concentrates the mind.

There was no money for grand gestures: the riots and debaucheries of the fictional terminal case. A thousand pounds were left over from the days in Malaya. Teaching was clearly impossible; no-one would employ a potential casket case. Burgess toyed (for how long no one really knows) with the possible options. When, at long last, he came down from his odious hospital bed to rejoin the intolerably lovely species of *homo sapiens sapiens,* it did not take him long to make up his mind. He would, unseduced by debauchery and death, hammer away at the typewriter keys and transmute black typeface to gold. His plain duty was to leave his wife an estate. To hell with the Shavian notion that the true artist lets his wife and children starve. Many a husband has done worse.

He distrusted the diagnosis, doubted the prognosis ("I didn't feel bad enough"), but prudently behaved as if the doctors were right. Then began that curious, exhilarating year (1959-1960) in which, under sentence of death by the quacks, Burgess quickly wrote five remarkable novels in one year (**Inside Mr. Enderby, The Wanting Seed, The Doctor Is Sick, The Worm and the Ring** and **One Hand Clapping**). His wife Llewela took the thousand pounds they had brought with them from Malaya and bought stocks on margin. In a few years, she doubled and quadrupled the original sum. The small profits on the stock market helped them to live through the year in the sea-side city of Hove some few miles west of Brighton.

Burgess is perhaps vaguely conscious of imminent bankruptcy dating from this period of his life. It was, despite the troubled budget, a curiously happy time and Burgess was "probably happiest when I was least known, when I had a year to live. Nobody knew me, I was never besieged by editors or telephoned by anybody, and I just got on with the job of writing." He developed staying power in front of his desk and wrote hours a day for seven days a week.

Heinemann, faced with the job of promoting five novels written by one author in a very short period of time, suffered a genteel failure of nerve. They assumed Burgess' prolific production would alienate the critics. Hence, they issued **Inside Mr. Enderby** and **One Hand Clapping** under the pseudonym Joseph Kell. The decision was a small publishing disaster. ANTHONY BURGESS had established a small audience of his own. That unknown JOSEPH KELL had to endure all the fanfare, jubilation and acclaim so well known to first novelists. The predictable result was that **One Hand Clapping** fell from the presses almost unnoticed, while that uproarious, cunningly confessional (but certainly far from wholly autobiographical) **Inside Mr. Enderby** did little better.

The publisher's diffidence had one agreeable consequence. Burgess was asked to review the work of that obscure novelist Joseph Kell and, madcap son of a madcap father in a madcap line, did so. He was then a paid reviewer for the **Yorkshire Post** (four pounds a week) and there, by God, was his own book. The dogs at the **Post** would have their review.

> . . . I wrote a novel called **Inside Mr. Enderby**, which came out under the name of Joseph Kell. One day, instead of getting the usual parcel of novels for review, I received a single novel in a single parcel, and this was my own, **Inside Mr. Enderby** by Joseph Kell. I assumed that the editor wanted a bit of a joke — wanted me to review this, but didn't want to make this request in writing. So I reviewed the book, and I said,

> if I remember, that this was not a book that I would put into the hands of a child, it was rather a dirty book, but it had certain compensating qualities . . . . No writer would be such an idiot as to merely use review space for puffing his own work. I think he would be much more inclined to see what is wrong with the work — and that is why I think probably it is the best review that the book ever had.[38]

The review is, in fact, free of all puffery. More, the relevant section (after the inevitable plot summary) is cunningly just.

> This is, in many ways, a dirty book. It is full of bowel-blasts and flatulent borborygms, emetic meals ("thin but over-savoury stews" Enderby calls them) and halitosis. It may well make some people sick, and those of my readers [the word almost gives the game away] with tender stomachs are advised to let it alone.
>
> It turns sex, religion, the State into a series of laughing-stocks. The book itself is a laughing stock.
>
> And yet, and yet and yet. How thin and under-savoury everything else seems after Enderby's gross richness.[39]

That judicious oxymoron sums up the situation very fairly. So, in the period spanning 1959 through 1968, Burgess lived the life of the literary outsider first at Hove and later in the small village of Etchingham, Sussex. From his public letters — he was continuing to write journalism to pay the bills — we have an account of Etchingham. The people were dour and unliterary. Kipling's ancestral home was only two miles away, but no villager was able to come up with memories about the man. To Burgess, who values a writer's ability to make a lasting impression on the local popular imagination, it seemed a damnable deficiency.

Work, Work, Work (with Interludes)

A spy observing Burgess at work at about this time would have given the following report:

> He gets up grudgingly and shows no haste to face the daily damnation of writing. He listens to William Walton's 'Portsmouth Point' overture; follows it up with the 'Crown Imperial March'; wanders dejectedly about the house and gives his black dog an amiable kick and tells it that it is a lazy black bastard; the dog shakes its tail with appreciation but shows no other impulse to move. The early morning passes quietly in idle chitchat, reading, jokes, riddles, familiar and comfortable exchanges with his wife. About ten, he puts his back into the job. His method is simply to work eight hours a day, seven days a week. It is by following this routine which, he claims, leads to hemorrhoids, excessive smoking, dipsomania, impotence, over-reliance on caffeine and dexedrine, dyspepsia and chronic anxiety, that he produces the many books which prompt envious wags to ask him if he has written his monthly novel yet? a charge that leads to a shrug of annoyance. He argues that the Forsterian quincunx has been unjustly established as a literary norm. Let us not, he says from time to time, consider costiveness laudatory.
>
> The conditions in Etchingham are primitive. He lives on the select side of the street, where the inhabitants have cesspools. On the other side, the practise is to defecate in buckets and bury the ordure in the back garden. 'This,' he says, 'is very difficult in winter when the earth is frozen: one feels like asking Graham Greene to arrange for the dispatch of pneumatic drills.' Greene's reply has not been intercepted.[40]
>
> The general ambiance of his Etchingham residence is very literary. He is grasping at journalism to pay his way, and review copies litter his study floor, and they accumulate on the treads of the stairs until he feels the need for buckshee money and a day in London, the swinging London of Mary Quant's miniskirt. Here is a typical jaunt of the kind which fully conveys the debauchery of the man. One morning, he packed a suitcase full of brilliantly new review copies and staggered off to the railway station. The villagers were at one time convinced that trips of this kind meant that he was leaving his wife again. Then, one morning, they saw one of the

suitcases break open; brilliant new novels littered the road, and they became convinced that he was involved in an obscure crime which was vaguely bookish, smuggling pornography out of Sussex. As he says, 'a very improbable notion.'

The review copies are bought by a bookseller very near Chancery Lane. The bookseller invariably pays him in cash. I have heard him say to a pubmate: 'This is important, this is the only cash I ever receive from anyone, this is the one segment of my income that escapes the scrutiny and penal impost of Her Majesty's Department of Inland Revenue. This is, to use a once popular army term derived from the Arabic, *buckshee* money. It cries out to be spent on cigars, out-of-season fruits, bottles of Cordon Bleu cognac, luncheons at the Cafe Royal. I become, until the 4:20 train that takes me back to Sussex, a part of Swinging London.'[41]

Swinging London does not, for him, swing. He admires the miniskirts, pays mental homage to delectable cruppers and chooses, if that is the term I want, to consort with the help of three dexedrine tablets and a beerglass full of gin-sauced ice. literary to be seditious. I have heard him intone the line 'Lord Snow is old-fashioned; Golding has plucked the last feathers off the bird of Evil; the Catholic converts are starting to bore.' There is a good deal of grumbling about the state of British criticism; they claim it is a sub-craft poorly paid and badly stinted as to permissible wordage, and triumphantly conclude that no writer can tell, on the basis of a few rushed or crowded words, whether he has written well or ill, etc., etc. (Malcontents, the lot of them, if you ask me. It is, after all, universally acknowledged that writers lead a soft and easy life.)

Although I must say, judging from my few glimpses into the unpreposessing Etchingham cottage, that our man labors long and hard. I have found the drafts in his wastebasket remains, a mountainous midden of discarded ms., mostly false starts buried under ash and old fag ends. He is resourceful and adaptable. When the country racket becomes insupportable, and the sheep bleat that they are 'bare,' or the teenage laborers make the day hideous with their transistor radios, he works at night with the help of three dexedrine tables and a beerglass full of gin-sauced ice.

His rate of production in one Christmas holiday period will be a standing reproach to most other writers who prefer, as the universal assumption has it, *dolce far niente*, and so on. It may not, as these things go, set an international record, but it is a respectable example of the Grub Street impresario cunningly transmuting typescript to gold. Here is how he put it, cunningly conveying an impression of weariness, of course, for the benefit of his American readers.

> I Christmassed in the country and did a lot of rather bizarre bread-and-butter literary work (God, how like **Fors Clavigera** this sounds already, except that Ruskin never had to do bread-and-butter literary work). I mean: fifteen thousand words on the Grand Tour; a popular essay on precognition; a study of the American Jew as Voice of the Nation; a little piece on Mark Twain and **Finnegans Wake** (Ph.D. thesis material there, lads); a short story about talking blood; articles on Malcolm Lowry, the Pre-Raphaelites, and the Modern View of Milton; other things I've forgotten.[42]

His method on the literary slag heaps — the boundless deprivations and many humiliations suffered by Richard Savage are never far from his mind — is to work on the first page until it is finished. This may mean that twenty or thirty drafts of the first page fill the waste paper baskets. Then he goes on to the second page and repeats the process. He claims that this working method was inculcated by his work as a composer; that scoring paper is very expensive, and it is best to use the paper to best advantage, but this reply, while superficially convincing, is not very logical for he plainly wastes a great deal of paper. In the evening, he watches television.

This daily practise is no mere self-indulgence; he is, after all, the television critic of

the **Listener** (a post he filled from May 23, 1963 to July 4, 1968) and it is the lot
of the poor Celt to work hard at both his primary craft (fiction) and his primary
source of income (journalism). So bound and shackled to work and wife, he seems
a reasonably happy man. He may groan about hemorrhoids and dyspepsia, and so
on, but he is, on the whole, and not making too fine a point on it, a reasonably contented, happily married man. The household includes dogs, cats and possibly the
abomination of guinea pigs. It is very curious that children are missing in this very
domestic menage. His wife drinks a lot, but he probably drinks more. In any case,
drink is the curse of the writing classes. Did not H.L. Mencken say that no man who
does not like to drink can write worth a damn?

Sober reality soon set in. After the 1943 assault, Llewela Burgess was never really quite the same.
"The gynecological complex begot its own psychological aura. Things never got really right again. And
so she just resigned herself to the idea of wanting to die and drank steadily. I couldn't stop her. Finally
she got what she wanted."[43] Although it is, in my view, unjust to this woman to write her history only
in terms of an extended medical note, the present Burgess biographer has no other choice. In 1960 the
couple went on a vacation trip to Leningrad (Burgess acquired material which later found its way into
Honey for the Bears and **A Clockwork Orange**) where, like Belinda in **Honey for the Bears**, Llewela
Jones had a breakdown. She was treated and released. In the following year she tried to commit suicide.
In 1967 she, "having lost several gallons of blood from a duodenal ulcer that, to use the fashionable
pentagonologue, escalated," was admitted to the hospital in Hastings.

The hospital is staffed mostly by immigrants from the liberated British colonies, and
these are refreshingly free from bedside syrup. They say, accusingly, "You have bled
too much" or "You have damaged your liver." Well, who hasn't? I travel every afternoon from Etchingham (train and bus) and back again (bus and train) to see her.
We both gain a perverse satisfaction from the knowledge that we are getting some
return at last from our forced contributions to the National Health Service. That,
I suppose, is the wrong attitude.[44]

There was a momentary remission of symptoms. In late February or March 1968, Llewela Burgess
visited the passport office to arrange for the renewal of her passport where she is told by a "petty
official" that her official name was now Llewella (not Llewela) and that "this . . . was the right spelling, the new reformed spelling, a legitimate child of the state however spawned out of carelessness,
and she would now have to change her name by deed poll to the name some snotty little penpusher
had accidentally given to her."[45]

The trip she was planning to take, with or without her husband, never took place. The damage to
her liver was irreversible and fatal, and she died some time in March 1968 of cirrhosis.

Burgess came back from the hospital at four thirty in the morning (the taxi-driver
insisted on playing his radio, which featured a song from a group called The Grateful
Dead), knew that I could not set any of the necessary processes in motion till about
nine o'clock, saw a half-finished article in my typewriter and did the only thing it
was proper for a writer to do — finished it. I made an error in the article, accusing
the author under review of misquotation, only to discover later — when the reprov-
ing letters came in — that the misquotation was my own and had been unconsciously
forced upon me by emotions I was keeping down. 'He a little tried/ To live without
her, liked it not, and died.' It should, of course, be 'she' and 'him.'[46]

After her death, Burgess married Liliana Macellari, a teacher of linguistics at Cambridge, Italian
translator of Lawrence Durrell, and a woman of charm, vivacity and force who now acts as his literary
agent; let publishers beware. He also reached the decision to leave England for good or, as he told
Anthony Lewis,

The last few years have been pretty tough. That's why I wrote so much — to get
a little pleasure out of life. It's a pity you can't begin to enjoy life when you're young
. . . . I've had a long period of unhappiness and over-responsibility and guilt, but
now I think probably this is coming to an end. The end of the period of guilt is being

signalized by the entry to the sea, which has never really known guilt. The Mediterranean, the middle wave. And Liliana.[47]

In late 1968 Burgess was forced to leave England for tax reasons. It was all the more galling for the preceding period of relative deprivation. In 1960, his first year as a professional writer, his royalties amounted to an unroyal 800 pounds. In 1964 he groaned in a review of J.W. Saunders' **The Profession of English Letters** that the profession "remains a difficult one."[48] By 1966, Burgess' improved finances provided the dubious luxury of tax problems. Inland Revenue demanded a thousand pounds. There was no ready cash to pay the bill; Burgess refused to sell shares of ICI at a loss. He expressed his puzzlement at this situation to his readers in the **Manchester Guardian.**

> I don't really know how all this came about. I do not live extravagantly. I smoke a lot (but that's a patriotic duty to the Exchequer) and very occasionally take a taxi, but I don't run a car. I have three suits. I try to drink only beer. I work seven days a week. The real answer is to work less, like other people dedicated to our economic recovery. This is also, in some cases, a means of obtaining a tax-free grant from the Arts Council. I've missed the boat somehow.[49]

Burgess, who can get furiously angry at a petty official who has the temerity to spell his first wife's name Llewella rather than the correct Llewela, now denounced his apparent oppressor. Labour was in power; levied taxes on wines and the C_2H_5OH that cheers; put draconian limits on exportable cash. Burgess blamed the ruling government for his troubles.

> There was a time when I believed that evil and incompetence could not inhabit the same body. Socialism, which is a great reconciler of contradictions, has taught me that they can, just as it has taught me that the finest encouragement is discouragement, and that an economy can best be saved by being strangled . . . . There is less and less to work for. It is as sinful to drink whisky as to look for a fortnight's sun. Ambition is more and more brutally penalised . . . . Socialism is based on a tangle of false premises: human beings are totally different from what Socialists think they are. But Socialism can at least modify the human make-up: we are all becoming bitter, disillusioned, obsessed by politics — which should be as unobtrusive as drains. For God's sake leave us alone and let those of us who want to work get on with it.[50]

Six months later his sense of grievance remained undiminished:

> I have never before, in all that part of my life that has consciously been coloured by public affairs, embarked on a new year with no hope at all, or else a number of mean and even treasonous hopes that derive from possessing no hope. I don't hope for the Government to fall: the job of Mr. Wilson's administration is less to govern than to exist. I have dreams of assassination, multiple air-crashes and so on, but these are improper. The most evil and incompetent government my generation has seen will still be puffing away at the beginning of 1969.
>
> If I could hope, I would hope that the trade unions rationalised themselves, coming to terms with the new age of technology (God, that sounds Wilsonian), that our leaders ceased to be frightened of them, and that their members learned corporate responsibility. I would hope that the workers stopped listening to ignorant demagogues and took a stand against victimisation for not toeing the imposed line. I would hope that everybody got mad at each new encroachment on personal liberty . . . .
>
> I would hope for common sense about censorship, a liberalising of the law of libel, something done about library charges to help authors, and a chance for authors to spread their tax liability over more than a single year. In my moods of blackest despair (what used to be called wanhope), I hope that the process of national dissolution will be so accelerated that at last citizens will feel genuine alarm and seek a change of government through loud words and even public violence. What I know (as opposed to what I would hope if I had hope) is that the pound will be further devalued in the new year, wage claims flourish, government by edict come nearer and (by the law of sympathy which most patently operates when Labour is in power) the weather be atrocious.[51]

His tax troubles, formerly a minor irritant, became a major source of worry in 1968. For in that year Burgess earned some real money. His script on the life of Shakespeare was sold to Hollywood; he earned some reasonable advances from his other books. Her Majesty's Department of Inland Revenue gallantly prepared to seize almost the whole of this sum.

Burgess, who has utterly no taste or inclination for practical affairs, now studied the issue at first hand. His friend Kingsley Amis, asked for advice, sounded a noble note. "If the Chancellor of the Exchequer made me pay ten thousand pounds a year for the privilege of staying in England, I'd gladly pay it."[52] All well and good, of course, but one must have the ten thousand pounds, and not all writers can afford endearing gestures on that scale. Another friend, less well-heeled, gave more useful advice.

> A writer I know spent twenty-five years struggling to earn a living with his typewriter. His annual earnings averaged 600 pound — $1,440. Strictly speaking, he was doing somewhat better than most free lances, but his standard of living was still well below that of the railway porter or bus driver. After these hard twenty-five years he suddenly hit the jackpot. A book of his was picked up by the American Book-of-the-Month Club; the film rights fetched a very handsome sum. In this twenty-sixth year — an *annus mirabilis* — he earned something like 80,000 pounds — $192,000. Her Majesty's Department of Inland Revenue immediately stepped in and claimed everything except about 5,000 pounds — $12,000. It was useless for him to protest that this was not really a year's earnings — it was the reward, very belated, of a quarter of a century's hard slog. Useless to point out that an *annus mirabilis* comes once only in a lifetime, if one is lucky. The tax men were adamant. All that my friend could do was, very sadly, to take his money to some dull paradise like Guernsey or Malta.[53]

Exile seemed the only choice, and Burgess prepared to join that distinguished group — Ovid, Dante, Hugo, Mann, Silone, Brecht, Lawrence, Joyce, Nabokov, to say nothing of Byron, Shelley, Dan Jacobson, Peter Porter and V.S. Naipaul — for a new reason. He was prepared to go; he was not prepared to go quietly. The debasement of British standards invited condemnation, and Burgess is not the sort of man to shirk his duty when the old high culture (and literature in particular) suffered from seemingly calculated official insults.

> Britain does not like her writers very much [he told his readers in the **Sunday Express**]. It humiliates them in its Honors List. A man who sails around the world gets a knighthood, and all poor Evelyn Waugh ever wanted was a knighthood. Of course, he never got one. All Muriel Sparke was given was the O.B.E. [Order of the British Empire] — which is what Mary Quant got for inventing the miniskirt.[54]

The detestable Beatles, much reviled by Burgess ("is Beatle the badge of an achieved *kharma* or one still to come?"), were making obscene profits while British writers, all 7,000 strong, earned 87% of them, less than 1,500 pounds a year. The honors went, then and later, not to the practitioners of literature, music and the arts, but to jockeys of disc and turf, showbiz paladins, female impersonators and inglorious time-servers of all kinds. Loyalty to literature entailed a secondary disloyalty to country.

And so he moved abroad, partly to escape Great Britain's penal taxation, and partly because, as a Lancashire Catholic Saxon Celt, he perceived England as vaguely foreign and vaguely inimical. Exile is an expensive business ("I leave behind me a trail of unsaleable properties and irrecoverable libraries"), but the British State duly allowed him to move to Malta.

In Malta, he encountered an ancient and entrenched theocracy which made his life intolerable with many minor irritations. The postal censorship threatened to bar inflammatory titles like Desmond Morris' **The Naked Ape**. Dull horror films sailed through to edify the Maltese; the genuine films were barred from entry. Towering intellectuals like Barbara Cartland were dissected by the literati. In short, Maltese Catholicism resembled the most dour and book-burning Calvinism. Burgess soon spoke up.

> Surely Malta's paternalism [Marie Said asked in a central question] has been a good thing — no drug addiction here, no sexual perversion, not much violence?

> We can eradicate any public evil we wish most efficiently [Burgess replied] if we employ dictatorial methods. The secret of government, as of private morality, is to balance

individual freedom of choice with what is considered to be a necessary apparatus of repression. Lead us not into temptation. But it's only to God that we pray so; it's not up to the State to keep away the occasions of sin. There should not be any protection at all; it's up to us as individuals to engage temptation, and try to conquer. That's what free will is about. Malta would try to do away with the concept of the Church Militant altogether and see this theocratic community as a trailer of the Church Triumphant. No fight against sin; no athletic struggle of the soul. Just the flabbiness of virtue achieved through sheer repression. If you can call such virtue virtue.[55]

In Malta, he finished his biography of Shakespeare and then prepared to go to Italy and Rome. At one point after he had left the island, he protested at the apparent confiscation of his Maltese home by the government. Unpaid taxes were evidently at the heart of the dispute; tax troubles, once they begin, entail a seemingly Sisyphean defense. He took on a series of teaching jobs at various American universities (North Carolina, City College, Princeton) for the money, and then entered the world of showbiz, publishing some novels on the side to keep his name before the public.

Pleasures of Showbiz

Screenwriters — this dark wisdom comes from John Gregory Dunne, himself a member of the tribe — are the niggers of the film industry. They have, as the phrase suggests, no real power to control the final product, what people in the industry call the picture. Ordered to commence work, often for a moderate/reasonable/extortionate fee, there is no guarantee whatever that the final picture, if any, will embody their labors. Other screenwriters may alter, amend, bowdlerize, and otherwise render null and void the work of the original author. What the author or authors have joined together, the *auteur* may put asunder. Finally, some modern Genghis Khan in the corporate suite may torpedo the whole project so that mere bubbles rise to the oily surface.

The history of Anthony Burgess in these treacherous waters is a fairly typical one; it has put money in his purse (but not a millionaire's amount) and done little to advance his literary reputation. The reasonable fees for the film rights and the moderate fees for the filmscripts of his **Enderby** and "Shakespeare" project ($25,000 for the latter) gave him his first (unaccustomed) year of affluence in 1968. Neither film has yet been produced, a fact which demonstrates that the celluloid Bitch Goddess continues to make her royal profligate progress in style. My own paperback copy of **Tremor of Intent** slyly reminds me, on the back cover, that it is SOON TO BE A MAJOR MOTION PICTURE. That boast was never fulfilled; and the book, which is eminently filmable, has never been filmed at all.

Burgess has also written screenplays of the lives of Moses ("The Lawgiver"), Michelangelo and Jesus Christ. "Fascinating in the first flush of writing, these have gradually become a bore, chiefly because of the need to defer to other people's conceptions of the projects, and the final, screened product will not be wholly mine."[56] All very true.

The remarkable thing is that, after the disillusioning experience with **A Clockwork Orange**, Burgess did any writing at all for the silver screen. Burgess wrote the book in 1961. It was first published in 1962 — and generally greeted with poor, disparaging, or worried and moralistic reviews. The anonymous genius of the **Times Literary Supplement** was a weary, blunt dictator superior to the whole artefact, and oblivious to its music — or its meaning:

> "A viscous verbiage . . . which is the swag-bellied offspring of decay . . . . English
> is being slowly killed by her practitioners." Lord Hailsham's lament might be applied
> to **A Clockwork Orange**, except that here the killing seems intentional. Mr. Burgess
> is an accomplished writer, who has set out, in the peculiar slang of 'nadsat', the
> autobiography of a teenager from fifteen to eighteen.[57]

And so on. The remainder of the review, a short thing, seems to be based on the blurb. Somehow, without any promotion or direction (certainly not on the part of Burgess) the book made its way up from obscurity in what is called the underground: chiefly American college students chortling away at a good read, who pass the book on to a buddy, etc. Years later Terry Southern, screenwriter and satirist ("Dr. Strangelove") gave a copy to Stanley Kubrick, who read it when he had finished his labors on **2001**.

Kubrick's first impression of the book was generous ("It seemed to me to be a unique and marvellous work of imagination and perhaps even genius") and so he set about the solemn business of obtaining the rights. His choice of subject is carefully considered ("I'm very, very careful about this . . . . A great narrative is a kind of miracle")[58] and shortly thereafter, in various fits and starts, the reading world had its first alarming look at the economics of one writer's trade.

Burgess, it seemed, had sold the rights to Mick Jagger of the Rolling Stones, with the wild and inimitable Mick intended for the starring role. Further, those who assumed that Burgess, ex-Catholic, ex-writer, was now edging his way into the debauched circle of the world's millionaires, were dead wrong. Burgess had reportedly sold the rights for the laughable sum of five hundred dollars.

The truth was less picturesque, but still a depressing spectacle for those who like to see authors make a legitimate profit from their work. Burgess' agent sold the rights to one of the film's executive producers, Si Litvinoff, for the still laughable sum of five hundred dollars. The edifying scenario when then unfolded is worthy of the talents of some future Balzac of the film industry. The film, released with much ballyhoo, much damned and much acclaimed, earned rental income of $15,400,000 from 1971 through January 1977. Burgess received, by way of ex-gratia payments, the additional staggering sum of $2,500.

The whole transaction raises some very interesting questions. Why did Burgess ("I needed the money") not sell the **option** rather than the rights? This course is, after all, the common procedure. A friend of mine, a novelist with a niggardly record of profits from his published works, and in most respects a man of advanced honor who detests the very idea of profits, meticulously confined the sale of his "property" to the option. His rigorous motto seems to be: bite the silver bullet, but keep the secondary rights.

Why Burgess did not do the same is a difficult question. Part of the answer appears to be that Burgess, son of a small shop-keeper, has reacted strongly against small shop-keeping element. He takes pride in his carelessness about the financial aspects of writing for a living. Burgess is also burdened with a very Catholic humility. Wilfrid Sheed was not very far wrong when he observed that

> "Humility is hammered perhaps a little too roughly into young Catholic skulls. I have known more promise gone to waste for want of a doting Jewish mother than history will ever hear about. After this boot training in self-abnegation, you may find that no matter how hard you come to believe in the secular world and what needs doing there, you will retain this reflex about yourself: I must not use it for my own glory — even if what it needs is my own glory."[59]

If Burgess had handled the issue with even a minimum regard for self-preservation, he would never have had to worry about money matters again. I suspect that this notion, if it has ever occurred to Burgess himself, has been dismissed out of hand. Perhaps not. It is hard to tell. He is sometimes bitter at the prospect of writing eight hours a day seven days a week; at other times he seems to consider this drudgery his reason for existence.

> There is no escape from me in the external world, or in drink or drugs. I had better start learning to live with myself. The only way I can live with myself, I find, is to justify my being here at all, and the way of justification is the way of work. I feel guilty when I am not writing, and so I do write.[60]

Burgess' response to Kubrick's film of **A Clockwork Orange** depended on circumstances. When he first saw it in the company of his wife and literary agent (who were all for walking out after ten minutes) his initial impression was one of fear. Early in 1972, soon after the film's introduction, he believed that its excellence derived from its faithful adherence to the book.[61]

At about the same time, he considered the film to be "technically brilliant, thoughtful, relevant, poetic, mind-opening" and observed that "What hurts me, as also Kubrick, is the allegation . . . that there is a gratuitous indulgence in violence which turns an intended homiletic work into a pornographic one . . . . It looks as though I must go through life as the fountain and origin of a great film, and as a man who has to insist against all opposition, that he is the most unviolent creature alive. Just like Stanley Kubrick."[62]

In about the middle of 1972, he edified the readers of **Rolling Stones** by observing that Mick Jagger was the original choice for the role of Alex. He records that he is pleased with the film but begins to sound more like *echt* Burgess — brisk, breezy, stoical at the deprivations of life:

> Apart from being gratified that my book has been filmed by one of the best living English-speaking producer-directors, instead of by some pornhound or pighead or other camera-carrying cretin, I cannot say that my life has been changed in any way by Stanley Kubrick's success. I seem to have less rather than more money, but I always seem to have less.[63]

Right. He also observed that "drug-taking was so much part of my scene that it automatically went into the book." The pertinent drugs are probably dexedrine and gin; it hardly needs to be added that gin and dexedrine have never by themselves, in isolation or baroque combination, written a good book.

At the same time, in mid-1972, he faced the issue of Kubrick's great financial reward from the film and his own trifling one. George Malko observed that "One of the practical consequences of the film is that Stanley Kubrick is being made very rich." Burgess' response is marked by a simplicity which verges, considering the disparity between his own reward and that of others, on an almost faultless magnanimity:

> And I'm not. We all entertain the dream of being rich sometimes and I'm fascinated by the thought that Kubrick himself is being made a millionaire by this film, literally a multi-millionaire without any doubt, because of the percentage of the gross he will take. I'm not envious of that. I daresay I will make a little from sales of the book, but what I make will be nugatory. I feel a curious sense of elation, or power, that a thing of mine can make money, that it can work in this big world which people take so seriously.[64]

That final sentence, it seems to me, strikes the authentic Catholic humble note, and the existence of this deep-seated trait is probably the best explanation for the existence of the disastrous contract. It is fair to say that anyone in this prayerful state of mind ('O Lord, I am not worthy'), who starts a negotiation so hobbled, will never be the J.P. Morgan of the literary world.

Still, there are reasonable limits to human magnanimity and even Catholic humility, and some time in 1972 a law suit was begun for the purpose of compelling Kubrick and probably Warner Brothers (I have not seen a record of the proceedings) to pay Burgess a more reasonable sum. The lawyers argued that the filmscript bore a remarkably close resemblance to the published book. The court decided in Burgess' favor, and he duly received a percentage, probably a very small percentage, of the total earnings.

In mid-1973, the first serious note of irritation entered Burgess' public discussion of the film. The newshounds, it can be assumed, were constantly on his trail and inviting him, known to be the source of good copy, to defend the film against the moralists who were attacking it on the ground that it was an incitement to, rather than a reflection of, the violence in society.

Burgess, who has confronted this argument many times in the course of his career, and who knows the arguments, both *pro and con,* backwards — was forced to advance across this no-man's land of wearying assertion again and again. If we ban the violence in books, we must ban many good books, beginning with much of the Old Testament, and many of the works of William Shakespeare (especially his **Titus Andronicus** — described in unexpurgated, gory detail later to the Maltese Library Association).

In any case life, not art, is responsible for the violence in art. He was personally sickened by the violence of **A Clockwork Orange** (an assertion made as early as 1964) but then, he had every right to be. It was *his* first wife who was assaulted and battered by American G.I. deserters in the course of World War II, and it was his wife who, as far as he could reasonably judge based on the medical evidence, suffered the aftereffects of that assault for years. The novel was intended as an exercise in charity, and a practical demonstration of the injunction to forgive thine enemies. Alternatively, he saw it as a "straightforward allegory — or a straightforward piece of homiletics — designed to show the importance of free will."[65]

In August 1973, beset by smuthounds and increasingly badgered by newshounds, he hit back with a cogent plea.

I think [Kubrick's film] is a remarkable work, and [it] is as truthful an interpretation of my own book as I could ever hope to find. But I am becoming increasingly exasperated by the assumption of guilt that it is my duty to defend the film against its attackers and not merely my book. It is surely the duty of the maker of the film to speak out for his own work. This may not be strictly relevant, but I am inevitably somewhat tired of the general assumption that **A Clockwork Orange** is the only book I have written. I'm the author of nearly 30 books and I should like some of these to come under attack or at least read.

Most of the statements I'm alleged by journalists to have made have in fact been distortions of what I have really said. This can be blamed on the difficulties of telephonic communications between Rome, where I live, and London. But it can chiefly be blamed on the scrambling apparatus which resides in the brains of so many journalists.[66]

In fact, Kubrick defended his work against one attacker, and argued, plausibly enough, that far from purveying the essence of fascism, the film worries about the new psychedelic fascism of eye-popping, multimedia, quadrasonic, drug-oriented conditioning of human beings by other human beings. That one defense done, he retired to his wife, children, dogs, computers, chess, and formidable reading list. He was presumably protected from an inquisitorial world by an impenetrable screen of accountants, lawyers, secretaries and myrmidons.

Then Kubrick did a strange thing. The object of friendly salutes from maestro Burgess ("To Stanley Kubrick: maestro di color" — dedication in **Napoleon Symphony**) who also observed that **Clockwork** sold a million copies in paperback "thanks to dear old Stanley," he published a book called **A Clockwork Orange**, a collection of stills from the film. He was dear old Stanley no more. Burgess, asked to review Kubrick's impertinence, resurrected the snarling young hoodlum, Alex deLarge, to make an unanswerable point on a question of simple human decency. The review, given here in full, must be one of the most remarkable in recorded literary history.

"Our starry droog [old friend] Kubrick the sinny veck [sinful man] has, my brothers, like brought forth from his like bounty and all that cal [shit] this kniggiwig, which is like all real horrorshow lomticks [marvellous pictures] from His Great Masterpiece [the film] which would make any fine upstanding young malchick smeck [boy laugh] from his yarbles and keeshkas [balls and guts]. What it is like is lashings of ultra-violence and the old in-out in-out, but not in slovos [words] except where the chellovecks [i.e. actors] are gavoreeting [talking] but in veshches [things: i.e. pictures] you can viddy [see] and not have to send the old gulliver to spatchka [head to sleep] with like being bored like when you are on your sharries [ass] in a biblio [library]. And you can like viddy [see] as well that the Great Purpose in his jeezny [life] which this veck Kubrick or Zubrick, that being the Arab eemya [name] for a grahzny veshch [dirty thing: the sense is surely that of 'dirty bastard'] is like now at last being made flesh and all that cal, was to have a Book. And now he has a Book. A Book he doth have, O my malenky [little] brothers, verily he doeth. A Book. Righty right. It was a book he did wish to like make, and he hath done it, Kubrick or Zubrick the Bookmaker. But, brothers, what makes me smeck like bezoomny [laugh like crazy] is that this like Book will tolchock out into the darkmans [throw out into the darkness] the Book what there like previously was, the one by F. Alexander or Sturgess [Burgess, of course] or some such eemya, because who would have slovos when he could viddy real jeezhny [see really clearly] with his nagoy glazzies [naked eyes]? And so it is like that. Righty right. And real horrorshow. And lashings of deng [cash] for the carmans [pockets] of Zubrick. And for your malenky droog not none no more. So gromky shooms [loud noises] of lip-music brrrrrr to thee and thine. And all that cal. — Alex [Anthony Burgess][67]

So Burgess, in his usual quiet way, addressed a Bronx cheer to the boy from the Bronx. Given the circumstances, flesh and blood could do no less.

* * * * * * * * * * * * *

Then, in the mid seventies, he moved to Monaco where banks take the place of boutiques, the dowagers play, cars growl like rutting beasts and the Chief of Police gave him a cheerfully sardonic greeting: "I know all about men of letters, Mr. Burgess. Be careful." So what does he do all day in the rich eye of the needle principality? admire the girls, visit the yachts of rich admirers, gourmandize in the cafes, spend lazy afternoons among the bougainvillaea waving a wicked cane? Not in the least. He grumbles and groans as he puffs on his Schimmelpenninck under the signed portrait of Sophia Loren in the land of bronzed taxdodgers.

> There's an exquisite appropriateness in the fact that *monaco* is the Italian for "monk."
> I have to stick to my cell in my hairy robe and painfully get on with the manuscripts.
> The roulette wheel spins, unheard by me. Crepes suzette and peches Melba are consumed in the Hotel de Paris, their home of origin. I hammer the keys, unseduced.
> I never thought the onset of old age would be like this. Now I see that for a writer who wasted too much time in his youth, the seven-day week and the twelve-hour day were inevitable. To be so engaged in a place given over to sloth and dissipation has its own piquancy.[68]

All of which is strangely reassuring, for Burgess lives and groans and agonizes still, and that should mean that the inimitable voice of Anthony Burgess will be heard from again, humble as he is. Humble? the devil you say? Oh, yes.

> **Interviewer**: Have you given any thought to your epitaph?
> **Burgess**: I've always been in love with a particular epitaph that may or may not be appropriate, but I'm determined to have it. You'll find it in the pseudo-Homeric poems, fragments of Greek poetry including an **Ode to Pan**: "Him the gods have made neither a digger nor a plowman, nor otherwise wise in ought, for he failed in every art."
> **Interviewer**: But you haven't.
> **Burgess**: Yes, I have. It's humble because it's true. We *do* fail if we attempt art. We're happier if we can do things like digging and plowing, just putting our hands to the ground, reaching Walden Pond. You can do that successfully because you have nature's help. But all artists fail.
> **Interviewer**: That's a rather sad note on which to end.
> **Burgess**: The sadness is in **life**. One loves life regardless of its sadness, perhaps because of it. It's summed up in a line by Virgil: "*Sunt lacrimae rerum; et mentem mortalia tangunt.*" (There are tears in things and all things doomed to die touch the heart.) What one loves about life are the things that fade. It's a sense of things passing — so regretful, regretful — of things being beautiful and yet mortal, that makes life worth living.[69]

Notes

1. Seymour-Smith, Martin. **Funk & Wagnalls Guide to Modern World Literature**. New York: Funk & Wagnalls, 1973, p. 303.
2. Burgess, Anthony. "You've Had Your Time: Being the Beginning of an Autobiography." **Malahat Review**, no. 44 (1977) pp. 11-12.
3. Ibid., p. 11.
4. Burgess, Anthony. **On Going to Bed**. New York: Abbeville Press, 1982, pp. 19-20.
5. Burgess, Anthony. "Don't Cook Mother Goose." **New York Times Book Review**, 5 November 1967, p. 1.
6. Burgess, Anthony. **Enderby**. New York: Norton, 1968, p. 26.
7. Lewis, Anthony. "I Love England, But I Will No Longer Live There." **New York Times Magazine**, 3 November 1968, p. 64.
8. Burgess, Anthony. "You've Had Your Time." **Malahat Review**, no. 44 (1977) p. 12.

9. Burgess, Anthony. "Pourquoi nous aimons les usurpateurs." **Paris-Match**, no. 1680 (August 7, 1981) 14.

10. Burgess, Anthony. "On Being a Lapsed Catholic." **Triumph**, v. 2, no. 2 (February 1967) 31.

11. Burgess, Anthony. IN **The God I Want**. Ed. by James Alexander Hugh Mitchell. London: Constable; Indianapolis: Bobbs-Merrill, 1967, p. 57.

12. Burgess, Anthony. "Silence, Exile and Cunning." **Listener**, v. 73, no. 1884 (May 6, 1965) 662.

13. Burgess, Anthony. "Lore and Disorder." **Spectator**, v. 222, no. 7347 (April 18, 1969) 512.

14. Burgess, Anthony. "On Being a Lapsed Catholic." **Triumph**, v. 2, no. 2 (February 1967) 31.

15. Burgess, Anthony. "Woman and Women." **Vogue**, v. 154 (October 1, 1966) 262.

16. Burgess, Anthony. "Dr. Rowse Meets Dr. Faustus." **Nation**, v. 200 (February 1, 1965) 117.

17. Burgess, Anthony. "Letter from Europe." **American Scholar**, v. 38, no. 4 (Autumn 1969) 685.

18. Burgess, Anthony. **Re Joyce**. New York: Norton, 1965, p. 18.

19. Burgess, Anthony. **Enderby**. New York: Norton, 1968, p. 24.

20. Burgess, Anthony. **Vision of Battlements**. New York: Norton, 1966, p. 27.

21. Burgess, Anthony. **On Going to Bed**. New York: Abbeville Press, 1982, p. 43.

22. Malko, George. "**Penthouse** Interview: Anthony Burgess." **Penthouse**, v. 3, no. 10 (June 1972) 116.

23. "**Playboy** Interview: Anthony Burgess." **Playboy**, v. 21, no. 9 (September 1974) 70.

24. Malko, George. "**Penthouse** Interview," p. 118.

25. Burgess, Anthony. "Private Dialect of Husbands and Wives." **Vogue**, v. 151 (June 1968) 118.

26. Ibid., p. 119.

27. Lois H. Fisher. **A Literary Gazeteer of England**. New York: McGraw-Hill, 1981, p. 22.

28. Burgess, Anthony. "The Emigrants: Malaya." **Punch**, v. 254, no. 6666 (June 12, 1968) 852.

29. Burgess, Anthony. "The Emigrants," p. 852.

30. Burgess, Anthony. "The Emigrants," pp. 853-54.

31. Burgess, Anthony. "The Emigrants," pp. 853-854.

32. Burgess, Anthony. "Powers that Be." **Encounter**, v. 24, no. 1 (January 1965) 71-76.

33. Burgess, Anthony. "Genesis and Headache," IN **Afterwords; Novelists on Their Novels**. Ed. by Thomas McCormack. New York: Harper, 1968, p. 57.

34. Burgess, Anthony. "Corruption of the Exotic." **Listener**, v. 70, no. 1800 (September 26, 1963) 465.

35. Burgess, Anthony. "Singapore Revisited." **Spectator**, v. 224, no. 7406 (June 6, 1970) 742.

36. Letter to author dated June 25, 1978.

37. Burgess, Anthony. **On Going to Bed**, p. 70-71.

38. Burgess, Anthony. "Anthony Burgess — On Being a Lancashire Catholic." **Listener**, v. 96, no. 2477 (September 30, 1976) 397.

39. Burgess, Anthony. "Poetry in a Tiny Room." **Yorkshire Post**, 16 May 1963, p. 4.

40. Burgess, Anthony. "Letter from England." **Hudson Review**, v. 20, no. 3 (Autumn 1967) 454.

41. Burgess, Anthony. Letter from England." **Hudson Review**, v. 19, no. 3 (Autumn 1966) 456.

42. Burgess, Anthony. "London Letter." **Hudson Review**, v. 20, no. 2 (Spring 1967) 99-100.

43. "**Playboy** Interview: Anthony Burgess." **Playboy**, v. 21, no. 9 (September 1974) 70.

44. Burgess, Anthony. "Letter from England." **Hudson Review**, v. 20, no. 3 (Autumn 1967) 454-58.

45. Burgess, Anthony. "Views." **Listener**, v. 79, no. 2032 (March 7, 1968) 295.

46. Burgess, Anthony. "Foreword." IN **Anthony Burgess: A Bibliography**, by Paul Boytinck. [Norwood, Pa.] : Norwood Editions, 1977, pp. viii-ix.

47. Lewis, Anthony. "I Love England, But I Will no Longer Live There." **New York Times Magazine**, 3 November 1968, p. 64.

48. Burgess, Anthony. "Review of **The Profession of English Letters**," by J.W. Saunders. **Listener**, v. 72, no. 1862 (December 3, 1964) 896.

49. Burgess, Anthony. "Letter to a Tax Man." **Manchester Guardian**, 28 December 1966, p. 12.

50. Burgess, Anthony. "**Spectator** Symposium." **Spectator**, v. 217, no. 7205 (July 29, 1966) 138.

51. Burgess, Anthony. "**Spectator** Symposium on 1968." **Spectator**, v. 219 (December 29, 1967) 804.

52. Burgess, Anthony. "London Letter." **American Scholar**, v. 37, no. 4 (Autumn 1968) 647.

53. Burgess, Anthony. "London Letter." **American Scholar**, v. 37, no. 4 (Autumn 1968) 647.

54. Quoted in Lewis, Anthony. "I Love England, But I Will No Longer Live There." **New York Times Magazine**, 3 November 1968, p. 39.

55. Said, Marie. "Anthony Burgess Interviewed by Marie Said." **Sunday Times of Malta**, 7 June 1970.

56. Burgess, Anthony. "Foreword." In Boytinck, Paul. **Anthony Burgess: A Bibliography**. Norwood, Pa.: Norwood Editions, 1977, p. vii.

57. Anon. Review of **A Clockwork Orange**. **Times Literary Supplement**, 25 May 1962, p. 377.

58. Houston, Penelope. "Kubrick Country." **Saturday Review**, v. 44, no. 52 (December 25, 1971) 42 + .

59. Sheed, Wilfrid. "The Politician as Professor." IN **The Morning After: Selected Essays and Reviews.** New York: Farrar, Straus & Giroux, c1971, p. 129.

60. Burgess, Anthony. "Letter from Europe." **American Scholar**, v. 41, no. 1 (Winter 1971-72) 139-42.

61. "Anthony Burgess: The Author of **A Clockwork Orange** Now Switches His Attention to Napoleon's Stomach." **Publishers Weekly**, v. 201 (January 31, 1972) 182-183.

62. Burgess, Anthony. "Clockwork Marmalade." **Listener**, v. 87, no. 2238 (February 17, 1972) 199.

63. Burgess, Anthony. "Juice from **A Clockwork Orange**." **Rolling Stone**, no. 110 (June 8, 1972) 52-53.

64. Malko, George. "**Penthouse** Interview: Anthony Burgess." **Penthouse**, v. 3, no. 10 (June 1972) 83.

65. Malko, George. "**Penthouse** Interview: Anthony Burgess." **Penthouse**, v. 3, no. 10 (June 1972) 83.

66. "Burgess, Originator of 'Clockwork,' Says 'Let Kubrick Defend Film'." **Variety**, v. 272 (August 1973) 2.

67. Burgess, Anthony. "Burgess on Kubrick on 'Clockwork'." **Library Journal**, v. 98, no. 9 (May 1, 1973) 1506.

68. Burgess, Anthony. "Saturday Review: Outlooks." **Saturday Review**, v. 5, no. 14 (April 15, 1978) 96.

69. "**Playboy** Interview: Anthony Burgess." **Playboy**, v. 21, no. 9 (September 1974) 86.

Preface

This guide, intended for the reader, student and scholar, has three different purposes: 1) to give some idea of the critical reception of Burgess' fiction and non-fiction; 2) to convey some notion of the range of his literary and journalistic output; and 3) to provide an account of the scholarly writings about Burgess in both journals and books.

The scope of the work extends from the year 1956 (when Burgess published his **Time for a Tiger**) to roughly the end of the year 1981. To my regret, some items have so far escaped the bibliographical net, and I am aware of the following gaps. First, Burgess' contributions to his college paper entitled **The Serpent** were not recorded. I have also been unable to find his published contributions in **Queen.** Finally, it is my impression that Burgess published some incidental pieces in Malaya. Any of his readers who would like to remedy these gaps for inclusion in a later, more definitive edition, are invited to send me the material so that the **lacunae** can be made good.

A word about the annotations is in order. They are, for the most part, reasonably dispassionate; and I have tried, in order to convey the nuances and emphases of the reviewer or critic, to adopt the diction of the reviewer or critic concerned. The syntax, necessarily more compressed, is of course my own. When the quoted text has included errors, I have generally preferred bracketed corrections to the censorious 'sic.' Occasional editorial comments are few. When they occur, the material is put in brackets as well. I have tried, when the reviewer has advanced an argument (not simply a plot summary) to convey the salient points of his or her case. In general, when the annotation consists chiefly of a quotation, or set of quotations, it should be assumed that these passages represent the fair, full and complete views of the author. If there are depths which cannot well be conveyed by a conventional annotation, the fact is noted as part of an editorial comment.

The arrangement, partially suggested by the work of Jeutonne Brewer, has been chosen to suit the needs of both students and scholars. The first part of the work, which relates the critical reception of Burgess' work from **Abba Abba** to **The Worm and the Ring** is in alphabetical order; there is, in other words, no necessity to consult either the Table of Contents or the Index. On the other hand, Burgess' essays, and the labor of the scholars, have been put in chronological order. This arrangement will please some and displease others. Ultimately, some choices must be made. It is probable that the only really useful arrangement is one which the user can define to a computer which jumps instantaneously at every command. Until that happy day comes, judgments and sacrifices must be made.

Finally, here are some miscellaneous comments. Burgess' manuscripts are deposited in the Mills Memorial Library, McMaster University, in Hamilton, Ontario, Canada. They are all without exception scrupulously neat examples of professional typescript without any Balzacian intercalations in margin, gutter or verso. I am not aware of any depository collections of letters and other biographical material of any kind. If any of my readers would care to acquaint me of their existence, the information will be gratefully noted and duly acknowledged in a later edition.

My gratitude extends to the following individuals and institutions: Mr. Wendell Smith, Provost, Bucknell University, for his generous support of this work; Susan Schmertz for her always cheerful assistance; Marge Heine of the Freas-Rooke Computer Center for guiding me through the intricacies of the CP-6 processor; the librarians at Bucknell, Ron Daniels, George Jenks, Helena Rivoire, Mary Jane Stoneburg, for bringing yet another delightful addition to my attention; the librarians at Penn State for their helpfulness, patience and forbearance; the librarians of the Library of Congress for their kind permission to browse in the stacks at will (those in the Newspaper Division must be among the most harried people in the profession); Marie Said, formerly of the Malta Library Association; Professors Geoffrey Aggeler and Samuel Coale; the editor of the **Yorkshire Post**; Anu Manu and Lynn Betts of the University of Alberta; Michael Kryzytski for some help with *nadsat*; Sherry Brooks of Media Services; James Muchler and Peggy Harris of Administrative Services. Still, in the last analysis, a bibliographer owes most to other bibliographers, and it is a compulsory duty and corresponding pleasure to record my many debts to Jeutonne Brewer, Beverly R. David, Carlton Holte, Jean E. Kennard, Wallace Coyle (bibliographer of Stanley Kubrick), and Samuel Coale. Finally, my thanks to Anthony Burgess for clearing up some biographical questions in the *Ratskeller* of the Nittany Lion Inn and talking with his usual fine candor.

Abba Abba

1 London: Faber and Faber, 1977.

2 Boston: Little, Brown, 1977.

3 London: Corgi Books, 1979. Pbk.

Reviews

4 Adams, Phoebe-Lou. Review of **Abba Abba**. **Atlantic**, v. 243, no. 4 (April 1979) 99.

"The novella about the doomed and resentful Keats is poignantly convincing. The appended translations from Belli (also by Mr. Burgess, although he chooses to pretend otherwise) produce a curious effect. Their content is antitheological and, because there is simply no English equivalent for Belli's Roman street argot, their style suggests Byron trying, with no great success, to talk Cockney."

5 Amis, Martin. "A?" **New Statesman**, v. 93, no. 2413 (June 17, 1977) 821-22.

Burgess distinguished (in **Joysprick**) between the "A" novelist who emphasizes character, motive, moral argument and the "B" novelist who values wit, ideas and language. This work is an appropriate mixture of "A" and "B". The title refers to this division as well as others [examples given]. Belli's sonnets in the second "B" part of the book, despite their much plugged earthiness and scurrility, are not much fun to read. Worse, the rhymes are impossibly lazy. In the first "A" part Burgess falls into some obvious traps. There are crassnesses, startling indecorums of speech and an awful, insistent lustiness supposedly characteristic of the age as well as a tendency to present writers as unrelenting epigrammatists. But the book's principal gamble, the description of the death of Keats, pays off handsomely.

6 Anon. "Fiction." London **Times**, 2 June 1977, p. 9.

[Plot summary which probably profits from Ricks's review in the **Sunday Times** (London). See #18.] "It is an ingenious, allusive book, but those who lack the patience or the appetite for this slightly self-indulgent kind of literary codebreaking may find themselves baffled and unmoved, overawed by the pyrotechnics but guiltily wondering exactly what they are all in aid of."

7 Anon. Notice of **Abba Abba**. **Observer** (London), 26 June 1977, p. 29.

"Ingenious and exuberant invention about Keats's dying days in Rome, full of Burgess's usual linguistic bounciness." [Complete text of notice.]

8 Anon. Review of **Abba Abba**. **Publishers Weekly**, (January 29, 1979) 112.

An extravagant and preposterous confection which shows off Burgess' quirky brilliance at its peak. "Exactly what the English poet has to do with the Roman poet, critically speaking, is a puzzle that could provide hours of literary speculation for the curious and the able. The genre here is tour de force — a dazzling display of all Burgess's tricks packed into a very few pages. This is a centaur of a book, so strange and wonderful that a lesser writer than Anthony Burgess could maintain his reputation on it alone."

9 Anon. Notice of **Abba Abba**. **Observer** (London), 25 February 1979, p. 37.

A virtuoso performance which weaves an exuberant fantasia around the dying days of Keats.

10 Anon. Review of **Abba Abba**. **Booklist**, v. 75, no. 18 (May 15, 1979) 1419.

[Review signed EB.] The sly title of this little entertainment refers to Christ's cry on the cross (Abba = father in Aramaic] and the octave of a Petrarchan sonnet. "The two poets [Keats and Belli] unknowingly share the realization that the sonnet form transcends language and might indeed be conceptualized as a construct of deity in its universal power. The second half of the book consists of, significantly, 69 of Belli's 2,279 sonnets about Roman life, in Roman dialect. . . [and] the exuberant, blasphemous cleverness of the sonnets does not save them from ultimate dullness, but they preserve a vision of Rome's earthy lower strains that should be heard. As an entertainment, the Burgess project is certainly worth a quick read, and Keats dying is always a moving set piece."

11 Anon. Review of **Abba Abba. Choice**, v. 16, no. 4 (June 1979) 526.

"Both Keats and Belli, in Burgess' projection, are akin in that each is torn between the need to conform to a prosy morality and an instinctive irreverence and earthiness. In the second part of these imaginary conversations. . . [Burgess] translates into English some of Belli's sonnets. The translations, on the whole, show that the language of the original is, indeed, untranslatable. Belli's irreverent and blasphemous treatment of sacred matters does not shock an English-speaking reader as it must have a Roman living in the shadow of St. Peter's. Burgess's idea is ingenious, but it suffers in the sketchy performance. One wonders, too, if the imaginary encounter is little more than a pretext for offering a set of translations."

12 Bromwich, David. "John Keats Meets Giuseppe Belli." **New York Times Book Review**, 29 April 1979, p. 14.

[Review of paperback ed.] The agnostic Keats while briefly in Rome during 1820-21, buoyed only by his faith in the holiness of the heart's affections surely did not die, as Shelley and Byron suggested, merely of his critics' venom. Burgess' fondness for Keats's poem on Mrs. Reynold's cat takes us from the narrative to the sonnets. "The sonnets are pretty bad, and there is no getting around them. Any quick or cunning reader, however, will find some way to stop short of them, aided by bold reconnaisance and word-of-mouth report." The portrait of Keats is witty, facile, allusive and unimpressed by the loftiness of a poet's life. The book has a beguiling archness not refined into tedium. Burgess will perhaps produce a sequel called CDCDCD which will return Keats to London.

13 Driver, C.J. "Dying to be Told." **Manchester Guardian Weekly**, 12 June 1977, p. 12.

[Omnibus review.] "The death of Keats is most movingly recorded, the idiocy of his treatment (starvation and blood-letting) savagely seen; the contradiction in Belli's sensibility convincing; and yet one feels the novel could have been bigger . . . . Burgess. . . has more talent in his little toe than most of our contemporaries in their carcases; and yet one has a sense that his witty intelligence restrains him from the novels he is capable of."

14 Enright, D.J. "Junkets." **Listener**, v. 97, no. 2511 (June 2, 1977) 729-30.

"A book by Anthony Burgess, fictional or otherwise and **Abba Abba** is both) is likely to be tricky — and harsh almost to desperation, moving and funny." Gives examples of the book's word-play, both playful and painful. Speculates if J.J. Wilson of part II can be related to J.B. Wilson [i.e. Burgess] and concludes: "There can be small doubt that Anthony Burgess is the father of this enlivening and distressing little book."

15 Hilts, Philip J. Review of **Abba Abba. Washington Post Book World**, 4 March 1979, p. 75.

[Review of paperback ed.] In this short book Burgess deftly exposes the holy and unholy parts of man and how they might fuse to make a modern philosophy. The atheistical Keats meets the blasphemous Belli and together they suggest a "compound of blasphemy and belief that is a good tonic for his, and our own pessimism about the modern world."

16 Morgan, Edwin. "The Thing's the Thing." **Times Literary Supplement**, 3 June 1977, p. 669.

An entertaining and thought-provoking work based on the speculation that Keats might have met the Roman poet Belli. The characterization of Keats is somewhat sympathetic but not wholly convincing. In any case, Burgess' real interest lies in his convictions that the nature-loving English Romantic poets forgot how to think in their worship of truth and beauty, and that they could also have benefited from some down-to-earth immediacy. Burgess initiates some interesting trains of thought; he does not, however, pursue them very far. The translations of Belli's poems are pungent and ingenious. "They are coarser than the Scots versions of Robert Garioch, and one word is so fucking pervasive as to become wearisome. They are much tighter. . . than the American versions by Harold Norse." The translator is, of course, Burgess himself.

17 Paulin, Tom. "Incorrigibly Plural; Recent Fiction." **Encounter**, v. 49, no. 4 (October 1977) 82-85.

A subtle and remarkable novella in which the normal laws of time are unobtrusively suspended. It is marked by a mythic dimension, an absence of sentimentality, and an insistence on the monistic relation between mind and coarse matter (see, for example, the low tavern debauchery) that recalls the later poetry of W.B. Yeats. But Burgess is able to fuse Keats's emphatic awareness of the grossly physical within his essentially religious point of view. Note, for example, Belli's meditation on the platonic idea of the sonnet form and Keats's dying vision of Christ on the cross. The complex fusion of suffering, prayer, art and grossness "justifies his title which isn't an example of merely tricksy punning, but an absolutely appropriate naming of his subject. If the translation of some of Belli's sonnets which Burgess adds as a coda to his story are disappointing, **Abba Abba** is nevertheless a brilliant achievement, the work of a wise and subtle visionary."

18 Ricks, Christopher. "The Abracadabra Man." **Sunday Times** (London), 26 May 1977, p. 41.

[Interesting review. Inset biographical sketch claims Burgess was in the Far East during his army days. Not true: England and Gibraltar.] Genuine blasphemy is Burgess' serious concern. Witness the title: the rhyme scheme of the octave in a Petrarchan sonnet, the Aramaic for 'father' **and** the initials of Burgess himself. T.S. Eliot has said that blasphemy, as impossible to the complete atheist as to the genuine Christian, is a way of affirming belief. "What lifts it above being a sly tract is not just the affectionate warmth with which it calls up Keats. . . but its central imaginative decision: that the only way to make blasphemy genuine and real today is to move it away from religion to something else that has stayed sacred; in this case, poetry and particularly the lives of the poets . . . . A slim, robust volume, it fascinatingly combines so many of the things which most matter to Burgess: his sardonic love of England and Italy, his verbal exuberance devoted to great writers, and his unorthodox religious urgency."

19 Scheider, Rupert. "A Small Brilliance." **Canadian Forum**, v. 57 (March 1978) 34.

In any assessment of the major influences on the Modern Novel the same ten names (Nabokov, Graham Greene, Waugh, Powell, Patrick White, Bellow, Iris Murdoch, Mailer, Updike and Pynchon) would occur on most lists. Others (William Burroughs, Philip Toynbee, John Hawkes and Jerzy Kosinski) would warrant discussion for their experiments. Burgess should, by right, belong in the first group. It is the notoriety of the filmed version of **A Clockwork Orange**, as well as the diversity of his output, that "have prejudiced assessment and even prevented his being taken seriously." Provides a biographical sketch of Burgess for Canadian readers and gives synopses of his works. In Burgess' 38th book "Parallels are established between Keats and Belli: their youth, enjoyment of word-play and bawdry, anticlerical skepticism, an obsession with the relation between truth, naked brute fact, and beauty, and their fascination with the sonnet." Unfortunately, while Burgess' translations of Belli's sonnets are more inventive and entertaining (and include more ingenious rhymes) than the translations of Harold Norse, his latest book "results not so much from a need 'to express a fictional idea that **demands** incarnation' as from Burgess' innate curiosity and darting inventiveness. As a result it hasn't the formal brilliance of his **Malayan Trilogy, A Clockwork Orange, MF**, and **Napoleon Symphony**; but, ingenious, witty, suggestive, it has a small brilliance of its own. Unfortunately, however, it will do nothing to convince the skeptic that Burgess is not just a literary 'dandy,' but a contributor of primary importance."

20 Scott, Paul. "Kaiser Bill Reassessed." **Country Life**, v. 161, no. 4174 (June 30, 1977) 1849-50.

[Omnibus review.] The title of the book may suggest some Nabokovian fun and games. "The story of the dying Keats, which occupies just 84 of the beautifully written 127 pages of this interesting exercise in marrying fact and fiction, may be the best thing Burgess has so far done. I found it immensely exciting and infinitely moving, memorable. The translations of Belli's sonnets, which come at the end, are rumbustiously elegant — which sounds like a contradiction in terms but here is not because the language is perfectly modulated to accommodate both the beauty of the rhythms and the splendid coarseness of the images."

21 Thwaite, Anthony. "Galloping Consumption." **Observer** (London), 29 May 1977, p. 28.

Novels based on fanciful history normally leave him cold; this one is different. It is different and attractive by virtue of the possessed imagination behind it, "an exuberant and almost self-exploding blend of pedantry and poetry." The portrait of Keats — feverishly fanciful, mercurial, glowing with excitement, verbal hyperaesthesia and terminal consumption — is marvellously authentic. A good deal of it seems to be based on Robert Gitting's biography of the poet. "This is altogether a fascinating, eccentric, thoroughly self-indulgent venture by an inventive and unclassifiable genius."

22 Williams, David. "Paperbacks: Pick of the Month." **Punch**, v. 276, no. 7225 (April 4, 1979) 600.

Burgess dwells much on Keats's bold, frustrated sexuality. "This near-death-mask portrait is done with all Burgess's exuberance and verbal virtuosity — and he lays much fuller claim than Gittings, of course, on the biographer's right to guess. Undoubtedly here he justifies this claim. But Burgess, with all his gifts, never seems willing to give us tenderness, and tenderness needs to come into this somewhere. [Belli's] bawdy sonnets, seventy-odd of them, come at the end. Some are witty; some would go down well at an intellectual rugger-man's Saturday-night sing-song. Too many of them though."

The Age of the Grand Tour

23 London: Elek, 1967.

24 New York: Crown, 1967.

[A selection of extracts from 18th century travellers. Includes an introduction by Burgess on pp. 13-32. The full title of this elephant folio (35 x 49 cm.) reads: "The Age of the grand tour: containing sketches of the manners, society and customs of France, Flanders, the United Provinces, Germany, Switzerland and Italy in the letters, journals and writings of the most celebrated voyagers between the years 1720 and 1820, with descriptions of the most illustrious antiquities and curiosities in these countries, together with the story of such traffic / by Anthony Burgess, and an appreciation of the art of Europe in the eighteenth century, by Francis Haskell.]

Translations

25 French: **Le grand siecle de voyage**. Paris: Michel, 1968. Translated by Nicole Rey, Huguette Perrin and Gloria de Cherisey.

26 Italian: **La bella Europa**. Rome: Editalia, 1970. Translated by Francisco Mei.

Reviews

27 Anon. Notice of **The Age of the Grand Tour. Wall Street Journal**, 4 December 1967, p. 20.

"Anyone who has taken a package tour of Europe will be interested to know that, in the eighteenth and nineteenth centuries, our ancestors had a far better idea." [Complete text of notice.]

28 Anon. Review of **The Age of the Grand Tour. New Yorker**, v. 43, no. 40 (December 9, 1967) 246.

The gargantuan scale of the book is justified by its purpose of providing a series of brief and playful yet instructive glimpses of the Grand Tour. "Anthony Burgess has contributed a characteristically racy historical introduction (on the subject of Voltaire's willingness to speak English, Boswell turns out to be better informed than Burgess) and Francis Haskell learnedly places the painters for us."

29 Anon. "Big Books of '67 — Sumptuous and Serious." **Newsweek**, v. 70, no. 24 (December 11, 1967) 105.

"Opened up it's a yard wide. It has triple endpapers and the pages are made of stock almost heavy enough for the walls of a Japanese house. On them you will find. . . a sumptuous record of the great age of travel in Europe, the century between 1720 and 1820 . . . . Splendid introductory essays by Burgess and Haskell launch your three-star jaunt across the Continent."

30 Anon. Review of **The Age of the Grand Tour. Time**, v. 90, no. 24(December 15, 1967) 112.

"For size, sumptuosity, style and snob appeal, this resplendent volume wins any 1967 publishers' award for conspicuous good taste . . . . Avoiding today's exhaustive and exhausting travel writing, this volume combines 18th century illustrations with prose from the past." Burgess contributes a splendidly evocative preface.

31 Anon. "Milord Abroad." **Times Literary Supplement**, 8 February 1968, p. 131.

"To call this a handsome book would be a puny use of language . . . . Mr. Burgess's essay gives an adequate but somewhat arch review of the Europe that a well-found English traveller would have discovered in the 1670s . . . . Indeed most of the extracts, which fill the bulk of the text, hardly support the stereotype of the English *milord*, vacuously enjoying his extensive journey, acquiring inferior Italian pictures, and basking in the sunshine and social life. Sterne, Boswell, Gibbon, Smollett, Shelley, Hazlitt, Arthur Young, were travellers indeed, but their purses hardly bulged, and they do not correspond at all to the semi-educated gentleman of leisure apostrophized by Mr. Burgess."

32 Canaday, John. "Journey by Diligence." **New York Times Book Review**, 3 December 1967, p. 62.

Hazlitt remarked that travellers must take their common sense along, and leave their prejudices behind. The advice is still sound today. "Hazlitt's companions are a distinguished list that includes Boswell in a fawning and gossipy letter written to Rousseau from Italy; Smollett, 'troubled with an asthmatic cough, spitting, slow fever, and restlessness,' and hence not too happy on a tour of France, where he hated everything, including the food, and supplied a set of crotchety Tourist Tips for anyone foolish enough to get into the same situation; Madame de Stael, reporting on Germany and Austria, with her appreciation rising and falling in accord with the status of local respect of female intellectuals; Shelley on Pompeii; Goethe on the beauty of the Venetian islands and Byron on the opportunities for amorous adventures in the city itself." The illustrators could hardly be bettered. Combined with an introduction by Anthony Burgess, the letters and journal extracts vividly evoke the look and feel of their century.

33 Ford, Brinsley. Review of **The Age of the Grand Tour**. **Burlington Magazine**, v. 110 (August 1968) 470-71.

The introduction by Burgess is extremely lively and light-hearted, and it is clear that he would have made a delightful cicerone for someone more interested in literature than the arts. His sketch of the impressions that Voltaire and Rousseau made on their contemporaries is brilliant. His treatment of Italy and Rome is less successful, and when he falls back on the expedient of inventing a dialogue between two imaginary Englishmen, the attention wilts away. "In justice to Mr. Burgess it must be said that he has succeeded in recapturing much of the spirit of the Grand Tour, and the fact that he has approached his subject with the care-free, and sometimes capricious, attitude of a Beckford or a Byron, rather than with the single-minded zeal of a Winckelmann, has undoubtedly added a great deal of sparkle and an element of the unexpected to his essay."

34 Honour, Hugh. "Too Much of a Bad Thing." **Observer** (London), 8 October 1967, p. 26.

The grand tour was both the final stage of an Englishman's education, and a male initiation ceremony. The subtitle of this work has as many escape clauses as an insurance policy. The works selected (from Smollett, Boswell, Gibbon, the Beckfords, Goethe) are well known, not to say hackneyed. The illustrations, while well done, are occasionally off the point; and there is not a single reproduction of an antique statue. "The essay on the grand tour by Mr. Burgess is quite astonishingly ill-informed. His remarks on Bologna — where, he fondly supposes, the eighteenth-century traveller would 'take a rest from art' are alone enough to demonstrate his ignorance. Indeed, his contribution is of a naivety equalled only by that of the editors . . . ." In any case, it does not really matter; the book is surely too much of a bulky bundle for mere humans to read.

35 Levey, Michael. "Extensive View." **Studio International**, v. 175 (March 1968) 155.

Burgess' rambling, semi-facetious essay incorporates a device of paralysing ineffectiveness. "Somehow, the references to Hemingway in Venice and modern charter flights come more patly than suggestions that without the Grand Tour there would be no Adelphi (a somewhat unfortunate phrase, since the Adelphi no longer exists) and 'perhaps none of the influences of Palladio.' May Inigo Jones forgive Mr. Burgess; nobody else can." The eighteenth century Italy Burgess sees ("vinous, laughing, drenched in colour and song") is precisely *not* the Italy seen by English eighteenth-century travellers.

36 Perreault, John. "More Big 1967 Books." **Nation**, v. 205, no. 22 (December 25, 1967) p. 697.

"Its theme is set in an essay by Anthony Burgess that recreates without sentiment the sentimental journey through the Continent considered obligatory for the would-be English gentleman of the 18th century . . . . It is an extravagant book, totally unnecessary; but it will impress and delight both the extremely literate and the quasi-literate, the seasoned Continental gadabout, as well as the armchair traveler."

37 Rea, Robert. Review of **The Age of the Grand Tour**. **Library Journal**, v. 93, no. 1 (January 1, 1968) 77.

"For the connoisseur and lover of great, handsome, expensive books, this volume provides a treasure trove of scenes, both verbal and visual, of a Europe long disappeared."

38 Vansittart, Peter. "On the Hoof." **Spectator**, v. 219, no. 7279 (December 29, 1967) 815.

"One can extract entertaining snippets, about fairs, transport, holy relics, temptations, Genoese galley-slaves, disgusting hotels, great men behaving abominably, the Venetian state encouraging gambling (to get foreign currency), Madame de Stael's views on German women, Italian operagoers wearing hats, so as to be able to doff them to royalty, the 'excruciating cacophany' of papal castrati (Stendhal) French landlords offering 'an abundance of dirt and the most flagrant imposition' (Smollett)." It is a book with a mildly entertaining historical veneer.

Beard's Roman Women

39 London: Hutchinson, 1976.

40 New York: McGraw-Hill, 1976.

Translations

41 Spanish: **Llueve en Roma**. Buenos Aires: Emece Editores, 1977. Translated by Anibal Leal.

Reviews

41.5 Burgess on his own work: "That novel was written on commission. I didn't want to write it, but a young Bostonian had some very good photographs of Rome and came to me and said to me, would I write some text to go with his photos? I said yes. I couldn't write a text of the kind he wanted, and said: 'Let's see if we can combine fiction and photographs.' I must have been lacking in inventiveness at the time, so I fell back more than ever I would normally on the facts of my own life. I had been greatly disturbed in 1968, when my first wife died, with certain psychic phenomena, or psychological phenomena — I don't know what one really calls them — in which I was aware that this wife of mine had not really died and was still there." **Listener**, v. 96, no. 2477 (September 30, 1976) 399. Later, not to leave a critical stone unturned: "Incidentally, I recently published in the United States a short novel which I wished to subtitle 'a novelette.' Unsure of the propriety of this (the publishers were totally sure of the impropriety), I looked up *novelette* in this volume [**A Supplement to the Oxford English Dictionary**, v. 2] and found that A. Burgess said (1967) that 'novelette' disparages not only length but content. I think the description would have served." **Times Literary Supplement**, no. 3897 (November 19, 1976) 1443.

42 Adams, Phoebe-Lou. Review of **Beard's Roman Women**. **Atlantic**, v. 238, no. 4 (October 1976) [114].

Burgess devotes his awesome powers of invention to the creation of disasters. "Somewhere at the base of all the eerie farce is an idea about the various and insufficient forms taken by masculine love, but it is the clatter of incident and the suprising and amusing use of language that carry the tale."

43 Anon. Review of **Beard's Roman Women**. **Kirkus Reviews**, July 1, 1976, pp. 747-48.

[Chiefly plot summary.] Concludes: "It's been a clever performance but fades out quickly."

44 Anon. Review of **Beard's Roman Women**. **Publishers Weekly**, v. 210, no. 3 (July 19, 1976) 130.

A minor feast of cryptic fun based on the myth of Orpheus and Eurydice. The drunken Gregson is a conductor of souls to the underworld. "The story is short and rather slight, but it's certainly interesting, also, in some measure, suspenseful, and there's a scene in which Beard is raped by some modern Bacchantes that's a delight."

45 Anon. Review of **Beard's Roman Women**. **Booklist**, v. 73, no. 1 (September 1, 1976) 22.

[Chiefly plot summary.] "In this delicious situation touched with piquant ironies, the surface movement is woven into a richly textured background of dialogue and characterization with expert precision."

46 Anon. Notice of **Beard's Roman Women**. **America,**, v. 135, no. 9 (October 2, 1976) 196.

Burgess sets his traditional novel in Italy. [Complete text of notice.]

47 Anon. "Death and Transfiguration." **Economist**, v. 262, no. 6965 (February 26, 1977) 117.

Burgess is a prodigy known for his fecundity, versatility, erudition, dazzlingly felicitous technique, sheer energy and intelligence. The reason he is not a candidate for the Nobel Prize is simple: the prim mutter of 'pas serioux.' "The burden of [Burgess on death and judgment] is, bleakly, that the conscious acceptance of death will set you free, but what you leave behind you will be mauled and used for base purposes by the living. Orpheus, mourning Eurydice, is torn to pieces by the bacchantes; Shelley,

Mary and Byron by the lake are chopped up and rearranged post mortem by Beard . . . . dead Belli is ill translated; Rome crumbles and (the point of the photographs). . . its name is writ in water . . . . It is the best thing Burgess has done; it is not to be missed.''

48 Anon. Notice of **Beard's Roman Women**. **Observer** (London), 26 June 1977, p. 29.

''For all confirmed mental travellers, an indulgent travesty about post-marital sex, with generous verbal parlour games and a collection of lovely, oblique photos of Rome thrown in.'' [Complete text of notice.]

49 Anon. Review of **Beard's Roman Women**. **Virginia Quarterly Review**, v. 53, no. 3 (Summer 1977) ciii.

''Burgess' latest novels are all bravura and no heart. This one about hits the usual level. Ostensibly, it's about a widower coming to terms with himself and his sexuality after the death of his wife. The marriage had lasted 26 years and seems to have been held together by a dozen bottles of gin a week . . . . The novel never truly comes to terms with its material and leaves the reader dissatisfied, but it has the merit of being a spirited read.''

50 Breslin, John. Notice of **Beard's Roman Women**. **America,,** v. 135, no. 9 (October 2, 1976) 196.

[Not a review. The book's title is listed in passing.]

51 Korn, Eric. ''Reflections in a Puddle.'' **Times Literary Supplement**, 11 February 1977, p. 145.

''It's a supple, complex, unexpected and ferociously witty story; relaxed but compact, combining low farce and dense moral engagement, with room left over for bawdy carols and the sacrilegious sonnets of another Belli. Which still leaves me wondering about those pictures. Perhaps we should think of them as illuminations to a modern, unmorbid Dance of Death, which we only fully appreciate if we ever regain the knack of reading with both eyes.''

52 Lewis, Jeremy. ''Facing Up to Death.'' London **Times**, 24 February 1977, p. 12.

[Omnibus review. Chiefly plot summary.] ''. . . and much of this witty, subtle and immensely sympathetic novel is concerned with facing up to death — one's own, and those of the people one loves — and learning to live without the reassuring familiarities of 'a private language, a shared history'.''

53 Lodge, David. ''Death-Dealing.'' **New Statesman**, v. 93, no. 2395 (February 11, 1977) 194-5.

[Substantial plot summary.] Lists the biographical resemblance between Burgess and Beard and suggests that ''these autobiographical references are clearly deliberate, partly illuminating and partly disconcerting in postmodernist fashion, drawing attention to the complicated and reversible relationships that exist between art and life, as well as between life and death. Having finished it, one feels an irresistible urge to turn back to page one and read it all through again. The subject may be death, but the writing bubbles like life-giving oxygen.''

54 Loriot, Noelle. ''Les mortelles nostalgies d'Anthony Burgess.'' **L'Express Magazine** (Edition Internationale), no. 1445 (March 24, 1979) 84-85.

Reviews of **Beard's Roman Women** (''Rome sous la pluie'') and **Ernest Hemingway** (''Ce sacre Hemingway''). Introduces Burgess to French readers — brain tumor, death of his first wife, prolific production during so-called 'terminal' year — and remarks that Burgess' depiction of American film-makers, English alcoholic colonialists and vulgar Romans is marked by a dazzling intelligence.

55 Moynahan, Julian. ''Death Trip, by Anthony Burgess.'' **New York Times Book Review**, 10 October 1975, p. 8.

Dying seems to be the last frontier in modern literature. Mentions characters (Anna Karenina, Ivan Ilyich) and authors (Nabokov, Sylvia Plath, I.F. Sissman, D.H. Lawrence) in a brief survey of the literature of death. Refers to the death of Burgess' first wife in early 60's [i.e., March, 1968] and to the diagnosis, by Burgess' doctors, that he had only a year to live. Surveys the plot and concludes that Burgess, in his final chapter, is full of literary sleight of hand. The framing of the book's last scene has a musical setting of Dryden's 'Ode to St. Cecilia's Day':

      The dead shall live, the living die
      And music shall untune the sky.

"Now there is confidence! But whether the reader can be confident that Burgess in this book has unknotted the enigma of dying, I am not so sure."

56 Murray, Isobel. "Shades of Messalina." **Financial Times** (London), 11 February 1977, p. 35.

57 Murray, John. Review of **Beard's Roman Women**. **Best Sellers**, March 1977, p. 379.

"Beard — I should say Anthony Burgess — finally ends his Roman holiday by trying to squeeze his heart into cardiac arrest running up and down Paola's stairs. His story often is 'too deep for tears,' and I applaud the effort to rehabilitate a broken heart, but I do so with 'one hand clapping'."

58 P[rescott], P[eter] S. "Life in Death." **Newsweek**, v. 88, no. 17 (October 25, 1976) 110-11.

The coming fashion in fiction is women as sexual aggressors and, although Beard may conclude that men (who think of themselves as the users) are the used, the book is really about learning to die and the persistence of life in death. Burgess writes with *sprezzatura*, the art that conceals the magnitude of his effort. "Here, as in all his books, he is witty, inventive with language; unobtrusively, he has strewn his story with little signs and portents of death." Even the photographs by David Robinson are called a 'sort of ghost look at the city.' If this delightful story has a message it is that there's life in death or, perhaps, a lot of death in life.

59 Pritchard, William H. "Merely Fiction." **Hudson Review**, v. 30, no. 1 (Spring 1977) 147-60.

[Omnibus review: see p. 153.] A disheartening work. The photographs resemble modern blurred-chic and the text recalls the coarse joylessness of **Enderby Outside**. Burgess' career, after his rapid and miraculous beginning, has been a disappointment. "There is hardly a laugh throughout [the novel] and as Burgess trots out the old routines once more. . . the shrillness and tiredness of it all becomes apparent." Regrets these views; he had much critical soul invested in the earlier Burgess and looks forward to the substantial and composed novel in progress. [The reference is to **Earthly Powers**.]

60 Ricks, Christopher. "Faces in the Mirror." **Sunday Times** (London), no. 8016 (February 6, 1971) 41.

[Omnibus review.] "But it would be gravely wrong to treat this humorous and moving book as if it were slight; it seems to me one of Anthony Burgess's best novels, for some of the reasons that make **The Ordeal of Gilbert Pinfold** one of Evelyn Waugh's best novels. In both there is a self-attention, an autobiographical graphicness which is not self-absorption but is a brave self-interrogation. In both there is a comedy which is haunted and haunting, a play of a sturdy sanity and innocence against a burgeoning lunacy and guilt." The novel is endlessly fertile in detail, and its essential simplicity and modesty are not marred by the publisher's claim that the author is an acknowledged "literary genius."

61 Rogers, Pat. "On the Move." **Spectator**, v. 238, no. 7754 (February 12, 1977) 23.

"As always, Burgess' language crackles with life. He is good at violently worded quarrels where the underlying emotions aren't all that violent; good at interior monologue; sharp in dialogue . . . . The comedy is not really black; averted deaths outnumber actual deaths, and the sparkle of the writing offsets any impulse to melancholy — occasionally at the cost of verbal precision (each stride of Pathan's black mistress is 'an alexandrine jewelled with superbity,' which may be Burgess' way of saying that she's six foot and proud of it). But it's intensely readable, perfectly constructed and altogether superior in execution. David Robinson's moist-looking photographs are gilding the lily, but that is what they are there for."

62 Sage, Lorna. "A Roman Holiday." **Observer** (London), 6 February 1977, p. 31.

Burgess has the cheek and the talent to make the tricks of his master, James Joyce, seem part of a more relaxed and free-wheeling literary handyman. "Inventive and prolific at once, he has little of the self-centredness that gives stylistic experimenters a bad name. If he pursues puns and riddles, he does it with vulgar infectious delight, and if he lives in a world of art, it includes other people's creations." The book is somewhat of a hybrid, and the material gives the impression of being somewhat invented and mechanical, but "his kind of novel (like the pictures in this one) operates at one remove from its objects, in an exuberant mirror-world where all connections are temporary."

63 Sage, Lorna. Notice of **Beard's Roman Women**. **Observer** (London), 18 December 1977, p. 21.

One of the better books of the year. It "stands out for its casual skill, its verbal and visual promiscuity and its fuzzy humaneness."

64 Soete, Mary. Review of **Beard's Roman Women**. **Library Journal**, v. 101, no. 14 (August 1976) 1656.

"While not the best of Burgess, this novel offers much of what we have come to expect of him: playfully allusive in themes and cleverly tightened by ironic coincidence, it delights much more than it disappoints."

65 Stewart, Ian. "Recent Fiction." **Illustrated London News**, v. 265, no. 6945 (April 1977) 59.

We are invited to consider Beard's fate in terms of Greek myth (Orpheus and Eurydice). The resulting mixture of realism and surrealism seems modestly experimental by comparison with **Napoleon Symphony**. The work is "short, stimulating in ideas and language, and robustly amusing."

66 Tennant, Emma. "Burgess's Many Voices." **Listener**, v. 97, no. 2495 (February 10, 1977) 189.

Burgess claims to see the ghost of Henry James at his bedroom door, but when the phone rings, Kubrick (not James) is on the line. Burgess is plainly suffering from a crisis of identity. The characters in this book have all the impersonality of characters in an airport lounge. "We do not care at all about Beard, or his tough and beautiful mistress, Paola, or whether or not the wife is miserably resentful beyond the grave." The work conveys an embarrassed air of undigested experience. It is boring. "One way or another, a *zuppa inglese*, heavy with leftovers and alcoholic seasonings."

67 Theroux, Paul. "Angry Old Burgess." **Manchester Guardian Weekly**, 20 February 1977, p. 22.

Burgess' heroes in his latest fictional 'turns' are marked by an element of irrational rage. The book is extremely funny in a breathless and headlong way, but it is also full of rejection, anger and failure. "This book is full of enjoyment and a certain rueful wisdom, but as a Burgess fan I finished it not dissatisfied but with a feeling of incompleteness: I wanted more."

68 Tobias, Richard. "Fiction." **World Literature Today**, v. 51, no. 4 (Autumn 1977) 618-19.

A variation of the Orpheus-Eurydice legend. "Instead of climbing down into hell, Beard climbs the steps of a tall Roman apartment building. Hollywood is hell. His dead wife returns to him by telephone. The maenads are Roman street urchins. . . who snatch Beard's filmscript, tear off his clothes and rape him. Beard is as serious as Milton and funny as Offenbach, but his story is perfectly natural, imaginable and true." The photographs corroborate the text, but this novel of glorious words proves there is life in the wasteland yet.

69 Wade, Rosalind. "Literary Supplement." **Contemporary Review**, v. 230, no. 1335 (April 1977) 215-16.

[Omnibus review: see pp. 215-16. Chiefly plot summary.] "And then this eccentric and often degrading tale takes a surprising twist. [Beard] now knows that he is dying of an incurable disease. He writes to Paola in dignified, musical prose, thanking her for all she has done for him and then carries on for a final booze-up with Greg Greg, leaving the reader hovering between realism and fantasy, shaken, confused and conscious of a lost opportunity, despite the verve and pace of this extraordinary novel."

70 Wood, Michael. "The Ladies Vanish." **New York Review of Books**, v. 23, no. 15 (September 30, 1976) 40-42.

[Omnibus review. Also reviews Burgess' **Moses** and some other books.] The 'leakage' of Burgess' life into his fiction, along with his frivolity and intelligence, give his novels a sense of energy and complication. His themes are the death of his wife (hardly an 'episode' as the blurb claims) and Burgess' own postponement of diagnosed death. The book suggests that a belief in ghosts, given the events, is the only acceptable one. "The ghosts turn all of Beard's relations with women into versions of his selfishness and cowardice, and it is a virtue of the book that this point of view is put with some authority." However, Burgess lets Beard off the hook by making him such a likable, disorganized, drunken clown. It is a lively and shallow book, and we are more likely to remember its gags than its ghosts.

Beds in the East

71 London: Heinemann, 1959.

72 London: Heinemann, 1968.

Reviews

73 Anon. Review of **Beds in the East**. **Times Literary Supplement**, 1 May 1959, p. 262.

The book attempts to create comedy entirely through character, without verbal trickery or facetiousness. To succeed in this aim, the characters must convince. Unfortunately, Crabbe is the only successful creation. The supporting cast of eccentric Tamils, an infinitely complaisant Eurasian girl and Genuine Oriental Teddies, are sheer grotesques. "The passages of persuasive humour spring mainly from sardonic observation of racial foibles. But there is too little sympathy."

74 Smith, Peter Duval. "New Novels." **New Statesman**, v. 67, no. 1469 (May 9, 1959) 663-64.

[Omnibus review.] In this work, the third of Burgess's funny and touching stories about modern Malaya, he gives us some brilliant comedy. His most successful character is the unvirginal Tamil, Rosemary, an astonishing beauty black as pitch. This creature aims to marry a duke but is beset by local Lotharios. Rosemary's suitors are described with "an impartial generosity; and the steamy, noisy, confused world they live in is conveyed with knowledge and skill. Perhaps the book goes off rather at the end, but for once it is not beside the point to invoke Mr. Forster."

A Clockwork Orange

75 London: Heinemann, 1962.

76 New York: Norton, 1963, c1962.

77 New York: Norton, 1963. Book Club ed. With an afterword and glossary by Stanley Edgar Hyman.

78 New York: Ballantine, 1963. Pbk.

79 London: Pan Books, 1964. Pbk. (Pan Books, no. X321)

80 New York: Ballantine, 1965, c1963. Pbk.

81 New York: Modern Library, 1968. Bound with: **Honey for the Bears**.

82 New York: Ballantine, 1972, c1963. Pbk.

83 London: Heinemann, 1975, c1962.

84 New York: Ballantine, 1976, c1963. Pbk.

85 Harmondsworth; New York: Penguin, 1972, c1962. Pbk.

Recordings

86 Prose Readings. [Phonotape] New York: Norton, [197?] 1 cassette. Introduced by John Simon. Burgess reads from **Enderby and A Clockwork Orange**. (YW-YMHA Poetry Center series)

87 A Clockwork Orange. [Phonotape] Written and recorded by Anthony Burgess. Caedmon, c1973. CDL 51417.

88 A Clockwork Orange. [Phonorecord] Written and recorded by Anthony Burgess. Caedmon, [1973]. TC 1417. Program notes by Burgess and M. Mantell on slipcase.

89 Anthony Burgess reads from A Clockwork Orange [and] **Enderby**. Spoken Arts, [1974?] SA 1120.

Translations

90 French: **L'Orange mecanique**. Paris: Laffont, 1972. Translated by Georges Belmont & Hortense Chabrier.

91 German: **Uhrwerk Orange**. Munchen: Heyne, 1972. Translated by Walter Brumm.

92 Italian: **Un'arancia a orologeria**. Torino: Einaudi, 1969. Reprinted: 1972. Translated by Floriana Bossi.

93 Japanese: **Tokei jikake no orenji**. Tokyo: Hayakawa Shobo, 1971. Translated by Inui Shin'ichiro.

94 Russian: **Mekhanicheskii apel'sin**. [s.l.: s.n., 1977?] Printed in Tel Aviv by the "Or-Press." Translated by A. Gazov-Ginzberg. (Biblioteka Danielia Amarilia, no. 15)

95 Spanish: **La naranja mecanica**. Buenos Aires: Minotauro, 1971. 2d ed. Translated by Anibal Leal. Reprinted in 1973, 1977.

96 Spanish: **La naranja mecanica**. Barcelona: Minotauro-Edhasa, 1976. Translated by Anibal Leal.

97 Swedish: **En Apelsin med Urverk**. Stockholm: Wahlstrom & Widstrand, 1972. Translated by Inkeri Uusitalo.

98 Turkish: **Otamatic portakal**. Ankara: Bilgi Yayinevi, 1973. Translated by Aziz Ustel.

99 Yugoslavian: **Peklenska pomaranca**. Ljubljana: "Mladinska knjiga," 1974. Translated by Ferdinand Miklavc.

100 Yugoslavian: **Paklena pomorandza**. Belgrad: Beogradski izdavacko-graficki Zavod, 1973. Translated by Zoran Zivkovic.

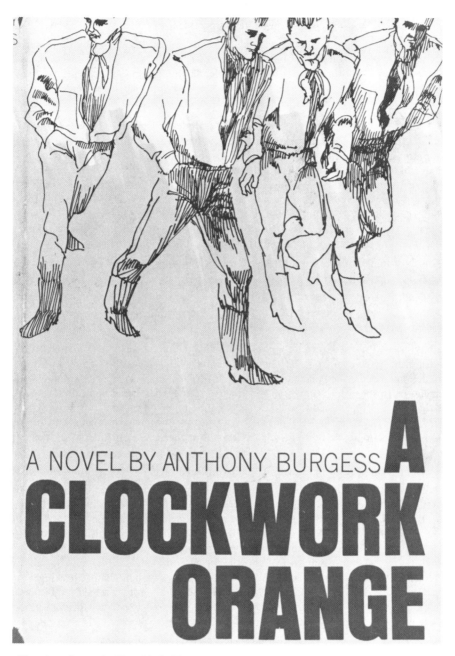

A NOVEL BY ANTHONY BURGESS A CLOCKWORK ORANGE

First American ed. (New York: Norton, c. 1962) of the novel which was later turned into a film (1971) by Stanley Kubrick.

Reviews

101 Anon. "Other New Novels." **Times Literary Supplement**, 25 May 1962, p. 377.

"A viscous verbiage. . . which is the swag-bellied offspring of decay. . . English is being slowly killed by her practitioners." Burgess is an accomplished writer who seems to have set out deliberately to
kill the language. The author's taste is questionable. The publishers promise picaresque villainy and
social satire, but satire implies hatred and this book sadly lacks any such viewpoint. "The author seems
content to use a serious, social challenge for frivolous purposes, but himself to stay neutral."

102 Anon. "The Ultimate Beatnik." **Time**, v. 81, no. 7 (February 15, 1963) 103.

It may look like a nasty little shocker, but Burgess has written that rare thing in English letters —
a philosophical novel. The point may be overlooked because the hero tells all in nadsat which serves
to put him where he belongs — half in and half out of the human race. "This pilgrim's progress of
a beatnik Stavrogin is a serious and successful moral essay. Burgess argues quite simply that Alex is
more of a man as an evil man than as a good Zombie. The clockwork of a mechanical society can never
counterfeit the organic vitality of moral choice. Goodness is nothing if evil is not accepted as a possibility."
Burgess' earlier **Devil of a State** gave little hint of the moral seriousness of **Orange**, where the brassily
orchestrated jive of nadsat is used to point up a grave philosophic theme.

103 Anon. Notice of **A Clockwork Orange**." **Best Sellers**, v. 25, no. 13 (October 1, 1965) 274.

"An off-beat and violent tale about teen-age gangs in Britain, written in much out-of-this-world gibberish." [Complete text of notice.]

104 Davis, Robert Gorham. "The Perilous Balance." **Hudson Review**, v. 16, no. 2 (Summer 1963)
280-84.

[Omnibus review. Preceded by reflections on sadism in literature.] Alex is a murderous Holden Caulfield
who lives in a badly controlled society, and he plainly steals, fights and rapes for the sheer sport of
it all. His actions are described in detail and with relish. The slang, which includes many Russian words,
has been chosen to suggest a brutal statism. Finally, after he has been conditioned to be "good," he
is released and brutally assaulted ("to an extent which is a libel on society") by those he has previously
injured. The novel clearly turns Alex into an articulate apostle of existential or even Christian freedom
and "By a perverse logic, images of violence are put at the service of a dreadful, dead-end concept
of freedom." 1,000w

105 Josselson, Diana. "Shorter Reviews." **Kenyon Review**, v. 25, no. 3 (Summer 1963) 559-560.

The slang, or nadsat, offers minor philological enjoyment. The work can be compared to Golding's
The Inheritors, but one loves Golding's Neanderthalers and hates his Modern Man. In the same way,
one hates the 'genial' Alex of Burgess' fiction. The source of the delinquency is never explained, and
the last chapter [21] in which Alex apparently outgrows his delinquencies is an incredible about-face.
". . . Alex isn't Penrod. Beatings, blindings, rapes, murders are not adolescent awkwardnesses to be
grown out of . . . . There is some sort of cheat involved in making the reader suffer all those painful
pages of terrible violence, only to have the perpetrators put away their chains and knives and knuckles
as childish things, and live as solid citizens ever after. So false a note is struck by this ending that the
whole book in retrospect seems false — a clockwork orange put together with mild ingenuity but to
no purpose and with no real vitamins." 800w

106 Levin, Martin. Review of **A Clockwork Orange**. **New York Times Book Review**, 7 April 1963, p. 36.

"With his tongue popping in and out of his cheek, Mr. Burgess satirizes both the sociological and
the penal approach to juvenile crime, literary proletarianism, and anything else in his path. Written
in a pseudo-criminal cant [it] is an interesting *tour de force*, though not up to the level of the author's
two previous novels." 130w

107 Moran, John F. Review of **A Clockwork Orange**. **Library Journal**, v. 88, no. 2 (February 15, 1963)
793-4.

"The ideas presented are thought-provoking, but the brevity of their treatment and the invented
language — for which, unlike Orwell, the author provides no glossary or explanation — often distract

from the narrative and will act as a barrier to the general reader . . . . For inclusive fiction collections only.''

108 Schickel, Richard. Review of **A Clockwork Orange**. **Show**, v. 3, no. 8 (August 1963) 39-40.

The work is a tour de force. When Alex, sadistic, amoral, animalistic, becomes the subject of a mechanistic form of rehabilitation decreed by the super-welfare state, it is clearly a projection of what Burgess sees as the trend of our time. ''Burgess is a novelist who knows what he thinks and knows how to find fictional correlatives for his beliefs. The result is a novel of striking style that is also a savage satire. A verbal joy, **A Clockwork Orange** offers a unique, forced perspective on the world we are creating.'' 180w

109 Talbot, David. ''Scream of Hate at a Mechanic World.'' **New York Herald Tribune Books**, v. 39, no. 21 (April 14, 1963) 7.

Alex is the last of a succession of sallow-faced rebels without a cause. The terrifying reality of Burgess' nightmare is due to nadsat, which has an emotional impact that transcends specific word meanings. He has looked into the blackness of totalitarianism and detected a macabre existential dilemma. ''In the shadowy non-world of the controlled society, man will be forced to love. But love cannot exist without the possibility of hate, and by forcing men to abdicate their right to choose one over the other, society turns men into automatons. Thus Burgess points his stunning moral: in a clockwork society, human redemption will have to arise out of evil.'' 200w

110 Taubman, Robert. ''Djunaesque.'' **New Statesman**, v. 63, no. 1627 (May 18, 1962) 717-18.

[Omnibus review.] The book, written in a combination of Jacobean English and nadsat, is a great strain to read. Although Alex undergoes a mental operation to reverse his responses ''There's not much fantasy here; Mr. Burgess works by keeping close to the way things are now, and the novel can be read, for instance, as straight satire on the indulgence of a good many current writers to their teenage heroes.'' 250w

111 Walters, Raymond. ''Say It With Paperbacks.'' **New York Times Book Review**, 4 December 1966, p. 60.

Announces the publication of five novels in paperback by this ''enormously talented and versatile British author.'' 60w

A Clockwork Orange (Film)

112 Kubrick, Stanley. **A Clockwork Orange**: A Screenplay. [s.l. : s.n.], 1970.

107 leaves. Photocopy of typescript. Shooting script, September 7, 1970. "Property of Warner Bros."

113 Kubrick, Stanley. **A Clockwork Orange**. Based on the novel by Anthony Burgess. New York: Abelard-Schuman, [c1972] "A complete, graphic representation of the film, cut by cut, with the dialogue printed in the proper place in relation to the cuts."

114 Kubrick, Stanley. **A Clockwork Orange**. Based on the novel by Anthony Burgess. New York: Ballantine Books, [1972]

Recordings

115 Carlos, Walter J. **A Clockwork Orange**. [Cassette. Selections.] Warner Bros., 1971. M5 2573.

116 **Music from the soundtrack. Stanley Kubrick's A Clockwork Orange**. Warner Bros., p1972. BS2573. [Authentic transcript from film.]

117 **Music from A Clockwork Orange**. [Sound recording.] Angel, [1972?] S-36855. [Authentic transcript from film.]

118 Carlos, Walter J. **A Clockwork Orange**. [Sound recording. Selections.] Columbia, [1972] KC 31480.

119 **A Clockwork Orange**. [Videorecording.] New York: WCI Home Video, 1980. 1 videocassette (137 min.); Beta format. Screenplay by Stanley Kubrick; produced and directed by Stanley Kubrick. Starring Malcolm McDowell, Patrick Magee.

Reviews: Kubrick's "A Clockwork Orange" (Book)

120 Anon. Review of **A Clockwork Orange** (by Stanley Kubrick). **Choice**, v. 10, no. 8 (October 1973) 1207.

In this work, Kubrick "attempts his own shot-by-shot analysis, with spoken dialogue accompanying the pictures at the appropriate point, so that what we have is an almost completely effective aide-memoire for the film, which is, after all, one of the principal reasons for publishing a screenplay in the first place." Remarks that, compared to the useful non-book which accompanied **2001**, Kubrick is perhaps less responsive to curiosity about the background of the film.

121 Burgess, Anthony. "Burgess on Kubrick on 'Clockwork.' " **Library Journal**, v. 98, no. 9 (May 1, 1973) 1506.

"Our starry droog [old friend] Kubrick the sinny veck [sinful man] has, my brothers, like brought forth from his like bounty and all that cal [shit] this kniggiwig, which is like all real horrorshow lomticks [marvellous pictures] from His Great Masterpiece [the film] which would make any fine upstanding young malchick smeck [boy laugh] from his yarbles and keeshkas [balls and guts]. What it like is is lashings of ultra-violence and the old in-out in-out, but not in slovos [words] except where the chellovecks [i.e. actors] are gavoreeting [talking] but in veshches [things: i.e. pictures] you can viddy [see] and not have to send the old gulliver to spatchka [head to sleep] with like being bored like when you are on your sharries [ass] in a biblio [library]. And you can like viddy [see] as well that the Great Purpose in his jeezny [life] which this veck Kubrick or Zubrick, that being the Arab eemya [name] for a grahzny veshch [dirty thing: the sense is surely that of 'dirty bastard'] is like now at last being made flesh and all that cal, was to have a Book. And now he has a Book. A Book he doth have, O my malenky [little] brothers, verily he doeth. A Book. Righty right. It was a book he did wish to like make, and he hath done it, Kubrick or Zubrick the Bookmaker. But, brothers, what makes me smeck like bezoomny [laugh like crazy] is that this like Book will tolchock out into the darkmans [throw out into the darkness] the Book what there like previously was, the one by F. Alexander or Sturgess [Burgess, of course] or some such eemya, because who would have slovos when he could viddy real jeezhny [see really clearly] with his nagoy glazzies [naked eyes]? And so it is like that. Righty right. And real horror

16

show. And lashings of deng [cash] for the carmans [pockets] of Zubrick. And for your malenky droog not none no more. So gromky shooms [loud noises] of lip-music brrrrrr to thee and thine. And all that cal. — Alex [Anthony Burgess]

Reviews (Kubrick's Film)

122 Alpert, Hollis. "Milk-Plus and Ultra-Violence." **Saturday Review**, v. 44, no. 52 (December 25, 1971) 40-41, 60.

Kubrick builds upon tendencies (the growth in youthful violence, the drug culture, an extraordinary increase in eroticism) already existing in today's societies. The opening close-up of the leering Alex sets a faintly sinister and satiric mood found throughout the film. "It is doubtful that *any* novel has ever been adapted for the screen as brilliantly as this one. Critic Stanley Edgar Hyman termed the book an 'eloquent and shocking novel that is quite unique.' Fully as unique, and as eloquent and shocking, is this film by Kubrick . . . . " Critics have been slow to get on his bandwagon, but Kubrick's record begins to look imposing indeed. He is the most important film-maker in the U.S., fit to stand beside Bergman and Fellini.

123 Austin, Charles M. "Stirring the Guttywuts." **Christian Century**, v. 89, no. 7 (February 16, 1972) 207.

[Chiefly plot summary.] 'McDowell's portrayal of Alex is superb, but the film is dominated by Kubrick, the consummate director. His social jabs abound in the film — the unctuous social worker, the vacillating, opportunist politician, the liberal writer who later becomes a ranting, panting parallel to Dr. Strangelove. And the film's visuals are as intricate as a symphony score . . . . " Although the film includes scenes of sex and violence, the triumph of the drug culture, and an image of the city as a vandalized garbage heap, the film is beautiful and "Kubrick's cry for a sane society goes beyond his own amazing creativity." 600w

124 Boyers, Robert. "Kubrick's **A Clockwork Orange**: Some Observations." **Film Heritage**, v. 7, no. 4 (Summer 1972) 1-6.

Kubrick presents us with a Dr. Skinner type, and the film is a discerning reflection of the age. Kubrick distances us from the horrors of the film, and his vision is both moral and religious: it is part of an authentic Old Testament moralism. We may not know what to do about the brutality, or the antipodal insistence on science and final solutions, but a civilized comfort is reflected in the views of the two **HOMES,** that of Alex's parents and the writer F. Alexander. In the former, we see the permissive contours of a home we have deliberately tried to create. These homes are consoling to their inhabitants and they assume mythic proportions. It is notable that Alex is displaced from both homes, and Kubrick's vision encompasses a vivid nostalgia for civility and stability. Notes that when Alex is treated brutally by his former victims, we share in the pleasure a little. 2,000w

125 Burgess, Jackson. Review of **A Clockwork Orange. Film Quarterly**, v. 25, no. 3 (Spring 1972) 33-36.

In times of trouble, people often look to the art for images of their despair, terror and interior violence. This film, reminiscent of battle-conditioning films of WWII, presents images of viciousness which obliterate the possibility of any humane context. Alex's brutality of the fist is made preferable to the slimy Home Secretary's brutality of law and order. Kubrick has turned Alex, not into a morally significant figure, but into a comic hero. The film is characterized by technical excellence, but this technique really celebrates the modish image of the sexually smoldering young brute, the descendent of Stanley Kowalski, slack-jawed, full-lipped, vaguely androgynous, crotch-swollen, capable of making grown men sweat and tremble with a sullen glance. Kubrick's statement that the film is satirical is ridiculous: the film explores a hypothetical question, and you cannot satirize a question, but only an answer, a condition, a status quo. The moral and psychological significance claimed for the film is nonsensical. The sanctity of man's right to choose evil is mere superstition. Kubrick's claim that the stylized violence shifts attention away from the mayhem is incorrect. The reverse is true. The fact is that Kubrick has long shown a horrified fascination with dehumanization. The laughter of satire is restorative and courageous; this film elicits a "mean and cynical snigger at the weakness of our own stomachs. Personally, I suspect that a weak stomach may do more to protect us against the horrors of the total state than any amount of medieval niggling about free will and natural depravity. A strong stomach is the first requirement for a storm trooper." 1,800w

126 Canby, Vincent. "**A Clockwork Orange** Dazzles the Senses and Mind." **New York Times**, 20 December 1971, p. 22.

"It is brilliant, a tour de force of extraordinary images, music, words and feelings, a much more original achievement for commercial cinema than the Burgess novel is for literature, for Burgess after all, has some impossibly imposing literary antecedents, including the work of Joyce." This adaptation of Burgess' perversely moral, Christian novel about the value of free will is essentially a British nightmare in its attention to caste, manners, accents and the atmosphere created by a kind of weary socialism. McDowell is splendid; Kubrick's cunning use of the wide-angle lens underlines the disconnection between people and their environment. 400w [For an opposing view by Clayton Riley, see #153.]

127 Canby, Vincent. "**Orange**-Disorienting but Human Comedy." **New York Times**, Section II, 9 January 1972, p. 1,7.

This 1971 winner of the New York Film Critics award is a brilliant but dangerous work. When Alex, who has all the cheeriness of a ratty Candide, triumphantly announces his cure we find it difficult to share his triumph. "It seems to me that by describing horror with such elegance and beauty, Kubrick has created a very disorienting but human comedy, not warm and lovable, but a terrible sum-up of where the world is at." The stylized violence is unlikely to corrupt adults, but qualified psychiatrists must judge the likely effect on immature audiences.

128 Ciglic, M. "Mechanicna oranza." **Ekran**, v. 11, nos. 104-105 (1973) 158-67.

129 Cocks, Jay. "Kubrick: Degrees of Madness." **Time**, v. 98, no. 25 (December 20, 1971) 80, 85.

[Includes some stills from the film.] The language may be strange, the setting unfamiliar, but Alex is the sort of man who would approve Charles Manson's credo: "Do the unexpected. No sense makes sense." The curiosity is that, in this evocation of a berserk future world, in which there are no real alternatives, only degrees of madness, Alex is surprisingly and undeniably engaging. "The political extremes in the film are both represented as the two sides of demagoguery. The Minister of the Interior is a kind of well-tailored Goebbels, an unctuous fascist. His opposite number is a radical writer. . . who is given to saying things like "the common people must be led! Driven! Pushed!" McDowell is sensational in the role of Alex, and Kubrick's work is stylistically flawless. "Yet, as with the novel, there is something troublesome about the film. **A Clockwork Orange** does not engage us fully on an emotional level. There is something about it a little too neat and too cold. The wit is there, and the ironic perception. It is funny and it is frightening, partly because of the world it presents but also because of the dispassionate attitude it adopts toward that world. One misses a sense of grief or of rage, and finally, a portion of humanity." [Followed by biographical sketch of Kubrick at home, en famille, surrounded by dogs, children, optical equipment, a computer . . . .] 650w

130 Comuzio, E. "Ludwig van e gli altri." **Cineforum**, no. 119 (January 1973) 75-78.

131 Costello, Donald P. "From Counter-Culture to Anti-Culture." **Commonweal**, v. 96, no. 16 (July 14, 1972) 383-86.

Woodstock, **Easy Rider** and **A Clockwork Orange** respectively define the counter-culture, warn against it, and predict its future course. **Woodstock** observed that the counter-culture virtues of love, peace and freedom were transmitted by sights and sounds, not by words; it is one of the most inarticulate films ever made. **Easy Rider** showed that the values of the counter-culture were becoming indistinguishable from those of the mainstream. Now this film completes the warning. In place of love, we have sex; in place of peace, we have violence; in place of freedom, we have compulsion. In Kubrick's ice-cold, uninvolved, primitive, dehumanized stand toward his materials we see a world in which there is no culture, no communal passing on of values. "The irrational tendency of the counter-culture defined so clearly in **Woodstock** has triumphed in **A Clockwork Orange**."

132 Crist, Judith. "A Feast, and About Time." **New York**, v. 4, no. 5 (December 20/27, 1971) 90.

This film produced by Kubrick is a stunningly original work which does full justice to Burgess' novel. Kubrick's harrowing vision extrapolates tomorrow's hell based on present social and moral decay. His film has made nadsat, a distraction in Burgess' novel, fully comprehensible. The total vision displays Kubrick's total mastery of every phase of his art. Musicology is Kubrick's hallmark and with the help of Walter Carlos he displays all its subtle variety. He has been able to tap all of England's acting talent:

McDowell now shows his full acting range, and Patrick Magee as the liberal writer is excellent, "each member is a facet in the brilliance of **A Clockwork Orange**." 250w

133 Daniels, Don. "**A Clockwork Orange**." **Sight and Sound**, v. 42, no. 1 (Winter 1972/73) 44-46.

Long analysis of the film in terms of psychoanalysis, with extended reference to the work of Franz Alexander. "Alex's roles are three. In attack he is the id's ever-renewing energies; in command he is the super-ego's ancient despotism, and in pain he is the neurotic ego." Includes some useful comments on Kubrick's comparison of Alex to Richard III (a red herring) and argues that Alex is much more comparable to Iago. 3,500w

134 Denby, David. "Pop Nihilism at the Movies." **Atlantic**, v. 229, no. 3 (March 1972) 100-104.

Describes the media hype which preceded the film's opening one week before Christmas. The film has been attacked by Pauline Kael [#143], Andrew Sarris, Richard Schickel [#108] and John Simon [#1791] but it has also been described as brilliant. The brilliance connected with this project properly belongs to Burgess. His fictional case for a voluntary ethics was marked by moral heroism. Kubrick's film panders to the youth culture. He conveys a contemptuous attitude toward art, caricatures all the adults and suggests that Alex is the true hero of the film. Burgess provided a rationale of freedom; Kubrick provides a rationale of a youthful thug's progress. His films have been notable for a progressive inhumanity and misanthropy. The role of the satirist has escaped him. Satire implies a structure of values and a standard of humanity by which inhumanity may be judged. Considers some recent violent films and observes that "Nihilism is well on its way toward becoming the complacent mass culture of our time." [Reprinted in #1776.] 4,000w

135 Fitzgerald, John E. "More Than a Product of Heredity." **Catholic News**, 30 December 1971, p. 4.

"And in the sinister and somewhat surrealistic world of glare and shadow in which **Orange** unfolds, producer-director Kubrick has chosen to use — even to exploit, but within context — the two most denounced elements of irresponsible moviemaking: sex, an expression of love, and violence, an expression of hate. All in an attempt to tell a tale, to create an adult-level nightmare, which is harrowingly humanistic, magnificently moral and chillingly Christian." The plot, with its artistic treatment of political, philsophical, psychological and theological issues, may convey much that seems irritating and repulsive, but Kubrick never loses his balance on his tight-rope walk to brilliance. He is clearly out to make an artistic and lasting impression rather than a cheap quick buck. Skinner has told us that man is but a grab-bag of conditioned reflexes. Kubrick shows us that man is more than a mere product of heredity and/or environment, and the film conveys the idea that redemption, a complicated thing, must be motivated from within, not imposed from without.

136 Frezzato, A. "Riproposta della vita." **Cineforum**, no. 119 (January 1973) 66-74.

137 Gambetti, G. "Due tipi de violenza." **Cineforum**, no. 119 (January 1973) 54-65.

138 Gumenik, Arthur. "**A Clockwork Orange**: Novel into Film." **Film Heritage**, v. 7, no. 4 (Summer 1972) 7-18, 28.

[Careful and extended examination of resemblances and differences between novel and film.] Burgess' concern is ultimately Christian; his interest lies in free choice and the human soul. Nadsat distances us from the novel's ultraviolence. Kubrick stylizes the violence and makes the victims utterly repulsive. Kael's attack on the film [#143, #1705] is the result of her environmental Utopianism. Kubrick departs from the novel by his emphasis on Alex's phallicism; his victims, by contrast, are impotent or homosexual. [This point is extensively documented.] Kubrick utterly fails to convey Alex's roles as a Christ figure and when, at the end, he turns Alex into a manipulator, a Machiavellian accomplice to government manipulation, he commits the ultimate sin.

139 H[art], H[enry.] "**A Clockwork Orange**." **Films in Review**, v. 23, no. 1 (January 1972) 51.

"Evil is the deliberate use of intelligence to debase man, and in this sense Anthony Burgess' **A Clockwork Orange** is an evil book and the film based on it, which was written, directed and produced by Stanley Kubrick, is an evil motion picture." Kubrick is truckling to today's alienated young and promoting nihilism for political purposes. The violence of the film is condoned and the establishment is derided. The script is an example of adolescent maundering. Kubrick is in pursuit of the big buck by means of graffiti, total nudity and sight-gags for perverts.

140 Hatch, Robert. "Films." **Nation**, v. 214, no. 1 (January 3, 1972) 28.

Burgess is a serious-minded writer with a tendency to kid around. His book's message is clearly that the effort to counteract brutal and obscene violence will facilitate the organization of a fascist apparatus. Burgess himself found the message not original and so embellished it with science fiction gadgetry, eroticism and an invented argot. Kubrick's entertainment should have presented the central proposition with less tinsel; he should have been less seduced by the oddities of Burgess' imagination. Found the violence titillating and outrageous. Confesses that the government's simplistic attempt at Pavlovian conditioning engaged his attention. McDowell as Alex is loathsomely attractive, but the film's da-glo color and omnipresent rouge on the actors are both objectionable.

141 Hiltmen, E. "Kenelle kellopeli soi." **Filmhillu**, no. 4 (1973) 20-22.

142 Hughes, Robert. "The Decor of Tomorrow's Hell." **Time**, v. 98 no. 26 (December 27, 1971) 59.

[Review by **Time's** art critic.] No film in the last decade (perhaps ever) has made such chilling predictions about the future role of paintings, buildings, sculpture and music. The decor is uniformly sterile. The femlins of the Korova milk bar are close parodies of the fetishistic furniture sculpture of Allen Jones. The immense phallus that kills the cat-lady is reminiscent of the work of Jean Arp. "The impression, a very deliberate one, is of culture objects cut loose from any power to communicate, or even to be noticed. There is no reality to which they connect." Kubrick disputes the popular nineteenth century idea that art conveys an ethical purpose, that it is Good for You, and provides a moral uplift. Kubrick's message is the opposite one that art has no ethical purpose; it exists to promote ecstatic consciousness. 650w

143 Kael, Pauline. "Stanley Strangelove." **New Yorker**, v. 47, no. 46 (January 1, 1972) 50-53.

Burgess' point of view is that of a humanist and Christian horrified by a clockwork orange society. Kubrick's Alex is a force pitted against society and, by making the victims more repulsive and contemptible than the thugs, Kubrick has learned to love the punk sadist. When Alex regains his will to evil, Kubrick clearly takes an exultant tone; he rejoices in Alex's triumph. Kubrick's Alex has been cleaned up: his taste for crushing small animals, raping ten year old girls and sadistic blood-lust are bowdlerized in the film. The violence inflicted on Alex is represented as far worse than the violence he inflicts himself. The worst fault of the film is not its corrupt morality, but Kubrick's leaden direction. The style of the film, although distinctive, is leering and portentous. The dialogue scenes go on forever and induce a stupor of inactivity. The movies are gradually conditioning us to accept violence and "How can people go on talking about the dazzling brilliance of movies and not notice that the directors are sucking up to the thugs in the audience?" 1,600w [Reprinted in #1776.]

144 Kauffmann, Stanley. "Stanley Kauffmann on Film: **A Clockwork Orange**." **New Republic**, v. 166, nos. 1-2 (Jan. 1-8, 1972) 22-23.

Kubrick sticks to a narrative, depicts character and opts for literary humanism. These virtues do not save the film. Its worst flaw is that its air of cool intelligence and ruthless moral inquiry is not fulfilled. His mistake was to select a novel which depends on words. Kubrick has to replace Burgess' linguistic ingenuity with a visual equivalent; his failure to do so leads to triteness and tedium. Burgess made his main point, the protest against an attempt to impose on man the laws and conditions appropriate to a mechanical creation, mildly interesting by virtue of his linguistic acrobatics. The opening sequence is striking; the Billyboy rumble is good; but a great deal of the film is banal or reminiscent. McDowell conveys energy and threat; Michael Bates is outstanding as the guard. "Something has gone seriously wrong with the talented Kubrick. I won't hazard guesses as to what it is. But the one thing that, two films ago, I'd never have thought possible to say about a Kubrick film is true of **A Clockwork Orange**: it's boring."

145 Kellogg, Jean. "The Cineast as Moralizer." **Christian Century**, v. 89, nos. 31-32 (September 6/13, 1972) 878-79.

The cinematic artist, agonizing on his isolated Golgotha over the evils of meaningless sex and brutal violence, inevitably must portray these vices. In the process, and in the teeth of his declared intentions, the mob rejoices in scenes of sex and violence. What set out as a morality play becomes a source of titillation. In films like **Carnal Knowledge, The French Connection** and above all, **A Clockwork Orange**, the same process occurs, and audience reactions support this contention. Today, the depiction of the cineast's loathing "feeds the very monstrosities it attacks, and the fact that it feeds them is known to the artist. When this happens, the whole historic thrust of art as guide and prophet becomes lethal, a driving toward a final thanatos of which the artist himself is celebrant." 950w

146 Khanuitin, I. "Koshmart na bdesheto." **Kinoizkustvo**, v.28 (September 1973) 50-63.

147 Kriegsman, Alan M. "**Clockwork**: Landmark or Wasteland?" **Washington Post**, Arts Section, 26 March 1972, p. K1, K4.

The film has polarized the movie public. Some hail it as a revelation and landmark; the others damn it as shallow and pernicious. Even those who damn the film, Sarris and Kael, give off some sour notes of half-hearted praise. It is somewhat like attacking **Wasteland** for its acerbity. Kubrick's megalomania, his sense of himself as an oracle, is repellent; but his films have added much that is new, striking and vital to the medium. The fighting point of the whole debate has been the film's violence. The Burgess-Kubrick idea that the freedom to murder and molest is preferable to scientific, totalitarian security is not the only possible interpretation. "It's possible to take the real horror to be the approach of a world where the only real option left for man is the choice between thugs and zombies . . . . ' Kubrick's belief in the violence of man is irrelevant to the appreciation of the film as cinematic art. One does not need to be a Nazi or Marxist to admire the work of Leni Riefenstahl or Sergei Eisenstein, and the **Clockwork** audience did not greet the film with hyena laughter as they did **Bonnie and Clyde** or **The Wild Bunch**. No point can be served by making Alex a loathsome baddie, or by mitigating the nastiness of his victims. "By making the victims unsympathetic, Kubrick forces us to question the nature of violence without the prop of simplistic diagrams, angels vs. devils. [If] You want to say that Kubrick is too brittle, too explicit and long-winded in making his points, that much of his humour is leaden and some of his imagery vulgar, I concur wholeheartedly. But this seems to me a fair price to pay for a film so searing in its vision, so dazzling in style and execution, so provocative in its confrontation with a subject of cardinal concern to all of us." [Reprinted in #1776.]

148 Mamber, S. "**A Clockwork Orange**." **Cinema** (U.S.), v. 7, no. 3 (1972) 48-57.

149 Marszalek, R. "Help!" **Kino**, v. 8 (June 1973) 42-49.

150 Millar, Gavin. "Treatment and Ill-Treatment." **Listener**, v. 87, no. 2234 (January 20, 1972) 93-94.

The novel is a one-idea book. Kubrick has produced an absorbing film, but he has had to push hard to do so. The prophetic edge of the book has been dulled. Urban violence, political and police corruption, brainwashing are now commonplace. Perhaps Kubrick's previous films have prepared us to accept this cynicism. The film has plainly sexed things up. "In view of the thinness of the theme and the melodramatic overstatement of the events, there might be a temptation to doubt Kubrick's seriousness. But no one who takes this amount of trouble can be joking, and it is in the end technique which pulls the film through into seriousness." Includes comments on some of the technical devices of the film.

151 Pechter, William S. "Peckinpah & Kubrick: Fire & Ice." **Commentary**, v. 53, no. 3 (March 1972) 79-81.

[Also reviews **Straw Dogs**.] Came prepared to like film on the strength of Kubrick's **2001** [extensively discussed] but concludes that the film is not interesting. It is striking, brilliant in a specious and repellent way, and it is definitely not the embodiment of Kubrick's startling vision. Burgess' thin and anecdotal fantasy of an imminent future is also devoid of a startling vision; it does not possess the reality, or the urgent ideas, of **1984** or **Brave New World**. The book includes, instead, platitudinous conjectures on the primacy of self-hood and the dubious goodness of those unable to choose evil. The loss of nadsat and a controlling voice cruelly expose, in the film, the book's paucity of narrative invention. Kubrick's **Clockwork** shows him declining into the art of interior decoration. McDowell's leering, smirking, swaggering Alex is misguided and, when Kubrick departs from the book, he indulges in bad Varsity humor and slapstick. The film shares all the sophomoric misanthropic humor of **Dr. Strangelove** and the misanthropy gives an impression of mere chic. Kubrick has been undone by his desire to be clever and photogenic. 2,000w

152 Ricks, Christopher. "Horror Show." **New York Review of Books,** v. 18, no. 6 (April 6, 1972) 28-29.

[Prolonged examination of the violence in the book and film.] Concludes that the book's violence is more nasty, sustained (and honorable) than that of the film. The violence inflicted by Alex in the film is muted, softened and blurred by eliminating details, excising some killings that conclusively demonstrate Alex's blood-lust, and the presence of sentimentalities and distortions. The violence inflicted on him in the film is more gory and believable and lovingly lingered over than the mayhem he himself inflicts. The sexual humor — and Kubrick has sexed things up — makes our hero seem a bit of a dog when he is actually one hell of a rat. Examines Burgess' and Kubrick's statements on the film (book) and makes pertinent and penetrating observations on their stated positions — complete with references to, or quotations from, Jonathan Swift, the Holy Ghost, T.S. Eliot, Dr. Johnson and the uses (and abuses) of the film art.

153 Riley, Clayton. "Or a Dangerous, Criminally Irresponsible Horror Show?" **New York Times,** Section II, 9 January 1972, pp. 1, 13.

[Reply to Canby's review. See #126] The symbolism is excessive and somewhat mindless; the title is unexplained. The work is a manual for every street gang in the U.S. Would the film still dazzle Canby's mind and senses if it depicted Blacks and Puerto Ricans roaming the Upper East Side in search of sexual assault? The book's thesis, emphasized by Kubrick, that the will to do evil is better than no evil at all, strikes Riley as criminally irresponsible and stupidly naive. The music by Europe's long-dead longhairs fails to turn a fraudulent mess into a Freudian Mass. If you liked the still shots of Mylai, you will hug yourself in ecstasy at the gory detail, the boot in the face, the third rape scene, the. . .

154 Samuels, Charles Thomas. "The Context of **A Clockwork Orange.**" **American Scholar,** v. 41, no. 3 (Summer 1972) 439-43.

The film takes a sardonic look at Alex. He is charming, but clearly not intelligent. This point is explicitly made in the gratuitous murder of the cat-lady. The narcistic, hypocritical poseur of a cat-lady suggests that lack of value in the adult culture facilitates teen-age violence. Kubrick's use of music is artful. He does not, however, emphasize the book's theme that goodness is unreal when not freely chosen. "Kubrick finds brilliant cinematic equivalents for Burgess' gimmicks, but he is limited by the original's intellectual and emotional thinness." Kubrick's earlier films tended to counter the American infatuation with mindless action which makes American film-makers seem like idiot-savants. He now threatens to go the way of his predecessors. 4,500w

155 Sarivonova, M. "Konfrontatsiia — Varsheva 73."' **Kinoizkustvo,** v. 28 (August 1973) 69-75.

155.2 Schickel, Richard. "Future Schlock and Family Affairs; Three Problems in Communication." **Life,** v. 72, no. 4 (February 4, 1972) 14.

Kubrick's failure to provide a visual equivalent for nadsat is a profound loss. The invented language provides an ironic counterpoint to the impoverished imaginative life of the future society. The wealth and wit of the language distance us from the violence and, most important, it enables Burgess to make an implicit demonstration of Alex's virtues as a human being. Kubrick works desperately hard to compensate for this loss of language, but without success. Cuteness marks Malcolm McDowell in the role of Alex. Worse, his victims are totally unsympathetic: old, homosexual or power-hungry. The loss of language means that "It is no longer a cautionary tale about how the bureaucratic rage for order creates a hopelessly banal social order and mindlessly murderous youthful rebel class." It is one of the most dishonest parables of the war between the generations and it shows what happens when moviemakers consider themselves intellectuals. 900w

156 Simonelli, G. "Arancia meccanica." **Cschedario,** no. 62 (February 1973) 53-63.

157 Strick, Philip. "Kubrick's Horrorshow." **Sight and Sound,** v. 41, no. 1 (Winter 1971/72) 44-46.

Argues that the film has borrowed the fun and vitality of the novel while rejecting the uncharacteristic milk-and-water ending of some editions. Observes that the language of the book is wholeheartedly adopted, and comments on the function of the dialogue in the film. Also compares it to **2001** and examines Kubrick's use of the camera to achieve his effects. "Movement is a vital part of each scene, a torrential, dancing flow that makes **2001** seem in retrospect to have approached the glutinous." Comments on the use of music, and praises the performances by Malcolm McDowell and Patrick Magee. Concludes that Kubrick "justly deserves his reputation as the cinema's greatest perfectionist." 2,200w

158 Walker, Beverly. "From Novel to Film: Kubrick's **Clockwork Orange**. **Women and Film**, v. 1, no. 2 (1972) 4-10.

Clearly the most misogynistic film of the year. Kubrick's view of female human beings is ugly, lewd and brutal. The violence committed by Alex is muted by various techniques; the violence inflicted on him is real by comparison, and we are now permitted to feel the pain of violence. A comparison of book and film reveals that Kubrick is responsible for the misogyny. Burgess' hoodlums are dressed in black; Kubrick chooses *white*. Burgess' teenyboppers are *raped*; Kubrick's girls are contemptuously depicted as teenage *sluts* who lick phallus-shaped popsicles. The intended victim of the Billyboy gang is ten years old in Burgess' book; in Kubrick's film she is an amply endowed woman, and after her breasts sway in a titillating display, she is discarded, having served the purpose Kubrick intended. Burgess' rape on the couple in the HOME is a gang-bang affair, and Alex slooshies cries of agony; in Kubrick's film her struggles are very moderate indeed. The femlins in the Korova milk bar, wholly Kubrick's invention, clearly convey the demeaning notion of woman as servant. Burgess' cat-lady is a dignified old woman; Kubrick's equivalent is a lewdie with a hard voice. A labyrinth of attitudes has conspired to keep women in a subservient position in America. Women must use all the means of protest, including the weapon of the boycott, to eradicate or change these attitudes. "An artist should be free to express what's on his mind, however kinky it may be. But we don't have to buy the product any more than we would a rotten orange."

159 Weinraub, Bernard. "Kubrick Tells What Makes 'Clockwork Orange' Tick." **New York Times**, 4 January 1972, p. 26.

[Interview.] Kubrick received copy of **Clockwork** from Terry Southern. He was excited by the plot, ideas, characters, language. Alex should normally be an unsympathetic, perhaps an abhorrent character, but, like Richard III, he undermines moral disapproval of his evil ways. The power of the story derives from its glimpse into the depravity of man. "One of the most dangerous fallacies which has influenced a great deal of political and philosophical thinking is that man is basically good . . . ." Describes Kubrick's obsessive working habits, his views on the director's role, and his low opinion of reviewers. "No reviewer has ever illuminated any aspect of my work for me." 1,500w

160 Westerbeck, Colin L. "The Screen." **Commonweal**, v. 95, no. 15 (January 14, 1972) 351-52.

Kubrick has produced a strained, visually cluttered film and all his trade-marks (backlighting, backtracking down long corridors) are unable to save it. In **Lolita**, as here, Kubrick broaches a theme which would be intolerable without the mediation of art. In Burgess' novel, nadsat makes a continuous statement; Kubrick's stylistic techniques are mere interjections. In the murder of the cat-lady (howlingly overdone), the rape scene and the hoodlum's rumble, Kubrick presents a world unable to distinguish fantasy from experience. He is moving beyond pessimism to cynicism, and the film (which nauseated Westerbeck) seems designed to rob the viewer of his moral choice.

161 Zimmerman, Paul D. "Kubrick's Brilliant Vision." **Newsweek**, v. 79, no. 1 (January 3, 1972) 28-33.

[Biographical sketch preceded by remarks on Kubrick's film.] The work, shorn of sentiment, works through brilliant ironies and dazzling dramatic ideas; it appeals to the intellect and the imagination; but it does not touch our hearts. It moves on many levels at once — social, psychological, moral and mythical. Alex is despicable but, like Richard III, redeemed by wit, energy and demonic imagination. Kubrick remarks that Alex, from his own point of view, is having a wonderful time. He wanted to portray this fact without the restriction of the conventional pieties. At its most profound level, the film is an odyssey of the human personality, the adventures of the id itself. Alex's resurrection at the end represents an ironic triumph of the human psyche over the forces of control. [Reprinted in #1776.]

Clockwork Testament

162 London: Hart-Davis, MacGibbon, 1974.

163 New York: Knopf, 1975, c1974. Illustrated by the Quays.

164 New York: Bantam, 1976, c1975. Pbk.

165 Harmondsworth, Eng.; New York: Penguin, 1978, c1974.

Translations

166 French: **Le testament de l'orange**. Paris: Laffont, 1975. Translated by Georges Belmont & Hortense Chabrier.

167 German: **Das Uhrwerk Testament**. Munchen: Heyne, 1974. Translated by Walter Brumm. (Heyne-Buch Nr. 5124)

Reviews

168 Adams, Phoebe-Lou. Review of **The Clockwork Testament; Or, Enderby's End. Atlantic**, v. 235, no. 2 (February 1975) 122.

"The arrangement permits a lambasting of street violence, urban filth, interracial rows, TV commercials, pseudo-intellectual talk shows, women's lib, undisciplined students, and people who write trash by mistake for poetry. Somehow none of the diatribe is as funny or perceptive as one expects the work of Mr. Burgess to be, and Enderby, dedicated artist and representative of traditional culture, is pretty much a surly old bore."

169 Allen, Bruce. Review of **The Clockwork Testament; Or, Enderby's End. Library Journal**, v. 100, no. 2 (January 15, 1975) 144.

"Burgess is an incomparable inventor, and this is all marvellous fun to read. But the novel is, palpably, 'message' more than life — and even its most delightful effects are a bit too desperately contrived."

170 Anon. "Beneath the Waves." **Times Literary Supplement**, 7 June 1974, p. 601.

Enderby is tiring of life, and Burgess has decided to conclude his saga with a last brief fling of protest against objects of his creator's scorn and dislike: most things in American civilization, and especially its protest culture. "For all the outrageous resource of Burgess's humour, this short book seems a slightly inadequate finish to poor Enderby's travails. The apologia for the **Deutschland/Orange** is an understandable exercise after all the rumpus, yet few readers who enjoy this novelist will feel any defence necessary . . . . Enderby's affirmations about literature are genuine enough, but tinged with a mixture of sadness and defiance which flamboyant joking does not conceal: a deep pessimist is grimly hanging on. Enderby deserved, no, not a nobler end, but something more thoroughly and zestfully in line with his beginning."

171 Anon. Review of **The Clockwork Testament; Or, Enderby's End. Economist**, v. 251, no. 6824 (June 8, 1974) 107.

"Mr. Burgess being Mr. Burgess, this scenario does not result in a large, serious novel with a message but in a short, funny one with several messages — about literary standards, nature imitating art, the pleasures of squalor, the separability of writers and their work, and much else. It is worth repeating that it is painfully funny, as well."

172 Anon. Notice of **The Clockwork Testament; Or, Enderby's End. Sunday Times** (London), 21 July 1974, p. 31.

"Return and departure of Enderby, poet extraordinary, film writer manque and one of Mr. Burgess's funniest creations." [Complete text of notice. Same notice repeated in **Sunday Times** (London), 1 December 1974, p. 40.]

173 Anon. Review of **Clockwork Testament; Or, Enderby's End. Kirkus Reviews**, December 1, 1974, p. 1266.

174 Anon. Review of **The Clockwork Testament; Or, Enderby's End**. **Publishers Weekly**, v. 206, no. 23 (December 2, 1974) 57.

"In what looks like his own testamentary farewell to New York and the American scene, Burgess is not only angry — his satirist's prerogative — but apparently tired. His story seems scratched together, his characters are clay pigeons to be shot at rather than people, his jibes at what he clearly considers the new barbarism. . . sometimes hit home and sometimes seem wild . . . . Burgess's main theme, as in his other 'Clockwork' story, is still the freedom to do evil; but there's something both sad and a little sour about this whole performance."

175 Anon. Notice of **The Clockwork Testament; Or, Enderby's End**. **Manchester Guardian Weekly**, 28 December 1974, p. 6.

"A farewell to arms for Burgess's memorable anti-hero Enderby, 'that much-abused creature of earth and air,' wrote Norman Shrapnel, 'who goes out with spirit, firing from every aperture'." [Complete text of notice.]

176 Anon. Review of **The Clockwork Testament; Or, Enderby's End**. **Saturday Review/World**, v. 2, no. 9 (January 25, 1975) 44.

"This novel is Mr. Burgess' answer to critics [of **A Clockwork Orange**] and a very good novel it is, too, though not for its retort on such things as the artist's culpability or lack of it (with regard to socially harmful themes), about which Mr. Burgess is apt to get quite tendentious. Far better than any of this is his superb splenetic assault on the destruction of language . . . . there are flaws in this many-sided and vastly entertaining work. Mr. Burgess's choice of satiric objects (New York City, crime, the activist-student lunkheads, the surly black maids) is a bit fashionable, and taking on the host of a late-night television talk show is like shooting fish in a barrel. Yet, it is all immensely well done, properly merciless, and full of sour pleasures, among them Mr. Burgess's unfailing ear for the way in which the enemy talks."

177 Anon. Review of **The Clockwork Testament; Or, Enderby's End**. **Booklist**, v. 71, no. 13 (March 1, 1975) 669.

"A brazenly funny, irreverent, and often vicious poke at individual and collective idiosyncrasies."

178 Anon. Review of **The Clockwork Testament; Or, Enderby's End**. **New Yorker**, v. 51, nos. 3-4 (March 10, 1975) 118-19.

A brilliantly funny novel that serves as a postscript for **A Clockwork Orange** and **Enderby**. This resurrection of F.X. Enderby in a gallant but doomed attempt to pit the spunky, eccentric individual against a world that reveres uniformity and right thinking is delightful. Enderby is beset by Blacks and Indians, journalists and assorted strangers. "Believing, evidently, that the best defense is a good offense, he responds with vehement homilies on art and original sin. Some of his arguments deserve better opponents than the cartoon characters Mr. Burgess provides, but Enderby's valiant form, flailing away at philistinism with all he's got, is utterly and hilariously endearing."

179 Anon. Review of **The Clockwork Testament; Or, Enderby's End**. **America**, v. 132, no. 16 (April 26, 1975) 320.

"This is simply Burgess at large, with his free-associating and often scurrilous imagination and his fantastic verbal skill." The summary may sound close to blasphemy, but movie makers, not Hopkins or nuns, are the true targets of this book.

180 Anon. Review of **The Clockwork Testament; Or, Enderby's End**. **Publishers Weekly**, v. 209, no. 3 (January 19, 1976) 104.

[Review of Bantam pbk. ed. Quotes sentences from earlier PW review. See #174.]

181 Anon. Review of **The Clockwork Testament; Or, Enderby's End**. **Washington Post Book World**, 20 May 1976, p. 8.

[Reviews paperback ed.] "The final work in the trilogy of the pet Enderby is a small volume but packed tight with action and meaning. At its core (and explaining the subtitle) is an apologia by the author of **A Clockwork Orange**, examining the process by which Hollywood can take a book whose subject is, essentially, the old theological debate about grace and free will, transform it into an epic of sex and violence and make a writer who was once poor and ignored instead wealthy and misunderstood.'' [The conclusion is an erroneous inference. Messrs. Litvinoff and Kubrick, as well as Warner Bros., profited from the film. Burgess profited only slightly by comparison; he did not become 'wealthy.']

182 Broyard, Anatole. "Poetry Can Kill a Man." **New York Times**, 1 February 1975, p. 25.

[Preceded by leisurely plot summary.] 'As Wallace Stevens said, poetry can kill a man. Because he is a poet, Enderby takes things to heart and the strain is too much for it . . . . For all his clowning and verbal dandyism, one gets the feeling that Mr. Burgess is reading us a moral in this book. It would not be the first time an eminent British visitor found fault with our national character and institutions. It is interesting to note that, in the latest edition of the Encyclopedia Britannica, Mr. Burgess wrote, in his article on the modern novel, that 'the glories and potentialities of American fiction are best summed up in the novels of Vladimir Nabokov . . . . ' You need a rather dark view of our life and letters to come to that conclusion."

183 Byatt, A.S. "All Life Is One." **Times** (London), no. 59,108 (June 6, 1974) 8.

"Burgess returns, with his own mixture of crude gusto and verbal intricacy, to a concatenation of themes: the freedom of the will, the nature of Good and Evil (and their difference from right and wrong) the relationship between art and morals, the proposition that all life is one." Refers to **The Wanting Seed** and observes that Burgess and Enderby see both Pelphase and Gusphase as extremes. Also refers to Enderby's early poem, 'The Pet Beast' and comments that "It may be that one needs a Catholic upbringing to appreciate the full urgency of Burgess's dichotomies . . . . **The Clockwork Testament** makes intricate connections between these themes, Hopkins, film and book of the **Clockwork Orange** and all sorts of aspects of contemporary art and life. It succeeds because it is ferociously funny and wildly, verbally inventive."

184 Edwards, Thomas R. "Academic Vaudeville." **New York Review of Books**, v. 22, no. 2 (February 20, 1975) 34-36.

[Omnibus review. For Burgess, see p. 36.] Burgess has perhaps more invested in Enderby than that Don Rickles of British Letters can sustain. It seems thinner, more local, than **Inside Mr. Enderby** or **Enderby Outside**. But let us not cavil. Burgess is one of our best and most serious fictional comedians. It may sometimes resemble transatlantic farce, but "It's also a stirring denunciation of the trivial, the second-rate, the mindless, and a continuously entertaining reminder of how much this marvelously generous — and for all his learning, unacademic — writer has given us in the past two decades."

185 Ehrmann, Hans. "Novel of Satire and Violence." **San Francisco Sunday Examiner and Chronicle, This World Section**, 16 February 1975, p. 28.

"At times convoluted and at times uproariously funny, Anthony Burgess' prose is like a ping pong match between a professor and and an anti-professor. Burgess loves learned literary allusions and rare words which do not necessarily appear in the dictionary (caecum, camiknicks, ithyphallus, dogmerd) . . . . Burgess is endlessly funny in this, the third of his Enderby novels. He seems to be playing a game of chicken with himself, driving to the very edge of facetiousness and backing away just in time for wit to prevail."

186 Foote, Timothy. "Wolf of God." **Time**, v. 105, no. 11 (March 17, 1975) 84-85.

Burgess, a man of wit and genius, has been inordinately fond of his fairly unprepossessing minor poet, F.X. Enderby. The reason he has written three books about him is that Enderby, with all his faults, is a strong booster of original sin in a society in which Pelagian perfectibility is the prevailing heresy. "Disaster, says Burgess. No original sin, no evil. No evil, no moral choice. No moral choice and human freedom becomes meaningless, man becomes a machine . . . . Burgess supports his dyspeptic Don Quixote through all sorts of polemical extremities. The reader is lashed with puns and offered poetic tidbits taken from Hopkins. But the book succeeds less as a novel than as intellectual program music." Enderby interprets the cruelty, vulgarity and violence of New York as a sign that man is still free and therefore in need of God's grace. Suggests that Enderby's failure to believe in the immortal soul makes his protest irrelevant.

187 Koltz, Newton. "Uncommon Wealth of Novelists." **America**, v. 132, no. 11-12 (March 22, 1975) 215-16.

Burgess' writing is fluent, witty, muscular and energetically gonadal. They are always a joy to read, but somehow they fail to come off because they tend to show more craft than substance. **The Clockwork Testament** makes the not very extraordinary point that men are better off when they are free to do evil than when they are forced to do good. This work is a series of bilious episodes. ". . . Burgess has set out to write, I think, a funny, brilliant, angry book about his weakened but still courageous poet-self in a last ditch stand against the besetting ills of our time — the diseases that have brought on decay of soul, decay of will, decay of sensibility, decay of language and the decay of New York. But what Burgess has actually done is make a funny, brilliant, malicious book. In the end, malevolence is much less memorable, much less of an achievement, than genuine anger. This is a disappointing book; still, two cheers for Burgess' energy and cunning."

188 Lhamon, W.T. "Recent Fiction." **New Republic**, v. 172, nos. 7-8 (February 22, 1975) 29.

"Never accuse Burgess of complicating our ideas about the world's workings. Oh! The world is so dumb. Only Enderby is still cultivated . . . . can there really be Burgess buffs? There must be, or else the publishers are losing a heap of money. Worldly but world-weary, committed but disengaged, passionate but juiceless: Burgess buffs must be human oxymorons. They must be interesting folks, but aggressive about their supposed superiority . . . . Burgess has mastered distaste. He loathes things and people involved with things . . . . The dialogues in **Clockwork Testament** are straw dialogues, set pieces that Enderby wins outright or wins covertly because the ostensible winners reveal their boorishness by their conquest . . . . But even the dialogues are sour, because they are steeped in Enderby's petty gloating over his petty wins. Having decided that the world is a loathsome place, what joy or seriousness or honor is there in proving the prejudice? . . . . Burgess and his editors must think there are more Prufrocks still buying books than I think there are."

189 Murray, John J. Review of **The Clockwork Testament; Or, Enderby's End**. **Best Sellers**, March 1, 1975, p. 523.

"Not since **Catch-22** in '62 has the reading of any book thrown me into convulsive hysterics . . . . Burgess strikes me as an ungentleized Thurber. Enderby's classroom lecture on a made-up Elizabethan dramatist named Whitelaw [i.e. Whitelady] is hysterical, and not only to a Francis Meres. The creative writing class (I think Burgess was visiting lecturer at CUNY) is a Juvenalian "University Days" wherein the wordloving wordsmith gets clobbered by an ethnic conglomerate of Boloncieewczs."

190 Nicol, Charles. "A Poet for Posterity." **National Review**, v. 27, no. 17 (May 9, 1975) 521.

Burgess often seems to be the only living novelist in England. Master of many languages and a lover of music, his prose bristles with knowledge and wit. He has not written a great novel, but his work proves that only Nabokov is his master, and only Burgess is in Nabokov's league. The belching, the flatulence, the unrestrained anality of Enderby plainly ridicule the Freudian position that the artist is a product of neurosis. The long poem compiled by Enderby is not, however, a convincing demonstration of his poetic genius. Its central argument over determinism and free will was better made in **A Clockwork Orange**. Still, "installing Enderby in New York City does allow Burgess to comment on teenage gangs, college students, women's lib, TV talk shows — all the crudities of America. If the urge toward autobiographical justification is at Enderby's expense, that price is still worth paying, for Enderby's hallucinatory experiences in New York between heart attacks are invaluable."

191 Nye, Robert. "A New Novel from 'Clockwork Orange' Author." **Christian Science Monitor**, 25 April 1975, p. 27.

Burgess is an author of extraordinary potential, and a critic of Joyce who fully understands the life that is in language, but his actual novels tend to be inventive failures. In this work the isolated peaks in the narrative occur when Enderby invents a fictitious Elizabethan author complete with selected soliloquies, and when Burgess satirizes the inanities of a television chat show. The problems of the novel are several. Burgess is plainly deriving much of the material from his own experience as the author of **A Clockwork Orange** — and there is not enough sustenance to keep the farce going. The text is shot through with references to the verse of Hopkins. What is the point, or relevance, of these quotations? "All the same, I don't want to finish on a curmudgeonly note. [He] is a novelist in the great tradition of energy which runs from Swift and Sterne to the present. His [energy or style] is perhaps even more like one of those careless Elizabethans — Thomas Nashe, say — who dashed off prose by the yard, careless, ambitious, witty, intoxicated with the English language. No single one of his books seems to me a satisfactory novel; but that is not to say that he is not a novelist of possibly major significance."

192 O'Hara, J.D. Review of **The Clockwork Testament**. **New York Times Book Review**, 2 February 1975, p. 4.

[Racy plot summary.] Observes that **Inside Mr. Enderby** can be read as "I'm Enderby," that the name Vesta Bainbridge includes two of Daedelus' detestations (bridges and baths) and that the initials of her name reverse the B.V.M. [Blessed Virgin Mary]. Fame has finally come to Burgess, not on account of his style, but because of a slick, coarse, and evil movie made from a moral and religious novel called **A Clockwork Orange**. The work "begins with a quotation from Seymour Bushe, rushes on to include Joyce, Borges, Nabokov, Shakespeare and Hopkins, and tumbles, slips, splashes and leaps happily in a welter of words until its all too quick end. Some of Burgess's wordy-gurdies are clotted with verbiage; this is not. It is grand, and purists can always ignore the message. Anyone considering a trip to the Big Apple should read it for its street scenes alone."

193 Ostermann, Robert. "'Enderby's End' is Manic but Triumphant." **National Observer**, 1 February 1975, p. 21.

Enderby (slovenly, coarse, bad-tempered, intolerant, rude in speech and manner, contemptuous of progress, fads, and fashion) is the finest creation of that versatile, prolific, audacious novelist, Anthony Burgess. It is a triumphant conclusion to a great work of fiction.

194 Prescott, Peter S. "Among the Yahoos." **Newsweek**, v. 85, no. 14 (April 7, 1975) 89.

"A fusty Gulliver among the Yahoos, Enderby stalks our murderous streets with a sword cape, denouncing complacency and vulgarity, defending art and human freedom . . . . Challenged to defend the ineradicable evil lurking in the world, Enderby takes on feminists, behaviorists, muggers, TV celebrities — all the simplicitarians of our ex-colonial civilization . . . . [This work] based on Burgess's own experience, is simply hilarious, not just for its satire but for its comic sense of timing and its celebration of the elasticity of the English language."

195 Prince, Peter. "Intramural." **New Statesman**, v. 87, no. 2257 (June 21, 1974) 894.

[Omnibus review.] It is not a very glorious exit. Burgess expresses his contempt for American culture and, more specifically, for the consciously chosen form taken by American higher education — the result of mainly conscious decisions about what role they should play in their society — and the sacrifices needed to attain it. Americans have openly debated the problems associated with an Open Admission policy. Enderby makes a very unimpressive as well as redundant prophet. "It is sad to watch his stature shrink in this alien setting. The egotism, the slovenliness, the indifferent poetry, which were all such fun in earlier volumes, seem rather dispiriting now that their possessor is actually proposing himself as an arbiter, even a model, of cultural excellence. And more seriously, Enderby's insularity and his racism. . . seem merely contemptible now that he has been translated from the easy-going bigotries of his native turf to this tense, angry city, one of the world's great black and Puerto Rican (and Jewish) capitals. It is all meant to be a jolly joke, of course, just part of Enderby's lovable British rumbunctiousness. Except it looks here like a case of incorrigible immaturity and loutishness, much more grave indeed than the mild juvenile iconoclams that Enderby diagnoses and deplores among his American students. And unhappily, as with his heart condition, it's clear that Enderby's at least is a terminal case."

196 Pritchard, William H. "Exile's Return." **Listener**, v. 91, no. 2359 (June 13, 1974) 776-77.

This, one of Burgess' shortest novels, alludes most directly to his recent life and previous fiction, and Enderby articulates disgusts and despairs for which he could never have found words in Morocco, or in Hove where he suffered notably in silence and eructations. The poet's life is still satisfyingly gross [quotes some passages of the novel concerned with food preparation] and it could be argued that the three Enderby novels are the richest and most verbally dazzling comedies Burgess has written.

Enderby's students at Manhattan U. are vicious, stupid and lazy, and there is no suggestion that the views of the novelist are any more complicated. So "In fact a case could be mounted against Burgess, as sharing enthusiastically his hero's self-pity and misanthropically slobbish grunts toward life — could be mounted, though, only by remaining resolutely impervious to moments of high entertainment and to the stylistic energies infusing them." Burgess is plainly not out of it at all.

197 Raban, Jonathan. "What Shall We Do About Anthony Burgess?" **Encounter**, v. 43, no. 5 (November 1974) 83-88.

[Omnibus review. Also reviews **Napoleon Symphony** and other novels. Preceded by informed remarks on **MF**.] Both books are about artists trying to scratch a vision on a rude and messy world. Both Napoleon and Enderby live in worlds covered with blood and shit. The novel takes the form of a scurrilous satire which jeers at American universities, the film and television industry, Black Power, and Women's Lib. He has created a grotesque society which has no use for art or history except as instruments of shallow and vicious propaganda. "Enderby, though dead, lives because he exemplifies the most important freedom of all — to keep one's own language alive . . . . The rage which boils inside **Clockwork Testament** is directed against any view of life which would set words beside swordsticks, as archaic curiosities. It's not that Enderby is dead, but that he must not be allowed to die." [See also #606.]

198 Shrapnel, Norman. "Clockwork Hero Meets His End." **Manchester Guardian Weekly**, 22 June 1974, p. 22.

"And it's perhaps time [Enderby] went. He deserves it. He's been a kind of fun for others, if not much for himself, but he doesn't belong any more — that's to say he's become the wrong sort of misfit. Poets are now totally unknown to all but a handful, in whose tiny circle they may well be heroes. Enderby belongs to the old victimised routine — bullied, debagged, mocked in **Punch**, ritually starved or exploited."

199 Smith, Godfrey. "Enderby in Manhattan." **Sunday Times** (London), no. 7,877 (June 2, 1974) 40.

"It is a chaotic little comedy, richly studded with Catholic and sexual imagery: part **Naked Lunch**, part **Hadrian the Seventh**, and will probably appeal most to those curious to gain a further insight into the mind of the extraordinary man who wrote **The Clockwork Orange** [i.e. **A Clockwork Orange**]."

200 Soule, Stephen W. Review of **The Clockwork Testament; Or, Enderby's End.Harper's**, v. 250, no. 1500 (May 1975) 55-56.

"Humorously, seriously, even didactically, Burgess examines the state of our culture. Americans are undernourished, physically and intellectually, their schools 'a whorehouse of progressive intellectual abdication.' Enderby — and Burgess — fight to maintain intellectual standards. **The Clockwork Testament** resembles Nabokov's recent novels . . . . Nabokov and Burgess are our two leading English-language novelists, and the convergence of their themes is intriguing. (Enderby, afraid that a lady out to kill him has erred, shouts, 'That's Nabokov. . . not me. **Pale Fire**, he clarified.') Nabokov and Burgess are both dedicated to words, to language, but Nabokov is detached and ironic, whereas Burgess/Enderby jumps right into the scuffle. Every battle Enderby fights is over words."

201 Theroux, Paul. "Shades of Enderby." **Washington Post Book World**, 9 March 1975, pp. 1, 3.

Confesses he has read **Inside Mr. Enderby** twelve times and memorized the passage that describes Enderby's stepmother. The persuasive detail about Enderby is that he is a good poet. "But there is a subplot, and for the author of **A Clockwork Orange** it was a piece of prophesy. Enderby's narrative poem, 'The Pet Beast' is stolen by a creepy hanger-on and Enderby has the horrifying experience of being responsible for another man's fame." This work should be read in conjunction with the other two Enderby books. "This is a combination of bad temper and elegance — an opposition Burgess handles well and there is no question that he is using his novel to fire a final broadside at the illiterate rabble who have associated him with the egregious movie of recent memory. It is a farewell to America, a good riddance to the cannibal temperament of mass media hacks, and a modest effort to clarify a Christian doctrine. It is also Enderby's end, a disorderly and uncelebrated death for the man who had such high hopes and fine lyrics in Volume One. Burgess's deftness with language is always a delight, but it is underpinned by sustained thought and a great satirical gift. Taken together, the three books that comprise the Enderby saga are a dazzling work, and very likely his best novel."

202 Toynbee, Philip. "Kicking the Bucket." **Observer** (London), 2 June 1974, p. 33.

[Also reviews **Ending Up**, by Kingsley Amis.] "It must be said that I think one of these books a very good novel indeed; the other a fairly bad one. To put it bluntly, Mr. Amis has never done better; I am not aware that Mr. Burgess has ever done worse . . . . My trouble with Enderby is simply that I like and admire him so much less than his creator seems to do . . . . He is rude about Negroes, Jews, etc., simply — or so I constantly felt — because he knows it teases. His views on literature are, to my mind, exemplary; but I wish he would make them sound a bit more interesting . . . . What is more he is a much worse poet than Mr. Burgess must (half-secretly) believe and hope. And the general argument about free-will and original sin which is conducted throughout the book has nothing perceptibly new or interesting to say about what should be a perennially fruitful topic."

Coaching Days of England

203 London: Elek, 1966.

204 New York: Time-Life Books, 1966.

Includes an historical commentary by Burgess, pp. 9-26. Both books have the same lengthy sub-title: "Containing an account of whatever was most remarkable for grandeur, elegance and curiosity in the time of the coaches of England, comprehending the year 1750 until 1850. Together with an historical commentary by Anthony Burgess, and in addition decorated and illustrated with a great number of drawings, prints and views in perspective gathered on purpose for this work."

Reviews

205 Annan, Noel. "Victoria Lives and Is in the Stacks." **New York Review of Books**, v. 8, no. 9 (May 18, 1967) 13.

". . . **Coaching Days of England** is surely a coffee-table book to end all coffee-table books. It should not have come to us straight from the printer and the bindery. It should have been sent to an automobile plant to have wheels put on it. An elegant coffee table would buckle beneath the weight. Hold it you cannot; you can only put it on casters and trundle around. [The book measures 39 x 53 cm.] Burgess' spirited and informative historical commentary proves he is no sentimentalist. He points out that the horses were brutally treated, the coachmen were blackguards, the frost and vomit intolerable. Veblen would have admired it as an object of Conspicuous Waste.

206 Hamilton, George Heard. "Panorama from the Palette." **Saturday Review**, v. 49, no. 49 (December 3, 1966) 33.

Most people brought up in the English-speaking tradition have an "ancestral" memory of the coaching days of England; the fiction of Charles Dickens is the cause. The book is continuously interesting. The portraits, genre scenes, hunting prints, posters and tavern signs record the coaching days with a wealth of detail and gesture. "If this is merely literary art according to contemporary theory, so much the worse for a theory too narrow to encompass a kind of art capable of communicating so much pleasure."

207 Rea, R.R. Review of **Coaching Days of England**. **Library Journal**, v. 92, no. 4 (February 15, 1967) 765.

A vivid account of the romance of the days of the brougham, phaeton and barouche. The reproductions of paintings by Hogarth, Rowlandson, and James Pollard are magnificent. Burgess describes the heyday of English coaching and links the extracts of writings by Fielding, Smollett, Burney, Young, Irving, Dickens, Nimrod, and Surtees. "The price [$32.95] dictates careful consideration before purchase."

208 Rosenberg, John D. "Plum Pudding." **Washington Post Book Week**, 11 December 1966, p. 5.

[Omnibus review.] It is less a book than a product. The introduction by Burgess is sprightly, but it is sumptuous packaging in search of an author.

209 Showers, Paul. "The Jumble Shelf." **New York Times Book Review**, 4 December 1966, p. 38-44.

[Reviews many books under one title. For Burgess, see p. 42.] It is an absorbing, immensely informative history of transportation and related subjects in England. The introductory survey by Burgess is as brisk and stylish as a park phaeton. "An elegant volume, it can be read with greatest comfort in a double bed, allowing half of the bed for the book. When open, it measures — cover edge to cover edge — about 3 ½ feet, which is also the wingspread of an adult peregrine falcon."

Cyrano! (Broadway musical)

209.2 [NOTE: Broadway musical comedy which opened at the Palace Theater, N.Y.C., on May 13, 1973. Ran for only 49 performances. Book by Anthony Burgess; adapted from Edmond Rostand's **Cyrano de Bergerac**. Music: Michael J. Lewis. Lyrics: Anthony Burgess. Staging: Michael Kidd. Sets: John Jensen. Costumes: Desmond Heeley. Not to be confused with **Cyrano de Bergerac** which played at the Guthrie Theater in Minneapolis.]

Recordings

210 Cyrano. [Selections. Phonorecord] A. & M. Records [1973] SP 3702. 4 sides, 12 in., 33 ⅓ rpm. Stereo. All lyrics by Anthony Burgess. Book based on Anthony Burgess' adaptation of Cyrano de Bergerac by Edmond Rostand. Music by Michael J. Lewis. CONTENTS: Overture. — Opening sequence. — Nose song. — Tell her. — From now till forever. — Bergerac. — No thank you. — Roxana. — It's she and it's me. — You have made me love. — Thither, thother, thide of the. . . — Pocapdedious. — Autumn carol. — I never loved you. — Epilog.

Reviews

211 Anon. "Palace 'Cyrano' Opens March 25." **New York Times**, 19 December 1972, p. 56.

[Play actually opened May 13, 1973. See below.] Brief news note. Describes principal actors, producer, fact that play will open first in Minneapolis, then Toronto, then Broadway. [Pre-Broadway tryout also took place in Boston at the Colonial Theatre.]

212 Anon. "Cyrano." **Harper's Bazaar**, v. 106 (March 1973) 153.

Plummer has performed the demanding dramatic role of Cyrano before to critical acclaim, but this new version of the play has a romantic hero who also sings. Newcomer Leigh Beery plays the part of Roxane.

213 Barnes, Clive. "Theater: Plummer Triumphs in Musical 'Cyrano'." **New York Times**, 14 May 1973, p. 37.

It is very good and partly excellent. The Burgess adapation is excellent and appropriately flamboyant. Michael Lewis' music stands nervously in the territory between the speech-song of "My Fair Lady" and the impassioned sentiment of "Man of La Mancha." Mr. Plummer as Cyrano is simply magnificent. The part suits him the way a sheath suits its rapier. His performance has a kinetic grace. He also accomplishes the considerable feat of making Cyrano a man without sentimentality. Leigh Beery as Roxana is delicate and yet passionate while Mark Lamos as Christian is bluffly attractive. The music may lack that overwhelming surge, but Mr. Plummer acts his heart out in one of the best performances of the season. [Includes credits, cast.]

214 Clurman, Harold. "Theatre." **Nation**, v. 216, no. 23 (June 4, 1973) 731.

Revivals of this play almost always repeat something of the original success. Henry James said he would not part with one inch of Cyrano's nose; George Jean Nathan thought it the most enchanting of all plays; and the tough-minded or hip young girl who saw it with him was reduced to unabashed tears at poor Cyrano's plight. *Ergo*, Cyrano has something. But Burgess' lyrics, in this version, are hard to hear; and the music hardly exists as expression. The triumph of the evening is Christopher Plummer. Unfortunately, even this spectacularly endowed actor does not invest the role with life. The performance is mostly brain and muscle.

215 "Cyrano." IN **New York Theatre Critics' Reviews**, v. 34, no. 12 (May 21, 1973) 272-76.

Collects and reprints the criticism of Martin Gottfried, T.E. Kalem, Jack Kroll, Douglas Watt, Richard Watts and Edwin Wilson. [For annotations, see surnames. Also includes very brief television reviews (not annotated) by Leonard Harris, Leonard Probst and Kevin Sanders.]

216 Gill, Brendan. "The Theatre: Please Do Not Touch." **New Yorker**, v. 49, no. 14 (May 26, 1973) 54.

It constitutes tampering with a very skilful play, and the songs and a few pattering dance steps interrupt the nicely calculated rhythm. "Rostand's bittersweet lightness of tone is made heavy by the explicitness of song; we get the uncomfortable impression that we are hearing everything twice, in a fashion coarser than our intelligence deserves."

217 Gussow, Mel. "To Plummer, Cyrano Is an Old Friend." **New York Times**, 17 May 1973, p. 52.

[Interview with Christopher Plummer who played the role of Cyrano.] The actor reflects on his role; recalls he played Christian to Jose Ferrer's Cyrano in 1951; explains why he turned down the role at the Guthrie; comments on the historical Bergerac; loves the swashbuckling of the play.

218 Gottfried, Martin. "A Musical 'Cyrano'." **Women's Wear Daily**, 14 May 1973, p. ?

The play probably defies musicalization on the ground that the story is so rich and familiar. Adaptors are fearful of editing it. Michael Kidd did not succeed in making the play musical enough. Praises Plummer as a formidably equipped, sensitive and magnetic actor. Sluggish adequacy describes the rest of the cast. Burgess' adapation is faithful, clean and often elegant even though he has a tendency to overuse the word 'God.' This musical version of the play is simply innocuous. [Reprinted in #215.]

219 Hughes, Catharine. "Tinkering with the Classics." **America**, v. 128, no. 22 (June 9, 1973) 538.

The performance is marked by a hectic drive which somehow detracts from the play. Burgess' clever lyrics are serviceable if not genuinely witty. Lewis' music, seventeen numbers in all, is exceptionally derivative. As for the cast, God knows that everybody works hard — which may well be part of the problem. The play proceeds at such a frantic pace that much of the poignancy and poetry is lost.

220 K[alem], T.E. "Coolheaded Gascon." **Time**, v. 101 (May 28, 1973) 55.

Cyrano is a sentimental favorite, and both the play and its hero are a trifle silly. The current revival is less than wholly satisfying because "For mystifying reasons, the play has been converted into a musical. Since the songs are clumsily inserted into the text, they simply interrupt the narrative flow. The music was composed by Michael J. Lewis and he has the soaring melodic imagination of a computer. The lyrics, supplied by Anthony Burgess, lean more toward economy than eloquence, and while Burgess' adaptation of the main body of the text is brisk and fluently idiomatic, it is emotionally reserved and poetically undernourished." [Reprinted in #215.]

221 Kroll, Jack. "Tin-Pan Cyrano." **Newsweek**, v. 81 (May 28, 1973) 83.

> Cyrano was the arch-romantic's dream,
> The Gascon poet, soldier, pioneer
> Of science-fiction, and to top it off,
> A lover with a comic tragic flaw —
> His big proboscis. What a tasty mix
> Of Villon D'Artagnan, Kurt Vonnegut
> And Schnoz Durante! He has never died.
> But nothing reaches immortality
> Until it's turned into a musical . . . .
> Plummer leaps over all the Broadway jive
> To burn the stage with poetry and power.
> Citizens, do not miss his Cyrano.

[Reprinted in #215.]

222 Watt, Douglas. "'Cyrano' Could Be a Lot Funnier." **Daily News** (New York, N.Y.), 14 May 1973, p. ?

The producers have added more flourish to a play that is all flourish and the result is an awesomely silly musical. Of course, Michael Lewis and Anthony Burgess are enormously less gifted at this sort of thing than Rodgers and Hammerstein. You get the feeling you are watching a melange of musicals past. Michael Kidd has staged the play as if he wanted to get it over as quickly as possible. "Even so it's a long evening and, as I have said, a silly one, though probably not silly enough to make it truly worthwhile." [Reprinted in #215.]

223 Watts, Richard. "The Big-Nosed Romantic." **New York Post**, 14 May 1973, p. ?

It has now opened in New York after a successful trial run in Boston. Not improved in the transition, it provides an interesting evening thanks largely to the presence, full of dash, charm, acting skill and dramatic authority of Christopher Plummer. He dominates the evening. "'Cyrano' didn't seem to me the masterpiece advance reports had suggested, but, with a special bow to Mr. Plummer, I enjoyed it." [Reprinted in #215.]

224 Wilson, Edwin. "Musical Cyrano Comes a Cropper." **Wall Street Journal**, 15 May 1973, p. ?

Burgess' translation of Rostand's play proved to be the best-attended production in the history of the Tyrone Guthrie Theater in Minneapolis. Then someone decided that Rostand's play and Burgess' words were not enough. They should have stopped while they were ahead. When the production stays with Rostand, and Plummer is allowed to play pure Rostand, he is little short of magnificent, and it is worth seeing the play to observe his performance alone. [Reprinted in #215.]

Cyrano de Bergerac

225 New York: Knopf, 1971. By Edmond Rostand. Translated and adapted for the modern stage by Anthony Burgess.

Reviews

Burgess on his own work: 'We must distinguish between **Cyrano de Bergerac** and **Cyrano**. The first the play in my translation for the Guthrie, produced with my own music. The second a Broadway musical with music by Michael Lewis. First a success, second a near-flop (running costs, superior attractions of Watergate on TV, etc.'' [Also Burgess on the sluggish sale of the book, etc.]: ''. . . my next task on this last Saturday was to go to Rizzoli's bookshop on Fifth Avenue to sign copies of a book of mine and to reward, if that is the term, the buyers of the book with a mini-lecture about the hardships of authorship. The book was my translation of Rostand's **Cyrano de Bergerac** which, in a very beautiful edition, came out in 1971 . . . . So my wife got to work and Rizzoli was agreeable, and the result was that I signed and sold forty-odd copies in an hour and a half — not a lot, but more than the book has sold since 1971.''

226 Adams, Phoebe. Review of **Cyrano de Bergerac**. **Atlantic**, v. 229, no. 1 (January 1972) 97.

Burgess' version mixes prose with a variety of verse forms. The method works very well in the comedy scenes, but the romantic arias seem as long-winded as ever. Burgess also removes Roxane, coach and horses from the battlefield. ''Mr. Burgess justifies it on the grounds of increased realism and the need to make the play available to 'good amateur companies.' He is right on both points, in regard to his own accomplishment. One is entitled to wonder, however, whether realism really benefits the peculiar *fin de siecle* romanticism, part sweet champagne and part wormwood, that underlies the play. As for those good amateur companies, Cyrano was written for a virtuoso professional, a notorious dazzler of an actor, and only Thalia knows how many audiences have been protected from an evening of ineptitude by Roxane's rig.''

227 Barnes, Clive. ''Stage: Langham Revitalizes the Guthrie Theater.'' **New York Times**, 20 September 1971, p. 31.

''The 'Cyrano' deserves many bouquets, but the first and most important must go to Mr. Burgess, who, in his translation and adaptation of the original, has taken daring liberties and yet emerged triumphant with a romantic comedy for our time. Mr. Burgess has given the play a positive blood transfusion of wit, imagination, and Cyrano, the perfect embodiment of gallant folly, that conspicuous expenditure of the heart, becomes a strangely contemporary hero.'' Paul Hecht is a bluff and clever Cyrano, more soldier than poet, who carries the play with the finesse of a fencer and the strength of a bull elephant. He never gives you time to think that Cyrano would never fall in love with such a ninny as Roxana, or, love's eloquent surrogate, woo for the tedious Christian. ''. . . I was fascinated to note that Mr. Burgess, in addition to everything else, composed his own attractively flamboyant music.''

228 Szogyi, Alex. Review of **Cyrano de Bergerac**. **New York Times Book Review**, 26 December 1971, pp. 6, 15.

Observes that each new generation deserves a new interpretation of a work, and the myth of Rostand's hoary valentine has been more salubrious for Americans than the life of Willy Loman. Burgess, that eclectic epicurean, has a view of life amusingly Cyrano-esque in flavor. His translation is virile and ingratiating. ''It is also quite noticeably prolix and unfaithful to the letter while attempting to garner the spirit of the original. It is not the work of a subtle poet: its alliterations are aggressive and grating and its penchant for repeating words three times is naive.''

Devil of a State

229 London: Heinemann, 1961.

230 New York: Norton, 1962, c1961.

231 London: Heinemann, 1971, c1961.

232 New York: Ballantine, 1968. Pbk.

233 New York: Norton, 1975, c1961.

Reviews

234 Anon. Review of **Devil of a State**. **Kirkus Reviews**, (November 1, 1961) 979-80.

"Life in the colonies in a jaundiced light, this lacks the direct focus of the earlier books."

235 Anon. Review of **Devil of a State**. **Times Literary Supplement**, 17 November 1961, p. 829.

"This novel would have been improved by more fact and less laboured fantasy . . . . Mr. Burgess catches the peculiar drifting squalor of a life like Lydgate's very well; but with comedy, his chief purpose, he has less success. Characters waver uneasily between satire and fantasy. The book does not even work up to a climax: a *dea ex machina* just holds up a police-womanly hand and stops it dead."

236 Anon. Review of **Devil of a State**. **Publishers Weekly**, v. 192, no. 24 (December 11, 1967) 48.

"Mr. Burgess leaves no joke unspurned in this 1961 novel about a new African state, a caliphate in East Africa that has a fortune in uranium concessions to dispose of to the highest bidder. As usual in a Burgess novel, the plot is part black humor, part satire and part English music-hall, and the author takes every opportunity to bite large holes in his characters with his wicked, witty teeth." [Complete text of review.]

237 Gross, John. "La Noia." **New Statesman**, v. 62, no. 1602 (November 24, 1961) 801-802.

[Omnibus review.] The novel is an altogether more genial offering than **The Hard Life**. "Pidgin English and multi-racial jokes are worked pretty hard; they'd seem funnier if Mr. Burgess hadn't been Scooped long ago. He is obviously inventive and sharp-eyed, but the whole book needs pruning and tidying up." [The reference is to **Scoop**, a novel by Evelyn Waugh.]

238 Jebb, Julian. "Savages at Large." **Time and Tide, v. 42, no. 44 (November 2, 1961) 1850.**

[Omnibus review.] "**Devil of a State** is pretty harsh stuff — as if **The Heart of the Matter** had been re-written by Peter Simple . . . . There is very little warmth in his portraits of the insanely polyglot inhabitants of the Caliphate of Dunia, but his brisk and careful analysis of their different ways of being ludicrous is accurate and funny. Best of all is a Chinese taxi-boy who entertains his customers with an endless Joycean enumeration of car numbers, lamp posts and bars."

239 Jennings, Elizabeth. "New Novels." **Listener**, v. 62, no. 1709 (December 28, 1961) 1133.

[Omnibus review.] In the best English comic fiction, a passive or semi-passive character becomes the victim of an unjust or fatuous society. Witness Paul Pennyfeather in **Decline and Fall**, and William Boot in **A Handful of Dust**. Burgess has learned narrative pace, an eye for detail, wit and love of the absurd from Evelyn Waugh. He has eschewed — and this may be an advantage to him as an original writer — the element of pure fantasy. "This riotous novel ends when Lydgate is foiled in an attempt to escape from his second wife, mistress, and complicated professional life, and finds his first wife waiting for him, 'about sixty, thin, lined, very brown, dry hair, quite grey. . . fingers like bones.' It is a fitting end to a book which often succeeds in making the near sublime very nearly ridiculous."

240 Keown, Eric. "New Novels." **Punch**, v. 241, no. 6323 (November 15, 1961) 731-32.

[Omnibus review. For Burgess, see p. 732.] An adroit satire on white men struggling on in Africa. It is a "light novel that is always readable and sometimes very funny. Mr. Burgess whips them up expertly, and his knowledge of the effects of heat and whisky on frayed nerves comes through with authority."

241 Levin, Martin. "Reader's Report." **New York Times Book Review**, 25 February 1962, p. 40.

In the uranium-rich, water-poor, East African caliphate that Mr. Burgess delineates with such dazzling brilliance, it is decidedly not easy for the characters to behave properly. Cites examples of misbehaviour on the part of characters in the novel. "Mr. Burgess is blessed with a magnificent ear for speech; he is possessed of the clear, skeptical and slightly bilious eye of the true satirist. All this — and a degree of technical artistry that keeps **Devil of a State** snapping, crackling and popping like a bowl of breakfast food down to the last spoonful."

242 Mitchell, Julian. "Wracks of Empire." **Spectator**, v. 207, no. 6958 (November 3, 1961) 636.

[Omnibus review.] "Mr. Burgess makes these people not only horrifying credible and brilliantly appalling, but also symptomatic of the collapse of the tradition they are hopelessly trying to prop up. His venom is sprayed with the speed and accuracy of machine-gun bullets on exploiter and exploited alike, and those foolish enough to get caught between naturally get badly hurt."

243 Price, Martin. "Bands of the Human Spectrum." **Saturday Review**, v. 45, no. 11 (March 17, 1962) 27-28.

[Chiefly plot summary.] "The book has a dark cast; but it is also written with a kind of wilful hilarity. Mr. Burgess lets no joke pass, nor does he fail to repeat many; the wit is often fine, but it is indiscriminate and too insistent. As a result, the book is heavily facetious and too pointlessly sardonic. It never decides whether to be farce or parable, and, inventive as it is, it never escapes the shadow of earlier and better works of a similar kind."

244 Rogers, W.G. "Among Recent Novels." **New York Herald Tribune**, v. 121, no. 42,095 (March 4, 1962) 13.

A rollicking extravaganza set in a distraught, chaotic land that brings real happiness only to the reader.

245 Quigly, Isabel. "Places of the Mind." **Manchester Guardian**, 10 November 1961, p. 6.

[Omnibus review.] "Outrageous but somehow not improbable, the novel steers a curious and and original course between — indeed among — farce, pathos, jokes of every colour, including some pretty black ones, and even at times tragi-comedy. Certainly it is unclassifiable. A description of its events and characters makes it sound like too many other satirical japes, but its flavour is all Burgess's, and its variety is not so much confusing as richly grotesque, many sided."

The Doctor is Sick

246 London: Heinemann, 1960.

247 New York: Norton, 1960.

248 New York: Ballantine, 1966. Pbk.

249 New York: Ballantine, 1973. Pbk.

250 London: Heinemann, 1977.

251 New York: Norton, 1979. Pbk.

252 Harmondsworth, Eng.: New York: Penguin, 1979. Pbk.

Translations

253 Finnish: **Pipopaa Potilas**. Hameenlinna: A.A. Karisto, 1973. Translated by Inkere Uusitalo.

254 German: **Der Doktor ist Ubergeschnappt**. Tubingen: Erdman, 1968. Translated by Inge Wiskott.

255 German: **Der Doktor ist Ubergeschnappt**. Reinbek bei Hamburg: Rowohlt, 1970. Translated by Inge Wiskott.

256 Spanish: **El doctor esta enfermo**. Buenos Aires: Editorial Sudamericana. Translated by Floreal Mazia.

257 Swedish: **Doktorn ar sjuk**. Stockholm: Wahlstrom and Widstrand, 1974. Translated by Caj Lundgren.

Reviews

258 Anon. Review of **The Doctor is Sick**. Punch, v. 239, no. 6275 (December 21, 1960) 909.

"The fantastic adventures of a philologist awaiting an operation for a brain tumour. *Con.* — it's at least 50 pages too long, and the dialect humour is as heavy as lead; but *pro.*, it abounds in gay invention, and at its high points is very funny indeed." [Complete text of review.]

259 Anon. Review of **The Doctor is Sick**. Times Literary Supplement, 23 December 1960, p. 825.

[Omnibus review.] "By way of contrast, **The Doctor is Sick** is very much a picaresque romp, very much a la mode London-style, 1960, full of crooks and aberrations and cafes and 'kinkys.' Certainly bits of it are very funny indeed, but Mr. Burgess is apparently so anxious to be up to date that he is out of date already. Every gimmick known to the ad-men is here, including a television contest for the handsomest bald-head in London. No end of japes in other words, and then our Ph.D. in linguistics, escaped patient from a hospital, mixing with mobsters and girls and so on, makes a final deflating discovery." [Virtually the complete text of the review. It ends in mid-air as given.]

260 Anon. Review of **The Doctor is Sick**. Kirkus Reviews, March 1, 1966, p. 266.

"A cinematic British comedy in which Thurber-Man is pitted against London riff-raff, this doesn't give the full range of Burgess' Promethean verbal wit but it is hilarious . . . . The night before the operation he is given a massive dose of sedatives, then falls out of bed. The body of the novel tells of his sneaking out of the hospital in his pajamas, slippers and a stone overcoat and of his three-day odyssey through the bohemian and criminal underworlds of Soho in search of his wife. During this flight from the surgeon's knife, he sheds the timid Spindrift and becomes the dynamic big spender of counterfeit money, whipper of a flagellant, winner of the Bald Adonis of London Contest . . . . A stack of mad climaxes, all wonderfully operative."

261 Anon. "The Riddle of Reality." Time, v. 87, no. 17 (April 29, 1966) 114.

Burgess spent six weeks in London's National Hospital undergoing tests for a suspected brain tumor. "In most men, the experience would have produced no more than a sigh of relief. In Burgess, it excited the wild flight of imagination that produced this novel." Followed by plot summary in racy **Time**-style. "A late-blooming novelist whose thoughts invariably run deeper than his plots, Burgess, 49, seems to be rekindling the nominalist argument that ignited scholars in the Middle Ages: does a thing achieve reality only after it has a name? Answers are not vital to the enjoyment of Burgess, who heaps on surface treasures of such antic richness that to plunge too far below them carries the risk of reducing their flavor. In other novels — **A Clockwork Orange, A Vision of Battlements, Honey for the Bears** — Burgess demonstrated truly impressive staying power: once read, a Burgess novel is never quite forgotten. It sticks to the palate like a good wine. **The Doctor is Sick**, published in England six years ago, is of the prime Burgess vintage and has only improved with age."

262 Anon. Review of **The Doctor is Sick. Choice**, v. 3, nos. 5-6 (July-August, 1966) 407.

"Burgess is as intoxicated with language as Nabokov, though not yet the master stylist that Nabokov is. But he is always imaginative, bold, Rabelaisian, and every novel is a fresh experience." Is the work a wildly comic Keystone cops caper, or a mordant commentary on London low life? "The reader will decide, and he will, incidentally, be given a lot of information on the nature of language and the life and death of words containing the very essence of reality. Burgess' Joycean wit, his microcosm of a delerious, sometimes sordid, dubious world as the anteroom of the scholar's monastic cell make this novel a prime requisite for academic libraries which should also have **The Clockwork Orange** [sic] and **Nothing Like the Sun**." [Review of Norton paperback ed.]

263 Anon. Review of **The Doctor is Sick. Publishers Weekly**, v. 191, no. 6 (February 6, 1967) 77.

"A good Burgess novel, part thriller, part satire, part spoof and very literary. And entirely original. The **New York Times Book Review** called Burgess 'Britain's answer to Vladimir Nabokov,' and Ballantine is doing well with its $3 boxed set of 'Five Novels by Anthony Burgess.' Now that his most recent novel, **Tremor of Intent**, has been sold to the movies, this fine author may be coming into his own at last." [Complete text of review.]

264 Baumbach, Elinor. "Professor's Pajama Games." **Saturday Review**, v. 49, no. 19 (May 7, 1966) 95.

"Dr. Edwin Spindrift has been bumbling contentedly along, immersed in his consonant blends and comparative dialects. His lack of sexual appetite seems a distasteful but irrelevant fact. . . Unfortunately, in this case the [horrific comic vision Burgess handles with consummate skill] ultimately fails. It is black enough to suit our time, and certainly funny; but Spindrift does not have sufficient weight. His predicament behind the comic situation is not serious enough. Celine once said that futility is the intellectual's vice. Convinced as we are of Edwin Spindrift's futility, we need more than grotesqueness to persuade us of his redemption . . . . Throughout Edwin's travel there have recurred commercials for a new cleaning device, the 'Spindrift.' This joke is emblematic of a deeper flaw in the book as a whole. Its milieu throughout is a shade more picturesque than exacerbating — a failure, it would seem of Burgess's generally mordant intention. When Edwin emits his four-letter expletive, the word is described, not quoted. This sort of evasion might produce comedy, but not the Swiftian revelation that has become a Burgess trademark."

265 Blakeston, Oswell. "Malayan Comedy." **Books and Bookmen**, v. 17 (August 1972) ii, iv.

[Review of Penguin pbk. ed. Also reviews **The Malayan Trilogy**.] After the Malayan book, Burgess relied more on his wonderful gusto than on exotic incident. Observes that **Doctor** is a transitional work. "The schoolmaster, after collapse with a failure of libido, is rushed back to England for an operation on a brain tumour; and then the author has a bang at too many targets: medicine, adultery, beauty contests, and so on. One feels he was just practising for his mighty second wind, belching almost. Not, then the best of Burgess; even if Burgess can never be less than a passable read." Pleads for a public performance of Burgess' musical works. "I am certain there is no end to the miracles of this remarkable man who once wrote a review which rightly highly praised one of his own novels written under a pseudonym." [Burgess did not highly praise his own book. See #448.]

266 Bowen, John. "A Matter of Concern." **Time and Tide**, v. 41, no. 48 (November 26, 1960) 1445.

The work has the same sort of picaresque structure (or lack of it) of **Under the Net** and **Hurry On Down**. He enjoyed the book. "Somewhere beneath the laughter and the decorated surface of this book, you may find a kind of appalled pessimism. Structurally (though of course it's not there for any reasons of structure) it's important, because it gives the book a depth which distinguishes it from something like, say, **The Foxglove Saga,** which just has a surface of funny cruelty and nothing beneath. It's a quality of *concern* that makes the genuine meringue from white of egg, not horse lymph.''

267 Donoghue, Denis. ''Experiments in Folly.'' **New York Review of Books,** v. 6 (June 9, 1966) 20-22.

[Omnibus review. For Burgess, see p. 20.] Henry James was right. Nothing so loses our interest in a novel so quickly as a fool in the center of things. **The Doctor is Sick** tries to circumvent this law and fails. ''The theme which holds these adventures together is the ambiguity of life and words. Spindrift is the name of a detergent; it is also the name of a film: the word appears in poems by Kipling and Hart Crane. The general notion is that people who are skilled in words are innocents abroad in life. Mr. Burgess works this theme for more than it is worth, pointing up the rift between Spindrift the word-man, and Spindrift the fool, thief, liar . . . . . Mr. Burgess is a lively writer, though the quality of the life is not the highest. One of the more innocent pleasures of the book consists in spotting the sources, other novels invoked for imitation. Basically, it is a **Lucky Jim** book, with comic incidents sometimes indebted to **Our Man in Havanna.** And there is the inevitable touch of **Ulysses.**''

268 Grigson, Geoffrey. ''Four Fantasies.'' **Spectator,** v. 205, no. 6909 (November 25, 1960) 860.

[Omnibus review.] ''Fantastic fantasy, which does not work — partly for a reason explained in an excellent (if dangerous) poem of D.J. Enright's saying that 'peacock' is a poor substitute for 'the thing that makes a blue umbrella with its tail,' and berating those who teach us more respect for words than regard for things, 'those older creatures and more real.' A Ph.D., a philologist whose being is word-symbols, has a tumour on the brain. He escapes under anesthetic from bilabial fricatives and the assimilation of *girasole* to 'Jerusalem Artichoke' into a loony sequence of those activities, etc., words are really about. A comic idea, but it does not translate. The words this novelist employs just don't produce things, or cohere, or make credible, in a sub-smart funniness (quotations from Webster, Eliot, Auden) I found not at all funny.'' [Complete text of review.]

269 Keeney, Willard. ''Ripeness is All': Late, Late Romanticism and other Recent Fiction.'' **Southern Review,** N.S., v. 3 (October 1967) 1050-61.

[Omnibus review. For Burgess, see pp. 1058-59.] ''The problem of identity, or more precisely, the post-Joycean definition of the problem of identity, also lies at the heart of Antony Burgess' **The Doctor is Sick.** The problem arises, Burgess seems to tell us, from the distance between abstract 'counters' (i.e. words) on the one hand and concrete things on the other. Identity is, therefore a problem in semantics — commit yourself too thoroughly to the word, the abstraction, and you lose touch with 'reality.' It is a problem in art as well, of course, a problem Burgess seeks to solve as Joyce did, by sheer multiplicity of incident . . . . On the whole, the comic episodes succeed very well; too well, in fact, to permit more than the minimal unity usually found in the picaresque novel. That, finally, is what **The Doctor is Sick** amounts to — a good picaresque novel.''

270 Lindroth, James K. Review of **The Doctor is Sick. America,** v. 114, no. 18 (April 30, 1966) 630.

''This novel, the author's ninth to be published in America, reveals the same satiric and metaphysical bent, plus a talent for comic inventiveness that places him in a class with Wodehouse, the early Anthony Powell and Evelyn Waugh at his best . . . . Beneath the picaresque comedy and social satire, however, Burgess explores a metaphysical problem: the meaning of human experience. Spindrift's adventures — whether dream, or reality — reintroduce him to the real world. His ivory tower crumbles, and at the end of the book Spindrift leaves the world prepared to face reality. Burgess' strength lies in the fact that he recognizes man's potential for change, thus his potential for dignity. His characters may be unsure of the choices they make, but choose they will.''

271 Malin, Irving. Review of **The Doctor is Sick. Commonweal,** v. 84, no. 9 (May 20, 1966) 260-61.

The novel begins with an opening question (''And what is this *smell?*'') which, ambiguous and terrifying, introduces us to a world of deception. Edwin is an emotional cripple who wants to contain reality in words; he has destroyed his own vital humanity. When he leaves the hospital for the London underworld, he is reborn and bruised by common humanity. The publisher's claim that the novel is exhilarating is partially right in that adventure follows madcap adventure. ''. . . we feel that Burgess cannot *stop.* He becomes word-intoxicated; he sacrifices the personality of his hero — as 'sick' as it may be — to the healthy rush of language. We are depressed and uplifted. There is a related problem. Because we have been so conditioned by Burgess to see reality as *dream*, we find it difficult to understand the game. Is he playing seriously? Does he intend us to get his message? Is he merely frivolous? Such questions are raised by the uneven quality of the adventures. We are left, finally, with the belief that there is less to this novel than meets the eye. Now we resemble Edwin who regarded reality in the same way. Or do we?''

272 Maloff, Saul. "A Matter of Words." **New York Times Book Review**, 24 April 1966, p. 5.

In the opening sections, we have fine, sly, rich comedy. The varieties of English speech spoken in the hospital ward is recorded with marvelous and hilarious accuracy. Even flesh is essentially a linguistic problem, and the hero devotes more time to words like "nude," "naked" and "love" than the realities these words stand for. "His body and brain transformed into an inert object of study by hordes of technicians, Spindrift rebels at being thingified, and escapes. Thereupon, the novel collapses into yet another figuration of the problem of illusion and reality, the ancient and contemporary delusion that the world out there may be all in the head. Where before Burgess had moved easily and gracefully through the ward, he now labors hard, his heart not really in it, propelling Spindrift through a series of bizarre, familiar, transposable episodes bordering on dream, on nightmare . . . . A fine comic conception — used imaginatively in the early sections of the novel — gets snarled in another and inferior novel, and is emptied of its possibilities long before the novel is finished.''

273 Ostermann, Robert. "Burgess' Newly Published Works Reveal Love of Language, Life." **National Observer**, 9 May 1966, p. 25.

[Also reviews **A Vision of Battlements**.] **Doctor** includes all the puns, paradoxes and parallels we have come to expect from Burgess. "Edwin must decide [if the picaresque adventures could, or could not, have happened]. And his decision, which is a surprise, transforms **Doctor** from the tired, trite, what-is-the-real-reality novel it might have been into a work worthy of the comic invention that is lavished through it. The sick doctor of philology discovers what Mr. Burgess, in **Re Joyce**, insists the patient reader of Joyce can find: 'An embarrassing joy in the commonplace, seeing the most defiled city as a figure of heaven, and assuming, against all the odds, a hardly supportable optimism'.''

274 Ready, William. "But the Patient Is Fine." **The Critic; A Catholic Review of Books and the Arts**, v. 25, no. 2 (October-November 1966) 114-16.

274.2 Richardson, Maurice. "New Novels." **New Statesman**, v. 60, no. 1551 (December 3, 1960) 888-90.

[Omnibus review.] "I've missed Anthony Burgess's serio-comic trilogy about the English in Malaya. If **The Doctor is Sick** were a first novel I should greet it as a promising curiosity. As a fourth it has to be labelled an interesting misfire . . . . The hospital part is very well done with exact observation, but the picaresque second half gets a bit laboured. Part of the trouble, I think, is that a cerebral tumour is not a subject a novelist can monkey about with; only a philosophical picaresque vein would have suited.''

275 Rosofsky, H.L. Review of **The Doctor is Sick**. **Library Journal**, v. 91, no. 8 (April 1, 1966) 1920.

Describes Sprindrift as a doctor of philosophy in entymology [i.e. etymology]. "The author spins a tale which cleverly enmeshes the reader, but it all turns out [well?] in the end. In all an amusing book, written with great competency and a rather oblique point of view.''

276 West, Paul. "Diction Addiction." **Washington Post Book World**, 15 May 1966, p. 14.

"It doesn't resound much from an apocalyptic viewpoint, but it does resound phonetically all the time with the raves and plaints of the swingingest city south of Liverpool. There's just one trouble: sometimes Mr. Burgess renders talk in such frenetic phonetics that you get held up puzzling things out.''

Earthly Powers

277 New York: Simon and Schuster, 1980.

278 London: Hutchinson, 1980

279 New York: Avon Books, 1981, c1980. Pbk.

Reviews

280 Amis, Martin. "Burgess at His Best." **New York Times Book Review**, 7 December 1980, p. 1, 24.

This long novel earns its amplitude by the complexity of the demands it makes on the reader. Asserts that Burgess left England, not for sexual or artistic constraints, but because he found its artistic caution uncongenial. [A singularly wrong-headed assertion. Burgess found its taxes confiscatory.] The book, filled with manic erudition, garlicky puns, omnilingual jokes, owes its neo-Victorian vigor to the modern American novel (Herman Wouk, Saul Bellow), and it meshes the real and personalized history of the 20th century more earnestly and intimately than E.L. Doctorow's **Ragtime** or Tom Stoppard's **Travesties**. Toomey, who is ubiquitous and knows everyone, acts as a lightning rod for the evil energies of the century and "The ultimate moral, or theological — or theodicean — irony (whereby divine intervention preserves the life of the future cultist mass-murderer) is stark and ferocious; it is the kind of challenge that the literary Catholic enjoys throwing out to the world, as if to testify to the stubborn perversity of his belief. Graham Greene did it in **Brighton Rock**, Evelyn Waugh in **A Handful of Dust**; but Mr. Burgess is more vehement than either." The affirmation that is possible in Toomey's grimly determinist world is that of artistic creation, man's only god-like act. The novel "is a considerable achievement, spacious and intricate in design, wonderfully sustained in its execution, and full of a wary generosity for the errant world it re-creates. As a form, the long novel is deeply flawed and approximate; and this book contains plenty of hollow places beneath its busy verbal surface. But whatever its human limits, it shows an author who has reached his earthly powers."

281 Anon. Review of **Earthly Powers**. **Publishers Weekly**, v. 218, no. 17 (October 24, 1980) 35.

"The problems of good and evil, free will and the use and abuse of power loom as large in Burgess's latest novel as they did in **A Clockwork Orange**, but here they are treated explicitly and discursively rather than allegorically and dramatically, with a notable loss in readability and tension . . . . There's some excellent satire, and Burgess's polymorphous learning is as much on display as ever; but the story is flat, and strangely irresolute regarding the great moral issues it nags away at so constantly."

282 Anon. Notice of **Earthly Powers**. **Human Events**, v. 40, no. 44 (November 1, 1980) 16.

"Sure to be talked about is the big new novel by Anthony Burgess, **Earthly Powers**. The two central figures are an aging, eminent, homosexual novelist (Andre Gide? [i.e. W.S. Maugham]) and a pope (Paul VI [i.e. John XXIII]) who is a shrewd manipulator of people and becomes the architect for revolution in the Church." [Complete text of notice.]

283 Caute, David. "The World and the Word." **New Statesman**, v. 100, no. 2388 (October 24, 1980) 22-23.

"**Earthly Powers** marks Anthony Burgess's triumphant ascent from the prodigal (lavish or recklessly wasteful) to the prodigious. In this marvellous epic an overflowing talent has at last been called to order." Observes that to make Toomey a compound of Maugham, Comptom Mackenzie and Nevile Shute is a shrewd move on Burgess' part. Toomey's narrative, by contrast with the rebarbative style of F.X. Enderby, is emotionally dripdry, aloof and sardonic. Some of the episodes in which he takes part are incredible ("one doesn't believe a word of it"), and his view of the world is marked by consistent patrician recoil. Although Toomey is tempted to re-enter the comforting womb of the Church, the Pelagian position of Carlo Campanati (evil is external, not internal; the Church is God's only broker, and only its intervention enables man to reject evil) does not strike him as credible. The infliction on Toomey of an insurmountable, if bitterly accepted, homosexuality is part of Burgess' design: the condition is neither the work of the Devil nor the fault of Toomey himself. It is part and parcel of Burgess' brooding on the question of free will. Describes the scene of buggery, involving sailors and violence, as one of great comic power. Toomey's violent outburst against his sister's fornication is not only the mark of hypocrisy: incest with his sister is the only means by which Toomey could have joined the ranks of the sexually normal. [Sic.] Followed by more plot summary. Remarks on Carlo's, now John XXII's [XXIII] diatribe against the nation's repellently ignorant spotty kids in jeans. "Be he the bard of the counter-counter culture, an unashamedly bourgeois individualist and all that, Burgess has written a novel epic in its sweep, subtle in its portraiture, graceful in its unforbidding exploration of ideas and brutally funny."

284 Clark, Jeff. Review of **Earthly Powers**. **Library Journal**, v. 105, no. 22 (December 15, 1980) 2586.

"**Earthly Powers** is an ambivalent summa of Burgess' Manichean vision . . . . [Toomey's] journey, devoid of high drama, is as exhausting as it is exhaustive. But the strategy pays off in the rich sense of a world concocted of antic loss and savage humor, which confounds all its inhabitants' sustaining convictions."

285 Davies, Robertson. "And God Created Them Both." **Washington Post Book World**, 23 November 1980, pp. 1, 13.

Burgess' fictional powers seem to be stretched to their uttermost extent. His great gifts — wit and energy — have led a part of the public to mistake a stern moralist for a funny-man. Now Burgess calls God to the bar of judgment. "For that is what it seems to me he tries to do in **Earthly Powers**. God moves in a mysterious way, His wonders to perform, and in the course of performing them He wreaks utter hell on all sorts of unoffending people. What does God imagine He is doing? Is He really frivolous, capricious and malign? Explain Yourself, Immensity, and You'd better make it good." God creates a people's pope — who then sets out to destroy the Church; saves a man's life by an apparent miracle — but the man so saved destroys 2,000 souls in a fit of religious enthusiasm; afflicts Toomey with homosexuality — who, as a Catholic, can only pursue his sexual bent in sin. "These problems are explored brilliantly, and the incidental discussions are deeply interesting. To what degree are homosexuality and artistic gifts allied? If it is true that God permits evil in order that man may have freedom of choice, why does He make evil so frequently attractive and good so dull? To what degree of heat may religion attain before it is super-heated and becomes what theologians condemn as 'enthusiasm'? Would American divorce be better described as serial polygamy? What is the source of the malice that pursues public figures? Which revenge is worse — that of talent overextended or talent betrayed?" The reminders of current history are sometimes too intrusive: we come across another real name and feel as if we had bitten on a stone in a cherry pie. But he is refreshed by the extravagant logodaedaly in Burgess' romances, and "Here is a fine, angry book for anyone who has ever given thought to the incalculability of God."

286 Dennis, Nigel. "No Holds Barred." **New York Review of Books**, v. 27, nos. 21-22 (January 22, 1981) 27.

The first 100 pages of this novel give the impression of being a grim study of the gay life. *Fuck* appears but not *cunt*. *Tits* mean falsies. A clitoris is part of a blunder (wrong bed, while stoned.) Only the men are naked. All sexual intimacies exclude the female. Hortense makes a promising heterosexual start, but soon goes over to the lizzies. Delmonico's six marriages are nothing but the neurosis of a frantic eunuch. When a normal heterosexual pair shows up, they are butchered by enthusiastic Black converts to Christianity. Later it seems that the book is concerned with the struggle between evil and muscular Christianity. Burgess is undoubtedly serious about religion, and his theme is the world-wide evil in its most monstrous forms that the united churches of the world will have to grapple with. He evokes his different historical periods very well, but the real problem is the Burgess mentality: the light and the heavy, the pious and the scabrous, the tough and the tender. "The reasons [these attributes are not reconciled or harmonized] is that brute force is really the only prime mover with which Mr. Burgess is at home. His approach to his subjects and his readers is brutishly dictatorial: the neatness and cleverness with which he handles words and constructs sentences would be pretty to see if an infintely boorish spirit were not to be felt behind them. All's well when it's a randy baronet buggering an able-bodied seaman on a quay . . . . But why should such a talent for indelicacies be allowed to handle more sensitive material? . . . . Of his limitations as a novelist Burgess lives in perfect ignorance: it is plain to see that his forte is the short, scabrous incident and, above all, mimicry and the comic aspects of conversation . . . . The reader who finds himself dismayed and distressed by Mr. Burgess may take heart from the fact; it proves that there is still some good in him and that the times have not robbed him completely of his sensitivity.''

287 Jones, D.A.N. "My Friend, the Pope." **Listener**, v. 104, no. 2684 (October 23, 1980) 544.

The opening sentence gives fair warning. Any reader who would prefer not to know about the homosexual experiences of an octagenarian and his relationship with the Catholic Church should stop now. The description of Kenneth Toomey is reminiscent of W. Somerset Maugham. Later he takes on some of the talents and characteristics of Noel Coward. The career of Carlo Campanati, and especially his one successful exorcism, suggest that this deed (and some of Carlo's papal reforms) put him in the company of evil-doers. The book is full of much exciting stuff; it is not surprising that the book was short-listed for the Booker prize. Of the real people who appear (Henry James, Joyce, Kipling, Pound and Hemingway) the most important is Dawson Wignall — presumably modelled on Sir John Betjeman — whose Christianity has a certain fascination for Roman Catholics like Burgess and Graham Greene. There are many who believe that religion is not important. This work is about the *dangers* of religion and it is "nearer in spirit to the serious *enemies* of religion, like Nicolas Walter, than it is to those who would dismiss the supernatural with an easy, modern, un-natural smile.''

288 Kendall, Elaine. "Novelist/Essayist at Ambitious Odds in a Grand Tour de Burgess." **Los Angeles Times Book Review**, 14 December 1980, pp. 1, 14.

"There are great rewards in **Earthly Powers**, but there are also unnecessary trials along the way. Burgess leaves travelers few options and his itinerary makes no concessions. The novel includes Campanati's program for the reorganization of the Catholic Church, and while that's a tour de force few lay writers would attempt, the device brings the novel to a virtual standstill . . . .'' The digressions, brilliant as they are, need to be integrated into the novel. Subsidiary characters are dropped, and attractive people are led off stage after they have said their pieces. "What begins as a delightful social encounter slips into propaganda, and the most promising characters turn out to be mere spokespersons for one cause or another. Instead of providing needed continuity and structure, they go separate ways and take pieces of the novel with them . . . . [The novel] is crammed to the turrets with souvenirs of the author's intellectual, spiritual and geographical travels . . . . Though Burgess never has kept his essays and his fiction entirely separate, the books since **A Clockwork Orange** show an increasing tendency toward collaboration with himself. **Earthly Powers** is a further extension of that teamwork, often dazzling as fiction, sometimes equally impressive as lecture, but always verging on disintegration into isolated segments.''

289 King, Francis. "Life and Times." **Spectator**, v. 245, no. 7946 (October 25, 1980) 22.

The opening sentence is brilliant and it recalls the career of W.S. Maugham, the man who can claim to have seen it all, done it all, met them all. But Maugham, master of cliché, would have been incapable of producing an autobiography in a style of such variety, richness and vigour. The book includes errors (those relating to the careers of Keynes, Martinu, and the House of Worth), but its greatest defect is that Burgess is unable to get his hero's sexuality into proper focus. "Another title for this novel might have been 'The Ragtime Exorcist.' Like Doctorow's best-selling fiction, it makes repeated use of real people or of characters in whom real people are adumbrated. Like Bladdy's best-selling fiction, it deals sensationally and (to me at least) rather absurdly with demonic possession.'' Burgess, a hugely talented novelist, was presumably asked to produce something really big by a hypermanic publisher. The novel is big all right. Taking it to bed is like bedding a tombstone; it is not a big novel in any other sense. "One has a sense of a high-speed train of prodigious power lapping mile on mile of countryside, its lights all blazing; but it has strangely little aboard and one can only guess at its destination.''

290 Klein, Julia M. "Burgess' Latest: Battle of Values Ending in a Tie." **Philadelphia Inquirer**, 21 December 1980, p. 18I.

The novel consists of a dialogue between Toomey, who believes in predestination, and Carlo Campanati, who sees life as a splendid battleground between good and evil. It is a novel of ideas that elicits intellectual rather than emotional engagement with its characters. "It takes Toomey 600 pages to unravel the meaning and mystery of [the alleged exorcism.] In between, he sodomizes young men, writes bad novels, loses his faith, falls platonically in love with a doctor, marries off his sister Hortense to Carlo's brother, Domenico, writes bad operas with Domenico, watches Domenico and Hortense cheat and leave each other and generally observes things coming apart. All the while, Carlo keeps insisting that man is good, that God is good, that evil is real but vanquishable.'' The intellectual debate between Toomey (who denies the ability of man to choose his fate) and Campanati (who insists on the mightiness of evil) is a draw. Chalk up a modest triumph for Burgess.

291 Leonard, John. "Books of the Times." **New York Times**, 19 November 1980, p. C33.

With this novel Burgess has made a remarkable recovery from the series of indifferent fictions that began with **MF**. Toomey is a brilliant pastiche of W.S. Maugham, Norman Douglas, Noel Coward and E.M. Forster, with a dash of P.G. Wodehouse and Graham Greene. Observes that the heterosexuals in the novels fare as badly as the homosexuals; the latter range from the opportunistic to the nasty. In the context of the novel they seem to deserve their misery. Serves up some plot summary (very brief) and mentions that the usual Burgess obsessions (food, linguistics, Joyce, Dante, Shakespeare, the Far East and the Mediterranean and the movies) are deployed in the service of a meditation on the nature of evil. If this sounds daunting [food in the service of a meditation on the nature of evil?] he hopes not. Observes the presence in the novel of an opera on the life of St. Nicholas, a musical comedy called "The Blooms of Dublin," and hilarious synopses of the stories of Toomey and the sermons of Carlo Campanati. "Mr. Burgess is prodigal. He intends to woo us on behalf of the traditional novel, while making fun of the traditional novelist and at the same time sending up the postmodernism which junks coherence and guilt, which would make of empirical reality a dull linoleum. He has written an entertainment about God, after the laughter stops . . . . Mr. Burgess is also quite serious. He is telling us that St. Nicholas was cheated; that if God is the Father we have come to know, we desperately need a Mother Church; that neither art nor propaganda can outshout senseless evil; that the 'horror of surfeit' [the Nazi pogrom] makes even language throw up. Still, certain words oblige us to cry, and he names them: home, duty, love, faith, shame, pity, death . . . . 'My destiny,' says Toomey, 'is to create a kind of underliterature that lacks all whiff of the subversive.' Mr. Burgess, in his best novel, subverts.''

292 Levin, Bernard. Review of **Earthly Powers**. **Critic**, v. 39, no. 4 (February 1981) 4-5.

The contemporary novel is timid, narrow and introspective because the dominant mode of thought is relativist, Cartesian and phenomenological. Burgess will have none of this mewling and puking and posits the idea that the responsiblity for everything we do must be judged by standards quite independent of us. The result is a long novel in which enormous imagination and vitality are applied to themes that concern all of us. It is strong meat, a book about evil (which Burgess strongly believes to exist) and free will (about which he has terrible doubts.) His theme is that man is born free, and everywhere he is in chains. This theme, or argument, is firmly anchored against a background of political and social reality. "Mind you, Mr. Burgess's prose, as always, boils over from time to time: 'Carlo was busy sucking an orange as a weasel might suck a brain' and 'The moon was like a round of Breton butter with fromatical veins' are both going straight into my forthcoming monograph, 'Improbable Similes, Their Cause and Cure,' and Mr. Burgess is so anxious to demonstrate that he knows more words than we do that he trips himself up: a 'mephitic hogo' is a tautology, meaning only a stinking stink. It can't be helped; with this author it is always necessary to take the hispid with the glabrous, and the credit balance is overwhelming. The historical sweep, the range of the enquiry, the immense wealth of illustrative allusion, the explosive energy with which the book is crammed, the giant appetite for event and description, the brilliance of the parodies, the iron control over at any rate nine-tenths of the material, the colour and daring, the relish of the true creative artist for his creation — all these combine with the theme to make **Earthly Powers** an achievement which any living writer would be proud of, and no dead one ashamed. In every sense of the phrase, a huge book.''

293 Nordell, Roderick. "Burgess's Big, Grating Mixed Bag of a Novel." **Christian Science Monitor** Monthly Book Review, 12 January 1981, p. B4.

Burgess' novel is in the service of two themes. The first is the centrality of free choice as a human attribute to be cherished. The second is the question of participation in life as opposed to 'this standing on the periphery and sneering.' The narrator is a homosexual who combines both themes; his homosexuality is imposed, not chosen. "Can it be that God had to create the devil in order to provide the free choice that would be denied mankind if only good and evil were available? Since God is, by definition, the creator, does this mean He cannot destroy anything He has created, including the devil? Such questions go counter to the biblical concept of God as good, unable to create anything unlike Himself and thus leaving evil in the realm of illusion. They are the kind of questions to send readers to consult their own religious experience rather than a literary phantasmagoria in which there is often a nagging doubt about the line between strong drama and cruel sensationalism.''

294 Prescott, Peter S. "Child of the Century." **Newsweek**, v. 96, no. 21 (November 24, 1980) 105, 108.

A man of talent gets the job done well; a man of genius gets it done in a definitive way. He has long been convinced of Burgess' genius, but this interminable new novel, alternately delicious and tedious, proves that a man less inspired would show a greater sense of his own limitations. Burgess is determined to pack the novel with the detritus of the 20th century, swamps us with theological speculation from the heretical school of Pelagius [i.e. the Manichean heresy], and many of the characters (with the exception of Toomey, a marvellously complex creation) exist only to represent an attitude. "We have, then, a novel that is twice too long, studded with dismal sermons and lectures on linguistics, a story that ends in sentimentality and outrageous coincidence. And yet I can't dismiss it; the first hundred pages are as fine as any Burgess ever wrote. Throughout, there are many hilarious, bilious, bitchy encounters — Burgess can't stay serious for long. His parodic synopses of plays, an opera, the sort of stories that Maugham might have written at various times, a withering spoof of John Betjeman and his verse, a homosexual reconstruction of the Garden of Eden story; these are worth the time spent hewing through the rest. As always, Burgess plays games with language with a skill no other living writer can equal; his mastery of the homosexuals' campy banter is itself a thing of wonder.''

295 Steiner, George. "Books: Scroll & Keys." **New Yorker**, v. 56, no. 8 (April 13, 1981) 156-162.

Praises, in a long preliminary passage, the breadth of Burgess' accomplishments and talents. Sample: "**Enderby, Nothing Like the Sun** and **Abba Abba** form a sparkling trio. They are studies of the writer's odd condition, of the pathologies and carnival of poetic inspiration. The first is a wry mirroring of Burgess himself; the second is just about the only convincing fictional recreation we have of the young Shakespeare; the third is a witty but also moving evocation of Keats in the season of his passing.'' **Earthly Powers** is an omnium-gatherum of Burgess' preoccupations and recent literary learning, and its opening sentence is a rococo masterpiece. It is a memorable study of an immensely successful middle-brow Willie Maugham with just enough lucidity to comprehend the final fiasco: the ephemerality of his most acclaimed works. The fictional canvas is crowded with writers, popes (John XXIII) and dozens of subplots. It is a taxing novel: the language is learned and allusive; the fictional aim — to reclaim for the novel modes of intellectual debate, political modelling, formal and anarchic religiosity, adult confrontations with humbling sexuality — is ambitious; the blending of fact and fiction creates an uneasy hybrid. On a first reading Steiner is not sure if the venture has come off, if it has become a breathing organism. Notes some small errors. Concludes: "There is here, and past cavil, a feat of imaginative breadth and intelligence which lifts fiction high. The whole landscape is the brighter for it.''

296 Theroux, Paul. "Burgess' Masterpiece." **Saturday Review**, v. 7, no. 15 (November 1980) 60-61.

About 14 years ago Burgess promised us a novel of Tolstoyan proportions. He promptly resumed his prolific literary activities and produced explosive, language-loving works expressing his "dissatisfaction with labour unions, literary cliques, the Catholic hierarchy, social hoodlums, corruption, human weakness, greed, moral sneakery, sinister bureaucracy, and a failure of will that has produced cheating art and a kind of cultural arteriosclerosis on a global scale. They are Tolstoyan sentiments, but none of the novels has been of Tolstoyan proportions." Now he has shaped a major novel which is huge, symmetrical, very funny and "It is such a pleasure to see such a grand edifice of intelligence, humor, ambition, and imagination, that it is impossible on reviewing it to appear less than rapturous.'' The resemblance between Toomey and the Queen of the Villa Mauresque [W.S. Maugham] is very slight. Toomey is much less reclusive, and shows a far greater interest in the Pelagian heresy. Quotes a passage from the novel which deals with the unreliability of a writer's memory. Considers the Malayan episodes among the best in the book. "Like two Tamburlaines on the prowl, they [Toomey and Campanati] seek the glory of an earthly crown, and in their separate ways they fail as men by succeeding in their art. But the novel is much more than the story of two men. It is about the course of literature, politics, popular culture, and religion; it contains fascinating discourses on food and language — it is full of meals and monologues. It is, in all ways, a remarkable book.''

297 Towers, Roderick. "The Prince of Darkness is Pope." **New Republic**, v. 184, nos. 1-2 (January 3 & 10, 1981) 32-34.

Demonic possession and exorcism seem to be taken seriously by Burgess. Has he been possessed by a scribbling demon? The novel has been hailed as a Tolstoyan masterwork [see #296]. Is it perhaps Luciferian? Lists some of the incidents in this novel and observes that Toomey is reminiscent of Upton Sinclair's Lanny Budd series. "Some of this [welter of incident] is entertaining, but there are disadvantages to the method. The namedropping is incessant and finally, as in real life, a bore. Too often the dialogue becomes portentous, weighed down by the necessity of speaking for history." The character of Toomey seems less an agent in his own right than a reactor to the rapidly unfolding events. Further, the ready-made association with Maugham ("the loneliness in the midst of wealth, the betrayals endured, the self-deprecation of his art") are too familiar to interest or move us. The postures of world-weariness, irony and knowingness are burdensome to sustain over hundreds of pages. Toomey's male lovers are tedious delinquents gifted only with elaborate bitchiness, just the sort of thing to give buggary a bad name. Carlo Campanati is a more complex creation than Toomey. Can it be that he is a secret agent for Lucifer? "Is **Earthly Powers** to be read as a covertly reactionary attack upon the whole Johannine revolution . . . . ? That would be to take the whole performance with undue gravity. Sensationalism — not moral or religious profundity — is what Burgess has to offer. For thick, greasy, loathsome detail, the scenes of exorcism in **Earthly Powers** match anything to be found in **The Exorcist**. 'Meaty,' 'fruity,' 'fatty,' . . . 'flatulent' — such were the gustatory and alimentary adjectives that came to mind as I made my way through the most 'oral' of novels, one in which every meal is described in loving detail and in which every spiteful impulse is fully voiced.''

298 Treglown, Jeremy. "The Knowledge of Good and Evil." **Times Literary Supplement**, 24 October 1980, p. 1189.

An enormous and enormously impressive new novel. It is Burgess' 'A Portrait of the Artist as an Old Man' in which Toomey is modelled on Maugham, though Toomey's conscience is closer to Greene than Maugham. The novel, complete with the introduction of real people, engages the events, ideas and problems of the century in a way that invites immediate re-reading. Provides a plot summary that focusses on the difficulty of recognizing evil, and the moral ambiguity of Carlo Campanati. Quotes and praises a parody of Betjeman as well as other descriptive passages, and observes that the natural world is conveyed with an indulgent Joycean rhetoric. Suggests that other aspects of the novel, Burgess' sensitive and unsentimental close-quarters treatment of homosexuality, his knowledge of music, and his ability to circumvent the limitations of the first person narrative, could well deserve extended treatment. "**Earthly Powers** is a big, grippingly readable, extraordinarily rich and moving fiction by one of the most ambitiously creative writers working in English.''

The End of the World News: An Entertainment

298.2   London: Hutchinson, 1982.

298.3   New York: McGraw-Hill, 1983.

Reviews

298.4   Reed, J.D. "Dividing Gall into Three Parts." **Time**, v. 121, no. 12 (March 21, 1983) 76.

Anthony Burgess, 66, has gone out on some strong limbs to avoid repeating himself [and this novel] offers a trio of plots linked by irony and caustic satire. Gives a brief summary of the novels about Freud, Trotsky and the science fiction theme. Concludes that Burgess is warm, wayward, imperfect, adaptable. "After blast-off, the fictional narrator who has combined the 'televisualized' Freud, the tin-pan Trotsky and the Shakespearean **Star Trek** starts to muse. In the future, as in the past, he decides, only one question has real pertinence: What aspects of civilization are worth carrying on? One implicit answer: the ability to wring harmony from dissonance, to create a work of the imagination from disparate and unpromising materials. Example: **The End of the World News**, a trio made from the detritus of history and sci-fi. True, the author has abused his poetic license; he is often perverse for perversity's sake, and he can be more outrageous than illuminating. Even so, he has produced a highly original volume — his 41st book in 27 years. Carry on, Burgess."

298.5   Wilson, A.N. "Faith and Uncertainty: Recent Novels." **Encounter**, v. 60, no. 2 (February 1983) 65-71.

[Omnibus review. For Burgess, see p. 70.] All Burgess' novels are hectically stylish, but the present one, which recalls Dr. Johnson's dictum that 'nothing odd will last long,' is really three novels in one: a vivid, fictionalised life of Freud, an extraordinarily feeble script for a Broadway musical based on Trotsky's visit to America along with a piece of science fiction. "It seemed impossible not to feel that Mr. Burgess had not served up three half-finished books from his desk drawer, all wildly disparate in character and stirred together carelessly . . . . [The novel] is almost insolently unpolished."

298.6   Wood, Michael. "A Love Song to What Would Be Lost." **New York Times Book Review**, 6 March 1983, pp. 3, 25.

Burgess is not an author but a phenomenon, and this work is his third published book in a matter of months. It appears to be chaff (an 'entertainment' he calls it, borrowing a term from his Riviera neighbour and sparring partner, Graham Greene) which is intended to parody the forms of writing that might survive the death of literature: the libretto, the novel ripe for a television series and science fiction. "The stories are not all the same, and they are not exactly about the end of history. But they are all about dreams of ending, about old worlds that go off with a bang, not a whimper, leaving us with less history than we thought we had but maybe more than we can manage . . . . The world won't end tonight, and Anthony Burgess doesn't think it will. His is not the scorching apocalypse of Lawrence or Yeats but a love song to what would be lost if the world went away: all its colors and tastes and smells and finally forgivable mistakes. It is an old song but a good one, made attractive not by its newness but by its steady virtue and the liveliness of Mr. Burgess' arrangement of it. 'This is the end of the world,' a character in the book says. 'I presume anybody can join in.' Sure. And we can also, in the words of Sam Goldwyn, include ourselves out."

Enderby

299 New York: Norton, 1968.

300 New York: Ballantine, 1969. Pbk.

[Includes **Inside Mr. Enderby** and **Enderby Outside**.]

Recordings

301 **Prose Readings**. [Sound recording] New York: Norton, [197?] 1 cassette. Introduced by John Simon. Burgess reads from **Enderby** and **A Clockwork Orange**. (YW-YMHA Poetry Center series)

302 **Anthony Burgess Reads from A Clockwork Orange** [and] **Enderby**. [Sound recording] 1 disc. Spoken Arts [1974?] SA 1120.

Translations

303 Italin: **La dolce bestia**. Torino: Einaudi, 1972. Translated by Floriana Bossi.

304 Swedish: **Enderby**(?) Stockholm: Wahlstrom & Widstrand. Translated by Caj Lundgren.

Reviews

305 Anon. Review of **Enderby**. **Kirkus Reviews**, April 1, 1968, p. 415.

"The novel is picaresque, obstreperous, hugely vital with an energetic comic gift. It derives its hyper-manic strength from one redolent character and Mr. Burgess' own prowess with words which could easily fell any trained lexicographer. Strong publisher promotion as his work most likely to succeed with a wide audience."

306 Anon. Review of **Enderby**. **Publishers Weekly**, v. 193, no. 4 (April 1, 1968) 34

"Burgess' treatment of the conflict between an older, traditional poet and a demoralized mod world is often hilarious, full of irony and excruciating circumstance, and is consistently powerfully written . . . ." *Major advertising and publicity*.

307 Anon. "The Poet as Anti-Stereotype." **Time**, v. 91, no. 24 (June 14, 1968) 93-94.

"Author Burgess is sounding again an ancient warning of his trade: that the poet's natural enemies remain varied and dangerous. The hostile forces manifest themselves as rich but tasteless patrons, pop singers, and even other poets, one of whom steals the Minotaur theme and turns it into a screenplay for **Son of the Beast from Outer Space**. But the poet, Burgess also warns, is a dangerous man — one of life's great survivors . . . . Enderby may not have the gift for living, but, concludes Burgess, 'poets, even minor ones, donate the right words' that enable others to live." Burgess is a superb writer whose serious novels are also his entertainments. This novel serves both his favorite lightweight tone and one of his favorite heavyweight meanings. "Here, with the most offhand, scurrilous charm, he illustrates as well as preaches that the artist is the man who expresses for all men their unbuttoned true selves."

308 Anon. Review of **Enderby**. **New Yorker**, v. 44, no. 19 (June 29, 1968) 87-88.

[Brief plot summary.] "The black satire is ferociously amusing, and the language superlative."

309 Anon. Review of **Enderby**. **Choice**, v. 5, nos. 5-6 (July-August 1968) 620.

"Beneath the surface, Enderby could represent the rise, the fall, and the restoration of the creative force inherent in the English language. In his black humoured best, Burgess stresses his view of man doing his best — composing poetry while sitting on the toilet. **Enderby** is not Burgess' tightest work but is profound and funny as well as an aesthetic via a persona. Appendix includes some of Enderby's collected poems. For all fine fiction collections."

310 Anon. Review of **Enderby**. **Booklist**, v. 64, no. 21 (July 15, 1968) 1263.

"The trials of a minor poet caught up by commercialism and unwanted fame are described in an

First American ed. (New York: Norton, c. 1968) of this novel. Includes *Inside Mr. Enderby* (Book I) and *Enderby Outside* (Book II). The seat, fittingly, is made of wood.

early rambling novel which forecasts the author's mature examination of language and the foibles of personality.'' [Brief, non-committal review.]

311 Baxter, Ralph C. Review of **Enderby**. **Best Sellers**, June 15, 1968, p. 126.

The novel is the best of comedy. Singles out the following scenes for their high comedic quotient: Enderby taking the drunken Rawcliffe home; Enderby seeing the film of 'L'Animal Binato' in company with Vesta Bainbridge; Enderby deserting a quick lay to pursue the sullen craft of poetry. ''If nothing else, the novel is a fantastic exercise in elaborate punning, etymology, taxonomy, and coinings. The greatness of Burgess' skill lies in the fact that this is a most appropriate method of development in a novel about a poet — a word-maker . . . . The feeling one has after reading a Burgess novel is, consequently, that there is nothing more — it is like experiencing a perfect artifact, simple and complete as possible with no superfluity.''

312 Bergonzi, Bernard. ''A Poet's Life.'' **Hudson Review**, v. 21, no. 4 (Winter 1968-69) 764-68.

Considers the publication history of the two Enderby books and draws attention to the Joycean influence in Burgess. Like Joyce, Burgess was brought up and raised as a Catholic. Quotes from Burgess' article ''The God I Want'' [see#1320] to demonstrate both Burgess' Catholicism and the depth of his feeling that the world is irredeemably sinful and corrupt. Then begins one of the longest plot summaries of **Enderby** cited in this section. Emphasizes the Catholicism of Enderby, his fear and hatred of his stepmother (who also symbolizes the Church). ''**Enderby**, which starts magnificently, dwindles by degrees into a rather ordinary fictional artifact, full of the depressing habits of a wide range of modern English fiction . . . . The second part of **Enderby** lamentably degenerates into a series of comic picaresque adventures of the kind that English reviewers often approvingly describe as a 'romp,' or even a 'glorious romp'.'' Considers the extent to which Burgess plunges into the episodic in this, and in other, novels and hopes that, with Burgess in Malta, his fiction will move into a new and impressive phase. ''The fact that he has not, for several years, made full use of his novelistic gifts does not lessen my confidence that he can still surprise us with them.''

313 Broadwater, Bowden. ''A Glob and His Girls.'' **Washington Post Book World**, 9 June 1968, p. 13.

''In Anthony Burgess' novels his typical masochistic, gray-collar British 'heroes' are liable to smacks in the kisser that leave them gap-toothed or, as dictionary-driven Burgess might say, diastematic. **Enderby** likewise asks for a jab.'' Praises three of Burgess' novels (**A Clockwork Orange, The Wanting Seed** and **Honey for the Bears**) but damns this one. Enderby is ''An older, incomparably less sexy Lucky Jim and a younger, infinitely less engaging Gully Jimson . . . .''

314 Davenport, Guy. ''Fiction: Parnassus the Hard Way.'' **National Review**, v. 20, no. 24 (June 18, 1968) 613-15.

[Also reviews **Narcissus and Goldmund**, by Hermann Hesse.] ''So it goes, as lively as a Mack Sennett comedy, from scrape to scrape. After 406 pages of Enderby, alias Hogg, is in charge of a bar in Tangiers frequented by the likes of William Burroughs and Peter Orlovsky . . . . For Burgess art is a joyous gift, like grace, that is as likely to turn up in Enderby as Shakespeare . . . . It is by now widely known that Anthony Burgess is no ordinary novelist. There are novelists who could have created Enderby; there are fewer novelists who could have written Enderby's poetry for him — poetry that we aren't quite certain isn't parody; there are very few novelists who could have topped this and invented a Muse who reels off top-notch textual criticism of the densest of Enderby's poems . . . . Add to this Mr. Burgess' rolling prose rhythms and his canny aptitude for languages (such as the slang of expatriate Englishmen in Morocco), and the category in which we can place Mr. Burgess seems to contain Mr. Burgess alone.''

315 DeMott, Benjamin. ''Gag Into Vision.'' **New York Times Book Review**, 30 June 1968, pp. 5, 34.

When Burgess created **A Clockwork Orange** he created a character, never once left him, and out of his superb verbal resourcefulness and wit found a bearable route into a crazed will which insisted, through the medium of nadsat, 'Keep your head, reader, keep your head.' Burgess has now emerged as a novelist of readable and engaging fictions, one of the most likable journalists in England, and an extraordinary rate of production that leads his most subtle critics, Christopher Ricks and William H. Pritchard, to throw catalogues at the reader. This work opens with a strong evocation of the working poet's inner mind, but chapters that promise patterns end in scrambles, jokes are overworked and several gauzy delicate ideas turn gaudy-maudlin in execution. "The air of the half-baked, which Brigid Brophy once claimed oppressed this *oeuvre* [for her review of **The Wanting Seed**, not the *oeuvre*, see #934] on occasion does hang thick. But time and time again it is cleared off by Enderby's splendid rages against poetasters and plagiarists." Burgess, through Enderby, protests that "if all tastes are equal, all hier-archies of value phony, and all pop art, where, pray, does a man stand when he wants to cool a riot or stop a thief? There is a Burgess who merely larks on, word-spins, conks out in 'satire' under insuffi-cient provocation, rifles his Orwell and his Dennis (Nigel) and his Cary, brushes Nabokov's teeth, pumps and puffs the book machine pedals to no end save survival. And there is another nearly too various for full belief — beefy, genial, evenhanded — curious, funny, intense — superbly unsolemnly deep. At its best, **Enderby** is news that, undaunted beneath a ton of 'copy,' the *vrai* Burgess is alive and living in keenness. A wonderfully welcome word."

316 Hicks, Granville. "Poetry as a Defense." **Saturday Review**, v. 51, no. 23 (June 8, 1968) 37-38.

Observes that Burgess spent his so-called 'terminal' year writing novels to provide for his wife. Briefly refers to **Inside Mr. Enderby**. The novel is about the life of a good poet who is no great shakes as a human being. "Burgess has no trouble in portraying Enderby's ridiculous aspect, in making him grotesque and yet not wholly unlikable. The problem, of course is how to convince us that he is a poet. Burgess does it the dangerous way — by quoting Enderby's poems — and he is himself a good enough poet to get away with it." Burgess has a way of raising religious problems though he never takes a positive position. It is probable that Burgess, like Enderby, believes that humanism always leads to totalitarianism. "If one cannot accept the Church, Burgess apparently believes, the poetic imagination is the best defense against the allied forces of technology and commercialism . . . . It is also a funny novel and a lively one, not quite so lively as **Tremor of Intent**, but exciting enough."

317 Lask, Thomas. "Books of The **Times**: Poet on the Loose." **New York Times**, 11 June 1968, p. 45.

Describes the character and filthy habits of Enderby, and observes that other creative men have wallow-ed in filth. "Mr. Burgess is, as his readers know, a technician of surpassing brilliance and he has a holiday in this book showing what happens in the caldron of creation. There is a great deal of travesty and exaggeration; a lot of it is ludicrous. But history is full of men who did more than Enderby to guard their talent. Beethoven's squalor was as great as Enderby's. And Specht gives us a picture of Brahms walking in the country once when he was struck by a musical idea and tells how he rushed home through the field, dragging his coat on the ground and making animal noises lest he lose what had just been given him." The book undoubtedly includes hidden meanings and symbols, but it is possible to have a good time with the book without troubling about these matters. Briefly observes the decline of interest or energy in the second half of the book.

318 Malin, Irving. Review of **Enderby**. **Commonweal**, v. 89, no. 7 (November 15, 1968) 262-63.

Enderby, who largely flees from relationships, refuses to earn a living, and battles orthodox religion lives his poems as he creates them. Burgess tempts his character with sex, money and violence; he shut-tles him from London to Tangier. The relentless pace is exhausting, and we may object that these peo-ple or places seem stylized, grotesque and frenetic. "This is Burgess' overwhelming purpose — he wants us to view the 'outside' world as 'way out' — as the exotic existence Enderby must tame and shape in poetry." The comic vitality of the novel is undeniable, but ultimately we are forced back to Art, Death, and Love — the ultimate concerns. Quotes part of the concluding section of the novel and cites it as proof of Burgess' brilliance in creating the poetic task.

319 Morris, Robert K. "The Flatulent Poet." **Nation**, v. 207 (July 22, 1968) 58.

Looks for and finds the "symbols" mentioned by Lask [see #317]. In slightly under a score of wildly productive and creative years, Burgess has concocted some of the purest fuel for literary rockets. **Clockwork** is a philologist's dream and a Socialist's nightmare, and Burgess is hip to the ways in which society attempts to subsume personal freedom to corporate happiness. The same theme, in a happier but no less morally indignant satiric vein, is the theme of **Enderby**. Psychiatry (Dr. Wapenshaw), romantic love in the person of Vesta Bainbridge, raw sex represented by the obsessive, nauseous Miranda Boland, and the professional pander to mass culture (Rawcliffe) all take part in the ultimately vain attempt to put an end to Enderby and cause him to entropy into a nonentity. "On a small but magnificent scale **Enderby** is an epic of the potential Eden within man."

320 O'Malley, Michael. "Bid and Made." **Critic**, v. 27, no. 2 (October/November 1968) 95-99.

[Omnibus review. For **Enderby** see pp. 97-98.] The novel concerns a lyric poet whose talent may be running out. He is taunted by Rawcliffe who cheerfully steals Enderby's great new theme and turns it into an Italian skin flick (well within the gentlemanly limits of the craft). It includes the best description — weird, irrational, credible — that O'Malley has read. "The story is vintage Burgess: nothing predictable, nothing sure, Enderby storming at existence with that ebullient drive and verve Burgess seems to have distilled from J.S. Bach . . . . After his psychiatric rehabilitation, [Enderby] is Piggy Hogg, an amiable bartender with little interest in poetry. Whether Piggy is somehow related to the tavern-keeper of **Finnegans Wake**, Humphrey Chimpden Earwicker, whose name alliterates with the '**Here Comes Everybody**' of that novel, I don't know. I don't think so, but 'Enderby' and 'Everybody' are close enough. . . to make me wonder . . . . Burgess' Enderby is always, like the rest of us, behind the door when they're giving away gold or glory or good sense."

321 Ostermann, Robert. "Expanded Version of **Enderby** Tells of the Poet's Lot." **National Observer**, v. 7, no. 26 (June 24, 1968) 19.

"**Enderby** can be taken as an affirmation of poetry, as a defense against the deadening neuterism of contemporary life. But it can also be taken as a case against *poetry*, for Enderby the man writes his poetry seated on a toilet and has deliberately turned away from all normal expressions of human love. Is the truth, then, that all is illusion and there is no meaning? The author doesn't tell. But if one may conjecture on Mr. Burgess' behalf, he would say that **Enderby** is Enderby and you must take of the book and the man whatever you can at the time of reading. And whatever the individual reader does make of it, **Enderby** remains a novel of enigmas and surprises, brilliantly and cunningly crafted, an exciting addition to a body of work that must some day win Anthony Burgess the acclaim he deserves."

322 Pettingell, Phoebe. "This Boor Joyce." **New Leader**, v. 51, no. 17 (September 9, 1968) 20-21.

[Long review. Considerable plot summary which makes the point that Rawcliffe is the worst of Enderby's enemies after Vesta Bainbridge and Doctor Wapenshaw.] Enderby is a kind of Prufrock or Polonius. ". . . **Enderby** the novel has most of the faults of Enderby the poet. It is much too long and involved (the complexities of the plot are astounding), and it is inventive at the price of being over-ingenious. The book abounds in cute references to writers . . . . One gets the uneasy sense that the book is a giant acrostic or puzzle of literary references. Furthermore, **Enderby** has either too much meaning, or not enough . . . . As in Enderby's poetry, too many meanings are possible, none arising directly out of the book . . . . I wish Burgess' 17th novel had been tighter, but he is certainly one of the funniest writers alive, particularly when he is attacking the contemporary scene . . . . If **Enderby** lacks the tightness of **A Clockwork Orange**, it is certainly much less pretentious than the recent **Tremor of Intent**. Burgess writes too many books, but I do not see that he has written himself out by any means . . . . **Enderby** is the most appealing of Burgess' books so far, and by far the most amusing."

323 Pritchard, William H. "Burgess vs. Scholes." **Novel**, v. 2, no. 2 (Winter 1969) 164-67.

[Omnibus review. Also reviews Burgess' **The Novel Now**. For **Enderby**, see pp. 166-67.] Quotes the passage which describes the death of Rawcliffe ("With the conventional accompaniment of rattle and postlude of rictus and liquidity"). "As the saying goes, this is no doubt darkly comic, black even; it makes a sudden and I think quite moving point about how one's poems are and are not one's own. . . it also works dramatically as a load off Enderby's shoulders and a way towards his own comic acceptance of himself as a minor poet who will persevere in trying not to lose his own poems . . . . [Burgess'] comedy nevertheless stems from a verbal exploitation of that reek of the human, of the deeds and language of men which Ben Jonson promised his comedy would choose. . . rather than from the fancier and I'm convinced more arid delight in ideational or philosophical structures there for inspection in Mr. Scholes' [his **The Fabulators** is also reviewed] favorite books. And it's for this reason that Burgess, in his latest effort, for all his fabulative propensities, remains very much and very satisfyingly a novelist."

324 Solotaroff, Theodore. "The Busy Hand of Burgess." **New Republic**, v. 159, no. 8 (August 24, 1968) 20-22.

Burgess writes with the lilt, blarney and the roving eye for earthy detail typical of the Irish. "He has also been playing the Irish role on the English literary scene, which is to pepper and stir the pot:

to be amusing about the things London takes seriously, such as status, and serious about what London finds amusing, such as sin.'' He shares many of the talents, and much of the point of view, of James Joyce. Burgess, pressed for money, and with something of the performer in him, has spawned creations rather than nurturing them. When Burgess does not resemble Joyce, he is apt to come close to Peter Sellers. **Enderby** tends to bear out this split. **Inside Mr. Enderby** is a magic brew of small beer about a minor poet lured out into the world. The bathroom fixation "functions as the core of a meticulously assembled portrait of a man who is both a mess and an artist.'' Observes that Enderby's inner life is dominated by the voice of his gross stepmother and the infinitely alluring voice of the muse. **Inside Mr. Enderby** is beautifully written and masterfully woven and it includes characterization that begins in sound psychology, and ends as art. **Outside Mr. Enderby** is another matter. It is clearly played for laughs; chance rules all; and only the slow death of Rawcliffe gives the prose a real occasion to rise to. "In the meantime there is **Inside Mr. Enderby**, with its fine insistence on making connections, on keeping its feet on the ground, on revitalizing the art of fiction instead of greasing the skids.'' [Reprinted in #1628.]

325 Tannenbaum, Earl. Review of **Enderby**. **Library Journal**, v. 93, no. 11 (June 1, 1968) 2257-58.

[Chiefly brief plot summary.] "Perhaps the book is overlong, but it is a virtuoso performance offering lagniappe examples of Enderby's poetry and insights to the creative process.''

326 Wain, John. "Puppeteers.'' **New York Review of Books**, v. 11, no. 3 (August 22, 1968) 34-35.

[Omnibus review.] Keats wrote that a quarrel in the streets is a thing to be hated, but the energies displayed in it are fine. In the same sense, Burgess's satiric extravaganza against all those things in the modern world hostile to poetry (and there are many) is full of fine things. "It is a 'quarrel in the streets,' a quarrel against our time carried on in public, very loudly, but there is a Gargantuan zest in it, a love of extravagance and proliferation, and a feeling for language, that makes its tone much more positive than negative. I was reminded more than once of Wyndham Lewis in **The Apes of God**, but I think Burgess' book is better.'' Finds that all the characters but Enderby are puppets; the style is marked by self-consciousness; the satirical targets are many and the book is long; and the premise of the book — a poet who cares for nothing except getting on with his poetry — is wildly unreal.

Enderby Outside

327 London: Heinemann, 1968.

328 Harmondsworth, Eng.: Penguin, 1971. Pbk.

[The second part of **Enderby**. SEE ALSO: **Inside Mr. Enderby.**]

Reviews

329 Anon. "Musings from Morocco." **Times Literary Supplement**, No. 3,457 (May 30, 1968) 545.

The mixture of the book is rich; there is a wealth of parody; and the scornful American literary artist in the Big Fat White Doggy Wog cafe is plainly William Burroughs. Despite all this, the actual structure so pleasantly festooned by Mr. Burgess is extremely thin. Gives an account of the events in Books I and II to document his case. Enderby's encounter with the muse (as the nameless girl must be presumed, somewhat embarrassingly, to be) suggests that not only Enderby, but also Burgess is lowering his sights and beginning to think of himself as a minor writer. "It would be a very great pity if Mr. Burgess too were content to think of himself nothing but a minor writer, because there is really no self-evident reason why he should not write a major book. Admittedly writers of slight and/or humorous works are seldom popular with the critics when they suddenly become more ambitious . . . . But then the critics can be insidiously mistaken. And if Mr. Burgess cannot somehow be induced to put all his talents into a work of that calibre then there is something sadly wrong with the English literary climate."

330 Anon. Notice of **Enderby Outside**. **Observer** (London), 15 August 1974, p. 18.

"The continuing adventures of the poet who was brainwashed 'for his own good,' into barman Hogg. The return of the Muse causes him to break out — to Morocco. Not a particularly pleasant tale; there is much to admire in the style, but precious little to relish." [Complete text of notice.]

331 Coleman, John. "Inside Mr. Burgess." **Observer** (London), 26 May 1968, p. 29.

"One must resist the lure to identify Burgess too narrowly with his Enderby: what's clear from some exact passages is that Burgess has a wonderful insight into the ramshackle way poems get made . . . . There are tough and excellent jokes everywhere, at the expense of holidaying spinsters, phoney psychiatrists, Burroughs-style writers; Enderby still has his rather emphatic bowel troubles (tiresome, that old business of doing his best work on the loo) . . . . As always with Burgess, there is a tremendous confidence with language and languages; he has probably the finest ear of our times. He is also very intelligent, sometimes to chilling or Nabokovian extremes."

332 Green, Martin. "Fiction." **Month**, v. 226, no. 1215 (November 1968) 286-87.

[Omnibus review.] It is a very fine piece of fiction compared to Muriel Spark's **The Public Image**. "In order to define what is good about it one has to make some preliminary concessions to the demon of high standards. With Burgess one always has *some* feeling that the effort is minor, a bit slapdash, a bit too reliant on the easiest of his talents, above all on his self-sustaining, solipsistic fertility." Burgess wanted to 'do' Morocco, and the plot was probably dreamed up in five minutes. But Burgess, like Amis, has the ability to put the reader at ease; the brisk, incisively contemptuous self-portrait is the probable cause. **Inside Mr. Enderby** is more brilliant, more of a virtuoso piece; the sequel is drabber, lower-spirited, perhaps more minor but more moving. "Burgess may well be one of the three or four contemporary writers who will endure, when fifteen or sixteen more aesthetically high-minded — who are now in the contemporary histories of literature — have disappeared."

333 Holmes, Richard. "Carnival." **Times** (London), no. 57, 266 (June 1, 1968) 20.

"It's a short, scintillating carnival of a novel, funny, cruel, immensely stylish. Underneath, unexpectedly like the Muse, it's grave . . . . Mr. Burgess has developed a deadly and fantastic eye, comparable only to Vladimir Nabokov . . . . Above all, he has developed Enderby, the mock-epic of his struggle between inner and outer worlds in love and poetry. And over him, that Muse, deliberate and delicious: 'You're frightened of the young and the experimental . . . you've never cared much for people, have you?' Enderby, a minor symbol of the times, low on the horizon, but a star.''

334 Kermode, Frank. "Poetry and Borborygms." **Listener**, (June 6, 1968) 735-36.

[Very long, dense review by critic Burgess greatly respects. Difficult to summarize or paraphrase; the meaning is embedded in rapid asides. Sample:] "The sea, the moon, death and women are now seen to be an important subtext in these books. Enderby at one point wrote 'All women are stepmothers' on a sheet of lavatory paper and flushed it. Later he says that the muse is 'all women.' The moon draws up tides in the sea and in women, in *la belle mere* and *la belle-mere*. The step-mother is the muse, death, the sea, even the moon or its goddess. Vesta: evening star, herald of the moon, stepmotherish glutton and burper — missing the point, Enderby recommends gin and hot water for menstrual pain. Miranda: learned in that brave new world the moon, waxing and waning, thin and fat, amorous and stepmotherish. Finally, naked and nameless, the moon-muse herself, at one with the sea and death. Rawcliffe died horribly, brave in the filth, and the muse consents to be wrapped in the robe he wore. She works on the volta of an Enderby sonnet, eats and drinks heavily, burps stepmotherly. Enderby loves her; he is almost, through Rawcliffe, ready for the life of a major poet. She gives him his chance, offers herself, having warned him that 'poetry isn't a silly little hobby to be practised in the smallest room.' But Enderby, 'not cut out for marriage,' never makes it with a woman in either book, and, middle-aged, withdraws from copulative majority into masturbatory minority. He can't take her 'ghastly young beauty' though his conventional worry about age is, she explains, only another instance of his cowardice . . . . ''

335 McDowell, Frederick P.W. "Recent British Fiction: Some Established Writers." **Contemporary Literature**, v. 11 (1970) 401-431.

[Omnibus review. For Burgess, see pp. 419-21.] Considers the tone of the book (somewhere between the mocking and sympathetic) and the way in which, although grubby and dessicated, Enderby has redeeming qualities (honesty, devotion to his art). "These Enderby novels, I feel, respresent Burgess at his best, the engaging novelist of **The Long Day Wanes, The Right to an Answer**, and **Honey for the Bears**, the writer aware of the profundities of our experience as well as of its absurdities, the writer whose comic vision promotes a detachment which is never devoid of sympathy.''

336 Nowell, Robert. "Horror Show." **Tablet**, v. 222, no. 6679 (May 25, 1968) 529-30.

Technically, Burgess is perhaps the most accomplished novelist writing in English today. His mastery over words enables him to describe his own particular and ambiguous world, in which we lurch from farce to tragedy. **Inside Mr. Enderby** is Burgess' masterpiece: it involved the creation of a genuine, credible poet. **Enderby Outside**, while self-contained, completes the work.

337 Price, R.G.G. "New Fiction." **Punch**, v. 254, no. 6664 (May 29, 1969) 794.

[Omnibus review.] "The mixture of seediness, poetry and jokes is much the same but it has clotted . . . . Loading every rift with ore is all very well; but it can be hard on the reader, and one doesn't want to trudge through what is obviously intended to be just an entertainment . . . . In the Malayan novels, the background was equal in weight to the literary interest. Here it seems dim. Attempts to raise it into relief by violence of language don't come off. Compared with the previous instalment of Enderby's adventure, credibility has leaked . . . . Thank heaven for a writer who, like Shakespeare, has such exuberant gifts that he can afford [near misses.]''

338 Rees, David. "Heroes of Our Time." **Encounter**, v. 21, no. 4 (Winter 1968-69) 74-76.

[Omnibus review.] "'. . . Mr. Burgess' new novel is a minor, complex masterpiece which fittingly carries on the Enderby story . . . . I have seen Mr. Burgess' literary talents, the sheer invention, the comprehension of language fused with the understanding of inner compulsion and outer necessity, compared with those of Nabokov. Perhaps. Rather, I feel, there is a Joycean felicity about **Enderby Outside**.''

339 Reynolds, Stanley. "Artful Dodger." **New Statesman**, v. 75, no. 1942 (May 31, 1968) 735-36.

[Omnibus review.] "Anyone taking a walk around the contemporary literary scene is bound to stumble upon Mr. Anthony Burgess, either as the universal expert criticising one form of art or another in any one of a number of newspapers and magazines, or crowding our bookshop shelves with novels, works of editing, or literary criticism and history. For years this artful dodger of critical pigeon-holes has been able to take subject and matter that in other hands would be mere romps, lightweight stuff

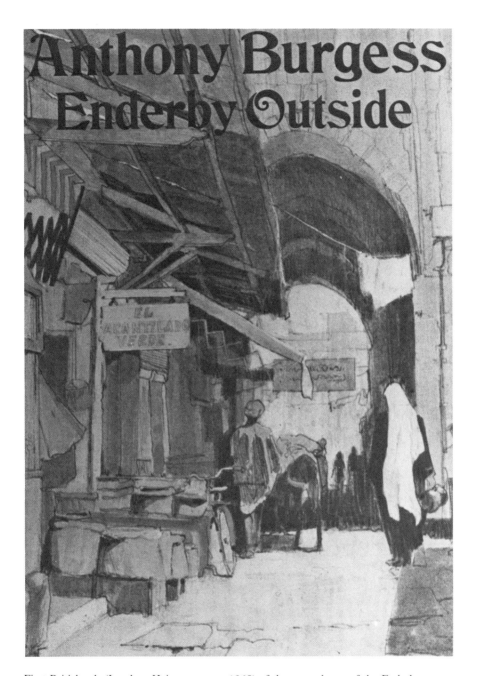

First British ed. (London: Heinemann, c. 1968) of the second part of the Enderby saga.

to amuse the invalid, and by sheer weight of numbers (five books published in one year) he has placed himself on equal footing with Graham Greene. But this is not fair. Certainly Burgess' stuff has some look about it of the lightweight entertainment, but there is more to it than that. There is tight construction and a dense, careful style that nevertheless glows once on almost every page . . . . Burgess is able to conjure with equal lush sensuality the texture of a stew or the taste of a Moroccan drink, and his scenes are ornamented with contemporary gargoyles as if to define the precise ambience, so that here Marshal McLuhan appears and there William Burroughs peers down grinning on the action.''

340 Shrapnel, Norman. "Productivity Burgess and Others." **Manchester Guardian Weekly**, 6 June 1968, p. 11.

[Omnibus review.] Given Burgess' fantastic output, his productivity is marked by excellent quality. This novel is vigorous, amusing and sensitive in the coarse-grained, no-nonsense fashion Burgess has made his own.

341 Waugh, Auberon. "Seat of Pleasure." **Spectator**, v. 220, no. 7300 (May 24, 1968) 745.

Sets down the stringent qualifications necessary to enjoy **Inside Mr. Enderby** (Catholic-educated, strong anti-populist sympathies, semi-serious despair for the Church swinging between atheism, militant anti-clericalism and hyper-ultramontanism, a certain sense of humor) and wonders at the generous testimonials to the first work plastered on its successor. The reviewer for the **Sunday Times** described it as 'a brilliantly fly [Brit. slang for knowing, sharp, smart, agile-minded] piece of work.' "How is it possible that such a grotesquely humourless reviewer could have appreciated the wisdom and wit, the originality, the pain and the exquisite, absolute justice of **Inside Mr. Enderby**?'' The sequel is beautifully written and tantalisingly close to being an obvious masterpiece. It snaps, crackles and pops with brilliant flyness and is far better than any other novel he has read this year. Outlines a Constructive Suggestion to fuse the two books into one true masterpiece and, that off his chest, thanks Burgess for another five hours of acute enjoyment.

342 Wood, Michael. "A Dream of Clockwork Oranges." **New Society**, v. 11, no. 297 (June 6, 1968) 842-43.

"Darkness descends like a team of heraldic apes. Banknotes rustle like pork crackling, a woman cackles like an old oboe, a fish sauce tastes like a clank of metal.'' Despite the characteristic flourish and violence of these images, the novel is a let-down. "There are fine comic scenes, but much of the satire is slack and clumsy, closer to Auberon Waugh than to Evelyn, and some of the writing is downright lumpish.'' In spite of these faults, it is too early to think of fatigue and flagging talent. Burgess has always been an uneven writer. A long, interesting essay review which quotes Burgess on literary fecundity (desirable), pays tribute to his learning, notes the echoes of Greene, and traces his one monumental debt to Joyce. "In his various threadbare disguises, peace-loving Bloom trots through all Burgess's violent fictions: human, cuckolded, put upon, mildly protesting, the faint voice of reason in the rising madness.'' Summarizes **The Wanting Seed, A Clockwork Orange, Honey for the Bears, Tremor of Intent** in terms of the dualism of good and evil in Burgess' work. "The attraction of a dualism is that it damns the neutrals, and Burgess, like Dante, hates neutrals above all things. Hence, I think, his sympathy for murderous young Alex . . . . Alex at least takes sides. He knows what evil is and he chooses it.'' ·

Enemy in the Blanket

343 London: Heinemann, 1958.

344 London: Heinemann, 1968.

345 London: Heinemann, 1972, c1958.

[NOTE: See editions of **The Malayan Trilogy** (British title) and **The Long Day Wanes** (American title) of which this work is a part.]

English Literature: a Survey for Students

346 London: Longmans, Green, 1958.

347 London: Longmans, 1966.

348 London: Longmans, 1974. New ed.

Translations

349 Japanese: **Igirisu Bungakushi**. Translated by Rikutaro Fukada and Hisashi Shigeo.

Ernest Hemingway and His World

350 London: Thames and Hudson, 1978.

351 New York: Scribner, 1978.

Reviews

352 Adams, Phoebe-Lou. Review of **Ernest Hemingway and His World**. **Atlantic**, v. 242, no. 4 (October 1978) 116.

"Perhaps because he is himself a novelist of deservedly high reputation, Mr. Burgess has been able to combine a just appraisal of Hemingway's importance with a tolerantly realistic view of his personal foibles to create a first-class short biography. The many photographs actually convey information which is not always the case in books of this type." [Complete text of review.]

353 Anon. Review of **Ernest Hemingway and His World**. **Kirkus Reviews**, (July 1, 1978) 723.

"Burgess shows respect for Hemingway's innovative prose procedures and sadness about his increasingly pathological life — all in that graceful Burgess style, not too tricky for once — but finally it's like a little wave too late and from too far away: a gesture, and of no consequence whatsoever."

354 Anon. Review of **Ernest Hemingway and His World**. **Publishers Weekly**, v. 214, no. 4 (July 24, 1978) 92.

"Told with the taut objectivity of a Hemingway story, this masterful, concise pictorial biography gives us a big hunk of Hemingway, shorn of self-made legend and myth." Underneath the tough-guy persona, there was a good deal of fraudulent posturing, but Hemingway's art is found to be as powerful as that of Fitzgerald or Faulkner.

355 Anon. Review of **Ernest Hemingway and His World**. **Booklist**, v. 75, no. 2 (September 15, 1978) 146.

[Review signed EB.] "Despite a decline in reputation following his suicide in 1961, Hemingway has never lacked for commentators, and this volume adds little to our knowledge about him or his work. The numerous photographs, however, some of which are published for the first time, offer a feast of unexpected revelations — the same cannot be said about the oddly flat, though competent, text by Burgess." [Complete text of review.]

356 Anon. Review of **Ernest Hemingway and His World**. **Critic**, v. 37, no. 10 (November 15, 1978) 7.

Burgess has no liking for Hemingway; he also tends to downgrade Hemingway's works. The book is reminiscent of Lillian Ross' notorious **New Yorker** profile. "As could be expected, Burgess writes with flair and the combination of his readable prose and a selection of appealing pictures cannot help but intrigue readers."

357 Anon. Review of **Ernest Hemingway and His World**. **Choice**, v. 15, no. 12 (February 1979) 1661-62.

"The pictures alone are worth the modest price; but in addition, the text is one of the best in the series. Anthony Burgess writes rings around any of Hemingway's other biographers, and his concise life has a sharpness and precision and sense of irony missing from Baker's massive but disappointing work. Burgess, resisting the fashionable trend to dismiss Hemingway's art because of his insufficiencies as a man, sees Hemingway steadily and sees him whole. His capsule criticisms of the most notable fiction and nonfiction are brilliant and incisive. Burgess adds few facts to the story of Hemingway's life, but his book is a pleasure to read and is valuable to students of both authors."

358 Beatty, Jack. Review of **Ernest Hemingway and His World**. **New Republic**, v. 179, no. 15 (October 7, 1978) 37-38.

An account of the life of Hemingway distilled from the book under review. Quotes Burgess on Hemingway's claim that he slept with Mata Hari (chronologically impossible); on Hemingway's poor record during the Spanish Civil War compared to George Orwell; on Hem's supposed sexual incapacity; and approvingly singles out Burgess' statement that Hemingway's greatest achievement was the introduction of a new prose style — a language of the nerves and muscles rather than the head and heart.

359 Bradbury, Malcolm. "The Wound and the Bow." **New Statesman**, v. 96, no. 2484 (October 27, 1978) 549.

[Omnibus review which compares the contrasted lives and achievements of Scott Fitzgerald and Ernest Hemingway.] Notes that Burgess, in his bouncy rewrite of the standard Baker biography, wounds Hemingway in the wrong leg. "Confession is a place where much of writing starts: a place of self-revelation, accusation, and attack. This we may contain by form, by the Jamesian panoplies or the more complex stoicism that Hemingway modelled for us. Books will be dramatised, completed, made secure as texts. On the other hand, we may, as Norman Mailer proposes, commit ourselves primarily to risking consciousness itself. Writing will then have raw edges, a sense of incompleteness, a quality of pained exposure."

360 Brudnoy, David. Review of **Ernest Hemingway and His World**. **Saturday Evening Post**, v. 251, no. 3 (April 1979) 88-89.

Hemingway has been imitated, derided, interred and disinterred. Here is a book for the general reader who wants to learn about Hemingway without the benefit of 10,000 footnotes. Burgess demonstrates that Hemingway was preoccupied with the sound of words and explains why the movies based on his books have fallen short of expectations. Burgess moves effortlessly back and forth — from the life to the books — to prove that Hem was something of a war-hero, anti-Semite, bully, vulgarian and snob. For all that, the short stories remain exquisitely wrought. "Those who must have their scandalous writers disinfected will come away from this book only partly satisfied. Not that Burgess prettifies his subject; he merely gets on with the business of exposition and exegesis, without lingering overlong on the gossip."

361 Caradine, K. Review of **Ernest Hemingway and His World**. **British Book News**, January 15, 1979, pp. 117-18.

Burgess' personality is stamped on every page of his cool, wry, and occasionally very funny 40,000 word biographical sketch. He is fun to read because he is ever ready to judge, even if some of his judgments seem questionable. Hemingway's **Toronto Star** pieces, far from displaying any self-effacement, reveal an extremely brash, offensively facetious wiseacre and red-necked personality. One sometimes wishes Burgess had more space to develop his ideas. His suggestion that the Hemingway prose is simple and direct, but always marked by melancholy, deserves expansion. The photographs are well chosen. Caradine's favorite is one of Alice B. Toklas holding an item of infant clothing as if it were about to explode.

362 Cosgrave, Mary Silva. "Outlook Tower." Review of **Ernest Hemingway and His World**. **Hornbook**, v. 54, no. 6 (December 1978) 669.

"In an admirably terse and incisive style Burgess has assessed Hemingway's literary achievement and reputation during his lifetime and afterward and has vividly drawn a portrait of the man — 'as much a creation as his books, and a far inferior creation' . . . . Burgess rates Hemingway at his best with Joyce, Faulkner, and Scott Fitzgerald; at his worst 'he reminds us that to engage literature one has first to engage life'."

363 Cross, Jack. "For Him the Bell Tolls." **Times Educational Supplement**, 20 October 1978, p. 24.

"There is no disguising the fact that Hemingway was a handsome, boozing, bullying braggart, self-deceptive and self-destructive, over-indulged most of his life, not least by his four long-suffering wives and a series of beautiful surrogate 'daughters'." Hemingway's greatest innovation was his style of description without decoration. It looks simple on the surface, but only because he produced it. Burgess' one paragraph on **The Sun Also Rises** is remarkably compressed and perceptive. However, it is probably untrue to claim, as Burgess does, that Hemingway's reputation has not noticeably diminished since his death. Hemingway's one genuine masterpiece remains his novella called **The Old Man and the Sea**.

364 Foran, Don. Review of **Ernest Hemingway and His World**. **America**, v. 139, no. 16 (December 2, 1978) 414-16.

Considers the Burgess style passionate and elegant, and quotes extracts (Burgess on the Paris of the 20s, and on **The Old Man and the Sea**) to demontrate the point. The work is true to Carlos Baker's comprehensive biography; it also includes strong critical judgments about the flaws in the man, and the effect of those flaws on the work. Burgess is quite right to see insecurity and even paranoia in Hemingway. It is remarkable that the perception of these flaws do not utterly undermine the insights into the author.

365 Kukacs, Paul. "A Fictional Self." **National Review**, v. 31, no. 13 (March 20, 1979) 428-30.

Hemingway became a legend in his own time. He was a big man, and the pose struck a chord in the American consciousness. The price he paid was an unwillingness to take risks in his fiction. This work is trying to be an. . . attractive summary of Hemingway's life, but Burgess never argues his central theme that "Hemingway the man was as much a creation as his books, and a far inferior creation." Worse, Burgess is a crude psychologist given to preposterous one-sentence conclusions. It is absurd to say that Hemingway's obsession with death and killing in **Death in the Afternoon** stemmed from guilt over a recent divorce. The book includes minor inaccuracies; it ignores Hemingway's literary achievement; it devotes too much space to the films. Hemingway's dilemma is expressed in 'The Snows of Kilimanjaro' where the dying writer regrets that "he had destroyed his talent by not using it, by betrayals of himself and what he believed in." Burgess is content to write about the legend, and he ignores the complex man beneath the persona.

366 Loriot, Noelle. "Les mortelles nostalgies d'Anthony Burgess." **L'Express Magazine** (Edition internationale), no. 1445 (March 24, 1979) 84-85.

Reviews of **Beard's Roman Women** ("Rome sous la pluie") and **Ernest Hemingway** ("Ce sacre Hemingway"). Introduces Burgess to French readers — brain tumor, death of his first wife, prolific production during so-called 'terminal' year — and remarks that Burgess' treatment of Hemingway conveys the impression that Hemingway exploited a popularity not justified by his uneven *oeuvre*, but that his influence ranks with that of Joyce and Faulkner.

367 Ott, William. Review of **Ernest Hemingway and His World**. **Library Journal**, v. 103, no. 14 (August 1978) 1510.

It is a coffee table book with spunk. Burgess finds much of Hemingway's personality offensive, but this distaste has not adversely affected his appraisal of the major short stories. The pictures seem fresh; they are more than **Life** retreads. "Of interest for public libraries; less important for research collections."

368 Shone, Richard. "Crack-Up." **Spectator**, v. 241 (November 25, 1978) 23.

[Also reviews **Scott and Ernest: The Fitzgerald-Hemingway Friendship**, by Matthew J. Bruccoli.] "All the more welcome then is Anthony Burgess's book, an excellent addition to an excellent series. He maintains that Hemingway was a bully, bore and fake. With suggestive precision and swiftness of language, we move from Oak Park, Chicago to the first World war in Italy; through four marriages, countless sporting exploits (and two plane crashes) to the Nobel-winning Papa, 'physically etiolated, profoundly psychotic,' who put a double-barrelled shotgun to his head in 1961 . . . . What is curious is that, in spite of the mauling his character gets (and often deserves), Hemingway emerges as an affecting, even invigorating figure — like his heroes, destroyed but not defeated."

369 Sternman, William. Review of **Ernest Hemingway and His World**. **Best Sellers**, February 1979, pp. 363-64.

Burgess has not so much interpreted Hemingway's work as recreated it in his own image. Witness what he has to say about **The Sun Also Rises**. Quotes a passage from Burgess' book and wonders whether he has muddied Hemingway's limpid story with Freudian fustian. "The passage quoted indicates another flaw in Burgess's biography. Although he has obviously done his research, given his subject some thought and come up with intriguing insights of his own, the very jerkiness of the book as a whole in itself hints at a longer manuscript that has been cut down to size to fit Scribners' picture-book format." It is, nonetheless, a valuable initiation to one of America's greatest writers.

The Eve of Saint Venus

370 London: Sidgwick and Jackson, 1964. Illustrated by Edward Pagram.

371 Rexdale, Ont.: Ambassador Books [1964?]

372 New York: Norton, 1970. Illustrated by Edward Pagram.

373 [Taiwan: s.n., 1970] Taiwanese piracy of 1970 Norton ed.

374 New York: Ballantine, 1971. Pbk.

375 New York: Norton, 1979, c1964. Pbk.

376 Feltham, Eng.: Hamlyn Paperbacks, 1981. With a special new preface. Illustrated by Edward Pagram.

Recordings

377 Anthony Burgess Reads from The Eve of Saint Venus and Nothing Like the Sun. [Phonodisc] Caedmon, 1974. TC 1442. Recorded June 4, 1974. Notes by E.P. Swenson on slipcase.

378 The Eve of Saint Venus and Nothing Like the Sun. [Phonotape] Caedmon Cassette, 1974. CDL 51442.

Reviews

Burgess on his own work: "Yet if remaining in print is a test of popularity, then Burton has remained quietly popular for the last century and a half. At this moment, though, his reputation seems to have suffered a certain depression. When I took the theme of a novella out of the **Anatomy**, there were certain critics who turned up their noses and murmured: 'Good God! He's old stuff, the sort of otiose bookwork most likely to be turned out of the Electronic Village; life is too short to settle down with a highball and Burton'."

379 Anon. Review of **The Eve of Saint Venus**. **Times** (London), no. 57,225 (April 13, 1968) 23.

[Review of Four Square paperback edition. Brisk plot summary in 75 words.]

380 Anon. Review of **The Eve of Saint Venus**. **Publishers Weekly**, v. 197, no. 13 (March 30, 1970) 61.

"This delectable trifle, written by Mr. Burgess in 1950 and not published in England until 1964, is deliberately a parody of a certain type of English drawing-room comedy of an earlier vintage . . . . There's just the right amount of light and fluffy nonsense attached to all this, with lovely Burgess-like word plays and ridiculous dialog along the way until the youthful lovers (real life) sort themselves out."

381 Anon. "Unavoidable Whimsy." **Time**, (April 27, 1970) 96.

"Whimsy is unavoidable. A dotty baronet has received a consignment of cut-rate statues from his alcoholic twin brother. The stone gods and goddesses include, naturally, Venus. A ring slipped on Venus' finger by a nervous bridegroom brings her to life, and love is reborn in a cold climate. The cast of characters, Burgess has explained, is drawn fondly from stock theatrical figures: 'The boneheaded gold-hearted country squire in plus fours, the pert and resourceful servant, the grim but reliable chatelain, the sweet guileless young lovers, the comic Anglican clergyman.' Only a writer who can bring such scarecrows to life would be willing to proclaim, let alone admit, that his characters come out of a fusty stage wardrobe. In **The Eve of Saint Venus**, this miracle is performed."

382 Anon. Review of **The Eve of Saint Venus**. **New Republic**, v. 162, no. 19 (May 9, 1970) 43.

It is high literary farce and the beginning evokes the social toughness of Congreve; then it dwindles to silliness. Sir Benjamin and the vicar display a marvelous sharpness of wit reminiscent of happier days for comedy. [Brief review for the NR.]

383 Anon. Review of **The Eve of Saint Venus**. **Booklist**, v. 66, no. 20 (June 15, 1970) 1262.

"A frothy, brief entertainment satirizing the conservative, insular, rural British aristocracy is a novella constructed somewhat in the style of the farces produced at the Aldwych Theatre in London, as explained in the author's foreword to the U.S. edition . . . . The accompanying illustrations add considerably to the delight of the book."

384 Anon. Review of **The Eve of Saint Venus**. **Choice**, v. 7, no. 9 (November 1970) 1229-30.

"Burgess intends the work to be an irreverent epithalamion supplying biting comment on life and love in the dingy English welfare state. American readers are likely to miss the satiric overtones and find, instead, a sophisticated entertainment. Burgess' classical erudition is pleasantly applied. His fondness for learned wordplay tends to grow tiresome, however. A novel like **A Clockwork Orange** (1963) has given Burgess a secure reputation on both sides of the Atlantic. But his early and, by his own admission, slight work will do little to dispel an American reader's impression of him as a clever writer rather than as someone to be taken — at this stage of his career — as a significant novelist. Recommended."

385 Anon. Review of **The Eve of Saint Venus**. **Critic**, v. 29, no. 3 (January 1971) 92.

"Credentials now established by a number of serious works, Anthony Burgess has released a 1950 *jeu d'esprit*, a light, witty tale of British rural aristocracy and a young man who on the eve of his wedding slips a ring on a statue of Venus with some engaging results. Burgess' book is after the manner of Wodehouse, which means plenty puns per paragraph. The effect is delightful." [Complete text of review.]

386 Anon. Review of **The Eve of Saint Venus**. **New Yorker**, v. 47, no. 4 (March 13, 1971) 135.

"Mr. Burgess tells us that he wrote this sparkling novel in 1950 but witheld it from publication because the gloomy mood of the time seemed to him unpropitious for a lighthearted work. He tells us, further, that his literary sources were two: English farce and an ancient legend of a man who married Venus by mistake. On these borrowings he has erected an edifice of laughter decorated with language. The work's serious message is that love — ordinary human physical love — is as important as such worthy activities as painting and prayer and politics." [Complete text of review.]

387 Baldwin, Barry. Review of **The Eve of Saint Venus**. **Library Journal**, v. 95, no. 11 (June 1, 1970) 2179.

"The novella is a frothy and somewhat academic jest (a knowledge of Latin is needed to grasp some of the humor); not a major work, nor intended to be, but a constant chuckle for a couple of hours."

388 Bolger, Eugenie. "Words, Words and More Words." **New Leader**, v. 53, no. 11 (May 25, 1970) 22-24.

[Reasonably long, thoughtful review.] Words often become Mr. Burgess' substitute for true characterization. **Enderby** includes many brilliant, perhaps dangerously precious passages. In **The Eve of Saint Venus** the sound, shape and infinite couplings of words are plainly the only reality. His characters are merely sketched in, and what happens to them, in what is admittedly a parody of Christopher Fry and T.S. Eliot, does not seem to matter. One senses the author chuckling in the background while he manipulates his creations; it is a disquieting sensation. He also displays an unfortunate tendency to underline, as when Sir Benjamin's swearing is described as too literary to be really offensive; the conclusion is clear enough, and the comment makes for condescension. The dialogue is sometimes more appropriate to a bookish author than his characters. His theme is the importance of physical love, but the message is not dramatically shown; it is merely reported. The fault is traceable to the scant respect the author gives his characters. "Where there is no characterization, where nothing truly engages the reader's attention, only words are left. In this case they are at least literate, bubbling, whimsical, and irrepressible."

389 Cook, Bruce. "Here's Mr. Burgess, Full of Swagger and Guilt." **National Observer**, 27 April 1970, p. 19.

[An interview and book review datelined Chapel Hill, N.C.] Burgess, swaggering around on the University of North Carolina in a jacket and black turtleneck, is a prepossessing figure. More, he is a genius. Witness his prodigious outpouring of some of the finest, quirkiest and most intellectually lively fiction

First English ed. (London: Sidgwick and Jackson, c. 1964) of this didactic entertainment.

written anywhere, his competence in linguistics and fluency in five languages. Quizzed on the point, he is humble about his musical career ("There was this awful agony at not being played as I thought I should be"). Briefly describes Burgess' career — Malaya, headaches, brain tumor, five novels in one year, his own review of his own **Inside Mr. Enderby** [see #448] in the pages of the **Yorkshire Post**. This novel, a little joke of a thing, has a neat, slightly contrived quality. Surely it was written for the stage? "Mr. Burgess owns up: 'No, not a play first, actually, but an opera libretto. It was done originally for BBC with Gion-Carlo Menotti in mind as the composer, and then Edmund Crispin was to be involved in the project. But nothing came of it. A disappointment, of course, but now I think I'll do the music myself'." Burgess describes his future plans. Less harried by journalism, he will now devote more time and pains to his novels.

390 Davis, L.J. "The Goddess Speaks with a Greek Accent." **Washington Post Book World**, 19 April 1970, p. 3.

"All of this is great fun and what used to be called a good read. It is not a major novel, does not pretend to be, and can be got through in a single evening. It is less about the 'importance of physical love,' as Burgess claims, than it is — in both structure and content — about England. It is an England that perhaps never existed but came close to reality, at least in the mind and heart. It was present in those old Aldwych farces — a basic decency, a humane optimism beneath all the silly goings-on, the entrances and exits and multiple deceptions that were, really, all in fun."

391 Dick, Kay. "Murdoch's Eighth." **Spectator**, v. 213, no. 7107 (September 11, 1964) 346.

[Omnibus review.] "Two short entertainments from two highly skilled professionals make a delightful exercise in contrasts. Mr. Burgess shoots off his glittering joke with great finesse. **The Eve of Saint Venus** is a very dashing plea for the lady's inclusion in the calendar of saints, and the pre-wedding antics which take place in a very U-county homestead are excruciatingly funny." [Complete text of review.]

392 Lindroth, James R. Review of **The Eve of Saint Venus**. **America**, v. 122, no. 20 (May 23, 1970) 565.

In this novella along the lines of the 'old Aldwych farces,' complete with its stock characters and somewhat artificial, literary prose, the figure of the English Lord remains amusing and interesting by virtue of his language alone. "The point that Burgess evokes in this world of light comedy is that man is humanized by love, and by love alone."

393 Morris, Robert K. Review of **The Eve of Saint Venus**. **Saturday Review**, v. 53, no. 30 (May 16, 1970) 48.

This comparatively light-weight addition to the substantial Burgess canon is derived from Burton's quaint and quirky **Anatomy of Melancholy**, and it features many of the stock characters of the English stage. Burgess' verbal and dramatic alchemy turns the dross of caricature into pure gold. "The divine succubus is everywhere attended by odors of fish, ozone, and the sea; the magic of love and beauty, fresh from the foam, penetrates barriers of brocades and morals and transforms the venerable state into a kind of Venusberg . . . . The theme of all this — with Venus providing the crucial link — is twofold. Just as the past continually feeds on the present, so earthly and heavenly love are manifestations of the same divine thing." If Venus is the heroine, the true hero is the English language. "The only predictable thing about Burgess is suprise. In **The Eve of Saint Venus** he loots the Elizabethan literary guild for echoes from Shakespeare, Ben Jonson, and Michael Drayton, ransacks Peacock's extravagances in **Crotchet Castle**, and plunders the techniques of Eliot's and Fry's verse drama; but the word-hoard is all his — and inexhaustible."

394 Murray, John J. Review of **The Eve of Saint Venus**. **Best Sellers**, May 15, 1970, p. 67.

If Sir Benjamin's recondite diatribe ("As for 'break,' 'break' is a trull of a word, it will take in everything . . . . ") is an example of linguistics fertilizing the novel, novelists may just as well leave it alone. Done as a play, it might prove amusing for students at Union Theological Seminary. "A slight modernizing and un-literaryizing of the dialogue, a huge slice out of the windiness of the characters, and the play might work, but it would still be only an interesting review skit or inter-commercial on TV."

395 Wall, Stephen. "New Novels." **Listener**, v. 72, no. 1850 (September 10, 1964) 401.

[Omnibus review.] The work is, to use the words of the blurb, a highly civilized joke which comes off thanks to the ebullient vitality of the language. "Some of the attendant characters have the air of doing a literary turn, but are sprightly and amusing enough — especially a fulminating baronet whose invective has a Falstaffian energy, and a Chaucerian nanny who makes a steaming cup of cocoa seem like the last word in lascivious potations."

Here Comes Everybody

396 London: Faber and Faber, 1965.

397 London: Faber and Faber, 1969, c1965. Pbk.

[Published in the U.S. under title: **Re Joyce**.]

Translations

398 German: **Ein Mann in Dublin Namens Joyce**. Bad Homburg: Gehlen, 1968. Translated by Gisela and Manfred Triesch.

Reviews

399 Anon. "Joycers Burgessbook." **Times Literary Supplement**, no. 3,323 (November 4, 1965) 972.

The ordinary reader scared off Joyce by the professors is unlikely to have the intellectual curiosity or persistence to get into Joyce. The best introduction to the later work is **Dubliners** — disposed of in one cursory chapter. The commentary on **Ulysses**, even when the commentator is intelligent, lively and enthusiastic, is unlikely to create a new audience for Joyce. Burgess' commentary on **Finnegans Wake** is free from jargon; it concentrates on the central themes and structural elements of the book. "For the new venturer in the long but never tedious exploration of **Finnegans Wake** this book supplies the basic equipment."

400 Anon. "Finnagain." **Economist**, v. 217, no. 6379 (December 4, 1965) 1095.

Burgess claims that this book is written for the average reader. In that case, only the average reader can judge his success — and no reviewer judged competent to review the book falls in that category. The average reader surely does not need help with **Dubliners** and its style of scrupulous meanness. **A Portrait of the Artist as a Young Man** needs no introduction: any reader so dull as to be put off by the stylistic unfamiliarity of the opening pages is beyond help. The major part of **Ulysses** is also comprehensible with a little patience. "That still leaves **Finnegans Wake**. Here we all need all the help we can get, but it is precisely here that Mr. Burgess is least able to be helpful. Here the scholars are indispensable, though there is a long, hard road ahead of those who set out to distinguish the good scholars from the bad. Sadly enough, they will have to throw out several of the writers who are mentioned by Mr. Burgess in his foreword and who have clearly influenced his own studies, for the worse. It is now surely known that much of the later study of Joyce has had to clear the ground of much misunderstanding and sheer nonsense in the earlier."

401 Donoghue, Denis. "Wortsampler." **New Statesman**, v. 70, no. 1801 (September 17, 1965) 402.

"Mr. Burgess wants to rescue Joyce from Professor X and give the whole *oeuvre* to you, mate." He is helpful on detail but nearly always wrong on the large assertion. To say that Joyce aimed at 'the ennoblement of the common man' or that his purpose was to 'glorify the Dublin of pubs and poverty' is to be guilty of unhappy formulations. "That Shem would have scorned both purposes never occurs to Mr. Burgess." He knows the books intimately, and loves them too well. Consequently he never asks himself the hard questions. He does not seem to realize that **Portrait** is a scrappy book with two great scenes and at least 50 pages of embarrassingly tumid writing. Argues that **Finnegans Wake** is not the sacred text on current show; that the arbitrariness of Joyce's language is an unresolved problem; and that the dream machine of the **Wake** enabled Joyce to fend off all responsibilities to people and things, and was designed for that purpose.

402 Furbank, P.N. Review of **Here Comes Everybody**. **Manchester Guardian Weekly**, 23 September 1965, p. 10.

403 Hart, Clive. Review of **Here Comes Everybody**. **Modern Language Review**, v. 62, no. 4 (October 1967) 714-15.

The book is a lucid summary of the events in the novels along with a certain commentary of a fairly simple kind. The really ordinary reader, if tempted by a work of criticism (unlikely) might well be fired by Burgess' evident delight in his subject. "Few people will quarrel with most of what Mr. Burgess has to say about Joyce in general, but in matters of detail the rather large number of inaccuracies may prove disturbing." Devotes a paragraph to these inaccuracies, and concludes that the book is too long and sometimes too strident. "The best things in it are its lucidity, its enthusiasm, and (for most of its length) its common sense."

404 Hodgart, Matthew. "Haveth Critics Everywhere." **Encounter,** v. 25, no. 5 (November 1965) 78, 80, 82.

"Mr. Burgess has now added his stone [to the *cairn* of Joyce's grave]: a rounded, pleasantly shaped and coloured, but otherwise rather unexciting pebble-sized pebble." He has not decided to compete with Richard Ellmann or T.S. Eliot — and the world has seen many excellent introductions to Joyce by Stuart Gilbert, Harry Levin, Frank Budgen, Campbell and Robinson and Adaline Glasheen. He does not add enough new material to distinguish his work from the lively, sensible and accurate criticism that went before. The chapters on **Ulysses** are humane and full of insights. Those on the **Wake** are substantially based on the **Skeleton Key to Finnegans Wake.** "He thus manages to give a rather false impression of the **Wake** on three counts: that it is decipherable, that it is equally good throughout and that in the last analysis it is a genial and humorous romp." [The remainder of this substantial review argues the opposite case on all three counts.]

405 Hollis Christopher. "James Joyce." **Tablet,** v. 219, no. 6546 (November 6, 1965) 1241.

Joyce, in company with Milton's Satan and Shakespere's Richard III, defied the claims of the Christian religion with a bold *non-serviam.* His works after **The Portrait of an Artist as a Young Man** were marked by an unpleasant extreme grossness and, in the case of the **Wake,** by unintelligibility which results from piling pun on pun. For Burgess to argue that Christ founded the Church with a pun is entirely misleading; He founded it upon one pun. For Burgess to observe that Joyce brought to us an 'almost insupportable optimism' is hard to understand. Vico's theory of eternal recurrence, if true, is not particularly optimistic. Joyce taught nothing in **Ulysses** and **Finnegans Wake** that he had not already conveyed quite simply in **Portrait.**

406 Peschmann, Hermann. Review of **Here Comes Everybody. English; The Journal of the English Association,** v. 16, no. 93 (Autumn 1966) 111-13.

It is surely only a form of inverted snobbery that **Ulysses** and **Finnegans Wake** are within the scope of everybody's assimilation. "While we have ceased to scream about their obscurity, blasphemy, and obscenity, it is high time we clearly admitted that they are very difficult; that they are, and are likely long to remain, minority reading — even though books like Mr. Burgess's should appreciably extend the minority who attempt them. He guides us expertly through what he calls the Labyrinth of **Ulysses** but to play down his scholarship in this conducted tour is absurd. This book is born of thirty years' study of Joyce and Joycean criticism; most of us have rather less time to spend."

407 Rodgers, W.R. Review of **Here Comes Everybody. Listener,** v. 74, no. 1911 (November 11, 1965) 767.

Joyce would warmly approve of this book, with its stated aim of rescuing his work from the professors and making it available to the ordinary reader. Burgess' pilot-commentary on **Ulysses** and **Finnegans Wake** is both useful and irresistibly enthusiastic in its discussion of Joyce's elaborate word-play, multiple meanings, and dazzling obscurity.

408 Salvesen, Christopher. Review of **Here Comes Everybody. Dublin Magazine,** v. 5, no. 1 (Spring 1966) 85-86.

Burgess is well qualified to write about Joyce but, despite the stress on Joyce's comedy and humanity, most of his time is inevitably devoted to exposition. "This should be compulsory procedure with Joyce, whose real difficulties are of the surface, a combination of Teutonic philologising and Celtic pattern-making. Mr. Burgess's commentary, though always straightforward, is forced to concentrate on Joyce's talent for Kellsification, the virtuosity at once obvious and reluctant to be unravelled. Mr. Burgess is good on the verbal fun, and clear about structure: but never quite dispels the feeling that elaboration for its own sake gets the better of whatever 'affirmation of man's worth' Joyce may be making.''

409 Seymour-Smith, Martin. ''Joyce the Great.'' **Spectator**, no. 7161 (September 24, 1965) 384.

''If we are all ordinary readers — and we ought to be if we aren't — then this is far and away the best book ever written on James Joyce.'' Burgess makes full use of the more important books, but his compressions and avoidance of dire pomposities improve on the work of his predecessors. The book, packed and suggestive, nevertheless demonstrates Burgess' modesty and enthusiasm. Argues that **Finnegans Wake** does not have as much to give the reader, and is not as good a book, as **Ulysses**. Nevertheless, Burgess ''performs the same humanising service for Joyce as Randall Jarrell performed for Whitman in his historic essay — where, defying all strictures and preconceived ideas, he set out to exhibit what Whitman could give. Mr. Burgess's book must at the least increase respect for Joyce, it explains him to the uninitiated, and is a tonic for critics.''

410 Toynbee, Philip. ''Joyce Without Tears.'' **Observer** (London), 3 October 1965, p. 26.

Dubliners and the **Portrait** have already become popular classics. **Ulysses** remains difficult and the **Wake** is almost impenetrable to all but very diligent readers. Hence, this book is unlikely to benefit the ordinary reader who loves books. That said, this work is an admirable introduction to Joyce. ''In fact this is the best study of Joyce that I have ever read — good-humoured and modest, learned but full of a considered enthusiasm which will make many of us turn back to **Ulysses** . . . . '' Observes that he cannot accept the contention that the **Wake** is the true transcription of a dreaming mind. The use of portmanteau words intended to convey many disparate meanings (the neologism ''venissoon'' supposedly unites ''very soon,'' ''venison,'' and Swift's ''Vanessa'') is one of the book's more dubious innovations. However, ''Mr. Burgess has written a brilliant and humane study of the most brilliant and humane of twentieth-century novelists.''

Honey for the Bears

411 London: Heinemann, 1963.

412 New York: Norton, 1964.

413 London: Pan Books, 1965. (Pan Book, X385) Pbk.

414 New York: Modern Library, 1968. Bound with: **A Clockwork Orange**.

415 New York: Ballantine, 1970. 2d Ballantine ed. Pbk.

416 London: Heinemann, 1972, c1963.

417 Harmondsworth, Eng.: Penguin, 1973. Pbk.

418 New York: Norton, 1978. Pbk.

Translations

419 German: **Honig für die Bären**. Tubingen: Erdmann, 1967. Translated by Dorothea Gotfart.

420 German: **Honig für die Bären**. Reinbek bei Hamburg: Rowohlt, 1971. Translated by Dorothea Gotfart.

421 Portugues: **Mel para os ursos**. Rio de Janeiro: Artenova. Translated by George Gurjam.

Reviews

422 Adams, Robert M. "Petit Guignol." **New York Review of Books**, v. 1, no. 11 (January 23, 1964) 7.

[Also reviews **The Wanting Seed**.] **Orange**, a minor bombshell, was also a flawed literary product. The main character was obviously mechanistic, and the book's clarity and point left something to be desired. Now **Seed** is a mechanically contrived and clumsy novel, but **Honey** is a novel for people. It is satiric comedy complicated by hard, fast and funny slapstick. All the machinery of exasperation and comic misunderstanding clanks and bangs away magnificently throughout the book. His high comic style is learned, vulgar, swiftly pictorial and dexterously psychological. Quotes some passages from the novel to prove his point.

423 Amis, Kingsley. "To Russia with Torment." **New York Times Book Review**, 2 February 1964, p. 5.

Burgess may seem a monster of fertility to American readers with his ten novels in ten years. Indeed, one of the buried (but nonsensical) assumptions of our times is that productivity is incompatible with seriousness. He has, like all good novelists, a strong comic sense. The book's homoerotic complications mean that "No doubt plenty of smut-hounds will be ready to denounce this book as obscene; it isn't. There's a vulgar error which confuses the **use** of sexual deviation and suchlike as (comic) material and its *glorification* for purposes of shock, pornography and so on. Mr. Burgess's witty astringency — or, if you like, simply his sense of humor — makes his account of these matters chastening, deglamorizing." His one reservation concerns the style. Burgess' insistence on verbal finish, while it produces some splendid effects, sometimes seems obsessive. "But this sort of thing hardly matters. There are so few genuinely entertaining novels around that we ought to cheer whenever one turns up. **Honey for the Bears** is a triumph."

424 Anon. "Going Red." **Times Literary Supplement**, no. 3,187 (March 1963) 213. 431

A good deal of the book is excellent. The language crackles and sparkles almost to the point of self-conscious virtuosity, while the metaphysical disgust with the absurdity of people and world is becoming increasingly Swiftian. "It is possible, in fact, that Mr. Burgess is writing too much too quickly, and that a more disciplined savagery would be even more effective, but this is perhaps a small price to pay for such vitality and inventiveness. Certainly it is long past time that critics stopped comparing Mr. Burgess, as they still do, with Evelyn Waugh and others. . . and saw him as a very considerable novelist in his own right."

425 Anon. "To Russia for Luv." **Time**, v. 83, no. 4 (January 24, 1964) 70.

"Burgess wrings some wry laughs from his hero's bumbling efforts to unload twelve dozen fancy 'drilon' dresses on the Russian black market. But alas, it turns out that Burgess takes his main joke [husband and wife both homosexual] seriously. He offers the perverted antique dealer as a disapproving symbol of Britain Today. Trying to be urbane about his (and England's) present predicament, the poor man says: 'You have no idea how pleasant it is not to have any future. It's like having a totally efficient contraceptive.' 'Or like being impotent,' says one Russian interrogator drily. The Englishman has the grace to blush."

426 Anon. "Schizoids in Leningrad." **Newsweek**, v. 63, no. 5 (February 3, 1964) 81-82.

It is Burgess' best work to date — funny, unbalancing and contentedly schizoid that reduces the cold war to an intimate kind of insanity. "Burgess writes, as always, with half-maniacal wit, and with uncommon attention to sight, smell, and sound. His beatnik Russia is a tawdry place, full of fakery, idleness, and, between slugs of Georgian muscatel, endless self-pitying comment about the Bomb. If the Englishman — and an expatriate American for that matter — seem to be right at home there, make the most of it. Burgess certainly does."

427 Anon. Notice of **Honey for the Bears**. **Books and Bookmen**, v. 18 (September 1973) 138.

[Notice of Penguin pbk. ed. For text of notice, see #879.]

428 Bowen, John. "New Novels." **Punch**, v. 244, no. 6395 (April 3, 1963) 498.

[Omnibus review.] The novel is funny and heartless while the writing is intelligent, daft and extremely inventive. Anyone who has studied an arts subject at a university would get a good deal of pleasure from the book. It is doubtful if non-arts students would do so.

429 Brooke, Jocelyn. "New Novels." **Listener**, v. 69, no. 1774 (March 27, 1963) 567.

[Omnibus review.] "Mr. Anthony Burgess seems to me to be the most gifted, intelligent, and entertaining novelist among those who have come to the fore during the last ten years or so . . . . How long will he be able to keep up a performance of such brilliance and gusto? . . . . The prose is as vivid, glittering, and allusive as ever (Nobody else — with the possible exception of Mr. Eliot — could have got away so neatly with the unacknowledged quotation from Hopkins on page 86). The Burgess territory has always marched with Greene-land: a certain romantic seediness is common to both, but the Burgess climate is less austere and altogether jollier. This is a vastly entertaining and exhilarating novel; it is also one of the most convincing evocations of contemporary Russia that I have read."

430 Gavin, William F. Review of **Honey for the Bears**. **America**, v. 110, no. 6 (February 8, 1964) 200.

Most of us demand distinctions in morality, politics, words and sex, but Burgess delights in finding similarities. The result is a study in the consolations of ambiguity. The final thirty pages are very funny, but he feels "it really doesn't make any difference if you read Burgess' book or not."

431 Gross, John. "Everything's Here But the Kievstone Cops." **Washington Post Book Week**, 9 February 1964, p. 6.

"A novel by Anthony Burgess set in the Soviet Union seems at first sight an unlikely proposition. Mr. Burgess is a prolific funny-man, quick-witted but wildly uneven — and Russia is Russia. Irrepressible joker meets immovable object?" The Russian scenes are well done; Burgess steers clear of direct political comment; and the Russian people are treated as unmysterious, ordinary people. The misunderstandings are likely to be cultural, linguistic or temperamental as much as political, and Burgess has written some of the most graphic and witty descriptions of contemporary Russia by an outsider since Truman Capote's **The Muses are Heard**. The secondary theme, the disintegration of the Hussey marriage, seems weaker than the rest. "Paul's wife is never a very interesting character, and the closing chapters are taken up with some transvestite high-jinks which I found too forced to be funny. But these are comparatively minor blemishes on a highly entertaining and intelligent book."

432 Hamilton, Alex. "Paperbacks." **Books and Bookmen**, v. 10 (July 1965) 47.

[Review of Pan pbk. ed.] **Honey** "is as funny as the first is frightening, a fantastic comedy developed about the commercial experiments of an antique dealer who chances his arm (and his American wife) in Russia."

433 Harvey, David D. "Muddle-Browed Faction." **Southern Review**, v. 5, no. 1, N.S., (Winter 1969) 259-72.

[Omnibus review. For Burgess, see pp. 263-67.] The novel is cause for encouragement. Burgess is someone whose poems would be atrocious, essays meretricious but who is all-on-going as a writer of fiction. The comic muse is the tutelary deity, and Burgess writes entertainments that can be described as sheer comedies. "The god of comedy presides, but there is no other god nor nostalgia for one in his work, hence no tyranny of the ironic or satiric motives. The way in which he has read Joyce, seeing that the most attractive and powerful force in Joyce is the natural freedom of comic expression, has influenced his own work very much indeed." He has pulled up the blinds as often as necessary to look at the mountain of achievement found in the work of Joyce. Burgess plainly lives in a world in which alienation and anomie, fragmented existences and totalitarian states, abound as painfully oppressive abstractions, but his tone separates him from most writers who capitalize on such abstractions. There is no underglaze of eternal and pointless suffering. He may not rival Joyce technically, but at no point is he technically incompetent.

434 Hoyt, Charles Alva. "Black Market in Red Square." **Saturday Review**, v. 47, no. 9 (February 29, 1964) 33-34.

It is one of the best-planned and most brilliantly executed books in a long time. The prose is marvelously compact, rich, juicy, every rift filled with ore. His logic may not always be sound and his understanding may sometimes seem unsound, but his sense of *programme* is almost perfect. He evokes an image of modern England "which to him is largely a tasteless and desperate degeneration, ghostly echoes of the past — the glorious, swaggering past of Shakespeare and Milton" [and in this work] there "are hollow sounds of great voices heard from afar, such as one sometimes catches in the antechamber of a vast museum. But the true voice of England, though it come from never so far, can yet summon a man to action."

435 Hyman, Stanley Edgar. "Well of Togetherness." **New Leader**, v. 47, no. 8 (April 13, 1964) 21-22.

[Omnibus review. For Burgess, see p. 22.] A farcical melodrama on the theme of homosexuality. It is funny at the expense of Soviet humourlessness. For Burgess, homosexuality is not furtive or glum, but open and comic. The ideal is carefree bisexuality, an enlargement of possiblity. Observes that much of the imagery is obsessively oral, and that this novel of a homoerotic masochist is written with comedy and style.

436 Ivsky, Oleg. Review of **Honey for the Bears**. **Library Journal**, v. 89, no. 3 (Feburary 1, 1964) 651-52.

"Some people can take their vodka straight and hold it like gentlemen; some cannot. Some can take in stride their Dostoevski, their 10 lessons in Elem. Russian Ib.36, and even their two-week trip to Leningrad; and some cannot. On the evidence at hand, Burgess belongs to the second category. What he learned on his trip is amusing, sharply observed, and delightfully told, though hardly new; but it fills barely a third of the novel. What he should have learned about Russia, the black market *modus operandi*, and a dozen other subjects, *prior* to writing, but did not, could fill a library. Painful evidence of this is present throughout the remaining two-thirds. The plot and situations of this alleged satire are silly but not funny (unless broken teeth, police tortures, and homosexuality are funny *per se*); background and atmosphere are as hopelessly mixed up as are all the characters, their motivations, and sexes (all five of the sexes). Particularly obnoxious are the constant parading of Mr. Burgess's nauseating brand of pidgin Russian and the habitual use of presumably authentic but barely intelligible R.A.F. slang spiced with a pathetic imitation of beat talk. For rental collections." [Complete text of review.]

437 Lodge, David. "Picturesque and Gawky." **Spectator**, April 19, 1963, p. 504.

[Omnibus review.] Burgess has a good target — the conventional idea of Russia as a sinister threat to the values of Western democracy. Unfortunately, he has permitted sentiment to invade a Waugh-like book. "Paul Hussey makes claims on our pity in a way Paul Pennyfeather never did, particularly when his homosexuality is in question. And there is a rather embarrassing letter from Belinda about Love which suggests that the author hasn't got the courage of his own lack of convictions. Still, this novel is good enough to send me back to the earlier ones."

438 Malin, Irving. "Sex in Print." **Antioch Review, v. 24, no. 3 (Fall 1964) 408-16.**

[Omnibus review. For Burgess, see pp. 414-15.] "Anthony Burgess. . . impressively relates sex to class. He apparently believes that contemporary life is so ambiguous that England, America, and Russia, men and women, are thoroughly unsure of their real being. Does sexuality create social systems? Burgess does not answer the question. But he views sex as 'political,' forcing unholy alliances which bridge the gap between countries, creating new boundaries. Let me clarify. Despite the odd workings of the Russian community as viewed by Westerners, East and West meet when Dr. Lazurkina and her patient, Belinda, fall in love. Their great social differences surrender to warm Lesbianism." Burgess is never solemn when he broaches the theme of sexual identity, but he plainly believes that homosexuality is the perfect symbol of our world: it is artificial, comic and mixed up.

439 Ricks, Christopher. "The Epicene." **New Statesman,** v. 65, no. 1673 (April 5, 1963) 496.

[Also reviews **The Novel Today**.] Burgess has the sort of fertility which makes one hopeful of a first-rate comic novel. Although **Honey** is oddly subversive both politically and sexually, he has not written it yet. The former because Russia turns out to be disconcertingly like America. The latter because the book intimates the "idea that being able to enjoy both [sexes] is to find more to enjoy and so to add to the public stock of harmless pleasure. That homosexuality is not wicked, not ethereally spiritual, not necessarily the source of anxiety or agony, not incompatible with other things, but a rather pleasant virtuosity — if this is not subversive, what would be?" Throughout his novels, Burgess has been trying to make up his mind about the epicene. Note, for example, the very uncensorious lilt in an early book as it observed the androgynous Ibrahim ("Undulating through the market, who so gay as Ibrahim?"). Burgess, like Fielding, clearly believes that many kinds of sexual immorality don't much matter. One advantage of this novel compared to the earlier **The Doctor Is Sick** and **A Clockwork Orange** is that Burgess is shedding the element of black realistic violence.

440 Salisbury, Harrison E. "End Papers." **New York Times Book Review**, 29 February 1964, p. 6.

"Anthony Burgess is a literary smart aleck whose novel, **A Clockwork Orange**, last year achieved a *success d'estime* with critics like William Burroughs, who mistook his muddle of sadism, teddyboyism, jive talk and Berlitz Russian for social philosophy. Now he tries again with a novel about a black market expedition to Leningrad by an ill-mated couple. The wife finds a more suitable partner in Sonya, her Russian doctor, and stays behind. The husband has some homosexual scrapes and is caught by the police trying to smuggle a Soviet citizen out of the country. The work offers no clue to Mr. Burgess's fixation upon things Russian. Nor to some critics' conviction that he is a first-rate satirist." [Complete text of review.]

Inside Mr. Enderby

441 London: Heinemann, 1963. By "Joseph Kell."

442 Harmondsworth, Eng.: Penguin, 1966. Pbk.

443 London: Heinemann, 1975.

444 Harmondsworth, Eng.: Penguin, 1979.

[Note: Issued by Heinemann under the pseud. of "Joseph Kell." Hence, not widely reviewed. The publisher's diffidence had one agreeable consequence. The editor of the **Yorkshire Post** invited Burgess to review his own book. An obliging Burgess did so. See #448 below.]

Reviews

445 Anon. Notice of **Inside Mr. Enderby**. **Observer Weekend Review**, 27 February 1966, p. 22.

"Middle-aged Enderby, a good minor poet, passes from neurotic creativity into bovine, uncreative sanity, via a disastrous and unconsummated marriage and attempted suicide. Ironic, and cruelly and touchingly funny." [Complete text of notice.]

446 Anon. Notice of **Inside Mr. Enderby**. **Books and Bookmen**, v. 18 (September 1973) 138.

[Marks publication of the Penguin pbk. ed. For complete text of notice, see #879.]

447 Brooke, Jocelyn. Review of **Inside Mr. Enderby**. **Listener**, v. 69, no. 1778 (April 25, 1963) 723.

[Omnibus review.] "It is an ironic tragedy, the real horror of which lies in the apparently 'happy' ending. The plot has its weaknesses, and Enderby's marriage is barely credible; but Mr. Kell writes with a sustained, poetic brilliance which strikes me as quite masterly. His prose is subtle and allusive yet muscular, and his command of language never flags. In most contemporary writing the pattern of the syntax is more or less predictable: given the first half of a sentence, one can guess, approximately, how it will end, just as certain musical progressions anticipate a foreseeable final cadence. Mr. Kell, however, is constantly springing syntactical surprises: the expected phrase suddenly modulates, as it were, into another key, or is varied by some wayward *appoggiatura* or adroit syncopation . . . . this novel seems to me, if not the best, at any rate the best *written* which I have read for some time."

448 Burgess, Anthony. "Poetry in a Tiny Room." **Yorkshire Post**, 16 May 1963, p. 4.

"This is, in many ways, a dirty book. It is full of bowel-blasts and flatulent borborygms, emetic meals ('thin but over-savory stews' Enderby calls them) and halitosis. It may well make some people sick, and those of my readers with tender stomachs are advised to let it alone. It turns sex, religion, the State into a series of laughing-stocks. The book itself is a laughing stock." [For an account of the circumstances which led Burgess to review his own books, **One Hand Clapping** and **Inside Mr. Enderby**, see #989, #1616.]

449 Platypus, Bill. "Bill Platypus's Paperbacks." **Spectator**, v. 230, no. 7566 (June 30, 1973) 819.

Notice of five new Penguin titles, including **Inside Mr. Enderby**, **MF**, **The Wanting Seed** and **Honey for the Bears** and **Urgent Copy**.

Joysprick; An Introduction to the Language of James Joyce

450 London: Deutsch, 1973. (The Language library) Pbk.

451 New York: Academic Press, 1973.

452 New York: Harcourt Brace Jovanovich, 1975. (A Harvest book, HB303) Pbk.

Reviews

453 Anon. "The Class 2 Novelist." **Times Literary Supplement**, 15 June 1973, p. 669.

Praises Burgess' translation of the opening of **Ulysses** into the language of the Class 1 novelist ("worthy of the Master of Parody") and observes that Burgess is himself a minor Class 2 novelist (obsessed with words, interested in ambiguities, puns, word-plays, centrifugal connations — all unlike the Class 1 novelist). Quotes Burgess on the differences between the Anglo-Irish and English pronunciation of words like "home, Christ, ale, master." Observes that Burgess' chapter on onomastics is interesting (although the surname 'Earwicker' existed in 1962!), and that his discussion of plebian obscenity is singularly competent, particularly when he observes that the word 'fuck' (cognate with the German 'ficken,' to 'strike') is not properly at home in the context of conjugal love.

454 Atherton, J.S. "Re-Joycing." **Manchester Guardian Weekly**, 23 June 1973, p. 26.

A guide to intelligent appreciation of prose useful to many students of English. Gives some examples of Burgess' critical technique and remarks that, as long as he confines himself to stylistic matters, Burgess is admirable. Burgess has not, regrettably, read any Joyce criticism in the last twenty years, and he does not acknowledge his debts to other scholars.

455 Chapman, Robert. "Jabberwocky and Joyce." **Books and Bookmen**, v. 18 (September 1973) 60.

Burgess has written an extremely useful book for those who consider his complexities worth exploring. It is not a dryasdust study of word frequency, but an exercise in linguistics, practical criticism, literary theory and biography. His distinction between the Class I novelist to whom language is a zero quantity, and the Class II novelist to whom it is everything is useful. He is also very good on the melodies of Joyce's prose, while comparisons with the poetry of Hopkins and the Jabberwocky of Lewis Carroll help to place Joyce's experiments. Burgess also demonstrates, by means of phonetic symbols and with reference to the Great Vowel Shift, that it is Stephen's **pronunciation** which signifies his alienation from such authority figures as the Dean of Studies. "According to T.S. Eliot, Joyce was 'the man who killed the nineteenth century' and, more than three decades after *his* death, he is still the most 'modern' writer in the language. Short of the 'ideal reader suffering from an ideal insomnia' that Joyce postulated for his work, Mr. Burgess will do. By concentrating upon the language — and thus going straight to the heart of Joyce's originality — this short critique is one of the best accounts of Joyce's place in a language revolution that still continues."

456 Eckley, Grace. "James Joyce." **Contemporary Literature**, v. 16, no. 4 (Autumn 1975) 504-15.

[Omnibus review. For Burgess, see pp. 505-07.] Burgess claims to have avoided scholarship, but his work is based on the work of real scholars: Clive Hart, Richard Ellmann, Campbell and Robinson, Edmund Wilson, A. Walton Litz. He appropriates the work of scholars without acknowledgment, which is bad enough. He also appropriates the mistaken notions of scholars, which is worse. He pays undue attention to certain details. In other places he is unbearably pompous. As an *introduction* to the language of James Joyce, the work may conceivably pass muster.

457 Fox, Jay. Review of **Joysprick; An Introduction to the Language of James Joyce. Modern Fiction Studies**, v. 21, no. 2 (Summer 1975) 264-67.

[Omnibus review.] Despite the disclaimer to scholarship, the scholarship is for the most part convincing and well-supported. His distinction between the Class I and Class II novelist is presented with the help of lucid examples.

458 Goldman, Arnold. Review of **Joysprick; An Introduction to the Language of James Joyce. Review of English Studies**, v. 25 (November 1974) 495-498.

Observes that Burgess has re-used material also found in his **Here Comes Everybody** (1965). Quotes Burgess on musicalisation in Joyce. Finds "no central thesis to **Joysprick**, and the whole unintegrated except by reference to a partly dutiful, partly self-indulgent *preludic* vamp through philologico — tropico — stylistico — linguistic modes. (Mr. Burgess plays cat-and-mouse with his 'Language Library' sponsor.) A scholar or no scholar, whatever escapes criticism best, he strings together introductory bridgework and imaginative (and sharply written) perceptions, whereby his own linguistic gifts may get the former taken for the later." Some of the perceptions are perceptive, illustrations invariably just, even if the book could do with more argumentativeness. "There is weak conventionality in Mr. Burgess's axioms, such as that Stephen will write **Ulysses** one day, or that he and Bloom have a 'mystical father-son relationship' though later 'no real father-son rapprochement is possible.' Burgess's critical prose suffers from 'loss of problems' (Wittgenstein). If there is no problematic in Mr. Burgess's analysis of Joyce's texture, there is finally a tonality, or overtone, and it is musical. It is the approach towards a formalization beyond sense and sight that matters most to him and is most approved, explained and justified. Perhaps even to an ideal lexical music beyond sound."

459 Luckett, Richard. "Richard Luckett on Joyce, Beckett and the Word." **Spectator**, v. 230, no. 7566 (June 30, 1973) 815-16.

[Also reviews **A Reader's Guide to Samuel Beckett**, by Hugh Kenner.] Quotes a punning passage from Smollett to demonstrate that the distinction between the Class I and Class II novelist is not airtight, and that a remarkable number of authors move from one technique to the other: Anthony Powell, or Burgess himself in his **Nothing Like the Sun**. "Mr. Burgess's problem, then, is that his brief has been to write on Joyce's language, the implication being that this can be treated as something apart from his work as a whole. He recognises this as the absurdity it is (though a semiologist might challenge the point) and gets down to talking about the way that Joyce uses language . . . . Barring ploys such as the class I and class II novelists the result is splendid. He identifies and isolates Joyce's use of Dublin demotic, of parody, of onomatopeia of all kinds, and he does this in a way that is always illuminating and never pedantic."

460 McLellan, Joseph. Notice of **Joysprick; An Introduction to the Language of James Joyce**. **Washington Post Book World**, 29 June 1975, p. 4.

"The Dubliner's distinguished disciple shifts here from the panoramic view of **Re Joyce** to minutiae, focusing chiefly on **Ulysses** (**Finnegans Wake** would require an encyclopedia) and noting the pervasive flavor of Dublin in its words, the varied private languages of individuals (two apiece, one for the world and one for inner monologue) elements of music in syntax, satire and parody in word choice, word blends and puns and linguistic gymnastics of all kinds. A lexicographer with a computer could (and will) do it more thoroughly, but Burgess offers, succinctly, a fellow craftsman's knowing tribute." [Complete text of notice.]

461 Ricks, Christopher. "Punditry." **Sunday Times** (London), no. 7829 (June 24, 1973) 38.

Burgess is a cogent elucidator of Joyce, but the moment he moves away from elucidation to special pleading his words no longer carry conviction. In the context of Joyce's ambiguity, the comic names are mere kidstuff. More important, what is the principle by which we can exclude or invalidate an interpretation of Joyce's wording? Burgess uses 'mad' frequently in his text to refer to madcap Lord Mayor's goonshow, but he never considers the real possibility that Joyce suffered from schizophrenia.

462 Toynbee, Philip. "Word Games." **Observer** (London), 24 June 1973, p. 32.

Burgess goes perhaps too far when he asserts that Joyce loved form above all things. Insofar as the remark is true Joyce was a creative linguist, not a novelist. Most of the book is about **Ulysses**, but he is also very good and persuasive in defense of **Finnegans Wake**. "Yet he makes, in reference to that dazzling monstrosity, a comment that is surely more damaging than he has fully recognised. 'The real problems of **Finnegans Wake**,' he writes, 'are not semantic but referential. Joyce loves to mystify, and the mysteries yield less to the language scholar than to the diligent inquirer into the fact of Joyce's life, or the lives of his friends.' Why is this any more tolerable than that practice of the thirties' poets — now generally recognised as intolerable — of constantly making private references to one another in the course of poems which were meant for public consumption? . . . . This is, in fact, a very fine book; and one which contributes still further both to our understanding and to our love of Joyce."

Language Made Plain

463 London: English Universities Press, 1964.

464 New York: Crowell, 1965.

465 New York: Crowell, 1969. (Apollo Editions, A-222) Pbk.

466 London: Fontana/Collins, 1975. Rev. ed.

Reviews

467 Adams, J. Donald. "A Common Heritage." **New York Times Book Review**, 28 March 1965, p. 26.

Clarity is the prime virtue of **Language Made Plain**, which "discusses words for their own sake, and takes some well-deserved pot-shots at grammarians. It ventures, with great common sense, into the fields of phonetics and semantics; it touches briefly and illuminatingly on the physiology of speech. It draws interesting contrasts between the language practices of the Western world and those of the Orient. Finally, praise be, it emphasizes the value of some acquaintance with languages other than one's own."

468 Anon. "Preaching Polyglottism." **Times Literary Supplement**, no. 3,243 (April 23, 1964) 337.

An attractive book written by a man of letters who draws upon his personal experiences at every turn. His thesis is that learning about the nature of language is the best way to learn them quickly and accurately. Accordingly his work devotes nine chapters to language in general and nine on languages in particular. Each of these chapters is happily conceived. Skillful exposition is evident, and his presentation of Pushkin's lovely eight line idyll "Ya vas lyubil" is a masterpiece of lucid and succinct exposition. [The reviewer devotes perhaps one-third of his review to a list of errors.]

469 Anon. Review of **Language Made Plain**. **Choice**, v. 2, no. 8 (October 1965) 480.

"A lively but shapeless introduction to the study of language . . . . It is in this potpourri of offerings, however, that the essential weakness of the book lies. Lacking design or sequence, and attempting to touch all bases, the book too often tidily disposes of concepts perplexing to the undergraduate (viz. his treatment of Grimm's Law). Its limitations are admitted in the preface: '. . . this book is a primer for amateurs by an amateur. It does not dig deep, and it is far from scholarly.' More reliable is Simeon Potter's **Modern Linguistics** (1957).

470 Anon. Review of **Language Made Plain**. **Publishers Weekly**, v. 196, no. 5 (August 4, 1969) 50.

"The famous British novelist and logophile has great fun and intellectual involvement here with the magic and mystery of language — what the historical, physiological, psychological and social elements are that go into the development of language and the creation of an alphabet. The audience for this may be small, but the book is an important contribution to a field cluttered with a lot of semantic jargon." [Complete text of review.]

471 Close, R.A. Review of **Language Made Plain**. **Modern Language Review, v. 60, no. 1 (January 1965) 84-85.**

An unscholarly work which also includes refreshingly well-written explanations of phonetics, phonemes, semantics and the concerns of linguists. The author's charge that dryasdust exposition marks many books about linguistics is noted. On the other hand, "In applying scientific method to a subject thoroughly confused by archaic logic, social prejudices and private associations, linguists are producing a new science which to the layman, brought up on the old grammar, seems a mystery; and the linguist, concerned with language, is bound to strip literary, and other, elements from the prime material of his study. Yet language concerns every member of society, and what Mr. Burgess has done is to try, with a good deal of success, to make the new mystery plain. He has also put life, allure, and a sense of humour into the dry bones of linguistic structure."

472 Cook, Margaret G. Review of **Language Made Plain**. **Library Journal**, v. 90, no. 11 (June 1, 1965) 2554.

"As a teacher and writer, he is concerned with grammar and sentence structure, and makes it very clear that few languages can be forced into the mold set by Latinists. The chief problems for the American reader are Mr. Burgess's references to Cockney, Lancastrian, and Welsh to explain phonetic symbols and other terminology designed to aid in pronunciation . . . . To be recommended to the student of language, this is another book concerned with widening our field of communication through learning the speech of other peoples, instead of expecting them to learn ours."

473 Dolbier, M. "On Language: An Amateur's Witty Primer." **New York Herald Tribune**, v. 124, no. 43,054 (February 8, 1965) 23.

"Mr. Burgess's service . . . is to write clearly and interestingly about a subject which, though it deals with such a simple thing as 'a mouthful of air,' has accumulated a technical terminology that tends to intimidate the general reader: phonemes and allophones, palatalizations and glottal stops, unvoiced alveolar plosives and voiced labio-dental fricatives." Gives some examples of Burgess' content and style. The book is enlivened by wit and conveys its author's own enthusiasm for his subject.

474 Gosling, Ray. "A Mouthful of Air." **Times** (London), no. 59,670 (April 3, 1976) 11.

"It is because Mr. Burgess revels in the petty parochialisms of English he's so good at making the learning of foreign language exciting. Each word we use has a history. Trace hocus pocus to *hoc est corpus* in the Mass. Palaver is Portuguese palavra meaning word . . . . It is fun this book. He turns a chore into an adventure: a bore into an amusing hobby. With breezy enthusiasm gives confidence to the timid, without in any way talking down to the reader or belittling his subject. It is a remarkable achievement . . . . Starting with everyday pithy specifics, he makes general principles. As gardeners do — and conjurers, he manages to make the amazing and impossible seem so simple and easy as A.B.C . . . . "

475 Harrison, Joseph G. "From the Bookshelf." **Christian Science Monitor**, 1 March 1965, p. 13.

[Preceded by some remarks on linguistics then and now.] The work "deals primarily, not so much with structural linguistics, as with many of the quirks and oddities which make language so fascinating. It is a very readable little book, and one which will leave the reader more intrigued than ever with his own and other tongues." [Virtually the complete text of review.]

476 Partridge, Eric. "Language at Work: Language at Play." **Books and Bookmen**, v. 21 (February 1976) 20.

Praises Burgess' **Nothing Like the Sun** ("a narrative and an interpretation at once profound and engrossing, torrential in its surging narrative, molten in its emotional impact, magistral in its employment of a style rich, vigorous, and deeply moving: a book that, leaving us stunned and exhausted, also and more importantly leaves us wealthy") and hopes it is the book by which he will be remembered. **Language** is a vivid and stimulating examination of language in general and languages in particular, and although Burgess is an alarmingly learned fellow, he almost never parades the learning. "The field and development of this subject have been deftly charted by Simeon Potter in his **Modern Linguistics**: and Anthony Burgess has notably and attractively furthered general interest in this intricate, far-reaching subject."

477 Scheib, M.E. Review of **Language Made Plain**. **Quarterly Journal of Speech**, v. 57, no. 1 (February 1971) 123.

An entertaining romp through phonetics, speech anatomy, comparison of foreign languages, comparative linguistics, historical linguistics, word derivation and foreign language learning. "The sting of such crass superficiality is considerably eased by the knowledge that the author obviously knows what he's talking about." It admirably succeeds in its aim to introduce the student to some general linguistic knowledge. Some of his examples of phonetic notation will confuse the General American speaker, but it is an informative analysis of language which makes for enjoyable reading.

The Long Day Wanes

478 New York: Norton, 1965.

479 New York: Ballantine, 1966, c1965. Pbk.

480 Harmondsworth, Eng.: Penguin, 1973. Pbk.

481 New York: Norton, 1977, c1965. (Norton Library) Pbk.

[NOTE: Includes **Time for a Tiger**, **The Enemy in the Blanket** and **Beds in the East**. See also the British title: **The Malayan Trilogy**.]

Reviews

482 Anon. Review of **The Long Day Wanes**. **Kirkus Reviews**, v. 33, no. 8 (April 15, 1965) 445.

"This is Burgess' earlier Malayan trilogy, which includes **Time for a Tiger, The Enemy in the Blanket** and **Beds in the East**, Burgess' comic valedictory to colonialism, centering around the experiences of an Englishman in the Education Service." [Complete text of notice.]

483 Anon. Review of **The Long Day Wanes**. **Time**, v. 86 no. 1 (July 2, 1965) 84.

"Author Burgess' witness to the waning of the imperial day is Victor Crabbe, a teacher in a multiracial prep school solemnly modeled by its British founders after Eton and Harrow (Burgess himself served for three years as an education officer in Malaya). Bemusedly, Crabbe sees that the system is crumbling, but the snobbery is not. Malays hate Indians, who hate Chinese. Every Asian hates the British, and secretly despises himself for not being British. Crabbe, who does not think himself superior to the Asians, is regarded as a madman. Who throws away superiority unless he is mad? The turnabout suggests what is wrong with the novel. Crabbe is truly without self-interest, almost without volition. It is very hard to write about such a hero." [Virtually the complete text of the review.]

484 Anon. Review of **The Long Day Wanes**. **Choice**, v. 2, no. 7 (September 1965) 383-84.

"This trilogy would seem to be the final word on the disintegration of British colonialism, and as good a picture trimmed in black as one could find of the mixture of races, colors, and creeds in Malaya: British, Chinese, Indian, Tamil, Malay, and Eurasian, not to speak of a Turk or two. Burgess is a keen portraitist, a remarkable novelist; one thinks of Joyce Cary, Graham Greene, and Evelyn Waugh, but Burgess is unique. He is a satirist, sociologist, psychologist, and philosopher, with an extraordinary ability to handle scenes ranging from burlesque to pathos to tragedy. This impressively informative, multilayered book ought to be required reading for State Department personnel, both British and American, and for any Peace Corps volunteer assigned to Asia."

485 Anon. Notice of **The Long Day Wanes**. **Best Sellers**, August 15, 1966, p. 188.

"Anthony Burgess' trilogy of Malayan life comes from Ballantine and should win the readers in the U.S. which the original titles did not when published from 1956 through 1959." [Complete text of notice.]

486 Anon. Notice of **The Long Day Wanes**. **Saturday Review**, v. 49, no. 39 (September 24, 1966) 40.

". . . Anthony Burgess is a product of the tradition of subtle high satire exemplified by Evelyn Waugh. **The Long Day Wanes** (Ballantine pbk. ed.), a trilogy in one volume, focuses on postwar Malaya during the declining years of British rule, when native leaders were preparing to govern their own land." [Complete text of notice.]

487 Anon. Notice of **The Long Day Wanes**. **New York Times Book Review**, 4 September 1977, p. 23.

[Notice of paperback ed.] "This trilogy, dating from the late 50's and here published in one volume, was Anthony Burgess's first fiction. He's surpassed it since, but its bright black-humor picture of a now-gone time assures it a lasting interest."

488 Bergonzi, Bernard. "Funny Book." **New York Review of Books**, v. 4, no. 8 (May 20, 1965) 15-16.

The term black comedy has been bandied about by the fashionable and ignorant in defense of a variety of repellent oddities. Comedy probably depends, to a different degree in different societies, on a withdrawal of symphathy for the victim. "Among contemporary writers no one is blacker, or more comic, than Anthony Burgess . . . . He combines a unique sense of humor with a desolate philsophical despair in a way that makes him one of the more remarkable of living novelists . . . . " Compared to the later, brilliant **A Clockwork Orange** and **Nothing Like the Sun**, **The Long Day Wanes** is a fairly unsophisticated piece of writing and it recalls the Evelyn Waugh of **Scoop** and **Black Mischief**. One of Burgess' subjects is racialism, or, more specifically, the profound contempt of the British, Malays, Chinese, Tamils, Sikhs and Eurasians have for each other; he suggests that human beings are that way. Burgess' contempt for his creations is sometimes disturbing. Victor Crabbe is stubbed out as casually as a cigarette, and the portrait of the demagogue, Mr. Bastians, suggests a degree of right-wing skepticism which projects the Jansenist flavor of certain English Catholic upbringings. His **A Clockwork Orange** is a superb tour-de-force. Its underlying assumption is that it is both better actively to do evil than to be spiritually dead. It is cruel, inescapably comical, and difficult to forget. Burgess brings to the novel a "genuine content of ideas, no matter how unfashionable and an extraordinary sensitivity to language."

489 Cruttwell, Patrick. "Fiction Chronicle." **Hudson Review**, v. 18, no. 3 (Autuumn 1965) 442-50.

[Omnibus review. For Burgess, see p. 449. Cruttwell remarks that he has some acquaintance with Malaya.] "The trouble here, I suspect, is over-rich material. For south-east Asia is enormously rich material — rich in colour, smell, sound, variety of races and cultures and faiths, relics living and dead of ancient diverse pasts, tragedy and farce — and Burgess splashes about in it all too loudly and joyously. Too many people, too many grotesque or horrific events, too much working hard for the belly-laughs. But the laughs are many and real — and it isn't, by any means, all exaggerated out of focus. Caricature, undeniably — but consistent caricature. What it does convey is a feeling of enjoyment — a feeling that in spite of all this is a wonderful and fascinating people and land."

490 [Fleischer, L.] Notice of **The Long Day Wanes**. **Publishers Weekly**, v. 190, no. 1 (July 4, 1966) 82.

[Review signed L.F.] "Early as they are, they already show the sardonic Burgess touch. Although not as experimental with language, they possess all the irony and bite that make many reviewers compare Burgess with Evelyn Waugh. In these three novels, the sun sets relentlessly and with bitter humor on the Malayan corner of the British Empire." [Virtually the complete text of notice.]

491 Gabriel, Brother D. Review of **The Long Day Wanes**. **Best Sellers**, July 1, 1965, pp. 150-51.

It is reminiscent of Evelyn Waugh, with its acid-etched sketches of colonial types and outlandish situations. It is also a "delightfully written, thought-provoking picture of what the British might have been going through in the breakup of Her Majesty's Empire and a proof that they have at least not lost their sense of humor."

492 Kauffmann, Stanley. "A Cycle of Cathay." **New Leader**, v. 48, no. 10 (May 10, 1965) 24-25.

Burgess is a current example of the British polymath and versatile creator who has also written the best novel about Shakespeare. There can be few writers who would not like to murder him. His fictional method is to see his characters from within in the context of an interwoven plot, and the method succeeds. His enormously varied, enormous cast could not otherwise be individualized so memorably. Burgess is a quick disciple of Waugh, although he is not yet up to the Waugh level. He is a keen observer of the Malayan human comedy. The book demonstrates his interest in language and phonetics, but he is not insufferably donnish. Observes that the source of the title is from Tennyson's **Ulysses**. An indication of Burgess' future novelistic aim, the attempt to probe deeper into the essence of the human personality, is demonstrated by his **Honey for the Bears**. "This trilogy, extraordinarily rewarding though most of it is, is inferior to his later work, but this, of course, is a happy fact. Those who are following this astonishing man's career must be grateful to his publishers for filling in some of his past and, despite the earlier work's flaws, heightening the astonishment."

493 Ostermann, Robert. Review of **The Long Day Wanes**. **National Observer**, 14 June 1965, p. 21.

494 Wheeler, Thomas C. "Twilight of Empire in the Malay States." **New York Times Book Review**, 30 May 1965, p. 14.

The work is that rare thing — an international novel that is a true novel rather than a string of episodes which dramatize the platitudes of foreign affairs. Burgess is entertaining; he is also a Rabelaisean writer afraid of very little; and his portraits of Chinese, Indians, Tamils and Malays become keenly alive. "A Moslem prays to Allah for a divorce. An Indian pursues independence like a jungle John Bircher. A phony sultan plans a Riveria [Riviera] exile a la Cary Grant . . . . this is a hugely informative book in which Asian hatred of Asian, a resentment of the white race stronger than any national bond, and the impulse toward national independence turning into a fantasy of self-indulgence become fictional truths." Burgess may not think highly of his own book, but it should be ". . . read — and pondered — in State Departments and Peace Corps camps. Here, conceivably, some Americans might emerge who could do in fiction what few Americans have — bring the political world and the private into a balance where, inevitable [inevitably], one invigorates the other."

495 Woodcock, George. Review of **The Long Day Wanes**. **Pacific Affairs**, v. 38, no. 2 (Summer 1965) 206-207.

The fate of Crabbe, the shabby English intellectual, is merely the continuing thread around which Burgess weaves a very complex web of sub-plots which involve literally hundreds of characters. "Burgess spent several years on the peninsula as an Education Officer and he has made remarkable use of his observations in creating vividly authentic types and a number of characters who are much more than types, such as the formidable, pathetic boozer, Nabby Adams, the old Indian army sweat whom the East has spoilt for life elsewhere, and whose gigantic, rumbling presence gives a comic power to **Time for a Tiger** which the remaining novels do not rival . . . . More than any other writer I have yet encountered, Burgess deserves to be regarded as the Balzac of the decline of colonialism."

A Long Trip to Teatime

496 London: Dempsey & Squires, 1976.

497 New York: Stonehill, 1976.

Reviews

Burgess on his own work: "I have tried it [the idea of marrying the aleatory and the imposed structure] myself, though I have never gone so far as to submit to pictorial images. Anybody interested may find a little book of mine around ostensibly for children, called **A Long Trip to Teatime**, in which an apparently free fantasy, on the lines of the Alice books, is actually under the rigid control of the E section of a small encyclopedia. The young hero's name is Edgar and he goes to Easter Island to hear about Eddington and Edison, and he ends up in the town of Edenborough. One of the tricks is to disguise the E initials, so that one wonders why Carlyle and Gladstone and Matthew Arnold are around, only to find the answer in the fact they they all contributed to the **Edinburgh Review**. And so on. And so on."

498 Anon. Review of **A Long Trip to Teatime**. **Booklist**, v. 73, no. 19 (June 1, 1977) 1483.

"Edgar not only returns in time for tea and the term's end, he comes back with an enviable grasp of the theory of relativity. Edgar is obviously Alice in Wonderland's twentieth-century male counterpart; in the Burgess canon, he is unique."

499 Atherton, J.S. "Edgar in Edenborough." **Times Literary Supplement**, 25 March 1977, p. 348.

Burgess' versatility merits polite applause. It is best described as Lewis Carroll on which a lively sprig of **Finnegans Wake** has been grafted. Doubts if the book is suitable for children; the work is likely to be bewildering and over-literary for the purpose. Relates some elements of the plot and observes that he enjoyed reading about Edgar's experiences.

500 Tennant, Emma. "Burgess's Many Voices." **Listener**, v. 97, no. 2495 (February 1977) 189.

[Also reviews **Beard's Roman Women**.] "Still, when narrative and semantic laughs are combined, it is fun to read, and more enjoyable than a lot of children's books."

501 Tovey, Roberta. "Two Children's Books for Adults." **New Republic**, v. 176, no. 22 (May 28, 1977) 41.

"Poor Edgar, caught in a children's book with possibly the worst story ever created: a series of entirely fortuitous incidents, all happening much too fast and connected only by historical and literary allusions, word plays and puns he cannot possibly understand . . . . Here too is wealth of very endearing (and deliberately) bad verse . . . . Purely as a vehicle for these games, the trip to teatime is sometimes as tiresome as it is long. The line drawings by Fulvio Testa, however, are wonderful. Perhaps we would be best off looking just at the pictures."

The Malayan Trilogy

502 London: Pan Books, 1964. Pbk.

503 Harmondsworth, Eng.: Penguin, 1973. Pbk.

[NOTE: Includes **Time for a Tiger**, **The Enemy in the Blanket** and **Beds in the East**. See also the American title: **The Long Day Wanes**.]

Reviews

504 Blakeston, Oswell. "Malayan Comedy." **Books and Bookmen**, v. 17 (August 1972) ii, iv.

[Review of Penguin pbk. ed. Also reviews **The Doctor Is Sick**.] The **Clockwork** film has made Burgess famous, but his own first review of **A Time for a Tiger** said as much some years ago. Quotes from that first review. Considers the main characters beautifully established. The second novel, **The Enemy in the Blanket** demonstrated an added adroitness in the story telling. "I loved the ways the Malays misinterpreted all the kindly gestures of the whites who had good will towards native ambitions. Reactions were so skilfully counterpointed that frustration and danger were inevitable for all concerned. This second novel convinced me that Mr. Burgess was better than his promise, a major addition to the ranks of novelists who offer employment to Genius."

505 Ratcliffe, Michael. "Fifteen Years On: A Comedy of Babel and Misunderstanding." **Times** (London), no. 58,517 (June 29, 1972) 12.

[Review of Penguin pbk. ed.] The trilogy will survive despite its flaws. Goes to the OED for the meaning of the names 'Crabbe' and 'Costard.' Observes that the end is appallingly bitter; the overall tone is much nearer to Waugh's **Black Mischief** and **Scoop** than Forster's **A Passage to India**. The two elements of anger and urbanity are in constant conflict throughout the novel. That urbanity wins out is one of its major flaws. The character of Crabbe is too dry and disappointed to hold the three novels together; only Burgess's extreme story-telling skill and huge controlled comic gift accomplish that aim.

Man of Nazareth

506 New York: Mc-Graw-Hill, 1979.

Recordings

507 Sir Lew Grade Presents Franco Zeffirelli's Production of Jesus of Nazareth [Videorecording] Written by Anthony Burgess, Suso Cecchi D'Amico, Franco Zeffirelli; produced by Vincenzo Labella; directed by Franco Zeffirelli. An ITC/RAI co-production. New York, N.Y.: RCA SelectaVision Videodiscs, 1981. 4 videodiscs. Duration: 390 min. CONTENTS: Disc 1. The promise. — disc 2. The ministry. — disc 3. The journey. — disc 4. The fulfillment. Performers: Robert Powell, Anne Bancroft, Ernest Borgnine, Claudia Cardinale, Valentina Cortese, James Farentino, James Earl Jones, Stacy Keach, Tony Lo Bianco, James Mason, Ian McShane, Laurence Olivier, Donald Pleasence, Christopher Plummer, Anthony Quinn, Fernando Rey, Ralph Richardson, Rod Steiger, Peter Ustinov, Michael York, Olivia Hussey. First issued as a television drama in 1977.

Translations

507.2 [Note: On this novel, first published in France (see below), Burgess based his filmscript for Zeffirelli's **Jesus of Nazareth**. The work was refused by American and British publishers. Burgess writes: "Curiously the work has been a bestseller in France, with book club, episcopal commendations and God knows what. This is an interesting example of the lack of universality of literature. What US loves is not necessarily what rest of world would even touch with its walking cane and vice v."]

508 French: **L'Homme de Nazareth**. Paris: Laffont, 1976. Translation by Georges Belmont and Hortense Chabrier of a work entitled "Jesus Christ and the Love Game."

509 Italian: **L'Uomo di Nazareth**. Milano: Editoriale Nuova, 1978. Translated by Liana Burgess [Burgess' wife.]

Reviews

509.2 Burgess on his own work: "I woke up one Sunday to see a book called **Jesus of Nazareth** [by William Barclay] heading both the hardback and paperback best-selling lists. It was made out of my own script for the Zeffirelli series, the script being a commodity bought by the production company, its novelisation assigned to a novelising hand not mine. This is life, this is big business." [Quoted from #1479.]

510 Adams, Phoebe-Lou. Review of **Man of Nazareth**. **Atlantic**, v. 243, no. 5 (May 1977) 94.

Those who fictionalize the gospels either paraphrase the Bible, or spring inventions and interpretations boring to the infidel and annoying to the devout. "Mr. Burgess has tried to get around the difficulty by lavishing attention on Roman politics and minor characters, an ingenious diversionary tactic which never really works. The book drifts into limbo — not quite fiction, not quite history, not quite orthodox, not (and very carefully) quite irreverent, not quite anything.

511 Anon. Review of **Man of Nazareth**. **Booklist**, v. 75, no. 16 (April 15, 1977) 1272.

"Burgess developed this impressive novel from his screenplay for Franco Zeffirelli's televised production 'Jesus of Nazareth' [see #507]." The author succeeds eloquently in depicting Jesus and his disciples as viable and their historic activities as perfectly congruous. The literary license Burgess ocasionally seizes may affront some readers with such inventions as Christ's brief marriage, celebrated at Cana; but the spirit and vitality of his creations and their linkage to prevailing concepts supply a crucial depth rarely achieved in religious history." [Complete text of review.]

512 Anon. Review of **Man of Nazareth. Kirkus Reviews**, v. 47, no. 4 (February 15, 1979) 206-07.

Burgess "also worries a variegated humanity from the supporting cast: Judas is a young vulnerable intellectual; Thomas is a **Downstairs** retainer; the Romans are cynically witty; the Zealots steely activists. His main thrust, however, is the portrait of Jesus as a good and brilliant man for whom the kingdom of heaven could be on earth: 'Enter the house of death and you leave time behind . . . . You may even say that kingdom is now, that heaven and hell are now.' Make of this what you will theologically — call it liberal Protestant or radical Catholic — but Burgess deserves A for effort in an impossible assignment.''

513 Armstrong, Marion. "A Reverent Tone." **Christian Century**, v. 96, no. 29 (September 19, 1979) 896.

The uniqueness of the book lies in its dry and rich literary style. The narrator, a Greek or Roman intellectual, is not guilty of a hyped-up emotionalism, and Burgess makes vibrant and plausible characterizations of the apostles. To make the marriage at Cana that of Jesus himself is a literary invention; a scriptural scholar of great note, quizzed on this point, ended the discussion with benign forcefulness. The description of a physically strong and virile Jesus able to tolerate unimaginable pain evokes an electrifying image of the Son of God. "And I am very glad that I did not see the TV rendition of this book, but I can't tell you how glad I am to have read **Man of Nazareth**. And as for the tone — that tone I would not forget — when all is said, the tone is reverent.''

514 DeMott, Benjamin. "According to Burgess." **New York Times Book Review**, 15 April 1979, p. 1, 20.

The tale opens with a cool Foucaultian account of a crucifixion followed by a Shavian declaration against 'this mode of punishing the state's offenders.' Much of the book deals with events recorded only sketchily in the Gospels and, while Burgess retains much of the Sermon on the Mount, he develops numerous conceits of his own, including a comparison between love and craft. Azur the narrator offers an amusedly secular interpretation of the injunction to love one's enemies: he argues that it is possible to do so only if one does not take life too seriously. Free dramatizations of the Gospels have served to revitalize Christianity, and the book gives evidence of imaginative energy (see the shade lubricous portrait of Salome, the depiction of Judas Iscariot as a political innocent), but it does not achieve the goal of lending solidity to the teachings of Jesus. "The reason is, I think, that the author is insufficiently concerned with the intellectual dimensions and power of the deeds at the center of the life of Christ. In recent decades writers of many persuasions, not merely crisis theologians, have come to understand this life in contexts different from that of other worldly salvation. They have seen it as charging christendom with the obligation of reconceiving human freedom as a choice for or against self-transformation in the here and now . . . . But **Man of Nazareth** misses the chance. It behaves throughout as though the secret of revitalization lay solely in lightness or off-handedness — in empty urbanity, breezy colloquialism and the rhetoric of skepticism and comical play.''

515 Kermode, Frank. "'Love and Do as You Please." **New York Review of Books**, v. 26, no. 13 (August 16, 1979) 44-45.

Burgess not only has many of the traditional skills of the novelist; he also has a taste for experiment. He sets himself puzzles that present difficult formal problems (witness **MF** and **Napoleon Symphony**), and much of this novel's interest lies in the deft solving of problems other writers would have left alone. Comments on the popularity of Lloyd C. Douglas' **The Robe**, a work marked by dullness and lack of literary quality. Speculates if these drawbacks endowed the Douglas *opus* with a certain purity. Burgess does not have that purity, and will not have millions of readers. Includes long and learned comments on Burgess' strategy in making Azor the narrator of the tale and, along the way, comments on Azor/Burgess' use of the gospels; the Temptation in the Wilderness; the impotence of Herod Antipater and the presence of two Salomes; the presence of two Jesuses (Jesus Bar-Abbas, and **Jesus of Nazareth**); Azor's anachronistic history; the presence of Jewish Zealots ('terrorists' or 'freedom fighters'); the subtlety of the innocent Judas; whether Jesus used *kamilon* (cable) or *kamelon* (camel) in his needle/camel mot. "I don't mean, by saying so much of Burgess' own trickery, to underplay the solid narrative virtues of his account. There is a lot of expert characterization and there are some well-imagined scenes, for instance in Herod's Palace, and in the Sanhedrin. His Jesus is a convincingly powerful athlete, a plainspoken godman. His soldiery is convincingly licentious and obscene. His Jerusalem, dangerous in the crowded days of the feast, is strongly presented. The prose is always full of life and interest. It is hard to think that anybody else could have done this job so well.''

516 Soete, Mary. Review of **Man of Nazareth**. **Library Journal**, v. 104, no. 8 (April 15, 1979) 972.

"It is a vigorous and gritty portrayal of Jesus as a man among his fellow men in a remote, dusty corner of the Roman Empire, married and widowed young, carpenter, teacher, miracle worker, fulfilling not only scriptural prophecy but the life of a man as well. Jesus as the bridegroom at Cana contriving, if not a miracle, a gently miraculous jest; or Gabriel filing his nails before the astonished Zacharias; or the wry storyteller-scholar's treatise on crucifixion, chilling in its tedious precision, the disciples chattering and chiding among themselves — these are aspects of Burgess the artificer at his best, firmly grounded in the Gospels and in history, but with an unerring ear for the accents of ordinary men and full of audacious invention and sheer fictive zest.''

517 Stauffenberg, Henry J. Review of **Man of Nazareth**. **Best Sellers**, June 1979, pp. 74-75.

A brilliantly sustained synthesis of canonical and non-canonical elements wholly worthy of Burgess. Burgess' treatment of the miracle of the Marriage at Cana is worthy of Chaucer's pardoner. "Although some aspects of **Man of Nazareth** might conceivably alienate conservative believers (e.g. the discharge of blood and water in 'as it were a lateral mode of describing the spearlike erection of the phallus of the newly expired') many of the non-canonical incidents recounted are no less bizarre than those found in the monumental Hennecke Schneemelcher **New Testament Apocrypha**, the M.R. James **Aprocryphal New Testament**, the Robinson **Nag Hammadi Library**, and the vast body of medieval religio-mythography. This reviewer (a believer) read **Man of Nazareth** several times and emerged from the experience unshaken in his personal convictions *and* his profound respect for the Burgess-ian aesthetic.''

518 Taliafero, Frances. "History Enhanced." **Harper's**, v. 258, no. 1549 (June 1979) 94.

A less than satisfying work by the heroic Anthony Burgess. For a reader of the gospels, the novel was unnecessary. It is a chronological account taken directly from the Gospels. "Burgess also leaps to a few dares. The complaisance of Joseph, married off to a woman already with child, is explained by his impotence: his testicles were crushed in his youth when an iron vise fell on him. The wedding at Cana was Jesus' own, to a young woman who died several years later. Salome, in her remorse over the death of John the Baptist, becomes a follower of Jesus. Judas 'betrays' Jesus in political innocence, believing that the high priests seek Jesus' best interests." Burgess' small fictions are far more persuasive than the labored guesses of scholars. The novel is a very literal prose translation which makes every attempt not to talk down to the reader or stretch his historical competence too far.

519 Twomey, Gerald. "Life Taken Whole." **America**, v. 140, nos. 23-25 (June 23, 1979) 517-18.

The Marian theology of the 50's has given way to the Christological studies of the 70's, and Burgess' novel succeeds admirably in depicting Jesus as both true God and true man. In many ways, it can be said that Burgess has written a 'fifth' Gospel. He is a masterly storyteller; his prose style is a joy; his command of language inspiring. He may get somewhat carried away in his treatment of Jesus' sexuality, but he has fully captured the humanity of Jesus. His insight that the Zealot party arranged for the death and execution of Jesus on account of His association with the Roman occupying forces is most profound. True to his lapsed Catholicism, Burgess places a high value on the worth of the human person and the role of free will. Certain passages may seem sexist — but only because Burgess is intent on a faithful reproduction of the contemporary Hebraic mind-set Jesus faced and confronted. It is a first-rate work, moving and inspiring: a perfect gift for summer reading.

520 Wilkes, Paul. "Jesus, East and West." **Commonweal**, v. 106, no. 18 (October 12, 1979) 574.

[Also reviews **A Life of Christ**, by Shusaku Endo.] Endo's book is marked by a slow pace, reverent tone, and interesting history. The reviewer, an old-school Catholic, found himself flagging and turned to Burgess. He found himself in the company of a much more talented writer who depicts a gouty Herod, a married Jesus and a bewildered Mary. It soon dawned that Burgess was concocting a meal made up of ice cream sundae. He returned to Endo and found himself in the company of an old friend who dispenses substantial whole wheat loaves. Burgess' book shares the fault of the television production: it features glaring superficialities turned into a biblical soap opera. Endo's book "will still be around and cherished when Burgess publishes his next dozen excesses — which shouldn't take him too very long.''

MF

521 London: Cape, 1971.

522 New York: Knopf, 1971.

523 New York: Ballantine, 1972. Pbk.

524 Harmondsworth, Eng.: Penguin, 1973. Pbk.

Translations

525 Portuguese: **Macho & Femea**. Rio de Janeiro: Artenova, 1971. Translated by E.G. Cerqueira.

Reviews

526 Adams, Phoebe. "Short Book Reviews." **Atlantic**, v. 227, no. 5 (May 1971) 114.

"A versatile and ingenious author, Mr. Burgess has confected an imaginary island, a number of peculiar characters, a mysteriously eccentric will, and a family with an inclination to incest — to mention merely the cream of an odd crop. The novel involves enough multilingual puns and puzzles to wake Finnegan and ends with a kind of detective-story explanation which, on the somewhat dubious assumption that I have not misread it, repudiates the whole enterprise as an example of art exclusively (that is, incestuously) generated from the more idiosyncratic areas of the artist's isolated imagination. This is an interesting idea, but in presenting it as a practical joke, Mr. Burgess may have outsmarted himself as well as the reader." [Complete text of review.]

527 Anon. Review of **MF**. **Kirkus Reviews**, January 1, 1971, pp. 16-17.

"It's Plautus and Terence by way of Frazier? Joyce? Borges? — heaven knows who else — and its hooting mythic obbligatos are delivered with the familiar prostrating technique. The rationale, in suitable question and answer form, appears to be: ". . . if nature does all the serious work, what is there left for man?" Simple: "We are all God's *jongleurs*; we play and tumble before His throne for His weary delectation." Burgess does something comparable for his claque and other readers with Olympian patience."

528 Anon. Review of **MF**. **Publishers Weekly**, v. 199, no. 6 (February 8, 1971) 78.

"There is an occasional air of strain, when Mr. Burgess pushes too hard, but on the whole this is good satire, very cheeky about the utterly permissive school of sexual writing and some classic manifestations of the incest theme."

529 Anon. Review of **MF**. **Booklist**, v. 67, no. 18 (May 15, 1971) 777.

"The possible complexities of human relationships from miscegenation to twinship to incest are all treated with sophisticated humor in a skillfully if somewhat bewilderingly designed novel complete with a surprise conclusion that affords a fresh perspective on all the events of the first-person narrative."

530 Anon. Review of **MF**. **America**, v. 124, no. 20 (May 22, 1971) 549.

"Any new book by Anthony Burgess should be an event — should, in fact, be a bigger event that this one is. Yet, though Mr. Burgess may simply be having his readers on and playing around with his great gift of invention, he still sets up, under his indecent title, an amazing set of characters and situations, and lots of linguistic fun. He is a very clever man." [Complete text of review.]

531 Anon. Notice of **MF**. **New York Times Book Review**, 6 June 1971, p. 3.

"Intricate, imaginatively daring — a young man's trip through toils of incest and coils of language." [Complete text of notice.]

532 Anon. "Higher Games." **Times Literary Supplement**, 18 June 1971, p. 693.

We are told not to look for meaning and that communication has been the whatness of the communication but, given all the indications of allegory, the reader can hardly be blamed for trying to find one. Compiles a list of Burgess' Latinate vocabulary, but decides that Burgess' poetic exactitudes of language are perhaps more rewarding. Concludes with a quotation from the book: "a sure sign of amateur art is too much detail to compensate for too little life."

533 Anon. Notice of **MF**. **New York Times Book Review**, 5 December 1971, p. 84.

Identical to #531 above.

534 Anon. Notice of **MF**. **Best Sellers**, May 1, 1972, p. 71.

"Anthony Burgess may just have been laughing with and at his audience in **MF** but he is always clever." [Complete text of notice.]

535 Anon. Notice of **MF**. **Books and Bookmen**, v. 18 (September 1973) 138.

[Marks publication of the Penguin pbk. ed. For complete text of notice, see #879.]

536 Cheshire, David. "Fiction." **Times** (London), no. 58,201 (June 17, 1971) 12.

A summary of this unruly novel is like trying to deep-freeze Niagara. The story apparently arose as a spoof of Levi-Strauss's link between riddles and incest and, while **MF** has a structure as awe-inspiring as DNA, in another sense it can be seen as an exercise in self-indulgence more reminiscent of Nashe or Lyly than the superficial resemblance elsewhere to Joyce or Nabokov. The author's tremendous relish has run to seed. Like the Elizabethans, Burgess seems more interested in the act of writing for its own sake — a "potential virtue which here, when the entertainment is wearing pretty thin, emerges unmistakably as professional vanity."

537 Chew, Shirley. "Mr. Livedog's Day: The Novels of Anthony Burgess." **Encounter**, v. 38, no. 6 (June 1972) 57-64.

[An essay. For full annotation, see #1659. Also includes brief review of **MF**. See pp. 63-64.] It is as ingenious as ever, but an air of contrivance now sits upon the invention. The hero is perhaps somewhat faceless, and it may be that "Burgess has fallen temporarily into Dr. Spindrift's predicament — becoming so absorbed by the fascinating life there is in words that he forgets they are 'part of the warm current' of a larger life. However, he has given fragments enough of his individual vision to convince us of its intensity and importance, and of the continuing vitality of his work."

538 DeMott, Benjamin. "God's Plenty in a Flood of Proper and Improper Nouns." **Saturday Review**, v. 54, no. 13 (March 27, 1971) 31, 39-41.

Quotes from the gluttonous eating contest scene in **Tremor of Intent** to demonstrate that Burgess' obsession with words is the primary force shaping his fictional world. This zany, slightly underworked novel is no exception, and Burgess' power of representing the rock culture at its most asinine and reclusive authors at their most fatuous is once again on bright display. At times, he seems to share the Conradian compulsion to make us see the fictional event; at other times, the intricate solidity of his description suggest a habitual incapacity to forego exact labels. The question and answer sessions in **Tremor of Intent** are functional; the one in this novel resembles a filler [quotes from both books]. Burgess' continual verbal fidgeting is sometimes pointless; at other times, it offers lovely examples of human ingenuity. Gives some examples of each. At moments of comic crisis, Burgess becomes a poet of life-profusion. Witness, for example, his description of a parade. Includes 300 word quotation. Wonders about the meaning of it all, and remarks that Burgess is not a master of moral intricacy or subtle psychological investigation. He is, in **MF**, praising the total variousness of life; he is telling the reader that the world is richer than we have believed; and his torrential fluencies, multiplicities beyond numbering, make him appear as a kind of literary Adam who shows us God's plenty as a flood of words.

539 Donadio, Stephen. "Anthony Burgess's Oedipus Rex." **New York Times Book Review**, 4 April 1971, p. 4.

[Plot summary with some heroic commentary.] The book is elegantly printed and bound. It is also fully realized. Of course, it does not yield its meanings easily. It will certainly not relieve the pressures of contemporary war-torn reality [the reference is to the Vietnamese Conflict]. It arouses the reader's prurient metaphysical interest [Donadio wrote this, dear reader, not me]. The plot is given. The remark is made that the plot continues to thicken. The narrative drive remains unrelenting throughout. Further, the story progresses clearly from point to point. Nevertheless, "the prose itself establishes its own closed circuit, which joins various times and places into a single here and now." [This quite remarkable statement is not enough, however. Therefore:] In this respect as well as a number of others (for the most part related to the transformations of language and the fascination with the pun as a kind of shuttle between various realms of experience [almost we have it all here]), the conception of the book is deeply Joycean [Aha!] The reader interested in pursuing the connection might begin with Burgess's reflections on the 'Proteus' episode of **Ulysses** in his **Re Joyce**." [You have now hit the ground running.]

540 Duffy, Martha. "Algonquin Legend." **Time**, v. 97, no. 12 (March 22, 1971) 80-82.

"In **MF** Burgess takes off from a Levi-Strauss contention that a universal connection exists between answering conundrums and committing incest. According to this view it was not by chance that Oedipus' unwitting incest occurred after he solved the riddle of the Sphinx . . . . Even for readers who have never read Levi-Strausss and think Algonquin legends are about Dorothy Parker, **MF** still works as a comic novel." [Last third of the review is devoted to an account of Burgess at Princeton.]

541 Horrocks, Norman. Review of **MF**. **Library Journal**, v. 96, no. 6 (March 15, 1971) 976.

"A contemporary novel full of verbal fireworks, puns, allusions, paraded erudition, and literary jokes . . . . Not really a novel for the prudish but an amusing-in-parts black comedy likely to appeal most to the Burgess devotees who will be prepared to tolerate and enjoy his exercise in self-indulgence."

542 Kavanagh, P.J. "Wordgames." **Manchester Guardian Weekly**, 3 July 1971, p. 19.

[Omnibus review.] "By the time we realise that the name of Faber's twin-double Llew is the last syllable of Nowell spelled backwards, the [that] Noel is the reverse of Leon and Sib Legeru is Anglo-Saxon (?) for incest and Castita is chastity (?) I for one was too exhausted to care. It is like trying to do a crossword under ether. By comparison **The Tower is Everywhere**, by Richard Jones, is splendidly unhysterical."

543 Kermode, Frank. "The Algonquin Oedipus." **Listener**, v. 85, no. 2203 790-91.

Burgess, an ingenious linguistician, has been boning up on semiotics. His new book, a complicated structure of riddles, cannot be understood without the help of Levi-Strauss's **The Scope of Anthropology** in which, on pp. 34-39, is found an Algonquin myth of riddling and incest. Burgess supplies great lexical profuseness, and one's first impression is of random invention powered by a remarkable riddling fantasy. "What. . . is one to make of it? It is a puzzle and on its own terms forbids solutions. But Burgess is rather movingly putting to use the self-begotten system of his own imagination and language to protest against spurious disorder in art and life. This is too solemn an account of a book so bewilderingly funny . . . . Its fertility is fantastic, and so is its ingenuity . . . . Perhaps all one ought to do is to characterise this book as a riddling Sphinx, and abstain from guessing further, but it should be added that it is a work of astonishing narrative and intellectual energy, and that everybody who thinks the English novel lacking in those qualities should read it, twice. Anthony has earned his place among the birds."

544 Learmont, Marina. "Anthony Burgess: **MF**." **Books and Bookmen**, v. 16 (July 1971) 45.

"Now Anthony Burgess offers us his own entertainment-version of the myth, in which Algonquin and Iroquois appear as the names of hotels, one of the drinks is called Clubfoot, and so on. Continuing his love affair with language, he writes in dense highly-mannered prose, with all sorts of language games thrown in, and the whole book is ridded with obscurantist, pedantic puzzles and palindromes. The trouble is that the riddles probably gave a lot more satisfaction to Burgess himself than they are likely to provide for any but the most besotted cross-word puzzle addicts among his readers. But there are intervals when he allows us to relax from the word-games, and then **MF** can be very funny."

545 Lehmann-Haupt, Christopher. "Incest in the Widest Sense." **New York Times**, 29 March 1971, p. 31.

"The moral being — insofar as this puzzle has a moral — that Miles's quest for freedom, both in surrealism and in defying one of mankind's oldest taboos, is chimerical . . . . Anthony Burgess is a puzzling writer — a brilliant literary machine, a Teletype tapping all of English literature . . . . He does do brilliant things in **MF** . . . . But too often Burgess seems merely to be manipulating the received literary past. And Dedalus' career notwithstanding, puzzles are not always art, and fancy falls short of imagination. Ultimately there is something too contrived about this novel. It is a mechanical bird, technically marvelous but secretly dead.''

546 Lindroth, James R. "Good Summer Fiction and God and Gospels on Trial." **America**, v. 124, no. 23 (June 12, 1971) 616.

The clues, in the form of three epigraphs, are thin but eventually "The mythic implications of Miles' 'riddling' ability become increasingly clear in the course of his journey. A young Oedipus in comic dress, he is twice threatened with death as the penalty for not correctly answering a riddle . . . . He neither dies nor transgresses this ultimate taboo [incest]: however, like Oedipus, he gains wisdom. At the beginning of his quest, Miles believes that absolute freedom, even the freedom to commit incest, is a basic human right. He comes to realize that the act of incest signifies, not freedom, but the 'breakdown of order, the collapse of communication, the irresponsible cultivation of chaos.' He learns that freedom has necessary limits . . . . Wild comedy, mythic portents, surreal adventure and biting satire combine to make **MF** the most enjoyable and interesting Burgess novel since **A Clockwork Orange.**''

547 McInerny, Ralph. Review of **MF**. **Commonweal**, May 28, 1971, pp. 290-91.

His prose verges toward the florilegium and the echoes, half-quotes, learned allusions and footnotes delivered on the fly that can make some readers hug themselves with joy. It has the same necromantic appeal as cryptography, but it communicates no emotion; therefore it is less than a success. With this book Burgess invites (perhaps demands) comparison with Nabokov and Joyce. "And yet, despite his exuberance and creativity and clear delight in all he does, he seems here to have chosen a roadway of fiction on which there is no mirror . . . . A novel like **MF** assumes language as its subject . . . . We are tugged, not toward the concrete or a simulacrum of it, but rather in the direction of abstraction, of bloodless cogitation . . . . Could this be said of Nabokov and Joyce? I think not . . . . Anthony Burgess is among the half-dozen most important English novelists writing today. He is surely one of the most intelligent. No writer can know too much but a writer's knowledge has to be assimilated and rendered almost visceral in order to count in a novel . . . . His facility and range are awesome and one toasts his fecundity and hopes for a multiple issue.''

548 Murray, John J. Review of **MF**. **Best Sellers**, April 1, 1971, pp. 15-16. (April 1, 1971) 15-16.

"The stewardess on Allegheny Flight No. 718 for Newark asked if the **MF** inscribed on the book-jacket of the novel I was reading referred to Male/Female, which only goes to show where the minds of stewardae are. I was only on page 17, pondering the meaning of *esculent* and *litotic*, but I was able to tell her, 'No. It refers to Miles Faber, the narrator's name, which, as any Burgess fan knows, means Soldier Maker, from the Latin, you see." Valiantly provides plot summary. Observes that Mr. Fonanta teaches Miles a lesson: "the easiest thing to do is to write and create in free association; any idiot can do it; all one has to do for recognition is to promote one's work in an aura of inaccessibility or shroud it in mystery. Burgess seems to be implying that this is precisely how he works, that his superficial talents, his undeniable mastery of the word and his rather potent linguistic skills at innovation, allow him to do as he pleases.''

549 Nash, Manning. Review of **MF**. **American Journal of Sociology**, v. 77, no. 5 (March 1972) 995-996.

The universality of the incest taboo has puzzled some of the best minds in social science (Tylor, Durkheim, Malinowsky, Radcliffe-Brown, Freud, Westermarck, Levi-Strauss and Parsons) and this polylingual feast of word play communicates a separable meaning to at least one professor. "Basically, Burgess is concerned with the dialectic of order and chaos in human life. There must be a delicate and continual interplay between them. In chaos there is creativity and freedom, while in order there is continuity and identity. Incest and exogamy pose this dialectic perfectly . . . . The only possible balance between chaos and order (or the synthesis of the thesis of incest and the antithesis of exogamy) is 'creative miscegenation . . . .' The book is great fun to read. Burgess is truly an *orang tukang*, and supremely *homo ludens* with symbol and word. The great Human meanings are not merely empirical. They are collectively existential.''

550 Nowell, Robert. "Words, Words, Words." **Tablet**, v. 225, no. 6839 (July 3, 1971) 650-51.

"It is indeed a brilliant performance." Nevertheless, "In all this there is a danger of people and their relationships with each other coming to play a merely secondary role to the battle of words, as if verbal pyrotechnics were a defensive screen against the world."

551 Ostermann, Robert. "In Puns, Riddles, and Coined Words, Mr. Burgess Discovers a Novel." **National Observer**, v. 10, no. 6 (April 19, 1971) 23.

This new extravaganza by Burgess features a three-ring circus and it is possible to follow any one of several possible trails. The deceptively simple title "are the initials of the novel's young hero Miles Farber [i.e. Faber]. But they also stand for the obscene accusation that probably was first hurled at Oedipus; and, meaning just that, they were carved on the gravestone of Miles Farber's [Faber again] grandfather." The novel is a modern version of the classical myth in which Theseus slays the Minotaur. The language is polysyllabic, the puns are time bombs which eventually explode, and the riddles clearly point the way to the author's fictional intention. The novel as art form is far from dead. "Here's a piece of fiction that challenges, stimulates, aims for the stars and gets beyond them, and generally makes tremendous good fun out of exceedingly serious ideas. This can't be said about too many novels. Don't miss this one."

552 Pritchard, William. "Stranger than Truth." **Hudson Review**, v. 24, no. 2 (Summer 1971) 366.

[Omnibus review.] Some years ago, Pritchard prophesied that Burgess would serve no master but language itself. **Enderby Outside** illustrated the point very well; it was a picaresque sequel to the more warmly depressed atmosphere of **Inside Mr. Enderby** — less humanly responsive to its hero, more concerned with piling up fantastic scenes created in spectacular language. In **MF** there is simply nobody to care about, and Burgess is free to concentrate on language to the exclusion of character. Quotes a section from the novel in which the hero disposes of maggoty meat and then comments: "This is brilliant, serving nothing but the language itself; but I was made uneasy and finally depressed by a novel that skates on such marvelous thin ice or freelances out along this razor's edge. Which is perhaps to say no more than that I've never had that much fun at **Finnegans Wake**, and that, with no right to urge it, I would love to see Anthony Burgess come more deeply and truly to terms with the surfaces of things he rendered so finely in books like **The Right to an Answer** or his early Malayan trilogy."

553 Raban, Jonathan. "Package Tour." **New Statesman**, v. 81 (June 17, 1971) 856-57.

". . . **MF** busily pecks away at the eyes and guts of that exhausted character, the novel; it aspires, in Barth's phrase, to be a footnote to the corpus of literature. Like so many recent exercises in auto-genesis and self-commentary, it sinks under the burden of its own cleverness." Castita (full of coincidences, plots, doubles, violence, riddles, etymologies and puns) is the place to which every novelist who tires of the resistance offered by a solid social world now offers to take us. "And Anthony Burgess is a cut-price tour operator; his powers of invention are neither as sustained nor as beguilingly obsessional as those of Borges, Flann O'Brien or Nabokov. What he offers is a frantic display of joke pedantry, colourful squibs and ingenious trick-constructions that look as if they've been made out of Meccano. When the resources of the fiction shelf fail him, he falls back on crapulous swivings . . . ." Burgess's adverbs and adjectives are on form: people smile saccholactically and look like presbyotic grannies. But as an exploration of *Siblegeru* (the word comes from Wulfstan's **Sermo Lupi ad Anglos**), the work is ineffective. "It's too pygobranchitic: meaning, roughly, that it breathes heavily through its hinder parts."

554 S., R.A. Review of **MF**. **Newsweek**, v. 77, no. 16 (April 19, 1971) 123.

Burgess has produced many books with furious, brilliant energy; but, in this work, the bookish side has all but stifled the novelist. "The prose is still fine, even spectacular in patches, but, for the most part, **MF** is a ragbag of murky linguistic riddles about incest uttered by a dessicated sphinx to a trivial Oedipus."

555 Thompson, John. "Words." **Commentary**, v. 52, no. 4 (October 1971) 108-109.

[Omnibus review.] "His latest fiction is **MF** (the title represents the initials of the hero Miles Faber, also the current term of Oedipal opprobrium, and doubtless much else as well). It is written in a series of puzzles and jokes and riddles . . . . The taste for this sort of thing is a special one which I do not happen to share." Quotes an excerpt that denounces Madison Avenue and describes the mugging of a rabbi. "To my ear, this prose has the loud empty noise of rock music, totally derivative of older and more authentic modes . . . . No one could doubt Burgess's extensive cleverness or his fantastic energy, but **MF** is mere public frenzy."

556 Wade, Rosalind. "Literary Supplement: Quarterly Fiction Review." **Contemporary Review**, v. 219, no. 1269 (October 1971) 211-15.

[Omnibus review. For Burgess, see p. 212.] "**MF** is not so much a fantasy as a completely different way of looking at familiar things which at times resembles an uneasy dream. His characters are grotesque — the fugitive Faber — the unappetising Erma into whose clutches he subsides all too willingly. A veritable gallery of characters, Charlie, Loewe and the rest prance through the small American townships where the heat is always unbearable and the people wear a grubby, used-up look."

557 Wall, Stephen. "Lexical Lark." **Observer** (London), 20 June 1971, p. 29.

It is a fantastic narrative on linguistic themes and, although it is ostensibly offered as a serious work, the narrative's witty turns bring many lively and exhilarating encounters. "[Faber's] admiration for the apparent disdain of meaning shown by the finally discovered works of Sib Legeru is dashed when he finds that the name is — as students of the hairier Old English texts will recall — Wulfstan's term for incest. Wulfstan feared for the end of his culture, and one of Mr. Burgess's morals (he offers several) may be that unreasonable desires for artistic freedom are dangerously incompatible with the artistic necessity for ordered communication . . . . **MF** has a great deal of comic brio, some of it coming from a tissue of literary references, often charmingly inappropriate to their new and usually grotesque context . . . . It is a further demonstration has Anthony Burgess is a man of parts and that **MF** deploys many of them."

558 Waugh, Auberon. "Auberon Waugh on New Novels." **Spectator**, v. 226, no. 7460 (June 19, 1971) 849-50.

"Any week which produces a new novel by Anthony Burgess must be ringed in gold on the reviewer's calendar." But is this esoteric novel not about word games and incest? coterie stuff? run the risk of exploiting what it condemns (incest presumably)? The argument of the new book is plainly this: reviewers are such dolts that writers must resort to word games and intellectual firework displays. The plot is preposterously baroque where it is intelligible at all. Provides plot summary and suggests Burgess did not seriously expect anyone to read the book. Still, the words redeem what the plot conceals. "All I can say is that in his happier moments — the first two-thirds of the book — Mr. Burgess demonstrates such a mastery of the English language and narrative form that if his plot were twice as absurd it could still be a delight to read. It can be read quite simply as a nonsense novel for its many excellent jokes . . . . Well, he has succeeded [in proving his superiority over the reviewer]. I can't make head or tale of it, but from the bits I do understand I can see it is jolly good. It only remains to thank him for the happy sensations which were excited by the many rare and beautiful words which ornament his prose, yes, like jewels in a monstrance, as I turned his later pages, one by one, in blissful incomprehension."

559 West, Paul. "A Trombone on Fire." **Washington Post Book World**, 21 March 1971, p. 3.

Denounces the sorry literary state of England. Where is the expansive tradition of Shakespeare, Marlowe, Byron, Carlyle, Dickens, Joyce, Dylan Thomas and Beckett? The baroque or ornate is disparaged as fancy or fruity by partisans of no-nonsense prose men passionately interested in politics, regiments and secondary education. Burgess, thank God, belongs to the minority tradition, and he is now delivering a verbal bombshell into the land in which Mrs. Harold Wilson is taken seriously as a poet. Followed by brisk plot summary. Followed in turn by commentary. "If none of this seems clear, then to hell with it; this is the pretext for the text, and the text, as a verbal tissue, is for the most part scintillating, ingenious, and impenitent." Declares it is also gratuitous, festive, delectably inexplicable. Provides some rich sample catalogs and inventive passages from the book and calls them invigorating verbal treasure troves.

560 Winter, Thomas. "A Protean Work." **Prairie Schooner**, v. 46, no. 1 (Spring 1972) 82-83.

"**MF** (mill finish? microfarad? *mezzo forte*? Master of Forestry?) is a misleading title. The hero's mother is left out entirely. It's his sister . . . . The book begins with our hero Miles Faber functionally naked, making love with a girl in front of the library as a 'yummy protest' against it-does-not-matter-what. It is, in fact, merely a *fortissimo* to engage the reader's attention . . . . Burgess's love of language is becoming proverbial, and this novel is a philologist's delight . . . . The significant names, with explanations, are a bit obtrusive . . . . **MF** also manages to be a book about poetry; it is, in short, a Protean work which all lovers of language will have to read. The only flaw is that a single, offhand sentence in the epilogue changes the complexion of the entire book. Are such clues as may exist a fair preparation for the reader, or did Burgess cheat and decide as an afterthought to bomb the reader with a cheap surprise? The book should be read carefully, no matter what the answer to the question.''

561 Young, B.A. "Smile, Please." **Punch**, v. 260 (June 30, 1971) 890.

[Omnibus review.] Sadly observes that he is not clever enough to appreciate the relationship between language and family structure mentioned by the publisher's blurb. "But the language! Mr. Burgess isn't content to gild his racy prose with words like margaric and rhodochrosite and hidrotic and onomastic; he gives us little lectures on Malayan word-formations and even invents a language of his own for his West Indian island, a kind of Slavified Romance. I recommend reading **MF** straight through twice, to pick up the nooscopic snarls the second time round that you missed the first.''

Moses: A Narrative

562 London: Dempsey and Squires, 1976.

563 New York: Stonehill, 1976.

Reviews

564 Anon. Notice of **Moses: A Narrative**. **Village Voice**, 29 March 1976, p. 42.

"Of the bullrushes — an unconventional 'imaginative' biography by the satirical lover of lingo." [Complete text of notice.]

565 Anon. Review of **Moses: A Narrative**. **Publishers Weekly**, v. 209, no. 26 (June 28, 1976) 91.

Burgess' use of narrative verse which, as he provocatively remarks, anticipates the cinema makes this work interesting in a technical and artistic sense. The work is dramatic, flowing, fresh — and it may enrich and enliven the Biblical text.

566 Anon. Review of **Moses: A Narrative**. **Booklist**, v. 73, no. 4 (October 15, 1976) 300.

"This epic took an interesting route to book form: it was originally used as the shooting script for the TV production **Moses**. In the fully realized poem, Burgess captures the flavor of dynasties and political movements, and brilliantly portrays historical characters as complex beings full of doubts and complaints. The brief autobiographical profile is an intriguing ending to the powerful achievement." [Complete text of review.]

567 Daiches, David. Review of **Moses: A Narrative**. **Times Literary Supplement**, 21 January 1977, p. 50.

[Written in narrative verse.] "Anthony Burgess, a gifted man with words,
Witty and bawdy and Joycean as we know he can be
— Composer too, and, as he tells us, a heavy smoker,
Also writes film scripts, film scripts.
(He likes repetitions like this.)
. . . And if I say that for myself, myself, I prefer the Bible,
The account in the Bible from the first Egyptian enslavement
To the death of Moses on Mount Pisgah
(and for that matter the Bible in its original language,
For I too have my linguistic obsessions)
— If I say that, Burgess cannot be offended,
Not offended, because after all he knows the splendours
Of that language as well as any of us
And leavens his own story with it at critical moments.
Interesting, then; commendable, even: a bit of a sport
In the garden of modern poetry. But none the worse for that.
I do not expect to see the TV series.
But mine eyes have seen Burgess's preliminary verse canter
As Moses saw the Promised Land from afar.
I am content."

568 LeClair, Thomas. Review of **Moses: A Narrative**. **Saturday Review**, v. 3, no. 21 (July 24, 1976) 27.

Burgess focusses on Moses the reluctant and embattled leader, and from exile to exodus, from Sinai to Pisgah, the pace is swift; the dialogue, short-winded; the magic, right. He imagines an engaging interior life for the minor characters, but not for Moses himself. "Poet Burgess shouldn't frighten away prose readers; **Moses** has less verbal display than many of his novels. As for epic ambition: instead of the ways of God to men, Burgess in his foreword seeks to justify publishing this poetic preliminary to a film script."

569 Soete, Mary. Review of **Moses: A Narrative**. **Library Journal**, v. 101, no. 21 (December 1, 1976) 494.

This epic poem based on Exodus, Leviticus, Numbers and Deuteronomy demonstrates the Burgess wit and style. It is a graceful and readable long poetic narrative complete with common and mythic touches which give the story wings.

570 Solomon. Albert J. Review of **Moses: A Narrative**. **Best Sellers**, v. 36 (November 1976) 264.

An acknowledged master of prose, Burgess the poet still has a way to go. The work is a blend of Cecil B. DeMille and John Milton. The character of Moses achieves a certain nobility, while Zimri and Balaam bear the mark of a novelist's eye. An interesting treatment of a monumental figure, it would probably have been better if Burgess had produced a prose epic.

571 Wood, Michael. "The Ladies Vanish." **New York Review of Books**, v. 23, no. 15 (September 30, 1976) 40-42.

[Omnibus review. Also reviews **Beard's Roman Women** and some other books. For Burgess, see p. 42.] "I hope our salvation doesn't depend on **Moses**, a rambling, amiable epic in loose verse, which Burgess used as the basis of his script for a television film starring Burt Lancaster. It is far closer to DeMille's **Ten Commandments** than it is to the Book of Exodus, and although it reiterates some of Burgess's favorite themes — the heavy burden of free will, the need to respect and yet to order the multiplicity of the given world — it is finally too much of a lumbering anachronism to be anything other than a curiosity. Its language sometimes catches an interesting rhythm and flow, and a man who can incorporate *verbatim* whole stretches of the King James version of the Bible without breaking his stride or his diction is clearly some sort of master of pastiche, but the verse of **Moses** is too often just sad doggerel."

Napoleon Symphony

572 New York: Knopf, 1974.

573 London: Cape, 1974.

574 New York: Bantam Books, 1975, c1974. (Bantam book, Y2045) Pbk.

575 London: Corgi, 1976. Pbk.

575.2 New York: Norton, 1980, c1974.

Translations

576 French: **La symphonie Napoleon**. Paris: Laffont, 1977. Translated by Georges Belmont and Hortense Chabrier.

577 Spanish: **Sinfonia Napoleonica**. Madrid: Ultramar Editores, 1976.

Reviews

Burgess on his own work: "The Napoleon novel I'm writing apes the **Eroica** formally — irritable, quick, swiftly transitional in the first movement (up to Napoleon's coronation); slow, very leisurely, with a binding beat suggesting a funeral march for the second. This isn't pure fancy: It's an attempt to unify a mass of historical material in the comparatively brief space of about 150,000 words. As for the reader having to know about music — it doesn't really matter much." Burgess on Boney circa 1972: "My preparatory reading for the novel has taught me that I had really been bludgeoned by the ruling classes into hating Boney, since the common man saw him as the liberator. So he was, of course, for a time. The novelist's attitude to him will only make itself apparent in the course of the writing of the novel: the end of a book is unforeseeable when one is at its beginning. The question I must ask myself now is: is the novel to be comic or tragic? I do not see how it can be tragic: what was the flaw, where was the sin? He took the Revolution, purged of its extremer features, to countries that needed it. He wanted a united Europe. England, having chopped down her forests and exhausted her iron to defeat him, is now entering the Napoleonic dream. It is, in a way, comic, but not meant for laughs. I suppose my Napoleon novel will have to be comic in that way too." — Letter from Europe, **American Scholar**, v. 41, no. 3 (Summer 1972) 428.

578 Ackroyd, Peter. "Cacophony." **Spectator**, v. 233, no. 7631 (September 28, 1974) 405-06.

"This is, in fact, a conventionally imagined book which makes use of the iron disunities of our time and which whips up its language to a frenzy for no particular reason. Mr. Burgess employs a variety of styles in an excessively self-conscious way, with the result that any dialogue between recognisable human beings seems a trifle cracked . . . . You could no doubt call the novel a 'sport.' Mr. Burgess being fanciful and inventive and outrageous, but it is only what the closing epistolary verse would call an 'orthodox success.' We are not particularly amused."

579 Anon. Review of **Napoleon Symphony**. **Kirkus Reviews**, March 15, 1974, p. 318.

580 Anon. Review of **Napoleon Symphony**. **Publishers Weekly**, v. 205, no. 12 (March 25, 1974) 50.

"We see [Napoleon] in four sequences, as emergent, triumphant, descendant and finished. Of these the last is the weakest; the rich linguistic fare (often gut-level or dreamlike) has thinned and there's an uncomfortable note of mockery that seems directed against subject and author alike. But from gut-teral snarls to breathings of passion to squeals of despair, the narrative swells with sound, complex, Joycean, organized like music; and the exercise as a whole is ebullient, entertaining and crammed with *live* history — what one might call a glorious limited success."

581 Anon. Review of **Napoleon Symphony**. **New Yorker**, v. 50, no. 20 (July 8, 1974) 80.

A coarse, energetic book on N's career from the Italian campaign to his death. The substance and tone of this book and the Eroica Symphony are worlds apart. "The music is noble and grand; the book, for the most part, is embarrassingly base. Mr. Burgess seems to have doubted his project from the start (he says at the end that it can't be done), and therefore to have abandoned himself to soldierly bluster and idle historical gossip. It is hard to believe that Mr. Burgess's zest — so evident in his previous novels — could become tiresome, but that seems to have happened in this misguided venture.''

582 Anon. Review of **Napoleon Symphony**. **Booklist**, v. 70, no. 22 (July 15, 1974) 1230.

''A tour de force based on Beethoven's **Eroica** Symphony blends poetry, dialog, and descriptive passages into a profile which contains opinions on Napoleon's life and fortunes by individuals on all levels of European society. Napoleon is seen as an upstart ambitious Corsican, an emperor dictating codes of behavior, a military genius decrying mistakes of subordinates and, simultaneously, as an impatient lover enthralled by war as well as women's affections. A long epistle in heroic couplets that explains the novel's origins is appended.'' [Complete text of review.]

583 Anon. ''Promethus Re-Bound.'' **Times Literary Supplement**, 27 September 1974, p. 1033.

Burgess has a triune passion for structure, music and heroes. The first point is self-evident; the second can be proved by reference to **Malayan Trilogy** and **The Eve of St. Agnes** [i.e. Venus]. The third point is proved by this work in which Napoleon is presented, not as ''un fou qui se croyait Napoléon'' (to quote Cocteau) but as a grotesque Punch with Josephine his Judy. The novel, like the symphony, is in four movements. The first two invoke Napoleon while the succeeding two deal with Prometheus. Considers some of the parallels between the **Eroica** Symphony and the novel. ''Most dazzling [in Burgess' novel] is the set-piece display in the last movement, where Beethoven's variations spark off some newly composed specimens (not parodies) of English prose styles contemporary with the Emperor's exile. There has been little like it since Joyce . . . . Is Mr. Burgess perhaps making a virtuosity out of necessity? His fireworks, for all their Promethean heat, seem rather lacking in human warmth . . . . In an avowedly non-tragic novel, however, we need some positive assertion of human or divine value as a redeeming feature. And there is none. God seems to be missing . . . . The voice of the common man, the Unknown Warrior, is heard in each theatre of war contributing his regular and raucous stage whisper in lines such as 'When do we get some fucking leave, how about our back pay. I've got this pain in the balls citizen sergeant.' Again the Joycean overtones are evident, but the lingo recalls the Home Guard more readily than the Old Guard.''

584 Anon. Review of **Napoleon Symphony**. **Economist**, v. 253, no. 6849 (November 30, 1974) 7.

[See the ''Survey'' section of this journal.] It does not provide the pleasure one expects from this enormously erudite and frighteningly prolific novelist. He is — searing indictment — too clever by half. Burgess deserves an Alpha for ingenuity, but dammitall, who can have the **Eroica** and the life of Napoleon filed in his head for ready reference? ''And if this sounds like the vindictive lash of envy, it is after all wielded by one who has not yet positively identified more than three of the stylistic sources for the brilliant series of pastiches (Mr. Burgess himself disclaims parody) that match the variations on the Prometheus theme in the finale of the **Eroica**, nor found the musical equivalent in Beethoven to the snatch of Arabic in Burgess' scherzo.''

585 Anon. Notice of **Napoleon Symphony**. **New York Times Book Review**, 1 December 1974, p. 70.

[Compressed reprint of earlier **Times** review. See #610.]

586 Anon. Notice of **Napoleon Symphony**. **Washington Post Book World**, 8 December 1974, p. 8.

''Fancy a cavalry charge through language, galloping off with Napoleon and Anthony Burgess, to the strains of the Eroica. A novel of Joycean virtuosity.'' [Complete text of notice.]

587 Anon. Review of **Napoleon Symphony**. **Publishers Weekly**, v. 208, no. 15 (October 13, 1975) 113.

[Review of Bantam pbk. ed.] Quotes and compresses the earlier PW review. See #580.]

588 Anon. Review of **Napoleon Symphony**. **Sunday Times** (London), no. 7,979 (May 16, 1976) 39.

[Review of Corgi pbk. ed.] ''Exuberant foray into historical fiction (1974) in four movements, suitably, with the St. Helena finals *adagio assais* the little man with halitosis and indigestion also has heartburn of another kind between (splendid) set-piece battles, for Josephine is misbehaving in Paris even as Buonaparte begins a most compromising relationship with the exquisite boy Czar, Alexander.'' [Complete text of review.]

589 Bayley, John. "From the Ridiculous to the Ridiculous." **New York Review of Books**, v. 21, no. 14 (September 19, 1974) 32.

In his habitual fertility, and his louche congenial knockabout confidence, Burgess reminds us of Nashe or Deloney. Like these Elizabethan writers, and unlike (say) James Joyce, Scott Fitzgerald or Anthony Powell, Burgess always seems to be in a literary workshop standing knee-deep in the shavings of new methods and grimed with the metallic filings of bright ideas. The symphonic stuff is easy to disregard; it is no more than bits of string. Burgess is immensely well read on the period; his interest lies in the psychology and motive of the Napleonic era that wooed, applauded and finally rejected Napoleon. His portrait of N. is variously reminiscent of the Bloomsian figures of his Shakespeare and Enderby: observant, civilized, distracted, victimized and endowed with a rich stream of consciousness. Burgess is an admirable popularizer of the techniques introduced by James Joyce. Quotes Napoleon's account of his meeting with the Queen of Prussia and comments that it is boneless stuff, with no skeleton of a point beneath it. The scene between N and Alexander is well done. So are certain scenes in which the grandiloquence of generals is juxtaposed to the pithiness of the foot soldiers. As for history, "Mr. Burgess is far too intelligent and thoughtful a writer not to have reflected on the curious fact that we can no longer render the past in terms of its pomp and cirumstance, the sublime as well as the ridiculous. We can only do it — perhaps we can only do ourselves too? — as creatures of fantasy and farce."

590 Blythe, Ronald. "Imperial Theme." **Sunday Times** (London), no. 7,894 (September 29, 1974) 39.

Burgess, like Wordsworth, is outraged by the spectacle of the republican Napoleon dripping with sceptres and diadems. The writing is audacious, bursting with energy and incessantly absorbing. The coronation scene is one of the most remarkable chapters in this very remarkable novel. "Burgess' great achievement is to have created a sparkling gloss on contemporary disillusionment with Napoleon. His build-up of the climate in which such heroics thrive, perfervid nationalism supported by sham notions of the Greco-Roman civilisations, etc., is often so exciting as to occasionally defeat its object . . . . As mere entertainment it is unique, as a tract it is salutary with a vengeance."

591 Chipchase, Paul. "Imperial Rag." **Tablet**, v. 228, no. 7014 (December 7, 1974) 1185-86.

"It is a dream novel, full of transformations, dreamed by an impassioned linguist . . . . [Burgess'] ingenuity is inexhaustible; there is no single page in the book which does not deserve some future scholiast's ravishment and annotation. And lest the reader should, without reading it, despise **Napoleon Symphony** as a boring book full of party tricks, let me say a) that is more *consistently* funny than any book of Mr. Burgess's that I know, and b) that it even makes the old Corsican gangster and tyrant interesting . . . . He is particularly good at deaths and means. And his own prose, when he is not being a ventriloquest, is invariably thick and solid and mouthfilling; he has proved himself the poet of all puzzled combatants 'coughing gunfog and thunder,' and about to die . . . . **Napoleon Symphony** is a rich vast growling narrative poem sometimes in prose. The thought that wove it never dropped a stitch."

592 Fawcett, Graham. "Symphonic Variations." **Books and Bookmen**, v. 20 (January 1975) 49-50.

Writers have long been fascinated by the idea of using musical forms, and by discovering what music and the literary arts have in common. Quotes Pope, Huxley, Gide, Strindberg, and Flaubert on the subject. "Readers who go to **Napoleon Symphony** [in the spirit that 'communication is the whatness of the communication'] will certainly be beguiled. By odd bars to start with: like 'amanuensal pencils', 'the horns wound louder', 'Tilsit ham and Niemen salmon,' 'water the plaudits of multitudes.' A roll-call of citizens (the same names) like trumpets leading to something else (always different). Soldiers gasping for breath, air, women, sleep, booze, moan in circles, oaths ringing like home-notes. Refrains in march-time whip up the pace. Three voices overhead speaking at once, the print changes case for each, it works. Weathercocks, being double-sided, swing round at the repetition of weathercock six times in seven lines. Fast writing makes sounds without vowels, acrostics run, double-takes stop dead ('the turning on the teller of the incredible believable'), tricks of sound and sight . . . . [Burgess'] dedication to a full use and extension of language and the intrinsic power of his subject-matter explain a consistent aim: to remind readers of the novel that the language still has enormous potential untapped by Englishmen; to entertain and not to bore; to use comedy as a toy weapon whose well set-up thrusts will make rhetorical address more acceptable (a lesson available for learning since Boccaccio); and to explode (again) the fallacy of experimental = meaningless by taking on the challenge of Joyce 'to exploit myth, symbol and language and to eschew contrivances of plot'.''

593 Glendinning, Victoria. "Hero Worship." **New Statesman**, v. 88, no. 2271 (September 27, 1974) 435.

[Omnibus review.] The heart sinks, the eyes glaze when faced with the prospect of reading Burgess; his writing sets up an initial hostility because it is so noisy. In this study of Napoleon, a violent amalgam of intellect and physicality, his debt to James Joyce is all-pervasive. In the final section, in which N talks to girls and ghosts of girls, something brilliantly special happens and Burgess fingers the wafer-thin membrane between the ridiculous and the sublime; she surrendered utterly.

594 Halio, Jay L. "Love and the Grotesque." **Southern Review**, v. 11, no. 4 (October 1975) 942-948.

[Omnibus review. For Burgess, see p. 948.] Napoleon is a comic grotesque, and Burgess' success is analogous to Byron's in **Don Juan**. Quotes from the "Epistle to the Reader." Observes that, to a man untrained in music, the four movements of the novel seem to have only the slightest relationship to the **Eroica**.

595 Heidenry, John Notice of **Napoleon Symphony**. **Commonweal**, v. 101, no. 9 (December 6, 1974) 239.

Nominates book as his best unread novel, but warns readers he has found other Burgess fiction gross.

596 Kermode, Frank. "The Burgess Emperor." **Manchester Guardian Weekly**, v. 111, no. 14 (October 5, 1974) 19.

"It is fair to say that one could read the novel with great pleasure without bothering too much about Beethoven, provided only that one has a clear memory of the main events of Napoleon's career; for me a rapid read through the biographies of J.M. Thompson and Felix Markham was a necessary pro-paedeutic, and there were still illusions [allusions?] I didn't pick up. But it's worth the trouble. The brio of the first movement is extraordinary . . . . The funeral march is a contrapuntal treatment of dreams and memories . . . . The finale mimics Beethoven's Promethean variations by means of parody, though the author, for some reason, expressly says in concluding epistle that this is not so . . . . People who know a lot about Napoleon and a lot about music as well will spot or explain a good deal that others may miss. I hope they don't make it seem laborious . . . . [Burgess] is writing very serious comedy and doing it with extraordinary resource, variety and pace. And if his imagination must, in the last analysis seem un-Beethovenian, those are still Beethovenian qualities."

597 Lennon, Peter. Notice of **Napoleon Symphony**. **Sunday Times** (London), no. 7903 (December 1, 1974) 39.

Lennon picks **Napoleon Symphony** as the best book of the year and gives it fifty words of comment.

598 McKenzie, Robb. Review of **Napoleon Symphony**. **Library Journal**, v. 99, no. 10 (May 15, 1974) 1406.

"The expected verbal roulades are abundant, together with the bawdy, the scatalogical, the witty. The English is liberally peppered with expressions from many other languages and the whole possesses an almost Joycean inventiveness. Few of the characters are particularly attractive, but they weren't in real life. They are complex and believably human, de Stael most of all. The retreat from Borodino reads with mounting horror, while the period of exile on St. Helena almost elicits pity. The novel is massive and innovative in plan, and though the execution is not wholly successful, it fails on a level far higher than most novels ever attain."

599 Mills, John. Review of **Napoleon Symphony**. **Queen's Quarterly**, v. 82, no. 2 (Summer 1975) 292-94.

Structurally, the novel starts, to use the language of John N. Burk, with an insignificant figure on the common chord. Then Burgess plunges into the *allegro con brio* which, to quote Burk again, gives the impression that the pencil can hardly keep pace with the outpouring thoughts. In the *scherzo* Beethoven introduced a theme he had already used in his ballet music **Prometheus**. Burgess, following Beethoven, introduces a play about Prometheus, which Naploeon watches with some suspicion. Burgess is not a didactic writer, and in this book his subject is language itself rather than its freakish central character [Napoleon]. It is not an analysis of history, but a script devoid of message and "crammed with a host of minor figures, all of them slightly mad — gourmets, con-men, courtesans, marshals, diplomats, queens, Napoleon himself — all of them driven by their bright, particular humours and seen from the outside and slightly above. . . . and given robust, idiosyncratic lines to speak while Burgess hops exuberantly across a linguistic gamut ranging from soldier's demotic to a gratuituous, extended and very funny parody of Henry James to present his true hero — the shaping spirit of the artist. There are more profound writers than Burgess in the canon but I can think of few who are so literate and no one who is as marvellously entertaining. **Napoleon Symphony** is, in my opinion, the best novel so far in his extraordinary career.''

600 Mirsky, Mark. "A Model Offering with Heroic Overtones." **Washington Post Book World**, 26 May 1974, p. 1-3.

"In an age of dull prose, jargon of sociology and psychology, incessant buzz of gossip, journal, the endless dribble of weepy-eyed ghetto hysterics, tin clatter of avant-garde mobiles, hollow academic puling: a reader who delights in succulent phrase, unctuous pap, the zest of word play and a saucy paragraph, must fall on each new work of Anthony Burgess with ravenous appetite." Some of his previous works have been mere dessert trifles; this is a full, groaning gourmand's table. It is arguably the truest form of biography; it compels us to believe we are in Napoleon's presence. By comparison, Tolstoy's portrait is stiff and prissy, and Burgess shows a dazzling generalship of his raw materials. The first 136 breathless pages bring us to Napoleon's coronation, while the next 160 are filled with melancholy and foreboding, and the emperor seems awkward, clumsy and confused when confronted by the naive, passionately nationalistic Stapps. "At the end the author stretches prose credulity to the breaking point in a set of parodies almost as elaborate as his real hero, First Consul James Joyce. Here in a final burst of fireworks, Burgess at his most characteristic, craziest, surpasses the high fun of the invented language in **A Clockwork Orange**. The emperor finishes as a chuckle in the divine symphony. A rococo performance of Prometheus, love-making in Poland, past battles, return to haunt Napoleon on St. Helena, as the author floats into a deft, rapid splicing of the hero's last fevered days, his life now all reflection and therefore all Burgess's, all dreams, all poetry.''

601 Morris, Robert K. "With Flourish of Hautboys." **Nation**, v. 219, nos. 1-3 (August 3, 1974) 87-88.

"Though writing under the pen-umbrage of Leo [Tolstoy] and [Henry] James, and under the longer shadows of Napoleon and Beethoven, Burgess has managed to elude them all and come up with an original, wild, picaresque extravaganza that is pure sunburst and probably his best novel . . . . Yet, oddly enough, the structures and techniques of **Napoleon Symphony** are not its greatest assets. A symphony after all unites to create one grand effect, and that effect here is Napoleon. *Pace* Tolstoy, Hugo, Ludwig, Segur, Caulaincourt, and innumerable other writers of biography and history and apocrypha, Burgess has given us a Napoleon for our time. He is N, *lui*, Napoleon, Bonaparte, Buonaparte, Nabuliune; he is lover, general, doting father, gourmandizer, whoremonger, cuckold, dyspeptic, tyrant, Emperor, genial Mafia cutthroat, martyr, myth. And on all counts he is Prometheus, the fire god; whether fired by passion, by the zeal for war, by his ambition, by the burning certainty of his morality and immortality, or whether chained to the promontories of history, his liver rotted from Courvoisier, his fingers probing the psychosomatic and physical wound . . . . In the long run, I suppose, it is Beethoven who gobbles up Napoleon and Burgess . . . . **Napoleon Symphony** is alive, lush, lyric, human, witty and wildly comic.''

602 Murray, John J. Review of **Napoleon Symphony**. **Best Sellers**, v. 34, no. 7 (July 1, 1974) 154-55.

Confines himself to two themes: the novel as musical composition and the novel as total dialogue. Burgess is almost overtrained to weave his grand artistic webs. He aims at the greatness of Mozart, but achieves the status of a witty but lesser John Cage. His conversational recitatives bear comparison with Landor's **Imaginary Conversations**; they are also a lot funnier. Witness Napoleon's night in bed with Josephine, N's tirade to his gutless "fighting 69th," his aspersions on Czar Nicholas' masculinity, and the political debate between N and Stapps. Quotes some dialogue to prove the second point. "The symphony ends, not with a dying fall, but with an autopsy upon the fallen dead. N's insides are dissected with the same kind of glee that historians of a psychoanalytic (Erikson) bent use in their dissecting, multi-volume biographies. All that's left of the poor Leone della Valle is a distended liver. Burgess' anti-eroica is also anti-war, in a co-see fan tutti fruity sort of way. Consider the following which is, I think, as good as Tolstoy, and almost as good as **Catch-22**.

> So snow and snow and everything was snow
> And slow in snowy woe the soldiers go
> Groaning at snowy woe and moaning: oh.

603 Nordell, Roderick. "Anthony Burgess' Experiment." **Christian Science Monitor**, 29 May 1974, p. 5.

A sometimes elegant, sometimes vulgar self-styled comic novel less reminiscent of music than cinema. "Contrary to the symphony's mood, Mr. Burgess simplistically relates Napleon's military adventures to his amorous ones . . . . The relentless military profanity sounds all too much like that of a later day, as do the foreboding references to gas chambers, secret police, and other elements of 20th-century tyranny." It seems destined to be a film script.

604 O'Hara, J.D. Review of **Napoleon Symphony**. **New Republic**, v. 171, nos. 8-9 (August 31, 1974) 32.

Gives an account of N's career, stresses the battles and the casualties, and N's execution of 4,000 prisoners. Observes that Burgess' N. dreams wistfully of sophisticated gas chambers and that N's violent attempt to unify Europe produced a backlash of irrational patriotism. Burgess must plainly labor to transmute his all too real ogre into a picaresque Punch. His medium is, of course, words. "He loves words, and allusions too. Here Josephine dallies in a gondola under T.S. Eliot's glum eye ('Lights lights'), Wordsworth writes of meeting Napoleon as a pudgy gardener on St. Helena, two soldiers plagiarize **The Nigger of the Narcissus**, a Jamesian sybil quotes Hopkins, Shem the Penman is everywhere, and of course there's lots of fustian, the literary equivalent of bombardment being bombast."

605 P[rescott], P[eter] S. "The **Eroica** Comedy." **Newsweek**, v. 83, no. 21 (May 27, 1974) 85-86.

Burgess writes with brio, with exuberance and sophistication and wit. His Napoleon is a bad lover, prone to deliver lectures on history and generalship, but he is not a clown. Burgess is clearly fond of him and treats him sentimentally. "Burgess appears to have had a grand time writing it, cramming into it jokes, puns, rhymes, lugubrious details and some marvelous special effects, yet he has kept it light and bouncy — good fun to read."

606 Raban, Jonathan. "What Shall We Do About Anthony Burgess?" **Encounter**, v. 43, no. 5 (November 1974) 83-88.

[Omnibus review. Also reviews **Clockwork Testament**.] It is as long, complicated and intermittently boring as the whole of the Old Testament. Burgess' Epistle to the Reader is indispensable to an understanding of the work, but the correspondences between Burgess' novel and Beethoven's Eroica, even if worked out in detail, will not make the work better or worse as a novel. The book is a vast exercise in parody and pastiche. "In battle and on the march, Burgess takes off from Joyce into a stream of something — not quite consciousness, exactly — but more a lot of get out of my line of fire before I spew, you prickless creampuff, etcetera . . . . The trouble is that [the ideas] have rather more force than the novel itself . . . . For Burgess has almost every talent needed by a great novelist — immense intelligence, inventive vigour, a wonderful sense of the play of language, a genius for pastiche — except one. He cannot make another human being come to life on the page. He has a single vivid character: an all-purpose *homme moyen sensuel* who goes under the name of "Enderby" or "Anthony Burgess," and farts and scratches his way through seedy cities and knockabout scrapes. The rest are sawdust . . . ." [See also #197.]

607 Ratcliffe, Michael. "Set to Beethoven." **Times** (London), no. 59,202 (September 1974) p. 10.

"The fact that, as Mr. Burgess himself remarks, the transliteration of musical sounds and forms into letters, words and sentences defeated the authors of **Point Counter Point**, the **Four Quartets** and **Ulysses** is not going to deter him from having a bash. The fact that a thing is known, preferably proved, to be impossible, has never deterred him from having a bash before; it is one of his most English, most Romantic and most likable qualities, and it will always be one for which he is consistently attacked as impertinent in England." Provides plot summary which compares the novel and the **Eroica**. Confesses he read the novel with the OED and his old Kleiber recording of the Symphony at hand, and observes that the novel is singularly short of any quality that could be called classical. It is often chaotic and clumsy, and the coarseness of the first two movements dulls the work and makes it heavy. "When, like Mr. Burgess, you are aiming for Nabokov, the lack of a truly fastidious wit is serious, and a distracting affection for Rabelais will only jog your arm. These two — the bringer of **Pale Fire** and the lord of Gargantuan misrule — have fought for possession of Mr. Burgess's talents before, but never so fiercely, or inconclusively, as here." It is a complex, ambitious and higly original novel. Burgess is often neglected on first publication. Who knows? in ten years the failure may not signify.

608 Sage, Lorna. Review of **Napoleon Symphony**. **Observer** (London), 29 September 1974, p. 31.

This celebratory autopsy on the long dead, long suffering Emperor demonstrates that Burgess gets a lot of horrid pleasure out of describing the megalomaniac energy that enables a man to treat the map of Europe as though it was written in the palm of his hand. The main effect of the Eroica on Burgess' fictional dialect is to send him off into exuberant pastiche. "A wonderful deadness: which is really the paradox of Anthony Burgess, as it is with so many of the writers who currently get the best fun out of the novel — he is original, inventive, idiosyncratic even, and yet the ingredients are synthetic, ready-made. His own attitude to this, so far as one can extricate anything so direct from [the novel] is determinedly, manically cheerful. Better the collective unwisdom of the verbal stew, he would say, than any tyrannous signature." [The meaning of this apparently profound passage is remarkably unclear.]

609 Sale, Roger. "Fooling Around, and Serious Business." **Hudson Review**, v. 27, no. 4 (Winter 1974-75) 623-35.

[Omnibus review. For Burgess, see pp. 627-28.] Quotes a passage ("I could practically feel my lower jaw dropping into my ball sack with the sheer fucking astonishment of it") and comments: "Not much Beethoven there, more like Pynchon, just as much of the rest is like Joyce. But Burgess isn't brilliant and sick like Pynchon, or willing to work at it for years like Joyce, or great like Beethoven. He will not discipline himself, and his 21st book is neither bad nor good and so ranks as a disappointment."

610 Sanborn, Sara. Review of **Napoleon Symphony**. **New York Times Book Review**, 9 June 1974, p. 5.

Burgess has endearingly deprecated his own work in the closing verses, and the novel is a curiosity: cacophonous confusing, claustrophobic. "There is little sense of historical time, place and condition; except for the musical tie-in, the novel could as well have been about Henry V or Bismarck. This is part of the point, though it is unlikely that the blandness of the effect was intended." Essentially, the book is not so much about Napoleon but about Anthony Burgess writing a novel. As such, it has many of the customary Burgess embellishments, but the linguistic flourishes often seem gratuitous "except of course for the fun of it. And that is saying a good deal. Even when we don't know what all the pyrotechnics are celebrating, we can still enjoy a good display."

611 Sheppard, R.Z. "Grand Illusions." **Time**, v. 103, no. 21 (May 27, 1974) 92.

In this work, variously reminiscent of Dickens, Tennyson and Wordsworth, with an occasional gash of Gerard Manley Hopkins' gold-vermilion, Burgess has reached for everything from kazoos to pipe organs. "On the broader screen of history, Burgess gets his effects by balancing the horrors of war with some of the absurdities of political power and private weaknesses . . . . Burgess grants Napoleon both genius and idealism, but has great fun exploring the Emperor's lack of moral sensitivity and aesthetic judgment. As the torch carrier of the Enlightenment, a kind of social engineer who believed man was perfectible through political institutions, Burgess's Napoleon ignores the intransigent nature of evil." Like Beethoven, Burgess appears to agree that N was not a hero and, in the final fugue of ideas in which N appears to confront Clio, the muse of History, it is made plain that the composer's art is more important than the general's military skill. [Also includes brief interview with Burgess in his Roman apartment.]

612 Tennant, Emma. "Josephine Wheels." **Listener**, v. 92, no. 2378 (October 24, 1974) 552.

The Burgess view of Napoleon the man transforms him into a creature of belches, afflicted by heart-burn and surrounded by the strong smell of garlicky Corsican sausage. The book makes use of film cutting techniques "to give the life, the mind, the sex, the liver of Napoleon Buonaparte, all running at the same time and, one feels by the end of the book, well into its fifth glorious year." The example of Dickens provides Burgess with lively coarse dialogue and characters, while Joyce has plainly influenced the long monologues, the puns, and the long descriptive passages. One aspect of the book, Napoleon's attempt to mould and twist the contours of Europe and Egypt into the desired contours of the Beauhar-nais body, is not successful. "In the effort to show the comic side of heroism, the farce of the conqueror whose loved one lies with a pretty officer while men lie groaning from dysentery and die bloated from the poisoned waters of the Nile, the imagery becomes strained, vulgar-Freudian.'' The account of the Egyptian campaign, and Napoleon's dinner for his family when the succession issue is settled, are minor masterpieces. The book includes small scenes in which the sense of reality is palpable, but **Napoleon Symphony**, like **The Wanting Seed** and **A Clockwork Orange**, reads like a nightmare future, and if Napoleon had never existed, Burgess would have had to invent him.

613 Trewin, Ion. "Highjinks." **Times** (London), v. 59,693 (May 1, 1976) 11.

[Omnibus review. Review of Corgi pbk. ed.] "In fact, it is a work of astonishing intellectual capacity, although I don't pretend to have caught all the allusions, all the nuances. Burgess sees Napoleon with a contemporary eye and all the hang-ups — hypochondria, image massaging and of course, Josephine. It's a novel I'm sure I will turn to again and again, finding new pleasures at each reading." [Virtually complete text of review.]

New York

614 Amsterdam: Time-Life International (Nederland), 1976. By Anthony Burgess and the editors of Time-Life Books. With photographs by Dan Budnik.

Reviews

615 Anon. Review of **New York**. **Publishers Weekly**, v. 211, no. 9 (February 28, 1977) 115.

"Burgess's colorful, witty, discerning and compassionate writing is sustained through chapters on Harlem, Broadway, street life, Manhattan's spires, its rivers, bridges, ethnic (and other) parades, Central Park, the outer boroughs — and the magic is doubled by the march of photos (mostly big and in color) by Time-Life staffers. It's a love song which may cause some New Yorkers to choke up."

616 Fisher, Antonia. "Tales of Two Cities." **Sunday Times** (London), no. 8030 (May 15, 1977) 41.

Burgess is quite accomplished enough to celebrate New York. The balance between text and illustration has been well drawn, and the book is very pleasant.

617 Loprete, Nicholas J. Review of **New York**. **Best Sellers**, v. 37, no. 4 (July 1977) 115.

It successfully captures the look, feel, pulse, pain, pleasures, failures and incomparable achievements of the world's premier cities. Burgess' text is succinct and perceptive, and gives us an expert guided tour of New York's group of neighboring communities. "I can think of no better moment for this book to appear than now when it is fashionable to snicker at New York's financial plight, shudder at its crime, condemn its huge welfare system. Perhaps Mr. Burgess' honesty and warmth, and the camera artists who have complemented his text with splendid and remarkable photographs will convince those of little vision that New York is not dead . . . ."

618 Rickleps, Roger. "A Blood-and-Bach Look at Gotham." **Wall Street Journal**, 6 June 1977, p. 16.

In Burgess' New York, men play Bach on clarinets while a mugged man's blood drains unheeded into the gutter. The blood and Bach image of N.Y.C. seems hopelessly entrenched. Then what of the other stereotypes that damn this Sodom and Gomorra. Does it lead to anxiety? Nonsense: to intellectual stimulus. The infamous flight to the suburbs? Nothing new, as Burgess well attests. Note, for example, the joys of Yiddish: the fearful curses ("A fire should burn in his heart, God forbid") sanctioned by nominal cancellation. The photographs are excellent; the problems are fairly explored (perhaps Burgess overplays the seamy and bizarre); and the time has come to recognize that New York is stimulating, blessed with a mild climate, excellent restaurants and fabulous cultural life. "But enough of this tirade. If Burgess feels an enthusiasm for New York that is slightly more qualified than my own, he clearly feels that the Bach outweighs the blood."

1985

619 Boston: Little, Brown, 1978.

620 London: Hutchinson, 1978.

Reviews

621 Amiel, Barbara. "The Unions and the Proles Are Watching You." **Macleans**, v. 91, no. 26 (November 26, 1978) 61-62.

In contrast to Old Etonian Orwell, lower-middle-class Burgess sees the working class as very ordinary: filled with the same greed, stupidity and envy that animates their upper-class counterparts. His novel is written with the power and intensity of a superb craftsman. His description of a totalitarian syndicalist society is less a prediction than the present transposed to the future: "the school curriculum of the women's — gay — multiracial -anti-intellectual libbers. . . is virtually identical with Canada's evolving 'progressive' educational guidelines."

622 Amis, Kingsley. "Orwell and Beyond." **Observer** (London), 1 October 1978, 34.

Burgess, that protean performer, has once again broken new ground, but what exactly he has done is not altogether so clear. Burgess' view that **1984** is a comic transcription of the drab conditions of post-war London is unjustified. His contention that Orwell's book must justify itself as literal prophecy is strange coming from a novelist as imaginative and genuine as Burgess. "Orwell was not prophesying; if he had been, the best — the only good — parts of the book would have been those few references to metrication, by which he meant not to predict, but to illustrate the homogenising and de-flavouring of life under Big Brother . . . . **1984** is as unaffected by its discordance with any possible **1984** as is **The First Men in the Moon** (1901) by improved lunar observation." His miscellaneous remarks on freedom, good and evil, right and wrong, the State, freedom, Bakunin and anarchism and youth are entertaining, but the novel **1985** suffers by comparison with **1984** and nothing can save him, in his foolhardy self-cleft stick, from being damaged by the Orwell comparison "not or not necessarily on grounds of merit but to the extent that ordered societies, like that of **1984**, differ widely, while states of chaos, as in **1985**, resemble one another. This is not new ground any more."

623 Amis, Martin. "A Stoked-Up 1976." **New York Times Book Review**, 19 November 1978, pp. 3, 60, 62.

Burgess' fiction was undoubtedly conceived in the year 1976 — when the pound was pitiably weak, the Arabs ("like the white gowns of a new and suddenly universal priesthood of pure money") were overrunning the city, the unions revealed that the unions ruled the country, and it was a sweaty time for all of us here. [The Europe of 1976 was notably warm: it produced an excellent vintage.] Something in Mr. Burgess wants his projected forecast to be accurate. Suspects that Burgess is depressed that the crisis turned out to be partial and temporary. The first part of this book, the evocation of London in 1948, when nothing worked, and cheap socks deliquesced beneath your feet, includes much of Mr. Burgess' sociopolitical musings. The second part makes one realize the extent of his nerve, or his nervelessness. He rejects a proven classic; he rejects his own critical dictum that the novelist only knows the past; and the result is a failure. Mr. Burgess' projection fails to interest, much less to terrify. "Alas, Mr. Burgess's failure is, vexingly, boringly, ineffably, a failure of language. [His] recent prose is characterized by professional haste and a desire to be a stylist. The result is a knotted, cadenced, bogus lustiness: every sentence is sure to contain some virile quirk or other, often (you feel) as a product of will rather than of inspiration or care." The best reason for reading **1985** is that it makes you want to reread **1984**.

624 Anon. Review of **1985**. **Kirkus Reviews**, August 1, 1978, p. 822.

625 Anon. Review of **1985**. **Booklist**, v. 75, no. 2 (September 15, 1978) 146.

"In an opening essay, Burgess considers Orwell's work not so much a moral fable of the future as a grim, comic commentary on postwar England; social criticism as well as literary interpretation is brought to bear in a playful yet provocative exegesis. The second part contains a short novel, which updates and revises Orwell with more contemporary observations as Burgess extrapolates his own vision of the future from present conditions.''

626 Anon. Review of **1985**. **Publishers Weekly**, v. 214, no. 12 (September 18, 1978) 161.

Burgess makes very clear how much Orwell's **1984** is indebted to London's year 1948. As we follow our hero's progressively ''picaresque and increasingly desperate adventures we may be entitled to a twinge of fear about what does indeed lie ahead for all of us. Anthony Burgess now lives in Monaco — no wonder.''

627 Anon. Review of **1985**. **Economist**, v. 269, no. 7050 (October 14, 1978) 144.

''It can be seen that Mr. Burgess' cacotopia is reasonably extrapolated from existing conditions. Maybe the trends it takes to a logical and horrible conclusion exist more strongly in newspapers — the exile's poison — than among people in England; but they are trends, not just the crapulous fantasies of somebody reacting to infrequent visits to our native squalor from congenial Monaco. On that basis **1985** needs to be taken seriously. Do not be fooled by the briskness and panache: unborn tomorrow is going to be unbearable. It was, after all, George Orwell who said (quoting Cyril Connolly) that intellectuals were always right about what was going to happen even if they were unreliable about when it would happen.''

628 Anon. Review of **1985**. **Choice**, v. 15, no. 12 (February 1979) 1662.

''His **1985** is a brilliant piece — and a frightening projection: an England tyrannized by the unions, held in fief by the Araba oil sheiks, its citizens' freedom — or will — to choose almost gone. His discussion of Orwell's premises and the plight of modern man is brilliant as well. Finally, his version of the workers' English, the officially sanctioned speech in **1985**, is a biting reduction to absurdity of the leveling — linguistic and otherwise — that threatens the very notion of excellence in our society.''

629 Deedy, John. ''Anthony Burgess: **1985**.'' **Critic**, v. 37 no. 12 (January 1979) 2-3.

The insights flash and Burgess admires his subject, but his assessment that **1984** is a comic translation of 1948 is unfair. The work conveys far more than that. Suggests that Burgess' view of the future will stand more revision than that of Orwell. There is a good deal of large satire and hyperbole in Burgess' vision of the future, and it is a fair bet that Orwell connects with the larger number of historical probabilities. Burgess is a strong social critic, but somewhat too hard on the younger generation. Wishes Burgess had explained his aside that Vatican II has drained Christianity and the West ''of solid and belligerent belief.''

630 Elledge, Jim. Review of **1985**. **Library Journal**, v. 103, no. 16 (September 15, 1978) 1765.

A masterful novella and an absorbing portrait of contemporary ills and fear projected into the future.

631 Fraser, G.S. ''Anthony Longmug?'' **Listener**, v. 100, no. 2582 (October 19, 1978) 517-18.

This story of a Britain ruled by tyrannical trade unions and tee-totalling Arabs, is decidedly thin, and the critical commentary on Orwell's **1984** does nothing to redeem the book. Orwell's novel is a cry of disgust and despair from a dying man and not, as Burgess claims, fundamentally a comedy. The discussion of good and evil, right and wrong, as if they were vulgarly secular matters, is nonsense both as ordinary philosophy and moral theology. His remarks on the fornication in **1984** are reminiscent of Lord Longford or Malcolm Muggeridge, but he is right in pointing out that Orwell's **1984** is really 1948. ''Orwell's imperfect book will always have some power over anyone who has felt that stinking sweat of fear [the fear of being a totally isolated target of hostility]. Perhaps Burgess has had the good luck not to. In any case, he fails to make our flesh creep.''

632 Granetz, Marc. Review of **1985**. **New Republic**, v. 179, no. 21 (November 18, 1978) 39.

Burgess' criticisms of **1984** are neither surprising nor subtle although some of his specific comments are of greater interest. One wishes Burgess, whose linguistic observations are always lively and often brilliant, had spent more on Newspeak. Burgess does not seem to value Orwell's book on any terms other than the accuracy of its predictions. As for Burgess' own novella and predictions: the prophecy comes rather easily; **1985** is only seven years off. ''Occasionally the prose sparkles. But the fiction is thin; a bunch of issues are discoursed upon by lifeless characters. And the issues, often bluntly expressed, are stale. Bev's call for punishment of bystanders who won't get involved is the minimally-rehashed

Kitty Genovese case, and his crusade is studded with banal exclamations; 'I'm a human being, not a bloody number,' 'closed shop is a fact of life,' and 'How can one man's truth prevail'?'' **1984** is artistic; **1985** is journalistic.

633 Hopkinson, T. Review of **1985**. **British Book News**, February 1, 1979, pp. 167-68.

Burgess' examination of the significance — and his analysis of the limitations — of **1984**, is the most searching to which that book has been subjected. It is hard to resist his conclusion that the forces which offer an effective challenge to state tyranny (religion and love) never appear in Orwell's book at all. The novella is another matter. "A thin thread of story runs through **1985** just as it ran through **1984**; but Burgess's explosive film-script style of writing renders it difficult to follow, and it is in any case unimportant. The meat of his book lies in his criticism of contemporary life and present-day values, expressed in the first half as argument and depicted by way of illustration in the second."

634 Irwin, Michael. "Tucland, Their Tuckland." **Times Literary Supplement**, 6 October 1978, p. 1109.

[Moderately good plot summary.] Crucial to the fable is the mistaken belief that 'liberty' has no role in public life — only in the private world of thought and imagination. But, although Bev Jones puts on a better show than Winston Smith (sharper, cheekier, more resilient), the whole cacotopia seems to lack commitment or imaginative energy. The essay on Orwell's **1984** is sometimes lively and shrewd, but it conveys little that is new. That Orwell was describing postwar London is a familiar fact; and Orwell's debt to Zamyatin's **We** was pointed out by Isaac Deutscher in 1954. Orwell conveys passion; Burgess intimates sport. "In its general effect the novel resembles a long preface by Bernard Shaw. It is witty, wide-ranging, often surprising, quite often wise — yet there is somehow a failure of seriousness or of coherence that makes the arguments unpersuasive."

635 Jamal, Zahir. "Kid Brother." **New Statesman**, v. 96, no. 2481 (October 6, 1978) 444.

The essay argues that Orwell's book is old religion: black comedy, a witty transcript of 1948 London. Easily the most readable parts of this essay are those where he lets himself drift back into the kind of mental state in which Orwell's book was first conceived. Considers how, as the ominous date approaches, Orwell's book is not likely to prove accurate prophecy. As for the fiction which follows, "Just how sorrily **1985** shoulders its imaginative duties is virtually impossible to convey. The setting in which Mr. Burgess has chosen to float his propositions could scarcely have been a grubbier amalgam of small worries and irritations. Enfeebled by its surroundings, a once-dextrous ingenuity struggles unavailingly with a narrative of surpassing silliness." An opportunity is missed when, in the form of the *Kumina* gangs, Burgess briefly weds culture to anarchy in a sly parody of the old Arnoldian antithesis. The decline of that unfortunate character Bev Jones might, in more caring hands, have been passably interesting. As it is, he is encouraged to mount the pulpit and descant on human dignity in a comic opera. "It's part of the ineptitude which distinguishes **1985** that it should add to its difficulties by picking on a book many times its size."

636 James, Clive. "Looking Backward." **New York Review of Books**, v. 25, no. 18 (November 23, 1978) 16-18.

Discusses **The Wanting Seed** and **A Clockwork Orange** and compares both books to science fiction written by Frederik Pohl and C.M. Kornbluth. Zamyatin, Huxley and Orwell surpassed the sci-fi writers. Does Burgess? In the first place, his essay demonstrates with marvellous thoroughness that he has misunderstood Orwell. By insisting that novels deal with sense data rather than ideas, he deludes himself that Orwell's book deals with the sense data of London in 1948 when Orwell's true aim is to demonstrate the essence of the totalitarian state. Orwell's main aim was to make the nightmare intelligible and hand on an instructive myth. He insisted that you must not only be anti-fascist but anti-totalitarian. Now Burgess is much the lesser man, who gives the impression that the world's irritants are directly aimed at his individualistic self. The novel is a scrap heap of ideas. It extrapolates left-wing tendencies; it disregards those of the right. He sounds like the union busters of the British managerial class and "**1985** is a yelp of annoyance, already out of date before it is published. **1984**, a minatory illumination of the darkest propensities in human nature, will be pertinent forever."

637 King, Francis. "Last Man." **Spectator**, v. 241, no. 7840 (October 7, 1978) 22.

Some small inaccuracies: there is no evidence that Orwell ever wanted to call his book 1948; second, it was conceived as early as 1943; third, the meat and tobacco rations in **1984** were more generous than

Burgess suggests. He is also wrong about the tepid reception of the work; it was widely praised at the time, and became an immediate success. Of Burgess' brilliance as a critic there can be no doubt, and Burgess' three basic judgements (Orwell was a poor prophet; he loved his country more than his party; he found it impossible to turn himself into a proletarian) are irrefutable. The novella proves that "Burgess believes passionately in 'the right of man to loneliness, eccentricity, rebellion, genius'; and it is with Swiftian indignation that he lays into the puny levellers who would like to abolish that right. Three cheers!" Compares the book to Kingsley Amis' **Jake's Thing** and observes that, while Amis' book is droopily depressing, Burgess' work is charged with intellectual energy and thrust. Gloomily doubts that Burgess' better work will make the same stir.

638 Lacy, Allen. "Burgess's **1985**: 7 Years to Cacatopia [i.e. Cacotopia]." **Chronicle of Higher Education**, v. 17 (December 1978) 13.

A unique combination of philosophical fiction with literary/social criticism in which Burgess pays extended homage to Orwell's **1984** ("an extended metaphor of apprehension, an apocalyptical codex of our worst fears") but observes that Orwell's work was founded in his disgust with the conditions of 1948. "Burgess writes: 'It was a bad time for the body. One asked for the bread of minimal comfort and was offered instead the stone of progress.' Thus **1984** was not so much a warning about a Big Brother in our future as it was a protest against cheap and oily gin, a grim projection 36 years forward of a present that was highly uncongenial to Orwell's spiritual need of creaturely comfort." Orwell plainly could not love the workers, and his contempt for the majority of mankind is embedded in his book, notably in Emmanual Goldstein's remark that they can safely be granted intellectual liberty because they have no intellect. Burgess grants **1984** high marks for its sense data, its success in capturing the gritty and greasy feel of life in postwar London, and Burgess' **1985** is a brave new world built, not on the premise of an inhuman lust for power, but on self-seeking stupidity that ends in a vision of universal social paralysis. "Since Anthony Burgess has twice explored the worst of all possible futures in. . . **The Wanting Seed** and **A Clockwork Orange** — he knows the territory well. Particularly in his commentary on Orwell and in his waspish distaste for much of contemporary culture, **1985** is fascinating and quirky."

639 McLellan, Joseph. "O Brave New Worlds." **Washington Post Book World**, 12 November 1978, pp. 5, 8.

Burgess now seems to believe that his **A Clockwork Orange** was too didactic, too linguistically exhibitionistic, too little understood. By contrast, and perhaps by design, there is little in this book not intelligible to the average reader on a quick first reading. "For most writers, it would be a highly commendable performance; from Burgess, one expects more depth, more ambiguity, a richer texture both in the choice of words and in the sights, sounds and actions that the words convey." While his book includes some improbabilities, it is a straight-line, short-term projection. "The basic problem is that Burgess foresees a rather dreary tomorrow and that he portrays that dreariness a little too accurately for comfort."

640 Nairn, Tom. "Burgess's Prole-Bashing." **Manchester Guardian**, 15 October 1978, p. 21.

Burgess' book makes the point ("Bring the pliers, Bert, this geezer's got a fair number of pegs in his cake-hole") that rule by the proles will be as bad as Orwell's mysterious and sadistic power elite. With all its prole-bashing passion balanced by a sub-Joycean verbal effervescence, the book reads like a parody (neither telling nor funny) of the English literary dystopia. Burgess claims to be melodramatizing certain existing tendencies; regrettably, since it falls into the bookshops after three years of trade union quiescence, mass unemployment and dropping living standards, Burgess cannot even get the tendencies right. The two propositions that **1984** reflects the conditions of 1948, and that it is essentially a comic book, couple half-truth and artful paradox and add nothing to Orwell criticism. The work is a petty, meandering rivulet in a once great river of contemporary English reaction.

641 Nordell, Roderick. "Beyond **1984** But Not Up To It." **Christian Science Monitor**, 13 November 1978, p. B15.

What Burgess leaves out of his fictional account of a Britain dominated by the Trade Unions is, by his own account, the good sense and humanity of the average worker. "He admits to melodramatizing certain tendencies. And one wonders if, by any chance, he or his editors realized he did not have much of a novel here — and therefore he added the surrounding framework of criticism, self-interviews, and the marvelously wry 'Note on Workers' English (WE),' with its observations, borne out by some of the dialogue in the novel, that former obscenities 'have full lexical status in WE'.'' A self-indulgent performance that has added yet another kind of book to the varied Burgess canon.

642 Prescott, Peter S. Review of **1985**. **Newsweek**, v. 92, no. 15 (October 9, 1978) 105.

"Shaw at his windiest never set one of his plays against an equal volume of didactic prefaces, but Burgess has no such compunction." In his cacotopia, the collective lust for slothful contentment has as effectively quelled the life of the mind and the spirit as the hate and fear under Orwell's hypocritically violent regime. "Despite the impedimenta with which it is encumbered, this is an entertaining story that hews more closely to probability than did Orwell's — and therefore lacks its predecessor's resonance."

643 Revzin, Philip. "'Tukland': Grim Alternate to Orwell's Future." **Wall Street Journal**, 21 November 1978, p. 24.

With just five years to go until **1984**, the race is on to evaluate and update Orwell's classic. Burgess' extrapolation hits home. "As this review is being written [in London] a bread strike is causing long lines at bakeries, intermittent railway strikes are causing chaos for commuters and wildcat strikes make trying to buy a newspaper a random gamble." The essays's central theme of individual freedom is well explored even if the analysis of heretical movements through the ages, from Morganatics to anarchists to behaviorists, is a bit hard to follow. With the Labor Party's potential move to the left, the theme is particularly relevant. He has perhaps underestimated the good sense and humanity of the average worker, and overestimated the sheep-like adherence to authority of most people. Still, the book is entertaining, especially in the section in which the affable, ineffectual Charles III addresses the crowd in Trafalgar Square.

644 Rieff, David. "Future Schlock." **New Leader**, v. 61, no. 23 (November 20, 1978) 16-17.

Burgess, that heroic Elizabethan who gives the impression that the editors hammer on the front door while the creditors howl out back, is almost superlatively equipped to write a really major work. His apparent unwillingness to do so is the worst kind of arrogance. His **A Clockwork Orange** sang: all his linguistic powers were put to the service of his art. His **1985** is reminiscent of the stuff cranked out by science fiction writers for years. More, it is an exaggerated version of a certain Tory rhetoric ("too many wogs, too much union power, too much crime, the country is going to the dogs") which finally suggests that Burgess understands almost nothing of politics, the totalitarian impulse and the totalitarian temptation. "His attempt to outdo **1984** is the undoing of **1985**. Unlike sadness or horror or foreboding or despair, indignation — particularly in sclerotic form — is a rather callow emotion. And while **1985** is rich in indignation it is poor in everything else. Burgess' cleverness is not enough to carry him through what is, by any reckoning, a project demanding a great deal of thought, and enormous sophistication and, above all, sobriety."

Nothing Like the Sun

645 London: Heinemann, 1964.

646 New York: Norton, 1964.

647 Don Mills, Ont.: Collins, [1964?]

648 New York: Ballantine, 1965, c1964. Pbk.

649 Harmondsworth, Eng.: Penguin, 1966. Pbk.

650 London: Heinemann, 1972.

651 New York: Norton, 1975, c1964. (Norton Library, N795) Pbk.

Recordings

652 Anthony Burgess reads from The Eve of Saint Venus and Nothing Like the Sun. [Phonodisc] Caedmon, 1974. TC 1442. Recorded June 4, 1974. Notes by E.P. Swenson on slipcase.

653 The Eve of Saint Venus and Nothing Like the Sun. [Phonotape] Caedmon Cassette, 1974. CDL 51442.

Translations

654 Swedish: **Intet ar som Solen. En Berattelse om Shakespeares Karleksliv.** Stockholm: Bonnier, 1964. Translated by Ake Oilmarks.

Reviews

654.2 Burgess on his own work: "**Nothing Like the Sun** was, I know, a literary task almost haemorrhoidally agonising, and it must have consumed yards of paper and thousands of cigarettes . . . . . One thing I can remember, and that is that nearly every page of typescript was commenced at least six times. I would tear up the sheet it was on and start again. I was not correcting so much as enriching . . . . The beauties of the plain style are often urged on me, the duty of excising rather than adding. But the Elizabethan spirit doesn't take kindly to the Hemingwayesque, the spare and laconic, nor does my own spirit. I don't think that **Nothing Like the Sun** has too many words; I think perhaps it has too few. One has to be true to one's own temperament, and mine is closer to that of the baroque writers than that of the stark toughies. To hell with cheeseparing and verbal meanness: it all reeks of Banbury puritanism." Alex Hamilton [see #1718] quoted Burgess' intentions as follows. "In his novel **Nothing Like the Sun**, he wrote about Will, with his Dark Lady, as if to make him mean something to Burgess's Malayan pupils of his Colonial Service days. He tried in various ways, the story the primary problem, realising he couldn't tell it as Shakespeare nor a contemporary Elizabethan observer, so he decided to pretend to be himself giving a final drunken lecture to a gang of Eastern students and the narrator ever drunker identifying himself with the dying Shakespeare. It was the improbable, but only way."

655 Anon. "Jakes Peer or Jacques Pere." **Times Literary Supplement**, no. 3,243 (April 23, 1964) 329.

Burgess' fertile, racy imagination has set itself the job of meshing the known facts about Shakespeare with his imaginative reconstruction. All in all, Mr. Burgess has won that game. He also, following Leslie Hotson, makes Shakespeare's Dark Lady a Malayan prostitute. "A great deal of the detail is very skilfully and attractively planted; WS's half-mad brother, Gilbert, produces many of the lines that are later to appear on Hamlet's lips, the gravediggers in **Hamlet** derive from the gravediggers at the burial of WS's own son, Hamnet, the repudiation of Falstaff is foreseen in WS's own fears of Southampton denying him . . . ." The deft language is an Elizabethan stream of consciousness that dispenses with Elizabethan syntax. Its modernity sticks out. The most provocative and personal part of the book is Burgess' treatment of the sexual theme, and Burgess would probably admit, if pressed, that this part of his book needed more subtle handling.

656 Anon. "A Pox on It." **Time,** v. 85, no. 2 (January 8, 1965) 71.

When Burgess, that prickly, unpredictable novelist writes a book about Shakespeare in a rich, impenetrable soup of pseudo-Elizabethan, normally intrepid critics approach it with extreme care and natter nervously about the inventiveness of the language. However, in this case, Burgess' "kind of fantasy must be entertaining, consistently intelligent and tasteful in order to maintain the illusion. Too often, Burgess is none of these things. He loads in the sex scenes but makes his Shakespeare a timid, ineffectual 'Stratford bumpkin,' afraid of impotence and baldness, who could hardly tell an iamb from his two left feet. He nonetheless calls the book an act of homage to Shakespeare."

657 Anon. Review of **Nothing Like the Sun. Choice,** v. 1, no. 11 (January 1965) 477.

"It is also an extraordinary depiction of a brutal, vital, corrupt age. Shakespeare's tangle of love, from a callow, fumbling first affair to his death in 1587, is explained by Burgess, who amplifies and illuminates the ambiguous sonnets and misogyny of the plays. Here is a Dark Lady, truly dark, brought back by Drake from the South Seas, mistress of both Shakespeare and his lover, Lord Southampton. The epilogue, Shakespeare's dying delerium, is writing of the highest order . . . ."

658 Anon. Notice of **Nothing Like the Sun. Observer** (London), 11 September 1966, p. 22.

"A novel which is a Shakespeare celebration all by itself. The Dark Lady, Mr. WH, play-making, politics, actors and the daily stuff of life wound together in Burgess Elizabethan, a dazzling prose style, spun from a boundless obsession with words, and pretty hard to read." [Complete text of notice.]

659 Buitenhuis, Peter. "A Lusty Man Was Will." **New York Times Book Review,** 13 September 1964, p. 5, 26.

"Neither the histrionic, the graphic, the touristic nor the scholarly celebrations of this quartercentenary year are likely to outlive this powerful novel." Burgess has taken up Ben Jonson's challenge to Shakespeare's engraver 'O, could he but have drawn his wit/ As well in brass, as he has hit his face' and his manufactured Elizabethan past is far more satisfying than the extrapolated future of **The Wanting Seed.** Burgess' case that Shakespeare's talent had its origin in his sexual drive, and that his words and works were powered by an immense libido is aptly confirmed by a reading of the sonnets. It is an astonishing performance: it has taken a poet to capture the inner life of a poet. "Bawdy, extravagant, word-drunk, **Nothing Like the Sun** is a piece of staggering cheek that comes triumphantly off."

660 Enright, D.J. "Mr. W.S." **New Statesman,** v. 67, no. 1728 (April 24, 1964) 642-44.

"**Nothing Like the Sun** is a clever, tightly constructed book, reminiscent in its smaller and more sensational way of Mann's **Doctor Faustus,** full of the author's old verbal ingenuity (with something of Shakespeare's to boot), and likely to be one of the most remarkable (though ambiguous) celebrations of the Bard's quatercentenary . . . . Only a gifted 'word-boy' could have managed an Elizabethan-style idiom which most of the time strikes one as being simply good lively English if rather gamy." There are some minor false notes, but his evocation of the period is marvellously discreet and rich. The major false note is the treatment of Shakespeare's sexual life. "Mr. Burgess's narrative might help to account for the rougher bits in the Sonnets, for Lear's remarks on the gentler sex, for Othello, Troilus, Leontes — but not for Hermione, Miranda, Imogen, Cordelia, nor exactly for that other dark lady, the serpent of the old Nile. WS's sexual history — love-life seems hardly the word — is not so much grim or terrible as horrific and grotesque." Burgess' conception of Shakespeare's vision is more in accordance with the work of Burgess than the works of Shakespeare. Examines some of Burgess' anti-flesh books (**Malayan Trilogy, The Doctor Is Sick, Honey for the Bears**) and announces that Burgess flays his characters so savagely that we turn at last against the creator.

661 Halio, Jay. "A Sense of the Present." **Southern Review,** v. 2, no. 4, N.S. (October 1966) 953-966.

[Omnibus review.] He not only invents a personality for Shakespeare, but gives him a Negro mistress, but "miscegenation does not awaken a sense of the present in the past, any more than Burgess' imitation of Elizabethan English awakens a sense of the past in the present. In short, **Nothing Like the Sun** is rather too much like costume drama . . . ." [Virtually the complete text of the review.]

662 Jennings, Elizabeth. "New Novels." **Listener,** v. 71, no. 1830 (April 23, 1964) 693.

[Omnibus review.] Burgess' novel is vastly inferior to John Brophy's **Gentleman of Stratford.** It makes claims that cannot be substantiated; it is written in a bogus archaic style; and it is pretentious since

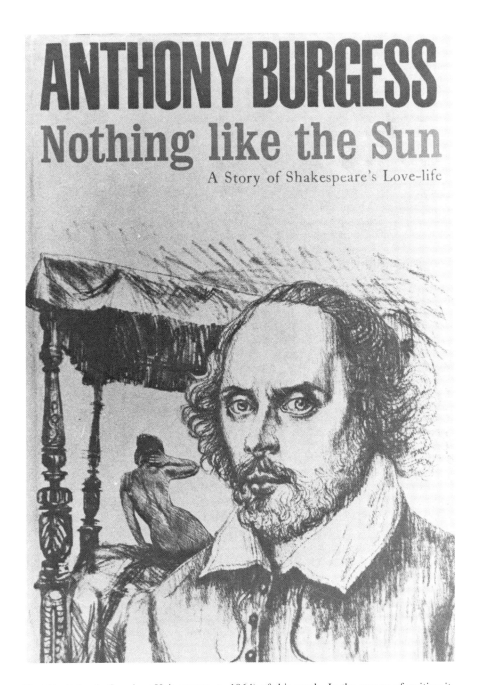

First English ed. (London: Heinemann, c. 1964) of this work. In the course of writing it
("I was not correcting so much as enriching") Burgess consumed yards of paper.

it is not possible to combine the novelistic farce with learned research. "It seems a pity that **Nothing Like the Sun** should be so disappointing . . . ."

663 Kauffmann, Stanley. "Filling in the Blank Verses of a Man on the Make." **Washington Post Book Week**, 20 September 1964, p. 5.

Burgess, who has skewered the vulgarities and strangulations of the present and the possible future, here turns his attention to Shakespeare's private life. His concern is with Shakespeare's emotional, sexual and social being for, as Shaw remarked, with the plays and sonnets in our hands, we know much more about Shakespeare than we know about Dickens or Thackeray, but we suppress it because the work proves Shakespeare unlike the conception of a god current in Clapham. The portrait of Shakespeare is apt. The style is marked by psychological intensity, an apt Elizabethan tumbling word-intoxication, and an occasional surge of Joycean streams, racing with interior fury. The book "contains what his readers have come to expect: distillation, subtlety, pungent wit; but, besides its freer form, it has another element not notable in his past novels: a positive passion as against the negatives of ridicule, disgust, ingenious dire prediction that have been his mainstays. What principally sustains this book is love, usually implied but no less fierce for that: of Shakespeare, of England and its language, of life as possibility: all expressed through a finely controlled but unembarrassed art . . . . Burgess's splashy but enthralling portrait may not be for all time but it will certainly serve for this age."

664 Lamott, Kenneth. "Burgess and Bellow." **Show**, v. 4, no. 11 (December 1964) 80.

The unfortunate Shakespeare threatens to be turned into a waxwork by the *Herren Professoren*, but Burgess' novel is an extraordinary piece of work, notable for its pyrotechnic brilliance in the evocation of Elizabethan England. Burgess' life is substantially based on the sonnets, and he does not spring any particular surprises on us. He identifies Mr. H.W. with Henry Wriothesley, Earl of Southampton. He also accepts the surmise that Southampton and Shakespeare contended for the favors of the inn-keeper's wife in the scandalous and anonymous **Willobie His Avisa**. It is a historical novel untainted by the modern plague of research, and it draws its fascination from Burgess' own view of life and his addiction to words. Warns that it is wrong to expect each new book to be an imperishable masterpiece. An author should be given a chance to shape a *corpus* by which he can be judged.

665 McCabe, Bernard. "No Bardolatry." **Commonweal**, v. 81, no. 6 (October 30, 1964) 174.

Those few snippets of fact, tricked out with fictional conjecture, surprisingly do not bore. Burgess conveys an extraordinarily vivid mock-up of Shakespeare's England, and the effect is not so much pastiche Elizabethan as pastiche Joyce. There are some lapses in a general atmosphere of deft sophistication, and Burgess is able to sound reasonably convincing while using an interpretation of the sonnet sequence as a text for his imaginative inventions. "The novel's central preoccupation is summed up in an Epilogue: 'Literature is an epiphenomenon of the flesh' — the pompous formulation is no doubt intended to convey ironical overtones, but it *is* what Burgess in effect keeps saying. (His Shakespeare has some of the air of a Rimbaud or Baudelaire plumbing the depths of experience in order to re-create it.) The trouble is that the flesh emerges as arid and brutal . . . . Further, although this novel if taken quite seriously does have something cold and ugly about it, a healthy wit and poise in the writing act as leaven."

666 Miller, Warren. "Enter Will, Dressed in Prose." **Nation**, v. 199, no. 9 (October 5, 1964) 196-97.

"Ave, lads, tha's done't again: another technicolor spectacular of lusty, brawling Elizabethan England: much ale and bosoms, broken teeth, plague, lechery, stinks, sores, quarterings and the now obligatory Eating Scene. And mystery. Not, who is Shakespeare? But, to whom did Burgess lend his name for the publishing of this very disappointing novel?" Groans that this is not the author of **A Clockwork Orange, Honey for the Bears** or that marvellous early book, **A Time for a Tiger**. Why, when Burgess can be a first-rate Burgess, has he elected to be a fifth-rate Nashe? There is the awful silliness of Shakespeare's mother denouncing his depraved poetic bent. The Dark Lady, more gold than black, talks like this: "who is dis Lesvia?. . . So what den do dey do?. . . We kiss not as you do. We have what is called de *chium*. It is done wid de nose." The name-dropping scenes are reminiscent of George Kaufman's description of Broadway historical drama. Burgess has produced a novel which, in the words of Billy Liar, is neither muckling nor mickling.

667 Pippett, Aileen. "The Sonneteer Was Not All Talk." **Saturday Review**, v. 47, no. 42 (October 17, 1964) 38.

This Shakespeare is no pensive, balding country gentleman in his best clothes, but a giant. The correspondence between the works and this work is a constant delight. The real-life models for Falstaff and that whole gallery of conniving rogues found in the plays exist in this novel, but nothing is dragged in for cheap effect and everything is relevant. "But it is not necessary to be learned to enjoy a brilliant book, for it all comes 'trippingly off the tongue,' including the atrocious puns and indecent allusions. It seems to have been written at top speed, yet the author never breaks down into blank verse, his style being taut and forceful. He is almost Joycean in the epilogue, which shows Shakespeare rich and respected in Stratford, having left the despair of Hamlet and the madness of Lear behind him . . . . If this is not truth it as close to it as we are likely to get. Come all the pedants in the world against us, the novelist is still the best witness to the reality behind the facts."

668 Raymond, John. "Paperback Monsters." **Punch**, v. 251, no. 6570 (August 10, 1966) 233.

[Omnibus review.] "For pure entertainment, Anthony Burgess. . . bears the bell away with ease. This story. . . is a real tour de force of the libido, with wit, reading and sheer uninhibited imagination running goat-footed in all directions."

669 Ryan, Stephen P. Review of **Nothing Like the Sun. Best Sellers**, v. 24, no. 13 (October 1, 1964) 259-60.

A fine, bold fictional treatment. The Shakespeare found in these pages is a vibrant human being tormented by the dual pull of the flesh and the spirit; he is certainly not the bland, rather stupid man who stares at us from the wall of Trinity Church in Stratford. Burgess is at his best in the evocation of the glories and horrors of Elizabethan and Jacobean England. "Not for the squeamish nor the puritanical, **Nothing Like the Sun** is a major novel; and the discriminating adult reader should not miss it. A final note: Burgess is a superb stylist; and in this novel he combines with uncanny skill an Elizabethan vocabulary with interestingly experimental contemporary techniques."

670 Sale, Roger. "Provincial Champions and Grandmasters." **Hudson Review**, v. 17, no. 4 (Winter 1964-65) 608-618.

[Omnibus review. For Burgess, see pp. 610-11.] By insisting on the intellectual and sexual querulousness of Shakespeare, Burgess manages his impossible task with considerable success. He has been clever enough to write a fiction that fits in all the known facts somewhere and the Shakespearese is fun as long as one concedes the author's questionable assumption that Shakespeare is rather like Anthony Burgess. Quotes a paragraph from the book and observes: "Not flawless surely, and all one can do with writing like this is count the hits and misses, but finally **Nothing Like the Sun** enhances one's admiration and hope for Burgess in ways no mere scutcheon can do."

671 Vansittart, Peter. "Primary Colours." **Spectator**, v. 212, no. 7087 (April 24, 1964) 561.

"Cuckolded by his brother on the second-best bed, poxed by the Dark Lady, scourged by alternate compassion and indignation, WS moves towards Cressida, Goneril, and hangman's hands, his bodily corruption reflecting a greater world poisoned at source. All this unlocks no secrets, though, ignoring the initial hopelessness of thus exploring or exploiting a major writer, the added details seem plausible enough. Groundlings may complain of the lyrical excess: critics may mutter about high-class fudge . . . . But one gets the feel of brutal primary colours, an age of kites, music, plague, conspiracy, filthy as a fox-hole, with its appropriate symbol, the jewelled, pocked, unwashed Queen, morbid and businesslike, shoving stinking breath on to elaborate mirrors long since painted over. As a jaunt through the more extreme reaches of language I found it highly enjoyable, at times suggestive; occasionally, as in the Tyburn scene, painful."

The Novel Now

672 London: Faber, 1967.

673 New York: Norton, 1967.

674 New York: Pegasus, 1970. Pbk.

675 London: Faber and Faber, 1971. New ed.

676 Folcroft, Pa.: Folcroft Library Editions, 1971.

Issued under title: **The Novel Today.**

Translations

677 Japanese: **Gendai shosetsu to wa naniki.** Tokyo: Takeuchi Shoten, 1970. Translated by Maekawa Yuichi.

Reviews

[The reviews of the American and British editions are combined in this section. The subtitles vary. The American edition reads **The Novel Now**: a Guide to Contemporary Fiction. The British edition is called **The Novel Now**: A Student's Guide to Contemporary Literature.]

678 Anon. Review of **The Novel Now. Observer** (London), 20 August 1967, p. 18.

In this guided tour to modern fiction, the omniligent (!?) Mr. Burgess makes an alert and stimulating cicerone, if also inevitably a breathless one. "In the house of fiction there are many mansions [sic], and he has managed to pay a flying visit to most of them, pointing out noteworthy features, drawing apt comparisons. A number of errors have crept in, and some of the omissions, from Pavese to Brian Moore, are highly debatable. But in general this is as useful and picturesque a handbook as the genre permits."

679 Anon. Review of **The Novel Now. Kirkus Reviews** (October 1, 1967) 1236.

Burgess' modest qualifications of this book make one hesitate to further question its utility. Nevertheless, college students will have outstripped the critical annotations while high school students will not have the time to spend on many of the minimal writers presented here. A modest work, already somewhat dated, which includes many charitable critical assessments.

680 Anon. Review of **The Novel Now. Publishers Weekly**, v. 192, no. 21 (November 20, 1967) 55.

"Anthony Burgess, an English novelist of great originality, writes a highly individual and selective survey of contemporary fiction, over the world [sic]. Because this book was specifically written for students, because Burgess' opinions are stimulating and sometimes electric, and because his style is something to admire and enjoy just for itself, this book stands a good chance of winding up in many college libraries." [Complete text of review.]

681 Anon. Review of **The Novel Now. New York Times Book Review**, 7 January 1968, p. 20.

It reads like a literary diary, and those who have read the books he discusses will find fresh insights into established authors like Proust, Lawrence and Joyce. His chapter headings, however, are idiosyncratic and even arbitrary; and there is little or no discrimination between the real writer and his popular facsimile. "A breathless performance, with some flashes of brilliance and perception, this is not to be mistaken for authoritative literary criticism."

682 Anon. Review of **The Novel Now. Booklist**, v. 64, no. 10 (January 15, 1968) 580.

". . . Burgess looks primarily at contemporary British fiction but does include some discussion of its Continental and American counterparts. The brief comments on each novelist's style, subject matter, and individual books are more descriptive than analytical yet this readable overview serves as introduction to more extensive and introspective studies."

683 Anon. "Contemporary Commentaries." **Times Literary Supplement**, 27 June 1968, p. 680.

The aim is the hospitable and unpretentious one of telling the reader something about novelists and their works. Burgess' (somewhat unnecessary?) remarks on the ancestry of the novel are sensible but desperately sketchy. "He runs breezily through a large cast of both British and foreign witers, and gives not always accurate lists of their works at the end of each section. There are some odd omissions (J.C. Powys, Roy Fuller, Brian Moore, Michael Frayn) and some unusual emphases. **The Old Men at the Zoo** is said to be the best thing Angus Wilson has done, but in the general atmosphere of tip and run these do not seem very culpable." Doubts if books of this kind are really necessary.

684 Anon. "Reader's Report." **Times Literary Supplement**, 21 April 1972, p. 439.

[Review of 1971 pbk. ed.] "Mr. Burgess tells us that this 'student's guide' was revised 'during the painful composition of **MF**'. . . but the interruption cannot have been great. Odd paragraphs have been infiltrated but the text is largely undisturbed. Said to be up-dated throughout, the new edition has caught up with recent Mailer, Nabokov and Durrell, but the author has not got around to the latest Angus Wilson, Patrick White or Kingsley Amis, and has clearly given up struggling with Iris Murdoch. Nor has he made good any of the first edition's omissions — Claude Simon, for example. However, the book remains readable and helpful within its limits."

685 Bergonzi, Bernard. "Fiction and Fabulation." **Hudson Review**, v. 25, no. 2 (Summer 1972) 355-57.

[Omnibus review.] Admires Burgess the novelist, but does not see much justification for this book. It consists of catalogs and plot summaries devoid of much critical speculation. It is unlikely to help the young. They have their own mysterious sources of information to guide their reading. Burgess displays all the skills of a practised reviewer. Some of the occasional judgments about Angus Wilson, Anthony Powell and Lawrence Durrell are welcome. The organization of his material is of dubious value. "A real book on the contemporary novel by Mr. Burgess would be worth having; and by that I mean a work that is genuinely selective, critical and personal in its approach, rather than a survey that provides a hollow comprehensiveness and no room for manoeuvre. Mr. Burgess' talents deserved better expression."

686 Hicks, Granville. "The Novel Today and Tomorrow." **Saturday Review**, v. 50, no. 9 (November 25, 1967) 33-34.

In this survey of 193 novelists, he deals not only with the giants of an earlier period — James, Proust, Joyce, Lawrence, Hemingway — but also some authors who belong to the pre-war era. To put Faulkner under the same heading as C.P. Snow and Anthony Powell ("The Novel as River") is to commit an error in classification. Yet Burgess often says more in a paragraph or page than most critics can do in a long article. His view that the true function of a writer is to produce a masterpiece is probably mistaken. Observes that the novel is not doing badly. When critics talk about the death of the novel, they have been affected by Connolly's attitude; they have also grown weary of doing the necessary reading. Burgess has a tremendous knowledge of the field, and a gift for making sharp, unambiguous judgments.

687 Hoggart, R. Review of **The Novel Now. Manchester Guardian Weekly**, 13 July 1967, p. 11.

688 Learmont, Marina. Review of **The Novel Now. Books and Bookmen**, v. 17 (April 1972) 61-62.

This sort of brief guide can be very indigestible, but in fact this one reads very easily. Women writers, however, are somewhat unceremoniously lumped in under the heading 'Yin and Yang.' Quotes Burgess on Doris Lessing's **The Golden Notebook**, ("a powerful expression of the resentment of the male"), Edna O'Brien ("a minor, near-popular, woman novelist who seems to blame male God for making woman what she is") and Brigid Brophy ("She can be witty and cruel, especially when exploding male pretensions, though some of her victims — including the present writer — are occasionally puzzled by a virulence that seems out of all proportion to the object of the attack"). The book includes fresh and stimulating opinions without much critical depth, and it left her wishing "that [Burgess] would write his novels as clearly and simply as he does his non-fiction works, instead of all too often getting bogged down in over-clever symbolism and word-games."

689 Lodge, David. "House of Fiction." **Spectator**, v. 219, no. 7260 (August 18, 1967) 190-91.

It runs to 200 pages; its pace is brisk; and it sometimes sounds like an extended Sunday omnibus review, but its true interest derives from the fact that Burgess ("one of our most talented novelists") addresses the novel form and his own aims as a writer. He reveals a confusion of values. On the one hand, he argues that one must write much in order to earn little. On the other hand, his critical enthusiasm for James Joyce, with *his* arrogant, intransigent, inexhaustibly patient and painstaking approach towards his art, is the "antithesis of the literary climate which Mr. Burgess inhabits, where we reassure ourselves with the Johnsonian maxim that 'no man but a blockhead ever wrote except for money.' I do not write this *de haut en bas*: I think most contemporary novelists are implicated in the dilemma Mr. Burgess rather confusedly reflects. But I think we should be honest about the choices involved. It is true that the house of fiction has always been at the same time a temple and a market-place; but it's no use pretending that there is no conflict of interest between these two functions."

690 Newlove, Donald. "The Contemporary Novel Through the Eyes of a Pro." **Washington Post Book World**, 3 December 1967, p. 32.

A bread and butter reference guide written with his left hand while the right was turning out the wonderfully gross **Tremor of Intent**. The sons of the Welfare State lust less after immortality than, in Burgess' view, the superior woman. He is exhilarated by the works of less sophisticated novelists from the United States. Regrettably, his flying typewriter fails to mention Celine, who died the same weekend as Hemingway. "For me, Celine's **Death on the Installment Plan** has the richest, most compelling, piercing, fearless and naked literary vision of the century, and events have only proven the validity of Celine's coal-black eyesight . . . . As a reviewer, Mr. Burgess is a professional violinist, who closes his case each evening and heads for his kitchen. If he saves his best energies and bravura for his own compositions, he's so much the wiser."

691 Sale, Roger. "Nothing Like the English." **Massachusetts Review**, v. 9 (Winter 1968) 181-84.

Praises Burgess' literary activity and records his unabashed amazement that Burgess has the time to catch up on his reading as a relaxation from writing **Tremor of Intent**. Gives names of some novelists omitted. Observes that critical judgments are restricted to flickers of doubt, or small surges of warmth. The book is the longest omnibus review on record. It is not stupid, infuriating or dull, and it is not (thank God) scholarly. More positive praise is hard to find. The book is not really suited for the young reader, and it is not apt for the older one. "The opinions are too polite, the values too thoroughly those of a relativistic and inveterate novel reader. C.P. Snow? He's OK. Rex Warner. He's OK, too. So is Olivia Manning, so is Pamela Hansford Johnson, so is Christopher Isherwood . . . . **The Novel Now**, thus, disappoints in the same way that Kingsley Amis' **New Maps of Hell** did a few years ago. Both are books written for no one. The man who knew how to write this kind of book was Frank O'Connor . . . ."

692 Simms, Theodore F. Review of **The Novel Now**. **Library Journal**, v. 92, no. 18 (October 15, 1967) 3642.

"Mr. Burgess's study of the novel seems the product of the casual reader who wishes to put his thoughts together to aid other casual readers. His critical judgments seem to lack a solid core; for example, he perpetuates the myth that Australian fiction begins with Patrick White. Also, his analysis of the great 'Moderns,' especially D.H. Lawrence, is too pat to be satisfying. His discussion of C.P. Snow's **Strangers and Brothers** is little more than a plot summary. This book does not pretend to be definitive; because of Mr. Burgess's relaxed approach, it seems unsubstantial."

693 Vonalt, Larry P. "Of Time and Literature." **Sewanee Review**, v. 77, no. 1 (Winter 1969) 164-70.

[Omnibus review. For Burgess, see pp. 164-65.] Burgess has set himself low critical goals. The work is bland, thoughtless and painfully dull. He includes, among his list of "Giants in Those Days," such dubious candidates as Hemingway, Fitzgerald, and Virginia Woolf. It is inexplicable and inconceivable that he omits Faulker from this section but includes Wyndham Lewis, E.M. Forster and Ronald Firbank. His classification scheme results in oddities. William Styron is classed as a war novelist. "The most interesting chapter is, however, the one on women novelists, entitled 'Yin and Yang.' It is not interesting because of its critical insights, but because of Burgess's bristling hostility towards 'female' novelists . . . . This book fails because it lacks critical intelligence and is carelessly written. For example, Burgess tells us that 'the big sex theme occurs in at least one' of Brigid Brophy's novels and that 'Faulkner is interested in the degeneration of representative white families in the South: that degeneration is part of history and sordid as it must be, it has to be recorded.' Such writing betrays itself to time."

Oedipus the King (Sophocles)

694 Minneapolis: University of Minnesota Press in Association with the Guthrie Theater, 1972. Translated and adapted by Anthony Burgess. With comments by Anthony Burgess, Michael Langham and Stanley Silverman.

Reviews

695 Constantinides, Elizabeth. Review of **Oedipus the King**. **The Classical World**, v. 68, no. 3 (November 1974) 211.

Burgess departs from Sophocles in making Oedipus blind himself on stage; this departure will strike the traditionalist as of questionable taste. The translation includes some feeble versions of familiar lines, and one occasionally suspects that Burgess had a Loeb translation at his elbow, but "barring a few inappropriate jingles, his versification is smooth, his language dignified in tone and at times moving in its directness."

696 Rendle, Adrian. "New Published Plays." **Drama; The Quarterly Theatre Review**, no. 110 (Autumn 1973) 81-85.

[Omnibus review. For Burgess, see p. 85.] "Mr. Burgess has welded together a highly dramatic text and his diversion from the original is responsible chiefly for bringing Oedipus on stage to take out his own eyes rather than relying on the Greek chorus to tell us about it for him." [Virtually the complete text of the review.]

On Going to Bed

697 London: Deutsch, 1982.

698 New York: Abbeville Press, 1982.

Reviews

699 Spurling, Hilary. "Roseleaves and Bedbugs." **Observer** (London), 22 August 1982, p. 28.

Burgess has slept in some depressing places (garrets, doss houses, barracks) and it is "No wonder Burgess's bed has now become, by his own account, a place for resting, reading, playing music, mixing stiff drinks and knocking off comparatively undemanding texts like this one." It amounts to 32 pages of large print and Burgess, perhaps the last man of letters, demonstrates a whimsicality and decorative pomp hard to distinguish from Robert Louis Stevenson. He can probably keep it up, full of roseleaves, literary asides, confessions, for ever — perhaps even in his sleep. "The good things in this book belong mostly to its darker side — nightmares, insomnia, bedbugs, alarm clocks; but, after reading his feeling account of the horrors of modern hospital beds, it would take a mean reader to grudge Burgess his roseleaf stuffings."

One Hand Clapping

700 London: Davies, 1961. As "Joseph Kell."

701 New York: Knopf, 1972.

702 New York: Ballantine, 1973. Pbk.

703 London: P. Davies, 1974.

Translations

704 Polish: **Klaskac jedna reka**. Warsaw: Czytelnik, 1976. Translated by Jadwiga Rutkowska.

705 Swedish: **Applad med en hand**. Stockholm: Wahlstrom & Widstrand, 1973. Translated by Caj Lundgren.

Reviews

705.2 Burgess on his own work: "Joseph Kell's first novel, **One Hand Clapping**, was a quiet and cunning female monologue that fell from the presses almost unnoticed. One Australian periodical acclaimed its virtues in a two-page review that, giving a thorough synopsis of the plot, must have made purchase of the book seem supererogatory." [Burgess made this observation in the pages of the **Yorkshire Post** (Leeds), 16 May 1963, p. 4, c. 1. In the same place, he accomplished the improbable feat of reviewing one of his own novels, **Inside Mr. Enderby**, also published under the pseud. of Joseph Kell. It is notable (and tells much about the chances of first novelists) that not one of the following reviews is of the 1961 ed.]

706 Adams, Phoebe. Review of **One Hand Clapping**." **Atlantic**, v. 229, no. 3 (March 1972) 108.

Why U.S. publication was delayed is a mystery. "One could make something pretentious of Howard as man destroyed by technology and of his wife as the indomitable life-force, but the notable point about the book is that it is ingeniously and devilishly funny."

707 Anon. Review of **One Hand Clapping**. **Publishers Weekly**, v. 200, no. 22 (November 29, 1971) 31.

"The initial quiet satire which lulls and amuses moves quite quickly into something more savage and shocking. This is not one of Mr. Burgess's major novels by any means, but it does enable him to get said skillfully some pointed things about the way life and our materialistic surroundings can affect us."

708 Anon. Review of **One Hand Clapping**. **Kirkus Reviews**, v. 39 (December 1, 1971) 1272.

Use both. It is a right proper little fairy tale, a right improper little horror story, and it could well be very photogenic.

709 Anon. Review of **One Hand Clapping**. **New Yorker**, v. 48, no. 4 (March 18, 1972) 154.

"Eleven years after its publication in England, this novel brings together some of the phrases of the alienated fifties — the title, for example, is from the Zen koan that J.D. Salinger used as the epigraph to **Nine Stories** . . . . His wife, fortunately, is a delightful little chatterbox, and she puts an end to all his worrying. A funny, pointed novel."

710 Anon. Review of **One Hand Clapping**. **Booklist**, v. 68, no. 17 (May 1, 1972) 752.

"The plot is at once an intricate and hilarious romp, a cautionary tale of the impact of sudden wealth, and, perhaps most importantly, a perceptive critique on the dichotomy between real life and the dramatizations presented on television."

711 Anon. Notice of **One Hand Clapping**. **New York Times Book Review**, 4 June 1972, p. 24.

"A British housewife and supermarket clerk is the narrator of this account of how her husband parlays his photographic memory into a small fortune on TV quiz shows — a 'witty and shrewdly joyful novel'." [Complete text of notice. Reprinted in #713.]

712 Anon. Review of **One Hand Clapping**. **Choice**, v. 9, no. 9 (November 1972) 1126.126.

"The thinness of this novel leads to the suspicion that, in this case at least, the protective pseudonym may well have been prompted by his own awareness of the book's weaknesses . . . . This narrative of basically tedious lives might have been enlivened by the zest for language shown in such works as **A Clockwork Orange** or **Nothing Like the Sun**. There is no lingual exuberance or inventiveness here, however, and as a result, **One Hand Clapping** is necessary reading only for those who feel compelled to read all the novels that Burgess has written.''

713 Anon. Notice of **One Hand Clapping**. **New York Times Book Review**, 3 December 1972, p. 78.
[Reprint of #711.]

714 Anon. Review of **One Hand Clapping**. **Publishers Weekly**, v. 203, no. 2 (January 8, 1973) 66.
This early novel by the brilliant Burgess is marvellous reading. The ending is pure, perfect Burgess.

715 Brickner, Richard P. ''A Mental Rigoletto.'' **New York Times Book Review**, 12 March 1972, p. 4, 37.
[Preceded by prolonged, rhapsodic plot summary.] ''Howard, though, is tortured by the cynicism and fury of one whose very kind of brain, he insists, suits him all too well for his time. Howard 'accepts,' in fact, much more easily than Janet does; he accepts to the point of succumbing to the worst the world can offer in order to justify his attempted revenge on it. Howard is a mental Rigoletto. Read this witty and shrewdly joyful novel. You'll like finding out what happens to Howard's attempted revenge, and be better for learning why the title is **One Hand Clapping**.''

716 C[ooper], A. Review of **One Hand Clapping**. **Newsweek**, v. 79, no. 10 (March 6, 1972) 78.
Burgess need defer only to Nabokov in translating bizarre comic vision into comic prose. Gives the whole of the plot away and comments that it will leave the reader with enough laughs to last the fortnight or so until Burgess publishes his nineteenth novel.

717 Degnan, James P. ''Fiction Chronicle.'' **Hudson Review**, v. 25, no. 2 (Summer 1972) 330+
[Omnibus review. For Burgess, see pp. 334-335.] Compared to J.M.G. Le Clezio's **The Book of Flights** the latest novel by Burgess gives an impression of classic greatness. It is not up to his best, but it is competent, readable, and funny. ''Told from the point of view of Howard's vulgar and ignorant (but not stupid) young wife — a point of view that enables Burgess to get in some funny and trenchant comments on contemporary British and American manners and morals — **One Hand Clapping** is easy to read and almost always entertaining. It is only when, for instance, Burgess allows the young wife to speak in a much more sophisticated and philosphical way than is credible for her that the novel, striking a dishonest note, stalls.''

718 Foote, Audrey. Review of **One Hand Clapping**. **Washington Post Book World**, 5 March 1972, p. 7.
[Plot summary which accurately conveys the tone of the book.] ''That superlative writing machine called Anthony Burgess doesn't hit a false note in this deadpan divertissement, which he probably scribbled down over a long weekend.''

719 H., V. ''Winners Weepers.'' **Christian Science Monitor**, 10 February 1972, p. 10.
''It's all told in the lingo of wife Janet, a girl with the conscience of an alley-cat, and a mind like a steel cliché. Mr. Burgess' uncanny apprehension of Janet's mental furniture is what provides this novel with its wild, wicked, witty tone.'' Includes some samples of Janet Shirley's opinions and remarks: ''If Janet sounds here like a kissing cousin of Joyce's Molly Bloom, read on. As the mayhem progresses she begins to look like a not-too-distant granddaughter of one of Macbeth's witches. Burgess buffs in America will be happy to have this book, which saw British publication in 1961, available. Its release has been timed to synchronize with the ticking of his **A Clockwork Orange** at your friendly neighborhood cinema.''

720 Moore, Harry T. Review of **One Hand Clapping**. **Saturday Review**, v. 55, no. 7 (February 12, 1972) 73.
Here Burgess turns his attention to the disintegration of values among young Britons at home, and he manages to remain mischievously amusing throughout most of this farfetched novel. Quotes two passages from the novel and observes that the play seen by the Shirleys sounds very much like John Osborne's **Look Back in Anger**.

721 Murray, John J. Review of **One Hand Clapping**. **Best Sellers**, v. 31, no. 22. (February 15, 1972) 514.

This little entertainment churned out by Burgess' furiously overworked typewriter is "a short, neat, professional way with a tale and an all-caution-to-the-wind willingness to experiment with voice. Here he deliberately chooses Janet's voice to tell all, just to see if he could pull off the challenge of male writing as a female. Janet's saying while thinking of lying with her lover, 'Sometimes it's no fun being a woman,' is merely Burgess' pixie voice saying 'Sometimes it's no fun trying to think like a woman and write like a man'."

722 Sayre, Ed. Review of **One Hand Clapping**. **Library Journal**, v. 97, no. 4 (February 15, 1972) 698.

A delightful work by a versatile and inventive craftsman. "While the diction is hardly Augustan, the narrative is witty and constrained, revealing the insights of a curiously intelligent but undereducated charmer. Highly recommended."

723 S[heppard], R.Z. "Clockwork Kumquat." **Time**, v. 99, no. 7 (February 14, 1972) 73-74.

"Although light years away in style and impact, **One Hand**, like Clockwork, is an example of Burgess's concern that modern man has all but shut himself away from spiritual joy . . . . Fortunately for the story, Howard's suicide plans include killing Janet. This provides Burgess with the opportunity to show a bit of his genius for drollery. Janet does in Howard first and with the aid of her poet-lover gets clean away. Howard, after spending weeks tucked in a trunk, literally ends up as a scarecrow. As the title suggests, though, Burgess is not satisfied to play at being Hitchcock. What is the sound of one hand clapping? What is the shape of a mind without soul?"

Re Joyce

724 New York: Norton, 1965.

725 New York: Ballantine, 1966, c1965.

726 New York: Norton, 1968, c1965. (Norton Library) Pbk.

727 Magnolia, Mass.: Peter Smith, [n.d.]

[NOTE: See also the British title for the same work: **Here Comes Everybody**.]

Reviews

728 Anon. Review of **Re Joyce**. **Kirkus Reviews**, v. 33. 33 (October 15, 1965) 1106.

"There is no air of speculation here, but a sureness of specifics and synthesis, an intelligence of imparting critical truths so that even if one were to differ, one would respect Burgess' approach. For an audience which finds Stuart Gilbert difficult, this makes Joyce accessible."

729 Anon. Review of **Re Joyce**. **Booklist**, v. 62, no. 8o. 8 (December 15, 1965) 393.

"One third of this immensely fruitful appraisal of Joyce's work is devoted to **Ulysses**, paralleled here with the the Odyssey; the remainder deals with **Finnegan's Wake** [i.e. **Finnegans Wake**] and Joyce's most important short fiction works."

730 Anon. Review of **Re Joyce**. **New Yorker**, v. 41, no. 48. 48 (January 15, 1966) 120.

"The most language-intoxicated of contemporary novelists is just the man to write a plain reader's guide to James Joyce. There are some things that Mr. Burgess does not know, and some things that he gets wrong, but he knows the big thing — that **Ulysses** and **Finnegans Wake** are moving stories about people, not puzzles. Mr. Burgess is particularly good on **Finnegans Wake** — in fact, his exegesis may be the best yet — but he should have been prevented from rewriting Joyce for further complexity." [Complete text of review.]

731 Anon. Review of **Re Joyce**. **Choice**, v. 3, nos. 5-6 (July-August 1966) 408.

It is most adequate in its account of **Ulysses**; less so with the poetry; and it is unconcerned with the metaphysical subtleties implicit in Joyce's work. It is one of the few books really adequate and richly informative on the musical elements in Joyce. It is brilliant and insightful, but not a scholarly work.

732 Anon. Review of **Re Joyce**. **Publishers Weekly**, v. 190, no. 15 (October 10, 1966)966) 75.

"Well-written, interesting to read and a genuine **must** for Joyce fans and students of lit."

732.2 Fremont-Smith, Eliot. "Through the Labyrinth." **New York Times**, 1 December 1965, p.45.

Burgess is one of the most imaginative, linguistically inventive and wide-ranging writers of our generation, but his book is a disappointment. It is just another analytical primer on **Ulysses** and **Finnegans Wake**, very much a jog-trot guide to the riches of the master. "Yet there are good things to say about Mr. Burgess's book. In its interpretation of the themes, antecedents, language and intricacies of construction of **Ulysses** and the less accessible great dream, **Finnegans Wake**, it is solid and resourceful. Mr. Burgess is particularly bright in his emphasis on the immense comedy, humanity and affirmation of man's worth that is in these books, and in his pinpointing of what it is Joyce's detractors complain about: 'It is the wealth of this mind that is most persistently attacked. Joyce's great crime, apparently, is to know too much.' And to have too much fun with it."

733 Hackett, Alice. Notice of **Re Joyce**. **Publishers Weekly**, October 10, 1966, p. 75.

Quotes Burgess' remark that his book does not pretend to scholarship.

734 Hatch, Robert. "His Fame Proceeds in Giant Steps." **Harper's**, v. 232, no. 1390 (March 1966) 142-43, 46.

"The irony of Joyce's position in modern letters is that from book to book his power and fame proceed in giant steps and from book to book his audience declines from a public to an elite to a circle."

Many enthusiasts make the arduous trek to the summit seem like a Sunday stroll. Burgess is no exception. The first seventy pages, up to the **Portrait**, consist of literary criticism enriched with biography and gossip. The next hundred pages constitute a kind of Baedeker to **Ulysses**, and here Burgess maintains his easy progress by throwing bridges of plausible generality at some of the most turbulent passages. When he gets to **Finnegans Wake,** he offers a synopsis for those who do not speak the language, and he is clearly going too fast. Observes that (*pace* Burgess) the Wake cannot be read like a book; it must be mined and coined word by word. "Joyce was seventeen years writing his last book and he is known to have thought that a man could do worse than spend seventeen years understanding it. That may well be so, but it is not a literary assignment; it is a career. I know some who have undertaken it and they have about them the contented air of men who know that they will not run out of occupation this side of the grave."

735 Kain, Richard M. Review of **Re Joyce**. Criticism, v. 9, no. 1 (Winter 1967) 102.

[Omnibus review. For Burgess, see bottom p. 103.] Burgess does not attempt to go far beneath the hitherto explored surfaces of the canon. His use of plot summary at the expense of text commentary is regrettable. He would have been well advised to provide an index, and to comment on the circumstances of publication.

736 Lewald, H.E. Review of **Re Joyce. Carleton Miscellany,** v. 7, no. 2 (Spring 1966) 124-25.

It "is not only another book about Joyce but one that ought to replace Stuart Gilbert's book in the libraries of those who read not **Ulysses** but the books about it, for this one is bright enough to drive or tease those readers to the Joyce novel itself. Mr. Burgess sees **Ulysses** and **Finnegans Wake** not as 'twin heavens for the scholars' or 'mystical codices' but as 'masterly novels intended to entertain.' In pointing out this obvious but sometimes forgotten fact, Mr. Burgess is himself masterly and entertaining. **Re Joyce**. Rejoyce. Concerning Joyce. Again Joyce. Back to Joyce. Read Joyce." [Complete text of review.]

737 Merton, Thomas. "News of the Joyce Industry." **Sewanee Review,** v. 77, no. 3 (July 1969) 544-45.

[Omnibus review.] One of the more useful and engaging of the recent books on Joyce. Burgess disclaims pretensions to scholarship; it is a pity he did not acknowledge his debt to professionals like Tindall, Kenner, Goldberg and others. The emphasis falls on the healthy catholicity of Joyce rather than on his allegedly sick Catholicism.

738 Noon, William T. Review of **Re Joyce. James Joyce Quarterly,** v. 3, no. 3 (Spring 1966) 215-19.

Observes that Burgess is out to rescue Joyce from the professors and to restore him to the ordinary people with heart. Considers the sentiment an insult to both parties. The ordinary people cannot understand Joyce because they "find themselves unable to cope with polyhedral puns in many foreign languages (Schweizerdeutsch, Russian, Danish-Norwegian, Old Gaelic, corrupt Galic, and so on), whose skill in anagrams, cryptograms, and acrostics is minimal, and who have only primitive knowledge of ancient Celtic folklore or of the pantheons of religions systems long since passed away." Lays on with a cane and lambasts Burgess for errors: **O Felix Culpa** is not derived from Augustine; the tenth appearance of the 'hundred letter' word for thunder has one hundred and one; if Joyce is the dreamer, as Burgess maintains, there are difficulties. If Burgess had learned more from the scholars [examples provided] his book would be more valuable. Burgess, nominally a Catholic, now a Manichaean, contributes little of value from the Catholic angle. His best comments are on Joyce as a musician. Gives the names of twelve scholars who write more informatively and wittily on Joyce today. [Note: Noon is a Jesuit.]

739 O'Dea, Richard. "Joyce Triumphant." **Southern Review,** N.S. v. 4, no. 1, (January 1968) 259-63.

[Omnibus review. For Burgess, see p. 260-61.] It is a lucid and chronological guide clearly intended for an English public which shares Shaw's suspicion of Joyce ("sheer madness"). His work is indebted to Edmund Wilson, and he helps to answer Wilson's own question: "Clever though this be, is it worth the effort?" "Decidedly for Burgess it is worth the effort, for Joyce cuts history down to size, measures it against the embarrassing necessities of the commonplace — a cold, a broken dental plate, the dust in a thumb-nail — and all these human necessities he announces with a language that glorifies them. To Joyce *nihil humanum alienum est* [nothing human is foreign to me]. Burgess concludes that none of us can read Joyce and ever be quite the same again, for 'we shall be finding an embarrassing joy in the commonplace, seeing the most defiled city as a figure of heaven, and assuming, against all the odds, a hardly supportable optimism'.''

740 Poirier, Richard. "No Invitation to Tea." **New York Times Book Review**, 9 January 1966, pp. 6, 46. 46.

Burgess assumes the role of a litterateur leading a peasant revolt on behalf of the 'average' reader against the professors. Who is this average reader scared off Joyce by professorial terrors like Harry Levin, Richard Ellmann, Robert Adams, Hugh Kenner and Father [i.e. William T.] Noon? In any case, Burgess' book reads like the dreariest of classroom paraphrases, uninvigorated by critical acuteness or personal temperament. Burgess boldly contradicts himself. What, in his preface is termed 'the appearance of difficulty in Joyce' becomes, on page 185, 'elusive and difficult.' The sad truth is that Joyce is not a writer for 'the people.' His literary relationships with Pater, Wilde and Arnold have been scandalously neglected. Further, Joyce deliberately puts some distance between Daedalus and himself, and Stephen's discussions of Aquinas are both intellectually pretentious and confused, "a fact that the average reader would be capable of recognizing even less readily than is Mr. Burgess." To say that it is 'safe' to put **Ulysses** into the hands of the 'devout believer', as Burgess does, is to ignore the liberating Circe episode, perhaps the greatest comic triumph in English literature. The episode demonstrates Joyce's marvelous human generosity, liberating comedy, rejection of all systems; but to infer, as Burgess does, that Joyce's lowly subjects are also his likely readers is a *non sequitur.* "The novels are about Joyce's chosen way of expressing his hatred of system and his love for ordinary humanity, a way that makes that love most available to those who perhaps need it most: to the quite learned, to the very smart, to the highly educated, to the very unaverage reader . . . ."

741 Porter, Raymond. Review of **Re Joyce**. **Catholic World**, v. 203, no. 1213 (April 1966) 61-62.

The book is intended for the average reader? That mythical mean will find nothing of interest in **Ulysses** or **Finnegans Wake**. "Joyce's thought and method preclude a cursory reading, which is what most average readers indulge in, and, perhaps, rightly so." It is a useful guide for the interested student but the treatment of the Eucharist in the 'Lotus Eaters' section is too brief, and there are nineteen divisions in 'The Wandering Rocks' section, not eighteen.

742 Sears, William P. Review of **Re Joyce**. **Education**, v. 87 (September 1966) 61.

"As the years pass, the glory and brilliance of James Joyce shines [i.e. shine] brighter and brighter. This book is both a scholarly and extremely sound and clear discussion of the works of the Irish master. The author recognizes the importance of **Dubliners** and **A Portrait of the Artist as a Young Man** in relation to the monumental **Ulysses** and the provocative **Finnegan's Wake** [i.e. **Finnegans Wake**]." [Complete text of review.]

743 Staley, Thomas F. Review of **Re Joyce**. **Commonweal**, v. 83, nos. 21-22 (March 4, 1966) 645-46.

Joyce, long the darling of American academic critics, now gets an unpedantic exegete. We are spared epiphanies, parallax, ancient heresies, Viconian theories, multistructured word origins, occult allusions and other such swamps. He relies on Stuart Gilbert and Campbell and Robinson's famous **Skeleton Key**, but neglects more recent studies by William T. Noon, W.Y. Tindall, A. Walton Litz, Clive Hart, R.M. Kain and Joseph Prescott. Despite this fault, Burgess' book is marked by an eloquent style, rich good humor, and its author's devotion to Joyce. His comment concerning the influence of the Church on Joyce's work is amazingly clear and accurate. "Hardly a page goes by that the reader will not be struck by the wry wit, the beautiful style, the bold statements, and the sheer exuberance with which Burgess approaches his subject. For him the book was clearly, as he suggests, a labor of love and he fulfills his purpose grandly; he has conveyed his great joy in reading a master of our century."

744 Sullivan, A.M. "The Sanctification of the Ordinary." **Saturday Review**, v. 48, no. 52 (December 25, 1965) 34-35.

The author is too modest about his scholarship and, while there have been numerous explications of Joyce, Burgess has placed Joyce's satire in its proper orbit. Refers to Burgess' discussion of Joyce and Hopkins, and then quotes Burgess on Joyce's perception of his priest-like function ("the solemnization of drab days, and sanctification of the ordinary"). Quotes Burgess on the Homeric parallels between **Ulysses** and the **Odyssey**, confides that he sometimes felt rebuffed by a superior and perhaps snobbish intellect [Joyce] and that if portions of **Ulysses** and much of **Finnegans Wake** still strain the reader's brain, Burgess has indicated where the clues are.

The Right to an Answer

745 London: Heinemann, 1960.

746 New York: Norton, 1961, c1960.

747 New York: Ballantine, 1966. Pbk.

748 New York: Norton, 1978, c1960. Pbk.

Reviews

749 Anon. "Local Boys Make Good." **Times Literary Supplement**, no. 3,040 (June 30, 1960) 349.

[Omnibus review.] "The tone of the book is comic, with some initial over-writing, but it takes a turn towards violence at the end. The likeliest scenes are in the local pub, but the Midlands town as seen by one who has become an outsider is sharply described. The reader, though, may well wonder whether the experiences recounted add up to anything of much importance."

750 Anon. Review of **The Right to an Answer**. **Kirkus Reviews**, v. 28 (November 1, 1960) 937.

"With a feeling for the ludicrous, for high-lighted characters and cumulatively heightened situations, this plays the 'angry' theme with adult modulations."

751 Anon. Review of **The Right to an Answer**. **Booklist**, v. 57, no. 9 (January 15, 1961) 292.

"The purposeless, amoral lives of Denham's new acquaintances deepen his frequently expressed dislike for modern England and his own feeling of aimlessness, but his subtle sense of humor fortifies him in most situations. For those enjoying novels of sophisticated disenchantment."

752 Anon. Review of **The Right to an Answer**. **Time**, v. 77, no. 4 (Jan. 20, 1961) 91.

It is a fictional sermon written in the form of a comic novel which reveals that Author Burgess, at 43, is still banging noisily on God's door, insisting on an answer to the riddle of existence. "Burgess writes comically enough about TV-induced catatonia, the god-awfulness of roast mutton, and the entanglements of adultery, but the reader feels compelled to check each incident with the solemn preamble — is such and such really putrid or merely pathetic, is it cause or merely effect? Despite such short-comings, the author's prose is graceful and precise, his wit is sharp, and he can complicate a comic situation to the point of inspired silliness."

753 Anon. Review of **The Right to an Answer**. **Times** (London), no. 57,184 (February 24, 1968) 20.

[Review of Four Square pbk. ed.] "Bitter and biting . . . . Mr. Burgess is clearly terrified lest the values of 'dull Midland towns' swamp the whole world."

754 Bliven, Naomi. "Books: Ordeals and Orgies." **New Yorker**, v. 37, no. 8 (April 8, 1961) 169-74.

[Omnibus review. For Burgess, see pp. 169-70.] Includes a long commentary on the character of Denham which suggests that he is foolish, self-deluded and victimized by his associates. Observes that, with the introduction of Mr. Raj, the novel becomes funnier, deeper and sadder. Notes that Raj, like Denham, changes before the reader's eyes: at first he is a butt, then a positive villain, and finally a victim of love. Burgess has surrounded these two with a number of other diverting figures. They, and their whimsical personalities, belong in the story and help to make it go. "Mr. Burgess has invented complex, varying people, and he has moved them well, giving them much to suffer and to do. The reader cannot outguess the plot, though he can believe in it. As a bonus, in the closing pages, Burgess has set off a wild joke in which all his themes — poetry, England, race, love — crackle and sparkle in a gloriously funny surprise . . . . the book is not a joke but a nicely controlled examination of some human predicaments that is cunningly disguised as entertainment."

755 Coleman, John. "Music Week." **Spectator**, May 27, 1960, p. 778.

[Omnibus review.] Not the best of Burgess' books. The inspired gaiety of **The Malayan Trilogy** is gone. "There are deaths and old J.W. reads more and more like that prissy joker, old Humbert Humbert: the poet's daughter, after four of her teeth have been smashed in by hoodlums, becomes the 'partially edentate Imogen.' Mr. Burgess might curb his inventiveness; he'd be a first-rate comic novelist if the camouflage of another little joke were down and he looked his subject squarely in the face.''

756 Fink, John. "Fabric of Question Marks and Quaint Paradoxes." **Chicago Sunday Tribune Magazine of Books,** 8 January 1961, p. 4.

"This is a brilliantly fashioned book. Its characters glitter in a satirical fabric woven of question marks and quaint paradoxes.''

757 Kenedy, A.R. Review of **The Right to an Answer. Library Journal,** v. 85, no. 22 (December 15, 1960) 4485-86.

[Burgess' image of England] ''is the usual right-wing one of amused despair given by writers who think of themselves as leftish. His hero, J.W. Denham, 40-year-old businessman returning from the East, surveys the British scene — a single quasi-philosophical motto his emblem: '[People] don't want freedom; they want stability. And you can't have them both.' (A highly debatable proposition; more erudite thinkers than Mr. Burgess have maintained that freedom is **stability . . . .**) Hardly taking time to breathe, the hero rushes off into a series of supposedly characteristic misadventures which are assumed to be funny — in which the publishers claim, the Kingsley Amis manner. Mr. Amis knows, however, his English language. The style of Mr. Burgess is often clumsy, seldom crisp, never biting. The story concerns a failed poet; an unfortunate printer, Winterbottom (referred to as Coldarse — for the sake of a joke); and a Ceylonese lecher. Human failure strikes our author as comic. So it may well be — when looked at with more passionate sympathy.''

758 Laski, Marghanita. "Morality with Heart." **Saturday Review,** v. 44, no. 4 (January 28, 1961) 17.

Concedes that the middle-class industrial suburbs *are* rather beastly today, but worries if foreigners should really be given this picture of England. Two-thirds of the way through his book, Burgess begins to show what is really a good heart and what follows is a nice exercise of morality. Little by little, more by good-heartedness than by mastery of the narrative art, Burgess persuades us that we are reading a worth-while book. "I may have made it all sound a bit tempestuous, but after page 183 a bit tempestuous is what it is. It's also great fun, not *very* good but *rather* good, and, for all its depressing beginning, a book made out of the author's own head and not from other Zeitgeist books. And I don't really mind foreigners reading it. Certainly it doesn't makes us look as if we're having it all that good, but it's not unlike what we are, and that doesn't turn out to be so bad after all.''

759 Nordell, Rod. "Fiction: The Comedy of Discontent." **Christian Science Monitor,** 19 January 1961, p. 5.

[Omnibus review.] "In the midst of a welter of self-indulgence [Denham's decision to end this standing on the periphery and sneering] may seem a rather small step in the direction of responsibility. But for the drifting junior intellectuals — or would-be intellectuals — for whom such books almost seem labeled, the decision to participate instead of scoff could be more than an academic matter.''

760 Peterson, Clarence. Notice of **The Right to an Answer. Chicago Tribune Books Today,** 27 May 1966, p. 9.

[Review of Ballantine pbk. ed.] "A satiric view of England today as two-bit America gone to sloth; peopled by poets and layabouts, middle-aged ladies hipped on sex, a lecherous Ceylonese, and the narrator, an Englishman recently returned from the Orient who says he's writing the story 'to clarify in my own mind the nature of the mess'." [Complete text of review.]

761 Price, R.G.G. "New Novels." **Punch,** v. 238, no. 6244 (May 25, 1960) 739.

[Omnibus review.] **The Right to an Answer** is probably the point in Mr. Burgess's literary career at which reviewers will be asking 'Whither now?' His Malayan trilogy established his strong individuality. A Burgess novel meant the seediness of an empire in decline, reminiscences of poetry written and read in Redbrick universities, critical pictures of the Succession States, very funny drunks and a good, swinging narrative. In his new novel the scene is a Midland suburb and the narrator is on leave from a commercial job in the Far East, where he has dreamed about home, which he now finds as seedy as Asia. I do not quite understand why everybody refers to Mr. Burgess as a funny man. He is as accurate and depressing as Gissing, though I agree he is a Gissing with a sense of fun and an eye for any comedy to be found in his ruined world.'' [Complete text of review.]

762 Raymond, John. "New Novels." **Listener**, v. 63, no. 1630 (June 23, 1960) 1111.

[Omnibus review.] One of the wittiest and slickest novels he has read in a long time. The Midland subtopia is excellently rendered and the hero-narrator is thoroughly likable and credible. "Mr. Burgess . . . is clearly out of the Smollett stable. He is an excellent judge of human horseflesh. Though his up-and-coming Babu barrister, Mr. Raj, is unworthy of the late F.A. Anstey, in some of his other characterizations he attains the velocity of a kind of supersonic Pritchett. One awaits his next novel with a very pleasurable interest."

763 Shrapnell, Norman. "Out of the Post-Atomic Caves." **Manchester Guardian**, 27 May 1960, p. 9.

"There is a portentous air about this writer which makes him a sort of music-hall Graham Greene ('I can feel damnation being broken in like a pair of shoes') but he has a wickedly accurate ear and eye and one of his characters, a man from Ceylon researching into race relations, is a memorable tragi-comic figure."

764 Talbot, Daniel. "A Wry and Comic Novel." **New York Herald Tribune Lively Arts and Book Review**, 22 January 1961, p. 32.

[Chiefly plot summary.] "In this wry and comic novel, Anthony Burgess displays a prodigious talent for narrative. His oddly mellifluous prose bites sharply into the mushy complacency of his world. This is a bitter indictment — all the more powerful because of the humor which has metamorphosed a statement of protest into a savage lyric satire."

765 Williams, David. "On Leave and On the Job." **Time and Tide**, v. 41, no. 24 (June 11, 1960) 679.

"This Mr. Raj is the best thing in a brilliant, uneven book. He is a Singhalese sociologist who attaches himself to Denham when the latter's leave is interrupted by an emergency call to Colombo, accompanies him back to England, and insinuates himself into the paternal semi where he enchants the old man with the suavity of his address and the richness of his curries. The book has plenty of sour, off-beat comedy, a sufficiency of wayward, mad-hatterish action, and more despair than 'an outstanding comic novelist' — this is the blurb's claim and I readily allow it — has possibly a right to."

Shakespeare

766 London: Cape, 1970.

767 New York: Knopf, 1970.

768 Harmondsworth, Eng.: Penguin, 1972. Pbk.

Translations

769 French: **Shakespeare** (?). Paris: Buchet/Chastel, 1972. Translated by Maud Sissung and Bernard Noel.

Reviews

769.2 Burgess on his own work: "Much of my time in Malta, since returning from the United States, has been spent in writing a new life of Shakespeare. New? — hardly, since there are no new facts, and one's style sets into an unedifying melange of the stock robust (ale, lice, wenching) and the timidly speculative, which is everybody's style when writing a Shakespeare biography. I ought to be ashamed, but I am doing it for the money . . . . The book will look very lovely when it comes out, full of colored pictures of Mary Fitton and the Earl of Pembroke, and it will stand, unread although regularly dusted, on several thousand coffee tables."

770 Adams, Phoebe. "Short Reviews: Books." **Atlantic**, v. 226, no. 5 (November 1970) 143.

"Mr. Burgess, admired by Professor Schoenbaum as the only person who ever wrote a good novel about Shakespeare, claims 'the right of Shakespeare-lover. . . to paint his own portrait of the man.' Admittedly speculative, thoroughly informal, the book is well illustrated, and the writing is animated by affection and an understanding of the creative imagination that only a creative writer can bring to bear." [Complete text of review.]

771 Anon. Review of **Shakespeare**. **Kirkus Reviews**, v. 38 (September 1, 1970) 1024.

"With a little highly educated guesswork but no invention, with great humor and infinite admiration, the 'nth' attempt to recreate the life and society from which the plays and poems stemmed, as well as to lend substance to the shadow of the man. Anthony Burgess as always contributes a stylish commentary . . . ." [Virtually complete text of review.]

772 Anon. Review of **Shakespeare**. **Publishers Weekly**, v. 198, no. 14 (October 5, 1970) 62.

A wholly attractive illustrated book in which Burgess makes engrossingly clear how completely Shakespeare was a man of his time and place. "Perhaps more than anything else, Burgess's book is an evocation of Elizabethan England, and particularly of London, as perhaps the most roistering, brawling, gossip-mongering and vitally creative center of history and culture that the world has known." It is a delightful and valuable book.

773 Anon. "A Novel Picture." **Economist**, v. 237, no. 6634 (October 17, 1970) 60-61.

The work is lavishly produced and expensively illustrated; the story is told with some verve; it is rarely dull; but it is plainly another one of Burgess' fictions. His Shakespeare is very much an Anthony Burgess character — lusty, hard-headed in money matters, and a word-reveller. He disclaims any attempt at 'genuine criticism,' but critical comments depressingly low in quality keep coming in. His scholarship is defective, and the chronological order of the plays is either based on outmoded, or crankily hypothetical theories. The literary opinions are wilfully odd and coarse; they suggest that Burgess is carelessly writing down for an ignorant public. [Examples document these charges.] "Describing the masques which Jonson wrote for James's court, he says: 'the anti-masque followed the masque as the jig followed the play.' Quite the reverse, actually, as he could have discovered by looking up any one of them."

773.2 Anon. Review of **Shakespeare**. **Best Sellers**, v. 30, no. 16 (November 15, 1970) 357.

A pleasant introduction to Shakespeare in a handsome volume complete with magnificent paintings, but the text flirts with inaccuracy and over-simplification.

774 Anon. Notice of **Shakespeare**. **Books and Bookmen**, v. 15 (November 1970) 40.

A sumptuous gift book in which one of the most able of modern novelists seeks to reconstruct the zest, energy, love of life and individualism in Elizabethan England.

775 Anon. "Shakespeare: The Works and the Worker." **Times Literary Supplement**, 11 December 1970, p. 1440.

Burgess has produced a narrative well-informed to the point of gossip, and he draws upon the good old literary convention that associates creative genius with sexual energy, and Shakespeare 'loved not wisely but too frequently.' "It seems, for instance, that he left Anne in Stratford rather than practise continence when the prospect of more children spelt poverty. In Mr. Burgess's right happy and copious industry, the adventures of Will Shagspere make eminently good reading, though the hero bears a closer resemblance to Ben Trovato than to Johannes Facscrotum." Perhaps Keats was right when he said that the poetical character has no identity of its own.

776 Anon. Notice of **Shakespeare**. **National Review**, v. 22 (December 15, 1970) 1358.

"A deliciously idiosyncratically Burgessian life-and-times book enhanced with pictures, mostly in color, of Elizabethan scenes, portraits, artifacts et cetera." [Virtually complete text of notice.]

777 Anon. Review of **Shakespeare**. **Booklist**, v. 67, no. 12 (February 15, 1971) 470.

"Thoroughly researched, elegant in format, and reflective of Burgess' infinite admiration as well as his honest humor concerning Shakespeare the text is a well-balanced consecutive narrative of the playwright's life."

778 Anon. Review of **Shakespeare**. **Contemporary Review**, v. 218, no. 1262 (March 1971) 168.

"It is a thoroughly enjoyable and penetrating book, written in delightful prose and garnished with superb illustrations."

779 Anon. Review of **Shakespeare**. **Virginia Quarterly Review**, v. 47, no. 2 (Spring 1971) lxvii-lxx.

"Scholars will be maddened and general readers charmed by this new life added to the canon of the bard." The splendidly illustrated biography is based on the known facts, Burgess' wide knowledge of literature, the internal evidence of the writings, the history of the period, and Burgess' conjectures. "The result is personal, controversial, and sometimes persuasive."

780 Anon. Notice of **Shakespeare**. **Books and Bookmen**, v. 18 (January 1973) 124.

"Revealing study of the *man*, his contacts, how his life influenced plays. An elegant quarto with nearly 100 black-and-white pictures, 48 in colour. 'It was a touch of near genius to choose Mr. Burgess to write the text' — David Holloway." [Complete text of notice.]

781 Brown, Ivor. "Shakespeare Panorama." **Drama; The Quarterly Theatre Review**, no. 99 (Winter 1970) 63-64.

The literary mandarins have studied the plays — and specialized subjects related to Elizabethan play production. Burgess wisely concentrates on the man and his times and "The new biographer's conjectures are bold and plausibly argued and his assurance is in likeable contrast to the usual scrupulous timidity . . . .and the pictorial side of this book is superb . . . .There is value for the money. From the elegance of the foppish milords and ladies to the sports and commerce of the common man, the grandeur, the squalor and the hardships of Shakespeare's world are on view with a new and exciting amplitude."

782 Butler, Francelia. Review of **Shakespeare**. **Library Journal**, v. 95, no. 20 (November 15, 1970) 3909.

"The most appealing part of **Shakespeare** is the obvious enthusiasm of the author for his subject. This biographical novel is full of conjectures evidently based on details lovingly gathered by Burgess over a very long period. Not strictly a biography and not strictly a novel, it belongs to that genre of fictionalized nonfiction which has special appeal to youth."

783 DeMott, Benjamin. "Will the Real Shakespeare Please Stand Up?" **Saturday Review**, v. 53, no. 45 (November 7, 1970) 31-32, 35, 46-47.

[Omnibus review. For Burgess, see p.46.] "The volume is a voluptuous affair of coated pages, luxo color portraits, and speculation doubling back on itself . . . . "Some of the fancies found in **Nothing Like** the Sun turn up here; there is some cryptographic dabbling intended to prove that Shakespeare had a hand in the King James Version; and there's an admirably determined effort to counter the absurdity that men write comedy when they're up, tragedy when down. "All that is painful is the implicit return to the Victorian 'burgher Shakespeare,' a brisk, cheerful, small-town jaycee: 'To see his face, we need only look in a mirror. He is ourselves, ordinary suffering humanity, fired by moderate ambitions, concerned with money, the victim of desire, all too mortal . . . . We are all Will'."

784 Eagleton, Terry. "Books: From Postcard-Length Data, a Wealth of Images and Legends." **Commonweal**, v. 93 (October 30, 1970) 129-31.

[Omnibus review. For Burgess, see p. 131.] "Anthony Burgess's **Shakespeare** is a lavish coffee-table affair, finely embellished with colorplates, but raised above the usual standard of such productions by a bright, racy, neatly intelligent text which compensates for its occasional fancifulness and facetiousness by packing a good deal of out-of-the-way information into its prose. It is knowledgeable and humorous, alternately sensible and quirky, and would make a good Christmas present." [Complete text of review.]

785 Fuller, Edmund. "Shakespeare, in Lively Fiction and Arguable Fact." **Wall Street Journal**, 20 January 1971, p. 14.

[Omnibus review.] One of the most beautiful books of the season. Also lively and contentious. Burgess pushes his conjectures to the point of invention [point not documented], and he has what the Elizabethans might have called a pretty wit.

786 Lask, Thomas. "The Making of a Monument." **New York Times Book Review**, 24 December 1970, p. 19.

[Also reviews **Shakespeare's Lives**, by S. Schoenbaum.] Burgess' suggestion that the 'Comedy of Errors' started as a Shakespeare translation of Plautus' 'Menaechmi' will raise the old issue of Shakespeare's knowledge of Latin, and the controversy over the order in which the plays were written. His solution to the duality of Anne Whately and Anne Hathaway is ingenious. "And he makes the most sensible remark about Shakespeare's wide knowledge and low social standing that I have read, one that ought to be a good answer to the anti-Stratfordians. The book is written in Mr. Burgess's usual bravura style . . . ."

787 Lewis, Naomi. "Shakespeare and the Readers." **New Statesman**, v. 80, no. 2075 (December 25, 1970) 870-71.

A wonderfully vigorous coursing through the Life, and Burgess' book "is always effective on matters that can be vouched for or reasonably guessed at: the nature of James I, the brutish details of Stratford life, bearpits, buboes, the methods of pirating plays, Jonson's part in the Gunpowder Plot, the School of Night, the dusky trulls in the Clerkenwell brothels, the lot of the child players, often 'pressed' into service, the tastes of the Southampton set when Will first entered the circle ('a mixture of Bedouin encampment, the well-appointed monastery and the Hellenic **agape**') and — in plausible reconstruction — a 'world premiere' of **Hamlet** . . . . What does bring the man and the time disturbingly near is the gallery of scenes and portraits: Marlowe, Donne, Essex, Southampton — all the embroidered courtly patrons returning our gaze with hard, ironic, melancholy eyes too well used to watching the unspeakable deeds touched off in the volume's text."

788 Lucy, Sean. "William the Silent." **Tablet**, v. 225, no. 6818 (February 6, 1971) 135.

A handsome volume, but a disappointment. The captions are coy, clever-clever, or muddled. Plain factuality would have helped matters. Burgess plainly does not know the religion of Shakespeare's home and district; and his groundless attack on Shakespeare's wife leads you to think that the biographer had known and hated her most of his life. One gets a strong feeling that Burgess had little heart for the work.

789 McLellan, Joseph. Review of **Shakespeare**. **Washington Post Book World**, 1 May 1977, p. 7.

[Review of paperback ed.] "Burgess (whose **Nothing Like the Sun** is one of fiction's most striking evocations of the young Shakespeare) returns to the subject with a novelist's skill, a scholar's careful dedication, producing a study of the life and works that is delicious in style and often brilliantly original in content."

790 Potter, Dennis. "Deep-Searched with Saucy Looks." **Times** (London), no. 57,979 (September 24, 1970) 15.

For this mere coffee-table book Burgess should be exposed to some of the bleaker lines of the bard. He flutters between the occasional flight of fancy and the gasping waddle of narrow fact. And the words soon give up healthy scholarship to be bandaged with pictures ("Study is like the heaven's glorious sun,/ that shall not be deep-searched with saucy looks") The illustrations are lavish; the setting is sumptuous; and the book as an object recalls Cleopatra's barge. "The insuperable difficulty is that there can be no adequate biography of Shakespeare. The greatest of all writers is the most elusive of all beings when we try to locate him too solidly in his own time and place, sitting at his own chairs and tables." The true features of the man are found in his plays. Still, nothing which Burgess touches can ever be totally dismissed, and there is a splendid sequence which puts down the pretensions of the Baconians by showing how the minds of professional writers work. "A cunning which the satirical rogue exhibits himself when he explains the lack of footnotes by claiming that beauty is preferable to scholarship ('Beauty provoketh fools sooner than gold')."

791 Prouty, Charles Tyler. Review of **Shakespeare**. **Yale Review**, v. 60, no. 3 (March 1971) 456.

Observes that this is a fine book, and praises the illustrations, particularly the plate of Queen Elizabeth dancing with the Earl of Leicester. Burgess' words, as opposed to the illustrations, tend to demonstrate Shakespeare's love of family. Observes that Shakespeare's Company also had a true familial relationship, and gives some reasons for that belief. Wishes that Burgess had been more guarded in presenting his conjecture that Shakespeare was involved with two Annes, Anne Hathaway and Anne Whately. Points out some minor inaccuracies, and concludes that these cavils do nothing "to alter my original view that this is a fine book which I am very glad to have in my library."

A Shorter Finnegans Wake

792 London: Faber, 1966.

793 Seattle: University of Washington Press, 1966.

794 Toronto: Macmillan, 1966.

795 New York: Viking, 1967.

796 New York: Viking, 1968.

797 New York: Viking, 1978, c1967.

Reviews

798 Anon. Review of **A Shorter Finnegans Wake**. **Kirkus Reviews**, December 1, 1966, pp. 1239-1240.

"No doubt pedants will object to the Burgess 'cuts' but since he has tastefully selected the more readable portions, accenting Joyce's robust lyricism and heartiest puns, and kept a good weather-eye open towards shaping the novel's outrageously double-dealing symbology, **A Shorter Finnegans Wake** may well prove to be a college favorite, and perhaps even seduce a few stalwarts into attacking the real thing."

799 Anon. "Funagain." **Time**, v. 89, no. 8 (February 24, 1967) 92.

Finnegans Wake is one of the longest wakes in history, and its comic genius is buried in a mountainous midden of language that is neither English nor Irish. Comments on Burgess's introduction ("admirable for clarity, good sense and erudition"), on the four-cycle theory of history devised by Giovanni Battista Vico and the meaning attached to the name Humphrey Chimpden Earwicker. Quotes the opening lines of the **Wake** and comments on the meaning buried there. Doubts if the **Wake** incorporates normal dream logic, and disputes the claim that Joyce's titanic creative labors liberated the language.

800 Anon. Review of **A Shorter Finnegans Wake**. **Booklist**, v. 63, no. 16 (April 15, 1967) 899-900.

Observes that Burgess has cut the **Wake** to one-third its original length.

801 Anon. Review of **A Shorter Finnegans Wake**. **Choice**, v. 4, no. 4 (June 1967) 422.

Burgess' attempt to cut the **Wake** to about one-third of its original length and filling in spaces with transitional synopses will be helpful to undergraduates.

802 Anon. Review of **A Shorter Finnegans Wake**. **New York Times Book Review**, 1 October 1967, p. 38.

"It was a risky undertaking for, as Burgess points out, **Finnegans Wake** 'contains not one word too many, and there is the danger that to pull at a single thread will unravel the entire fabric.' Provided one does not forget how passionately Joyce wanted his book to be taken on its own terms, one may regard this treatment as a teething ring to sharpen the bite for the main course. And if it makes the obscure masterpiece available to more readers, **A Shorter Finnegans Wake** is worth the price of Burgess."

803 Benstock, Bernard. Review of **A Shorter Finnegans Wake**. **James Joyce Quarterly**, v. 4, no. 2 (Winter 1967) 137-39.

Speculates for what audience this abridgment was intended, and examines Burgess' credentials for producing it. Refers to the feud over Burgess' **Re Joyce**. ". . . scholars who have been working with Joyce materials for some time now were offended by Burgess's disdain for scholarly approaches to the subject, particularly when he pilfered so liberally from these same scholars (his format avoided the clutter of footnotes . . . . Burgess picks up where the **Skeleton Key** leaves off, and remains there . . . . You will find an *uncanny* similarity between the **Skeleton Key** introduction and Burgess's." Burgess' claim to be basing his work on a direct reading of Joyce's work is hollow. He is ignorant of an important Joyce letter which explains both "wielderfight" and "Sosie = double." Burgess is essentially wrong when he claims that Earwicker's name is Porter; and he ignores a wealth of Chinese-Japanese wordplay. Benstock graciously lists some typographical errors. "Frankly, gentle reader, I doubt that you really exist at all, or that a Burgessized version of **Finnegans Wake** will serve as stepping-stone to larger pastures. But if you are there, **A Shorter Finnegans Wake** is available for you in all drugstores where LSD is sold."

804 Blish, James. Review of **A Shorter Finnegans Wake**. **Wake Newslitter**, v. 3, no. 4 (August 1966) 87-89.

Unlike the **Skeleton Key**, this work makes no attempt to simplify or paraphrase single sentences from the **Wake**. The summaries are well done, the discussion in the Foreword is elementary but also well done, and it is possible to read this edition of the **Wake** in one sitting! Provides an exhaustive list of the parts from the original **Wake** found in this version, and argues with Burgess' implication that the **Wake** is a coterie novel. "For my part, I vote for the experiment. It was worth doing, and Mr. Burgess has done it well."

805 Edel, Leon. "A Small Dose of Joyce." **Washington Post Book World**, 19 February 1967, pp. 12-13.

The **Wake** has seemed like gibberish to would-be readers. It is written in a kind of bric-a-brac English, an extravagant jumble of languages and jabberwocky words, outrageous puns and lilting word music which resembles the word-salads sometimes created by certain schizophrenic patients. Burgess' abridgment of the inaccessible masterpiece is a boon to lay readers as opposed to code busters. "Mr. Burgess offers a condensed 'plot'; and he elucidates the story of the pubkeeper and his family, their night's sleep and dreams by the banks of the Liffey. He offers sizable chunks of text, which still remain difficult, and require polyglot verbal alertness. I doubt whether Burgess intends this book to supplant the original, yet this is exactly what will happen. Not in the way that counterfeit drives out the genuine — for this is the genuine — only in smaller doses; but those interested are most likely to turn to the 'shorter Wake' because it is a practical and sensible way of overcoming the oddity of Joyce's performance, and yet sampling its flavor and complexity. At the same time the original remains undefiled, and available to those who want to pore over it endlessly, in its pure state."

806 Griffin, L.W. Review of **A Shorter Finnegans Wake**. **Library Journal**, v. 92, no. 1 (January 1, 1967) 134.

"Though it may be damned by snobs and fanatics, Anthony Burgess's abridgment of **Finnegans Wake**, with its interspersed commentary and its long introduction, will probably do more than any other work has done to bring to the serious general reader one of the most admired — and difficult — books of this century . . . . Highly recommended for both public and academic libraries."

807 Gross, John. Review of **A Shorter Finnegans Wake**. **Observer** (London), 19 June 1966, p. 27.

"And why not? Few of us can manage to spare the lifetime which Joyce demanded for the proper appreciation of his jabberwocky epic . . . . Mr. Burgess contributes a rousing and instructive prefatory essay. It may not dispel all your doubts about the streak of mad pedantry in Joyce's whole conception, but it convincingly reaffirms how many uproarious, sinister and oddly beautiful new effects he was able to wring out of the language."

808 Hodgart, Matthew. "Meanderthalltale." **Manchester Guardian**, 24 June 1966, p. 9.

Remarks that the **Wake** can be read in different ways by different readers. Gives some examples. "Mr. Burgess has made his selection with affection and skill; he has cut the text to less than half, adding an introduction and a dozen pages to provide continuity . . . . To avoid the introduction of new errors, the printers have reproduced photographically the pages of the current hard-cover edition, and Mr. Burgess has ingeniously fitted his commentary into the gaps . . . . My only other complaint is that Mr. Burgess follows in his commentary the old 'skeleton key' of Campbell and Robinson too closely: their work is still helpful but it is not the only way to interpret the mystery." [Reprinted in #809 under the corrected title "Meandertalltale."]

809 Hodgart, Matthew. "Meandertalltale." **Manchester Guardian Weekly**, 30 June 1966, p. 11.

[Reprint of #808 above. The title has been corrected.]

810 O'Flaherty, Gerard. "Books." **Dublin Magazine**, v. 6, no. 1 (Spring 1967) 94-95.

[Omnibus review.] "For those who know nothing of Vico's philosophy or **The Egyptian Book of the Dead**, this is an ideal introduction to what Mr. Burgess describes as 'one of the most entertaining books ever written.' While on holiday, I managed to read it straight through in a week without suffering from insomnia, and feel bound to agree with Joyce that there is lots of fun at **Finnegans Wake**."

811 Seymour-Smith, Martin. "Burgess's Wake." **Spectator**, v. 216, no. 7200 (June 24, 1966) 794.

The **Wake** is a responsible monument to irresponsibility, and it signed the death warrant of the avant garde novel. For Joyce, who had a strange and moving relationship with his schizophrenic daugher Lucia, it probably represented an agonizingly sane mirror of the insane. No one can deny its nobility and its gaiety in the face of many despairs. Mr. Burgess' abridgment is incomparably well done. His seventeen page introduction is a model of modest and straightforward criticism. His linking commentary, based on the **Skeleton Key**, threatens to supersede the **Key** itself.

Time for a Tiger

812 London: Heinemann, 1956.

813 London: Heinemann, 1968.

[NOTE: See also editions of **The Malayan Trilogy** (British title) and **The Long Day Wanes** (American title) of which this work is a part.]

Reviews

813.2 Burgess on his own work: "My first attempts at writing fiction were made in response to an exotic stimulus, and I have often wondered since whether this was right. I was living in Malaya in 1955, working for the Government and, in my spare time, carrying on with what I thought was my true artistic vocation — the composing of music. One morning I woke to hear the muezzin calling — 'There is no God but Allah' — and, as often happens when one first wakes, to find the names of my creditors parading through my mind, together with what I owed them. Something like this:

> **La ilaha illa'lah**
> Lim Kean Swee $395
> Chee Sin Hye $120
> Tan Meng Kwang $250
> **La ilaha illa'lah**

And so on. Here obviously was the beginning of a novel: a man lying in bed in the Malayan dawn, listening to the muezzin calling, worrying about his debts. So, out of this little *collage*, I began to write, with suspicious ease, my first published work of fiction."

814 Anon. "Burning Bright." **Times Literary Supplement**, no. 2,854 (November 9, 1956) 670.

[Omnibus review.] "It provides a number of amusing incidents, but because it is truthfully seen by the author as an arid and fatiguing society of mixed races in a hot country it does not offer the tenser conflicts that make a powerful story. Mr. Burgess, knitting loosely, cannot and does not give his people the chance to go through their emotional paces. They never really escape the burden of appearing to have been brought together artificially, of being expected by the novelist to strike sparks off each other. This they rarely do: there is too much drifting, drinking and droning — although Mr. Burgess is at his best in the drinking scenes."

815 Blakeston, Oswell. "New Novels." **Time and Tide**, v. 37, no. 43 (October 27, 1956) 1306.

[Omnibus review.] The imaginary Malay state of Lanchap is convincingly real. "Europeans eat with sucking noises, making every course sound like soup, moustached native pupils learn from a history book written by a woodwork expert ('History is a sort of story. The story of our country is a very interesting story.'), dogs truffle for fleas, terrorists (men called Lotus Blossom and Dawn Lily) indulge in gutting and garotting, and the dawn comes like a huge flower in a Nature film. It is a really brilliant presentation of a land that looks on logic as a Western importation . . . . But having got everything vividly set, Mr. Burgess does not seem to know what to do for a story. One cannot be convinced by the way his four central characters make a team and go off on dangerous picnics together. However there is enough colour and wit to keep the book alive."

816 George, Daniel. "New Novels." **Spectator**, no. 6696 (October 26, 1956) 582.

[Omnibus review.] "For the moment, Malaya seems to be the popular stopped-up sink of iniquity. [Burgess' novel] has received praise so excessive that it is armoured against critical pinpricks, and depreciation of its conformity to an established type of unsavouriness would be regarded as naive. As for declaring that one was not amused by it — unthinkable!" Complains that the characters are incompetent, silly, dipsomaniacal, ignorant and prejudiced, and that each page is littered with italicized words and phrases in Urdu, Malay, Arabic, Tamil, Hindustani and Chinese. "The reviewer who, according to the advertisement, said 'Mr. Kingsley Amis and the Red Brick boys will have to look to their laurels' may be right. Mr. Anthony Burgess may indeed, as another said, have 'literary gifts of a very high order.' We shall see."

Tremor of Intent

817 London: Heinemann, 1966.

818 New York: Norton, 1966.

819 New York: Ballantine, 1972, c1966. Pbk.

820 New York: Norton, 1977, c1966. Pbk.

Translations

821 Danish: **Martyrernes Blod**. Copenhagen: Spektrum, 1969. Translated by Harry Mortensen.

822 Dutch: **Mensen in etui**. Amsterdam: Arbeiderspers, 1976. Translated by Wim Dielemans.

823 French: **Un Agent qui vous veut du bien**. Paris: Denoel, 1969. Translated by Michel Deutsch.

824 French: **Un Agent qui vous veut du bien**. Paris: Gallimard, 1973. Translated by Michel Deutsch.

825 Portuguese: **A Ultima missao**. Rio de Janeiro: Artenova, 1973. Translated by Edith Arthens.

826 Spanish: **Tremula intencion**. Buenos Aires: Sudamerican, 1972. Translated by Patricio Canto.

827 Swedish: **Skuggan av ett Svek**. Stockholm: Wahlstrom & Widstrand, 1972. Translated by Caj Lundgren.

Reviews

828 Anon. "Spying for Laughs." **Times Literary Supplement**, 9 June 1966, p. 509.

"He has written a first-class knockabout thriller with erotic scenes that are little masterpieces of fierce delicacy . . . . Mr. Burgess often writes like Nabokov, with the same energy and delight in language, the same constant awareness of nuance and ambiguity in the words he uses; very Nabokovian too is the mixture of horror and comedy that reaches a climax in the scene where Roper and Hillier are confronted by the professional killer who has been appointed their executioner. Yet, for all its fine qualities, the novel does not wholly satisfy. The versatility and facility that dazzle and delight are also Mr. Burgess toughest handicaps, for they invariably leave one wishing for more concentration, a more relentless probing of idea, motive and situation. **Tremor of Intent** is a marvellously entertaining book but when the fireworks die away there is not much left in the cold darkness to warm or to sustain."

829 Kirkus Reviews, v. 34, no. 18 (September 15, 1966) 1007.

"Burgess again defies easy classification as a novelist, this time turning out a seriocomic Catholic spy novel in his richer style. It is occasionally mock-Joycean and will have the reader dipping in the dictionary, for Burgess never shirks the divine afflatus when he wishes to swell a scene or two . . . . The climax is a variation on the doublecross Le Carré used on Leamas, in which used-up hero is sent on an ersatz mission to effect his own doom. An entertainment from a writer's writer."

830 Anon. "Eschatology & Espionage." **Time**, v. 88, no. 16 (October 14, 1966) 125-26.

"The literary chromosomes of Graham Greene, C.P. Snow and Vladimir Nabokov are also traceable in this deliberate hybrid. But Anthony Burgess is not trying to imitate them. He has never written an unoriginal novel or an unlaminated one. Every Burgess surface conceals another, like Salome's veils, and they must all peel off to expose the author's naked core. In this exceptional book. . . the reader quickly discovers that Burgess has much more on his mind than international intrigue . . . . The reader may feel, however, that he has encountered some of **Tremor**'s eschatology before. Hillier's religious experience mirrors that of Richard Ennis in **A Vision of Battlements**. In **A Clockwork Orange**, Burgess emphasized the importance of free will, whether for good or evil. **Tremor** emphasizes it again, but perhaps less successfully . . . . Yet Burgess, stirring with memorable characterization and wit, has succeeded in serving up one of the best spy novels since **The Spy Who Came in from the Cold**."

831 Anon. Notice of **Tremor of Intent**. **America**, v. 115, no. 22 (November 26, 1966) 708.

This eschatological spy novel may strike some as also scatological: it has a definite preoccupation with sex. [The reviewer is playing with words. 'Scatological' does not mean that at all.] The work is marked by the author's peculiar gifts of insight, thought and style.

832 Anon. Review of **Tremor of Intent**. **Choice**, v. 4, no. 5-6 (July-August 1967) 530.

"Burgess, like Shakespeare, employs the trappings of a popular story vehicle (most of the gimmicks are here and embellished with some of the best parody to appear in the 1960's) to achieve his ends on many levels — 20th-century life is more of a game; good and evil are not distinct; and man's intent is just a timorous tremor. Neither as funny as **Honey for the Bears** nor as tragi-comic as **A Clockwork Orange**, but libraries will enhance their modern fiction collections with **Tremor**."

833 Anon. Review of **Tremor of Intent**. **Publishers Weekly**, v. 192, no. 11 (September 11, 1967) 71.

"Since the author himself describes this book as 'an eschatological spy novel,' the reader may be warned that, if he yearns for James Bond fare, he should pass this by. It's a spy-novel-cum-intellectual-exercise filled with Burgessian puns, obscure literary and philological references, satire, bawdiness and just about everything one comes to expect from Burgess, including obfuscations." [Complete text of review.]

834 Anon. Review of **Tremor of Intent**. **Virginia Quarterly Review**, v. 43, no. 1 (Winter 1967) x.

Burgess turns out a steady stream of finely carved gems, and this work is a very good spy story. "Working around such promising themes as the Profumo case and the fate of Sean Lemass (Burgess is a little close here), the author has produced a singularly well-written little vignette of cold-war intrigue salted generously with black comedy and sex."

835 Anon. Notice of **Tremor of Intent**. **Best Sellers**, September 1, 1972, p. 262.

[Review of Ballantine pbk. ed.] "Anthony Burgess' sex-filled, Roman-Catholic-Jansenist haunted spy novel of some six years ago." [Complete text of notice.]

836 Anon. Notice of **Tremor of Intent**. **New York Times Book Review**, 24 April 1977, p. 49.

It is described as an eschatological spy novel, but don't let that put you off, for there are touches of James Bond, Sterne, Joyce and Evelyn Waugh.

837 Bliven, Naomi. "Books: The Good Guys vs. the Bad Guys." **New Yorker**, v. 42, no. 51 (February 11, 1967) 159-62.

[Omnibus review. For Burgess, see pp. 159-60.] Readers of spy thrillers normally expect to be entertained and to be spared the pother of abstract ideas. The work is full of wonderful entertainment, full of scary surprises, and funny to boot. But here the deaths and survivals imply questions about the judgment of God and the nature of sin, and these theological ideas are artfully and unobtrusively woven into the narrative. Hillier's Manichaeanism (nobody can take that ancient heresy seriously any more) is more of a mood than a philosophical alternative. Argues that this mood ("The expense of spirit in a waste of shame is lust in action") is almost always a masculine one which springs from getting away with sins of the flesh. Wonders to what extent this mood is shared by the author, and suggests that his imagination is overflowingly funny in a way that suggests joy rather than hatred of the Creation. "I suspect that Burgess wants us to take Hillier's theological development a mite more seriously than I can; for me, the book's profundity is not the theology but the comedy."

838 Cook, Bruce. "Spying, the Cold War and Eschatology." **National Catholic Reporter**, 18 January 1967, p. 9.

839 Crinklaw, Don. Review of **Tremor of Intent**. **Commonweal**, v. 85, nos. 11-12 (December 16, 1966) 329-30.

An exhilarating display of literary craftsmanship in a work that combines an examination of the morality of espionage with an account of a soul's progress from unbelief to doubt and torment to purgation and final religious commitment. "The reservations which have in the past kept me from surrendering completely to Mr. Burgess' remarkable powers still persist, however, and some question arise: Isn't his language, for all its awesomeness, rather too tidy? Are his people people or cunningly contrived collections of attitudes and interesting psychological states? In short, do his books, except intermittently, come to life? The vitality of **Tremor of Intent** exceeds, I think, that of his earlier novels, yet there are places in which the author's verbal powers are both his glory and his downfall, the imagery seems to come from a combination of creative force and the poet's handbook, and the poetry of the grander scenes seems to belong to Burgess rather than Hillier.''

840 Cromie, Alice. "An Original Spy Tale." **Chicago Tribune Books Today**, 13 November 1966, Section 9, p. 17.

"Hillier and his fellow workers are as glittering in wit and devious intent as Deighton's **I Spy**, as full of bounce as Bond, and as bounce-backable. But using what by now are well-thumbed formulas of espionage fiction, Burgess has produced an original spy tale." Hopes that Burgess will now get his share of deserved attention in the U.S. Quotes some sections of the novel to demonstrate its merits.

841 Daniel, John. "Who's Your Agent?" **Spectator**, no. 7198 (June 10, 1966) 733-34.

In theory, the intellectual spy thriller offers rich natural material: debates on loyalty and personal behaviour while the spy's biography presents a whole archive of material on alienation and disaffection. Unfortunately, writers who attempt to exploit the mode tend to forget the split between action and thought. "For the action of the spy story is of a particular kind. It does not arise from character, but exists as a separate entity. It is anarchic, blazing, whirling, senseless. As such it offers perhaps a paradigm of our modern existence, but it is such a powerful and intoxicating draught that ultimately it doesn't matter a hoot whether the agents are married to German whores, from English Catholic schools or descended from a long line of Elizabethan martyrs." The last chapter does not link all the levels of the novel, as the publisher's blurb claims. "But [it is] a compulsively readable story, full of gore and lechery and money, in which Burgess's superiority over other writers of the genre emerges. His killings are better, his women are better, his evocation of places (especially the Black Sea ports) is better and his wit and *savoir-vivre* give his hero a smoothness beside which Mr. Bond is a provincial impostor."

842 Davis, Robert Gorham. "Invaded Selves." **Hudson Review**, v. 19, no. 4 (Winter 1966-1967) 659-668.

[Omnibus review. For Burgess, see pp. 666-67.] "**Tremor of Intent** combines immediate erotic and sadistic action of a totally uncommitted, daydreaming kind, with general sentiments against cruelty and betrayal that impose assent on the reader. But politically everything gets cancelled out. Religion does not complement politics; it replaces it. Hillier enters abruptly and unpersuasively a faith of which the reader has been given rather unsavory glimpses on a mostly metaphysical level. Eschatology does not figure at all."

843 Dolbier, Maurice. Review of **Tremor of Intent**. **World Journal Tribune**, 7 October 1966, p. 20.

844 Dollen, Charles. Review of **Tremor of Intent**. **Best Sellers**, October 15, 1966, pp. 254-55.

It is "an important novel, but not an easy novel to read. Since the reader has no way of knowing how important the many religious and philosophical conversations are, these tend to become boring. When sex seems to be over-emphasized just for sensationalism, that too is boring. Yet this book can definitely be recommended to the mature adult."

845 Duchene, Anne. "Playing the Game." **Manchester Guardian Weekly**, 16 June 1966, p. 11.

What plagues and aborts Burgess' writing is that Greene wrote just before him and pre-empted his themes, so Burgess plays the Catholic clown to sheer away from any too embarrassing likeness. Followed by plot summary. Then: "A bit of everything, then. And it is splendid entertainment, of course: outrageous ribaldry, lordly, lazy intelligence, all baked in the glorious thick crust of Mr. Burgess's exuberant language. Graham Greene used to distinguish between his 'novels' and his 'entertainments,' though. Mr. Burgess doesn't; and one can quite see why. It seems only properly respectful to regret it, too. Because this is a ridiculous book, really, to come from one so richly endowed."

846 Evans, Fallon. "The Ultimate Spy." **The Critic; A Catholic Review of Books and the Arts**, v. 25, no. 4 (February-March 1967) 78-79.

847 Gardner, John. "More Smog from the Dark Satanic Mills." **Southern Review**, v. 5, no. 1, N.S. (Winter 1969) 224-44.

[Omnibus review. For Burgess, see pp. 239-40.] It is a black comedy in the sense that what ought to be sad turns out to be grimly funny. In this work the characters are comically unable to make up their minds or get off their hind ends and assert themself for heaven or hell. Hillier considers his mission to bring Roper back as his last move in the thoroughly dirty game of spy and counterspy. "After this he will break out and turn honest. But Hillier is only a man; he cannot resist the force of truth drugs administered to him, and, once having assisted the enemy, however unwillingly, he cannot escape. Limited in a thousand ways by their tragicomic humanity, Burgess's characters can get no farther than the tremor of their noble intent." Burgess is a good writer, but not a great one. His characters do not fight toward the impossible with the same demonic intensity as those of Lagerkvist, and they are not cruelly broken when they fall.

848 Graver, Lawrence. "House of Burgesses." **New Republic**, v. 155, no. 16 (October 15, 1966) 25, 27.

This new novel, which proves that the house of fiction has many windows and that Burgess seems to have stared out of all of them, shows the strengths and limitations of Burgess' fiction. The element of play is outrageous and nearly always funny: see, for example, the duel combined with an orgy. Good jokes get better if you catch the allusions to Dante, Goethe, Joyce or Robert Graves, and the work is a kind of clown's **Wasteland**, but the serious ideas come on too casually and are never given sufficient articulation. The characters fail to rise above caricatures; hence their assertions are so much intellectual ballast. The denouement is so preposterous that one suspects a leg-pull: we are supposed to accept the Manichean heresy working comfortably within the established order. "Several weeks ago. . . Burgess discussed his work in progress, a novel about a middle-aged poet working as a bartender in a London hotel. Being called back to the mess of the real world sounds like a good omen."

849 H., P. Review of **Tremor of Intent**. **The Month**, v. 222, no. 1189 (September 1968) 154.

"Not for the squeamish or the prurient, Mr. Burgess' umpteenth novel is much subtler than its dustjacket. It looks like Bond out-Bonded and the pursuit, the gadgets, the inhumanly clever opponent, the lush girls are all there. But there is something more and it is rooted firmly in a 'Catholic background' which it would be totally mistaken to view as decor to add the spice of blasphemy to fairly routine 'sin'." Observes that the epigraph from Eliot applies to Roper. Quotes Hillier's speech on the battle between good and evil and remarks that Hillier creaks towards regeneration and, in a moment of apparent death, makes what would be called a perfect act of contrition in the old books. A dazzling comedy on the surface of things, it conveys a disturbing hint of the underdog clearly *pas pour les infants*.

850 Harris, Leo. "Novels or Thrillers?" **Punch**, v. 250, no. 6563 (June 22, 1966) 926.

[Omnibus review.] Crimewriters entertain; novelists expound, evangelise, and express themselves — which, rather unfairly, frees them from the salutary discipline of plot and plausibility. "Between polymath and know-it-all is but a fine dividing line; in **Tremor of Intent** Mr. Burgess funambulates expertly showering us with great coruscations of recondite facts (or *fictions*?), sparkling displays of wit, satire, parody and philosophy. Using the spy story — or, rather, **pastiche** spy story — as stalking horse he snipes, belabours, titillates — but never betrays his own position. "Is the ignorant, anti-semitic priest a parody of all those novels about Catholic education? Is the superb Deva's sexual technique really derived from the Tamil **Kama Sutra**, the **Pokam**? Is the Manichean thesis seriously intended? Does Theodorescu mean 'Son of the gift of God?' Should we *enjoy* the highly technical Rude Bits, just like the poor people, or can intellectuals be trusted (Gibbon left Rude Bits in Latin)?"

851 Hatch, Robert. "A Tour of the Pops." **Nation**, v. 203, no. 19 (December 5, 1966) 620-21.

[Omnibus review. For Burgess, see one paragraph on p. 620.] Valiantly observes that he has checked the meaning of the term eschatology; that the book is exceedingly erudite in a playful way; that the delicious sexual refinements of Miss Devi can probably be traced to their sources; and that Burgess equates lust with gluttony to an unsettling degree. "Otherwise, his narrative is alive with violent incidents and sudden encounters designed to expose and admonish the killer in us all."

852 Kitching, J. Review of **Tremor of Intent**. **Publishers Weekly**, v. 190, no. 13 (September 26, 1966) 131.

"There is an underlay of somewhat cynical humor, some very violent action, and intricate plots and counterplots to entice readers through a recondite suspense story — readers who might be put off at first by Hillier's intense analysis of his own motives and those of Roper."

853 Lejeune, Anthony. "Bond in Greene-Land." **Tablet,** v. 330, no. 6584 (July 30, 1966) 872.

"That Mr. Burgess is an exceptionally talented writer is a truth long ago proved beyond dispute. His wit and inventiveness ensure that his books are never dull. **Tremor of Intent** is not dull; its style gleams with sophisticated literary polish and the ideas embedded in it are solid enough to start a train of thought or two. But whether it was itself a good idea, whether the conception deserved the expenditure of so much talent, seems more doubtful . . . . Mr. Burgess has a tricky way of saying, or not quite saying, what he means; and his prose, normally so lucid, suffers occasionally from the baneful influence of James Joyce. **Tremor** moves — and moves briskly — along a knife-edge between narrative and parody, nonsense and profundity. Only a highly intelligent writer could succeed in so difficult an exercise: and it may be felt that a writer intelligent enough to achieve this feat would be better employed working within a less ephemeral frame of reference."

854 Levitas, Gloria. "No Fun and Games." **Washington Post Book World,** 12 November 1967, p. 23.

[Review of Ballantine pbk. ed.] An extraordinary spy novel. "The plot twists and turns engagingly. The hero has the proper credentials: a strong sexual drive and a brand on his thigh inflicted during some previous assignment. If that's not sufficient, Burgess should be read for his precise use of words, as breathtaking as his fast-moving plot."

855 Lindroth, James R. Review of **Tremor of Intent. America,** v. 115, no. 17 (October 22, 1966) 492.

It is a good-natured parody of spy fiction, a sermon on the seven deadly sins, a philosophic reflection on the nature of morality, a satirical thrust at the games people play — and, through Hillier's reflections on free will, morality and 'palpable, stinking evil' Burgess shows an eschatological concern with God, the Devil, Heaven and Hell.

856 Lord, John. "Slick Spy Story on Split Levels." **Life,** v. 61, no. 16 (October 14, 1966) 10.

It is time for Americans to catch on to the remarkable Anthony Burgess, whose 16 novels have made a fairly noiseless appearance in the U.S. He is the stunt man of the novel, and this parody of the spy novel is a real hunt'em down thriller which mocks the contemporary masters of the genre. "With the women lascivious, the weapons authentic and the locations exotic . . . . [the novel provides us] a cold and ironic look at current international politics . . . ." His thesis is that real evil lies in neutrality and the characters in his thriller are the personae of his allegory of good and evil. "Burgess writes with the urgency of a man in a condemned cell with dawn coming up. His mortuary humor, his narrative speed, his intellectual weight and the baroque brilliance of his verbal style should have brought him more fame here than he enjoys. **Tremor of Intent**, because it is sensational, may turn the trick. It deserves to succeed for better reasons. Not only is Burgess hopeful, which is a lot in these post-black-humorish days, but most important, he is honest."

857 Maloff, Saul. "Sin Was a Chronic Disease." **Saturday Review,** v. 49, no. 44 (October 29, 1966) 32-33.

The prodigally gifted Burgess begins with conscious cliché and ends the book in paradox — and all his will and narrative agility cannot synthesize the disparate elements. He fails to discover adequate metaphors for radical evil; hence, devoid of seriousness, the work degenerates into a kind of theological farce. The actual content with which Burgess invests his drama is so extravagantly ludicrous as to be ludicrous. Hillier (the name is allegorical) renounces the flesh by immersing himself in the vices of gluttony and satyriasis. Suddenly the spirit stirs within him, and Hillier is transformed into a priest. Unfortunately, ". . . Hillier simply cannot contain the burden of ideas imposed on him: the epiphany is merely asserted, and the proclaimed transformation is more shocking than startling, more depressing than elevating. And because he cannot contain the novel's willed ambiguities — heady stuff — they are in the end left to lie there, earth-bound reminders of Burgess' spiraling ambitions, fragments of two novels, neither wholly achieved, though both are brilliant, essentially frivolous gestures on the part of a novelist who is capable of anything."

858 Mayne, Richard. "Spy in the Sky." **New Statesman,** v. 71, no. 1839 (June 10, 1966) 852.

[Omnibus review.] Burgess seems to be playing for laughs as well as kicks; then gets interested in the mechanics of false identities; and finally turns his agent into a priest. "Along the way, in typical Burgess fashion, there are cryptographical and philological sidelights, an erudite bout of physical love-making with all the passion of a Swiss watch, a child prodigy strayed in from Salinger's trying Glass family, and a villainous heavy of the type played by Sig Ruman in the early Marx Bros. pictures.'' We're meant to be agog for the hidden depths but Burgess, unlike Graham Greene, is less successful at integrating the different levels of his stories, at blending the tonic with the wine. To paraphrase Kingsley Amis, Burgess may be good for you, but the others [Greene, Sterne] make you drunk.

859 Moon, Eric. "Joyous Cynicism." **Washington Post Book World**, 9 October 1966, p. 2.

Speculates if rapid-fire production and gadfly variety of themes, characters and backgrounds has kept reviewers and readers off-balance, and so prevented Burgess from being ranked with contemporary novelists like Amis and Sillitoe, Murdoch, Braine and Spark. This work of espionage proves that Denis Hillier has inherited his creator's somewhat joyous cynicism, and it also demonstrates Burgess' devotion to Sterne, Joyce and Evelyn Waugh. "A linguist and teacher of language, Burgess is one of the rare novelists writing today (Nabokov, Barth, Updike are others) in whose work the language and the style often seem too elaborate for the framework they are required to carry. He is a virtuoso with words, but his passion for them may also be his Achilles heel as a novelist. He caroms words and phrases off each other like Willie Mosconi at the billiard table. But the books as a whole are mostly a little too pat, too professionally packaged, too much tinkles thrown off with a very fluent left hand." Burgess is capable of more than mere entertainments in the Graham Greene manner, and his superb performances suggest an Olivier performing in vaudeville.

860 Ostermann, Robert. "Buoyant Bawdiness: **Tremor of Intent**, Proves Anew the Artistry of Anthony Burgess." **National Observer**, 31 October 1966, p. 20.

The suspicious reader, confronted by the buoyant bawdiness, satire and love of language that variously recall Laurence Sterne, Johanthan Swift, Evelyn Waugh and James Joyce, assumes that the effortless display of such riches may mean that the prolific author is not serious. But in this work the skeptic will find such wonders as the ravishing Miss Devi, the Trencherman Stakes between Hillier and Theodorescu and he will shortly conclude that "The pace is swift; the exposition of character and motive and meaning is conducted with dazzling sureness; the play of ideas is balanced and intricate." Burgess proves by his varied output set in different periods, countries and climates that "Neither time nor location matters; an artist can begin anywhere. And Mr. Burgess is an artist. For him anything is possible and everything becomes an invitation for a new voyage of discovery."

861 Pritchard, William H. "The Burgess Memorandum." **Partisan Review**, v. 34, no. 2 (Spring 1967) 319-323.

It is advertised as a James Bond spoof, a gloss on the Cold War, some meaty stuff about ultimate realities. At first acquaintance, we feel in the presence of the Catholic Satirist, not a particularly new or exciting thing to be in the presence of. But Burgess as a novelist is married to his cast, who confers on even momentary bit players momentary verbal splendor. Examines the description of Mr. Theodorescu, and observes that even Sidney Greenstreet can hardly live up to such magnificence. In some respects, examined closely, Burgess' prose is clearly better than that of Greene. The question is whether this superlative style can express Burgess' eschatological meanings: History a bloody mess, the modern world a terrible place, the musings on Ultimate Reality. Concludes that Burgess succeeds best when the eschatology does not advertise itself directly, but inheres in the situation; in, for example, the great, mad event, the eating contest between Hillier and Theodorescu. It is one of the most richly labeled social events since the wedding of Miss Fir Conifer in **Ulysses**. The fact is that the values testified by Burgess' prose refuse to be modified by or enlarged into any higher (eschatological, if you will) values. "**Tremor of Intent**, like Burgess' other novels is only as solid and satisfying on the whole as it is page by page. But page by page it is very satisfying indeed, asking to be reread and re-experienced, rather than pondered and then abstracted into a pungent message for our time . . . . Anthony Burgess, like Hillier in this novel, plays the secret-agent game of 'being a good technician, superb at languages, agile, light-fingered, cool.' But behind these ambiguous gifts, sentence by sentence, there stands revealed the man who wrote them, an extraordinary and attractive character whose like has been seldom seen."

862 Ready, William. Review of **Tremor of Intent**. **Library Journal**, v. 91, no. 19 (November 1, 1966) 5426.

"This bell of a book swings its clapper from a toll through a crash and clang to a dubious and tuneful carillon with such joy below that it tempers the swinging abandon, the salacity and improvident adventure

. . . . He is a Graham Greene with mustard . . . . There is more action and erotic jiggery-pokery in this book than it can contain without spilling over . . . . Here is a book for all, save children. Put it on Reserve. Buy many copies.''

863 Richardson, Maurice. "Burgess in Spy-Land." **Observer** (London), 5 June l966, p. 26.

Worries about Burgess trying to out-do Bond. The book crosses the border into nightmare-land, and the plot is meagre. "The underlying theological thesis about serving either God or the Devil, but not ourselves, seems to my simple mind neo-Papist, or possibly neo-Manichean, gas. Mr. Burgess is a nice-natured person, and though his wilder flights are bound to shock a lot of people into blue fits I don't find anything inherently noxious in them. He overwrites insanely. What I cannot understand is why a man who is so outstandingly clever should feel compelled to try too hard to be even cleverer.''

864 Saal, Rollene W. "Pick of the Paperbacks." **Saturday Review**, v. 43 (October 25, 1969) 42.

Notices that Ballantine has published **A Clockwork Orange**, **Enderby** and **Tremor of Intent** in paperback.

865 Schott, Webster. "A New Order of Things." **New York Times Book Review**, 16 October 1966, p. 4.

"Anthony Burgess silver-plates another piece of our cultural junk. Using the spy as missile-era folk hero, he creates a gleaming novel of ideas — troubling ideas about the survival value of ideology, the disease of our appetites, our malevolent innocence as we perpetrate incredible atrocities and feel no guilt. Brazenly clever, Burgess is Britain's answer to Vladimir Nabokov . . . . A facsimile of reality, his imaginary system reduces life and death, sex and belief, to a game. The game has dualistic goals. Support poles of strength, whether good or evil. To hell with neutralism. That's how to die. Choose strongly and live . . . . Burgess is nothing if not outrageous. Morality is urgency. 'We need new terms,' Hillier says in Roman collar near the end. 'God and Notgod, Salvation and damnation of equal dignity, the two sides of the coin of ultimate reality. . . we'd all rather see devil-worship than bland neutrality.' In his strange way Burgess likes mankind. He would see us monsters before he would see us give up life.''

866 Tisdall, Julie. "Fiction: Julie Tisdall on Two Outrages." **Books and Bookmen**, v. 11 (August 1966) 34-35.

This mixture of espionage and religion, part spoof Bondism and part philosophical thriller, includes some hilarious and unforgettable scenes, and it is "no mere spy saga. Hillier is a man seeking a philosophy, albeit enjoyable. Through all his adventures he is 'creaking towards a regeneration.' Taken as serious food for thought or merely as outrageous entertainment this book is bound to succeed. And deservedly.''

867 Tucker, Martin. Review of **Tremor of Intent**. **Commonweal**, v. 85, nos. 9-10 (December 2, 1966) 273-74.

"Burgess's sheer joy of words, his almost savory handling of adjectives, pervades his latest novel. It is no accident that puns abound in his work: Burgess is dedicated to the greatest pun-master, Joyce.'' The novel, described as an eschatological spy novel, gives food for thought on many levels.

868 Willett, John. "Burgess's New Novel." **Listener**, v. 75, no. 1941 (June 9, 1966) 849.

This fashionable spy thriller in the fashionable vein starts well. The opening scene, in which the shabby, tough, disgruntled British agent sets out for the Crimea on a gastronomic cruise, is the best and most Burgessian part of the book. The school scenes, and the portrait of the German wife, are well done. However, Burgess parodies the conventions of the thriller (see, for example, the great gastronomic contest between Hillier and Theodorescu, and the superfatted sensuality in which Hillier practises Kama Sutraesque exercises with Theodorescu's beautiful Indian companion), and it is not certain when the parody is meant to stop. We are not certain if the dingy, reverent conclusion of the story is to be treated solemnly, or if it parodies the Greene theology. "That the novel is well written, with enough cleverness and erudition for six ordinary authors, hardly needs saying to anybody who already knows Mr. Burgess' books. The trouble is that it is not worthy of his really quite remarkable gifts.''

Urgent Copy: Literary Studies

869 London: Cape, 1968.

870 New York: Norton, 1969, c1968.

871 Harmondsworth, Eng.: Penguin, 1973. Pbk.

Reviews

872 Anon. Review of **Urgent Copy: Literary Studies**. **Kirkus Reviews**, v. 37 (January 1, 1969) 36.

Burgess is a word-man and we can expect some sesquipedalian wonders. "What is unexpected is the general level of great good sense Burgess displays in his critical judgments: in style, he may have Joycean exuberance, but in evaluating everyone from Milton to Levi-Strauss and McLuhan he travels the broad middle ground so thunderously advocated by Dr. Johnson. Thus his vivid metaphors are counterbalanced by the essentially conservative cast of his mind, and the variety of his interest (he can be equally cogent on Kipling and pornography) are saved from dilettantism by the strict observance of scholarly rules and acumen. In short, a pleasure to read and to ponder."

873 Anon. Review of **Urgent Copy: Literary Studies**. **Publishers Weekly**, v. 195, no. 3 (January 20, 1969) 264-65.

Burgess the novelist, poet, authority on linguistics and composer — prolific author of five books in one year — writes reviews in his spare time. The best essays are his critiques of Shaw, Dylan Thomas and the postwar American novel.

874 Anon. "Beyond the Pleasure Principle." **Times Literary Supplement**, 13 March 1969, pp. 258-59.

[Omnibus review. For Burgess, see p. 259.] "One of the harshest attacks Mr. Grigson has made recently was on Mr. Anthony Burgess as a critic [see #885]. Certainly Mr. Burgess overstates the case when he subtitles **Urgent Copy**, his collection of reviews, 'Literary Studies.' Their weakness is too little study, too hasty an enthusiam or burst of bile, too quick a turning of attention to large, vague literary questions. . . and too quick a turning away from them again and rounding off with a joke or a genuflection. Mr. Burgess's real gifts, as seen in his novels, only come to the fore. . . when he is really worked up, or when he can tell a story rather than go on with judging the book."

875 Anon. "The Creative Man's Critic." **Time**, v. 93 (April 11, 1969) 108.

The novels of Burgess are distinguished by their Elizabethan prodigality of creation, and this work proves that he is also a good critic. His critical intelligence functions at many levels; he loves to play with words; his article against Brophy et al. is a masterpiece of robust derision and scholarly scorn. He also traces the worst modern vices (materialism, pragmatism and relativism) back to the influence of the English monk Pelagius. Such rigorous philosophical dogma is unexpected in English criticism. "Yet Burgess' prose never seems plodding despite his spiritual preoccupations. In any case, he is the kind of man who could write a light review of a heavy British Treasury tax form. Should he do so in the future, it will have to be written from Valetta. Anthony Burgess has transplanted himself from taxheavy Britain to Malta. This move is part of what the British deplore as the Brain Drain. Where Burgess is concerned, both the brain and the drain are considerable."

876 Anon. Review of **Urgent Copy: Literary Studies**. **Virginia Quarterly Review**, v. 45, no. 3 (Summer 1969) ci.

In this volume of reviews and slight essays Anthony Burgess, the best of the current wordsmiths, "offers sparks more than the formal essay can afford. Here are bits on novels, criticism, linguistics, and just sheer language. Burgess fans will enjoy their hero in bits and gobbets."

877 Anon. Review of **Urgent Copy: Literary Studies**. **Booklist**, v. 65, no. 19 (June 1, 1969) 1107.

"Essays on novelists, playwrights, artists, and poets, together with analyses of diverse literary themes, written with uncompromising taste and wit."

878 Anon. Review of **Urgent Copy: Literary Studies**. **Choice**, v. 6, no. 11 (January 1970) 91.

"Happily there are many moments in this incredibly sprightly book where he reveals himself fully qualified to judge (useful criticism of Dickens, Nabokov, Saul Bellow) and not always kind and cautious: see his contempt for Brigid Brophy's **Fifty Works of English Literature We Could Do Without** or his forthright disagreement with George Steiner's writings about Silence. These essays, plus many others, vindicate Burgess' claim that 'some fine nervous prose can be jerked out by deadlines.' Recommended."

879 Anon. Notice of **Urgent Copy**. **Books and Bookmen**, v. 18 (September 1973) 138.

"Essays, reviews by journalist Burgess who has uttered 'occasional sneers at writers who slap articles between hard covers and call them Collected Essays' but is now unrepentent, only half-apologetic because he knows his own are good." [Complete text of notice.]

880 Browne, Joseph. Review of **Urgent Copy: Literary Studies**. **America**, v. 120, no. 13 (March 29, 1969) 369-70.

The reader will find relief from the fear that literary criticism is dominated by compulsive punsters and pedants. The essays are consistently penetrating, provocative and objective; his exegesis of other authors is sympathetic and perhaps even excessively kind. "These essays are obviously the work of a man who is in love with literature; and in an age when it has become increasingly easy to be discouraged and often sickened by critics whose inverted values exalt only what is obscure and perverse, it is encouraging to learn that Anthony Burgess is alive and well in the literary world."

881 Cutler, Edward J. Review of **Urgent Copy: Literary Studies**. **Library Journal**, v. 94, no. 6 (March 15, 1969) 1147.

"Often Burgess' prose rises to the level of genuinely meaningful literary criticism in the fullest sense of the term; at all times it provides a graceful, witty, and enlightening examination of its subjects' worth."

882 Dick, Susan. Review of **Urgent Copy: Literary Studies**. **Queen's Quarterly**, v. 76, no. 2 (Summer 1969) 366-67.

[Omnibus review.] This volume demonstrates the same wit, impressive range of knowledge and highly readable prose found in Burgess' novels. We can be thankful that novelists find it financially necessary to write criticism. His explanation of Yeats's mythical system is both lucid and sensible, and the other articles on diverse subjects are moving, able and and full of energy. Quotes Burgess on the role of the artist. ". . . I regard the artist's trade as not merely the most honourable but also the most holy. The vision of unity, which is what the artist sells, is preferable to any mere religious or metaphysical manifestoes."

883 Doyle, Paul A. Review of **Urgent Copy: Literary Studies**. **Best Sellers**, April 1, 1969, pp. 3-4.

Essays on a seemingly infinite variety of subjects marked by fine insights and almost continuously amusing. He luxuriates in highly questionable generalizations (that the artist sells a vision of unity; pornography is harmless as long as it is not mistaken for literature), but they have the value of forcing the reader to think harder. His opening sentences are arresting. Here's richness, much thought, comedy and brilliant style and exquisite freshness; the book reveals a man one would be dazzled to know.

884 Feeney, William J. "Some Elegant Essays." **Catholic World**, v. 209, no. 1252 (July 1969) 190-91.

Enjoyed the delightful piece on the literary and linguistic achievements of the Grimm Brothers, the comparison of the Fitzgerald **Rubaiyat** with the Graves translation, and the essay on Hopkins "which takes the unusual course of clarifying the work rather than displaying the subtlety of the critic." But all the essays are bright and readable, and although Burgess faults himself for excessive mildness of judgment, he can be commendably harsh — demonstrated in his characterization of Brophy's **Fifty Works** as "ill-conceived, ignorant, and vulgar." He seems to be a liberal in the almost extinct sense of the term, and he calmly refutes the distorted criticism by doctrinaire 'liberals' like George Steiner and George Harrison. Regrets the absence of a bibliographical **apparat**. Burgess demonstrates the most enlightened kind of criticism, the informed good taste that deals with each work as it comes up.

885 Grigson, Geoffrey. "Insatiable Liking?" **Listener**, v. 80, no. 2067 (November 7, 1968) 618-19.

Abstracts sentences from the book and attacks them. Burgess is guilty of overstatement, silliness, exaggerated masculinity. "I have quoted [these sentiments] less because they are silly (but some of them are surely a trifle bizarre?) than because the words exhibit the quality of mind, a quality that no one will find other than coarse and unattractive, I should think, or hope. I find a desire to please, in rather an ignoble or sneaking way: the style that slaps its own back, and ours . . . . I suspect [Burgess'] anxiety to convince himself (perhaps more than others?) that an insatiable liking for words amounts to an ability to use them well and to distinct purpose. Only some such literary anxiousness coupled with energy could explain writing on and on with a badness at once so surprisingly defiant and so exceedingly obvious, or could explain the way Mr. Burgess throws about in such a mode references to the obscurity of his own scholarship . . . ." [For Burgess on the amiable Grigson, see #1369.]

886 Gross, John. "Poet, Professor and Novelist." **Observer** (London), 8 December 1968, p. 29.

"Basically [Burgess] is a novelist, for whom criticism is never more than a sideline — although naturally something of his novelist's inventiveness spills over into **Urgent Copy**, along with his characteristic humour and his one-man Berlitz School expertise."

887 Hughes, Catharine. "Burgess as Critic." **Progressive**, v. 33, no. 5 (May 1969) 48-49.

Most reissues of occasional reviews tend to be ephemeral, but Burgess has been farsighted or fortunate enough to review reprints of accepted classics, and the reviews are generally perceptive and interesting. His essay on the politics of Graham Greene may do little more than scratch the surface, but his short essay on pornography is refreshingly free from cant. "Good luck to Anthony Burgess, and to **Urgent Copy**, for its welcome reminder that literary criticism need not be either stodgily academic or petulantly narcissistic . . . ."

888 Lask, Thomas. "Good Talk." **New York Times**, 20 March 1969, p. 45.

He is a natural essayist. The style may be light, but the subjects are weighty. "He's deadly serious about literature and writing, but he's neither defensive nor belligerent about it and he assumes you share his mind if you are bothering to read his essays at all. The result is a lot of stimulating talk about books and the men who write them. And because he is so informal, the sharpest remarks are made almost as obiter dicta. Reading his book is like hitting all the right pubs with the best talk and the best brew."

889 Macauley, Robie. "Reviewing a Writer Who Writes About Writers Who. . ." **New York Times Book Review**, 30 March 1969, p. 4.

It is a first-rate book in spite of Burgess' prefatory disclaimer. Confesses he is dubious of Burgess' belief in the 'big bed' of Victorian criticism: American criticism needs more exactness, less paper and more precision. Further, **Urgent Copy** is an admirable demonstration of the art of writing short, and Burgess "uses the classic tactics of the essay — to grasp the subject quickly, to define two or three of its most salient qualities, and to comment succinctly on what they mean . . . . The insights usually have a clear relationship to some position Mr. Burgess has taken up for the moment. In other words, when he makes a value-judgment, he wants us to be sure from what standpoint he issues it. He is an old, original English Catholic as he discusses Evelyn Waugh; he is a good liberal when he talks about pornography and censorship. He is old fashioned and John Bullish when he talks about the pre-Raphaelites . . . . He puts on his academic robes (borrowed) and becomes a scholar of Persian when he writes about Robert Graves's neo-Rubaiyat." As an essayist he can be compared to George Orwell, a comparison to be taken very seriously.

890 McGuinness, Frank. "Special Notices." **London Magazine**, v. 8, no. 8 (November 1968) 110-12.

Burgess, a writer of enormous industry who has previously censured the whorish abandon with which reviewers clap their ephemera between hard covers, has written a book which contains some excellent articles (fine pieces on Joyce and Beckett, the American Jewish novelists, and a short essay on Graham Greene) but is little more than an assortment of weekend reviews masquerading as a serious work of literary criticism. "They are, in short, no more than competent pieces of journalism, which is to say, without under-rating them in any way, articles written to order, dispatched at speed, and so restricted by spatial requirements as to allow the writer little scope to develop his ideas or indeed do anything other than scratch the surface of the subject . . . . [Burgess] has resorted to such stock tricks of the trade as dressing up the obvious and elementary in the rags of mock scholarship, substituting mere fancifulness for originality, and passing the most sweeping judgments without benefit of evidence or argument. Nothing sharpens the critical faculty so much as the feeling that we are not getting the genuine article, and this, I fear, is all too true of this often entertaining but essential prefabricated work.''

891 Mitchell, Julian. "High Hack." **New Statesman**, v. 76, no. 1966 (November 15, 1968) 678.

Burgess' novels, 17 so far, are all of a consistent and high quality, but there is no masterpiece, and Burgess can probably write one. Observes that Mitchell gave Burgess some good advice: invent a prose of your own. Burgess replied there was no money in mere 'proses.' He would stick to the orthodox. Well, orthodox novels do not bring in cash — or Burgess would never have written so much orthodox hackwork in **Listener, Queen**, the **Sunday Times** (London) and **Observer** and theatre criticism for the **Spectator.** Burgess is a dazzler as a reviewer, but the lack of space has prevented this collection, first published in the periodical press, from becoming 'literary' studies. Hopes that now, freed from the necessity of hackwork by Shakespeare [a filmscript] and Hollywood, the talent of Burgess will burgeon in the sun and he will never have to review another book again.

A Vision of Battlements

892 London: Sidwick and Jackson, 1965. Illustrated by Edward Pagram.

893 New York: Norton, 1966, c1965. Illustrated by Edward Pagram.

894 New York: Ballantine, 1966, c1965. Pbk.

Reviews

895 Anon. "The Ennead." **Times Literary Supplement**, no. 3,318 (September 30, 1965) 850.

The illustrations by Pagram do not give the reader's imagination much of a slash across the rump. The work is supposedly based on the **Aeneid**, but Virgil really only helps with the broad story line. Lavinia, slim and cold, with hair of gold, is well done; so is Turner as Turnus. Not enough happens in the course of the novel — despite Burgess' sense that novels are made with words. "The trouble is that tedium and a borrowed structure do not lie easy in the same bed. With Turner's end the reader notes with some surprise that there are forty pages to go. Vignette follows vignette in the rambling tones of a soldier recalling the war on television. Ennis suffers from premature ejaculation with wife, Concepcion and Lavinia. This malady extends to the novel. Too many of the effects are consummated with premature and bootless speed . . . . For literary historians there is a bit of the anti-hero about old Ennis — he does teeter between Gumbril and Dixon; writing a passacaglia and paying an urchin to muck up the Major's quarters. But then, as Mr. Burgess remarks, the Welfare State rebels were anticipated by the Army rebels. Fuit Ilium; all Ennis could do was sit, a young man on a dry rock, waiting for rain."

896 Anon. "Virgil on the Rock." **Time**, v. 87, no. 5 (February 4, 1966) 107.

"It is a high-spirited cadenza amid the brassy cacophony of war, played by a born verbal musician. Among the fictional souvenirs of World War II, mostly heavy, khaki-colored, lugubrious and dull, this is a glittering bit of Fabergé loot — a bauble to defeat boredom . . . . If Ennis is not much of a Roman, he is fatally a Roman Catholic, a failed one, trying to get free of his faith . . . . **Vision** is a book to be read twice — once allegro and once more with allegory added. It is perhaps the conflict between classic fate and Christian eschatology which made the book so painful to Novelist Burgess that he suppressed it for so long. Yet he must have known that on the surface it was an amazingly successful first novel . . . ."

897 Anon. "Splat!" **Newsweek**, v. 47, no. 8 (February 21, 1966) 104.

The super-prolific Burgess showed tact by waiting sixteen years before publishing this novel; he could have shown more by waiting another sixteen. This novel of a bumbler in bed, and a mumbler in his cups struggles to reach the humor of **Mr. Roberts**. Burgess' real interest is to create verbal Silly Symphonies which capture the absurdity of human affairs. "But there's more than fun. Burgess comes closest to the moral of his story when Ennis, whose moony blather fails to overpower the worldly Lavinia, confides 'I must learn to grow up. I can't put it off much longer.' Yes, and the talented Burgess should have realized that the indiscretions of youth are best forgotten. Splat!"

898 Anon. "Books: Briefly Noted." **New Yorker**, v. 42, no. 11 (May 7, 1966) 186.

"There are fine comic moments, particularly between the hero, an addled British soldier stationed in Gibraltar at the end of the Second World War, and his barracks-mate, a kindly homosexual, who teaches him how to wash beind his ears, and take care of his clothes; the prose, swinging along behind Joyce, is occasionally inspired and always controlled; and the hero is probably the first of the Angry Young Men or, better, Funny Young Men. More important, Mr. Burgess hasn't stopped writing." [Virtually complete text of review.]

899 Anon. Review of **Vision of Battlements**. **Choice**, v. 3, nos. 5-6 (July-August 1966) 408.

"Burgess seems to have a talent for living a variety of lives from which the stuff of excellent novels has been distilled . . . . he undoubtedly understands the loneliness of that seemingly exotic, sternly enclosed, comparatively untouched base. Even in this first novel (written in 1949, and just now published), he shows the perceptive, wry, individual eye and ear of his later, more vivid works. Students may appreciate his attempt, as a lover of Joyce, to fit his plot into an epic-comic frame, in this case **The Aeneid**. A multitude of war novels written after 1949 treated themes of boredom, a dubious sexual career, contrasted British and Mediterranean mores; but few have bettered Burgess.''

900 Anon. Notice of **Vision of Battlements. Saturday Review**, v. 49, no. 48 (November 26, 1966) 40.

"New and noted: **A Vision of Battlements**, by that prolific Englishman Anthony Burgess; this novel, his first, written in 1949 but unpublished for sixteen years, mocks wartime Gibraltar, where not everyone was a hero.'' [Complete text of notice.]

901 Baumbach, Elinor. "Stranded on Gibraltar." **Saturday Review**, v. 49, no. 5 (January 29, 1966) 38.

Observes that Burgess' later work has become increasingly more sophisticated and complex, his humor darker, his language richer. In this early work, we have evidence of an absurd, grotesquely surrealistic universe in which the anti-heroes are clockwork heroes in a mechanistic universe. Burgess is at his best in his scathing portrayal of Major Muir. He also captures well the cool, nagging tone of Laurel Ennis, and the mindless ferocity of the troops responding to banal exhortation. "Unfortunately, the book as a whole gives us a sense of *deja vu*. The diminished epic framework (Gibraltar as Troy) does not add much resonance, even to a hero who is also a Cambridge wit. Ennis is less interesting than his land-scape, and his landscape is rather derivative of Waugh. Burgess found his real satiric voice in his seven later novels; but his sharp eye and acid pen are implicit in this.''

902 Brooke, Jocelyn. "New Fiction." **Listener**, v. 74, no. 1905 (September 30, 1965) 505.

Mr. Burgess may claim that he wanted to be a composer, not a writer of fiction, but it is plain that he is a born novelist. This story, confessedly autobiographical, in which the anti-hero Sergeant-Major Ennis, gets into trouble with drink, women, insubordination and seditious activities, makes Gibraltar sound pretty awful. "The passage I admired most was one in which [Burgess] starts off a chapter with a rhapsodic tribute to Spain in the best (worst) sort of travel-agent prose, then switches abruptly to the real thing: the drabness, the squalor, the vomiting drunks, the beggars, the used french letters in the gutters.'' With this first novel, stylistically more like the early Malayan books than his later, more richly orchestrated works, Burgess leapt at once into sudden artistic maturity.

903 Coleman, John. "Here Comes Burgess." **Observer Weekend Review** (London), 26 September 1965, p. 28.

[Omnibus review.] "Virgilian parallels were intended, 'a tyro's method of giving his story a backbone' in Mr. Burgess's own words, and they hardly come off. What does (where it does) is the tangy, late 'Penguin New Writing' absurdity of the well-meaning sergeant's encounters with military apes, queens and sheep. Often slapdash and wilful, the tale veers into several improbable puddles, but a certain intelligent élan steadily comes to the rescue. There is already the characteristic Burgess mixture of comedy and bitters: to such a degree that yet again one wishes this so nearly distinguished writer would concern himself more with the uses of snaffle and curb on his sprawling gift. The bloody horse is there all right. The novel is copiously illustrated by Edward Pagram in a manner reminiscent of thirties schoolboy annuals or contemporary Soviet book-art. Since drunks and naked ladies crop up here and there, a kind of tiresome piquancy results.''

904 Gardner, John. "An Invective Against Mere Fiction." **Southern Review**, v. 3, no. 2, N.S. (April 1967) 444.

[Omnibus review.] "The central character is a serious composer whose noble but inept attempts to manage where a Truth-man does not fit [i.e. the Army] throw comic light on both the impossible ideal (which we all the more earnestly affirm) and the social realities which keep the ideal out of reach. Not that the tale is a melodrama. The army is all too eager to be a friend of art, education, and all that: it joyfully makes lists, sends out directives, studies the appropriate and inappropriate regulations; but it is as hard for military system to adapt to art as for art to adapt to military system . . . . The language in **A Vision of Battlements** is not as ingenious as in the later Burgess novels, but it is sufficient, often very funny, rich in images which are at once clever and grimly appropriate.''

905 Hackett, Alice. Notice of **Vision of Battlements. Publishers Weekly**, v. 190, no. 15 (October 10, 1966) 75.

"It is a mock-heroic story, set in Gibraltar at the end of World War II, the anti-hero musician Sergeant

Ennis, a teacher in the Army Vocational and Cultural Corps. In the intervening years the author has written a number of novels, the latest **Tremor of Intent** to be published by Norton October 10.'' [Virtually the complete text of notice.]

906 Hoyt, Charles Alva. Review of **Vision of Battlements**. **Commonweal**, v. 84, no. 1 (March 25, 1966) 33-35.

The introduction reveals some of Burgess' preoccupations: a musician's love of sound combinations, both sweet and startling; a real erudition which fills his novels with literary references; and a vigorous and highly intelligent inquiry into the problems of modern England. ''I would add two items which he does not allude to in his introduction: a curiosity about homosexuality and a recurrent tendency towards unhappiness.'' This funny but frustrating story of an early anti-hero is perhaps as much of a *Bildungsroman* as we are likely to get from this unusual man. Briefly discusses some of Burgess' other novels: **The Right to an Answer**, **A Clockwork Orange**, **Nothing Like the Sun** and **Honey for the Bears**, unquestionably one of his finest novels. He is certainly a man to reckon with, and he deserves a large audience to cheer him on.

907 Knickerbocker, Conrad. ''Variations on an Antiheroic Theme.'' **New York Times**, 1 February 1966, p. 33.

''Mr. Burgess is best known in this country for **A Clockwork Orange**, a stunning, glittering novel that foresees tomorrow's world as an overpopulated hell shored up by legalized homosexuality and murder.'' [The reference is clearly to **The Wanting Seed**.] The book is a good thing, despite its hastiness of composition. Ennis is the kind of stumblebum who goes about Gibraltar as though he were a man with his foot permanently caught in a spittoon. Crowds inflate him with gusts of windy liberalism. He always begins his enterprises sanely enough; then his bumbling anguish, abetted by the evil spirit of Major Muir, turns the occasion into a shambles. The book's weakness lies in the repetitiveness of this same theme, its single anecdote, but it is saved by its style, the hot needles under the fingernail, the fierce, voracious, pitiless humor of Burgess's public point of view.

908 Ostermann, Robert. ''Burgess' Newly Published Works Reveal Love of Language, Life.'' **National Observer**, 9 May 1966, p. 25.

A Vision of Battlements, although written early in Burgess' career, by no means disgraces the author. It is a mordant, ironic work which is remarkably mature given its early composition.

909 Ricks, Christopher. ''Rude Forerunner.'' **New Statesman**, v. 70, no. 1802 (September 24, 1965) 444-45.

The illustrations by Pagram may well relegate the work to the level of facetious crudity, but the work itself is consistently entertaining and observant. It evokes the robust madness of military command; it communicates the brutally sardonic idiom of barrack-room talk; and the poor hero is trapped in various limbos. The framework of the book is a flop; they have no good effects and some bad effects. ''But the myth-manipulating can easily be ignored, and one is left with a vivacious truth-telling at which memory will appropriately flinch.'' The book also includes Burgess' later concerns: the epicene, the idea that artists are hermaphrodites, the notion that Russia and American are the same, and the interpenetrating opposites, Yin and Yang. Note, however, that Ennis uses Geoffrey Gorer's phrase (first published NS, 4 May 1957): 'the perils of hypergamy.' ''Most prescient of Ennis, though he does later visit a fortune-teller. But bear in mind that we have to do with a novelist who notoriously succeeded in reviewing one of his own novels [see #448] so it might be as well to accept this particular bit of crystal-gazing with respectful scepticism.''

910 Shuttleworth, Martin. ''New Novels.'' **Punch**, v. 249, no. 6528 (October 20, 1965) 588.

[Omnibus review.] ''. . . one can see why he didn't publish it then [16 years before], hear almost the shouts of wrath that would have gone up if he had for the Rock is a very small place and here it is, in war-time, imitated to the life. It's a dazzling novel, quite as funny as **Decline and Fall**, though more mature . . . . Here it all is: the drunken, browned-off soldiery of the democratic world; dumb society gearing itself in the dark for peace; the individual, baffled in his search for pattern and shape in his own life, finding consolation and oblivion in the comicality of present surfaces — a novel, in short, of wit, shape and importance, perhaps **the** novel of those years.''

911 Swanson, Stanley. Review of **Vision of Battlements**. **Library Journal**, v. 91, no. 8 (April 1, 1966) 1920-21.

"We see his early concern with words and their sounds, so apparent in later novels. An amusing, witty novel, with an especial appeal to men, it merits purchase by libraries having his later works."

912 Vansittart, Peter. "Rebels and Officers." **Spectator**, no. 7162 (October 1, 1965) 424-25.

[Omnibus review.] "Anthony Burgess's novels have unusual quality. This one is actually his first (1949) hitherto unpublished . . . . Time is not wholly kind to his tale, a Virgilian symbolism is too deeply buried to be noticed, but there is left much genial mockery of war-time militarism, tourist clichés, official attempts at moral uplift, together with a side-glance at colonial poverty, sardonic but compassionate."

913 Wheeler, Thomas C. "Intrigue on the Rock." **New York Times Book Review**, 30 January 1966, p. 32.

"This is an Army novel, without the foxhole or stockade, that succeeds in conveying a humanity where others dig into mire. The author's failing but never falling musician-sergeant (so obsessed by creative energy that even in the midst of a foolish philandery he 'worked out a passage of double fugue') is as fallible as the [Army] brass . . . . In this novel, the author puts man in his perilous place — but, in the confusion, the untouchables become real and likable. There is laughter here, but no scorn. And there is an unmistakable love for the human race, despite its faults."

914 Wood, Frederick T. "Current Liteature 1965: I. Poetry, Prose and Drama." **English Studies**, v. 47 (August 1966) 314-25.

[Omnibus review.] The work is in no way outstanding or remarkable, but it is an early example of the novel in which the anti-hero with few illusions rebels against the Establishment and achieves nothing.

The Wanting Seed

915 London: Heinemann, 1962.

916 New York: Norton, 1963.

917 London: Pan Books, 1965. Pbk.

918 New York: Ballantine, 1970. Pbk.

919 Harmondsworth: Penguin, 1973. Pbk.

920 London: Heinemann, 1973.

921 New York: Norton, 1976.

Translations

922 Danish: **Du Skal aede din Naeste**. Copenhagen: Schonborg, 1963. Translated by Michael Tjen.

923 French: **La folle semence**. Paris: Laffont, 1973. Translated by Georges Belmont and Hortense Chabrier.

924 Italian: **Il seme inquieto**. Milan: De Carlo, 1974. Translated by Valentino de Carlo.

925 Japanese: **Mikomi no nai shushi**. Tokyo: Hayakawa Shobo, 1973. Translated by Saito Kazue & Kuroyanagi Hisaya.

926 Portuguese: **Sementes malditas**. Rio de Janeiro: Artenova. Translated by Hindenburgo Dobal.

Reviews

927 Adams, Robert M. "Petit Guignol." **New York Review of Books**, v. 1, no. 11 (January 23, 1964) 7.

[Also reviews **Honey for the Bears.**] **Orange**, a minor bombshell, was also a flawed literary product. The main character was obviously mechanistic, and the book's clarity and point left something to be desired. Now **Seed** is a "mechanically contrived and clumsy novel; its gimmick is the population explosion, and it relies on no other allurements — neither plot nor character nor style nor atmosphere. All the foreseeable grotesque horrors are here; the teeming rabbit-warren cities with contraceptive dispensers at every street-corner, population police, castration-propaganda, a diet of plankton-cakes, mass murder, and mass homosexuality." The two main characters are paper dolls.

928 Anon. "The Hungry Sheep." **Times Literary Supplement**, no. 3,162 (October 5, 1962) 773.

Burgess has published nine novels to date. The first group, witty and light-hearted (**Malayan Trilogy**), was widely and rightly acclaimed. The second group involves an expatriate who anatomatises some vulnerable aspect of English life. Burgess "chooses some aspect of modern life, subjects it to all kinds of stresses and strains, caricatures it, mocks it, tortures it, and forces it to up to and beyond [the] breaking point." This novel, which fits in the second category, is wildly and fantastically funny, for all the bitter after-taste of many incidents. "Here too is all the usual rich exuberance of Mr. Burgess's vocabulary, his love of quotations and literary allusions . . . . This, then, is a remarkable and brilliantly imaginative novel, vital and inventive. Inevitably it will be compared with **1984** and **Brave New World**. . . but the comparison is not really helpful. Nor is the comparison, so often made, with Evelyn Waugh, for here only Mr. Waugh's **Love Among the Ruins** is really relevant, and this is a minor work, almost a squib. **The Wanting Seed** is most certainly neither."

929 Anon. "World Without Sex." **Newsweek**, v. 62, no. 18 (October 28, 1963) 101-02.

"This bilious comment on man's cyclical return to barbarism is hair-raising just as it stands, but it would be considerably more effective if Burgess had written a better novel. He has had the misfortune to tell his story with marionettes — a poor sap of a history teacher, his-soft-bellied wife, and her lover, who happens to be the teacher's brother. She bears twins — whose are they? — and the novel commences a quick slide straight into the nineteenth century. Burgess is an engaging stylist, with a fine sense of theory, but he ought to pay stricter attention to the people around him."

930 Anon. Review of **The Wanting Seed. New Yorker**, v. 39, no. 37 (November 2, 1963) 209-10.

"This imaginary world, which now and then seems to be more a bad dream of the present than a nightmare of the future, is peopled by Mr. Burgess mainly with caricatures but also with a few almost real men and women, among them a man named Tristram Foxe. The writing falls too often into easy, jeering lines and cheaply bitter antics, but Mr. Burgess's natural talent is in view at all times, and one cannot help feeling that a writer who is able to create the wistful, hardy Tristram Foxes should not limit himself to threats and warnings. The scene is England, with a short and particularly horrid episode in the West of Ireland."

931 Anon. "A Deadly Round." **Time**, v. 82, no. 23 (December 6, 1963) 123-4.

[Chiefly plot summary.] "The horror of this book is not that men breed, swarm and die like insects. It is rather that hope is always held out, and always perverted, as the world turns through its three-part cycle. Burgess' vision is both sophisticated and cynical, and there is not a line of it that seems impossible."

932 Anon. Review of **The Wanting Seed. Sunday Times** (London), 1 July 1973, p. 39.

"Four novels [**Seed, Inside Mr. Enderby, MF, Honey for the Bears**] and a collection of literary essays join other volumes including **A Clockwork Orange** already in Penguin." [Complete text of notice.]

933 Anon. Notice of **The Wanting Seed. Books and Bookmen**, v. 18 (September 1973) 138.

[Notes publication of the Penguin pbk. ed. For complete text, see #879.]

934 Brophy, Brigid. "Not Very Brave, Not So New." **Washington Post Book Week**, 3 November 1963, pp. 6, 25.

"'Half-baked' might have been invented to characterise the new Anthony Burgess novel. Not that Mr. Burgess himself would invent any such term. He would prefer 'hemicaust.' His prose glitters with shards of Greek — embedded, however, in mud, for apart from his Greekisms and a couple of words in Chinese script Mr. Burgess writes in pure, old-fashioned English clichés." He has borrowed a medical turn of description from Aldous Huxley. A flimsy copy of Orwell's vivid atmosphere of shoddiness, shortages and the synthetic hangs over his work. He also makes sly, but fatuous allusions to English literature as it appears in the academic syllabus. Literary digs (Jackie Priestly, Joan Wain) are brought in on the cabaret entertainer's assumption that the topical must be witty. His war of extermination between the sexes gives him his few good scenes. Although he seems to be stating the dangers of over-population, he sides emotionally — indeed mystically — with fertility. The best dystopian novels express loathing for the present through a nauseous future. Reading Burgess' book is reminiscent of those queasy days when you feel like vomitting, but can't actually bring anything up. Finally, he has stolen his last and moving sea-washed paragraph from the French. [For Burgess on Brophy, see #1228, 1291.]

935 Buitenhuis, Peter. "A Battle Between the Sexes Was the Answer." **New York Times Book Review**, 27 October 1963, pp. 4, 20.

It is an ambitious counter-Utopian novel; the theme is large; his treatment is comprehensively comic and gruesome detailed; the style is at once pedantic and knockabout. Unfortunately, the three major characters are essentially unreal, while the minor characters are about as memorable as a politician's orations. "Since we can't believe in his characters — and since he seems to be no more committed to a particular outlook on present events than he is to any definable view of what may come — we cannot, in the end, take his theme seriously."

936 Cayton, Robert F. Review of **The Wanting Seed. Library Journal**, v. 88, no. 17 (October 1, 1963) 3641.

"The satire is heavy-handed most of the way, but there emerges for the reader from the first page to the last a frightening thought for us today, foreseeing a time when there might be a need for wars to kill off surplus population and a need to have ministers of infertility and fertility. This book is a warning to us to do whatever must be done to plan a sound future world, but it also chides us never, under any circumstances, to try to kill man's need for love and fulfillment. Not entertaining fiction, but good reading."

937 Maguire, Clinton J. Review of **The Wanting Seed. Best Sellers**, v. 23, no. 15 (November 1, 1963) 277.

"Serious this is. Sensational it is also. But what it intends to establish is not at all clear. Doubtless, this intends to be the 1984 of what this author is worried about as THE enemy, over-population. He

The Wanting Seed

a novel by
ANTHONY BURGESS
the author of
A CLOCKWORK ORANGE

First American ed. (New York: Norton, c. 1963) of this novel.

lacks, however, the wit of Aldous Huxley in speculating on man's future; and he lacks, also, the bite of Orwell. This novel most nearly approaches Vonnegut's **The Sirens of Titan** and misses the maniac mordancy of that. Much effort and brilliance of language have gone into **The Wanting Seed**; but on the whole it is not funny, it does not realistically shock, and it is dull.''

938 Dempsey, David. ''Fe, Fi, Fo, Fum. . .'' **Saturday Review**, v. 46, no. 47 (November 23, 1963) 43-44.

Introduces Burgess to an American audience by way of a moderately lengthy commentary on **A Clockwork Orange**. In this Malthusian comedy, Burgess argues that reason itself will not save mankind. ''I doubt if Mr. Burgess is opposed to Planned Parenthood, but he is skeptical of the universal overplanning that seems to be creeping through the world as it fills up. The story is told through Tristram Foxe, a man for all seasons who is able to accommodate himself to the constant shifts of state policy without surrendering his integrity, an Everyman upon whose conscience, courage, and common sense the salvation of the future hangs. And what makes this future so terrifying is that it is such a clear extension of the present. Not everyone will share Burgess's pessimism, but there are few who will not enjoy his biting wit.''

939 Hamilton, Alexander. ''Paperbacks.'' **Books and Bookmen**, v. 10 (July 1965) 47.

[Review of Pan pbk. ed.] Burgess ''can be as funny as he is terrifying, as convincing as he can be fantastic, as intimate as he can be brutal.'' The book is macabre and chilling.

940 Keown, Eric. Review of **The Wanting Seed**. **Punch**, v. 243, no. 6371 (October 17, 1962) 575-76.

[Omnibus review.] ''Mr. Burgess's hero, an unhappy schoolmaster whose wife has stained the family honour with twins, lives through the great rebellion when cannibalism breaks out, the unpopular police are tinned, and Dionysian revels all over the country coincide with a renaissance of religion. Drafted into the army, he is the sole survivor of a faked war, inspired by a panic-stricken Government, in which forces of patriotic men and women exterminate each other in a remote corner of Ireland against a background of canned battle noises. This is at the same time a terrifying book and a highly amusing one. Mr. Burgess uses all his considerable skill in dialogue and narrative to give it life, and his comic invention is unflagging. But while one laughs it is hard to quench the uncomfortable thought, what is to prevent all this happening?''

941 Taubman, Robert. ''Prospects.'' **New Statesman**, v. 54, no. 1647 (October 5, 1962) 460-61.

[Omnibus review.] ''Compared with his recent **A Clockwork Orange**. . . this novel runs smooth and clear, if to no very obvious design . . . . The characters are slight, but Mr. Burgess bubbles over with ideas. Society is shown passing from a Pelagian into an Augustinian phase; optimism and pessimism, sterility and fertility, are celebrated in turn. The war is neither real nor imaginary but a prototype of modern war . . . . Mr. Burgess is unfailingly inventive and apposite; a tough-minded Augustinian himself, to judge from his horror at the way people and governments behave, but an Augustinian with a sense of fun; a protean stylist, specialist in English sound-changes and rare words, polymath, antiquarian, a bit of a Joyce even. But he bears it all lightly, and this is both a serious novel and unusually engaging.''

942 Wilkie, Brian. ''Satiric Ramble.'' **Commonweal**, v. 79, nos. 15/16 (January 17, 1964) 465.

It has no sustained purpose, and it is boring, pointless and silly. The macabre effects are heavy-handed, the humor seems mere pointless frivolity. It starts off as a parody of Orwell's **1984**, turns into broad farce and towards the end, includes a fairly powerful mockery of war as an instrument of extermination. Mr. Burgess' conception of good and bad are not conveyed. ''Liberals are apparently damned, so are conservatives; sex is ridiculed, as is the denial of sex — if, that is, any such judgments are compatible with schoolboyish giggling. What's the point? . . . . Worst of all, perhaps — at any rate, Mr. Burgess keeps coming back to it — races are mingled! Polynesians in the same elevators and apartment-houses with Anglo-Saxons! It is sometimes hard to say which of these prospects Mr. Burgess finds most frightening.'' The author has a certain stylistic flair, but he writes badly. His literary influences are evidently women's pulp fiction, second-rate whodunit-ese — vintage 1935 — and the more cleverly intellectual poetry written by undergraduates in 1940.

The Worm and the Ring

943 London: Heinemann, 1961. [Edition suppressed. See below.]

944 London: Heinemann, 1970. Rev. ed.

Reviews

944.2 Burgess on the suppression (a secretary believed she had been libelled) of the 1961 ed.: "In some countries, particularly Great Britain, the law of libel presents insuperable problems to novelists who, innocent of libellous intent, are nevertheless sometimes charged with defamation by persons who claim to be the models for characters in works of fiction. Disclaimers. . . have no validity in law, which upholds the right of the plaintiff to base his charge on the corroboration of 'reasonable people.' Many such libel cases are settled before they come to trial, and publishers will, for the sake of peace and in the interests of economy, make a cash payment to the plaintiff without considering the author's side. They will also, and herein lies the serious blow to the author, withdraw copies of a whole edition. Novelists are seriously hampered in their endeavours to show, in a traditional spirit of artistic honesty, corruption in public life; they have to tread carefully even in depicting purely imaginary characters and situations, since the chance collocation of a name, a profession, and a locality may produce a libellous situation." Quoted from "The Novel." **New Encyclopaedia Britannica in 30 Volumes**. 15th ed. **Macropaedia**, v. 13, p. 297. Chicago: Encyclopaedia Britannica, 1974.

945 Anon. "Sparing the Rod." **Times Literary Supplement**, no. 3,097 (July 7, 1961) 421.

[Omnibus review.] The theme of the peace-loving, anti-flogging headmaster at odds with the dense members of the Board of Governors is not a strikingly original one. "The especial distinction of this book is the treatment of the private life of the German master, Chris Howarth, a lapsed Catholic. The terrible dilemma of his small son Peter is described skilfully, tenderly, and slightly light-heartedly. Peter has to reconcile his love of God and the Roman Catholic Church with love for his father. His father praises Luther to him, leaves him access to uncensored books, commits adultery, and finally serves him bacon on a Friday. Mr. Burgess also has a gift for near-caricature which makes the damp grey atmosphere of his Midland town almost bearable."

946 Price, R.G.G. "New Novels." **Punch**, v. 140, no. 6302 (June 28, 1961) 989-90.

[Omnibus review.] "The trouble with Mr. Burgess's ebullient disgust is that he will overdo things." His pictures of a declining Great Power are often funny and horrifying, but the seediness and bitterness are excessive. Observes that Burgess' Grammar School entrants are near-illiterates, drooling delinquents. "There is no suggestion that there are many schools where learning and good manners are successfully implanted in the children of the working-class by modern educational techniques . . . . As usual the episodes leave a more vivid memory than the pattern as a whole. But now not much of the writing is even wryly funny [compared to **The Malayan Trilogy**.] Mr. Burgess is far too talented a novelist to become a whiner."

947 Raven, Simon. "Verdicts of Guilty." **Spectator**, July 7, 1961, p. 421.

[Omnibus review.] "The comedy is excellent, the moral rather sad: liberals are on the side of the angels, Mr. Burgess seems to say, but they make the mistake of seeing angels all around them — with the result that they are always making fools of themselves and are seldom fit to conduct enterprises of moment. This task they should leave to careerists and hard-faced men who have a taste for such things, and themselves retreat like Horace to his Sabine Farm, like him allaying their guilt (for guilt there must be) with jokes about their defection. I hope Mr. Burgess is wrong, but he makes a very good case."

Other Works by Anthony Burgess

948 Pelegri, Jean. **The Olive Trees of Justice**. London: Sidgwick and Jackson, 1962.

Translated by Anthony and Llewela Burgess.

949 Saint-Pierre, Michel de. **The New Aristocrats**. London: Golancz, 1962.

Translated by Anthony Burgess and Lynne Wilson [i.e. Llewela Burgess.]

950 The Novel Today. London: Published for the British Council and the National Book League by Longmans, Green, 1963. 56 pp. (Bibliographical series of supplements to British Book News) NOTE: Another work with this title issued in Folcroft, Pa., by Folcroft Library Editions in 1971 is apparently a reprint of Burgess' **The Novel Now**. See #676.]

951 Servin, Jean. **The Man Who Robbed Poor Boxes**. London: Golancz, 1965.

Translated by Anthony Burgess. Burgess on his translations: "I have done [translated] three French novels for money, such as it was, and only one was worth doing — Servin's **Deo Gratias**, which became **The Man Who Robbed Poor Boxes** . . . . Another novel, whose name I refuse to remember, was so indifferent in the original that I tried to transform as well as translate, and I gained wry satisfaction from seeing my own felicities ascribed by reviewers to the original author and praised as the sort of thing that English novelists could not do."

952 Bashford, Henry Howarth. **Augustus Carp, Esq., By Himself**. London: Heinemann, 1966.

With an introduction by Anthony Burgess, pp. 9-26.

953 Defoe, Daniel. **Journal of the Plague Year**. Harmondsworth: Penguin, 1966.

Edited by Anthony Burgess and Christopher Bristow, with an introduction by Anthony Burgess.

954 Peake, Mervyn. **Titus Groan**. London: Eyre and Spottiswoode, 1968.

With an introduction by Burgess, pp. 9-13.

955 Selby, Hubert. **Last Exit to Brooklyn**. 2nd., post-trial ed. London: Calder & Boyars, 1968.

With an introduction by Burgess, pp. xiii-xvii.

956 Chesterton, Gilbert Keith. **Autobiography**. New ed. London: Hutchinson, 1969.

With an introduction by Burgess.

957 Desani, G..V. **All About H. Haterr**. New York: Farrar, Straus and Giroux, 1970.

With an introduction by Burgess, pp. 7-11.

958 Mozart, Wolfgang Amadeus. **Don Giovanni. Idomeneo**. London: Cassell, 1971.

With an introduction by Burgess.

959 Collier, John. **The John Collier Reader**. New York: Knopf, 1972.

With an introduction by Burgess, pp. xi-xv.

960 Lawrence, D. H. **D. H. Lawrence and Italy**. New York: Viking Press, 1972.

With an introduction by Burgess.

961 Obscenity and the Arts. Valletta: Malta Library Association, 1973.

Printed version of a public lecture delivered before the Malta Library Association in 1970.

962 Jerrold, Douglas William. **Mrs. Caudle's Curtain Lectures**. London: Harvill Press, 1974.

With a foreword by Anthony Burgess.

963 Doyle, Arthur Conan. **The White Company** . London: Murray, 1975.

With an introduction by Burgess.

964 Puma. Universal City: Universal Studios, 1976.

[An unpublished novel. It is the property of Zanuck-Brown, and will probably not be published. Some printed copies of the original typescript or screenplay circulate in the rare book trade.]

965 A Christmas Recipe. Verona, Italy: Plain Wrapper Press, 1977.

[Recipe, in verse, for a trifle. Edition limited to 180 copies signed by Burgess and illustrator Joe Tilson. Quite expensive.]

966 Will and Testament; A Fragment of Biography. Verona, Italy: Plain Wrapper Press, 1977.

[A story about William Shakespeare. Edition limited to 86 copies signed by Burgess and illustrator Joe Tilson. Very expensive. List price in one dealer's catalog ca. 1981 ("A very impressive item from this important modern private press"): $1,250.00]

967 The Land Where the Ice Cream Grows. London: Benn, 1979.

Story and illustrations by Fulvio Testa. Told by Anthony Burgess.

968 Modern Irish Short Stories. Ed. by Ben Forkner. London: M. Joseph, 1981.

With an introduction by Burgess.

969 Joyce, James. **Ulysses**. New York: Book of the Month Club, 1982.

With a new foreword by Anthony Burgess.

970 Der Rosenkavalier: A Comedy for Music in Three Acts. By Richard Strauss; libretto by Hugo von Hoffmannsthal; story adaptation by Anthony Burgess; introduction by George R. Marek. Boston: Little, Brown, 1982.

[CONTENTS: Richard Strauss and Hugo von Hoffmannsthal, a reevaluation, by George R. Marek. The Cavalier of the Rose, by Anthony Burgess. Der Rosenkavalier: synopsis, by John Cox. Libretto, by Hugo von Hoffmannsthal.]

971 The End of the World News. New York: McGraw-Hill, 1983.

[A novel about Sigmund Freud and Leon Trotsky.]

Poems

972 "Five Revolutionary Sonnets." **Transatlantic Review**, v. 21 (Summer 1966) 30-32.

973 "The Sword." **Transatlantic Review**, v. 23 (Winter 1966-67) 41-43.

974 "Imagination is Your True Apollo." **New York Times**, July 21, 1969, p. 17.
   A single poem. At head of page: "Some Reflections of Man and the Moon at their Closeup Encounter."

975 "O Lord, O Ford, God Help Us, Also You'; poem. **New York Times Magazine**, 29 December 1974, pp. 6-7.

976 "On Christ's Nativity; Five Sonnets." **Times Literary Supplement**, No. 3854, January 23, 1976, p. 76.
   You Know the Day; Only a Few Weeks After; Mary Received, While Burning Joseph's Toast; Our Lady Had a Painful Christmas Day; King Herod Now, to Minimal Applause — poems by Giuseppe Gioacchino Belli; translated by Anthony Burgess.

Stories

977 Burgess on his own work: "More than anything, I know something of the management of the rhythm of a novella, a full-dress-novel, even a **roman fleuve**. But when it comes to trying to write a short story I am totally at sea. Its rhythmical problems are altogether different from those of even the shortest possible novel (which can never be a short story): I may know how to start, but I do not know when the climax, if any, should come, and I certainly do not know how to make a short story end. I've written stories only because I've occasionally been asked to write them, but they've been mere pieces of trickery, swollen anecdotes, or else fragments of novels." In "What Literature Is About." **Irish Press** (Dublin), 2 June 1977, p. 6.

978 "An American Organ." **Mad River Review**, v. 1 (Winter 1964-65) 33-39.

979 from "It Is the Miller's Daughter: A Novel in Progress." **Transatlantic Review**, v. 24 (Spring 1967) 5-15.

The sight of this extract in cold print turned Burgess against the work. There is, consequently, no novel entitled: "It is the Miller's Daughter."

980 "Muse: A Sort of SF Story." **Hudson Review**, v. 21 (Spring 1968) 109-26.

981 "Somebody's Got to Pay the Rent." **Partisan Review**, v. 35 (Winter 1968) 67-74.

982 "A Benignant Growth." **Transatlantic Review**, v. 32 (Summer 1969) 10-15.

983 "A Fable for Social Scientists; In Which Our Leading Practitioner of the Trade is Quickly and Painlessly Skinned." **Horizon**, v. 15 no. 1 (Winter 1973) 12-15.

A short story, somewhat in the mode of Aldous Huxley, which confronts and satirizes some of the notions of B.F. Skinner.

Burgess: Articles, Essays, Reviews, Etc.

984 "Who's Afraid of Thomas Wolfe?" **Country Life**, v. 143, no. 3720 (June 20, 1960) 1720-21.

Reviews of **Thomas Wolfe; A Biography**, by Andrew Turnbull; **They Made Their Name**, by Anthony Blond; **How It Happened Here**, by Kevin Brownlow.

985 "The Human Russians." **Listener**, v. 66, no. 1709 (December 28, 1961) 1107-8.

The Russians are an inefficient but warm people. Their apparent mendacity is perhaps a mere penchant for fantasy, and in their very inefficiency there is cause for reassurance. The beef stroganoff may be two hours late; the notion of serving available beer derided; the taxis non-existent; there is, at the same time, a reassuring absence of police. Manic-depression seems to be part of the Russian character and, while there is much drunkeness, and even more shabbiness, the people themselves are kind and likable. "If one expects to find a totalitarian state full of soft-booted, white-helmeted military police, conspicuously armed, one also expects a certain coldness, a thinness of blood, all emotion chanelled into love of Big Brother. You certainly find none of that in Leningrad. There is a tremendous warmth about the people, a powerful desire to admit you, the stranger, into the family and smother you with kisses." [Reprinted #992.]

986 "The Writer and Music." **Listener**, v. 67, no. 1727 (May 3, 1962) 761-62.

[Report of a talk given on the BBC Home Service.] Only Thomas Mann, in his **Doctor Faustus**, has described a composer from the inside. Romain Rolland's **Jean Christophe** gives us the composer as great lover and revolutionary. "There is not much room left for mere music." Among English writers, John Wain, Stanley Middleton, Robert Browning, Shakespeare, Samuel Butler, James Joyce and Aldous Huxley have, with varying success, incorporated music in their work. Argues that the novelist has much to learn from musical forms and concludes with a droll anecdote about Swinburne.

987 "Cain and Abel in Algeria." The **Yorkshire Post** (Leeds), 21 March 1963, p. 4.

Reviews of **The Fratricides**, by Maurice Edelman; **A City of Scarlet and Gold**, by Patrick Raymond; **Race of the Tiger**, by Alexander Cordell; **Three Cheers for Me**, by Donald Jack; **A Kingdom for a Song**, by Ira J. Morris; **The Island Is Full of Strange Noises**, by Angus Heriot.

988 "I Remember Grossmama." **Yorkshire Post** (Leeds), 18 April 1963, p. 4.

Reviews of **Before My Time**, by Niccolo Tucci; **Georgie Winthrop**, by Sloan Wilson; **Welcome to Thebes**, by Glendon Swarthout; **Forests in the Night**, by Jon Cleary.

989 "Poetry for a Tiny Room." **Yorkshire Post**, 16 May 1963, p. 4, c. 4.

[Burgess adds to the legend by reviewing one of his own books. The circumstances of this legendary but faintly scandalous affair were roughly as follows. **One Hand Clapping** was published under the pseud. of Joseph Kell. Burgess told **Yorkshire Post** staffers that he was the author. Somewhat later, he received a parcel of books to review for the **Post**. **Inside Mr. Enderby** by 'Kell' was one of the lot. Burgess assumed, somewhat typically, that editor Kenneth Young wanted a bit of a joke. Young was not amused, and Burgess was fired. Letters followed. Novelist Maurice Edelman protested Burgess' removal and described him as "the most original novelist writing today and a critic of integrity." Other accounts intimate that Burgess reviewed only his own book. That is not true. See below.] "This is, in many ways, a dirty book. It is full of bowel-blasts and flatulent borborygms, emetic meals ('thin but over-savoury stews' Enderby calls them) and halitosis. It may well make some people sick, and those of my readers with tender stomachs are advised to let it alone. It turns sex, religion, the State into a series of laughing-stocks. The book itself is a laughing stock." Also reviews **The Natural**, by Bernard Malamud; **A Penny for the Guy**, by Teo Savory; **Travelling People**, by B.S. Johnson. [For an editorial disclaimer, see "Burgess and — Kell." **Yorkshire Post**, 20 May 1963, p. 6.]

990 "Takeover." **Listener**, v. 69, no. 1782 (May 23, 1963) 884.

[Burgess replaces Peter Green as regular television critic.] On Mexico's Day of the Dead, a tour of Iceland by Mai Zetterling (a goddess), a televisual tour of Surinam and South America, and interviews with Jorge Luis Borges and Dino de Laurentiis "that God-haunted man whose name sounds like a thesis."

He is pushing on with his filming of the whole Bible, and he admits how much he likes being 'the boss'. Honesty is the best television.''

991 "A Place for Nature." **Listener**, v. 69, no. 1783 (May 30, 1963) 938-39.

[Television criticism.] On a somewhat misguided celebration of 'Nature Week,' a documentary on the steam engine, and a performance by soprano Lisa della Casa, who served sixty minutes of *Schlagobers*. "Of what stuff are they made, these polyglot beauties of ferocious dramatic and vocal talent, evidently incapable of ageing, devoted to dogs and husband, puffing away at a fag between arias, breathing adoration as if it were air? One sees why they are called *diva*.''

992 "The Human Russians." **Science Digest**, v. 51, no. 5 (May 1962) 33-37.

[Reprint of #985.]

993 "The Battering of Britain." **Listener**, v. 69 (June 6, 1963) 974-75.

[Television criticism.] On Australian aborigines, the British housing shortage and brain drain. "Here were cognate batterings. Four million slums and three million substandard houses, our apparent inability either to build homes or afford them; industry's unwillingness to apply new techniques; the frustration of self-exiling scientists; our feeling that efficiency is ungentlemanly and only all right for damned foreigners — everything added up to the picture of a malaise which calls for a more general documentary analysis.'' Also on Alan Taylor, who once marked a paper by the young Burgess: "Bright ideas insufficient to conceal lack of knowledge.''

994 "Grave Matter." **Listener**, v. 69 (June 13, 1963) 1012.

[Television criticism.] On the death of Pope John, the future of the Papacy and the Profumo affair. "We were reminded that Curzon and Lloyd George did, like Falstaff, in some sort handle women, but they never perpetrated any barefaced public denial. A Minister's sexual morality was his own affair; a Minister's lie was his country's. Worsthorne suggested. . . that the call-girl cult could be seen as an unworthy flower of a suspect and lopsided affluence." Also on Kwame Nkrumah.

995 "Thundering Text." **Listener**, v. 69 (June 20, 1963) 1050.

[Television criticism.] Lord Hailsham on "the Larger Ethics, a fulminant credo, a lay sermon on the general moral decline of which the Profumo affair may be regarded as a syndrome" was moving, even noble. Schweitzer reminded us that "ethics is a matter of reverence for life, not just of avoiding mendacity and fornication . . . .''

996 "Away From the Profumeira." **Listener**, v. 69 (June 27, 1963) 1086.

[Television criticism.] Evasive politicians elegantly stone-wall when asked to pick Macmillan's successor. A documentary on Spain is creditable. Another on Morocco is a taut and disciplined work of art.

997 "A Metaphysical City." **Listener**, v. 70 (July 4, 1963) 30.

[Television criticism.] On a tunnel from East to West Berlin, a lumberjack's trek to Alaska, and a confrontation between women writers and women critics. "Muriel Telford and Frances Glendenning, both educators [the critics], gently pointed out the wealth of cliche, poverty of language, excess of plot-manipulation in what the others regarded as the 'bread-and-butter' of literature . . . .''

998 "Leporine." **Listener**, v. 70 (July 11, 1963) 66.

[Television criticism.] On hares, the Lasry-Baschet musical instruments and Bellevue hospital.

999 "A Little Threepenny-bit." **Listener**, v. 70 (July 18, 1963) 104-5.

[Television criticism.] On the cotton workers of Lancashire, soccer, the fittingly enthusiastic reception of the London Symphony Orchestra in Japan and the position of the artist in Soviet Russia. It is hard to resist the conclusion that, "though the soviet leaders regard the artist as 'the wrecker of the status quo,' at least his own status is an adult one in the U.S.S.R.: he is a dangerous giant, not a harmless, long-haired epicine. Pasternak is ennobled by being attacked by Surkov; Khruschev, making three major speeches in one year on the subject of the arts, demands more strength-through-joy anecdotalism, fiddler's collectives, films about warm-hearted polcoms: at least he's aware of the devil of the sixth sense.''

1000 "Homo Aquaticus." **Listener**, v. 70 (July 25, 1963) 142.

[Television criticism.] An interesting program about Cousteau and his divers is followed by the pseudo-artistic posturings of some art students. These students were guilty of "as wretched a gallimaufrey of phoney aesthetics and scruffy-underdog whining as ever steamed up from the dog-end-littered floor of a Soho wine-club . . . . Anyway, said these students, in the last analysis we only paint to please ourselves. Gurt topfloor ararkis wertle dick-dock. That is written to please me, and to hell with communication."

1001 "Not So Plurabelle." **Listener**, v. 70 (August 1, 1963) 178-79.

[Television criticism.] A disappointing program on Ireland, a dull one on the great crested grebe, an ophiolater's delight on snakes, the war games of business execs, Oxford ponderously explained to the Americans, and politicians on the Test Ban treaty. "Political leaders are, on television, a kind of Jonsonian humours: predictable, identifiable with what they stand for, hardly worth interrogating. What general truths will they give us the keys to? Given! A way a lone a last a loved a long the"

1002 "Pere et Fils." **Listener**, v. 70 (August 8, 1963) 214.

[Television criticism.] A sensible program on farming, a solid one on housing, and a superb production of the ballet 'Checkmate.'

1003 "Formidable Navigators." **Listener**, v. 70 (August 15, 1963) 250.

[Television criticism.] On the precise metaphysic of businessmen and a reassuring look at construction laborers. "The men we met seemed grave, decent, mutually loyal, incurious about private pasts or even surnames . . . . Yet the main vice of the modern navvy-man remains drink — drink as an end, though, and not as a tool for more complex vices, and twelve pints are taken in the confidence that they will be quickly sweated out on the job. There are worse things, God knows: coffee bars, the Beatles, the cult of the disk-jockey, watching 'This is Your Life' for pleasure, giving some harmless ancient the boot for a giggle." A dull life of Harry Secombe was followed by divinely inspired agreement that the state should support sports. "I was reminded of an army-course discussion-group about whether or not the pubs should stay open all day: the theme was disposed of in thirty seconds flat."

1004 "Looking for Centres." **Listener**, v. 70 (August 22, 1963) 286.

[Television criticism.] Laments absence of a Jamesian center in a television program about the British in India and a Swedish look at Britain.

1005 "Guilt." **Listener**, v. 70 (August 29, 1963) 322-23.

[Television criticism.] "'Moansday, Tearsday, Wailsday, Thumpsday, Frightday, Shatterday' — so James Joyce rechristened in brine the days of a week laden with guilt and shame. After such a viewing week, with weather to match, I groan towards my typewriter as to an instrument of penance. Every image has been an accusatory one — Germans querulous about our continued beastliness towards them; American Negroes ranting, sorrowful, forgiving, prophetic of the downfall of Anglo-Saxon civilization; the innocent eyes of pheasants bred for rich men's guns; the face of a great dead rich man chiding me for my own inability to turn four pounds into many millions; the, to me, unattainable ideals of Yoga. *Mea culpa, mea culpa, mea maxima culpa*."

1006 "March." **Listener**, v. 70 (September 5, 1963) 360.

[Television criticism.] An anti-climactic March on Washington, and an unexpectedly charming agent for some pop singers.

1007 "Temporary Daughters." **Listener**, v. 70 (September 12, 1963) 398-99.

[Television criticism.] On *au pair* girls, Venezuela, Guatemala, Salzburg and a Bristol police inspector.

1008 "Symposia." **Listener**, v. 70 (September 19, 1963) 440-41.

[Television criticism.] Talk shows on the drama, the future of Hollywood and a documentary concerning a nursery school trainee.

1009 "Irritation." **Listener**, v. 70 (September 26, 1963) 482-83.

[Television criticism.] On Europe and Britain's attitude towards the Common Market, a lifeless shop steward, and some charming, humble physicists probing the nature of the atom. It appears that "the physicist's best work is, like lyric poetry, done in youth and neither he at forty-five, nor Chew at thirty-eight could expect again a phoenix-hour.''

1010 "The Corruption of the Exotic." **Listener**, v. 70, no. 1800 (September 26, 1963) 465-67.

[Long essay on the art of fiction.] On the genesis of his own **Time for a Tiger**. The novelist who writes with mere juxtaposition of two cultures is animated by an impure motive. The omnipresent temptation to falsify the environment and misrepresent the characters in the foreign environment must be strenuously resisted. It is tempting, for example, to impute godlike transformations to Malays, Chinese or Indians merely because they are different from Anglo-Saxons and Russians. The true subject matter of the novelist is the English here and now. When the dramatist and the screenwriter have captured the novelist's technique, the true function of the novelist is to revify old myths or create new ones. "The more banal, commonplace, everyday, the subject-matter of the novel is, the more the novelist is compelled to work hard at his craft . . . . One wonders how much true devotion to his art is shown by the novelist who expatriates himself because of income tax, disillusionment with English society, climate, or in search of greater sexual tolerance. It is the novelist's task to stay here and suffer with the rest of us. He can, through his art, lessen that suffering.'' [For a similar argument, see #1055. Burgess later decided that the exotic was not quite so corrupting.]

1011 "Weak, That Was." **Listener**, v. 70 (October 3, 1963) 520-1.

[Television criticism.] The return of 'That Was the Week That Was' proves to be "wholesome, high-spirited, unpretentious, humanly unbuttoned, often shrewd and amusing, and — above all — totally lacking in malice.'' Also on the Savoy hotel and a cybernetics expert.

1012 "Thanatos." **Listener**, v. 70 (October 10, 1963) 582-83.

[Television criticism.] On American morticians, and the suicide rate in South Wales. Also on Arezzo (Italy) and Hollywood musicals.

1013 "Monarchy in Abeyance." **Listener**, v. 70 (October 17, 1963) 626.

[Television criticism.] Spaniards are the most paradoxical, enigmatic, and lovable race in Europe, but this television documentary did not do them justice. The Beatles were shown to be decent working-class lads, but their fans were orgiastic and disgusting.

1014 "God in the Gaps." **Listener**, v. 70 (October 24, 1963) 668.

[Television criticism.] Churchmen inflict **Elmer Gantry** portentosities on us; the unbelievers are incisive. "In traditional Christianity, God has appeared in those gaps (so one speaker said) which reason has been powerless to fill. As reason has filled more and more of them, a less essentialist and more existentialist approach to God seems to have been found necessary to justify belief in a deity at all. . . but. . . the less essentialism the less Christianity; an existential theology is a self-contradiction.''

1015 "Laughter Close to Tears." **Country Life**, v. 134, no. 3478 (October 31, 1963) 1148-49.

Reviews of **Ninety Double Martinis**, by Thomas Hinde; **Scholars and Gypsies**, by Walter Startie; **Boswell's Journal of a Tour to the Hebrides**, ed. by F.A. Pottle and C.H. Bennett; **Henry of Navarre**, by Hesketh Pearson; **Concerte Guide**, by Gerhart von Westerman.

1016 "The Very Casques." **Listener**, v. 70 (October 31, 1963) 712.

[Television criticism.] A fine documentary on the Battle of Agincourt; the political commentators show skill and patience; Kingsley Amis showed good sense when he argued that the aim of a university is to serve a subject, not a student; a dull program on food; and a view of Nubia before its submergence.

1017 "At Table." **Listener**, v. 70 (November 7, 1963) 766.

[Television criticism.] On his total lack of interest in actors as critics (here discussing **Hamlet**), the inevitable but vacuous symposium on the Trend report, a program on food and on the pioneer flight of Alcock and Brown.

1018 "Gerontion." **Listener**, v. 70, no. 1807 (November 14, 1963) 804-5.

[Television criticism.] On pensioners in Bournemouth, a documentary on Sicily, a program on murdered royalty ("This is the sort of film that ought to be made and ought to be shown''), a study of the latest fashions in beds, and the 'Miss World 1963' contest. "I thought the standard of beauty in the contest was not so high as in other years — too much standardization of the coiffure, the inevitable false eyelashes twittering away. Let's have these girls judged, for a change, coming straight out of bed or emerging from a by-election tussle . . . ."

1019 "The Return to Reality." **Listener**, v. 70 (December 5, 1963) 956.

[Television criticism.] A brief report on Tangier (where he has been on holiday) is followed by the television response to the assassination of President Kennedy. Also on the Buchanan report concerning the future of British towns and a program in which Europe looks at itself.

1020 "TV on TV." **Listener**, v. 70 (December 12, 1963) 1000-1.

[Television criticism.] A look at television examining itself, a history of the London subway, a look at progressive Islam, a stereotyped view of the Sikhs as mere martial hoplites (they were more renegade and human in the East) along with an examination of Raoul Follereau and his work with lepers.

1021 "Shantih 3." **Listener**, v. 70 (December 19, 1963) 1042-43.

[Television criticism.] An excellent program on the poetry of T.S. Eliot, Hugh Trevor-Roper on Thomas à Becket, with a disquisition on the facial responses of television audiences that leads to an anti-Beatle diatribe.

1022 "Antenatal." **Listener**, v. 70 (December 26, 1963) 1080-81.

[Television criticism.] On a dull film about Siberia [see also #1030], the dangers of air travel, a mandatory symposium on the proposed entry into the Common Market, Kenya, Cairo and the history of Christmas, a holiday he loves.

1023 "Yuleovision." **Listener**, v. 71, no. 1814, (January 2, 1964) 34-35.

[Television criticism.] "The limit of frothy insubstantiality was reached on Christmas Eve with that incredible 'Elizabeth Taylor in London' — a waste of public money, an impertinence and an insult, an invitation to a feast of nothing . . . . The eponymous goddess. . . was a jaw-dropping vision of totally meaningless allure — Yves St Laurent icing, delectability of fairy gold, the poor little box of tricks of Zuleika Dobson." Also on the two best programs of the year (**The Picardy Affair** and **Britten at Fifty**), Thomas Birdsall, and a program which summed up the notable events of the year. "Nothing can prevent next year's television from standing or falling on the way it celebrates at least the first [the quatercentenary of Shakespeare] and third [the jubilee of World War I] of these events. We shall be watching."

1024 [Untitled Letter in Defense of William Burroughs] **Times Literary Supplement**, 2 January 1964, p. 9.

Burroughs is a serious novelist trying to extend the boundaries of the novel form. Life, not art, provides the nauseating subject matter of art. ". . . I do not always like what I write about: I was nauseated by the content of my **A Clockwork Orange** . . . . For heaven's sake, let us leave morals to the moralists and carry on with the job of learning to evaluate art as art." For short letters, see TLS, 9 January 1964, p. 27 (David Damant, Wilson Harris, Wilson Plant); TLS, 16 January 1964, p. 53 (Nicholas Bentley).

1025 "No Sense of Occasion." **Listener**, v. 71 (January 9, 1964) 90.

[Television criticism.] On the poor quality of year-end television, the curious predictions of the futurologists, the Holy Land and a profile of Pope Paul VI. "The early life of Giovanni Battista Montini would not, I think, predispose the average Briton to admiration or love — here was a sickly ungamesome boy, holy, a swot, with ten out of ten for conduct. The swift biography took fire when it got to his translation to the archdiocese of Milan; anyone then must warm to this man who brought spiritual sustenance to the workers in the workers' own terms and dedicated a church to Christ the Worker."

1026 "Probing the Probers." **Listener**, v. 71 (January 16, 1964) 128.

[Television criticism.] On probing surgeons who are themselves probed with questions that land them outside their speciality, the questionable literary propriety of David Storey's 'Death of My Mother', which assumes that Lawrence's Paul Morel can be equated with D.H. Lawrence, maritime treasure seekers and the Pope's recent pilgramage up the Via Dolorosa.

1027 "Flimsy Pretexts." **Listener**, v. 71 (January 23, 1964) 166-67.

[Television criticism.] On the dangers of tobacco smoking, automation and the future life of collective hedonism, the teaching of English in a multi-racial North London schoolroom, the disposition of British troops for greater Army preparedness and Erasmus.

1028 "Inspired Mismanagement." **Listener**, v. 71 (January 30, 1964) 208-9.

[Television criticism.] A well made program on the admirable Sir John Pope-Hennessy, Victor von Hagen's proposal to map the Roman road system, businessmen quizzing their politicians, Strindberg's **The Father**, the Swingle Singers' presentation of Bach and general election antiphonies.

1029 "A Long Drink of Porter." **Spectator**, v. 212 (January 31, 1964) 151.

Review of **The Collected Stories of Katherine Anne Porter**. Her **Ship of Fools** disappointed some of us. It was too close to the puddingy **Narrenschiff**, too self-consciously 'great' a work, a massive vessel with too many passengers and not enough engines. "Rope" is a short story which establishes its mood with economy and virtuosity, and it demonstrates that the secret of her short stories is "flow." Her masterpiece is **Pale-Horse, Pale Rider** in which the impact of the Kaiser's War on an American city is chronicled with a terrible cold passion.

1030 "A Rap from Moscow." **Listener**, v. 71 (February 7, 1964) 246.

[Television criticism. Burgess is criticised by Marxists for not thinking a film about Siberia interesting.] "I found that Siberian 'adventure' dull, but I am willing, even eager, to find Siberia itself undull. Let the U.S.S.R. publish some of my bourgeois novels and I undertake to spend my unexportable royalties on a trip to Siberia." Also on the ectoplasmic amiability of television "personalities," a tour of a pig farm, the great American sport of domestic murder, President Johnson, Jacqueline Kennedy, C.S. Lewis and the bats in the caves of Kuala Lumpur.

1031 "Mighty Lineless." **Listener**, v. 71 (February 13, 1964) 286-87.

[Television criticism.] Criticizes a misguided program on Christopher Marlowe, the philistine music policy of the BBC and growls at Beatlemania. Also on the pop art of Ben Rauschenberg, a Goya exhibition, and interviews with members of the working classes which treats them as stumbling oracles.

1032 "Pain." **Listener**, v. 71 (February 20, 1964) 326-27.

[Television criticism.] An unilluminating discussion of pain by Archbishop Bloom and Archrationalist Muggeridge (while Burgess suffered the 'lancinating pangs' of toothache), a crossing of the Sahara and a horribly graphic account of a police *ratissage* in a Congolese village, the ineptness of the Angry Young Man appellation and Sir Charles Snow's contention that his 1959 'Two Cultures' lecture prompted a heated response because the literary men fear the big egalitarian wind of modern science. "There are other forms of science [than the study of matter.] I can tell Sir Charles nothing of nuclear biology; can he define a phoneme for me?"

1033 "Treasures and Fetters." **Spectator**, v. 212, no. 7078 (February 21, 1964) 254.

Review of **The Little Girls**, by Elizabeth Bowen. Briefly compares male and female novelists and observes that, although women have a better natural fictional equipment than men, they lack the architectonic gift. Bowen has obviously been influenced by Henry James, who allowed the *yin* to overcome his *yang* principle. "Where James articulates a whole culture, Miss Bowen conserves a particular place at a particular time; this is a feminine gift . . . . It is a wonderful artefact, a triumphant Female Novel by one whose gifts release her from the more male duty of being just among the Just, among the Filthy filthy too, and of suffering dully all the wrongs of Man."

1034 "Home Thoughts." **Listener**, v. 71 (February 27, 1964) 368-69.

[Television criticism.] On youthful PM Wilson casually throwing his journalist interlocutors, a maddening interview of Evelyn Waugh by Elizabeth Jane Howard (Waugh had stipulated a 'pretty woman'), Galileo, egg sniffing prior to processing, Indian fertility and British infertility, and a mathematician explicating his arcane speciality. "All we learned was that mathematicians are decent ordinary chaps who play Mozart, have children, and are very important."

1035 "Jubilate." **Listener,** v. 71 (March 5, 1964) 406-7.

[Television criticism.] A remarkable program about viruses. "The sense of beauty and intricate organization (the tobacco-mosaic virus like the plan of a new city) strikes with such awe that we forget we are looking at the enemy. But Dr. Sanders did not let us forget." A profoundly moving film of Balinese dancers stabbing themselves while in a state of religious frenzy, a view of Leicester in the Midlands, and the effect of coloured immigrants from the Commonwealth on the coming election.

1036 "How Often is Diurnal?" **Listener,** v. 71 (March 12, 1964) 444.

[Television criticism.] An account of Europe's cultural influence on America, displaced persons in Germany and an extremely mixed bag: crime and criminals and the police, the threatened extinction of the golden eagle in Britain, Chinese pop songs, animal trainers and the Trinidadian aversion to marriage.

1037 "Nerves in the Afternoon." **Listener,** v. 71 (March 19, 1964) 494-95.

[Television criticism.] On soccer players, a hysterectomy, travellogues on Ladakh and Gibraltar, as well as an interview with Mr. Harold Wilson. "Religion has ceased to engage our imaginations, and now politics follows. The dark Satanic mills of Blake's poem meant churches and senate-houses, and the Jerusalem we were to build was a kind of city of the imagination — all light and creative madness. Why can't our television politicians temper their all-too-sane visions with a little poetry?"

1038 "The Alien Quorn." **Listener,** v. 71 (March 26, 1964) 530-31.

[Television criticism.] An account of fox-hunting. More concern should be expressed about the souls of the hunters than the fate of the fox which, "dapper, clever, handsome, a lone hunter, may well symbolize sexual success, a red Lord Byron to be destroyed in envy." Also on the Pitman alphabet and the reasonable views of Alex Comfort. "Here was the soothing voice of reason [Comfort] assuring us that violent art means non-violent living."

1039 "Easter 1964." **Listener,** v. 71 (April 2, 1964) 566-67.

[Television criticism.] On pilots, ballet dancers at class and a documentary history of Ireland. [For Huw Wheldon's comments on this review, see #1602.]

1040 "Entente Cordiale." **Listener,** v. 71 (April 9, 1964) 602-3.

[Television criticism.] On artistic depictions of Christ, a satire on hanging, Tennyson, the construction of the Concorde and the Battle of Clacton between Mods and Rockers.

1041 "An Age of Teen." **Listener,** v. 71 (April 16, 1964) 646-47.

[Television criticism.] On teenagers and their dubious right to rebellion, muscular Christianity, Martinique and Brazilian fishermen. "It is the stubborn resistance of the primitive Brazilians to sheer reason, let alone change, that has impressed me . . . . These fierce Christians cling to their suffering God, who exalts their own misery, rather than listen to the communist hucksters who promise an end of hardship; the lobster-fishers prefer the chance of an Atlantic death on their *jangadas* to motor-trawlers and safety. Something perhaps mad, but certainly human, is enshrined here."

1042 "The One and Only." **Manchester Guardian,** April 17, 1964, p. 8.

Review of **A Singular Man,** by J.P. Donleavy. "Mr. Donleavy's statistics belie his bulk. This is only his second novel, and it comes so long after his first that one can't talk about surmounting a hurdle: one is not even aware of the course . . . . The whole book is richly idiosyncratic. It is also very, though sadly, funny. It is also (but perhaps we can forgive this in so unprolific an author) about a hundred pages too long." [Reprinted in #1044.]

1043 "**Hic et Ubique. Listener,** v. 71 (April 23, 1964) 694-95.

[Television criticism.] On tributes to seventy year old Khrushchev, a debate between an arms merchant and a disapproving MP, taxes, Les Halles, and a rehearsal of **The Flying Dutchman** by Georg Solti.

1044 "A Man On His Own." **Manchester Guardian Weekly,** 23 April 1964, p. 11.

[Reprint of #1042.]

1045 "In Search of Shakespeare the Man." **Listener**, v. 71, no. 1830 (April 23, 1964) 670-1.

[Speculations later embodied in Burgess' **Shakespeare**.] Shakespeare was revolted by sex, cuckolded by his wife, wrote for the sake of money and advancement, lost his heart to Southampton and a Dark Lady. "Ultimately there is nothing there. Disturb the bones to find what spirit animated them, and the curse comes upon you — you are face to face with emptiness . . . . it is best to stop playing these games of reconstruction from a few bones and get down to reading the plays again. So, anyway, reason tells us. But is there one person living who, given the choice between discovering a lost play of Shakespeare's and a laundry list of Will's, would not plump for the dirty washing every time?"

1046 "What a Sight It Were." **Listener**, v. 71 (April 30, 1964) 730-1.

[The last of Burgess' weekly television criticism. He continued to write a monthly column called "The Arts" until June 3, 1965.] On the inauguration program of BBC2, a robbery, the Shakespearean life and vigor of Marshal Tito and a biography of Shakespeare. "It was scholarly. . . and uncontroversial . . . . Scholars don't regard their function this quater-centennial year as involving the stirring up of Fleet Ditch or of scratching pocky boils. Leave the dirt to the novelists. This programme moved me a great deal, brought hopeless tears, filled me with a damnable and unaccountable nostalgia. On which note I lay down my typewriter."

1047 "A Trauma from the Fens." **Spectator**, v. 212 (May 15, 1964) 667.

Review of **The Brickfield**, by L.P. Hartley. "The economy of the book is a wonder and the power to conjure past time while staying awake to the present as remarkable as one would expect. And, like his peer Forster and his master James, Hartley knows how to shaft out aphorisms that are barbed with personal shock, so that a fictional experience becomes as privy as a surgical operation."

1048 "A Pilot for Our Pain." **Manchester Guardian**, May 22, 1964, p. 6.

Review of **The Diaries of Franz Kafka**, ed. by Max Brod. The three philosophers who have presided over our own age are probably Kierkegaard, Sartre and Kafka. They help us to explain, without the benefit of revealed religion, the nature of things like free will, choice, evil, guilt. We are thankful to Kafka for his secular assurances that man's fundamental condition is one of helplessness and insufficiency. The guilt which saddled K. can be seen as the guilt of original sin. The interest of these diaries lies in Kafka's attempt to convert his private nightmare of guilt, isolation and frustration into public symbols. "The pain of the artist is a kind of pilot for the pain of community — a pain which is only properly felt when the artist has provided a terminology for it. There is certainly enough pain in these daily grapplings with the banalities of life." [Reprinted in #1050.]

1049 "The Arts." **Listener**, v. 71 (May 28, 1964) 899.

[Television criticism.] Television cannot bear the beatific or infernal vision of true art, no matter how humble. On a performance of **La Traviata** ("Mary Costa as Marguerite could take any number of comely close-ups, but that great rounding of the mouth to hurl notes at far galleries wasn't right for a medium made of mumblings and whispers"), the Royal Ballet's **Toccata**, performances by Britten and Pears and the series 'Music in Miniature' ("Paul Tortellier could fill two hours of screen-time and I should never object: his 'Master Class' on the Elgar cello concerto. . . was a great joy to me and helped to make a beloved work even more beloved"), but 'Writer's World' was disappointing ("It may be that the trade of writing engenders a weariness with words outside the study, while musicians, who are professionally locked in a golden dumbness, luxuriate in a chance to use the more direct medium"), and an excellent visual program on Shakespeare showed documents most of us are too lazy or diffident to search out for ourselves.

1050 "Pilot for Our Pain." **Manchester Guardian Weekly**, 28 May 1964, p. 11.

[Reprint of #1048.]

1051 "The Arts." **Listener**, v. 71, no. 1839 (June 25, 1964) 1042-43.

[Television criticism.] On Aaron Copland's **Music for a Great City**, Paganini's **Caprice XXIV**, a discussion of **Peter Grimes**, a documentary on Bela Bartok, and performances of **Houseparty** and **Peer Gynt**. "The trouble is Grieg ('bonbons stuffed with snow', said Debussy); Ibsen was right in finding his music inadequate to suggest or underline the bitter profundity of the drama. When the starting-point is Grieg, not Ibsen, and the **Peer Gynt** music leads to a cosy sleigh-ride through other of his works, a gibbering parody of a great poet is the inevitable result.''

1052 "Concerning Amation." **Manchester Guardian**, July 10, 1964, p. 7.

Review of **Erotic Poetry**. Ed. by William Cole, with a foreword by Stephen Spender. Also **A Literary Guide to Seduction**, ed. by Robert Meister. In the East, the act of sex is often regarded as an impersonal gateway to an aspect of ultimate reality while "with us in the West, the personality of the sexual partner is paramount — playing records before and making tea after — and hence we find it hard to achieve self-denying Eros. Agape, like Edward's cheerfulness, keeps breaking in." This anthology proves that the West has not done at all badly in the erotic line, and his favorite poets (Ben Jonson, The Earl of Rochester, Shakespeare) are all represented. There is little erotic verse by women, but that is due to a faulty literary tradition which has made many women writers wish to be regarded as auxiliary men. [Reprinted in #1054.]

1053 "We Call This Friday Good." **Spectator**, v. 213, no. 7098 (July 10, 1964) 59-60.

Review of **The Morning Watch**, by James Agee. The young hero tries to imagine the terrible reality of Christ's passion on Good Friday. The sophisticated adult can look back on pubescent religious fervor and recognize much of it as a glandular epiphenomenon of the flesh. Agee concludes, with Traherne, that growing up is growing down. His rich vocabulary attempts to find a verbal equivalent for a pre-verbal state, and Agee, often known as a big film man, has here written one of the best books about childhood ever written.

1054 "Amation Through the Ages." **Manchester Guardian Weekly**, 16 July 1964, p. 11.

[Reprint of #1052.]

1055 "The Novelist's Sources are Myth, Language, and the Here and Now." **New York Times Book Review**, July 19, 1964, p. 5.

[A somewhat revised version, to make it suitable for American consumption, of "The Corruption of the Exotic." For annotation, see #1010.] For letter by Robert S. Umans, see **New York Times Book Review**, 6 September 1964, p. 18.

1056 "The Arts." **Listener**, v. 72, no. 1843 (July 23, 1964) 138-39.

[Television criticism.] On a performance of Bartok's **Concerto for Orchestra**, Benjamin Britten's performance of his **Cello Symphony**, the Tortelier family and their interpretation of Bach. Also on interviews with Alfred Hitchcock and a middle-aged *pointilliste* painter. Debates what, if anything, television brings to music. "The act of producing music can be ugly and even absurd, what with beery men spitting down trombones and, during a **tacet**, draining the saliva off, the lambasting of kettledrums like round tuned enemies, grown men prettily tintinnabulating tiny triangles. Women do well with cool white arms over the harp-strings, but generally speaking the auditor ought to bury his head in his miniature score."

1057 "The Universal Mess." **Manchester Guardian**, July 24, 1964, p. 9.

Review of **The Novels of Samuel Beckett**, by John Fletcher. Beckett is both a French and Anglo-Irish writer. He abandoned English and adopted the French language not for the grounds stated ("it was more exciting for me — writing in French") but because he needed "austerer tools than that tortuous allusive English which is the loved and hated heritage of all intellectual novelists this side of the Channel." Mr. Fletcher's study defines the Beckettian man, a stoic creature which shambles from book to book, ugly, paunched, dirty, halitotic, his feet bad; the philosophy exemplified by this figure is a brave one. "It accepts a dualistic view of the universe and rejects all comfortable plausibilities about the possibility of body and soul fusing into a unity. The body is useless and sex is horrible and sensory perception inaccurate . . . . As for God, the wretched Beckettian exile needs Him, but Hamm sums up for everybody: 'The bastard! He doesn't exist'!" [Reprinted in #1058.]

1058 "Beckett's World." **Manchester Guardian Weekly**, 30 July 1964, p. 11.

[Reprint of #1057.]

1059 "The Arts." **Listener**, v. 72, no. 1847 (August 20, 1964) 282-83.

[Television criticism.] On the songs popular in World War I, the war poetry of Wilfred Owen, a performance of Britten's **War Requiem** and of Ravel's **Bolero**, Mozart's **Don Giovanni**. A program called

Brecht on Music "proved how neatly music will outlive ideology, bending to the doctrinaire as a bough will bend to the snow on it and then, when bent enough, dislodging the powdery burden." Jazz "is narcissistic and, far from rejoicing in true improvisation, it will slyly hoard effective tropes and bring them out again and again." Praises, in connection with the first program, a book called **The Sexual Cycle of Human Warfare**.

1060 "Iridectomy." **Manchester Guardian**, September 11, 1964, p. 10.

Review of **The Italian Girl**, by Iris Murdoch. It is a popular novel in the worst sense of the word. It is a "novel of the easy way out — psychological (or glandular) crises externalised into film-symbols, conventional characterisation, the pathetic fallacy. . . the flabbiness of the previous two novels persists, along with a notable lack of humour . . . . It is time to call Miss Murdoch's bluff. Her reputation is grossly inflated; this book should help to prick it." [Reprinted in #1062.]

1061 "The Arts." **Listener**, v. 72, no. 1851 (September 17, 1964) 440-41.

[Television criticism.] On the performance of works by Schumann, Mendelssohn, Walton, Elgar and Gilbert and Sullivan. Hugo Dyson's discussion of Shakespeare filled him with intolerable nostalgia and Robert Kee's reports from Edinburgh festival with depression. "The pubs close gleefully at ten and remain shut on Sunday; Edinburgh is a gastronomic hell. Life and art continue to be parallel worlds, incapable of engaging, and the vitality of the artists is pushed into the catacombs."

1062 "Iridectomy." **Manchester Guardian Weekly**, 17 September 1964, p. 11.

[Reprint of #1060.]

1063 "Wagner's 'The Ring'; Anthony Burgess on a Number of Interpretations." **Listener**, v. 72, no. 1851 (September 17, 1964) 419-21.

"When I wrote my first serious novel with an English **mise-en-scene** it seemed natural to base it on **The Ring** cycle and even call the book **The Worm and the Ring**. I opened out with the three Rhine-maidens turned into schoolgirls splashing through puddles, the horrible dwarf Alberich into an ugly, randy, eventually love-renouncing brat called Albert Rich . . . ." Records his first horror on finding out that Wagner was supposed to be responsible for the Nazi movement. "**The Ring** is symbolism, and only artists who are not sure what they believe indulge in it, since symbols are good at reconciling opposites, resolving ambiguities, suggesting archetypes . . . . The symbolism of **The Ring** can mean pretty well anything — anything, that is, except National Socialism trimphant." Quotes Wagner on the genesis of the opera, and describes the Jungian interpretation of Robert Donington, the Shavian twist of Bernard Shaw and Ernest Newman ("the greatest Wagnerian of them all") on Siegfried. Comments on the fragments of Wagner found in T.S. Eliot's **The Wasteland** and James Joyce's **Ulysses**.

1064 "Why, This Is Hell." **Listener**, v. 72 (October 1, 1964) 514.

Review of **A Single Man** by Christopher Isherwood.

1065 "The Arts." **Listener**, v. 72, no. 1855 (October 15, 1964) 602-603.

[Television criticism.] On the "incestuous" relationship between Ibsen and Emilie Bardach in a riveting documentary, the literature produced in World War II ("Let's be honest about the literature that came direct and hot out of that dull and necessary war; let's admit that little of it was any good"), a lumpish production of **Iolanthe**, and a performance of the Beethoven Concerto which confirms his impression that the work is a bore.

1066 "A Peck of Penny Wisdom." **Manchester Guardian**, October 16, 1964, p. 9.

Review of **The Faber Book of Aphorisms**. Ed. by W.H. Auden and Louis Kronenberger. An aphorism "is the hors d'oeuvre, the remove, or bonne bouche, a brightener and lightener of the solid work of masticating true argument or wisdom. The hard-pressed writer or speaker will, accordingly, welcome this book as a spice-shelf and not confuse it with a kitchen." [Reprinted in#1068.]

1067 "A Touch of the Apostasies." **Spectator**, v. 213 (October 16, 1964) 518.

Review of **Julian**, by Gore Vidal; **Anno Domini**, by George Steiner; **The 480**, by Eugene Burdick; **Kelly**, by Eric Lambert. **Julian** manages its huge cast well; the style is Graves-plain; the treatment is comprehensive. **Anno Domini** deals with war as sex, war as love-hate, war as self-revelation. There are flaws: the English dialogue is not always convincing, but the skill is considerable and the insight devastating. **The 480** deals with the mass-marketing that attends an American presidential election. It is skillfully done, but it will be stone-cold by Christmas. **Kelly,** about the Australian rogue Ned Kelly, is sub-Snow, but it needs no stylistic graces. "While the hangman tightened the noose, Kelly said, 'Such is life'."

1068 "A Peck of Penny Wisdom." **Manchester Guardian Weekly,** 22 October 1964, p. 11.

[Reprint of #1066.]

1069 "The Arts." **Listener,** V. 72, no. 1859 (November 12, 1964) 774-75.

[Television criticism.] On Britten's **War Requiem,** a Mozart concerto, a performance by Benny Goodman, an interview with theatre director Peter Hall and a discussion of Bach. "This, if you like, was a waste: there was everything except enough time. Figure to yourself, as they say — Leopold Stokowski, Michael Tippett, William Mann, John Amis, port on the table, most efficient putters-on of records, fine blown-up Bach portraits, and all we got was a mean, a criminal, half-hour. This cries to heaven for vengeance."

1070 Review of **My Life and Loves,** by Frank Harris. **Listener,** v. 72, no. 1859 (November 12, 1964) 769.

"When Mozart was four, he wrote minuets; when Frank Harris was four — or, not to make him appear too precocious, 'between four and five' — he touched a girl's legs. Each, then, chose his art early, or was chosen by it." It is difficult to dismiss Harris as a lecherous egoist, tasteless bore or crude groper. He was no stylist or scholar; he lacked the power of selection; he was devoid of humor. "Ultimately, though, Harris seems to be on the side of the gods. Whatever his faults may be, meanness of spirit and ungenerosity of emotion are not among them."

1071 "Cream and Offal." **Spectator,** v. 213, no. 7116 (November 13, 1964) 643.

Review of **Girls in Their Married Bliss,** by Edna O'Brien; **Better Dead than Red,** by Stanley Reynolds; **One Man, One Matchet,** by T.M. Aluko; **The Cool Meridian,** by Sarah Kilpatrick; and **The Main Experiment** by Christopher Hodder-Williams. O'Brien's novel, closely examined, is illogical and inept ("Kate has to get married because she is ten months pregnant. Now, let's either have the Salinger touch of a million years pregnant or else observe the biological facts of gestation"). She is plainly a man-hater. "Seduction is a big theme, however, and it seems to be introduced primarily to demonstrate how horrible men are — selfish, effete, kinky . . . . Despite its pornographic elements, no book could well be less pornographic: a few more books like this and one could be put off sex forever. The act is described with a sort of indulgent sneer . . . . The final effect is of a dish of ill-cooked offal topped with sour cream from O'Hanlon's Dairy. Miss O'Brien is revealed as a member of that literary sorority dedicated to the deflation of piss-proud man. This is a big job; it requires a bigger talent." Reynolds has written a savagely funny book; Aluko a solid, Snovian one; while Kilpatrick has reinstated the theme of emotional agonies of complex people with considerable skill. Hodder-Williams has written a fine thriller which gets its distinction from the moral seasoning.

1072 "On the End of Every Fork." **Manchester Guardian,** November 20, 1964, p. 9.

Review of **The Naked Lunch,** by William Burroughs. "It's amazing how little is needed to slake the thirsts of the pornographic-hounds, the prurient sniggerers, the protectors of public morals. From the title of Mr. Burrough's masterpiece they will be led to expect something illicitly agapoid, a sort of phallic Laocoon, and they will be disappointed. What they will find, on the other hand, is a palimpsest of obscenity so emetic that no amount of casuistry will be able to justify a charge of inflammation and corruption. This, God help us, is no **Fanny Hill** or **Lady Chatterley's Lover.** It is a picture of hell, and hell is not corrupting. The obscenity is not of Mr. Burroughs's devising: it is there in the world outside . . . . The meat on the end of every fork is revealed as the guts and blood of our fellow-men." Burroughs may well be compared with Swift, and **Naked Lunch** is a very important piece of literature. "It will make the rest of the autumn's offerings look remarkably lumpish or puny." [Reprinted in #1073.]

1073 "On the End of Every Fork." **Manchester Guardian Weekly,** 26 November 1964, p. 11.

[Reprint of #1072.]

1074 "Saying or Screaming Their Say." **Manchester Guardian**, November 27, 1964, p. 15.

Review of **The Speakers**, by Heathcote Williams. This study of four Hyde Park speakers attempts to answer questions once posed by Sean O'Casey: where they come from, how they live and where they go when they have had or screamed their say. "None of these has a creed or message to be summarised. The real nature of their protest against society belongs to some prearticulatory region of the brain. The wound, whatever it is, doesn't heal; words — and it doesn't much matter what they are — are a kind of pus. Wisely, Heathcote Williams attempts neither diagnosis nor judgment. These men are what they are — dirty, paranoid, lunatic missionaries, teachers with nothing and nobody to teach; they are also a fringe of society which society would be unwise to try to snip off . . . . Some of their demented epigrams stick like burrs ('Lomas says that reason is an emotion for the sexless')."

1075 "Dear Mr. Shame's Voice." **Spectator**, v. 213, no. 7118 (November 27, 1964) 731-32.

Review of **Joyce's Portrait; Criticisms and Critiques**, ed. by Thomas Connolly; **A New Approach to Joyce**, by Robert S. Ryf; **The Art of James Joyce**, by A. Walton Litz; and **Joyce's Benefictions**, by Helmut Bonheim. American scholars, endowed with time and money, are busy plucking the Joyce-bird down to the last microscopic feathers. What worries him is the gratuitous scholarship devoted to Joyce's **Portrait**. The professors seem intent on reducing a work of naturalism to a mere collocation of symbols; and they miss the obvious in their restless search for the esoteric. When they argue that the symbolism of the **Wake** drowns the naturalistic they are flying in the teeth of Joyce's intentions. "**Finnegans Wake** is a costume-ball whose motif is Guilty Love — Swift and Stella, Parnell and Kitty O'Shea, Ibsen's Master Builder, Tristram. The incest-theme is no mere intellectual *donnee* but the stuff of true fiction." He is grateful for the sweat and poring and ingenuity of the American professors, but feels "the time has come for Joyce — a demotic writer if ever there was one — to be released from the Babylonish captivity of the professors and presented to the people as one of the great comic writers of all time."

1076 Review of **The Profession of English Letters**, by J.W. Saunders. **Listener**, v. 72, no. 1862 (December 3, 1964) 896.

"When writers get together they rarely talk about writing. They usually talk about advances and royalties and the best places to sell review copies." Pope drove hard bargains with publishers, but Johnson got only 400 guineas for his **Lives of the Poets**. Byron asked 3,000 pounds for his poems largely because Moore and Campbell got 3,000 for theirs. Scott boasted that he could write ill enough for the present taste; he was the first writer to be corrupted by money. Contemporary British writers, some 7,000 strong, earn (87% of them) less than 1,500 pounds per year. "Mr. Saunders praises the hard and various writer, like David Holbrook, who will tackle anything from a hymnal to a ballad opera. Your present reviewer he totally neglects — five novels written in 1960, one of them a Book Society Choice, as well as reviews and God knows what else. Things ease a little when the paperbacks come or America starts a minimal vogue. But the profession remains a difficult one . . . ."

1077 "Multilingual." **Observer Weekend Review**, 6 December 1964, p. 2.

Review of **The Mother Tongue**, by Lancelot Hogben. English inherited a broad basis of grammar and vocabulary from the original Low German settlers. It absorbed a vast Romance vocabulary from the Normans along with a great number of learned Latin and Greek terms. Much of this book derives from the earlier **The Loom of Language** and the work is notable for a total unwillingness (perhaps cowardice) to present the facts of speech in scientific terms by means of phonetic notations. "Hogben. . . is either scared of phonetics or else thinks we are scared . . . . Professor Hogben seems to think that the eye is enough and totally neglects the ear." He learned Dutch from the earlier **Loom** book, and gained a pen-pal from The Hague but, due to the absence of notation, never dared to speak the language.

1078 "The Arts." **Listener**, v. 72, no. 1863 (December 10, 1964) 950-51.

[Television criticism.] On Winston Churchill as amateur painter, a number of interviews in the **Monitor** series (Jonathan Miller interviewing Peter Brook and Susan Sontag) the Bolshoi Opera Company in a performance of **Prince Igor**, Klemperer's interpretation of Beethoven's Choral Symphony, and a performance of Michael Tippett's Concerto for Double String Orchestra. "I'm still unhappy about the brevity of the **Music Forum** sessions. The one on Beethoven was like eating plum pudding for breakfast

— no time to savour the richness, the certainty of dyspepsia. With so little time, the quiz aspect will get the better of the expert discussion. One should be able to feel what Beethoven called *aufgeknöpft*." [Lit. unbuttoned; i.e., relaxed, at ease]

1079 "Polycarpic Polnay." **Spectator**, v. 213, no. 7120 (December 11, 1964) 820-21.

Review of **The Plaster Bed**, by Peter de Polnay; **The Night in Lisbon**, by Erich Maria Remarque; **The Boy Who Wanted Peace**, by George Friel; and **The Honey Bird**, by Stuart Cloete. "Mr. de Polnay is always very good on the margin. He turns his back on the plates spinning on poles (the impetus is so powerful that the central plot can get along very nicely on its own) and busies himself with fascinating subsidiary tricks — deracinated drunks in Majorca, pub anecdotes, the terrible girl-friend Beulah. The canvas is busy with life; the artfully plain style shoots off intensity when we least expect it; the whole thing is a devastatingly accurate picture of our times. If novel-readers were less scared of prolificity, they would recognise in Peter de Polnay one of the most brilliant entertainers of the age. But the spare quincunx of E.M. Forster remains the ideal of an *oeuvre*. I personally am quite sure that Mr. de Polnay has another twenty-four novels in him, and I thank the life-force for it."

1080 "Chekhov For Ireland." **Spectator**, v. 213, no. 7121 (December 18, 1964) 848.

Review of **Collection Two**, by Frank O'Connor. O'Connor admits to being a perfectionist driven to rewrite his short stories. One wishes he would polish less and publish more. His 'Guests of the Nation' says, in a few words, all that needs to be said about the Troubles. His 'Darcy in the Land of Youth' concerns an Irishman who consents to the rituals of guiltless pre-marital sex with an English girl and it demonstrates that the Irish are different. "O'Connor catches [the Irish] in an epoch of change and bewilderment, coping with new forces, trying to understand themselves, God-centred but fundamentally hopeless." He is a considerable artist in his own right.

1081 "Waugh Begins." **Encounter**, v. 23 (December 1964) 64-68.

Review of **Waugh Begins; The First Volume of an Autobiography**, by Evelyn Waugh. Waugh obviously inherited some of his father's limited literary tastes (if not his style). The accuracy of the book is often in doubt. Gulosity appears; lust does not. "An academic failure, indecisive in his choice of vocation, inclined, like St Augustine himself, to debauchery . . . . [Waugh] sought a sempiternal quietus in the waters of the North Wales coast. The jellyfish stung him and sent him back to the future; the sea proved lustral, not lethal. Naturally, we rejoice. We look forward to reading about the larger learning, a lifetime's lesson on how not to repine." Reprinted in **Urgent Copy**.

1082 "Shakespeare in Music." **The Musical Times**, v. 105 (December 1964) 901-2.

Review of **Shakespeare in Music: A Collection of Essays** by John Stevens . . . [et al.]. Ed. by Phyllis Hartnoll. "Shakespeare is a god, but he was also a man of the theatre, and he knew which words would set and which would not. Simplicity — even conventionality — of theme, variety of vowel and diphthong, concentration on voiced consonants rather than unvoiced — these are the big lyric secrets. Sometimes, as in 'Take O take those lips away,' meaning is not greatly missed. Once, in Pandarus's dirty song in **Troilus and Cressida**, the sound of orgasm only comes to shocking life when we hear the setting: it looks like mere harmless nonny-nonny on the page." Also discusses some works by Vaughan Williams, Mendelssohn, Schubert, Berlioz, Elgar, Verdi and Benjamin Britten.

1083 "Powers That Be." **Encounter**, v. 24, no. 1 (January 1965) 71-76.

Review of **Corridors of Power**, by C.P. Snow and **Late Call**, by Angus Wilson. Lord Snow's novel exemplifies a kind of latter-day neo-classicism. Snow would agree with Dr. Johnson's Imlac that the business of the imaginative writer is to examine the species, and not the individual. Regrets the abstractions, the moves towards generalized experience in Snow's novels and argues that "The minutiae that make real novels are the taste of eggs and bacon, the bad tooth, and the pang of heartburn . . . . More novels like **Corridors of Power** and the novelist must be admired more and loved less." Snow has deprecated the Dickensian talent for mimicry and argued that it represents a flight to the periphery of a story. The phrase is a a disturbing one and "There is a sense in which all genuine fiction represents such a flight. All of Dickens' novels have a hard centre, but by an artistic paradox, we can only come to know it after vigorous and joyful no-hands cycling round on the perimeter." Wilson plainly delights in his talent for mimicry and parody, and it enables him to make points which could not have been stated with austere directness.

1084 "The Arts." **Listener**, v. 73, no. 1867 (January 7, 1965) 30-31.

[Television criticism.] John Betjeman attends a Children's Christmas party. Philip Larkin reads his verse ("here is a poet who is going to be major"). Susan Sontag interviews New York architect Philip Johnson. The Royal Ballet's **Coppelia** is magnificent. Yehudi Menuhin's performance of the Elgar Concerto ("the greatest, surely, ever written") made him brim with pride and tears. A survey of what composers have done with Shakespeare confirms his impression that composers want to enclose rather than serve Shakespeare. "As Christmas is becoming a Negro feast, so New Year is now reserved for either pop-maniacs or Scots — both, I think, minority sects. Let's have fair play for the majority. My new Year resolution is to form a new *Davidsbund* to fight the Philistines, the disc-jockeys, the intellectual adulators of pop-tripe, the negritudinizers, and the grovellers before the slack-mouthed youth. Founder-members forward. You won't, alas, get crushed in the rush."

1085 "Rare Plants Under a Frosty Moon." **Spectator**, v. 214, no. 7124 (January 8, 1965) 47.

Review of **The Multiple Modern Gods and Other Stories**, by Stanley Berne; **Kaliyuga**, by David Stacton. Berne seems to argue for more structural bricks and less syntactical mortar ("she spread and lower pants of his soul from before asked and knocked and asked her to break her virgin to seek safe and pill and kill the juice acid") but words must be set in structures, however minimal. Mr. Stacton attempts a novel in which his suburban and bored married couple are transformed into Kali and Siva, but his characters are too dimpling and nice to achieve the apotheosis.

1086 "Cast a Cold Eye." **Spectator**, v. 214, no. 7125 (January 15, 1965) 73.

Review of **The Vast Design: Patterns in W.. B. Yeats' Aesthetic**, by Edward Engelberg; **W.B. Yeats: Selected Criticism**, ed. by A. Norman Jeffares; and **Yeats**, by Peter Ure. Yeats found his symbols in Theosophy and Rusicrucianism and he stood for the whirlpool, Madame Blavatsky and the yogibogeybox, but the content of his verse "resolves itself into the common stock of all poets — the opposition of the moving river to the static stone, the agony of transience, the need to build something on which to rejoice." His achievement was an astonishing rhetoric or grandiloquence, and the true Yeats scholar should try to work out the secrets of his verbal magic. Yeats is an untrustworthy judge of the work of other writers (witness his edition of the **Oxford Book of Modern Verse**) but he is the greatest poet since Hopkins. Reprinted in **Urgent Copy**.

1087 "Fraynetic." **Manchester Guardian**, January 22, 1965, p. 7.

Review of **The Tin Men**, By Michael Frayn. This novel about computers who ape men follows the **Observer** technique of most satisfying *feuilletons* unified by a a tenuous plot and a few contemporary humours. Computers write newspapers. One computer named Samaritan, on a raft with another survivor extends calipers, finds the skull to be human, and throws itself overboard. "One knows, sourly, that this book was going to be funny; one did not see how it could be so continuously funny; the book-humorist's problem lies in preventing periods of recovery between jokes from becoming mere *longueurs* . . . . The fun of **The Tin Men** is outrageous because it's so serious — which may not be the right thing to say as the effervescence tickles one's throat, but I say it."

1088 "The Arts." **Listener**, v. 73, no. 1870 (January 28, 1965) 161.

[Television criticism.] "T.S. Eliot's death should not have come as the shock it did. If his youthful poems were studies in calculated senescence, his middle-aged poems were preparations for the journey into the dark — viaticum after courteous viaticum." Reviews some obituary television programs and laments absence of adequate film footage of great writers. The program on Alasdair Gray, an obscure Glasgow poet and painter, was a shocking hoax. Also on composer Michael Josephs, performances of Mozart and de Falla conducted by Edward Lockspeiser, and the reminiscences of writers on their schooldays.

1089 "From the Inside." **Manchester Guardian**, January 29, 1965, p. 10.

Review of **The Working Novelist**, by V.S. Pritchett. This collection of essays from the **New Statesman** by the best story writer of our age is as remarkable for its range as for its range of sympathy. He shows an unfailing ability to find the apt instance which is felt as an epiphany of his subject's essence. His qualified praise of Durrell is worth more than all the French and American gushing. It is, all in all, an admirable work. [Reprinted in #1090.]

1090 "From the Inside." **Manchester Guardian Weekly**, 4 February 1965, p. 11.
[Reprint of #1089.]

1091 "Dr. Rowse Meets Dr. Faustus." **Nation**, v. 200 (February 1, 1965) 115, 117-18.

Review of **Christopher Marlowe**, by A.L. Rowse. Confesses that Marlowe struck him, in 1940, as a tortured fellow renegade. "I was a renegade Catholic who mocked at hell but was still secretly scared of it, especially as it might come any night now. I felt, despite all the biographical evidence, that Marlowe himself might be such a man, his blasphemies and beery jags the true voice of imperfect emancipation." Gives an account of **Tamburlaine, The Jew of Malta**, and **Dr. Faustus**. Observes that Dr. Rowse does not seem to believe in hell, or perhaps the concept of the soul; that his biographical part is no better than that of other scholars; that his criticism is based on fiat rather than fact. "I think Marlowe's quatercentenary, cast into deep shadow by that of his longer-lived junior [Shakespeare], called for a better book than Dr Rowse's — something less opinionated, more sensitive, more — in a word — Marlovian. Will we have to wait till 1993, quatercentenary of a dagger through the frontal lobes and a swearing death, before we get it?" Reprinted in **Urgent Copy** under title: "Dr. Rowstus."

1092 "Past Time and the River." **Spectator**, v. 214, no. 7128 (February 5, 1965) 176.

Review of **Mallabec**, by David Walker; **Patterns of Three and Four**, by Hubert Nicholson; **Sheba's Landing**, by Thomas Baird; **The Cockpit**, by Paul Bourquin; **The Hat of Authority**, by John Sanders.

1093 "Idiophone Book." **Times Literary Supplement**, 11 February 1965, p. 112.

Review of **Systems of Prosodic and Paralinguistic Features in English**, by David Crystal and Randolph Quirk. The study of linguistics can palliate the average bookman's guilt about the Two Cultures. Science has become inordinately specialized and prohibitively expensive, but the scientific study of language remains accessible to every literary person. Only Shaw took phonetics seriously enough to create a phonetician, even though he was not one himself. Argues that the literary man should be prepared to make use of a scientific notation of speech sounds when it is needed by his text. It is shameful that linguistics men are interested in literature, but literary men shoo away linguistics as a horrid science. [Original review unsigned but reprinted in **Urgent Copy** under title: "The Proper Study of Literary Man."]

1094 "The Arts." **Listener**, v. 73, no. 1873 (February 18, 1965) 274-5.

[Television criticism.] On the death of Winston Churchill, the poetry of William Empson, a program on art appreciation, the music of Wagner, Brahms and Chopin and a performance of **Beauty and the Beast**. "Churchill's greatness would have thrust itself out of the screen even more tellingly if it had occasionally been qualified. I don't mean the pig-headed ungraciousness of the **Daily Worker** nor the disparagers of Churchill's prose (they will be back again shortly). I mean the articulate artists who have their own voices and their own valid summations of the Age of Churchill."

1095 "Take a Wound, Take a Bow." **Spectator**, v. 214, no. 7132 (March 5, 1965) 305.

Review of **A World Elsewhere**, by John Bowen; **The Monkey Watcher**, by Robert Towers; **Love from Venus**, by Max Catto; **The Satyr and the Saint**, by Leonardo Bercovici; **Across the Sea Wall**, by Christopher Koch.

1096 "The Arts." **Listener**, v. 73, no. 1876 (March 11, 1965) 381.

[Television criticism.] Responds to Huw Wheldon's article entitled "Television and the Arts" [see #1602]. On two ballets (**The Firebird** and **Las Hermanas**), the music of Verdi, a program called **Muses with Milligan** (execrable), a demonstration of what the artist can learn from science (depressing) and literary exiles. "Perhaps the scope was too great — Ovid, Dante, Hugo, Mann, Silone, Brecht, Lawrence, Joyce, Nabokov, to say nothing of Byron, Shelley, Dan Jacobson, Peter Porter, and V.S. Naipaul. Practically everyone who has ever written seemed to have joined the exiles' ranks . . . ."

1097 "Not So Gentle Craft." **Spectator**, v. 214, no. 7133 (March 12, 1965) 329-30.

Review of a performance of **The Shoemakers' Daughter** by Thomas Dekker and the Theatre Club production of **Hippolytus** by Euripides.

1098 "Coves and Morts." **Manchester Guardian**, March 19, 1965, p. 11.

Review of **The Elizabethan Underworld; A Collection of Tudor and Early Stuart Tracts and Ballads**. Selected and edited by A.V. Jones. "As a sociological study this book is admirable; as popular literature it lifts up the heart. So much do we incline to the devil's party (knowing it, too) that we're not likely to wish any of these long-dead rogues in hell. A spell in purgatory, perhaps, and then an eternity with the false dice or other cony-catching. We've enough to do cursing our own criminals and trying to reform them. Can they be reformed? History gives a pessimistic answer."

1099 "Cobblers." **Spectator**,, v. 214, no. 7134 (March 19, 1965) 364.

Review of a performance of **Hobson's Choice**, by Harold Brighouse. "It was cobblers for my first week (**The Shoemaker's Holiday**) and it is cobblers again for my second. Is this a sort of warning that I ought to stick to my last? Anyway, it's unlikely that cobblers will turn up any more unless — as seems possible in this job — I shall need terms of defiance and abuse." Also reviews Brecht's **Happy End**. "I think the Brecht cult has gone on long enough. Even a touch of that name, like a rub of garlic, is supposed to be enough to give a flabby charade distinction. It's a confidence trick. A lot of us put up with Brecht for the sake of Weill, but this is far from being his best score . . . . I left the Royal Court enraged. Who are they to drag me out, limping with thromboangitiis obliterans, crammed with great expectations which, Michael Geliot must well know, are not going to be fulfilled? Every prospect displeases; the only man is Weill — and second-rate Weill, too. Cobblers."

1100 Review of **Memoirs of a Malayan Official**, by Victor Purcell. **Listener**, v. 73, no. 1878 (March 25, 1965) 461.

"Great colonial officers must expect this — the ignorance of the sweet stay-at-home, their portion of the collective sneer of the progressive paper or television programme, the statue melted down for guns by the manumitted natives . . . ." Dr. Purcell chose to specialize in Chinese, and back in Malaya, he spent 30 years protecting the Malayan Chinese. He also saw to it that they behaved ("too many brothels, strong-arm gangs, secret societies, anti-British text-books in the schools, the first cobra's nests of communism") and this work is one of the ornaments of Malayan scholarship.

1101 "Lawful Ambitions." **Spectator**, v. 214, no. 7135 (March 26, 1965) 391.

Review of performances of **Inadmissible Evidence**, by John Osborne; **Widowers' Houses**, by Bernard Shaw; and **Return Ticket**, by William Corlett. Nicol Williamson's performance as Maitland, the man afflicted by wanhope, the big despair of the theologians, is one of the wonders of the English stage. Shaw's interest lies, not in Rachmanism itself, a practise which has been going on since before the ancient dawn of rents, but how people will trim their philosophy to continue raking in the profits of slum landlords. Why Londoners like the anaerobic **Return Ticket** is one of life's mysteries.

1102 "What Now in the Novel?" **Spectator**, v. 214, no 7135 (March 26, 1965) 400.

D.H. Lawrence, the pale Galilean, would be delighted. "We have got over that infantile concentration on streams of consciousness; we don't worry overmuch about form; we take the provincial lower orders seriously; we clear people's minds of cant; we try to make new myths out of the deep dark bitter belly-tension of man and woman, man and man; we go abroad." The post-war English novel was the soldier's revenge (less cant, cultural pretentiousness, Mozart — more beer and fags and superior women) but, if the time for lashing out at society is over, and we lack Golding's concern with moral profundities, what is left for the novelist to write about? Suggests the young novelist should experiment with form and language. "It means expending the resources of literature in an attempt to find out more about the whole human complex, the roots on which societies are built. Only through the exploration of language can the personality be coaxed into yielding a few more of its secrets." Reprinted in **Urgent Copy**.

1103. "The Arts." **Listener**, v. 73, no. 1879 (April 1, 1965) 498-99.

[Television criticism.] On Sir John Barbirolli, Henry Livings, the art of South African homeowners, the architecture of Leicester University's Department of Engineering, the poetry of Robert Lowell, interviews with Robert Shaw and David Jones ("a great artist") and a performance of the ballet **Romeo and Juliet**. "Ballet is the most dangerous of all the arts, the art that most approaches beautiful mindlessness. What can one say of Fonteyn and Nureyev except that they were exquisite and had nothing to do with Shakespeare?''

1104 ''A New Turn on the Old Ferris Wheel.'' **Spectator**, v. 214, no. 7136 (April 2, 1965) 447.

Review of **The Destroyer**, by Paul Ferris; **Lunch with Ashurbanipal**, by Wallace Hildick; **Powdered Eggs**, by Charles Simmmons; **Yes From No-Man's Land**, by Bernard Kops. The book by Ferris is finely contrived and moving. Hildick shows an interest in formal experiment, but the theme is too bookish. Simmons reveals a combination of wit and innocence which makes his work a very acceptable piece of post-Salingerism. Kops's style has a power and idiosyncratic unity under the remarkable variety of tone.

1105 ''The Trouble with Racine.'' **Spectator**, v. 214, no. 7136 (April 2, 1965) 442.

Review of performances of **Andromaque**, by Racine; **Le Pieton de l'air**, by Eugene Ionesco; **Ne te promene donc pas toute nue** — all performed by the Theatre de France. ''I followed much of **Andromaque** with the text and a torch, swallowing great gobbets whole and then coming up for air, action and sheer listening and looking. This, though, was regarded by my neighbours as vaguely anti-social.''

1106 ''Made in Heaven.'' **Spectator**, v. 214, no. 7137 (April 9, 1965) 476.

Review of **Le soulier de satin**, by Paul Claudel and **The Platinum People**, by Ian Messiter. ''Why does time pardon Paul Claudel? (The answer is not given by Auden. 'Pardons him for writing well' refers to Yeats.) Perhaps time forgives his faults because he fills great slabs of it with eternity.'' The claims made for Messiter's play are excessive. ''Two young men next to me roared their heads off. I claudicated home feeling old, sour, and unloved.''

1107 ''Mysteries.'' **Spectator**, v. 214, no. 7138 (April 16, 1965) 506.

Review of performances of **The Wakefield Mystery Plays** and **La Bugiarda**, by Fabbri. ''All the appurtenances of a tart, though a fundamental core of Catholic innocence, are brought by Rossell Falk to the part of Isabella in Fabbri's **La Bugiarda**. The Aldwych curtain went up to Isabella's strip-teasing **sola**, and these tired glands responded gratifyingly. The Falk is totally enchanting, the play as sweet and frothy as Asti Spumante . . . . The final triumph was Rossell Falk's — a kind of pledge that the lucid mysteries of femininity can never, thank God, be exhausted.''

1108 ''The Arts.'' **Listener**, v. 73, no. 1882 (April 22, 1965) 610-11.

[Television criticism.] On Baudelaire as art critic, a production of **The Pied Piper of Harlow**, some opera singers on their craft and a poetry reading by Stevie Smith. [This column also includes William Trevor's review of Burgess' own **Silence, Exile and Cunning**. See #1115] Trevor: ''More than anything else, this was a display of one man's enthusiasm for the work of another . . . . It was, I think, as close to Joyce and as close to his Dublin as a film of this kind can be. Its economy sharpened the grey, dry grittiness that is there in the city always, side by side with the flow of words or the pawky reticence. The treatment of Molly Bloom's last speech from **Ulysses**, magnificently spoken by Sheila Manahan, was as delicate and moving a small-screen item as any I can remember.''

1109 ''The Living Language: Novels Are Made of Words.'' **Times Literary Supplement**, April 22, 1965, p. 317.

Describes his bewilderment at the resistence of novel readers to terms derived from linguistics. He has used 'rhotacismus,' 'obturator' and 'bilabial fricative' in his fiction. They have elicited gnat-noises of complaint; fists have occasionally been shaken. ''I cannot at all understand why novel-readers will lap up references to bleeder-screws, distributor-arms and all the technical magic of Shuteland, while denying the novelist the right to bring exactness of description to processes fundamental to an art based on dialogue.'' Then observes that some of his paralinguistic expressions (''war awe warthog Warsaw'' to describe a yawn) have caused trouble for translators. Discusses his decision to invent an Anglo-Russian dialect in **A Clockwork Orange** and the fact that an auditory impulse lay behind his novels about Malaya. Also refers to his novel-in-progress (**Tremor of Intent**) and **The Right to an Answer**.

1110 ''Cloud-Cuckoo-Land.'' **Spectator**, v. 214, no. 7139 (April 23, 1965) 534.

Review of **The Birds**, by Aristophanes.

1111 "Crisis in Gibralter." **Spectator**, v. 214, no. 7139 (April 23, 1965) 528.

The Gibraltarians are no fools. The conditions of well-being are free or duty-free. Their stock is compounded of Genoese, Maltese, Moroccan, Portuguese and British elements. Their first language is Spanish, but they have no sense of ethnic identity. They are determined to be British, not Spanish. They have recently protested the failure of the Spanish government to allow altar wine to pass through customs. They have now determined their political future in the 1964 election: participation in domestic and municipal affairs is theirs. The sovereignty of the island rests with the Queen. The recent proposals of the Gibraltarians themselves (suppression of smuggling, granting Spain a base on the Rock) demonstrate that they are "responding with reason and dignity to the vindictiveness of Spain. One expects no less from British people."

1112 "Man of Letters." **Manchester Guardian**, April 23, 1965, p. 9.

Review of **Correspondence of Jonathan Swift**. Ed. by Harold Williams, vols. IV and V. Swift, the man of the world and of affairs, friend of the great, aristocratic democrat, involved in politics, tortured by guilt and love, continues to live in his letters. This ultimate monument of devotion to a writer who amply repays devotion shows us a man who prized his friends but was also capable of listing them as ungrateful, grateful, indifferent and doubtful. The heart was warm and vulnerable, but his immense intellect got in the way. Here we learn many and curious facts: that Swift attributed his giddiness to eating a hundred golden pippins at a time; that he whipped a servant for breaking a lobster's claws between door-hinges; and that Richard Bettesworth, victim of a verse, came after the Dean to cut off his ears. The compilation of letters and notes is a miracle of scholarship and ample proof of devotion.

1113 "Spring and Fall." **Spectator**, v. 214, no. 7140 (April 30, 1965) 563.

Review of performances of **Spring Awakening**, by Franz Wedekind; **Present Laugher**, by Noel Coward; and **The Persians**, by Aeschylus.Wedekind, in a play marked by the vitality of its content, is an expressionistic dragon who uses drama to indict hypocrisy and stupidity. **Present Laughter** is one of the most actable and enjoyable light comedies produced in the present century. **The Persians** rightly stresses the importance of the chorus. That Aeschylus presents the Greek victory at Salamis from the viewpoint of the vanquished is a matter for mild surprise. "The fact is that the dramatic categories had as yet no room for dithyrambic **Henry V** type plays, and, comedy being out, tragedy was the only available medium . . . .Let then the vanquished lament, and let the author sneak in pride for the Greek victory."

1114 "Vengeance as a Corrupter." **Spectator**, v. 214, no. 7140 (April 30, 1965) 575.

Review of **Throw**, by Anthony Bloomfield; **One by One**, by Penelope Gilliatt; **Giant Dwarfs**, by Gisela Elsner; **The Pond**, by Robert Murphy; and **Nefertiti**, by Nicole Vidal.

1115 "Silence, Exile and Cunning." **Listener**, v. 73, no. 1884 (May 6, 1965) 661-63.

The text of Burgess' television program on James Joyce in the **Monitor** series. Joyce's world is a strange fusion of the lowly and exalted; his "language combines the banalities of the streets of Dublin and the pubs and the humble houses with the majesty and gravity of Catholic ritual and liturgy." Gives an account of **Ulysses** and the effect it had on him (an anguished renegade) at the age of sixteen. Briefly describes the mythological structure of both **Ulysses** and **Finnegans Wake**. "So many things draw me to Joyce, the dignity of the exile, the silence that will not complain nor explain. Most of all, the miracle of the language. And I also admire, more than I can say, the manner in which Joyce has transmuted the ordinary stuff of life, the lowly, to something glorious and eternal." [For William Trevor's review, see #1108.]

1116 "Word, World and Meaning." **Times Literary Supplement**, May 6, 1965, p. 350.

Review of **Language, Culture and Society; A Reader in Linguistics and Anthropology**. Ed. by Dell Hymes. "Linguistic anthropologists are at least asking questions about language which pull that phenomenon down from its cold noosphere back into the warm current of social living. 'Whatever else language does,' says A.L. Kroeber, 'one of its patent uses is to convey information.' In other words, meaning ought to be enthroned as the central concern of linguistics, however important the phoneme or morpheme may be. We cannot doubt that it is through the type of inquiry exemplified in Dell Hymes's monumental reader that the next great advances in linguistic science will be made." Reprinted in **Urgent Copy**.

1117 "Ghost at the Wedding." **Spectator**, v. 214, no. 7141 (May 7, 1965) 599-602.

Review of **Dybbuk**. To ask us to believe, as this play does, that ghosts can play a part in dramatic motivation, is carrying things too far. "It's not a story I'm prepared to accept, since there's a limit to what one can be expected to take on trust. I don't mean just the existence of dybbukim or the lethality of a dose of the Cabbala, but the human elements which are the true drivers of a plot."

1118 "The Two Shaws." **Spectator**, v. 214, no. 7141 (May 14, 1965) 635-36.

Review of **The Complete Plays of Bernard Shaw** and **Complete Prefaces of Bernard Shaw**. Shaw, a life-long adolescent, inveterate rationalist and optimist, was afflicted by a dramaturgical instinct so powerful that it threatened to rob him of his identify; hence he constructed a finger-pointing, beard-wagging statue called G.B.S. The emotionally cold adolescent may prefer the prefaces; the adult prefers the plays (perhaps second only to those of Shakespeare) whose readability may outlive their actability. The prefaces show evidence that Shaw learnt from too many masters. "Express Darwinianism or Bergso-nianism or Sweetism or Webbism in that prose which Pitman taught to flow, a prose variously reminis-cent. . . and you seem to get the quintessence of a new thing called Shavianism. But Shavianism is not a philosophy . . . . Shavianism are things said by an unforgettable voice, associated with the look of a 'milk-fed satyr' (Eric Linklater's phrase) and a persona recognizable chiefly by idiosyncrasies like left-foot and right-foot socks, vegetarianism, 'rational' clothes, and the postcard-sending habit." Reprinted in **Urgent Copy**.

1119 "The Arts." **Listener**, v. 73, no. 1885 (May 13, 1965) 718-19.

[Television criticism.] On Anglo-American writers, Dorothy L. Sayers, a public tribute to Sir Malcolm Sargent, Berg's Violin Concerto, a ballet and the Swingle Singers again. The celebration of the Shakespeare quatercentenary has been disappointing; an interview of Norman Mailer by Jonathan Miller and Malcolm Muggeridge leads to worry. "What chiefly worried me, seeing that these three discutients are all in-tellectuals, was their inability to invoke an exact terminology or even to relate the Mailerian Manichaeism to traditional theology or quasi-theological literature."

1120 "Blues For Mr. Baldwin." **Spectator**, v. 214, no. 7142 (May 14, 1965) 632-33.

Review of **Blues for Mr. Charlie**, by James Baldwin; **The Solid Gold Cadillac**; and **Portrait of a Queen**. "Approaching James Baldwin's play totally without prejudice, I was no more surprised to find it bad than I would have been to find it good. What did surprise me was the fact that it was so ordinarily bad — the dialogue undistinguished, the construction loose, the situations stock, the resolutions ob-vious, the characters cardboard, the message banal." **Solid Gold** is stale bread. **Portrait** depicts royal anabasis of Queen Victoria from tremulous bride to cantankerous grandmother. It is not, of course, a play.

1121 "The Blackness of Whiting." **Spectator**, v. 214, no. 7143 (May 21, 1965) 664.

Review of **Saint's Day**, by John Robert Whiting; **The Three Sisters**, by Chekhov; and **Mother Courage**, by Bertold Brecht. The first work is a genuine play; the second static ("there was no sense of real *fin de siecle* Russia: if we were anywhere at all, it was in a doomed South waiting for a terrible slow sword"); and the Brecht play embodies a very feeble concept. "Here we have the very nub of that 'epic' didac-ticism which hammers away at the self-evident and, because it's concerned with pain and waste more as doctrinal propositions than as properties of human experience, is finally vicious and life-denying."

1122 "Just Like the Ivy." **Spectator**, v. 214, no. 7144 (May 28, 1965) 691.

Review of **A Heritage and its History**, dramatization of a novel by Ivy Compton-Burnett. Miss Compton-Burnett writes witty novels about incest, murder, adultery and forgery. She "reminds me of a dance-team I once worked with in concert party. . . their music varied from season to season, but their routine never changed." There is nothing quite like this play anywhere. "My run as **Spectator** theatre critic has been short, though not so short as the run of many a play I have had to see. Not having written a book for several months, I feel guilty about it. Also I am not well. I now take my guilt to the country (would that our rulers would do the same) along with an indisposition I acquired in the Colonial Service 'serve you right, the progressives will say)."

1123 "Pushkin and Kinbote." **Encounter**, v. 24, no. 5 (May 1965) 74-78.

Review of **Eugene Onegin**, by Alexandr Pushkin. Translated and with a commentary by Vladimir Nabokov. Nabokov's literal translation conveys the feeling of a literary experience and "These four volumes (beautifully made, and each one with a bookmark) represent the very perfection of scholarship, though a scholarship that suggests no parallel talent to the one exhibited in the (now one comes to think of it) Pushkinesque novels. The Nabokov we know is very much here. I know of no other work which, ostensibly serving no higher purpose than to ease the way into an unknown piece of great art, itself approaches great art.''

1124 "The Arts.'' **Listener**, v. 73, no. 1888 (June 3, 1965) 837.

[Television criticism.] A much trumpeted, daring film of Debussy turned out to be deadening. "All that emerged of historical ruminability was what a swine Maeterlinck was. May cats now be shooting at him in whatever pink impressionist hell he inhabits.'' Filming the recording of Wagner's **Ring** left him "stricken by a new awe and I felt the power of Wagner as I had not felt it since I was a boy. When the principals were briefly interviewed they all spoke good sense and rightly poured scorn over the heresy that Wagner was responsible for Hitler. Wagner, like Merlin, is an uncovenanted power.'' Also on David Holbrook's disappointing poetry lecture. Announces his resignation as regular television critic for **The Listener**.

1125 "The Pattern and the Core.'' **Spectator**, v. 215, no. 7149 (July 2, 1965) 20, 22.

Review of **The Towers of Trebizond** and **Told by an Idiot**, by Rose Macaulay; **Pleasure of Ruins** by Rose Macaulay (text) and Roloff Benny (photographs). **Towers** is one of the twenty best books of the century. It is based on a belief in Anglicanism (and his family has resisted Anglicanism for centuries) but it is at least based on a belief in **something**. **Idiot** is one of the great comic travel-books.

1126 "Joyce Industry in the United States.'' **Atlas**, v. 10 (July 1965) 51-53.

[Reprint of #1075.]

1127 "Koestler's Danube.'' **Spectator**, v. 215, no. 7162 (October 1, 1965) 418-19.

[Review prompted by the Danube editions of **The Gladiators, The Yogi and the Commissar and Other Essays** and **Thieves in the Night**.] "Koestler frightened us not just because he brought in the freezing wind of totalitarian experience in Europe; he used his third language with as much confidence as Conrad; he virtually invented the 'political novel'; his intellectuality was ferocious, earnest, not just a donnish game.'' Nevertheless, these three books convey a strong smell of failure; they do not convey that air of perennially fresh surprise we expect from true works of art. Only in **Darkness at Noon** does Koestler achieve a balance between his literary and didactic impulses. Reprinted in **Urgent Copy**.

1128 "The Perfect Shavian.'' **Spectator**, v. 215, no. 7163 (October 8, 1965) 452.

Review of **Collected Letters of Bernard Shaw**, ed. by Dan Lawrence. Shaw's letters are marked by a consistent devotion to work and a consistent egoism. "The letters never for one instant touch on ennui, self-doubt, depression. If it is all an act, it is an act well-sustained; if only it would let up and be human, crapulous, dyspeptic, sexually repressed.'' It is conceivable that the revulsion caused by the letters is a sinner's response to the Shavian sanctity, but the letters give us Shaw the pure-oiled busy sewing-machine. The machine claims to lust after Ellen Terry, but behind the gallantry, wooing poses and show of appetite is Shaw the cool rationalist saint devoted to Jaeger and wool, apples and milk. "Every hair of the beard of a saint must however sour-facedly, be cherished, every scale of the bandersnatch.''

1129 "Sins of Simony.'' **Spectator**, v. 215, no. 7164 (October 15, 1965) 491-2.

Review of **Friends in Low Places**, by Simon Raven; **The Egyptologists**, by Kingsley Amis and Robert Conquest; **Games of Chance**, by Thomas Hinde; **Sweet Morn of Judas' Day**, by Richard Llewellyn; and **A Suspension of Mercy**, by Patricia Highsmith. Mr. Raven is building a Jonsonian humour-epic, and his *roman fleuve* probably needs really big (or nice) characters. Amis and Conquest have written a good and funny book. Mr. Hinde has been making agony-bordering-on-dementia his astringent literary speciality, and the time has now come for him to look for another theme. Llewellyn carries on synthetic Irish whimsy for 488 pages, but the book has a peculiar and haunting distinction. Highsmith has written a thrilling and plausible work.

1130 "Said Rudyard to Rider." **Spectator**, v. 215, no. 7166 (October 29, 1965) 550.

Review of **Rudyard Kipling to Rider Haggard: The Record of a Friendship**, ed. by Morton Cohen. This correspondence shows a lack of obsession with art. "Both writers skirt, with a kind of British embarrassment, Paterian obscenities like aesthetic values; their skills are in the service of entertainment or national and imperial reform." Neither man captured the imagination of the local populace in Etchingham, Burwash or St. Leonards. By contrast, old yokels in Adderbury talk of the Earl of Rochester as though he had died only yesterday. The correspondence is touching, sometimes very interesting, but rarely memorable. Reprinted in **Urgent Copy**.

1131 "Golding Unbuttoned." **Listener**, v. 74 (November 4, 1965) 717.

Review of **The Hot Gates** by William Golding. "The fact is that Golding is one of those great men with a deep and narrow talent. He has made a kind of patent out of the reality of human evil and he possesses — which is very rare — the skill of the true fabulist. But he has hardly an original idea in his head, and, once his prose loses the charge of a terrible message, he writes like Evelyn Waugh's father."

1132 "The Pringles All Entire." **Spectator**, v. 215, no. 7167 (November 5, 1965) 591.

Review of **Friends and Heroes**, by Olivia Manning; **A Second Home**, by Brian Glanville; **Hurry Sundown**, by K. and R. Gilden; **Night of Camp David**, by Fletcher Knebel; **The 38th Floor**, by Clifford Irving; and **the Penetrators**, by Anthony Gray. "With Miss Manning's **Balkan Trilogy** at last completed, it would be frivolous to begin with one of those general literary exordia which reviewers, wistfully trying on the critic's full regalia, like to primp in before, with a sigh, getting down to their cataloguing."

1133 "Kipling: A Celebration in Silence." **Spectator**, v. 215 (November 24, 1965) 833.

Review of **The Art of Rudyard Kipling**, by J.M.S. Tompkins. The Kipling centenary (1965) passed in silence. Kipling had the epic poet's equipment, but he did not write a great novel. "Kipling did not have the architectural gift. Looking at a collapsed empire, we feel that it ought, in its greatest days, to have been recorded in some huge Tolstoyan unity, and that Kipling ought to have been the man to do it. He was too small, however; the halo of greatness which his devotees make sit on him is really an emanation of the vast wasted subject-matter." His poetry is marked by a technical professionalism which marks him as undubitably minor. Ultimately, he witheld something of himself and so we feel vaguely cheated in reading his verse. Yeats, by comparison, is always himself: he never pushes a mere persona — whether tommy, high priest, or bard — at the reader. That helps to explain the silence. Reprinted in **Urgent Copy**.

1134 "A Litre of Shandy." **Manchester Guardian**, November 26, 1965, p. 15.

Review of **Laurence Sterne: From Tristram to Yorick**, by Henri Fluchere. Translated and abridged by Barbara Bray. Dr. Fluchere finds an analogue to Sterne in Proust (not Joyce). Proust waits for the flux to dissolve, while Sterne shakes the enemy till its teeth fall out, and Sterne is the first novelist to give us, not objective time, but 'subjective duration.' Locke, not Bergson, was Sterne's philosopher. "Locke, enemy of ideas, symbols, abstractions, taught that the philosopher's proper study was not the 'external world' of Aristotle but the intelligence which surveyed it. **Tristram Shandy** is, in its way, the sort of honest record of the mind's activities that Locke would most approve, though Sterne, being an artist and not a philosopher could not go to the end of Locke's road."

1135 "These Canapes are Great!" **Spectator**, v. 215, no. 7170 (November 26, 1965) 706-7.

Review of **Winter's Tales**, ed. by A.D. Maclean; **Going to Meet the Man**, by James Baldwin; **The Smell of Bread**, by Yury Kazakov; **Stories, 1895-1897**, by Anton Chekhov; **Voices: 2**, ed. by Michael Ratcliffe; **The Wedding Party**, by H.E. Bates; **Collected Short Stories**, by Robert Graves; **The Hospitality of Miss Tolliver**, by Gerald Kersh; **Famous Tales of the Fantastic**, ed by Herbert van Thal; and **Great Short Stories of the World**, ed. by Whit and Hallie Burnett.

1136 "Sisters Under the Skin." **Listener**, v. 74 (December 2, 1965) 914.

Review of **Talking to Women**, by Nell Dunn. On women's lib. Burgess reviews the work in question and answer form. Concludes that the book is trendy, shallow, inconsequential, rambling and easily dismissed.

1137 Review of **The Language of the Law**, ed. by Louis Blom-Cooper. **Listener**, v. 74, no. 1917 (December 23, 1965) 1044.

"As none of us really thinks he deserves to escape whipping, we approach any book about law as potential defendants. 'He were a right bastard,' said one hardened criminal to me once, referring to a judge who had sent him down a couple of times, 'but he appealed to my sense of humour'." The book disarms us by convincing us of the humanity and humility of judges and so persuades us to admire their legal reasoning, rhetoric and persuasion.

1138 "W. Somerset Maugham: 1874-1965." **Listener**, v. 74 (December 23, 1965) 1033.

[Obituary.] "Perhaps one of Maugham's finest creations was the first-person narrator who is almost, but not quite, the author himself. Here again was something that English fiction needed — the dispassionate commentator, the *raisonneur*, the man at home in Paris and Vienna but also in Seoul and Djakarta, convivial and clubbable, as ready for a game of poker as for a discussion on the Racine alexandrine, the antithesis of the slippered bookman."

1139 "Required Reading." **Spectator**, v. 215, no. 7174 (December 24, 1965) 846-47.

Review of **Fiction and the Reading Public**, by Q.D. Leavis; **A Guide to English Literature**, by F.W. Bateson.

1140 "The Postwar American Novel: A View from the Periphery." **American Scholar**, v. 35 (Winter 1965-1966) 150-56.

American novelists have the courage to deal with big themes thrown up by contemporary history; the English, their art charming but calligraphic, tend to be too satisfied with provincial subject matter — class, hypergamy, suburban adultery. The war novel in English was generally written by Americans (Mailer, Vidal, Heller, Burns). One can perhaps grumble that American authors tend to be one-book novelists (Heller, Salinger, Ellison) and that satire seems to be foreign to their nature (an American surely should have written **The Loved One**), but the British in their turn no longer produce the massive single novel associated with Proust, Dickens or Joyce. The American novel is taken seriously because American literary criticism is taken seriously. Reprinted in **Urgent Copy**.

1141 "Bagehot on Books." **Spectator**, v. 216, no. 7176 (January 7, 1966) 15.

Review of **The Collected Works of Walter Bagehot** (vols. 1, 2). "Reviewers would like reviewing better if they could engage their whole personalities in it, revel in real exhibitionism: the art of love is best learned at night in a big bed, not through a furtive ten minutes in a back alley." Bagehot has sometimes been accused of promiscuously liking too many disparate books, of liking to read books and write about them, but his judgments of Clough, Dickens and Shakespeare were sound. Those judgments were written in the 20,000 word essays, a Victorian amplitude now totally lost. "It is civilized and humane writing, of a kind that has long disappeared." Reprinted in **Urgent Copy**.

1142 "The Recovery of Mandelstam." **Manchester Guardian**, January 7, 1966, p. 7.

Review of **The Prose of Osip Mandelstam**. Translated by Clarence Brown. For him, the poetry of Mandelstam conveyed an excitement comparable to Mallarmé and Rilke, and the death of the poet in a Vladivostok corrective labour camp is "as appalling as anything of that regime of knout-armed philistinism . . . . A great deal of the wry delicacy of Mandelstam comes through in Professor Brown's translations. It is a quality that modern Russia has suppressed: Mandelstam is a dirty name. But the world outside is beginning. . . to learn something of a delicate genius for which a brutish Utopia could find no place but a Siberian labour camp." [Reprinted in #1143.]

1143 "Poet and Victim in Russia." **Manchester Guardian Weekly**, 13 January 1966, p. 11.

[Reprint of #1142.]

1144 "The Triple Thinker." **Spectator**, v. 216 (January 14, 1966) 47-48.

Review of **The Bit Between My Teeth: A Literary Chronicle of 1950-1960**, by Edmund Wilson. On literary matters, it is dangerous to disagree with Mr. Wilson. He has helped to banish mere parochial criticism and to introduce polymathy and cosmopolitanism into critical judgments. His insistance on reading books in the original language is sound. The two essays on the Marquis de Sade are superb, and his distinction between Swinburne the good prose writer and bad poet is enlightening. "The range of his fifteen years of explorations is very wide, and nothing is dull . . . . He is, finally, so generous to modern British novelists that when he mentioned the 'Warwickshire burgess Shakespeare' I felt that this was too much of a good thing. But then I spotted the lower-case letter and breathed again." Reprinted in **Urgent Copy**.

1145 "New Fiction." **Listener**, v. 75, no. 1921 (January 20, 1966) 109.

Reviews of **The Ghosts** by Kathrin Perutz; **The Velvet Bubble**, by Alice Winter; **There Goes Davey Cohen**, by Wendy Owen; **Last Exit to Brooklyn**, by Hubert Selby, Jr.; **Love on the Dole**, by Walter Greenwood; and **Snapshots: Towards a New Novel**, by Alain Robbe-Grillet. "Hubert Selby Jr.'s study of drag-life in the sickest part of New York is certain to bring out the well-worn OBSCENITY banners, but no book could well be less obscene. We are spared nothing of the snarls and tribulations of pimps, queens, and 'hip queers', but the tone is wholly compassionate though sometimes whipped by the kinesis of anger. But the ultimate candour does not necessarily make for great literature, and too much of **Last Exit to Brooklyn** is logorrheal typewriterese, often with the shift-key jammed down."

1146 "Exhausted Wells." **Spectator**, v. 216, no. 7179 (January 28, 1966) 111.

Review of **H.G. Wells; Journalism and Prophecy, 1893-1946**, ed. by W. Warren Wagar. Some of Wells's military predictions on the nature of air warfare, the value of the tank and the devastating potential of the atomic bomb, have come true. Others, notably his expectation of a nuclear war by 1958, and his prophecies of a rational, socialist future, have not. Wells's later novels were gallimaufries pretending to be novels. He was a superb imaginative writer till about 1918. "Then he began to confuse the world of realised fancy with the world of recognised fact. That brought his own mind to the end of its tether."

1147 "Guide to G. B. S." London **Observer Weekend Review**, 30 January, 1966, p. 26.

Review of **Shaw in His Time**, by Ivor Brown. Mr. Brown has chosen to instruct new devotees and, since Shaw yields better to category treatment ("Shaw and Women," etc.) than most other writers, Brown's superb expository style does justice to the man. "The best chapter is the one called 'Things Believed.' A lot of nonsense has been assumed about Shaw's atheism or agnosticism — both of them anti-systems too negative for a creative artist. Shaw was a Creative Evolutionist who saw the point in Christianity and, if he rejected God, rejected only 'the tribal god of the Old Testament.' Christ. . . is a vessel of the Life force. The Shavian liberalism, unlike that of Wells, was capable of a heartening irrationalism and of an optimism that, looking beyond mere human history, could not turn to sour disappointed despair."

1148 "New Fiction." **Listener**, v. 73 (February 3, 1966) 181.

Reviews of **The Comedians**, by Graham Greene; **A Man of the People**, by Chinua Achebe; **The Emperor of Ice Cream**, by Brian Moore; **Langrishe, Go Down**, by Aidan Higgins; and **Second Skin**, by John Hawkes.

1149 "Language, Myth and Mr. Updike." **Commonweal**, v. 83, no. 18 (February 11, 1966) 557-59.

Review of **Of the Farm** with extended comments on **Rabbit, Run** and **The Centaur**. "When I read and reviewed [**Rabbit, Run**] I made a judgment that I have since had no cause to revise — that Updike was guilty of a sort of democratic heresy in pouring the riches of language on characters and situations so trivial." **The Centaur** was a noble attempt to call on ancient myth in the attempt to add fresh dimensions to a contemporary story. Updike's interest in language is a healthy sign that language means something to him, but when individual passages are subjected to analysis, the imagery is shown to be imprecise and self-conscious, but he is one of America's most exciting talents, with much of the excitement still to come. For letter by Updike, see **Commonweal**, v. 84, no. 5 (April 22, 1966) 160-61. Updike defends himself against the charge of imprecision and maintains that nothing interests him about language but its possibilities for precision.

1150 "The Lower Depths." **Manchester Guardian**, February 11, 1966, p. 8.

Review of **Journey to the End of Night**, by Louis-Ferdinand Céline. Translated by John H.P. Marks. The grudging rehabilitation of Céline, Jew-hater and Nazi-lover, slowly proceeds. He is often, wrongfully, classed with Henry Miller and Genet, but he has nothing in common with the phallic sage or the criminal saint. "Both Miller and Genet promote, however perversely, a respect for life: Céline sees what is low in humanity and — instead of fumigating it with Rabelaisian language or sweetening it with flowers — makes it appear lower still.'' In this piece of glum picaresque, Céline finds images of human degradation in African jungle, battlefield, Paris gutters, Detroit slum; and we read on eagerly and (we think) not at all morbidly. The novel says things about humanity which sometimes have to be said, and it says them eloquently and sardonically. It provides a corrective to the dimpling nice view of life. ''Rodin, says Auden, must have found the Thinker in the lavatory: Céline finds the lavatory in the Thinker.''

1151 ''Yards and Yards of Entrails.'' London **Observer Weekend Review**, 13 February 1966, p. 27.

Review of **Nova Express**, by William Burroughs. Much *avant-garde* writing sounds thrilling in the manifesto stage. The actual results, on cold paper, make for a dullness inaccessible to the orthodox. Burroughs' intention is to make people aware of the true criminality of our times but what he really likes is the fact of war: he delivers a commentary on a lively Manichean duoverse. His prose is non-Aristotelian, devoid of logical cause and effect, and much influenced by the cinema-film. The result is a kind of prose collage in which the unit is not the individual word but the line of type. The work tends to monotony. It repeats motifs of significance only to the author; the sexual images symbolize outrage; and it is full of the jargon derived from drugs, technology and metaphysics. A sad verbal poverty is present, and ''. . . for the most part, each man his own Genêt we take the 'yards and yards of entrails irrevocably committed to the toilet' with the weary smile of one who is given a tired violet.''

1152 ''New Fiction.'' **Listener**, v. 75 (February 17, 1966) 253.

Reviews of **Mrs. Bratbe' s August Picnic**, by Jacqueline Wheldon; **The Cold Country**, by Jennifer Dawson; **Excursion**, by Francis Pollini; **Cool Change Moving North**, by Royston Morley; **The Aerodrome**, by Rex Warner; **South Riding**, by Winifred Holtby; and **Our London Office**, by Thomas Armstrong.

1153 ''Camus at His Exercise.'' **Manchester Guardian**, February 18, 1966, p. 7.

Review of **Carnets 1942 — 1951**, by Albert Camus. The book includes, along with pensées, lengthy and knotty explorations of aspects of the human condition. ''His writings derive much of their power from our knowledge that the writer is involved in the world, is urgently forced into constructing a philosophical system that is the analogue of a bicycle, typewriter, or gun, not of a Fabergé toy.'' The philosphy of Camus is a rock-bottom one: man derives his majesty from being down and out. These notebooks give us a private view of one of the most candid minds of the age. [Reprinted in #1155.]

1154 ''Candid Camera.'' **Spectator**, v. 216, no. 7182 (February 18, 1966) 201.

Review of **Exhumations**, by Christopher Isherwood. This hodge-podge of reviews, sketches and little stories will keep the fire burning until the coalman comes. Isherwood proves he is not a poet, but he is very good on Auden and when he gives his candid camera eye impressions of London in the ghastly winter of 1945-47 (''when soldiers fought the frost with flame-throwers'') he is at his best. He should have taken these bits and pieces and worked them up into another **Down There On a Visit**.

1155 ''Thoughts for the Age of Assassins.'' **Manchester Guardian Weekly**, 24 February 1966, p. 11.

[Reprint of #1153.]

1156 ''Manicheans.'' **Times Literary Supplement**, no. 3340 (March 3, 1966) 153-54.

Art provides us with some foretaste of Ultimate Reality. Admittedly, there is some danger that art's devotees will serve beauty, and not goodness or truth: Salisbury Cathedral or Bach's Mass in B minor do not necessarily induce prayers. The art of the novel least excites ecstatic twinges, and the novelists show very little interest in writing about religious experience. Mr. Isherwood may argue that every action of the saint is a genuine act of free will, but common sense counter-proposes that the saint offers little material for fiction. He lacks color, conflict, variety, libido. Considers some of the saints in the fiction of Aldous Huxley, and believes that the sinner turned saint is a legitimate source of fictional fascination. Discusses, in this context, the fiction of Graham Greene. ''What the religious novelist often seems to be saying is that evil is a kind of good, since it is an aspect of Ultimate Reality; though what he is really saying is that evil is more interesting to write about than good. After all, a novelist has to purvey thrills, and good never thrilled anybody.'' Briefly discusses Evelyn Waugh, William Golding and some other novelists. Observes that it is very doubtful if a novel can possess any vitality without an implied set of values derived from religion.

1157 "New Fiction." **Listener**, v. 75 (March 3, 1966) 325.

Reviews of **A Touch of Red**, by William Fennerton; **A Stone Man**, by Daniel Curley; **Castle Keep**, by William Eastlake; **Hall of Mirrors**, by John Rowan Wilson; and **The Ulcerated Milkman**, by William Sansom.

1158 "The Great Gangster." **Listener**, v. 75 (March 17, 1966) 401.

Review of **The Anti-Death League**, by Kingsley Amis. "This long story strides along with a kind of grey stoical vigour; the large cast is wonderfully managed, though the women (including the polyandrous Lady Hazell, soldiers' friend) have more life than the men."

1159 "How Well Have They Worn? Ulysses." London Times, 17 March 1966, p. 15b.

After its first publication, on February 2nd, 1922, **Ulysses** was accepted as the dirtiest book in the world. Now, thanks to the fictional candour Joyce initiated, the book seems reticent and restrained by comparison. It proclaims the glory of family relationships. Unfortunately, it is still widely considered unintelligible. Most readers, baffled by the absence of plot, fail to understand that Joyce's aim was to exploit myth, symbol and language and to eschew the contrivances of plot. "From the average reader it demands an exorbitant interest in language, one that the reading of most other fiction does nothing to promote. But perhaps, very slowly, that interest is coming. Outside a pub in Wales, one night last summer, a pork butcher looked up at the sky and turned to me to remark: 'The heaventree of stars hung with the humid nightblue fruit'." Reprinted in **Urgent Copy**.

1160 "The First J.J." **Spectator**, v. 216, no. 7186 (March 18, 1966) 332.

Reviews of **Twelve and a Tilly — Essays on the Occasion of the 25th Anniversary of Finnegans Wake**, ed. by Jack P. Dalton and Clive Hart; **A Question of Modernity — Essays on Writing with Special Reference to James Joyce and Samuel Beckett**, by Anthony Cronin; and **James Joyce in Paris — His Final Years**, by Gisele Freund and V.B. Carleton. The twelve essays on the **Wake** are light-hearted and they illuminate mysteries. Cronin's book is valuable: he is not only a Joyce scholar but a Dubliner. The book on Joyce in Paris consists chiefly of photographs and not particularly apposite texts from the master.

1161 "New Novels." **Listener**, v. 75 (March 24, 1966) 445.

Reviews of **Totempole**, by Sanford Friedman; **Flesh Wounds**, by David Holbrook; **The Watchers on the Shore**, by Stan Barstow; **The Second Stone**, by Leslie A. Fiedler.

1162 "The Great American Visionary." **Spectator**, v. 216, no. 7187 (March 25, 1966) 365.

Review of **Leaves of Grass**, by Walt Whitman. Whitman has only one subject, acceptance of — and reverence for — the life-death cycle, and his language is an idiosyncratic compound of the colloquial and the technical. His quality of uncompromising acceptance makes him antipathetic to many Europeans who take it for granted that the poet should be sick, and not eupeptic. Whitman's sensuality is omnifutuent rather than homo-erotic: a tribute to friendship in the terms of sexual love. "The catalogues of 'Song of Myself' are magnificent; the unremitting detail of 'Drum Taps' makes it probably the finest long war-poem of all time. Perhaps only an American poet could see the rhetorical possibility of this enumerative technique; the immense plurality of the United States is made for this kind of celebration . . . ." Reprinted in **Urgent Copy** under title: "The Answerer."

1163 "Depraved Humanity." **Manchester Guardian**, March 31, 1966, p. 5.

Review of **Rogue's Progress. An Autobiography of "Lord Chief Baron" Nicholson**, by Renton Nicholson. Ed. by John L. Bradley. Nicholson was a small-time Victorian criminal whose crime was mostly debt, although he had the appurtenances of a decent all-round criminal. He was president of the Judge and Jury Society which conducted mock trials of alleged sexual offenses in an atmosphere that pandered (in the words of one observer) to the lowest propensities of depraved humanity. "This London of dark alleys, cheap gin, rags, and desperate crime is ghastly — though Nicholson's unfailing facetiousness and seedy courtliness drag us away from overmuch identification with society's victims." He is the necessary "obverse to Brunel, the Great Exhibition, Mendelssohn and the Queen herself, doling out morality which mean nothing to the London poor." [Reprinted in #1164.]

1164 "Depths of Depravity." **Manchester Guardian Weekly**, 7 April 1966, p. 10.

[Reprint of #1163.]

1165 "Stryne Agyne." **Listener**, v. 75, no. 1931 (March 31, 1966) 480.

Review of **Aussie Slang**, by John O'Grady. "I had a dekko at this book this arvo while killing a snake in the toot or dyke or dunny, needing it after more than one beaut drop, or, to be exact, several middies of fifty." The trouble with this book is that the author does not provide an analysis of Australian phonemes; the phonemic system, close to Dickensian cockney, deserves professional study.

1166 "New Fiction." **Listener**, v. 75 (April 7, 1966) 515.

Reviews of **The Russian Interpreter**, by Michael Frayn; **The Fetch**, by Peter Everett; **Horse Latitudes**, by Keith Walker; **Shooting Script**, by Gavin Lyall; **Everything that Rises Must Converge**, by Flannery O'Connor; and **The Smile at the Foot of the Ladder**, by Henry Miller.

1167 "Evelyn Waugh, 1903-1966. The Comedy of Ultimate Truths." **Spectator**, v. 216, no. 7190 (April 15, 1966) 462.

[Obituary on Evelyn Waugh.] ". . . no Christian could ask more than to die on Easter morning — suddenly, without fuss, having just celebrated the truth of Christ's, and hence man's resurrection." Waugh actively prepared for death, and his work records the encroaching barbarism of the modern world. "The good man retires from the world, cherishing fragments from an incorrupt past, cultivating style, assuming stoical poses that are not without a certain discreet self-mockery." His **Decline and Fall** has survived because it records the right of the decent man to find decency in the world. Tony Last's innocence in **A Handful of Dust**, appropriate to a younger son, is properly fatal to a small aristocrat with large responsibilities. **Brideshead Revisited** remains the record of "a soldier's dream, a consolation of drab days and a deprived palate, disturbingly sensuous, even slavering with gulosity, as though God were somehow made manifest in the *haute cuisine*." Waugh will be remembered as a comic novelist with a Shakespearean hunger for order, and mere authors will continue to despair of their ability to approach the perfection of his prose style. Reprinted in **Urgent Copy**.

1168 "Parallel Spatial Matrix." **Manchester Guardian**, April 15, 1966, p. 9.

Review of **The Crystal World**, by J.G. Ballard. "It is this lack of human interest that deeply wounds all of our best science fiction: H.G. Wells's early romances spread science on the Dickensian world; today's men come straight from the laboratory or the poetry seminar (which, as at Cambridge, can be the same sort of thing) and arrive at the typewriter without having noted adenoids or bunions on the way. Admittedly, Ballard explicates with great cunning the ambivalence of his cancerous crystals: some run screaming from 'the fantastic disease of time'; others greet it in wonder as a restored Eden. But these are postures illustrating concepts; they don't seem to spring out of real people."

1169 "Sage and Mage of the Steam Age." **Spectator**, v. 216, no. 7190 April 15, 1966) 471.

Review of **Robert Browning: A Collection of Critical Essays**, ed. by Philip Drew. "His subject-matter is wide and his passion considerable; he is metaphysically knotty; he controls a big word-circus; his range of civilisations is matched only by Pound in the **Cantos**." Despite all these apparent advantages his verse seems stuffed and stuffy. The big Browningian theme of optimism rings sourly today. His monologues never sound like real people talking. The rhythms are wooden, the contractions archaic, and the near-rhymes are mere eye-stuff. His true ability lies (*vide* **The Ring and the Book**) in the organisation of massive story-telling structures.

1170 "New Fiction." **Listener**, v. 75 (April 21, 1966) 588.

Reviews of **Of the Farm**, by John Updike; **Journal from Ellipsia**, by Hortense Calisher; **Zones**, by Alexis Lykiard; **The Camp**, by Gordon M. Williams; **The Green Man**, by Henry Treece; and **The Soul of Malaya**, by Henri Fauconnier.

1171 "Enduring Saturday." **Spectator**, v. 216, no. 7192 (April 29, 1966) 532-533.

Review of **The Testament of Samuel Beckett**, by Josephine Jacobsen and William R. Mueller. "And so Beckett's enduring Saturday is the one that comes between Good Friday and Easter Day, except that time has a stop after Christ's crucifixion. Saturday refuses to become Sunday, and we are stuck with 'a large measure of despair and a small measure of hope.' The thing to do is to wait, even though we can be quite sure that the waiting will not be rewarded. Life is a wretched grey Saturday, but it has to be lived through . . . . Things are inexplicable; the scientific mirror lies; we know nothing. His aesthetic is dedicated to the stripping off of illusion, showing what is left after the dissolution of shape, colour, habit, logic." Reprinted in **Urgent Copy**.

1172 "The Writer's Purpose." **New York Times Book Review**, May 1, 1966, p. 2.

Attends a session of Long Island University's Writers' Conference on the subject: should literature have a social purpose? Concludes, after considering the pros and cons of the issue, that literature should serve an aesthetic, not a utilitarian function.

1173 "New Fiction." **Listener**, v. 75 (May 5, 1966) 659.

Reviews of **The Nightclerk**, by Stephen Schneck; **The Magus**, by John Fowles; **The Judge**, by Alan Thomas; and **The Seahorse**, by Anthony Masters. On Schneck: "The author uses language kinetically — to move, not merely inform, the reader; the result is obscene . . . . That this slick little abomination should have been granted a major international literary award [the Prix Formentor] is a major international literary disgrace."

1174 "A Raven on the Aerial." **Spectator**, v. 216, no. 7193 (May 6, 1966) 574-575.

Review of **Royal Foundation and Other Plays**, by Simon Raven. "Among serious writers, Raven has come out of the TV mangle fatter than any; most of us have long given up trying to give the damned medium what it thinks it wants." His dramas, studies of conflict on points of principle in closed military and academic societies, constitute a kind of streamlined Snow.

1175 "Dark Disease as a European Tradition." **Commonweal**, v. 84 (May 13, 1966) 231-32.

Review of **Incubus**, by Giuseppe Berto. Reprinted in **Urgent Copy**.

1176 "Italus the Swabian." **Manchester Guardian**, May 13, 1966, p. 8.

Review of **Italo Svevo: The Man and the Writer**, by P.N. Furbank. Italo Svevo (Ettore Schmitz) is at last being recognized as a fictional innovator, and the ineffectual heroes of his fiction are representations of modern man. There is much more to **The Confessions of Zeno** than an attempt to give up smoking. "Zeno over-smokes, bringing on bronchitis, to punish himself for wanting to kill his father. It is desirable to achieve the 'last cigarette,' but, in Furbank's words, 'last cigarettes taste better than any other'." In this biography, Zeno's creator "is revealed, with his self-mockery, his wit, capacity for love and loyalty, as one of the most likeable characters in modern literary biography. But liking the man is not enough. The books are available to British readers, and British readers must read them."

1177 "New Fiction." **Listener**, v. 75 (May 19, 1966) 733.

Reviews of **Memoirs of a New Man**, by William Cooper; **The Opoponax**, by Monique Wittig; **That Awful Mess on the Via Merulan**, by Carlo Emilio Gadda; **Frost**, by Andrew Hall; and **A Willing Victim**, by Harriet Grierson. On Cooper: "It is the enlivening of the Snow world with the leaps and comic shuffles of a stick-dance that makes the whole entertainment so ghoulish."

1178 "Lewis as Spaceman." **Spectator**, v. 216, no. 7195 (May 20, 1966) 640-41.

Review of the Penguin ed. of **The Apes of God**, by Wyndham Lewis. "His works are huge monsters frozen in the act of snarling or clawing, the children of manifesto rather than real impulse." Lewis's dogmatic insistence on the Great Without, the external approach, results in a kind of literary brushwork more frozen than fluid. Writers without painting talent have produced the best word-pictures. His satire, directed against dabblers, dilettantes and racketeers of the art world, breaks butterflies on a wheel. Nevertheless, **Apes** draws on a vast vocabulary, expresses a great, if pig-headed British personality, and its visual concentration is a corrective in an age of careless and perfunctory description. Reprinted in **Urgent Copy**.

1179 "The Big Daddy of the Beats." **Observer** (London), 22 May 1966, p. 26.

Review of **Desolation Angels**, by Jack Kerouac. Kerouac gives an impression of sheer goddam niceness, and it records the good quiet life, a pot session after a hearty breakfast, seeing a bit of the world, doing no harm to nobody. The niceness itself may be a kind of art. Unfortunately, the movement is in danger of being debased by its unkempt fringe. "And the Kerouac way of writing, though frequently deplorable, is occasionally to be seen as an analogue of the jazz solo, aleatoric, punctuable only with dashes like breaths, capable of describing the banal. . . without tedium . . . .'' His philosophy, the message that eternity and the present moment are the same thing, and must be enjoyed to the utmost, is good. Digs this man.

1180 "The Meaning of Meaning." London **Observer Weekend Review**, 29 May 1966, p. 22.

Review of **The Oxford Dictionary of English Etymology**, ed. by C.T. Onions. Etymology tends to prove that original meanings run off the rails over time, and any etymological work must be supplemented by your old, tattered defining dictionary. "The science of phonetics deals with shaped air, but that is far more solid than the subject-matter of semantics. As this dictionary shows us, there is no single direction of change. A meaning can contract ('deer' was once any animal) or expand 'bird' used to mean only a young bird), become pejorative (a cretin is really a Christian) or ameliorative ('nice' comes from *nescius*, Latin for 'ignorant'). A word has to have a very solid referent indeed if it is not itself to turn to liquid." It is, all in all, a very fine etymological dictionary, but remember the caveat.

1181 "Great Vowel Shift & All That." **Encounter**, v. 26, no. 5 (May 1966) 70-73.

Review of **The Story of Language**, by Mario Pei. The student of literature is concerned with legitimate aesthetic inquiry; the philologist derives little masturbatory satisfactions from his esoteric knowledge of word origins (witness Mr. Bevis in Huxley's **Eyeless in Gaza**). Gives evidence of the entertainment to be derived from recherché etymologies ("nice" is derived from "stupid, unknowing." Chaucer's "harlot" once meant "maid-servant") and observes that language is in a constant state of flux. It is ultimately made, and the rules are grounded on, the actual speech of women in the supermarket and men on the factory floor. Suggests that the educated have long stopped using a spoken form of the language; their conversation derives from the written word. "Dr. Johnson was probably the misguided pioneer of book-talking, killer of those purely social elements in speech which Malinowski called 'phatic'." What probably chills the humanist about linguistics is its apparent lack of human reference. Only semantics includes the living world; the aim of phonetics is to examine the functioning of a machine. Linguistics can explain how, but not *why*, a given linguistic change in speech habits occurs. Observes that the two important linguistic concepts of our time are the phoneme and the morpheme.

1182 "Twelve Hundred Pages and Four Marbles." **Listener**, v. 75 (June 2, 1966) 804.

Review of **Miss MacIntosh, My Darling**, by Marguerite Young. Advises readers to avoid this 1,200 page opus. "If you have all that reading time available, fill it up with **Don Quixote, Tom Jones**, and **Tristram Shandy**, with perhaps the New Testament as makeweight. Miss MacIntosh would have been a bit of a bore in a decent eighty thousand words; in all these millions she is a Medusa." Also reviews **The Solid Mandala**, by Patrick White. Finds it a moving work, an exercise in pathos.

1183 "Work and Play." **New York Times Book Review**, June 5, 1966, p. 1.

[Authors are asked how they plan to spend their summer holidays.] "I shall be in East Sussex, two miles from the village where Rudyard Kipling lived and 15 miles from the coastal town which, with no gaiety and little ice in the pubs, will this year be celebrating the 900th anniversary of the Norman Invasion. I shall be writing a novel but, at the first hint of sun, I shall be out there on the lawn with my wife, playing demon croquet (forfeits for knocking balls into flowerbeds). In the evenings we shall play shove-ha'penny or sit bemused in front of the TV. I shall play jazz on the piano and Elgar on the record player. It will be thoroughly, vegetably, rustical. I shall get drunk occasionally and knock hell out of the philistines."

1184 "From London to Hastings." **Country Life**, v. 140, no. 3618 (July 7, 1966) 50-51.

Reviews of **Letters from Jack London**, ed. by King Hendricks and Irving Shepard; **The Unrepentant Pilgrim**, by J.P. Smith; **The Hunger to Come**, by John Laffin; **The Battle of Hastings**, by Patrick Thornhill.

1185 "A Very Tragic Business." **Spectator**, v. 216, no. 7198 (June 10, 1966) 731.

Review of **Modern Tragedy**, by Raymond Williams. Argues that, although Williams is prepared to widen the meaning of the term 'tragedy' to include sad and shocking events (including those caused by war, famine, work, traffic, politics) his own preference is for the strict, traditional definition derived from Aristotle. "If man is a tragic figure (or 'absurd,' or comic), all his art is the same, and hence it is inappropriate to talk of tragic art as a separate category. So we have to start all over again, and we might as well use 'tragedy' for a narrow compartment of art, one which sees the human dichotomy as terrible rather than ridiculous, accepts the need for sacrifice to the power that has cursed man by making him what he is, and knows that *hubris* must be punished. Delimitation is no bad thing." Reprinted in **Urgent Copy.**

1186 "New Novels." **Listener,** v. 75 (June 16, 1966) 883.

Reviews of **The Family Moskat,** by Isaac Bashevis Singer; **The Beginners,** by Dan Jacobson; **Death on the Instalment Plan,** by Louis-Ferdinand Céline; and **The Diary of a Chambermaid,** by Octave Mirbeau. "Céline's pessimism is, nevertheless, somehow life-enhancing. A world in which everybody is both torturer and victim has the nasty vitality of a head of hair ridden with fleas, but it is better than bourgeois death."

1187 "The Long Fountain Pen." **Spectator,** v. 216, no. 7199 (June 17, 1966) 764.

Review of **Writer by Trade: A View of Arnold Bennett,** by Dudley Barker. "I find [Bennett's] work mostly unreadable, mainly because of an insensitivity to language, a lack of poetry, which was seen by some, and is still, as a commendable no-nonsense plainness. But I admire him as a worker and tend to venerate him as the patron saint of men who write to live."

1188 "Key Personalities." London **Observer Weekend Review,** 26 June 1966, p. 27.

Review of **At the Piano,** by Ivor Newton; **In Pursuit of Music,** by Denis Matthews. Both men have written chatty and informative books about their crafts. Both also show evidence of modest charm and an unbreakable enslavement to art. Matthews' portrayals of the prima donnas he has accompanied on the piano sometimes give one pause. ". . . we begin to wonder who the hell they think they are. After all, they didn't compose the music, and they would have been lost without Newton behind them. The big executants — mounds of flesh and exuberance encasing a larynx — can be a bit of a bore." As for Newton, his book would have been better if he had told us a bit more about himself. What is it like to be in tails on the piano-stool, making Mozart sound like a liquid miracle? Both Matthews and Newton give us a very fair and often amusing prose, marred only by facetiousness, the musician's greatest failing.

1189 "New Novels." **Listener,** v. 75 (June 30, 1966) 955.

Reviews of **Gentlemen in Their Season,** by Gabriel Fielding; **The Second Inheritance,** by Melvyn Bragg; and **In the Absence of Mrs. Peterson,** by Nigel Balchin.

1190 "Anthony Burgess on **Strine.**" **Australian Book Review,** v. 5 (Summer 1966) 215-16.

Review of **The Australian Language,** by Sidney Baker. Comments on his early speech habits as a resident of Manchester and on his accent. "I have lived for some time now in the great poofter-speaking literary community of London, and I have found it convenient to drop my native accent (though I can switch it on again when I want to) in favour of what is sometimes called Received Standard English." Observes that to point out what makes Australian English different from Pom English is to emphasize inessentials. Distinguishes, following the practise of Saussure, between *la langue* and *la parole* where the first is the whole potential body of language, and the second a specific instance encoded in particular speech-events. Comments on the Australian accent and its derivation from the Cockney. Admires the lexical content of the Australian language, particularly that anti-establishment instinct which cuts pomposity down to size. Speculates if Australia does not, perhaps, like its writers very much since they tend to opt for exile in London. Concludes that Australian is a sub-dialect and not a language.

1191 "He Wrote Good." **Spectator,** v. 217, no. 7202 (July 8, 1966) 47.

Review of **Papa Hemingway,** by A.E. Hotchner. Also notices **Green Hills of Africa, Across the River and Into the Trees, The Torrents of Spring, The Fifth Column** and **A Moveable Feast,** all by Ernest Hemingway. Hotchner presents Hemingway's last years (paranoia, fears of poverty) with ruthless compassion. The famous Hemingway prose was inspired by Stein, but perfected by the disciple. It was developed at a time when Western man was unhappy at the civilization he had made; consequently it has the tone and rhythm of liturgy. Hemingway's achievement was to create a style exactly suited to the exclusion of the cerebral. "Reconciling literature and action, he fulfilled, for all writers, the sickroom dream of leaving the desk for the arena, and then returning to the desk. He wrote good and lived good, and both activities were the same. The pen handled with the accuracy of the rifle; sweat and dignity; bags of *cojones.*" Reprinted in **Urgent Copy.**

1192 "New Fiction." **Listener**, v. 76 (July 14, 1966) 65.

Reviews of **Moderato Cantabile**, by Marguerite Duras; **Not the Defeated**, by Peter de Polnay; **Asylum**, by Colin Spencer; and **Octopussy and the Living Daylights**, by Ian Fleming. [Last of Burgess' omnibus reviews of fiction in the **Listener**.]

1193 "Funferall." **Manchester Guardian**, July 15, 1966, p. 8.

Review of **Joyce-Again's Wake**, by Bernard Benstock and **The Joyce Paradox**, by Arnold Goldman. Gardien-weaders (as Joyce probably called them in his palincestuous mysterpeace) will not need to be reminded that **Wake** represents the dream of Finn about the dream of Humphrey Chimpden Earwicker. Professor Benstock believes that the **Wake** is about the **Wake**, and what Joyce laboriously put together is now unravelled, as other codexes have been unravelled; and a living organism threatens to be transformed into a piece of mere morphology. Dr. Goldman has written a pretty, though humourlessly, enlightening work. "What worries me is the dissolution of great works of fiction. . . in the face of heavy philosophical batteries . . . . Soon we may be taught that Joyce, like the Bible, is blasphemed against if enjoyed. I am tired of Bloom as Christ or the Holy Ghost; I like him best as a Jewish advertising canvasser with a sexy wife."

1194 "Exhausted Wells." **Country Life**, v. 140, no. 3620 (July 21, 1966) 186-87.

Reviews of **The Experiment in Autobiography**, by H.G. Wells; **Gordon, Martyr and Misfit**, by Anthony Nutting; **Eleanor: Portrait of a Farjeon**, by Denys Blakelock; **World of Strange Animals**, by V.J. Stanek.

1195 "Where is English?" **New Society**, v. 8 (July 21, 1966) 100-1.

Discusses some of the differences and similarities between American and British English. Gives examples of some Yiddish and American negro contributions to American English. Examines some representative samples of standard expository writing, and believes the passages do not betray their provenance. Concludes that we should try to create a sort of ecumenical English.

1196 "Enemy of Twilight." **Spectator**, v. 217, no. 7204 (July 22, 1966) 124.

Review of **Collected Works** (vol. 2: Prose), by J.M. Synge ed. by Alan Price. Irish anger at an Irish author is a good test of closeness to the people. By this test, Synge's **Playboy of the Western World** demonstrated his closeness to the Irish earth, as opposed to the Irish mist. 500 police kept order on the final night. "His crime was to find murder condoned in County Mayo and as much poetry in the real country libido as in the fancied country soul." Aran was the making of him as a writer. It gave him his plots as well as a rich, uncorrupted vernacular. Reprinted in **Urgent Copy**.

1197 "Notes, But Also Letters." **Manchester Guardian**, July 22, 1966, p. 10.

Review of **The Letters of Mozart and his Family**. Translated and edited by Emily Anderson. Leopold Mozart knew he had fathered a genius and determined to write his biography: hence the existence of the letters. They show a Mozart with the likeability of Keats along with a very un-Keatsian scatological side; but they reveal an exuberance and affection that refuse to yield to depression, ill-health, ill-luck. His sister-in-law wrote that she had never seen Mozart in an angry temper. "That is the impression we gain from these letters — the kindest man alive, with none of that temperament which became the sick glory of the romantics, a man too big for self-pity, vindictiveness, or pettiness, and at the same time just small enough to contain a human share of harmless weakness." [Reprinted in #1198.]

1198 "Mozart Compositions." **Manchester Guardian Weekly**, 28 July 1966, p. 11.

[Reprint of #1197.]

1199 "Spectator Symposium." **Spectator**, v. 217, no. 7205 (July 29, 1966) 138.

"There was a time when I believed that evil and incompetence could not inhabit the same body. Socialism, which is a great reconciler of contradictions, has taught me that they can, just as it has taught me that the finest encouragement is discouragement, and that an economy can best be saved by being strangled . . . . There is less and less to work for. It is as sinful to drink whisky as to look for a fortnight's sun. Ambition is more and more brutally penalised . . . . Socialism is based on a tangle of false premises: human beings are totally different from what Socialists think they are. But Socialism can at least modify the human make-up: we are all becoming bitter, disillusioned, obsessed by politics — which should be as unobtrusive as drains. For God's sake leave us alone and let those of us who want to work get on with it.''

1200 "Science Fiction." London **Observer Weekend Review**, 31 July 1966, p. 21.

Omnibus review of **Dune**, by Frank Herbert; **The Last Refuge**, by John Petty; **All Fool's Day**, by Edmund Cooper; **The Fury Out of Time**, by Lloyd Biggle, Jr.; **The Menace from Earth**, by Robert A. Heinlein; and **SF6, an Anthology**.

1201 "Making de White Boss Frown." **Encounter**, v. 27 (July 1966) 54-58.

Review of **Uncle Tom's Cabin**, by Harriet Beecher Stowe. Ed. by John A. Woods. Mrs. Stowe's protest novel led to the crumbling of the 1850 Compromise and, although marred by sentimental slush (importations from Scott and Dickens), the book has a considerable vitality of its own. Reprinted in **Urgent Copy**.

1202 "A Biographer for a Biographer." **Manchester Guardian**, August 5, 1966, p. 7.

Review of **James Boswell: The Earlier Years, 1740-1769**, by Frederick A. Pottle. An urbane and erudite scholar has given us a delightful portrait of a moderate satyromaniac and a born literary artist with a great gift for mimicry. Boswell in effect created Dr. Johnson. Without him, we would have **Rasselas** and the Dictionary, but not the Grand Cham himself. "This book is a great delight . . . . Its portraits of Voltaire, Rousseau and his mistress (who also became Boswell's, but who did not?) Wilkes, the Auld Laird of Auchinleck himself, and — like the other side of the moon — the great muttering rolling scrofulous tender supreme graduate of Grub Street are works of considerable humour, delicacy and shrewdness." [Reprinted in #1203.]

1203 "A Biographer for a Biographer." **Manchester Guardian Weekly**, 11 August 1966, p. 10.

[Reprint of #1202.]

1204 "The Seventeenth Novel." **New York Times Book Review**, 21 August 1966, pp. 2, 14.

He is working on his seventeenth novel [**Enderby Outside**] and feels that he is in danger of repeating himself. "I have created so many characters, major and minor, that I am in danger of completing the roster and having to go back to the beginning again." Looks with wistfulness at the fictional experimentalists who, let us face the fact, experiment because they are bored. He has considered writing novels in the form of a newspaper, a mock biography, a small encyclopedia. But warns "that the new shapes are not really enough. Sterne had Uncle Toby and Mr. Shandy; Nabokov has Kinbote; Joyce had both Bloom and Earwicker. There are certain things that the novel cannot do without, and the greatest of these is character." [Reprinted in #1378.]

1205 "On English in English." **Spectator**, v. 217 (August 29, 1966) 233-34.

Review of **The English Language: Essays by English and American Men of Letters, 1490-1839**. Selected and edited by W.F. Bolton. These essays by early students of language (Caxton, Camden, Hobbes, Defoe and Johnson) proves that they knew a lot, worried about the variety of written and spoken English and "one of the small joys of watching these philologists at work — from Caxton to de Quincey — lies in seeing the continued autonomy of what they would all like to control" and "One thing we can learn from all these pleas for academies, imposed uniformities, the enactment of stasis, is their utter hopelessness." Reprinted in **Urgent Copy**.

1206 "Curry and Claret." **Listener**, v. 76 (September 8, 1966) 360.

Reviews of **An Anecdotal History of Old Times in Singapore**, by Charles Burton Buckley and **Our Tropical Possessions in Malayan India**, by John Cameron. "There have been periods of effeteness and stupidity [on the part of the British in Singapore]; there was the shameful time when the guns pointed the wrong way and the Japanese, almost unresisted, poured in from the north; but the record of colonial rule may be called exemplary and reviewed with wistful pride."

1207 "Fleurs du mal." **Spectator**, v. 217 (September 9, 1966) 326.

Review of **The Reactionaries**, by John Harrison. Harrison argues that Yeats, Wyndham Lewis, Pound, Eliot and Lawrence belonged to an anti-democratic intelligentsia and that there is an intimate connection between their politics and their art. They all believed art and *demos* to be incompatible, and so leaned towards authoritarianism in politics. They were probably misguided in thinking that one type of society must necessarily breed better art than another, but it is perhaps silly and pointless to look for a nexus between misguided political beliefs and supreme works of literature. "What puzzles me is that [Mr. Harrison] should think it necessary to survey ground neither arable nor suitable for building. It's waste-land; it doesn't matter . . . . It is the work, it is the work that counts." Reprinted in **Urgent Copy**.

1208 "Late Tribute." **Spectator**, v. 217 (September 16, 1966) 354.

Review of **Siegfried Sassoon: A Critical Study**, by Michael Thorpe. Sassoon is a minor poet. Much of his work is marred by Marshianism — the limpid regularity and sloppy post-Swinburnianism Sir Edward Marsh considered poetic virtues. The merit of Sassoon's war poetry is that the easy rhymes and jog-trot rhythms were put to the service of satire. His later poetry gives us the vague language of conventional devotion following Sassoon's conversion to Catholicism. It, too, is unfortunately marred by Marshianisms, and the virtue of this book is that it firmly puts Sassoon in a minor niche.

1209 "Carry on Jack." London **Observer Weekend Review**, 18 September 1966, p. 26.

Review of **The Moment and Other Pieces**, by J.B. Priestley. This collection of reviews culled from the **New Statesman**, speeches and popular pundit's rhetoric, argues for a better world very reminiscent of solid and stable Edwardian comfort. "He loathes cant, the decay of the theatre through anaemic telly addiction not furious Puritanism, the fact that pubs close just at the time one wants to start drinking, the windy mockery of international conferences, personality as a substitute for talent . . . . He loves smoking and scoffs, rightly, at the lung-cancer doom-prophets. The gusto is of the traditional unqualified kind."

1210 "Matters of Romance." **Spectator**, v. 217 (September 23 1966) 384.

Review of: **Of Other Worlds: Essays and Stories**, by C.S. Lewis. Ed. by Walter Hooper. Lewis had an interest in fairy tales and science-fiction and, pre-occupied by the marvellous, the coincidental and the fantastic — elaborated his theory of Story. Lewis "regrets, and rightly, I think, the subordination in modern fiction of 'the series of imagined events' to idea and character, and he naturally looks for the despised element. . . in literary forms which the Leavisites might not regard as serious." He was a good critic but one not capable of the memorable *mot*; perhaps that explains why he is not one of the great ones.

1211 "Augustus Carp Addresses a New Generation of Sinners." **Bookseller**, September 24, 1966, p. 1768-69.

1212 "The First Madame Bovary." **Spectator**, v. 217 (September 30, 1966) 414.

Review of **November**, by Gustave Flaubert. "Flaubert, the sedentary bachelor, rejecting even love for literature, agonizing in unnatural seclusion over the *mot juste*, blueprinting his books like complex pieces of machinery — is it not right that life should take revenge on such a man and refuse to lodge in his works? . . . . The big bouncing Balzac took less care, but how instinct with life (presumably precisely because he took less care) all his characters are!" Reprinted in **Urgent Copy**.

1213 "An Electric Grape." **American Scholar**, v. 35, no. 4 (Autumn 1966) 719-20.

Invited to respond to the Spring number of the **American Scholar**, he finds, after three nights of over-stimulated insomnia, that Roger W. Wescott's "Introducing Coenitics" is a reminder that linguistics has been elevated to an austere science; that he cannot come to terms with cybernetics; that **Understanding Media** is one of the seminal books of the age, but while there is a lot of communication about language, there is very little mention of values. "Charles Snow, speaking of the Two Cultures, mentioned the old-fashioned humanist, ignorant and distrustful of science, trying to warm himself in the tattered rags of his outmoded learning. I feel rather like that — not willfully embracing my inertia, but wondering if it is not perhaps too late to learn the new things . . . ."

1214 "Letter from England." **Hudson Review**, v. 19, no. 3 (Autumn 1966)

Describes life in the village of Etchingham, Sussex ("the people are dour and unliterary") and gives a cheerful account of a trip to London to sell review copies. The swingingness of London is much exaggerated, and the middle-aged are gently excluded from the swinging life. The writers meet, instead, to lament the state of contemporary British writing. "Lord Snow is old-fashioned; Golding has plucked the last feather off the bird of Evil; the Catholic converts are starting to bore." Laments the parsimoniousness of British reviews, the neglect of literature by the State, the virtual impossibility of knowing the response of the British reading audience. "One ends, then, by writing in a void, throwing words into an emptiness. And yet one goes on writing." Considers the limited subject matter available to the British writer and speculates if a concentration on supra-national ideas may represent a new approach. "The organisation of words into meaningful patterns — it represents, against all the odds, a sort of salvation."

1215 "The Jew as American." **Spectator**, v. 217, no. 7215 (October 7, 1966) 455.

Essay prompted by the Penguin editions of **Dangling Man, The Victim, The Adventures of Augie March, Henderson the Rain King, Seize the Day**, and **Herzog**, by Saul Bellow. The modern American hero belongs to the towns, and the Jew is America's great urban expert. Pre-war Jewish writers had the death-urge; after the sustained European pogrom they were neurotic, obsessed, self-pitying, paralysed. Only Malamud and Bellow have demonstrated staying power. Bellow, unlike some American novelists who seem primarily to be moralists, is concerned with creating literature, and the extraction of social messages from his work is not easy. The vitality of his heroes derives from his language, his combination of rich, crazy poetry, a juxtaposition of high and low style, elegance and slang. This natural, but extravagant literary dialect is the true answer to the careful etiolations of the Hemingway style. In his maturer work, Bellow "has opted for the delineation of a complex dissatisfied personality, a heaving centre with a periphery glittering with near-hallucinatory detail. Man seeking self-definition is plot enough." Reprinted in **Urgent Copy**.

1216 "Naked Mr. Gibbon." **Spectator**, v. 217, no. 7217 (October 21, 1966) 521.

Review of **Memoirs of My Life**, by Edward Gibbon. Ed. by Georges A. Bonnard. "A re-reading of this opulent and altogether satisfying edition confirms what we expected to be confirmed — namely, that this is the best British autobiography there is. But why? After all, nothing happens. There are no Cellini amours or Berlioz transports. The accounts of Gibbon's spiritual vicissitudes lack the African magic of Augustine's, and there is none of the emotional allure of those other **Confessions**. But the sense of intellectual control, of a life somehow grasped as a concept, is unmatched." He sums up the brother-sister relationship for all time; the Augustan generalities do not smother the careful delineations of character; the perfection of the prose style knows neither decline nor fall.

1217 "Behind the Law." **Listener**, v. 76 (October 27, 1966) 616.

Review of **A Law Unto Themselves**, by C. Northcote Parkinson.

1218 "Soil and Flower." **Spectator**, v. 217, no. 7218 (October 28, 1966) 554.

Review of **The Novel and Society**, by Diana Spearman.

1219 "The Panel Game." **Times Literary Supplement**, 3 November 1966, p. 1003.

Letter to the editor. Doubts if he would accept an Arts Council grant on the terms breezily outlined by Mr. Day Lewis. It is stated that the work must be "good work" which confers "prestige." This stipulation surely means that one must please Day Lewis and the members of his panel. Second, if an author's impecuniousness is a criterion, surely snoopers will peer through cob-webbed windows at fireless grates? "A state award for writers implies too many kinds of unseemliness — unseemly snooping, unseemly obligation (is not the needy writer's sponsor supposed to look over his shoulder and report progress?) unseemly discrimination (writers being what they are). Let all available money go to the Royal Literary Fund and be paid out to authors' widows or widowed authors. That is where the real need lies."

1220 "The Writer as Drunk." **Spectator**, v. 217, no. 7219 (November 4, 1966) 588.

Review of **Brendan Behan, Man and Showman**, by Rae Jeffs. Both Brendan Behan and Dylan Thomas were pubmen with an ancestral memory of the word-man's social function, the bardic job; but Dylan was proud and alone in the pursuit of his craft, the drafts piling high to reach a peak of impossible perfection. The dangerous and damning thing about Brendan was that he cried for help in his art. Brendan, at the end, when the drink got to him, was reduced to the tape recorder and the help of Mrs. Jeffs; he lost the properties of art — shape, precision, economy. The result was half-art, art indubitably minor. He was one of those Falstaffian figures that must be destroyed in this pursed, prissy age. "Brendan may have been a nuisance, but he was alive, and he proclaimed to a large public that the art of letters, however minor its practice, belonged to life and not just to libraries." Reprinted in **Urgent Copy**.

1221 "Coming to the Crunch." **Manchester Guardian**, November 4, 1966, p. 6.

Review of **Nature and Human Nature**, by Alex Comfort. This reasonable man, fit to join Machiavelli, Voltaire, or Bernard Shaw, has the unnerving, predatory look of a cant-hunter. His remarks about the human species are apt and reasonable. He knows that the prospect of death brings wretchedness, that art and religion have a biological function, and he deplores the Western inheritance of the Roman *severitas* rather than the Greek spirit of moderation. Athenians knew that man was rational and irrational, Appollonian and Dionysian. "The exponential curve of population growth seems to presage a doubling of the world population in sixty years; man is living longer; the survival of the species will depend on revolutions in our attitudes to fertiliy, food supplies, morals which — with our powerfully developed aggressions — we seem so far to be unwilling to make." [Reprinted in #1223.]

1222 "Rock of Ages." **Manchester Guardian**, 9 November 1966, p. 18.

He returned to Gibraltar for a visit. He was insulted by a waiter; the breakfast was cold. Franco, of course, is a hypocrite: Spain has plenty of colonies overseas. He was worried about the Gibraltarians. Their Britishry seems superficial, their culture derivative, their ambition restricted solely to commercial profit. In the event of a showdown with Franco's Spain, it is possible that they would acquit themselves well at the barricades even though, during the war, they were reluctant to be soldiers. "One hopes so. One likes to think well of the British."

1223 "Coming to the Crunch." **Manchester Guardian Weekly**, 10 November 1966, p. 10.

[Reprint of #1221.]

1224 "His Ain Folk." **Spectator**, v. 217, no. 7220 (November 11, 1966) 621.

Review of **The Company I've Kept: Essays in Autobiography**, by Hugh MacDiarmid. "Much can be forgiven a man who is, at one and the same time, the Grand Old Man and *enfant terrible* of Scottish literature. And, for many admirers of his poetic achievement, there is quite a lot to be forgiven — an anglophobia that doesn't disdain a Civil List pension, a willingness to celebrate the Russian invasion of Hungary by getting back into the Communist party, a smugness rather unseemly in a writer of seventy-four, an unashamed capacity for dealing out some of the worst prose of the decade." His dream of independence for Scotland is right: the Union killed Scottish culture. He properly loves Pound, Sean O'Casey, Willie Gallacher, John MacLean and Kaikhosru Shapurji Sorabji. MacDiarmid must be *simpatico*. It is a pity his book does not demostrate the fact.

1225 "The Wearing of the Greene." **Manchester Guardian**, November 11, 1966, p. 8.

Review of **Graham Greene**, by John Atkins. It is an acute and clever treatise by a man who hardly ever genuflects to his subject. Mr. Atkins, not a Catholic, does not seem to like Greene's heterodox Catholicism, and he worries about Greene's theology. "He can find little basis in either statistical fact or orthodox morality for supposing that a Catholic, however much he sins, emerges as better — i.e., possessing a true grasp of *caritas* — than a merely right-doing Protestant. Mr. Atkins shows how bad and uncharitable Catholics can be. Greene protests that to do evil is to engage in an ultimate; right and wrong are mere shadows. Both he and Mr. Atkins seem to have missed the fact that the Greenean theology is closer to Kant than to Aquinas; the *noumenon* is real, the *phenomenon* is only apearance. Evil is an aspect of the *noumenon* as seen morally." [Reprinted in #1227.]

1226 "Daltonian Prejudice." **Manchester Guardian**, November 16, 1966, p. 20.

He first contributed a drawing to the **Manchester Guardian** when he was eleven years old; wonders if he was actually paid five guineas for this contribution. His ambition was to be a great pictorial artist. Then, at fourteen, he discovered he was color-blind. So determined to be a composer: the ear would make up for the deficiency of the eye. Protests against the state's proposed technique of teaching reading based on color recognition. This technique (only males are color-blind) will ensure that the girls will do all right, but a lot of the boys won't.

1227 "The Wearing of the Greene." **Manchester Guardian Weekly**, 17 November 1966, p. 11.

[Reprint of #1225.]

1228 "Yin and Bitters." **Manchester Guardian**, November 18, 1966, p. 7.

Review of **Don't Never Forget**, by Brigid Brophy. She is much too pretty to be an author ("That girl was made for love" as an American friend of his once growled) but her logic never falters. It is hard to disagree with her on censorship, the rights of animals and women, masturbation, matrimony. She is a *yin* author at war with a *yang* world and a *yang* God. Many of these collected reviews are insultingly short when put between covers, but "the parade of sense, erudition and rationality is ex-hilarating, though the personality that emerges is not made for love — at least, not the love of a *yang* reader. She knows too many of the answers . . . ." [Reprinted in #1230.]

1229 "Rationality in Drinks." **Manchester Guardian**, 23 November 1966, p. 16.

Laments the high cost of tonic, and the practise of dispensing it in a large bottle. When there is tonic left over, as there always seems to be, he is tempted to order more gin. [The trick here is to drink the tonic without the gin?] Recounts his difficulties with a home soda-making machine. Green chartreuse, as Fleming observed, gives the best results per fluid ounce, but it is hard to get. "When the barman is not busy he will consent to mix me a Hangman's Blood, and I recommend this for a quick, though expensive, lift. Into a pint beer-glass doubles of the following are poured: gin, whisky, rum, port, and brandy. A small bottle of stout is added, and the whole topped up with champagne or champagne sur-rogate. Then it is dispensed into wine-glasses. It tastes very smooth, induces a somehow metaphysical elation, and rarely leaves a hangover." Also laments the absence, in England, of a rough and powerful cheap drink for the regular, as opposed to festal, cheering of the heart.

1230 "Yin and Bitters." **Manchester Guardian Weekly**, 24 November 1966, p. 11.

[Reprint of #1228.]

1231 "Here Parla Man Marcommunish." **Spectator**, v. 217, no. 7222, (November 25, 1966) 674-75.

"Languages in contact, as Mario Pei reminds us, are bound to mix." Provides examples of loan words in other languages ("This last word [the Russian word **loder**] which means 'lazybones,' comes from 'loader': visiting Russians were greatly struck by the slowness of the stevedores on British docks") and then takes aim at Labor's regrettable drift towards Europe. "Mr. Wilson, if it is he who is going to lead us into the Common Market, will no doubt be found equal to the linguistic demands of the inauguration ceremony. He will have two alternatives. First, he can tell the europeans that the britannic nation [Burgess has just delivered an argument against capital letters] has emerged from a *mauvaise epoque* in which the *Lumpenproletariat* rendered torpid by *la noia* of the *ancien regime*, with its *Unrealpolitik* of *il faut cultiver notre jardin*, possessed no viable *Weltanschauung*, has, *nel mezzo del cammin* of the socialist *renaissance* rediscovered, through *Sturm und Drang* and the *empressement* of the *Zeitgeist*, its élan vital and is, *con brio e con amore e molto accelerande*, becoming *au fait* with the *nouvelle vague politique, fatigué* as it is with the *faux-naiveté* of *passé* chauvinistes and the *verloren hoops* to whom *laissez-faire* was the *dernier cri*."

1232 "Man and Artist." **Spectator**, v. 217, (November 25, 1966) 693-94.

Review of **Selected Letters of Dylan Thomas**, ed. by Constantine Fitz Gibbon; **The Craft and Art of Dylan Thomas**, by William T. Moynihan; and **A Garland for Dylan Thomas**, by George J. Firmage and Oscar Williams. The letters convey an impression of irresponsibility to everything except his art. The expository letters, in which he defines his poetic aims, have assumed the status of public aesthetic manifestoes. Others are artful, and still others record the distance between the impressions of the man and the impulses of the artist. "I have no new items to add to the legend, except that he once played me a few bars of Scriabin in G flat and that he would cow his stomach with lime juice for breakfast in the Richmond station bar." Reprinted in **Urgent Copy**.

1233 "The Wide-Eyed View." **Manchester Guardian**, November 25, 1966, p. 14.

Review of **The Mind of the European Romantics**, by H.G. Schenk. "Mr. Schenk rightly sees Nietzsche as the heir of romanticism: 'Dissonance, that characteristic of the Romanic movement as a whole, was the keynote of Nietzsche's own personality.' But are there not later and more significant heirs? How about D.H. Lawrence, totally unmentioned? **Finnegans Wake**, strangely, gets a mention as a 'cul-de-sac of Romanticism,' since it tries to use language to probe the unconscious. One ends up, frankly, by being less sure at the end than at the beginning as to the nature of the movement. We had better take it that art and thought have been romantic for the past two millenia, except for a brief sunlit era when 'Augustus on a guinea sat up straight'.''

1234 "Humor and the Real." **Manchester Guardian**, November 30, 1966, p. 16.

He tends to niggle about accuracy and probability even in areas of mere entertainment. In this helpful spirit, he once commented on the propriety of naming a Roman lady 'Diddius' in an army review. In this same spirit, he observed certain solecisms in the musical "My Fair Lady." Argues that even the wildest farce must have its own internal logic, and then condemns the ignorance and inverted snobbery of certain inept popular entertainers who fail to meet this elementary axiom.

1235 "Shem the Penman." **Spectator**, v. 217, no. 7223 (December 2, 1966) 726.

Review of **Letters of James Joyce**, vols. 2-3, ed. by Richard Ellmann. "But, after the image of grave formality that emerges from the Gilbert letters, an image corroborated in Ellmann's biography, we are not prepared for the satyr that leaps out in the newly published letters to Nora Barnacle. The God of creation has ceased to stand indifferent above his work, paring his finger-nails; he has entered the flesh of Leopold Bloom." Nora Barnacle's letters to her husband reveal pages of authentic Molly Bloom. The letters of his mother, marked by a faultless simplicity, show the young Joyce to be a monster of a son, and the mother a heroine. Reprinted in **Urgent Copy**.

1236 "The Book Is Not For Reading." **New York Times Book Review**, December 4, 1966, p. 1.

An account of his reading habits. Laments inability to tackle Jane Austen. His preferred fiction as a "strong male thrust, an almost pedantic allusiveness, and a brutal intellectual content." For letter by Marion Citrin, see **New York Times Book Review**, 1 January 1967, p. 21.

1237 "The Irish in Me." **Manchester Guardian**, December 7, 1966, p. 16.

The atavistic grumbling of his Finnegan blood is prompting him to learn Irish. It is a hellishly difficult language. Compared to Gaelic, spoken Chinese is nothing at all, the Indonesian tongue is a toy for kittens. Unfortunately, the primer is no help at all. He wants to tell the Aer Lingus stewardesses that a large whiskey with ice would hit the spot, but the primer suggests such exquisite haikus as: sea-water is warmer than spring-water and Did the priest believe the boys? "My big moment of revolt has just come with: 'Where is the cow-byre? It is beyond the turf-rick.' Try that over a champagne cocktail in the Gresham Hotel."

1238 "Song in the Mist." **Spectator**, v. 217, no. 7224 (December 9, 1966) 762.

Review of **The Early English and Celtic Lyric**, by P.L. Henry. [Burgess significantly includes a passage on exile for quotation and discussion.]

1239 "Matter of Manners." **Manchester Guardian**, December 14, 1966, p. 18.

As he gets older, his temper in certain minor matters becomes more volcanic. Does the waiter suggest bread and cheese after a meal? He rages that he wants some exquisite concoction which does justice to those elaborate kitchens and temperamental chefs. The other day, his digits buried in a scholarly text to collate some facts, the impertinent telephone rang. It was a wrong number and he vented his rage on the poor neutral phone. The next day, he held open the door to his bank and a long queue of customers marched through without a word of thanks. They got an earful. Laments the rotting away of simple courtesy and tells a story of a grateful New York City taxi driver who, asked to go to Riverside Drive *please*, was charming and ingratiating in return.

1240 "ANA." **Manchester Guardian**, December 16, 1966. p. 7.

Review of **Observations, Anecdotes and Characters of Books and Men**, by Joseph Spence. Ed. by James M. Osborn. Spence endeared himself to Pope by a long, precocious essay on the poet's work; he was soon in a position to add vastly to the world's Popeana. Did not Dr. Johnson suggest "ANA" as a suitable synonym for Spence's ponderous title? This new edition replaces the former Singer version, and the handsome work exemplifies everything that is admirable about American scholarship. Gives some succulent morsels from the present edition: Pope's alkaline constitution, the Duke of

Montagu's kind but eccentric fondness for ugliness, the custom of Spanish nuns to ask their spouse's [i.e. Christ's] pardon for any future adultery, the tendency of Spanish whores (great Mariolaters) to ask the Blessed Virgin to drum up trade . . . .

1241 "Damned Dot. . ." **Manchester Guardian,** 21 December 1966, p. 12.

A polemic against decimal coinage and the decimal system in general. Decimal numbers are hard to add up in your head. A dollar is not divisible by three. "The real horror of a decimal coinage comes when you try to split a dollar (or new pound) three ways." Liters and kilos are the most unmanageable units of measurement ever devised. Remember the old man in Orwell's dystopia who says: "Why can't I have a proper pint? All these litres keeps me running?" [Pints and quarts will have the same effect. Reprinted in #1242.]

1242 "Down with Decimals." **Manchester Guardian Weekly,** 22 December 1966, p. 12.

[Reprint of #1241.]

1243 "Dickens Loud and Clear." **Spectator,** v. 217, no. 7226 (December 23, 1966) 817.

Review of **Oliver Twist,** by Charles Dickens. Dickens was heavily influenced by the rampant Victorian melodramatic tradition and heavily under the influence of Christian evangelism that allowed big unqualified moral gestures. "We lack enthusiasm and are embarrassed by moral fervour and grandiloquence alike. This is why our attitude to Dickens is ambivalent — nostalgia mixed with distaste, *nausee* in the presence of the spreading chestnut tree." Dickens' effective early "rhetorical" punctuation shows that he was working in an auditory tradition. "The tyranny of orthodox rules [of punctuation], as exerted in most modern Dickens editions, hammers the words flat and blows out the stage candles." Reprinted in **Urgent Copy.**

1244 "Letter to a Tax Man." **Manchester Guardian,** December 28, 1966, p. 12.

He received, just before Christmas, a scrawled demand from the taxman for 1,000 pounds on or before January 1. The pertinent question is: how will this sum be raised? To sell his shares in ICI now at a loss would be foolish. To ask for advances on royalties would be improbable. Nobody knows and nobody cares. "Nobody will say. . . that this freelance writer has choked up his lungs with smoke, gone without sleep, developed callouses on his two typing fingers, sacrificed style to speed, all in order that a thousand pounds that nobody really cares about should to to an ungrateful fisc." Soon there will be hard questions about the other installments. "I don't really know how all this came about. I do not live extravagantly. I smoke a lot (but that's a patriotic duty to the Exchequer) and very occasionally take a taxi, but I don't run a car. I have three suits. I try to drink only beer. I work seven days a week. The real answer is to work less . . . . I don't regard you tax people as faceless monsters. One evening in the Café Royal I saw some of you junketing with your wives, many of whom were very gay (there had been a tax people's dinner or something). You looked decent enough. But you stopped Evelyn Waugh from writing and you helped to kill Dylan Thomas."

1245 "Three Sterling Islands: 1. The Rock." **Listener,** v. 76 (December 29, 1966) 965-66.

On Gibraltar. "And so you will enjoy a fair simulacrum of a Mediterranean good time by going to Gibraltar's night clubs, but you will look forward to the diamond morning, the sun, a little bathing, the flowers in the Alameda Gardens, the changing of the guard outside the Convent, the moderately cheap drinking in the bar of the Sombrero on Cornwall's Parade, the chicken or swordfish, the siesta. Despite the night clubs, a sort of British ennui descends in the evening. Gibraltar's main commodity is the sun."

1246 "Kipling and the Kuch-nays." **Spectator,** v. 218, no. 7228 (January 6, 1967) 18-19.

Review of **Kipling in India,** by Louis L. Cornell and **Rudyard Kipling,** by J.I.M. Stewart. The richness of Kipling's English can be seen as the ex-colonialist's compensation for the loss of Hindi, and his early mistreatment in England at the hand of Mrs. Holloway confirmed him in Anglo-Indian attitudes he never lost. His Indian writing was rooted in the need to notate the actual ("After all, one needed an audience, and that audience was the club . . . .he wrote for Anglo-Indians as Shakespeare wrote for Elizabethans"). His sympathies lay with the ruler and the ruled. For both the Indian and English middle classes he had nothing but incomprehension and dislike. And so, "he wrote for a minor autocracy.

But a member of that autocracy, back home in England, is nothing more than a *kuch-nay* — a middle-class nonentity. By a terrible irony, the *kuch-nays* of England, praying for ten per cent, made him their own poet.'' Reprinted in **Urgent Copy**.

1247 "**Spectator** Symposium on 1967.'' **Spectator**, v. 218, no. 7228 (January 6, 1967) 6.

[Burgess contributes his hopes for the new year.] Political unarmed combat against one of the worst governments of the century. The Wilson oligarchy to consult its electorate, not party ideology. National referenda on major innovations. No decimal coinage. MPs to consult their constituents, not their consciences. More trees. Good bread. "The appearance of a poem as good as **The Waste Land** and a symphony as good as Elgar's Second. And — but one takes this for granted — an honourable settlement in Rhodesia and the end of the Vietnam nonsense.''

1248 "Television.'' **Listener**, v. 77 (January 12, 1967) 71.

[Television criticism.] On an adaptation of Evelyn Waugh's **Men at Arms** (superb), Joan Henry's **Person to Person** (pointless), the ecumenical movement, Pakistani minorities in Britain, the death of Donald Campbell in **Bluebird**, British population growth and a tolerable sitcom called **Till Death Do Us Part**.

1249 "Watch Your Language.'' London **Observer Review, 15 January 1967, p. 26.**

Reviews of **The Treasure of Our Tongue**, by Lincoln Barnett; and **Personalities of Language**, by Gary Jennings. Barnett is an amateur at a time when the study of language has become increasingly cerebral, cold and repulsive. Like many an amateur, his love of language includes an element of awe. He is therefore tempted to legislate a state of linguistic stasis complete with Fowlerian concepts like 'correctness' and the study of 'grammar.' He fails to understand there is no available legislation for promoting this linguistic health. Nevertheless, his book is a warm and eloquent tribute to the Anglo-American language. Jennings is best in the great junk-shop of oddities which conveys an overall air of the joyous slapdash. One needs the academic dryness of a few scholarly citations as a corrective.

1250 "Europe's Day of the Dead.'' **Spectator**, v. 218, no. 7230 (January 20, 1967) 74.

Review of **Under the Volcano**, by Malcolm Lowry. With an introduction by Stephen Spender. Also reviews **The Selected Letters of Malcolm Lowry**. Ed. by Harvey Breit and Margerie Bonner. **Volcano** is a book about a dipsomaniac; it is also a book about heaven and hell and the necessity of choice between them. It was a critical and financial success in the U.S. and Europe, but not in England. "Despite its British hero, it was apparently not considered provincial enough here; the study of evil and human degradation was too profound and detailed, the exploitation of myth and language asked for very strenuous engagement.'' Lowry wrote a letter in which he argued that the defect of the work is its essentially poetic conception. It is plainly intended as another **Inferno**, and Lowry wrote the novel Conrad Aiken, for lack of an architectonic gift, failed to write. Geoffrey Firmin is a giant character whose vices (sloth, alienation from life, inability to love) ironically etch the desired virtues. Lowry's life was adventurous but hard: critical success, when it came, nevertheless doomed him to the twentieth-century writer's hopeless struggle to make ends meet. That he is one of the great dead major novelists there can no longer be any doubt.

1251 "The Brotherhood.'' **Spectator**, v. 218, no. 7231 (January 27, 1967) 106-7.

Review of **Rossetti and the Pre- Raphaelite Brotherhood**, by G.H. Fleming; **Millais and the Ruskins**, by Mary Lutyens; and **The Professor; Arthur Severn's Memoir of John Ruskin**, edited by James S. Deardon. "We talk of art as the mirror of life, but here was one aspect of life that — thanks to a taboo still unbroken — art was unable to teach John Ruskin. The whole business is acutely embarrassing. Ruskin had admired classical statues and closely examined the paintwork on nudes, but gross human reality horrified him. Little girls — who were innocent, made no sexual demands, and had no pubic hair — were later to help reconcile him to the female form worshipped by painters, but ultimately Ruskin stands, on his own admission, as a man unmovable by anything except copies of life and abstract stone artefacts.'' Reprinted in **Urgent Copy**.

1252 "What's Going on There.'' **Manchester Guardian**, 27 January 1967, p. 7.

Review of **The New Writing in the USA; African Writing Today; Italian Writing Today; German Writing Today**. There is no excuse now for Ukasians to remain ignorant of contemporary foreign writers.

"No excuse now, except the familiar one about buying British and, even in that field, having one's work cut out to keep up with the output of such native authors as are not protected from fecundity by the Arts Council."

1253 "Books Wanted in 1967: A Dream of Publishing." London **Times**, 2 February 1967, p. 16b.

[Books Burgess would like to see in print.] An Augustan satire in impeccable heroic couplets which would lead to mass remorse among the country's rulers; a novel written entirely in carefully disguised Petrarchan sonnets; a novel which chronicles the history of the British stage and combined the talents of Chaucer, Sterne, Fielding and Joyce and featured unrequited love every generation; a book so funny that it would cause the deaths of many readers and compel Parliament to issue the Control of Risibility Act, 1967; and he would also republish **The Sexual Cycle of Human Warfare**, Ford Maddox Ford's **Parade's End** and some other, very funny novels.

1254 "Levitating a Little." **Spectator**, v. 218 (February 3, 1967) 140.

Review of **The Heat of the Sun**, by Sean O'Faolain. ". . . no man has done more to render Irishry as a contemporary commodity, not a harking-back to mists and leprechauns."

1255 "Television." **Listener**, v. 77, no. 1976 (February 9, 1967) 206-207.

[Television criticism.] For Zeffirelli's **Much Ado About Nothing** he has nothing but "anger and contempt . . . ." [Zeffirelli] doesn't understand Shakespeare, therefore. . . he tricks it out with an intendedly piquant anachronistic setting, a broth of inconsistent accents, a pitiful display of pseudo-comic 'business' . . . ." Jim Allen's **The Lump** includes inbuilt tapes of Leninist oratory, but conveys a sense of life. **Great Expectations** suffers by comparison to the David Lean film. A telebiography of Malcolm Lowry fails to evoke his **Under the Volcano**. "Geoffrey Firmin, British consul in a Mexican town, drinking himself to death on the Day of the Dead, is more than a hopeless petty Faust bent on self-destruction: he sums up the suicidal Europe of 1939."

1256 "Soft-Shelled Classics." **Spectator**, v. 218 (February 10, 1967) 171.

[Extremely brief reviews of some paper-back books.] **The Man of Property, In Chancery, To Let**, all by John Forsyte; **John Christopher**, by Romain Rolland; **Martin Eden**, by Jack London; **The Bostonians** and **The Golden Bowl**, by Henry James; **Emma**, by Jane Austen; **David Copperfield**, by Charles Dickens; **Death in the Afternoon**, by Ernest Hemingway;**The King Must Die**, by Mary Renault; **The Golden Warrior**, by Hope Muntz; **Fathers and Sons**, by Turgenev; and **Vendetta and Ziska**, by Marie Corelli.

1257 "English as an America." **Encounter**, v. 28 (February 1967) 67-71.

Review of **Modern American Usage**, by Wilson Follett. Edited and completed by Jacques Barzun and others. The aim of this book is to promote a clear, dignified, unambitious expository standard of English which has little to do with art but much to do with journalism. When these authors, or pundits, write about the split infinitive (sometimes admissible in writing, but not in speech), the inadmissibility of the word "enthuse," or "togetherness," they are clearly seen as somethat conservative and pedantic guardians of the language, and the reader should rebel at some of their rulings. "If we go to Fowler or Follett for guidance, it should be guidance in the narrow zone of linguistic etiquette, on which — in our superstitious way — we are always ready to be instructed, as in the movement of a religious ritual. But all the fulmination, scorn, querulousness and cold reason of the pundits can do nothing to stop the current of language from going its own way." Also reviews **The Random House Dictionary of the English Language**. Reprinted in **Urgent Copy**.

1258 "Gibraltar." **Holiday**, v. 41, no. 2 (February 1967) 71, 86-87, 92-93, 126-127, 129.

Gibraltar, that mass of Jurassic limestone, with the biscuit colored beauty of the girls and the gold-toothed business drive of the men is, in his mind, three islands. In 1943, when he was an army sergeant, it represented a bitter barrack incarceration. Later, in middle age, it became a pleasure town. Finally, it is a bone of contention between the Spanish, who yap for it, and the British, who hold it down with an uneasy paw. Gives his impressions of Gibraltar as a great living thing. Describes the Barbery apes who snarled at him when, a soldier, he explored the island. Anthropoids now photograph the simians and ignore, rightly, old Gibraltarian customs; for there are none; the inhabitants are chiefly dedicated to the careful making of money. Relates the capture of the Rock by Admiral Rooke during the War of the Spanish Succession. His Gibraltar friends, modestly prosperous, are prepared to defend the "free association" with Britain *con valor churchiliano* even while they feel the temptations of Spain. He, glorying in human diversity, is quite prepared to endorse the *status quo*. It has, for all its diversity, a domestic coziness of a city like Dublin. Quotes James Joyce on Gibraltar and remarks that it is like that.

1258.2 "On Being a Lapsed Catholic." **Triumph**, v. 2, no. 2 (February 1967) 31.

Observes that he was the first in the family to apostasize from the Catholic Church. Describes his family's reactions to his loss of faith, and confesses he wants pagan night. The reason is not the prospect of interminable pain, but that he wants "Anthony Burgess blotted out as a flaw in the universe: a terrible sin of presumption, orthodoxy might counter, for who am I to question my worth to God? That I do question it is a fact, and no amount of earnest expostulation seems able to change the position." He has no quarrel with any aspect of the Catholic doctrine granted the ignition spark of faith. Laments the current slackness, cheapness, ecumenical dilutions taking place in Roman Catholicism, and describes his response to other religions. He wants to believe, but finds it impossible to do so.

1259 "Slangfest." **Listener**, v. 77 (March 2, 1967) 299.

Review of **A Dictionary of Slang and Unconventional English**. Vol. 2: The Supplement, by Eric Partridge. "A wonderful read, as well as a mandatory aid to travellers in the unbuttoned world, and gamy with the long-basted personality of its compiler."

1260 "The Purpose of Education." **Spectator**, v. 218, no. 7236 (March 3, 1967) 247.

Teachers tend to be devoted to niggling and useless detail; he shares the vice himself. The true teacher should be passionately interested in the examination and transmission of values. "And the personality of the teacher will be a sufficient witness to the desirability of the values he teaches — vital, hungry for truth and beauty, probably eccentric, capable of depression, crapula after euphoria, the unpredictable rage, the unaccountable tolerance. He must, in short, be a fully rounded human being, not a cold and competent technician.

1261 "Singer at the Feast." **Manchester Guardian**, 3 March 1967, p. 7.

Review of **Short Friday** and **In My Father's Court**, by Isaac Bashevis Singer. Concerning the first book, "even the contemporary Jew must find difficulty in accepting as naturalistic fiction (for so they seem to be offered) short stories about demons, witches, the world of the dead, a ghost at a wedding, evil forces that make witches come horribly true." The second work is another matter, for "Young Isaac was brought up in an atmosphere of bizarre spiritual problems, acts of fantastic litigation, instances of impossible heroism, and incredible vindictiveness — all to be solved, adjudicated, deliberated in a home parlour. May a man sleep with his dead wife to avoid being eaten by the rats on the floor? Why shouldn't an aged wife show her love by making her husband get married to a younger woman? . . . . There's no end to the Solomonic skills required of Singer's father . . . . Few *goy* writers provide feasts as rich as this."

1262 "Death and Abduction." **Country Life**, v. 141, no. 3653 (March 9, 1967) 554-55.

Reviews of **Matters of Felony**, by Margery Weiner; **Rhodesia and Independence**, by Kenneth Young; **The Thought Revolution**, by Tung Chi-Ping and Humphrey Evans; **Orbit of China**, by Harrison E. Salisbury; **The Fon of Bafut**, by Pat Ritzenthaler.

1263 "Television." **Listener**, v. 77 (March 9, 1967) 335.

[Television criticism.] On installments of **Beyond the Fringe** and **Till Death Do Us Part** (toilet taboo broken in both), Japanese population growth control, a documentary on Michael Faraday (good) and an infuriating drama about a young schizophrene. Infuriating ("I will rage, hit my head on the wall, or, more sensibly, go out and drink myself insensible") because the program created concern but failed to discharge it in artistic fashion. Also on the unalluring people who deal with computers, and the heart-breaking business of making a start as a novelist.

1264 "Open and Shut Case." **Spectator**, v. 218, no. 7237 (March 10, 1967) 281.

Review of **The Turn of the Novel**, by Alan Friedman. "And so, with delicacy and occasional bursts of gusto, he shows how form and moral outlook are interconnected. In the modern novel we don't close in to a heartening though cosy stasis. There is, said Lawrence, 'no end, no finish, only this roaring vast space.' Mr Friedman, less rhetorically, sees in the modern novel a model of the modern cosmos, ever-expanding, and 'racing away fastest at its outmost reaches.' It is a stimulating thesis, and most of the demonstrations convince.''

1265 "Now Thank We All. . ." London **Observer Review**, 19 March 1967, p. 27.

Review of **The Cambridge Hymnal**, ed. by David Holbrook and Elizabeth Poston. "As a Catholic, I was brought up on very bad hymns, like 'Faith of our Fathers' and 'Hail, Queen of Heaven' and (a real shocker) 'Soul of my Saviour'." The hymns of the Reformed English Church naturally intimate special Grace and Favour. He has tried most of them on his small electric organ (a devotional activity that induces impotent rage in his neighbours) and finds some unfamiliar while others are charming.

1266 "Poet and Pedant." **Spectator**, v. 218, no. 7239 (March 24, 1967) 336-37.

Review of **Speak, Memory**, by Vladimir Nabokov. Nabokov is arguably the last of the literary dandies: the *mot-juste* sits like a Brummel cravat, locutions as rings, puns wink like Fabergé curiosities. He does not appreciate any of the unwritten laws about rhetoric and reticence, and it appears that the special task of the English-writing Slav is to remind us of the gorgeousness of the English language. In this autobiographical work he tells a bad tale of treachery and disposession with stoicism, even with aristocratic *hauteur*. The trait is evident, for example, in his tendency to condemn those more concerned with soul (Dostoevsky, Balzac) than style (Pushkin). It seems just and wholly inevitable that so exquisite and scholarly an artist should have become America's greatest literary glory. American novelists can turn out jumbo artefacts like Bruckner or Mahler symphonies; but, unlike Nabokov, they have little apparent aptitude for the rococo concerto. Nabokov's work is characterized by love, intelligence, erudition, elegance and pride. Reprinted in **Urgent Copy**.

1267 "Caprine Messiah." **Spectator**, v. 218, no. 7240 (March 31, 1967) 369.

Review of **Giles Goat-Boy**, by John Barth. The book "impresses more with its concept than (sheer mastery of length apart) its execution. And the concept is available to any clever undergraduate. On the other hand, self-criticism is built into the book, and any disparagement of mine has already been well taken care of. It makes much contemporary British fiction look very lightweight. Interpret that in what sense you like." Reprinted in **Urgent Copy**.

1268 "Letter from England." **American Scholar**, v. 36, no. 2 (Spring 1967). 261-65.

On the imminent introduction of decimal coinage in Britain, a glum production of **Alice in Wonderland** ("admittedly clever but wholly misguided perversion of a profound and funny book") and the new puritanism among youthful Britons. "The young seem to have all the sex they need, but sleeping together has an aura of duty about it (stern daughter of the voice of God); little joy and, I should imagine, little skill."

1269 "London Letter." **Hudson Review**, v. 20, no. 1 (Spring 1967) 99-104.

Gives an account of his impressive literary production over the Christmas holidays, describes his return to London to drink in the wisdom of the pubs and London literary life. The London working class, Tory in pubs, Labour in the voting booth, is taking kindly to the visit of Mr. Kosygin ("cozy gin") and this reflection leads to the description of a lively sitcom featuring xenophobia and the tele-execration of wogs and nignogs ("a harmless expression of a melanophobia that rarely seeks action"). [The reference is to **Till Death Do Us Part**. The American imitation is called **All in the Family**.] Comments on the disappearance of the race-theme from contemporary British literature and the way in which British newspapers approach writers through their dipsomania and other follies. "The cult of the scandalous writer serves, in effect, as a substitute for a concern with literature itself." The disaffection of the British young tends to mimic their California mentors. Describes the charges of obscenity against **Last Exit to Brooklyn** and his role in the court proceedings. "In a review of **Last Exit**, [see #1145] I suggested that 'no book could well be less obscene.' A prosecution witness wittily put forward **Pride and Prejudice** for my consideration in this respect. I submitted that it might corrupt the impressionable more, since all the Bennet sisters (with the possible exception of Mary) are very attractive, which is more than can be said for any of the characters in **Last Exit**. But nobody wishes to argue the matter out, and one may predict confidently that the Old Bailey will resound with highly charged shibboleths as a substitute for reason.''

1270 ''Two National Disgraces.'' **Country Life**, v. 141, no. 3657 (April 6, 1967) 810-11.

Reviews of **Banned! A Review of Theatrical Censorship in Britain**, by Richard Findlater; **The Dreyfus Affair**, by Betty Schechter; **Horace Sippog and the Sirens' Song**, by Su Walton; **Caviar for Breakfast**, by Ray Pierre Corsini; **Greece — A Classical Tour with Extras**, by George and Lucile Brockway.

1271 ''Television.'' **Listener**, v. 77 (April 6, 1967) 471.

[Television criticism.] On a damnable production of **Alice in Wonderland**, Ray Lawler's **A Breach in the Wall**, the sorry fare on Easter Monday (''Separate a holiday from its religious significance and this is what happens'') the Sinatras (father and daughter) and British political heckling.

1272 ''Other Edens — Anthony's Eden.'' **Punch**, v. 252, no. 6605 (April 12, 1967) 535-36.

Burgess describes his ideal island. Covers the landscape, the climate, inhabitants, health, diet, dress, languages, currency and religion.

1273 ''Below the Burma Road.'' **Manchester Guardian**, April 14 1967, p. 7.

Review of **The Source of the River Kwai**, by Pierre Boulle. Boulle, after Henri Fauconnier, gives us the best French view of Malaya and surrounding countries. This book gives an account of the author's adventures in China, and his misadventure in Indo China, where he was imprisoned by a colonel loyal to Vichy France. The first part of it is amusing; the second is gripping.

1274 ''Blood in the Matzos.'' **Spectator**, v. 218 (April 14, 1967) 424.

Review of **The Fixer**, by Bernard Malamud. Malamud does not come out well of a comparison with Saul Bellow or Isaac Bashevis Singer. ''This is only because he has, unlike Bellow, failed to turn the American Jew wholly into an American, and, unlike Singer, failed to stay uncompromisingly in the East European ghettoes.'' It is a moving and harrowing book; it is the finest fictional evocation of Slav Jew-hatred; but the book raises the suspicion that the brilliance is that of the cold and deliberate technician. ''The elation of contriving a trick piece of Jewish-European literature must have cathartized in advance the anguish of the subject-matter. The pity and terror, totally unpurged, are left to us.'' Reprinted in **Urgent Copy**.

1275 ''A Return to Polemics.'' **Country Life**, v. 141, no. 3659 (April 20, 1967) 962-63.

Reviews of **MacBird**, by Barbara Garson; Confronting Injustice, by Edmond Cahn; **A Substantial Ghost**, by Violet Powell; **Put Out More Flags**, by Evelyn Waugh.

1276 ''More Comedians.'' **Spectator**, v. 218 (April 21, 1967) 454.

Review of **May We Borrow Your Husband? and Other Comedies of the Sexual Life**, by Graham Greene. ''Mr Greene, who, being a great writer, is also a modest one, will not ask us to make too much of this little book of stories . . . . Behind the smallest productions of Greene there is a whole civilization, one that can be observed through the windows of the novels (whether saying 'SALOON BAR' or chromatically depicting the Scriptures) and squinted at through the chinks of these wholly admirable stories.''

1277 ''The Milton Revolution.'' **Spectator**, v. 218 (April 28, 1967) 487-88.

Review of **Milton: The Modern Phase**, by Patrick Murray and **Milton**, by E.M.W. Tillyard. T.S. Eliot, Ezra Pound and F.R. Leavis reviled **Paradise Lost** as a monstrosity of genius, a diabolically skilful engine for the torturing of English and the elevation of sound above sense. In fact, Milton stressed the Romance element of English, and he introduced shock value by interpolating an Anglo-Saxon word in a Latinate context. The normal practice, in Shakespeare and Eliot, is to reverse the process. He has been disliked for his theology, ethics and politics: his regicidal republicanism and the arrogance of his hates are difficult to like, but ''The picture of a thin-lipped Brownist, intolerant of fleshly indulgence, does not tally with the praise of married sex in **Paradise Lost** . . . . It is impossible not to be moved by this Samson beset by Philistines, fury tamed into resignation, sniffing the corruption of a Gaza that has brought him low, the hopes dead whereon he expended his sight to the utmost.'' Reprinted in **Urgent Copy**.

1278 "Politics in the Novels of Graham Greene." **Journal of Contemporary History**, v. 2 (April 1967) 93-99.

Greene's Catholicism approaches Jansenism, the heresy which argued that original sin expressed itself in the depravity of nature, appetite and concupiscence. A religion should beget its own politics and a Catholic should look with suspicion on a political ideology that rejects original sin and believes in moral progress. It is the Jansenist strain in Greene that leads him to places where the squalor of sin is exposed in its rawest forms. Greene's fiction often expresses anti-American views, and he is assumed, by pro-Americans, to be anti-democratic and pro-communist. Greene is anti-American because America wraps up her materialistic doctrines in the language of spiritual aspiration. She transmits her power, promotes her trade, and pretends to be crusading; this practise is the unforgivable hypocrisy. Communists actively promote material welfare, signally fail to achieve their stated aim, and actively resist spiritual values. Hence they may be guilty of incompetence, but not hypocrisy. "A place that seems to breathe sin is, paradoxically, spiritually healthier than an aseptic garden city." [Reprinted #1295, 1379; also in **Urgent Copy**.]

1279 "Television." **Listener**, v. 77 (June 1, 1967) 727.

[Television criticism.] On the high standards of British actors when compared to their American counterparts, a sketch by Pinter, an interview of Laurence Olivier by Kenneth Tynan, **Drums Along the Avon** (an abortion) and regrettable adapations of **The Divine Comedy** and **Lucky Jim** while **Russia: Beneath the Sputnick** was very impressive. "I had to keep reminding myself that, despite all the scientific achievements, you still can't get ice in Leningrad bars or lunch in under two hours."

1280 "Reading Your Own." **New York Times Book Review**, June 4, 1967, p. 6.

[Vonnegut, Barth, Burgess and Herbert Gold are asked to name their favorite books. The question induces, in Vonnegut and Burgess, a near coma of modesty.] He would settle for **The Long Day Wanes**. "I remember very vividly the writing of it — in the hot Malayan, and then Bornean, afternoons, when everybody else slept. The typewriter keys grew slithery with sweat; my forehead dripped sweat onto the paper. But I sweated words: my verbal pores were open. I tried very rapidly to encapsulate the period in British imperial history through which we were passing. I, as a colonial officer, was in the middle of it, concerned with training the new rulers of a protectorate that was raising its own flag . . . . But there would be a lot of poignancy in a rereading — the things that can never be relived, the friends gone for good, my own idealistic late youth, the pepper-tree in the garden, the snakes under the bougainvillea. Spare me the rereading; let others do the reading."

1281 "Summoned by Bell." **Spectator**, v. 218, no. 7250 (June 9, 1967) 682.

Review of **Collected Poems, 1937-1966**, by Martin Bell. "No postures, exact locution, a hypersensitive ear: he has all the talents and embodies all the temperaments — from the ribald to the vatic. All he needs now is acclamation."

1282 "Hindu Crush." **Spectator**, v. 218, no. 7251 (June 16, 1967) 714.

Review of **A Meeting by the River**, by Christopher Isherwood. [Plot summary written in the form of a letter to "Tony" and signed "Love from Burgy."] It is a very nice, moral little book. "It would make a very accepable tract to advertise the Beauties of Hindu Contemplation. I remember there used to be stories like this one issued by the Catholic Truth Society, but of course that wasn't to turn anybody into a Hindu; just the opposite, really."

1283 "Television." **Listener**, v. 77, no. 1996 (June 29, 1967) 862-3.

[Television criticism.] On **The Reluctant Romeo** (implausible and weak), an episode of the **Frost Report** (witty: well-paid writers), **Misleading Cases** (reasonably funny). Also a drama on the *mafiosi*, an indictment of smoking, a ballet on a confrontation between Mods and Rockers, and three separate tributes to Bach in as many programs. The program on "cancer and smoking. . . came as near as I ever feared any programme would to a definitive indictment of coffin nails as coffin nails. It was frighteningly well done, but my own fright soon dissolved into resignation. I can't write without smoking; the damage is done already; I have had a fair life; I keep a *cache* of barbiturates."

1284 "Gun and Pen." **Spectator**, v. 219, no. 7254 (July 7, 1967) 15-16.

Review of **Blasting and Bombardiering**, by Wyndham Lewis. The prose style is unattractive; too many exclamation points follow unremarkable asseverations; there is heartiness incompatible with the postures of the aesthete, and there is too much talking down. This work gives the impression of animated sculpture filled with plenty of linguistic bloat.

1285 "Master Beckett." **Spectator**, v. 219, no. 7256 (July 21, 1967) 79-80.

Review of **No's Knife**, by Samuel Beckett. Also reviews **Beckett at Sixty**. "Beckett's mastery of a kind of poetry of deprivation has a quality of miracle in it. His heroes have nothing but sores, smells, poverty, impending dissolution, but their language is rhythmically rich and their cries thrill like trumpets." The courage and remorselessness of the man are impressive.

1286 "Television." **Listener**, v. 78, no. 2000 (July 27, 1967) 123.

Television criticism. On cooks and cooking, witch doctors in Central Brazil, a potted biography of Richard Crossman and another one on Khrushchev in exile. Crossman was praised, by left and right, for a brilliance which Burgess was dying to see in action; it never really came. Khrushchev in his *dacha*, without the charisma or mana of power, proved a dull speciman. A contest of one family pitted against another was intended to prove what? something about genetics? Brien's quiz show proves that writers care about the work of other writers. Burgess has this dream of being the only one to answer the question: "Who wrote: 'Honuphrius is a concupiscent exservicemajor who makes dishonest propositions to all. . . '?" **Melodies for You** proves that badly chosen *Schlagobers* make one thirsty for pop. The master-class on Verdi's *Falstaff* was full of art, life, insight. The program on hypnosis with that riveting *Kaiserschnitt* was fine stuff. He is in no hurry to sample the delights of color television: "we will glory in the sensuous bliss of it all and become uncritical of the human content."

1287 "Et Ego in Arcadia." **Spectator**, v. 219, no. 7258 (August 4, 1967) 133-34.

Review of **O Canada: An American's Notes on Canadian Culture**, by Edmund Wilson. Samuel Butler saw that the Canadian repressive moral tradition, which distrusted joy and feared the flesh, would prove inimical to art. The book shows Englishmen and Americans the sound work that has been done, and it is the only useful handbook on the whole complex political and intellectual situation in Canada. "The bitter and touchy French Canadians, as distrustful of France. . . as of Anglo-Saxondom. . . are forming their committees and planting their bombs. Mr. Wilson provides us with a very useful history of their intransigence."

1288 "Discussing 'Coronation Street'." **Listener**, v. 78 (August 10, 1967) 186-87.

[Television criticism.] On **Coronation Street, The Big Killing**, television news and programs about an air crash, a young woman in a geriatric hospital, human behavior and Mick Jagger. "My heart warms to anyone [Jagger] who pleads the rights of the individual to do what he wishes so long as he doesn't harm the community: Jagger's logic was as sound as an amplified guitar, while the others sounded a bit querulous."

1289 "Auden's Minor Birds." **Spectator**, v. 219, no. 7259 (August 11, 1967) 161-62.

Review of **Nineteenth Century Minor Poets** ed. by W.H. Auden. When Victorian poetry is irretrievably minor it is implausible, egocentric and filled with moral lessons — the obvious tarted up as the gnomic. Charles Tennyson Turner is the worst offender of the lot. Also includes comments on Michael Drayton, Thomas Hood, Clough, Housman and Hopkins. "There was a time when I knew all [Hopkins'] poems by heart — the one instance in literary history of a major poet having an *oeuvre* small enough so to be encompassed."

1290 "Views." **Listener**, v. 78, no. 2005 (August 31, 1967) 261.

[Burgess, in the words of the cover, celebrates his illnesses.] Suffers from haemorrhoids, dyspepsia, *Thrombo Angitiis Obliterans*. Harley Street later thought the trouble was classical if premature arteriosclerosis. "The diseases of the old are dull, but those of the middle-aged are, surely, interesting. I often visit public bars for my medicine (Harley Street says that alcohol is an efficient vasodilator)" and gives news of some hair-raising pub pathology. From *Krankheit* he moves to crankhood and opposes the tyranny of a decimal British monetary system. Then recalls an old man who, in his innocence of the new racial taboos, happily tried to teach little black children a song about ten little n****r boys.

1291 "The Democracy of Prejudice." **Encounter**, v. 29 (August 1967) 71-75.

Review of **Fifty Works of English Literature We Could Do Without,** by Brigid Brophy, Michael Levey and Charles Osborne. He has never encountered such bloody arrogance. The authors have published an ill-conceived, ignorant and vulgar book. Their hunger for notoriety leads them to attack **Beowolf**. They fail to see that literature is a continuum; that Anglo-Saxon verse contributed the technique of head-rime to Middle English literature; and, blissfully ignorant, they condemn the Middle English York Mystery plays, learnedly arguing that alliteration is the mark of intoxification. Their condemnation of Jonson is devoid of proof; their dismissal of Hopkins is riddled by mindless confusion and mere empty prejudice. Observes that contemporary reviewers are too bitchy by half and parodies the authors' style in hilarious mock condemnations of Jane Austen and Mozart. Reprinted in **Urgent Copy**.

1292 "The Artist as Martyr." **Manchester Guardian**, 1 September 1967, p. 5.

Review of **Flaubert: The Making of the Master**, by Enid Starkie. Dr. Starkie is occasionally pedestrian, but her virtues (diligence in locating illustrative texts, sexual candour and scholarly tidiness) lead to a portrait of Flaubert that qualifies the abiding image of a mother's boy bachelor devoted only to his art. His early baldness was due to mercury treatments for syphilis. He had a tempestuous affair with Louise Colet. "For a prose-writer to put his art first was a new thing then, and the self-lacerations of the stylist must still strike some as the dementia of an unnatural sublimation. If Balzac wrote badly, was careless about form and contemptuous of probability, all was forgiven because of the vitality of his characters . . . . [Flaubert] sacrificed everything to a very demanding art and set standards in it which continue to shame those of us who call ourselves novelists. He had the humility of the priest, not the arrogance of the self-apotheotised."

1293 "Surprise from the Grove." **Observer** (London), 3 September 1967, p. 22.

Review of **The Third Policeman**, by Flann O'Brien; **Dubliners**, by James Joyce.

1294 *"Deja Vu."* **Listener**, v. 78, no. 2006 (September 7, 1967) 315-16.

[Television criticism.] Most television on national holidays is dull stuff. **Way Off Beat** was a repeat. **The Big M** and **Angel Pavement** were promising, fair stuff. Also on a program about the making of the Concorde. He has another try at a dispassionate evaluation of the Beatles but finds "the faces of the performers. . . brutish, wet-lipped, prognathous, and I can't hear their words in order to have a good slam at them. What I chiefly loathe is the *instant* quality of everything, the lack of concern with skill, the horrifying absence of anything approaching comeliness." Records that studio audiences have groaned at his ignorance on panel shows. Disposes of a critic who believes television reviewers should preview their stuff without the benefit of *literary* exercises.

1295 "Politics of Graham Greene." **New York Times Book Review**, September 10, 1967, p. 2, 32, 34.

[Reprint of #1278.]

1296 "Officers and Gentlemen." **Listener**, v. 78, no. 2007 (September 14, 1967) 340-41.

Long review of **The Blast of War** by Harold Macmillan. There is, it appears, one war for gentlemen politicians and another for the enlisted man. For Macmillan, the war was evidently a "great war for epigrams, literary allusions in communiqués, trips round ruins, mess discussions about Herodotus, the maintenance, even with Vyshinsky around, of the gestures of a civilised elite." Reports that, as a former other rank, the war was "mostly an over-long, sometimes dangerous, often boring parenthesis — a sentence within a sentence."

1297 "Thoughts on the Thoughts." **Spectator**, v. 219, no. 7264 (September 15, 1967) 322.

"The point about the Thoughts [of Mao Tse-Tung] is their wholesome near-nullity, their decent harmlessness, their mild boy scout values, their total evasion of the revolutionary, their pleonastic wilsonicity. You can read without being engaged: you don't have to knot your brow, as you do with Marx or Lenin, over metaphysical rugosities. It is like a series of sips, as many or as few as you like, of well-filtered warmish water."

1298 "The Antis: The Weasels of Pop." **Punch**, v. 253, no. 6628 (September 20, 1967) 430-31.

Describes his own experience as a professional musician. Speculates if the rise of pop coincided with the loss of the parlour piano and the introduction of the electronic guitar. Observes that he can tolerate the noises of pop and even the fatuities of its practitioners, but that he detests the burblings of the intellectuals, the prating adults, about it. When these vacuous, trendy critics begin their spiel, he gets sick. When they indiscriminately use the word 'great,' they shame language ("when such mean and cheap janglings are 'great,' what term do we reserve for **Tristran** and the **Choral Symphony?**"). "Do they [these adults] merit vitriol, even a drop of it? Yes, because they corrupt the young, persuading them that the mature world, which produced Beethoven and Schweitzer, sets an even higher value on the transient anodynes of youth than does youth itself. For this they stink to heaven."

1299 "Gash Gold-Vermilion." **Spectator**, v. 219, no. 7265 (September 22, 1967) 326-27.

Review of the **Complete Poems** (4th ed.) by Gerard Manley Hopkins. Hopkins' revision of his work was over-influenced by Bridges, a man who was very small beer as a poet. Finds it unlikely that James Joyce, Cummings or Dylan Thomas were decisively influenced by Hopkins. Considers some of the accidental similarities between the constructions of **Finnegans Wake** and Hopkins' poetry and discusses the influence of music on Hopkins' work (rhythm, heavy head-rimes, the solidity of content of a sequence of chords). Hopkins is a religious poet of the highest rank, perhaps greater than Donne, certainly greater than Herbert and Crashaw. "The devotional writer deals in conventional images of piety; the religious poet shocks, even outrages, by wresting the truths of his faith from their safe dull sanctuaries and placing them in the physical world." Reprinted in **Urgent Copy**.

1300 "Together Again." **Spectator**, v. 219, no. 7266 (September 29, 1967) 363-65.

Review of **The Company She Kept: Mary McCarthy, Herself and Her Writing**, by Doris Grumbach; **A Prelude: Landscapes, Characters and Conversations from the Earlier Years**, by Edmund Wilson. A sharp, perhaps cruel critic, later a heavily autobiographical novelist, McCarthy's stories and novels are works of moral criticism. Wilson's **Memoirs of Hecate County** showed a love of candor for its own sake. "This is the essence of good autobiography, as of good criticism: when we read Wilson on other authors we know there'll be no covering up of ignorance, or of erudition either."

1301 "Letter from England." **Hudson Review**, v. 20, no. 3 (Autumn 1967) 454-58.

His wife is in a hospital suffering from a duodenal ulcer, but the demands of the writer's trade continue. He finds it murderously difficult to find the right ending for his **Enderby Outside**. Meanwhile authors are asked to express their commitment on various issues. Since writers spend their professional lives qualifying their answers and responses to life, it is hard to give a mere yes and no answer. Discusses the disclosure that **Encounter** has been financially supported by the CIA and argues that it is impossible to distinguish between clean and dirty money. Kingsley Amis has done a painful and courageous thing: he has publicly declared against Labour. Observes that never in his youngest and fieriest days did he have any hopes for socialism. "In 1945 I voted Labour, because it seemed that Winston Churchill wanted to keep us in the army forever, and I'd already had six frustrating military years . . . . My political views are mainly negative: I lean towards anarchy; I hate the State. I loathe and abominate that costly, crass, intolerant, inefficient, eventually tyrannical machine which seeks more and more to supplant the individual. The more State we have, the more wretched we become . . . . The Socialists erect a great State tumulus, and it remains when they go out of office. They nationalised the railways and committed the Tories to making that nationalisation work." Expresses his profound distrust of Harold Wilson.

1302 "London Letter." **American Scholar**, v. 36, no. 4 (Autumn 1967) 636-38.

Praises British Rail and recalls, with horror, an American train trip. Observes that the young are becoming more homogeneous, less class-conscious, and approves of the fact. Finds marijuana harmless; opium, for him at any rate, is not addictive. Severe punishment for the possession of soft drugs is excessive, but the drug-taking of the young, like their passion for pop and photography ("it's not an art but a *tissage* of little tricks") testifies to their desire for instant gratification. "A generation that seems to be revolting against the mechanical disciplines of adult life is itself very much in the grip of the mechanical. What I miss in the young is self-reliance."

1303 "The God of the Beatles." **Listener**, v. 78, no. 2010 (October 5, 1967) 447-48.

[Television criticism.] On documentaries of Trappist Cistercians, the steamship **Queen Mary** as well as a drama on the expectations and frustrations of British youth. Also on an interview with the Beatles and their Maharishi. "There was George Harrison going on about immanent deity and the proper use of the *mantra*, and John Lennon saying that God was inspissative like electricity, and both believing in metempsychosis (is *Beatle* the badge of an achieved *kharma* or one still to come?). But the real point of their evidence was that a daily dive into the timeless brought them up again fighting fit and tingling with energy, saying (Lennon's words, I think): 'Where is it? Let's get at it.' Meaning more pop and dollars and the OBE next time. There are perhaps safer varieties of religious experience.''

1304 "The Modicum is the Messuage." **Spectator**, v. 219, no. 7268 (October 13, 1967) 427.

McLuhan is drawing a respectable income out of a modest principal of ideas. He was probably influenced by the Cambridge aesthetic of the 30s which taught that, in a work of art, the form is the content, the medium is the message. "Applying the Cambridge aesthetic to all the communication media, he is led to distort it in a very interesting way. He deliberately refuses to distinguish between a medium as the determinant of an art-form and a medium as a transmissive device . . . . McLuhan is absolved from the need to get to the core of a communication-process by his deliberate identification of the artistic 'message' with the purely informative or didactic one." His observations concerning, say, the influence of the typewriter on the art of authorship are suggestive. His insistence on the worthiness of the advertisement is probably right, but some of his distinctions between "hot" and "cool" media are nonsensical, and his refusal to accept the fact that ideas are stronger than media invites skepticism.

1305 "Beyond the Oxgrave." **Spectator**, v. 219, no. 7270 (October 27, 1967) 493.

Review of **A New Canon of English Poetry**, by James Reeves and Martin Seymour-Smith. Praises the book and includes selections from the poems.

1306 "Commercials." **Listener**, v. 78, no. 2014 (November 2, 1967) 583-84.

[Television criticism.] On television commercials, **The Prisoner**, an adaptation of Aldous Huxley's **After Many a Summer** ("Judith Arthy was a suitably bathycolpous and callipygous Virginia with a nice line in post-coital languor"), **A Black Candle for Mrs. Gogarty**, a study of some women vagrants who assert the right to be underprivileged, and an episode on the David Frost show ("that once nice boy is beginning to deserve a bit of a clobber").

1307 "Sins of the State." **Listener**, v. 78, no. 2018 (November 30, 1967) 730-31.

[Television criticism.] The Oxford Union debated the motion: "The Roman Catholic Church has no place in the 20th century." The pig-headed Ian Paisley, by endorsing the motion, helped to defeat it. Also on a dramatisation of the Sinyafsky-Daniel trial ("animated by a noble indignation"), the State's denial of pensions on the curious ground that the recipients are *too* old, a performance of Gounod's Faust ("faintly preposterous") and a tribute to Benjamin Britten.

1308 "Why All This Fuss About Libraries?" **Spectator**, v. 219 (November 3, 1967) 529.

Large libraries are antipathetic. Gives an account of some of his own unhappy experiences in large libraries as boy and man and proposes, in a moment of Johnsonian speculation, to consider books as members of a harem. "A book should be a whore, not a lady. Except, of course, that the place of a book is in the home: there the image breaks down. Let us say, then, that one's personal library should be a kind of harem." The large libraries induce agoraphobia. "That some libaries should actually house such millions is monstrously unnecessary, like the stars . . . . And this same trade [of Burgess the novelist] will flourish best if I stop myself thinking of all those millions of volumes in the British Museum Library and the others that haven't yet caught fire from Caesar's ships or Caesar's fear of the honest spirit of inquiry of his subjects. The writer has to think of himself as a lone star. To know that he's a mere speck in the galaxies of Bloomsbury [site of the BM] is dispiriting and inhibiting. No writer is great enough for the great libraries." [Reprinted in #1334.]

1309 "Don't Cook Mother Goose." **New York Times Book Review**, November 5, 1967, p. 1, 48, 50.

Argues that nursery rhymes, for all their apparent blood-and-thunder content, are better crafted (and better for children) than commercial TV jingles. At their best, they are literature, an exploitation of ambiguity, mystery and verbal magic. Includes many verses, both traditional and contemporary, to present his case.

1310 "A Bit of a Sissy." **Punch**, v. 253, no. 6636 (November 15,1967) 757.

Review of **The Infirm Glory**, by Godfrey Winn. The author is an inveterate name-dropper, a people's crusader who hobnobs with the nobility, and he does not deserve the coveted title of being a good craftsman. "Clichés, invertebrate sentences, images imperfectly visualised — these are cognate with an impatience with form, even chronology . . . . Gossippy discursiveness is his line."

1311 "The Good Companion." **Spectator**, v. 219, no. 7273 (November 17, 1967) 609.

Review of **The Oxford Companion to English Literature**, ed. by Paul Harvey, revised by Dorothy Eagle. It is a charming work, full of oddities, and fortunately devoid of the impartiality and impersonality of the encylopaedia. "It's more like reading a Michel Butor novel than a cold work of reference." The principle of selection of the post-Harvey entries is curious. Many moderns are entered; many moderns are excluded. "As for Anthony Burgess, I am reconciled now to seeing the name survive only as that of a seventeenth century divine who wrote too many sermons on the one text from St. John." Concocts a fanciful plot based on entries in the book. "There is no end to the uses of Harvey, as I know. As I very well know. As I know as well as any literary man living." Reprinted in **Urgent Copy**.

1312 "If Oedipus Had Read His Levi-Strauss." **Washington Post Book World**, 26 November 1967, p. 6.

Review of **The Scope of Anthropology**, by Claude Levi-Strauss. The book demonstrates that territories far separated share archetypal myths. There is, in the Algonquin and Iroquois Indian legends, a close connection between riddling and incest, just as there is in the myth of Oedipus. "If Oedipus [after correctly answering the riddle of the Sphinx] had read his Levi-Strauss, he would have known that incest was on its way. The man who solves the insoluble puzzle has, symbolically, disrupted nature. Since incest is the ultimate perversion of nature, nature is shocked to death." Examines the riddle/incest theme of **Finnegans Wake** and and of his own **MF**. [This article should be mandatory for all readers of **MF**.]

1313 "What Is Pornography?" **Spectator**, v. 219, no. 7275 (December 1, 1967) 683-84.

The banning of **Last Exit to Brooklyn** on the ground that it is a pornographic work is a sorry and disquieting affair. Argues that pornography depicts social acts of sex, often of a perverse and fantastic nature, and without regard to the limits of physical possibility. Under this head, **Last Exit** is clearly not pornographic. It does not conduce to a desire for masturbation; therefore it is not pornographic and twelve good men have made an error of classification. They have confounded an emetic work with a pornographic one. The judgment is a "sorry and disquieting affair. It is not only a question of the inability of the law to encompass matters of aesthetics . . . . It is a matter of the law's apparent inability to cope with the semantics of its own terms of reference." [Reprinted in #1401.]

1314 "Books They Liked Best." **Washington Post Book World**, 3 December 1967, p. 16.

A list of favorite books of the year. Burgess lists **Poems of Gerard Manley Hopkins; The Ambidextrous Universe**, by Martin Gardner; and **The Scope of Anthropology**, by Claude Levi-Strauss. On a separate page under the heading "Books They Liked Least," Burgess cites **The Infirm Glory**, by Godfrey Winn. [For the review see #1310.]

1315 "Prompt Book." **Spectator**, v. 219 (December 15, 1967) 751-52.

Review of **The Oxford Companion to the Theatre**. 3d ed. Edited by Phyllis Hartnoll. The work includes Osborne, Whiting, Ionesco, Joan Littlewood, Arnold Wesker. Some players are also included; but others, notably Donald Pleasence, Maggie Smith and Ernest Milton, the greatest Hamlet of this century, are bafflingly excluded. "The article by Owen Rutter on the Malay *wayang kulit* — to take one of the two kinds of recherché drama of which I can claim some knowledge — is wonderfully concise and accurate . . . . This is altogether a good **Companion**, and no library — however private and constricted — should be without it."

1316 "Japanese Pillow Pattern." **Spectator**, v. 219, no. 7278 (December 22, 1967) 782-83.

Review of the **Pillow Book of Sei Shonagon**, translated and edited by Ivan Morris. Includes comments on the absence, until recently, of English lady novelists. The joys of this author are set in a closed, civilized world; she evinces an almost pathological worship of the royal family and a detestation of the lower orders which suggests the hypnopaedia of **Brave New World**. "We can forgive her callousness towards her social and intellectual inferiors when she shows such feeling for the natural world, such zest in ritual, colour, and the minutiae of civilised life. She seems as close to the modern reader as his own pillow. It is hard to think of her sleeping in her day-clothes and, following the fashion, making her teeth black."

1317 "Reflections on a Golden Ring." **Listener**, v. 78, no. 2022 (December 28, 1967) 858-59.

[Television criticism.] Television coverage of musical events introduces irrelevant distractions ("when I put that symphony — conducted by Karajan — on my record-player, I keep seeing Bernstein capering and smirking between me and it") and concludes, after much brooding on the subject, that radio is the only substitute for the concert-hall experience. Notes the declining interest in the arts on television. Also on an adaptation of **Vanity Fair** and a program called Dante's Inferno.

1318 "**Spectator** Symposium on 1968." **Spectator**, v. 219 (December 29, 1967) 804.

[Six of the **Spectator's** contributors venture their hopes and fears for the new year.] Regrets that "The most evil and incompetent government my generation has seen will still be huffing away at the beginning of 1969." Hopes that the trade unions will see reason and come to terms with the new age of technology. Comments on censorship, law of libel, library charges and income tax averaging to help authors. "I hope that the process of national dissolution will be so accelerated that at last citizens will feel genuine alarm and seek a change of government through loud words and even public violence. What I know (as opposed to what I would hope if I had hope) is that the pound will be further devalued in the new year, wage claims flourish, government by edict come nearer and (by the law of sympathy which most patently operates when Labour is in power) the weather be atrocious."

1319 "Steinerian Agony." **Encounter**, v. 29 (December 1967) 79-82.

Review of **Language and Silence**, by George Steiner. Dr. Steiner's message that language cannot properly cope with the horrors of Auschwitz and Buchenwald should not be met by a silence which appears to be acquiescence. Argues that the quantitative arguments can be discounted. "To make one Jew, or Catholic, or Lutheran, or free-thinking intellectual, drown, flayed, in a bath of human ordure is as much a token of the existence of evil as the world needs." Further, Dr. Steiner's other argument that German is the language of evil, and music the language of silence, ought to be resisted or questioned. Reprinted in **Urgent Copy**.

1320 [Untitled Essay on the Nature of God] In **The God I Want**, edited by James Alexander Hugh Mitchell, p. 57-70. London: Constable, 1967. Indianapolis: Bobbs-Merrill, 1967.

[Cast in the form of Socratic discussion between "Anthony" and "Burgess."] His youthful God was a big vindictive indivisibility. "The thing to do was to avoid hell, and it seemed impossible." Burgess is interested in God as a paradigmatic essence, not the anthropomorphic God of the Irish or Malays. The God he wants is a free and independent essence who does not give a damn about humanity. Argues that God, if we look for a human reference, is more apt to resemble a human artefact (a bridge, a symphony) than the human artisan. Considers the extent to which truth, goodness and beauty are all part of Ultimate Reality. "Here's where God differs from a sublunary symphony or picture. He's a work of art that appreciates itself. Infinitely beautiful and infinitely appreciative of His own beauty. If you like, a work of art equipped with infinite intelligence and infinite sensibility, but all directed towards this infinite enjoyment of its own infinite essence." Observes that traditional religion has held back social progress, and that the God he wants is actively needed by an affluent society.

1321 "Sleepbox." **Listener**, v. 79, no. 2026 (January 25, 1968) 122-23.

[Television criticism.] On the phatic and reassuring elements in television ("the screen adds to its dream properties a very comforting set of functions — nightlight, the world going safely on, guardian angels ensuring that death won't suddenly leap (this only happens in the total dark, in total loneliness). I've had some very comfortable sleeps thus protected.") Also reviews **Jamie On a Flying Visit** and an adaptation of **The Portrait of a Lady** ("a very large triumph.")

1322 "Murder Most Fair — by Agatha the Good." **Life**, v. 63 (December 1, 1967) 8.

Review of **Third Girl**, by Agatha Christie. "Agatha is Greek for 'good.' Paradoxically, it's a sense of the fundamental goodness or wholesomeness of the world that emerges from all these studies of crime and detection . . . . The non-highbrows among us are delighted to be merely pleased by being puzzled, entering a world that, though full of danger and nastiness, is fundamentally as wholesome as a Berkshire apple, and engaging the perplexities of people who, though very real, are set in patterns as cool and intellectual and abstract as a Euclidean theorem. It is in the nature of Agatha to continue to be good."

1323 "Graves and Omar." **Encounter**, v. 30 (January 1968) 77-78.

Review of **The Rubaiyyat of Omar Khayaam**. A New Translation with Critical Commentaries by Robert Graves and Omar Ali-Shah. It is well known that Fitzgerald traduced Omar Khayyam: he misrepresented the poet as a material epicurean opposed to sufism. Now Graves, with the help of an accurate manuscript provided by Ali-Shah, attempts to set the record straight. His poetic reworking of a literal translation from the Persian is regrettably devoid of rhyme, lacks much associative magic and "The task of achieving a true glamour that will drive out Fitzgerald's false is evidently still there for some poet's undertaking." Reprinted in **Urgent Copy**.

1324 "My Country, 'Tis of Thee." **Spectator**, v. 220, no. 7287 (February 23, 1968) 228.

"When Dr Johnson called patriotism the last refuge of a scoundrel, he undoubtedly had politicians in mind." Excoriates Prime Minister Harold Wilson's record, denies Wilson's right to speak for the country, or to invoke the term patriotism. Examines his own responses to patriotic stimuli. The term Britain leaves him cold. England amasses a Christmas parcel of sentimental perceptions, but it also evokes repressive English history. One of his ancestors was burned at the stake. The annual celebration of Guy Fawkes is a vindictive commemoration. Drake's piracies were merely immoral and English colonial history is a sordid record of gin and Bibles. English literature and music present a sound claim to sentimental attachment but to fight for them would be absurd. Dismisses the notion that England is a place full of kindness, fair play, political freedom, freedom of the printed word, courtesy or civility. Argues that the really important faiths best flourish in small nations and expresses his fear of the new cold economic agglomeration [the Common Market]. "Words mean what the demagogues want them to mean; we must refuse to be moved. If 'Britain' means the Labour party, I glory in my lack of patriotism."

1325 "Future of Anglo-American." **Harper's**, v. 236, no.1413 (February 1968) 53-56.

The future development of English will be determined by the scientific and technological domination of the future society. The names for many things, species of birds, the names of plants, will be largely forgotten, and vast technical lexica (perhaps not well understood) will be common. Since generalization, both in common speech and scientific applications, involves lying, there is a danger of total state control of the language along the lines of Orwell's **1984** in order to prevent chaos, arguments about meanings, verbal speculations generally. This outcome, the development of some future Newspeak, is unlikely. Slang, the pale substitute for poetry, which the young have tried to hurl at the growing corpus of abstract language, is vague, ephemeral and ineffectual. American pronunciation will be the received standard wherever English is spoken. The grammar of English in 2067 will be spare. "We shall have to cherish our poets in the future far more than we have ever done in the past. It is only they who will be able to bring back the flavor of the particular to words that — cut off from nature — will be gray neutral counters. They will have the job of reminding us that words relate to things, not to abstract ideas."

1326 "Vieux Chapeau." **New York Times Book Review**, March 3, 1968, pp. 4-5.

Review of **Les Belles Images**, by Simone de Beauvoir. Translated by Patrick O'Brien. The French think too highly of their cuisine, couture and prowess in amour. An Englishman or American may Create a modest short story, not dreaming of an accolade; the French publish their bloated short stories and reward them with many and vainglorious prizes. This book is a dismal nullity. Its description of a married couple in the Eden of Parisian *chic* and affluence in which the heroine rejects what the world calls health in favor of what the world calls disease (sense of sin, desire for reality) has been better done in T.S. Eliot's **The Cocktail Party**. De Beauvoir is serving up yesterday's mashed potatoes with the flourishes of an Escoffier. "She ought to visit the big world outside France, where they manage these things better — meaning the novel of domestic frustration, dead souls, affluent despair, and all the cognate fictional subjects which (dare one whisper it?) are growing just a little stale."

1327 "Portrait of the Artist in Middle Age." **Nation**, v. 206, no. 10 (March 4, 1968) 309-310.

Review of **Giacomo Joyce**, by James Joyce. Edited by Richard Ellmann. This work is not really a serious part of the Joyce *oeuvre*, but more of an essay in private onanism occasioned by his infatuation with a young, rounded, voluptuous Jewish student. The work is a finger exercise. Joyce was learning a prose technique suitable for Stephen in **Ulysses**.

1328 "Protestant Catholics." **Punch**, v. 254, no. 6652 (March 6, 1968) 357.

Review of **Songs of Irish Rebellion**, by George-Denis Zimmermann. "Dr. Zimmermann, whose scholarship in this field is formidable, even mad, is a Swiss, and hence one of the bloody foreigners who were never worth a roasted fart to Ireland. But his subject needs a rabid application to sheer historical fact; it needs neutrality, and his nation has for a long time specialised in neutrality." Zimmermann has well conveyed the glamour of all the bad times of oppression and the more heartening days of struggle in this well-made Swiss box.

1329 "Views." **Listener**, v. 79, no. 2032 (March 7, 1968) 295-96.

On his difficulties in getting a passport renewed, and his wife's shock on learning that her official name was now Llewella (not Llewela). She was told by a "petty official that this . . . was the right spelling, the new reformed spelling, a legitimate child of the state however spawned out of carelessness, and she would now have to change her name by deed poll to the name some snotty little penpusher had accidentally given to her." Announces the dismal news that decimal time will soon follow the damnable innovation of decimal coinage. Predicts the imminence of the regraduation of the circle from 360 old degrees to 100 new in the service of a hypergallic logic.

1330 "State Favoritism in Literature." **Sunday Telegraph**, 12 March, 1968, p. 14.

1331 "Dare to Be a Catman." **Spectator**, v. 220, no. 7290 (March 15, 1968) 330-31.

Long reminiscence of a Siamese cat named Lalage ("She attached herself like a limpet to my wife and decided to hate me . . . . She insisted on sleeping in the bed and lying, like a sword, between my wife and myself") leads to an appreciation for the reissue of Christabel Lady Aberconway's **A Dictionary of Cat Lovers**. The book does not answer the question why some people adore, and others abominate, cats. "I am sure, however, of this, that cats have nothing to do with moral character. They go beyond good and evil and are hence probably closer to ultimate reality than the dogs we make in our own image . . . . We can't imagine God as a dog, but He may well be a cat with (Old Possum's words) an ineffable name."

1332 "A Good Man Destroyed — Hilariously." **Life**, v. 64, no. 2 (March 15, 1968) 8.

Review of **Cocksure**, by Mordecai Richler. This is probably one of the funniest books of the year in the service of a satirical intention: to depict the contemporary Anglo-American ethos in which promiscuity is a substitute for passion and anti-racist committees take the place of human charity. "Some readers will consider this novel obscene, so I'd better forestall them. It contains a large number of obscene elements . . . . The human body becomes Swiftianly nasty . . . . But nothing is dwelt on with depraved fascination: we are conducted so rapidly through the contemporary sewers that the trip seems positively bracing. Anyway, the obscenity belongs not to the book but to the world it lacerates. But, please remember, it's a funny book, gorgeously so. I wish I'd written it myself."

1333 "London Letter." **American Scholar**, v. 37 (Spring 1968) 312-15.

Considers the banning of **Last Exit to Brooklyn**, examines the meaning of the word pornography, finds that banning some books will lead to the banning of nearly all books but the most staid, and concludes that "There is never any justification for censorship. It doesn't protect us from corruption; it merely anesthetizes, blinkers, dehumanizes." Considers the gloom and doom found in the daily papers and describes the **Daily Mirror** for his American audience. [The first part of this letter is a somewhat revised version of "What is Pornography?" See #1314, 1401.]

1334 "What's All This Fuss About Libraries:" **Library Journal**, v. 93 (March 15, 1968) 1114-15.

[Reprint of #1308.]

1335 "Paperback Tiger." **Spectator**, v. 220, no. 7292 (March 29, 1968) 410..

Review of **The Making of a Publisher**, by Victor Weybright. "The audience for such a book may be regarded as a rather specialised one — publishers who want to see what is said about them by a confrére, as well as how the NAL [New American Library, founded by Weybright] described, integrity-wise, its Spenglerian parabola; authors who want excuses for distrusting publishers even more than they do, or even want to learn to like them."

1336 "Pukka Trumps and Lost Char-poys." **Spectator**, v. 220, no. 7294 (April 12, 1968) 499.

Review of **Hobson-Jobson** [an Anglo-Indian glossary], by Henry Ule and H.C. Burnell. "We threw the Empire away before it was ripe for abandonment, and we threw away a great linguistic and folkloric heritage at the same time. I mean, of course, a living and continuing heritage, not a museum. *Competition-wallahs* and servants of John Company did not spend all their time beating the natives. They turned themselves into very competent amateur philologists and anthropologists, and what they have preserved for us they have preserved out of love."

1337 "Romantic Ireland's Dead and Gone." **Punch**, v. 254, no. 6660 (May 1, 1968) 651.

Review of **The Irish**, by Donald S. Connery and **1916 — The Easter Rising**, ed. by Owen Dudley Edwards and Fergus Pyle. The Irish, like the Russians, have a tendency to manic depression, a desperate bibulosity, an inability to cope with what the unimaginative term the truth. The factories are now going up, the priests have less power, and Ireland is likely to profit from the mistakes of other industrialised societies. **1916** provides the raw meat, the source-stuff, of history. It is the more welcome for that. "We have had enough romantic evocations."

1338 "Think-tank." **Spectator**, v. 220 (May 3, 1968) 598-600.

Review of **The Year 2000**, by Herman Kahn and Anthony J. Wiener. Wells was the last of the utopian futurists; after him, the fictional prophets, Orwell and Huxley, were dystopian and dyspeptic. Wiener and Kahn predict a world of progressive computerization, genetic control, cheap contraceptives: a world of megacities with national defence lines in outer space. "It is very sobering to observe how small a part Great Britain is going to play in the plastic, computerised, sterile future. A dead power, swallowed up in the concept of Europe. . . increasingly bizarre in our juvenile behaviour-patterns, a cold but colourful buffer between American and Western Europe, neither of which will take us seriously." The book contains no surprises, and he hopes it will have dated terribly by the year 2,000.

1339 "Russian Roulette at 4:30 A.M.." **Listener**, v. 79 (May 9, 1968) 614-15.

[Television criticism.] Praises the quantity of television available in Beverly Hills at 4:30 A.M. and wishes that both British quality and American quantity were equally available. Records shock of American film producers at low cost of British productions. Also on **The Man Behind You, No Easy Walk, The State of the Jews** and **The Lion and the Dragon**.

1340 "Let Your Son Be a Spy." **Punch**, v. 254 (May 15, 1968) 708-10.

[Prompted by remarks of Louis Hagen as reported by the **Sunday Times**. "If I had a son, and he seemed reckless and intelligent, then I would tell him to go in for the intelligence service. Really, it's one of the safest jobs in the world."] Burgess pretends to be a teacher-counsellor who delivers a flavorful and slightly risqué harangue on spying as a career to a dull student.

1341 "Enjoying Walton." **Listener**, v. 79, no. 2045 (June 6, 1968) 750-51.

[Television criticism.] On William Walton's music (the **Portsmouth Point Overture** and **Crown Imperial March** help him to adjust to the daily damnation of writing), on nuns who have thrown off the medieval robes which derive from Islamic dress, a program on American electioneering ("American politics seems to have a sweaty meeting-tent quality of revivalism about it that justifies the simple appeals to fundamentalist morality") and some miscellaneous dramas.

1342 "The Emigrants: Malaya." **Punch**, v. 254, no. 6666 (June 12, 1968) 852-54.

Dissatisfied with a penurious life, he applied for a teaching post to the isle of Sark. On regaining sobriety, he discovered that he had applied to the Colonial Office for a job in Malaya. Describes the worried, harried moments of departure, the trip to Malaya on the Dutch ship **Willem Ruys**, the beginnings of his love for Malaya. Expresses shocked dismay over the mere hedonistic exile, the man who loves Malaya merely for its creature comforts, and chooses to learn nothing about "the fascination of Malay syntax, Islamic divorce-laws, the matriarchal traditions of Negri Sembilan, the eating habits of elephants, the temperament of hamadryads, the techniques of Chinese acupuncture." Also describes his eventual return to England. "For my wife and myself there would never again be the old frustrations, voiced over draught cider and five small cigarettes a day. I had learned my own new tricks, and I would get money for performing them."

1343 "Private Dialect of Husbands and Wives." **Vogue**, v. 151 (June 1968) 118-19.

Fears that his own kind of kidding may be the death of him. Confesses he once gave a fictitious lecture on Grasmere Tadworth (1578-1621). Worse, he once listed his wife as his hobby, and now feels called upon to explain the fact. Observes that a marriage is a civilization in miniature; it is broken up at the peril of one's soul. Language is the essence of a civilization and gives examples of private communication between himself and his wife. "I think I have a vocation for gaining the maximal social fulfillment, which means communicative fulfillment, which means even a kind of spiritual fulfillment, out of living with a particular woman. But, frightened of the big words, and also incurably facetious, I have to talk of my wife as a hobby . . . ."

1344 "Frenglish." **Encounter**, v. 30, no. 6 (June 1968) 75-78.

Review of **Mots d'Heures: Gousses, Rames**, by Luis D'Antin van Rooten. "I am all for the George-Herbert-type poems about the double significance of J and C, sonnets whose lines are single anapaests, acrostics, monstrous baroque conceits, riddles like the Anglo-Saxon ones, grossness disguised as decency and *vice versa*. When politicians debase language, it is up to the writers to restore its dignity . . . . The macaronic dilettantes and crossword compilers are nearer the heart of language than they probably know."

1345 "The Calamity of Authorship." **Country Life**, v. 143, no. 3722 (July 4, 1968) 56-57.

Reviews of **The Author's Empty Purse and the Rise of the Literary Agent**, by James Hepburn; **The Women in Shakespeare's Life**, by Ivor Brown; **John Dee**, by Richard Deacon.

1346 "Televalediction." **Listener**, v. 80, no. 2049 (July 4, 1968) 27-28.

[Television criticism.] Laments suicide of Tony Hancock, a promising comic, and looks back on 5 years of television reviews. Praises the BBC for its quality, integrity and daring. "The best thing for me in a whole decade has been **An Age of Kings**, the next best the adaptation of Ford Madox Ford's **Parade's End** . . . ." Announces his imminent departure from Britain for tax reasons. "Many years of hard slog and small earnings are sometimes suddenly rewarded with a year of exceptional affluence — a year that comes only once in a lifetime. Unfortunately, that year is treated by the taxman like any other, and the state gulps nearly all the cake."

1347 "Wowsers Join Larrikins." **Country Life**, v. 144, no. 3724 (July 18, 1968) 190-91.

Reviews of **Southern Exposure**, by David Beal and Donald Horne; **Encyclopaedia of Ireland**; **Stable Management and Exercise**, by M. Horace Hayes.

1348 "Johnson(?) on Johnson." **Horizon**, v. 10, no. 3 (Summer 1968) 60-64.

An irreverent, parodic biographical sketch of Dr. Samuel Johnson, the English lexicographer, critic and man of letters.

1349 "Involvement: Writers Reply." **London Magazine**, v. 8 (August 1968) 9.

[Writers are polled on the question of political involvement. For the complete text of Burgess' response see below.] "It's not the job of the creative writer to be a polemicist. To be committed to anything more sectarian than a belief in total individual freedom is to subscribe to something less than the truth. If I have political views, these are held in a private capacity, and I would not associate my creative persona with them. Organizers of public opinion have always been failed creators — demagogues, minor poets, pamphleteers."

1350 "Thoughts of a Belated Father." **Spectator**, v. 221, no. 7315 (September 6, 1968) 322.

His son, now four, communicates reasonably well. Told that "The wort fulderbill in spurgeous plumchucks spries most corpily when fritched on its netherwise frimtips" he responds with "You did but I didn't" or "that's rude." etc. He has a seemingly endless capacity for producing instant squalor; he also shows a demented creativity. Burgess can do without Paolo Andrea at his present stage. "A child is just something that has to be turned into an adult, and the quicker it's done the better for everybody." Darkly doubts if paternity or maternity are good for the soul. "I once knew a girl with whom I carried on a delightful intellectual correspondence. Such wit, such taste, such treasurable *mots*. Then she had a baby and became an idiot. This was biology at work."

1351 "Easy Money: Brought With the Wind." **Punch**, v. 255, no. 6681 (September 25, 1968) 428-30.

Gambles a ten-shilling note found in St. Leonards-on-Sea. After one day of betting on the horses, the sum is transformed into 40,000 pounds. It is invested in the publishing firm founded by one Reginald Horsley. Poor Horsley publishes a ghost-written book about a pop-star; finds himself sued for libel; loses all. Burgess now drops occasional ten-shilling notes to study peoples' reactions. Most are unimaginative with the windfall. [This entire account is, of course, largely fanciful; the betting facts are probably accurate.]

1352 "London Letter." **American Scholar**, v. 37, (Autumn 1968) 647-49.

Announces he will leave England. The taxes imposed on writers are extortionate. Gives the example of a writer friend who earned $192,000; the Exchequor claimed $180,000 of this sum. Feels that, for the sake of his art and his family, he must go into exile. Discusses his work on a film adaptation of the life of Shakespeare, tells an amusing story [see #1356] about Dr. Johnson's distaste for salads to a stewardess (who does not understand the point) and comments on the current temper (strikes, student protest) of life in England.

1353 "Amis and Enemies." **Listener**, v. 80, no. 2063 (October 10 1968) 475.

Review of **I Want It Now** by Kingsley Amis. Amis shows an emergent moral philosophy, and his invectives against the rich are marked by a virulence verging on hatred.

1354 "Fed Up to Here." **New York Times Book Review**, October 20, 1968, p. 66-67.

An open letter to the **New York Times**. Holds that far too many cook-books are being published. Ridicules exotic foods featured in most cook-books. For letters by B.H. Fussell and D.E. Waldo, see **New York Times Book Review**, 10 November 1968, p. 52.

1355 "Joyce Cary's Heroic Journey Up." Life, v. 65 (October 25, 1968) 15.

Review of **Joyce Cary** by Malcolm Foster. Cary "fell into the error of all literary tyros: he thought it possible to write great novels with one hand and salable bosh with the other. It didn't work: a whiff of greatness infected the stories, and the **Post** didn't want them any more. From then on, it is the old story of laudatory reviews and wretched royalties — until belated fame came with **The Horse's Mouth**."

1356 "Views." **Listener**, v. 80, no. 2068 (November 14, 1968) 634.

On American stereotypes of foreigners and his failure to interest British salesmen in the act of selling him a Bedford van. On a plane trip which features some contrived Britishry, he confronts a stewardess who asks him for his favorite salad dressing. "I asked her to sit down, which she did gingerly. Then I asked her if she had heard of Dr Johnson. (No.) He was a great lexicographer. (Huh?) His recipe for salad was: take a lettuce, wash it, dry it, season it, and then — (Yes?) Throw it away. But why, asked this delicious girl, after a very long pause, did he want to throw it away after taking so much trouble over it? I muttered to myself over more Olde Milwaukee Ayle . . . ."

1357 "A Colonial Christmas." **Punch**, v. 255, no. 6691 (December 4, 1968) 801-802.

Describes the Christmas festivities in a place called "Tahi Panas" — complete with satirical carols, bibulous members of the Islamic faithful ("So the Muslims are happy to celebrate along with the Christians — no pork, this being *haram*, but plenty of alcohol, this being also *haram* but not quite so much"), a stranded Land Rover on a beach with the North China Sea ebbing in, rescue from the crocodiles, and the award of a third prize as a castaway in a costume party.

1358 "Brothers Grimm and Their Famous Law for Linguists." **Horizon**, v. 10 (Winter 1968) 66-72.

Gives an account of the brothers Jacob and Wilhelm Grimm, their interest in fairy tales and philology, and explains Grimm's law. Observes that the fairy tales, far from being distinctively German, record the myths of all lands and all people. The nightmare element in them is partly justified by the fact that the stories are lay moral sermons; they instil a profound sense of the pre-Christian moral order, and an offense is soon followed by an inexorable apparatus of punishment. Reprinted in **Urgent Copy** under title: "Snow White and Rose Red."

1359 "Introduction." In **Last Exit to Brooklyn,** by Hubert Selby, Jr. 2d [post-trial] ed. London: Calder and Boyars, 1968, pp. xiii-xvii.

Gives an account of the book's arraignment under the Obscene Publications Act, and quotes the opinion of Mr. Leo Gradwell that the book would tend to deprave and corrupt. Argues that, although the burden of proving the book's capacity to corrupt rested with the prosecution, no such proof was offered; mere pious expressions of horror were sufficient to ban the book. **Exit** describes the actions of a set of misfits, perverts and predators in a symbiosis that makes Dante's hell seem paradisal. It conveys, with machine-like transcriptions of actuality, variations of *fellatio* and *anal coition* without any of the literary condiments to inflame the reader. The characters are sufficiently individualized so that their brutal careers and destinies invite compassion. The reader wants to change the society in which this brutality occurs. The book is therefore kinetic; it leads to the impulse for reform. To that extent it is a lesser work than true literary creations in which the emotions are discharged within the book itself. "How this honest and terrible book could ever be regarded as obscene (that is, designed for depravity and corruption) is one of the small mysteries of the decade."

1360 "Genesis and Headache." In **Afterwords; Novelists on Their Novels.** Ed. by Thomas McCormack. New York: Harper, 1968, pp. 29-47.

Describes the plot of the book and the literary and historical issues raised by the novel. "**Nothing Like the Sun** was, I know, a literary task almost haemorrhoidally agonising, and it must have consumed yards of paper and thousands of cigarettes . . . . One thing I can remember, and that is that nearly every page of typescript was commenced at least six times. I would write a sentence, even a paragraph, and then tear up the sheet it was on and start again. I was not correcting so much as enriching . . . . The beauties of the plain style are often urged on me, the duty of excising rather than adding. But the Elizabethan spirit doesn't take kindly to the Heminwayesque, the spare and laconic, nor does my own spirit. I don't think that **Nothing Like the Sun** has too many words; I think perhaps it has too few. One has to be true to one's own temperament, and mine is closer to that of the baroque writers than that of the stark toughies. To hell with cheeseparing and verbal meanness: it all reeks of Banbury puritanism."

1361 "Did Shakespeare Mean That, or Is It a Printer's Error." **Chicago Tribune,** 12 January 1969, p. 5.

Review of **The First Folio of Shakespeare.** Prepared by Charlton Hinman. Shakespeare, the dramatist who wrote for money (not posterity), probably did not care whether or not his plays were published. And yet, probably groaning, he permitted quarto editions of his plays to appear in his life-time to foil the pirates. The first folio of Shakespeare's plays was put out by Hemminge and Condell, fellow players, in 1623. Thanks to their act of devotion, we have Ben Jonson's tribute to his fellow playwright. We also have many plays that would otherwise have been lost to posterity. Quotes three lines from **Troilus,** and asks if the error is a printer's error. Imagines that Hemminge and Condell rescued the manuscripts from the flames which destroyed the Globe theatre in 1613. Records his gratitude to the men who first issued, and then re-issued, this edition ("the finest present any bookman could wish to have").

1362 "Letter from Europe." **American Scholar,** v. 38, no. 2 (Spring-Autumn 1969) 297-99.

Essay on Malta. The Church is too powerful, the bureaucracy is maddening, but the language is fascinating.

1363 "Lore and Disorder." **Spectator,** v. 222, no. 7347 (April 18, 1969) 511-12.

Review of **The British Folklorists: A History** and **Peasant Customs and Savage Myths,** both by Richard M. Dorson. Folklore implies the quaint, the picturesque, the harmless. In fact, folklore, as Edward Clodd demonstrated, is pure dynamite. "If God had wished to demonstrate the whole range of available paganism, he could not have done better than to will Christianity into being. It is all there — vegetation god sacrificed and resurrected, water-worship in the form of baptism, solstice ceremonies, absorbing the substance of the god by eating him." Remarks that, as a youth, he was given Grant Allen's **Evolution of the Idea of God.** The purpose was to snuff out his inherited Christianity; the book had quite the opposite effect.

1364 "Troubled Bubbles." **Spectator,** v. 222, no. 7351 (May 16, 1969) 655.

Review of **Secret Laughter,** by Walter de la Mare. "On the whole, the Walter de la Mare world is a sinister one. The cobbler says 'Grill me some bones.' A fish in a frying-pan speaks and then lies wearily back in the hissing fat. The mould in the cellar turns into a creature called John Mouldy (though not in this volume). Often this quality seems imposed rather than genuine . . . ."

1365 "Views." **Listener**, v. 81, no. 2095 (May 22, 1969) 709.

Chicken pox and influenza alter his neural chemistry. "The smell, texture, whole concept of bacon became not merely gross but somehow immoral, even evil." Debussy's **Arabesques** convey a quality of evil. On the other hand, he apprehends parts of **Uncle Tom's Cabin** and the whole of 'Hugh Selwyn Mauberley' more directly; scenes and lines become palpable as objects. Also on the bizarre notions of literary propriety in Malta.

1366 "The Reticence of **Ulysses**." **Spectator**, v. 222 (June 7, 1969) 748.

Written in Malta, where the censorship nibbled at one of his blameless works [**Tremor of Intent**] and barred ingress to Desmond Morris' **Naked Ape**. Argues that the obscenities in **Ulysses** are strategically necessary to achieve different artistic aims. The Tommies who explode into mindless obscenity in the brothel scene suggest mindless violence. Believes that Lawrence, in **Lady Chatterley's Lover**, made the semantic mistake of using army language in a context of love and tenderness. "For, as every ex-soldier knows, once you admit verbal obscenity you admit it everywhere. It becomes debased, it loses all force and, worst of all, it ceases to have much aesthetic value." Suggests that, in these days of the new freedom, writers try a little self-imposed, ingenious restraint.

1367 "A Good Read." **New York Times Book Review**, 15 June 1969, p. 2.

Comments on lack in much current literature of books that are good reads — i.e., books that are meant to be read in spare time and have a general uplift. Humorously suggests that modern day criticism will replace such reads.

1368 "Swing of the Censor." **Spectator**, v. 222, no. 7356 (June 21, 1969) 820-22.

Review of **A Long Time Burning**, by Donald Thomas; **Books in the Dock**, by C.H. Rolph; **The End of Obscenity**, by Charles Rembar. Censorship takes different forms in different ages. "*Cunt* and *bugger* can get on the literary bus only because *kike* and *nigger* have been ordered off." In the U.S., thanks to the first amendment, literary sex can go as far as it likes. In Britain, in the late 20s and early 30s, the Polish Count de Montalk was sentenced to six months in prison for using four letter words in his poems. James Douglas was among the worst of the wowsers. It is best to insist on the existence of an unwritten British first amendment rather than to qualify or dilute an anti-censorship position. Demonstrates the absurdity of censorship by referring to his experience in Malta. The French copy of his **Tremor of Intent** was held up by the snufflers; the Danish copy, entitled **Martyr's Blood**, whizzed through the post-office almost with an official blessing.

1369 "Partridge in a Word Tree." **Encounter**, v. 33, no. 1 (July 1969) 51-55.

Review of **A Dictionary of Slang and Unconventional English from the Fifteenth Century to the Present Day**, by Eric Partridge. Observes that Geoffrey Grigson has called him a bad writer [see #885] and traced the cause to Burgess' fondness for words. Discusses some of the more complicated doings in linguistics, and remarks that the making of dictionaries is still a true field of language study. "There is a New Zealander in England who follows Samuel Johnson in making lexicography a one-man calling and keeping it personal, healthily prejudiced, flavoursome and full of fun. This man is Eric Partridge, to whom, quite apart from his generosity to myself and my own work, I owe more hours of pleasurable uplift than I can well count." Praises Partridge's candid erudition in dealing with the so-called taboo words and also discusses a reprint of his **Shakespeare's Bawdy**. [Burgess also published a biographical sketch of Partridge under the same title. See: #1558.]

1370 "Seeing the Shape of Things to Come." **New York Times Book Review**, 3 August 1969, pp. 1, 18.

Review of **H.G Wells; His Turbulent Life and Times,** by Lovat Dickson. Wells was very small beer as a thinker — on a level with Dickens, a grade higher than Shaw. Thinking is a job for our servants: the politicans who don't, and the philosophers who do. Imagination and sensuality are the twin redeemers of thought. The great virtue of Dickson's work lies in its exhibition of the demonic element and the strong libido during the late 90s when Wells was turning away from his career as a novelist to become a prophet and teacher and a seeker after sexual satisfaction. Wells was an astonishing prophet who foresaw the atomic bomb and World War II; his half-mad gifts sprang from an overweening libido. Although he became rich and famous, he remained the child of the British lower classes who are celebrated with intense and exact detail in his early books. "The Wells of the brain is all too forgettable; the Wells of the imagination and senses is memorable with memorability of greatness."

1371 "Letter from Europe." **American Scholar**, v. 38, no. 4 (Autumn 1969) 684-86.

Feels saddened and bored by the conformity of North American students. The manifestations of Black Power are depressing, and the notion of Black Studies is absurd. "A course that encloses St. Augustine, Toussant L'Ouverture, Coleridge-Taylor, Paul Robeson and Papa Doc, because they are all black, is as absurd as one that deals with Robert Louis Stevenson, Joseph Stalin, Mark Twain and Salvador Dali because they all had moustaches." Contrasts the attitude of the protesting students with those of his own generation and comments on his own hard-won education. Foresees that student indiscipline, victimization of the faculty and the elevation of racial rights above the demands of scholarship will result in the degradation of educational standards at some institutions, while the real work is done in real universities. Observes that the heroic student protest is going on behind the Iron Curtain. Comments on his own forthcoming biography of Shakespeare.

1372 "From A to ZZZ." **New York Times Book Review**, 21 September 1969, p. 2.

Reviews merits of some American dictionaries.

1373 "Woman and Women." **Vogue**, v. 154 (October 1, 1969) 194, 262-63.

Women are specific persons in space and time. Woman is the paradox of a gorgeous sensuous abstraction. The woman of the year 1969 conveys, by her dress and posture, a new aggressiveness that inevitably discloses something of the male. "The sensuality of this new, spare, unpampered body of the fashion advertisements is a world away from the dreams of my moaning adolescence — the harem houri, plump, pouting, perfumed from a spout not a stopper, her embracing fingers sticky with Turkish delight." The woman of the late 60s uses the sharp aggressive vocabulary of men; she swears and tells men in crisp detail what she wants. "This is admirable. . . but it is somewhat unaphrodisiacal. Lust and light are deadly enemies. Shakespeare said that, and Shakespeare was never wrong." The female voice, pitched low and soft, with the timbre of an oboe d'amore, remains a potent instrument of sexual attraction. In Britain, the sexes seem to be growing more alike. Speculates if this may be nature's way to check fecundity by weakening the polarization of the sexes. It is when women are found behind the alluring facade of woman that the knees of men crack and the act of worshipping comes before the act of possessing.

1374 "Seen Any Good Galsworthy Lately?" **New York Times Magazine**, Section VI, 16 November 1969, p. 57.

Galsworthy received every honor Britain can confer on an author and yet, as a novelist, he hardly exists when compared to Joyce, Lawrence and Conrad. Galsworthy was a Whig gentleman, given to good manners and the postures of chivalry, and he first made his name with plays notable for their humanitarianism. "This profound yet simple humanitarianism. . . is wholly admirable; that it does not make admirable art is another matter, and it is perhaps ungentlemanly to raise it." The Forsyte values are money values and Galsworthy, who started out by castigating these values in superb shafts of irony, later identified himself with the change-hating Forsytes. This change of direction does not affect the central issue: **The Forsyte Saga** is an astonishing creation — but not great literature — because the writing is not distinguished and the characters are not, in the perceptions of both Virginia Woolf and D.H. Lawrence, free autonomous beings. "They are creatures of society, not their own inner demons . . . . **The Forsyte Saga** is a great television triumph, since the Galsworthian conception has the near-coarseness, the near-melodramatic simplicity of superior soap opera . . . ." For letter by David A. Kahn, see **New York Times Magazine**, 21 December 1969, p. 26.

1375 "The Professional Viewpoint." **Twentieth Century Studies**, v. 1, no. 2, (November 1969) 109-30.

A 500 word passage on the inadequacy of language to deal with sexual matters. Also comments on the sexual descriptions in **A Clockwork Orange** and **Tremor of Intent**. "In writing both sections of the books I was more moved than I wished to be: I could have dipped my phallus in the ink . . . . The result, anyway, is not pornographic and that's all the reader should be concerned with."

1376 "Our Bedfellow, the Marquis de Sade." **Horizon,** v. 11 (Winter 1969) 104-9.

An account of de Sade's career — complete with brief accounts of sodomy, flagellation and self-flagellation, torture of prostitutes and the long imprisonment of the Marquis, intently watched by the police, in various prisons and mental institutions. Argues that de Sade's works should not be banned: when there is a will to cruelty and murder, the pretext of a literary example is supererogatory. Besides, his image of man as a creature given to cruelty, is unfortunately more realistic than that of Rousseau or the Church. We are all touched by the sadomasochistic impulse. "There is some obscure neural liaison in the brain between the sexual urge and the desire for domination — and the latter phrase I have deliberately left ambiguous." His unexpurgated works, devoid of an interest in people, include dollops of farinaceous inedibility. His true influence has been on popular writers who have diluted his message and made it palatable to suburban minds: Ian Fleming, say, and the misanthropy conveyed by William Golding's **The Inheritors.**

1377 James Joyce's Dublin: A Documentary on the Work & World of a Masterful Writer. [Phonotape] Tucson, Ariz.: Motivational Programming Corp., 1969. 1 cassette. Duration: 27 min.

1378 "The Seventeenth Novel." **Page 2: The Best of Speaking of Books from the New York Times Book Review.** Ed. by Francis Brown. New York: Holt, Rinehart and Winston, 1969, pp. 85-89.

[Reprint of #1204.]

1379 "The Politics of Graham Greene." **Page 2: The Best of Speaking of Books from the New York Times Times Book Review.** Ed. by Francis Brown. New York: Holt, Rinehart and Winston, 1969, pp. 284-91.

[Reprint of #1295.]

1380 "Words." In **The English Language.** Ed. by Whitney French Bolton and David Crystal, v. 2. London: Cambridge University Press, 1969, pp. 294-304.

A chapter from **Language Made Plain.**

1381 "Language as Movement." **Encounter,** v. 34, no. 1 (January 1970) 64-67.

Reviews of **Changing English,** by Simeon Potter and **Tudor to Augustan English,** by A.C. Partridge.

1382 "To Be or Not to Be in Love with You." **Show; The Magazine of Film and the Arts,** v. 1, no. 1 (January 1970) 75-80.

When Warner Bros. summoned him to work on a musical based on the life of Shakespeare he was not outraged. He is, after all, not a scholar, but a novelist and therefore a kind of showbiz man himself. Quotes some of the lyrics from the proposed musical. However, Joe Mankiewicz wanted the richness of the period recorded without benefit of added musical riches. Ergo, his "songs lie mouldering on archived tape and disk." Discusses the revised script. Shorn of its music, the watchword was motivation and the problem was language. "T.S. Eliot said that plot was a bone that a burglar threw to a dog while he got on with the job of rifling the silver. True." Quotes section from the screenplay which describes the death of Marlowe and provides a sample from the screenplay itself. [Note: This work, with a working title of 'The Bawdy Bard,' was never produced.]

1383 "Smooth Beawties." **Spectator,** v. 224, no. 7389 (February 7, 1970) 179-80.

Literary men who are also musicians rank high in his scheme of things; for that reason Campion has always been one of his favorites. Campion's achievement in verse can only be understood by those who understand his achievement in the dual art of song. His songs, "I care not for these ladies, When to her lute Corrina sings, Till cherry ripe themselves do cry" are notable for taste, fragrant wit and subtlety. Campion was not only a Jacobean, "He was also an Elizabethan, which is more acceptable, and this well-edited volume is a fine monument to that almost manic concern with beauty which flowered under Elizabeth and went sour and putrid under James."

1384 "Great Mogul Beethoven: Genius Got in the Way." **Vogue,** v. 155 (March 15, 1970) 132-33.

Both Beethoven and Dr. Johnson were brought up in traditions which made artists and scholars humble beggars of bread from noble lords. Both fiercely asserted their independence. Gives an account of Beethoven's early musical education, and finds that Beethoven's father may have helped to foment the son's rebellion. ". . . Beethoven's father was so drunken a sot, so weakly tyrannical and sickeningly irresponsible, that Ludwig could not easily be persuaded that deference to elders and so-called betters was part of the rational order.'' Beethoven studied under Haydn, who recognized his talents and called him the Great Mogul. Beethoven was never bemused by political greatness, as he demonstrated when he tore up the Eroica (third symphony) dedication to Napoleon when the First Consul elevated himself to Emperor. Gives an account of Beethoven's life which emphasizes his deafness, personal squalor and unscrupulousness. ''He would willingly sell the same piece to two or three different publishers.'' With him music ceased to be a mere artifact but became a miraculous emanation of the human spirit.

1385 ''Durrell and the Homunculi.'' **Saturday Review**, v. 53, no. 12 (March 21, 1970) 29-31.

Essay review of **Nunquam**, by Lawrence Durrell. Durrell is a considerable lyric poet, and his novels show the lyric virtues: verbal exactness, wit, color, memorability, the sensorium dew-washed, the feet light. Unfortunately, the lyric gift is not enough for the novelist, who must also create credible characters animated by credible motives. **The Alexandria Quartet** was a commercial success because it included great lashings of sex, cruelty, evocations of the exotic, the sense of sin as understood by a Thirties shopgirl educated by **Poppies Paper**. Durrell also included rape, sodomy, incest. The reader jumped, and he thought it was the characters moving. The striking lyric line must be justified by striking events. In both **Tunc** and **Nunquam** Durrell has come to terms with his total incapacity for including real life in his fiction. ''Durrell is a light entertainer equipped with a poetic faculty, a singer of clever-silly ribaldries supported by a Wagnerian orchestra.'' **Nunquam** is the usual Durrell loose parcel which contains tawdry costume jewelry mixed up with genuine gems. For real fiction, it is necessary to ''Go to writers without an ounce of poetry in their arteries but with whole blood banks full of human concern.''

1386 ''Moses in a Lounge Suit.'' **Spectator**, v. 224, no. 7395 (March 21, 1970) 374-375.

Review of **The New English Bible: The Old Testament**, by the Joint Committee on the New English Bible. The translators of this new version are all acceptable names, but none is exactly formidable. The bible of the King James version was almost Shakespearian; this new version is reminiscent of the work of Nevil Shute, all lucid, factual, contemporary narrative at its best. The translation does well enough with the prohibitions of Leviticus and brings the Law ('You shall not have intercourse with your father's sister, etc.') home to the suburbs. Unfortunately, it does not do justice to the passages of prophecy and poetry. Cites passages from both the Jacobean and the modern version and finds the latter grossly inadequate in selected sections. ''Let me finish with captiousness . . . . The New Testament, which came out in its new form in 1961 and sold even better than **Lady Chatterley's Lover**, released unexpurgated at about the same time, has relevance to our age and that age needs the message in plain, not in an antique code. The Old Testament works best in a remote and magical language; with its taboos, savagery, and violent poetry, it is awkward in modern dress, like Moses in a lounge suit.''

1387 ''The Novel in 2000 A.D..'' **New York Times Book Review**, 29 March 1970, p. 2.

If the novel is dead by 2000 A.D. it will be for lack of technical problems which sustain the writer's interest in the genre. **Naked Came the Stranger** demonstrates how a novel of sorts can be written by teams of journalists each writing a different chapter. Dialogue nowadays is easy to reproduce; we all have tape recorders. Facile psychological depth via interior monologue is shamefully easy to supply. The novelist is expected to produce clichés; he does so by the very nature of his calling. Predicts that English in the future will simplify its structure and augment its vocabulary. The literary novel of the year 2000 will consist of straight dramatic dialogue ''And then the film-script format gives place to a page or so of prose as elaborately and painfully composed as a piece of 12-part counterpoint for strings'' — full of irony, humor and pathos and allusiveness. The best-seller of the same year will be much like the best-seller of today.

1388 ''Mirable Annals.'' **Encounter**, v. 34, no. 5 (May 1970) 65-68.

Review of **The Literary Life**, by Robert Phelps and Peter Deane. Compiles a long catalog of the remarkable literary events of the miraculous year 1922, comments on female novelists notable for their beauty (the prize goes to Rebecca West) and ugliness (Amy Lowell, Gertrude Stein), the tendency of male novelists to hunt, smoke and soldier on (''no author dies of cancer of the lung'') and describes the book, originally compiled for private pleasure, as a long toast to the practitioners of literature.

1389 "Singapore Revisited." **Spectator**, v. 224, no. 7406 (June 6, 1970) 742.

Invited to show their gratitude for the title of his first book, **Time for a Tiger**, the brewers of Tiger beer cautiously declined, observing the book, if obscene or seditious, might damage sales. "I was very hurt [he only wanted a wooden Tiger-advertising clock found in the *kedais*], and showed this in an emendation I at once made in the text. My hero wins the Federation Lottery first prize of $350,000, and it is suggested that a celebratory case of Tiger be sent out for. 'No,' he says, 'make it Carlsberg. It costs a bit more but it's a better beer'." The **Trilogy** was prophetic, not obscene. Malays and Chinese are regrettably killing each other in fact and not fiction, and the racial feuding seems likely to continue. Compares the Singapore of today with the town of yesteryear, and concludes that, provided you forget the tyrannical pragmatism of its politics, Singapore is the most sense-oriented place on earth. The climate is pleasantly hot, the food is edible and the women are mostly exquisite. Unfortuntely, for all its cosseting of the body in the service of puritannical production, it produces no culture or ideas.

1390 "Gladly My (Maltese, George) Cross I'd Bear." **Punch**, v. 258, no. 6772 (June 10, 1970) 860-61.

The State taxes the few fat years without taking into account the many lean years. He needs daylight; his sight is deteriorating. Britain provides no subject matter for the novelist. For all these reasons he left Britain for Malta. "Fill up to a spumous overflow with death duties and tax on the living. Drink it all down and, drunk, convince yourself that the world needs your writing. Then scuttle or sneak or run." Discusses the advantages (and many disadvantages) of living in Malta, including the cost of living, the state of Maltese Catholicism, censorship, the films on tap, the middle-brow reading habits of the Maltese and the prevailing complacency.

1391 "The Price of Gormenghast." **Spectator**, v. 224, no. 7408 (June 20, 1970) 819-20.

Review of **A World Away**, by Maeve Gilmore. It is impossible not to be moved by this memoir of Mervyn Peake. He [Burgess] wrote the introduction to **Titus Groan** to show his admiration for this novelist and artist who died at an early age of Parkinson's disease. **Titus Groan** has the kind of three-dimensional solidity shown by Wyndham Lewis and often found in pictorial artists, and it is one of the most important works of the imagination (along with **Gormenghast** and **Titus Alone**) of the 40s. The extreme penury of the Peakes makes moving reading. It also proves that the productive artist is ignored by the Arts Council. "Perhaps Peake had too many talents to please the fates or the British public . . . . Meanwhile the minimal talents go on being disproportionately rewarded. What can we do about it? Not very much . . . . Those of us who are critics can perhaps learn to temper our jealousy of the creative artist. For the rest, the moral of [this] exquisite and poignant book is what we already know — that life is hell, but we had better be grateful for the consolations of love and art, human creations that owe nothing either to the State or the Destroyer. There is probably nothing else in the world worth bothering about."

1392 "Reflections on a General Election by Six Independent Contributors." **Spectator**, v. 224, no. 7408 (June 20, 1970) 812-13.

In Malta and Italy, he is very left wing ("who but a fascist swine could support the political pretentions of the clergy and their unwillingness to allow civil marriage or divorce?") but in England he is a Tory. It is true that Mr. Heath, a bachelor choir-master giggler, does not personify all the Tory virtues and the probable result of this improbable choice of leadership is that Labour, under Mr. Harold Wilson, will win the election. [Other contributors include Kingsley Amis, Lord Beeching, Trevor Grove, Stuart Hood, and Tibor Szamuely.]

1393 "Culture as a Hot Meal." **Spectator**, v. 225, nos. 7410-11 (July 11, 1970) 13-14.

Review of **The Raw and the Cooked**, by Claude Levi-Strauss. "Structuralism is about the structures that the human brain imposes on the world about it. Nowadays we neither follow Berkeley in holding that the world has no existence independent of the perceiver, nor, with Dr. Johnson, confute such idealism by kicking a rock." Followed by a fairly detailed examination of structuralism and the judgment that Levi-Strauss "is one of the few men writing today who dare not be ignored." [Structuralism is pertinent to an understanding of **MF**.]

1394 "Joyce Can't Really Be Imitated . . . ." **Books and Bookmen**, v. 15 (July 1970) 8-9.

[Not examined.]

1395 "Letter from Europe." **American Scholar**, v. 39, no. 3 (Summer 1970) 502-4.

Gives some impression of the American South as a place in which to eat and drink. On going to Mallorca to assist in the establishment of the American Institute of the Mediterranean in Deya he is oppressed by American students who wear jeans, espadrilles and torn maillots. "In Deya their dress looks like a mockery of the circumambient poor and their lying around while these poor scratch their living from the rocks or dredge it from the sea is, to say the least, an indiscretion." Considers some of the differences between these American students and the European temperament, laments Maltese philistinism and praises the food, entertainment and ambience on tap in Rome.

1396 "Bless Thee, Bottom. . ." **Times Literary Supplement**, September 18, 1970, p. 1024-25.

He has translated **The Wasteland** into Malay, some French novels into English [see #948-49, 951]. Translators have a hard time of it in this world. Cites passages from **Tremor of Intent** and compares the original English with the elegant French of Michel Deutsch. Also cites passages from **The Doctor is Sick** and compares the English and German versions. The Italian version of **Clockwork** makes the whole thing sound like a story about Milanese thugs. It would be child's play to translate the work into Russian, but "official Russia notices my work only to condemn it: they had the nerve to sneer at my interpretation of Shakespeare's character in **Nothing Like the Sun** on Moscow Radio. On the other hand, a furtive message has informed me that I have a small underground readership in the Soviet Union, and that pleases me more while paying me no less." Observes that he and his wife are translating **Finnegans Wake** into Italian. The working title is **pHorbiCEtta** which means earwig. For letter by Michael Donley, see TLS, 25 September 1970, pp. 1094-95.

1397 "Anatomy of Melancholy." **Horizon, v. 12, no. 4 (Autumn 1970) 48-53.**

Burton's **Anatomy of Melancholy** is one of the greatest works ever written on the subject — and one of the longest. The surviving portraits show us the face of a man shy, thoughtful, intelligent, diffident and genial. "He accepted his melancholy as part of the Adamic inheritance and made the best of things." The book is one of the great comic works of the world. Quotes Burton on the ill-favored mistress ("heavy, dull, hollow-eyed. . . gubber-tushed, rotten teeth, black, uneven, brown teeth, beetle-browed, a witch's beard, her breath stink all over the room . . . ."). Burton on love melancholy exhausts its subject and very nearly its reader. His prescription for a bout of depression is sound and "Burton's strength, and the ultimate cause of his cheerfulness, lies in an incapacity for disappointment: he already knows the worst. All that remains to be done is to attempt cures where cures are possible, and where there is no cure, to seek what palliatives art and nature provide. Let us relieve the fundamental melancholy that is woven into the human fabric by partaking of the infinite solace of the world — wine, venery, the bad language of bargees, talk, tale-telling, and most of all, books."

1398 "Honoring a Prophet in His Own Country." **Tri-Quarterly**, v. 19 (Fall 1970) 60-63.

Edward Dahlberg is great — and greatly ignored by the plain people if not the intellectuals. His autobiographical **Bottom Dogs** committed the crime of conveying a distrust of coarse and venal Marxists. His anti-Nazi novel, **Those Who Perish**, sold a derisory 200 copies. Those 200 copies were a virtual death sentence. The public, which does not read his anti-flesh books, **The Sorrows of Priapus** and **The Carnal Myth**, is frightened by unpopular doctrines, archaisms and the carefully chiselled sentences. "Beneath the glitter there's a solid and enduring pessimism — the mark of a writer who thinks so highly of the human potential that he cannot but be let down by the human actuality. But there's plenty of comfort in words, words, words."

1399 "Is Shakespeare Relevant?" **New York Times**, 11 December 1970, p. 47, column 4.

Decides to explore if the younger generation finds anything of relevance in Shakespeare. Observes they know very little. But when you describe Shakespeare's appearance, the students sense a somatic and sartorial kinship. "He had long hair and a beard, wore earrings and showed the shape of his legs and his bottom. Nothing uptight there . . . ." Observes they know the plots of **Romeo and Juliet** and **Hamlet**. Comments that all the plots of Shakespeare are pregnant with present relevance and gives some examples ("Black is beautiful — **Othello** and **Cleopatra** — but Mister Charlie does for them.") Argues that they need more than the plots; they need the poetry as well. Concludes with an account of a lecture on Shakespeare delivered before detestable hippy-types in Deya.

1400 "Letter from Europe." **American Scholar**, v. 40, no. 1 (Winter 1970-71) 119-22.

Singapore under the reactionary pragmatism of Mr. Lee Kuan Yew seems somehow unclean and nasty since the British departed. Mr. Lee does not repine at the departure of the humanists in the English Department. Australian parochialism is cracking under the influence of the Nyu Orstrylians, but the light is marvellous, the beer cold, the oysters cheap and it is a wonderful place for bringing up big, brown, baretoed children. **Kangaroo** is still hated; no Australian, Owld or Nyu, has managed to produce anything as good or true. Cites examples of Australian speech, or "Strine," and comments on the Australian penchant for mateship. "Sex has been sublimated into sport, the joys of malereek and pubfug, the stupor of marine sun relieved with the occasional cracking of a frosty (or opening of a bottle of cold beer)." Describes some of the differences between the national characteristics of Australians and New Zealanders. Argues that the republican system is unsuited to the genius of the English speaking world, and states the case for a limited monarchy.

1401 "What Is Pornography?" In **Perspectives on Pornography**. Ed. by Douglas A. Hughes. New York: St. Martin's Press, 1970, pp. 4-8.

[Reprint of #1313.]

1402 "John Bull's Other Language." **Punch**, v. 260, no. 6800 (January 6, 1971) 1819.

The Irish have a passion for phatic communication without a separable content. They talk about their novels in pubs; the actual writing becomes supererogatory. The proposal of the Irish government not to tax artists and writers ("with mad sane Irish logic it is evidently foreseen that there'll be no income to pay tax on") is not a serious reason to settle in Ireland: Dublin is parochial and the Irish, who have never liked the books written about Ireland, tend to regard the writer as colourful property to help the tourist trade or a black soul to be threatened with exorcism. "Looking for James Joyce's father's grave in Glasnevin, I was told: 'Ah, now he was a decent man, something in the Castle at one time, not like that bitch of a son of his' . . . . Joyce, as always, was right: **The Book of Kells** is the true work for the Irish — three or four Latin words to the page, all the rest curlicues and flowers and pictures of Our Blessed Saviour."

1403 "Coming Soon: Hilton-Upon-Stratford." **New York Times**, 11 March 1971, p. 39, c. 4-6.

The prosperity of present-day Stratford is ironic: Stratfordian Shakespeare made his fame and fortune in London. Provides the new Stratford Hilton with a fanciful Shakespearean menu. Notes absence of housing for poor students.

1404 "The Canterbury Tales." **Horizon**, v. 13, no. 2, (Spring 1971) 44-47, 57-59.

An introduction to Chaucer's **Canterbury Tales**. Briefly considers the publication history of the tales, Chaucer's use of East Midlands English, the pronunciation and the language of the period. "The heartening thing about the Middle Ages, as that long and complex period is expressed in Chaucer, is what T.S. Eliot would call a community of sensibility: the aristocratic intellect does not despise the grosser plebeian sensorium." Observes that Chaucer, by comparison with Boccaccio, insisted on an exact characterization. His men and women are sharply contrasted individually as well as socially. Comments on the tales of the Miller, the Monk, Pardoner. The story of the Pardoner is one "that I have told to the least literary, even the least literate, of scholastic or social groups (on guard duty in the army, for instance), and I have never yet known it to fail to move its audience." The Parson's tale is flat, stale and platitudinous. "One fears that Chaucer was of the devil's party without knowing it. Certainly he never seems, with any conviction, to be on the side of the cenobitic virtues: he is all for the rich, sensuous, bawdy variety of the world." With drawings by Z. Blum.

1405 "Mulligan Stew; Irving Wallace Rewrites **Ulysses**." **New York Times Book Review**, 6 June 1971, pp. 5-6.

Parody. Rewrites the muscular opening paragraphs of **Ulysses** in the more discursive (and flabby) style of Irving Wallace.

1406 "Letter from Europe." **American Scholar**, v. 40, no. 3 (Summer 1971) 514-20.

Reports that his organization has lost the fight against decimal coinage. He is rapidly becoming the very image of a conservative, imperialist Englishmen, a comic fossil. Records his antipathy to some

American usage (the detested "Hi" and "wow") and the confusion caused by the absence of a received pronunciation. Also comments on his Creative Writing courses at Princeton and Columbia. The poor quality of American television turns him from a good guest into a snarling ingrate. Why all the "editing?" Why does some great Federal corporation not take over the job of adult communication? Notes that ordinary tommies and erks had no great love for the cigarred, V-signing, bricklaying, hard-swearing aristocrat (Churchill) who Understood the People. Churchill's election addresses, in which he proposed to fight the new menace from beyond the Iron Curtain, was a mark of great political ineptitude.

1407 "Love Story (19th Century Style)." **New York Times**, 27 April 1971, p. 43, c. 4-6.

Debunking account of love affair between Robert and Elizabeth Barrett Browning. Makes a case for saving the Casa Guidi in which they lived for fourteen years.

1408 "Glamour Under the Elms." **Travel and Leisure**, October-November 1971, pp. 6-10.

[An irreverent Burgess on the Writer-in-Residence and the writer as a teacher of a Creative Writing Course.] The true reason why Fossell Manningtree, his "photographs show a middle-aged man with a loose mouth and lewdly promising eyes, the hair thinning but still untamed, the body not yet wrecked by the rumored drinking" is invited to become a Writer-in-Residence is that he is expected to confer glamour on the college which issues the invitation. To be asked to write, as innocent students sometimes do, far away from the domestic necessities and the battered 1926 Webster, is to be asked the impossible. He will not be allowed to teach the work of others; his influence may be seditious to the instructor's truth. He is not qualified to talk about his own work; he only laid a moderately golden egg which others are more fit to interpret than he himself. So one Burgess was stunned to learn, from a brilliant exegete in North Carolina, that R. Ennis spelled "sinner" backwards. As for teaching creative writing, the Creative Writer is the first to acknowledge that the art, which requires the same dedication as that of a carpenter or student of medicine, cannot be taught. The Creative Writer suspects that he was issued the invitation to write about the college. "They don't want a writer-in-residence really; they want residence in a writer."

1409 "Is America Falling Apart?" **New York Times Magazine**, 7 November 1971, pp. 99-102.

America spoiled him with its consumer comforts but, living as he did in New Jersey without a car, he came up against the nastier side of the consumer society. The trains are squalid; the home, that bulwark of private independence, is dependent on great impersonal corporations; consumption itself is turning insipid; education of the young is conscientious but without spark or daring. Argues that Americans, with the Vietnam war and the Mylai horror, are discovering that they are as subject to original sin as sinful Europeans. Argues that crime, the preying of the opium eaters on the working community, must be controlled; the citizens and the police must be disarmed. A measure of socialization, pension and sickness benefits, nationalized transport, should be national priorities. "American politics, at both the state and the Federal levels, is too much concerned with the protection of large fortunes, America being the only example in history of a genuine timocracy. The wealth qualification for the aspiring politician is taken for granted; a governmental system dedicated to the promotion of personal wealth in a few selected areas will never act for the public good." A sense of sin is a good thing; it must not be allowed to degenerate into a neurosis. He finds America more stimulating than depressing, and he will be back there again. [Reprinted in #1443.]

1410 "Letter from Europe." **American Scholar**, v. 41, no. 1 (Winter 1971-72) 139-42.

He is now genuinely in Europe, in Bracciano, housed in a hovel ("probably originally a scullion's hovel or nest for a cast-off mistress") and fascinated by fragments of ancient Latin. On the ship **Michelangelo** the gluttony of nouveau-riche Italian-Americans and the sight of fat hairy bellies wambling about proudly in the sun brought out a thin-lipped puritanism. He and his wife dined modestly and worked on their Italian translation of **Finnegans Wake**. Reports that he has completed his work on **Cyrano de Bergerac** (translation and music) and is now working on a Brechtian-type musical based on Joyce's **Ulysses**. Includes some observations on the death of the dollar and the unstable political situation in Italy. Solipsism threatens again. "There is no escape from me in the external world, or in drink or drugs. I had better start learning to live with myself. The only way I can live with myself, I find, is to justify my being here at all, and the way of justification is the way of work. I feel guilty when I am not writing, and so I do write." And so on to Rome, and the beastly Romans. Then discusses an Italian version of **My Fair Lady**.

1411 "Review of **My Life and Times**, by Henry Miller." **New York Times Book Review**, 2 January 1972, pp. 1, 10, 11.

Today's naked generation has learned nearly everything from Miller, but not his bookishness, his capacity for recapturing innocence, his sense of wonder or his sense of words. Miller's works are heavily erotic, *not* pornographic, but those Donna Giovannas who believe that Miller demeans women may be right. "They are right, I think, because, though Miller respects ladies like Anais Nin, he cannot help making woman the sexual instrument come before woman the human entity." He belongs in the logorrheal tradition of Rabelais, Sterne and Burroughs. He has produced autobiography that begs at the door of fiction and, although he has cleansed the dialect of the tribe, Orwell did better and more enduring work in that vein. "A cigarette-smoking, gin-drinking octogenarian, he is a fine advertisement for the longevital virtues of regular sex" but industry and longevity are no substitute for genius. For letter by Joseph Schrank, see **New York Times Book Review**, 27 February 1972, p. 22.

1412 "Clockwork Marmalade." **Listener**, v. 87, no. 2238 (February 17, 1972) 197-199.

Feels himself involved in the controversy surrounding Kubrick's **A Clockwork Orange** ("technically brilliant, thoughtful, relevant, poetic, mind-opening.") The title derives from Cockney slang. "It was a traditional trope, and it asked to entitle a work which combined a concern with tradition and a bizarre technique." Recalls the concern with criminality in the late 50's and various influential theoreticians who proposed the use of aversion therapy to condition criminals into 'goodness.' The limited stock of free will is too precious to encroach on. The novel was intended to be a tract, or sermon, on the importance of the power of choice. Alex is evil, not merely misguided. Theologically, evil is not quantifiable, but it is possible to argue that the wish to diminish free will is the sin against the Holy Ghost. "What hurts me, as also Kubrick, is the allegation. . . that there is a gratuitous indulgence in violence which turns an intended homiletic work into a pornographic one." Observes that the work is an act of catharsis and charity; his own first wife was robbed and beaten by three G.I. deserters in 1942. The language of the book, Nadsat, was deliberately adopted to turn the book into a brainwashing primer. "It looks as though I must go through life as the fountain and origin of a great film, and as a man who has to insist against all opposition, that he is the most unviolent creature alive. Just like Stanley Kubrick."

1413 "The **Ulysses** Sentence." **James Joyce Quarterly**, v. 9 no. 3 (Spring 1972) 423-435.

An essay on the syntax and diction of **Ulysses**. Later incorporated into Burgess' in the chapter headed "The Joyce Sentence." See pp. 69-81 of **Joysprick**.

1414 "Viewpoint." **Times Literary Supplement**, 21 April 1972, p. 446.

On the squalor and seedy desperation of reviewers. Put to the test for hard copy, they paraphrase blurbs. Reviews become criticism only when the word count goes up in the thousands. Argues that the typical writer knows his own faults as well, or better, than the reviewer. "The fairest review that any novel of mine ever received was one I wrote myself." [See #448, 989.] Reviewing is a more corruptive craft than fiction.

1415 "Said Mr. Cooper to His Wife: You Know, I Could Write Something Better Than That." **New York Times Magazine**, 7 May 1972, p. 108 +

Cooper was thirty when he published **Precaution**, a work of parody and criticism in which he packed all the genteel bourgeois Englishry that had been bedeviling American fiction. With the publication of **The Spy** "Cooper. . . spewed all the Englishry out of American imaginative writing in one quiet but devastating act. After it, real American fiction-writing could begin." Gives a brief account of Cooper's life, and then discusses the "Leatherstocking Tales." These novels are masterly. Their one disadvantage is that they did not have the benefit of a course in post-Hemingway typewriterese, and much of the dialogue sounds "artificial, staid, pedantic, pseudo-poetic, apter for the theater than for the haunts of beavers and chipmunks, but it is in a convention that most of Cooper's contemporaries had to subscribe to, since there was no other fictional idiom available."

1416 "Juice from a Clockwork Orange." **Rolling Stone**, no. 110 (June 8, 1972) 52-53.

Mentions that Mick Jagger was the original choice for the role of Alex. Discusses nadsat with the help of two examples: horror show and gulliver. He is pleased with the film, but "Apart from being gratified that my book has been filmed by one of the best living English-speaking producer-directors, instead of by some pornhound or pighead or other camera-carrying cretin, I cannot say that my life has been changed in any way by Stanley Kubrick's success. I seem to have less rather than more money, but I always seem to have less.'' Comments on the drug-taking in the book (''drug-taking was so much part of my scene that it automatically went into the book'') and the three qualities that make Alex human: his love of aggression, language and beauty. Quotes from the ending of the first Heinemann (1962) ed. and observes ''America prefers the other, more violent, ending. Who am I to say that America is wrong?''

1417 "Letter from Europe." **American Scholar**, v. 41, no. 3 (Summer 1972) 425-28.

Reminded by the **Scholar** about summer deadlines, and the need to write his letter from Europe, he first compares the art of writing to the art of composing music. His life is utterly uneventful. However, his family was a recent guest at Claridge's courtesy of Warner Bros. The Queen was lunching with the King of Afghanistan in the same hotel. It was all accomplished with quiet efficiency. ''No shrieking of sirens, roar of motocycle escorts, menace of polished holsters and oiled guns. This is the old England, but not many people can afford it.'' Regrets the monetary decimalization now on public view and speculates if ''progress'' is not weakening British national decency. Observes that he was interviewed by the London **Evening Standard** on the subject of **A Clockwork Orange**. His speculation that the attack on his wife by a gang of G.I. deserters might have contributed to her comparatively early death is transformed to the sensationalistic headline: "**CLOCKWORK ORANGE GANG KILLED MY WIFE — AUTHOR.**" It is depressing to encounter the assumption that the issues raised by **Clockwork** are now important because they are embedded in the demotic medium of film. However, the channels for publicising public and private wrongs are laudably open: minor and indisputable cruelties and nuisances are promptly corrected. He would feel happier about the English if they felt more strongly about the bloody mess in Northern Ireland. Discusses a national coal strike and confesses his panic in the arctic Minneapolis climate. Then talks about his preparatory reading for **Napoleon Symphony**.

1418 "Viewpoint." **Times Literary Supplement**, 4 August 1972, p. 916.

Italians rarely or never read British fiction. They tend to read American fiction for its political quotient. ''In Italy, as in France, every novelist has to have a political affiliation. . . and this is taken into account even in purely aesthetic evaluations of his work . . . . My crime [he was called a reactionary] is to be distrustful of progressive shibboleths and to say that we are all sinners.'' Examines the low opinions of current British fiction expressed by Frederick R. Karl's **A Reader's Guide to the Contemporary English Novel**, and explores the influence of Italian on Joyce's **Ulysses** and **Finnegans Wake**.

1419 "Blimey!" **New York Times Book Review**, 13 August 1972, pp. 4, 5.

Review of **Blimey! Another Book About London**, by Donald Goddard. The fact that so many books have been written about London means, not exhaustion of the subject, but inexhaustibility of subject matter. Goddard introduces London to New Yorkers. He is up to date on the planning horrors that will demolish the capital more effectively than either the Blitz or the fire of 1666. He observes, quite properly, that the London food is probably the best in the world; that the music is plentiful; that the pubs are excellent; that the Londoners genuinely believe in equality, but in an equality within a structure of rules. The deference is shown to the office, not to the man. An excellent book, which should be supplemented by the street-guide called "A to Z," and then London will belong to you.

1420 "Sober City to Lift Your Heart." **Daily Telegraph Magazine**, 29 September 1972, p. 52+

1421 "Viewpoint." **Times Literary Supplement**, 13 October 1972, p. 1224.

Announces that he is off to America to teach and work on a musical (''A failed musician and an even more failed poet, I am left with a residual capacity for verbal engineering''). The amount of detail that goes into discussions of **Cyrano!** puts much scholastic wrangling to shame. Quotes sample lyrics from the work, and includes his comments. Also observes that he has completed the book, lyrics and music of a work called "Blooms of Dublin."

1422 "Anthony Burgess Meets New York: Cucarachas and Exiles, Potential Death and Life Enhancement." **New York Times Magazine**, 29 October 1972, pp. 28, 32-39.

A description of New York City — complete with *cucarachas* or cockroaches (''They suggest a vivarial pageant of some Latin republic, poor but vital''). Includes facts likely to interest the reader of **Clockwork**

Testament ("James Drought, the Hibernico-Chericee author, has sent me many long scarifying letters, telling me that I am a penilambent parasite and that the British have achieved nothing in 2000 years"). Comments on his difficulties with credit cards, the spray can graffiti, the readiness of the great Republic to tax him even when he has no vote, but declares that he finds the city *simpatico* because it is seething with exiles. For letter by A.H. McCormick, Jr., see **New York Times Magazine**, 19 November 1972, p. 34. Burgess replies in the same issue.

1423 "My Dear Students; a Letter." **New York Times Magazine**, 19 November 1972, pp. 20, 22, 30, 32.

Feels he has known his students a long time. Observes that the dress and behavior of American students are copied all over the world. "I love you all dearly because you are decent, serious, concerned, worried to death." Their rejection of the past worries him. Although fascism had its roots in Augustan Rome, he learned to know the language of Virgil, Homer and the myths of ancient Greece and Rome. He is disturbed that students want to study Vonnegut, Kesey and "God help us, even my own work." Comments on the deprivations and harrassments of City College students, set in a milieu where fear stalks among the dogmerds. Observes that the open admission policy is leading to the admission (and graduation) of unqualified students. Notes that the humanities (*not* the scientific and technological subjects) are the first to be corrupted by low standards and expresses his concern. Gives examples of some slangy and imprecise English constructions concocted by his students. Ends with this exhortation: "For the moment, I would ask you only to expand your vocabulary, develop a minimal grace of style, think harder and learn who Helen of Troy and Nausicaa were. And for God's sake, stop talking about relevance." For letter by Horace A. Porter, see **New York Times Magazine**, 24 December 1972, p. 32. Remarks that he asked for "relevant" courses, and lobbied for Black Studies. He does not regret the fact: the price of progress is action.

1424 "Viewpoint." **Times Literary Supplement**, 1 December 1972, p. 1458.

The University of Rochester marks the death of J.C. Wilson, father of Xerox. The students cheer the widow, but not a performance of the last movement of Beethoven's Ninth symphony. Observes that one can understand the motivation behind the snarls ("Money-loving America. Dollar charisma") of dead Uncle Ez [Ezra Pound]. Also comments on the trials and strains of the American lecture circuit, some American writers whose first language is not English, graduate students in his Creative Writing course and the violence he has witnessed in New York City.

1425 "Letter from Europe." **American Scholar**, v. 42, no. 1 (Winter 1972/1973) 135-38.

Rome, a beautiful city, is made hideous by noise and depressing by the essentially political approach of the journalists who sip his whisky. "If, in an interview, I diffidently mention the faith of my fathers, with its intellectual dignity and its fixed but reasonable dogmas, the antifascist sneers begin, and I shudder at the impending columnar venom." On the ship **Rafaello**, outward bound for New York, he is not impressed by the cuisine or his travelling companions. At a performance of **Random Harvest**, the *mafiosa* next to him is audibly moved by the sweet and intelligible decency of it all. No-one has read any of his books. "All this serves me right for travelling first-class. Next time I shall learn my place and travel with the lean intellectuals in tourist . . . . Two keen-eyed immigration officers, young men from Columbia, recognize me and say, "Welcome to New York, Mr. Burgess." A moment far sweeter than the denouement of **Random Harvest**. The lady with the writer friend in Manhattanville hears. Two of the Mafia men hear. Nobody welcomes *them*."

1426 "The Waste Land Revisited." **Horizon**, v. 14, no. 1 (Winter 1972) 105-9.

Describes the effect **The Wasteland** had on him when he was a boy of fifteen ("I took in with relish the horns and motors and the throbbing taxi, the fishing by the dull canal, the carbuncular small house-agent's clerk"), gives a summary of the poem, and compares the literary techniques of Eliot and Joyce. "The twentieth century has seen bigger and more ambitious poems than **The Wasteland** — the still unfinished **Cantos** of Pound, the **Anathemata** of David Jones, the **Anabase** of Saint John Perse — but none has been a more miraculous mediator between the hermetic and the demotic."

1427 "Hamlet — World Premiere." **Stratford Papers**, 1968-69, p. 75-84. Ed. by B. A. W. Jackson. Shannon, Ireland: Irish University Press, 1972.

Describes the insurrection and execution of the Earl of Essex and then tries to imagine what it was like to witness the first performance of **Hamlet** in 1601 ("Let us now eschew known facts and enter a world of pure speculation").

1428 "Just $10.00, Please For My Mugger." **Vogue**, v. 161 (January 1973) 112.

He finds it very difficult to get a credit card in spite of his professorial position, reputation as a kind of international author, solidity and his age. Spent nearly five weeks trying to open a bank account in New York. Traveller's checks are suspect. Large bank notes are cautiously scrutinized to detect possible forgeries. "I suppose what I'm observing in America is the growth of a collective distrust so massive that even money, that traditional American idol, is beginning to be doubted."

1429 "Viewpoint." **Times Literary Supplement**, 19 January 1973, p. 64.

On American television. In quantity it leads the world, but it lacks the good European tradition of drama written expressly for the medium. Also on the addictiveness of turning literary texts into musicals. He has in mind musicals based on Thomas Mann's **The Transposed Head** and other works. Delivers a lecture on Joyce before the Celtic section of the Modern Language Association, and feels cheap, unlearned and ineloquent in the learned company. On his teaching methods. When asked to give a style-kit, he lists selected works by Ford Maddox Ford, George Eliot, Henry James, Max Beerbohm, James Joyce . . . .

1430 "The Offshore Islanders." **New York Times Book Review**, 28 January 1973, p. 4.

Review of **England's People from Roman Occupation to the Present**, by Paul Johnson.

1431 "In the Other England, the Land of Cotton, Nobody Says 'Baaaaath'." **New York Times**, Resort and Travel Section, 28 January 1973, pp. 1, 13.

[Celebrates Lancashire as a better vacation alternative than London.] Includes samples of Lancashire dialect, tells a coarse joke of death and sodomy, praises the local cuisine (fish and chips, tripe, cowheels, hot pot), describes the Saturday night pub life and his own experience as a pub pianist. For short but appreciative letters by Nat Halebsky, Otto Janssen, Stephen L. Johnson, Mrs. Robert N. Manning, and Leslie Rebanks, see "Pubbing and Dubbing in the Baaaaalmy 'Other England'," **New York Times**, Resort and Travel Section, 25 February 1973, p. 4. Burgess replies.

1432 "Boo." **New York Times Book Review**, 11 February 1973, p. 2.

An omnibus review of current Gothic and supernatural fiction available in paperbacks. He is respectful of Thomas Tryon's **The Other** and Peter Blatty's **The Exorcist**, but has exuberant fun with what he calls "femfic" — the cliché-ridden gothic fiction written mainly by women for women. For letter by Joan Cleworth, see **New York Times**, 1 April 1973, p. 36.

1433 "Viewpoint." **Times Literary Supplement**, v. 72 (March 23, 1973) 322.

On **Cyrano!** Musicals are expensive: natural wastage and restrictive union rules are the cause. Gives account of a woman admirer, probably mad, who believes that his work is a personal attack on her ("an urge to rape her mind, take over her cerebrum and fill it with my own ideas, rhythms, even tone of voice") prompted by lethal malice [cf. **Clockwork Testament**]. The cops who hauled her out put their own broad interpretation on the affair. Also on his cogent and reasonable denunciations of Blackspeak which resulted in the (empty) threat of violence. Worries about the ease with which America induces and rewards the lesser talent of talking, performing and making a fool of oneself (**vide** Mailer and Capote), his statelessness, the fact that he has not worked on his novel-in-progress since last August . . . . For letter by Neil Corcoran, see TLS, 30 March 1973, p. 353. Corcoran observes that Burgess misquotes Eliot. The line reads "Old men ought to be explorers." For relatively long letter by Joyce Carol Oates, see TLS, 13 April 1973, p. 420. Burgess' view that the writer must take responsibility for the consequences of his written words, while moving, bears examination. The role of the artist is to give coherence and form to unconscious emotions. Burgess also fails to understand the theatrical and exhausting nature of American society, which makes it necessary for the virtuous to advertise their virtue.

1434 Review of **Places**, by James Morris. **New York Times Book Review**,8 April 1973, p. 28.

The book is an example of a genre, once popular and even moderately lucrative near-art form: the old-fashioned book of travel richly laced with good organic British creamy charm. It is marked by thoroughgoing optimism; it includes solid information; and it captures the spirit, if not the smell, of most of the places visited. Literary men use their travels, not for belles-lettres, but to include in their novels. Often they invent foreign places they have not even visited and they have shown (Pynchon, Joyce, Bellow, Kafka, Burgess) considerable skill in doing so.

1435 "Focus on Theatre: Lorelei and Roxane — Two Enduring Dumb Blondes." **Harper's Bazaar**, v. 106 (April 1973) 98, 128.

[Burgess on Edmond Rostand's **Cyrano de Bergerac** and his own adaptation under the title **Cyrano!**] He has taken the liberty of changing the name of Roxane to Roxana, partly to evoke Defoe's fictional naughty lady. Gives the plot of the play and observes of Roxane/Roxana: "Can one find in all dramatic literature a more implausible chunk of Eve's flesh?" Since no modern audience is willing to accept the Platonic convention that exists at the heart of the play (the preference of Cyrano's wit and spirit to Christian's dumb, worshipping physicality) his version has transformed Roxana into a sort of psychiatric case. The bourgeois Roxana associates crude protestations of love with dirty old men full of wine and blue blood; *ergo*, she needs the more poetical and refined Cyrano. Briefly comments on the proverbial and irresistible appeal of the dumb blonde "But no woman, except Roxana, is ever really stupid in the important things — pleasure, mink, holding a man. Intellect, *pace* Femlib, has always been a little supererogatory."

1436 "Viewpoint." **Times Literary Supplement**, v. 72 (May 11, 1973) 526.

On misquotation in daily life, and the role of literary allusion in literary practice (with a glance at a passage in **Enderby**) and his experience as a teacher of American university students. The students are devoid of historical information (who is Holofernes? no answer), contemptuous of style, exclusively interested in content. Their literary tastes reduce their professors to tears. Also relates some of the troubles pertaining to his musical, **Cyrano!**, now running at the Colonial Theatre in Boston and almost ready for Broadway. "And everybody is saying how marvellous Sondheim's lyrics are in the rival musical **Little Night Music**, and how Burgess had better watch out." Student evaluation of their teachers are the result of democracy, anti-elitism, student power; professors are reduced to the status of entertainers.

1437 "Viewpoint." **Times Literary Supplement**, v. 72 (June 22, 1973) 718.

On the nausea induced by an undignified graduation ceremony at Fordham ("And so I end my nine months as a writer-academic having to hear **Godspell** and watching people reach-out-and touch at what should have been a dignified ceremony") and his attempt to sell copies of **Cyrano de Bergerac** at Rizzoli's bookstore. Sold 40 copies in an hour and a half. Bowed by the hardships of writing and tempted by the professorial life, the ghosts of Henry James and Dr Johnson dissuade him. The first tells him to get on with his novel; the second exudes the nobility of shabby independence. Jealously contemplates the literary success of some graduates of his creative writing courses. For letter by Brian Stone, see TLS, 6 July 1973, p. 779. American students (*pace* Burgess) are kind and considerate. Their faults are due to an open admission policy. For long letter by George W. Shea, see TLS, 20 July 1973, p. 834. Shea, Dean of Liberal Arts College, Fordham, charges Burgess with mercenary motives and unforgivable rudeness at Fordham graduation exercises. His behavior deserves to be censured clearly, loudly and publicly. For defence of Burgess by Leo Hamalian, see TLS, 10 August 1973, p. 931. Hamalian, Director of the Creative Writing Program, City College, observes that Shea is wrong on several counts. Burgess had no private secretary at City College. Further, to intimate that this generous spirit is moved to give an address only in return for a fee of $500 is false.

1438 "For Permissiveness with Misgivings." **New York Times Magazine**, 1 July 1973, pp. 19-20.

Books and films like "Deep Throat" are denounced as obscene and pornographic. Since the obscene is, by definition, merely disgusting and the pornographic leads to masturbation (not yet illegal), why all the fuss? Comes out on the side of total permissiveness ("though who is doing the permitting?").

Freedom is always a terrible responsibility. The arguments against permissiveness are all aesthetic.   The bad artist, or the money-grubbing sub-artist, will exploit sex and violence since these things interest people most, and goes on to argue that a repressive state encourages aesthetic ingenuity. "It is certain that literature thrives best when its practitioners are disciplined, reticent and ingenious. Writers nowadays do not have to describe the sexual act through the devices of symbolism or the significant lacuna. They can put it all down, dripping with sweat and semen, and they are no better off — artistically speaking — for the freedom that their betters Joyce and Lawrence so dearly bought." Ingeniously points out that Judge Joel J. Tyler's objection to "Deep Throat" is probably based on aesthetic rather than legal grounds. For letter by William Gleneak, see **New York Times Magazine**, 29 July 1973, pp. 2, 4.

1439 "Viewpoint." **Times Literary Supplement**, v. 72 (August 24, 1973) 976.

Harried by heat and noise in Roman apartment ("noise every night, with me living in the middle of it and Saint Cecilia resting indifferent") he is contractually bound to work on a six part television series on the life of Moses. Briefly discusses the plot and the point of **Clockwork Testament**. Observes that censorship proposals always begin with secular, not sacred, literature. The Bible, however, has prompted some strange and bloody murders. Writes about the trials and sorrows of the free-lance writer and will, henceforth, issue more novels and less "Viewpoints." For letter by Norbert F. Gaughan, see TLS, 7 September 1973, p. 1028. Burgess is a great joy to read. Letters from stuffy Deans [see #1437] are a dime a dozen. Keep Burgess on the payroll!

1440 "Ameringlish Isn't Britglish." **New York Times Magazine**, 9 September 1973, p. 86+

Comments on some differences in usage and pronunciation. Opposes "hopefully" ("Use 'hopefully' to mean the parenthetical 'one hopes' and you are deprived of the opportunity of saying, 'It is sometimes better to travel hopefully than actually arrive'."), "disinterested" as a synonym for "uninterested," (a language blunter which kills meaning). Observes that the American taste for the laconic derives from the myth of the frontiersman; the British tough guy myths derive from the days of Elizabethan England, when a fighter could also be an orator or a poet. Abominates the use of "Hi" in response to a greeting. "This vocable represents to me the ultimate in assumed ease and synthetic palliness." Recommends Alistair Cooke as the model speaker of Ameringlish: Cooke also comes from his home town, Manchester. For letter by Louis T. Milic, see **New York Times Magazine**, 30 September 1973, p. 8.

1441 "An Ancient Kickaround (Updated)." **Time**, v. 104, no. 2 (July 8, 1974) 39.

[An editorial note explains that the momentous events of the 1974 World Cup soccer competitions strain conventional reporting techniques of factual description. What was needed was the fictional reach of a novelist.] The Kempinski Hotel in West Berlin served World Cup cocktails. "The spirit of internationalism was stretched so far that even selected chain gangs from the workers' paradise over the Wall were clanked into the corruptive world of blue films and blue jeans, then — on the final whistle of the match they witnessed — knouted off again." The British invented the game and, in fact, codified the rules of gentlemanly rugby in 1863, but soccer is a traditionally crude game, and it attracts roughs, drunks and roarers. "The *Fussballweltmeisterschaft* has brought nations together in unlethal rivalry, and that cannot well be shrugged off as a lot of fussball about nothing." [**POSTSCRIPT:** the Dutch team, popularly known as the 'Clockwork Orange' from the perfection of its graceful passes, lost to the West Germans.]

1442 "The Case for Diversity." IN **New Movements in the Study and Teaching of English**. Ed. by Nicholas Bagnall. London: Temple Smith, 1973, pp. 115-24.

1443 "Is America Falling Apart?" IN **The Norton Reader; An Anthology of Expository Prose**. 3d ed. Ed. by Arthur M. Eastman. New York: Norton, 1973, pp. 424-29.

[Reprint of #1409.]

1444 "The Novel." **New Encyclopaedia Britannica**. 15th ed. Chicago: Encyclopedia Britannica, 1974. **Macropaedia**, v. 13, p. 276-98.

1445 "Michelangelo: The Artist as Miracle-Worker." **Sunday Times Magazine** (London), 2 February 1975, p. 24, 32, 34-36.

Shakespeare and Michelangelo have this in common: both sons of the bourgeoisie, they abandoned money for art. Observes that the Florentine Buonarotti family was the more aristocratic of the two.

The young Michelangelo "could not be thrashed into learning either Latin or the mercantile virtues." Gives an account of Michelangelo's relations with the court of Lorenzo the Magnificent. When Savonarolans damned art, M. demonstrated his true allegiance by making a Cupid of almost frightening allure. After his work on the Pieta ("The work still excites mixed feelings. Few are happy about the excessive youth of the mother who holds on her lap the son taken down from the cross") he worked on the statue of David ("and one so epicene that it invokes unpleasing visions of Michelangelo's slavering over male beauty"). Gives the history of the tempestuous relations between M. and Pope Julius II and relates that it was the jealousy of his fellow artists that prompted them to ask the Pope to commission M. to work on the Sistine Chapel ("What we are disposed to think of the work is much conditioned by our knowledge of the agony entailed in creating it, with Michelangelo up there on the scaffolding for four years"). Then relates M.'s tribulations in working on the Church of San Lorenzo — the pope and popes capricious and avaricious throughout poor M.'s career. In the sonnet form, M. unlocked his heart and recorded his Platonic relationship with Vittoria Colonna and Tommaso Cavalieri, a youth of beauty and no mean intelligence. M. seemed incapable of creating a nubile female; only his men and boys are creatures in whom sexuality is admissible. M. is the "romantic paradigm of the heroic maker, fighting againt odds, achieving much against incredible opposition. His devotion to art, which he sometimes presents as a devotion to religion, seems absolute, totally unqualified by opportunism or compromise, and it admits little room for vice and ungenerosity." [Reprinted in #1451.]

1446 "On the Hopelessness of Turning Good Books Into Films." **New York Times**, Arts and Leisure Section, 20 April 1975, p. 1.

Observes that "The Exorcist," "The Great Gatsby" and "**Ulysses**" ("part of the fascination of Joseph Strick's travesty was the variety of his failure") were all inferior to the books, and argues that brilliant or successful film adaptations are based on fiction of the second or third class. Further, a film director who is fully the equal of Henry James will prefer not to interpret another artist. "The worlds of Bunuel, Fellini and Godard are totally unbookish . . . . This is why literature is superior to the other arts and, indeed, why there can be a hierarchy of arts, with ballet at the bottom and sculpture a few rungs above it." Believes that Kubrick's adaptation of **A Clockwork Orange** was marked by a major directorial style, but that the book, with its peculiar home-made idiolect, an anti-pornographic technique, muffles the violence. Expresses disatisfaction with the degree of collaboration common in the film/television world, and announces he will return to writing books. For letters by Bernard F. Dick, Warren Kronemeyer and Miles Montemore, see **New York Times**, Travel and Leisure Section, 18 May 1975, p. 19.

1447 "Writing in Rome." **Times Literary Supplement**, 31 October 1975, p. 1296.

He approaches most Italian fiction with indifference. Italian writers fail to write good novels for two reasons: the presence of numerous Italian dialects ("dialect seems diminishing and parochial to the serious writer") and their political commitment, which turns them into polemicists. Observes that he is translating some of Belli's richly obscene and blasphemous sonnets into English and provides an opening passage of his translation of Joyce's **Wake** into Italian. Fears that his murderous labor on the latter project may be interpreted as sheer frivolity by the committed Italian writers. For letters by Edwin Morgan and J.M. Edelstein, see TLS, 7 November 1975, p. 1332 and 21 November 1975, p. 1388. Both Morgan and Edelstein make a similar point. Selected poems of poet Belli *have* been translated into English.

1448 "On Lengthy Matters." **New York Times Book Review**, 14 December 1975, p. 39.

Discusses the length of the American novel compared to the thin British counterparts. Economics has nearly everything to do with it. "Our position is basically that of Dr. Samuel Johnson, forced to write the novella **Rasselas** in a week in order to pay for his mother's funeral." The one great British theme, the rise of the Empire, has been shamefully nibbled at. Still, is it not true that the best American novels have been relatively short? Contends that the long novel is easier to write than the short, and announces that he began working on a long novel [**Earthly Powers**] two years ago; he now has thirty pages in a sun-bleached folder.

1449 "How I Wrote My Third Symphony." **New York Times**, Section II, 28 December 1975, pp. 1, 19.

Describes his first symphony (he still shudders at its Vaughan Williams folksiness) and his second (it was called the 'Sinfoni Merdeka' and had been intended to celebrate Malaya's independence, and the less said about that the better) and now describes the performance of his third symphony, the Symphony in C. Invited by Jim Dixon of the Iowa University Symphony Orchestra to present a work for performance, he was suitably gratified. "But it worked. The work worked. I was, and remain, overwhelmed. I had written those noises. That was me, that great web of sonoritities being discoursed by those hundred handsome kids under that big man on the rostrum. I have written over 30 books, but this was the truly great artistic moment. Evanescent, of course." Also includes a brief review of the work by the Iowa City Press Citizen.

1450 "A Mingled Chime." **Times Literary Supplement**, 16 January 1976, p. 50.

Review of **Cyrano de Bergerac**, by Edmond Rostand. Translated by Christopher Fry. The translation is too loose, too lax, and it would probably benefit from a formally strict approach to the French verse.

1451 "Michelangelo. Pt. I. The Artist as Miracle-Worker." **The Critic**, v. 34, no. 3 (Spring 1976) 12-22.

[Reprint of #1445. Pt. II consists of Sir John Pope-Hennessy's analysis of Michelangelo's work. There is, consequently, no pt. II by Burgess.]

1452 "The Magical Madness of Flann O'Brien." **Saturday Review**, v. 3, no. 14 (April 17, 1976) 25-27.

Review of **Stories and Plays**, by Flann O'Brien. The time has come to praise O'Brien. Only when he has been praised to excess will it be the turn of the captious critic. His **At Swim-Two-Birds** owes a lot to Joyce, but it avoids the massivity of **Ulysses**. He avoids action, sexual confrontation, the fruits of mindlessness, and concentrates instead on parody, extracts from ancient heroic annals, newspaper reports, dreams, drunken phantasmagorias. This avoidance of action "seems like a limitation, but it grants scope for the only kind of extension that means much to the Irish writer — extension of fancy, of language. Your average best-seller gives you violent action and simple language. Joyce and Flann O'Brien assault your brain with words, style, magic, madness, huge vocabularies, and unlimited invention. In other words, they are literary writers, which loads the dice against their popular acceptance. Sex and dirty language helped Joyce's reputation; Flann O'Brien is as clean and unerotic as a boiled Wicklow egg . . . . Of all the neglected truth-tellers of our age, Flann O'Brien is perhaps the most considerable. He shows what life is really like when the damnable abstractions are scrubbed away. You *have* to read him."

1453 "Music at the Millennium." **Hi Fi**, v. 26, no. 5, (May 1976) 46-49.

An attempt to describe the kind of music which will be composed in the year 2001 or before. "The looked-for synthesis of the end of the millennium is a composer of personality strong enough to create an individual language out of the century's three main heritages — the diatonic, the serial, and the polytonal — *without* the aid of *literary* texts."

1454 "Dirty Words." **New York Times Magazine**, 8 August 1976, p. 6.

On words like hunkies, niggers, micks, kikes and spinsters. Argues that "harm cannot properly reside in a word, only in the attitude that animates it. You can't outlaw attitudes by outlawing words. You drive the word into an area of private darkness where it becomes more obscene." Considers "Mistress" usage preferable to "Miss" or "Ms." Readers respond. For letters by Helene Hanff, Sheila Taub and Nancy Swann, see **New York Times Magazine**, 29 August 1976, p. 46.

1455 "This Our Exile." **Spectator**, v. 237, no. 7734 (September 18, 1976) 13-14.

He moved abroad, partly to escape Great Britain's penal taxation, and partly because he is a Lancashire Catholic Saxon Celt who perceives England as vaguely foreign and vaguely inimical. The British State duly allowed him to move to Malta. He reviled the prevailing censorship and harassment of writers and found himself reviled in turn as a low-tax paying foreign ingrate. "It soon became time to move on to Italy where, having loudly reviled the Second Vatican Council and refused to accept Pope John as a Communist saint, I was frequently billed in newspaper headlines as **BURGESS IL. FASCISTA**." Exile is an expensive business ("I leave behind me a trail of unsaleable properties and irrecoverable libraries") and London is always delightful, but British fiction is becoming more and more parochial and unadventurous. He hopes he will be sometimes remembered; he is certain he will not be forgotten by Her Britannic Majesty's Commissioners of Inland Revenue.

1456 "The Long Road to Nzima." **Times Literary Supplement**, 19 November 1976, p. 1443.

Review of **A Supplement to the Oxford English Dictionary**. Vol. 2: H-N. Ed. by R.W. Burchfield. The work is an example of devotion, precision and elegance in a world of slipshod artifacts and insolent artificers. Dr. Burchfield stated his public view that no word would be excluded from this work on the ground that it might be offensive to a given group. "These conclusions are admirable enough, but I feel disquiet at the notion that it should seem necessary to arrive at them." A lexicographer should only consider one offense; that against the gods of accuracy. Considers some of the words in the dictionary (mavrodaphne, juvescence [which ought to be juvenescence], jamrag, Jesuit, James Bond, ludic, novelette) and delivers some quibbles. "The **Supplement** is respectfully dedicated to Her Majesty the Queen, and the existence of one of the most glorious achievements of her reign is thus a fact that the Executive may not ignore. The ennoblement of Dr. Burchfield and selected members of his staff should at least be seriously considered while the next honours list of jockeys (disc and turf), showbiz paladins, female impersonators and time-servers is being compiled."

1457 "A Resonant Bellow." **Spectator**, v. 237, no. 7744 (November 27, 1976) 26.

Review of **To Jerusalem and Back**, by Saul Bellow. "The propriety of awarding [Bellow] the Nobel prize is, to me, proved by the fact that he has evinced no new line of development since the ten-year old **Herzog** . . . . He is a long-settled, totally achieved artist, and to such men the Nobel prize must go. He joins Rolland, Galsworthy and Matilde Serao as a prizewinner from whom it would be indecent to expect literary surprises." The notable things in this book include the portrait of Teddy Kollek, the conversation with Henry Kissinger ("Ah, if only the Bible had been written in Uganda. Everyone would have been so much better off") and the enjoyment of the minutiae of daily existence proper to a novelist.

1458 "Provincial Gothic." **Spectator**, v.237, no. 7746 (December 11, 1976) 21-22.

Review of **Havergal Brian: The Making of a Composer**, by Kenneth Eastaugh and **Havergal Brian: The Man and his Music**, by Reginald Nettel. "Inevitably the music-making of Brian's Potteries was provincial in the pejorative sense. The musicians sprang, as Brian himself did, out of the working-class: there was no tempering of skill with aristocratic taste, and it would have been hard for a Fauré or a Ravel to come into being among the horny-handed choristers and fiddlers. Facetiousness had to substitute for wit . . . . The **Gothic Symphony** is both a horror and a wonder."

1459 "Kidney-Stealing Harmlessly." **Times Literary Supplement**, 17 December 1976, p. 1576.

Review of **Norman Douglas**, by Mark Holloway. "**South Wind** remains as a delight, though a steadily diminishing one. It belongs with, say, **Sinister Street** and the early novels of Somerset Maugham and perhaps **His Monkey Wife** as a kind of mule literature which cannot beget and stubbornly resists dislodgement . . . . This book is so well done that I doubt if it will ever have to be done again."

1460 "All Too Irish." **Irish Press** (Dublin), 13 January 1977, p. 6.

Review of **James Joyce's Disunited Kingdom and the Irish Dimension**, by John Garvin. Despite two books on Joyce, a shorter **Finnegans Wake** and a Broadway musical called "The Blooms of Dublin," he feels unqualified to read Joyce's deeper meanings. Dr. Garvin's knowledge of Dublin is large, but his approach to Joyce may well cast out love.

1461 "Choosing to Die." **Times Literary Supplement**, no. 3905 (January 14, 1977) 33.

Review of **Black Sun; The Brief Transit and Violent Eclipse of Harry Crosby**, by Geoffrey Wolff. "He ranged the world of sensation as sedulously as any good pupil of Lord Henry Wotton and began to learn about diminishing returns. There is a limit to what the body can do. The Mind knows no limits, and the same is true of art, but one may deduce from Harry's dicta as much as his writings that both his taste and his intelligence were severely circumscribed."

1462 "Homo Sibilans." **Times Literary Supplement**, no. 3906 (January 21, 1977) 65.

Review of **Whistled Languages**, by R.G. Busnel and A. Classe.

1463 "Reputations Revisited." **Times Literary Supplement**, no. 3906, January 21, 1977, p. 67.

A paragraph. Some writers are overrated (Gide, Hesse, Forster); others are underrated (Ford Maddox Ford, Conrad Aiken).

1464 "Up the Monument." **Spectator**, v. 238, (January 22, 1977) 20-21.

Review of **Shakespeare: The Man and his Achievement**, by Robert Speaight. It is a model of factuality, fine critical exposition and lucid prose, but it errs in the direction of overcautious conservatism. Rowse's proposed identification of the 'Dark Lady' is cautiously weighed. G.B. Harrison's proposal that the Dark Lady was black is not even mentioned. Wishes Speaight had said more about the occasions for which the plays were written. Doubts if Speaight's suggestion of a harmonious matrimonial life can be accurate with Shakespeare away in scortatory London much of the time. Regrets that Speaight does not consider the sounds of Elizabethan English.

1465 "A $200 Million Erector Set." **New York Times Magazine**, 23 January 1977, pp. 14-22.

An account of the Centre national d'art et de culture Georges Pompidou. Also includes some of Burgess' incidental brooding about the role of the state in subsidizing the arts.

1466 "A Lion's Roar." **Library Journal**, v. 102, no. 3 (February 1, 1977) 327-29.

[A squib reprinted from the Annual Report of the New York Public Library.] Describes the life of a student in the future. Books are abolished. Microfiche books are the norm, and to conserve space, logograms replace words. Learning, since there is so much to learn, will be done through hypnopedia. Students will be prodigies of learning. When asked if they are happy, they will reply: Indubitably, apodictically, incontestably, no. By the year 2051 all languages but Anglo-American were abolished. Those who protested about their inability to read Racine and Goethe in the original were liquidated as TCEs (Trouble Causing Esthetes). Laments the stylistic infelicities of his earlier books, and dreams of destroying the microfiches of his works, but fears the electronic liquidators will do him in. "And, as my dust is carried off triumphantly in a box, those ancient lions will roar satisfaction. ntny brgss. Poughkeepsie, June 16, 2976."

1467 "Blood Groups." **Irish Press** (Dublin), 10 February 1977, p. 6.

Review of **Dreams of Revenge**, by Kevin Casey. The plot, bloody and glamorous, suggests the cinema; but the literary distinction of the book is that it effectively transcribes the language of love. "Here on the page we can only have breathy cliché, yet the cliché is rhymically [rhythmically?] so well disposed that it sounds like the world's first lovers. Or the second, or third." Casey also does well with the Irish disability, the fact that Joyce and O'Casey and Flann O'Brien have made Dublin the most magical city in the world, and he successfully neutralizes his town as if it were set in the Balkans.

1468 "A Shrivel of Critics; Modest Proposals for Reviewers." **Harper's**, v. 254, no. 1521 (February 1977) 87-91.

Advice to book reviewers prompted by acid or incompetent reviews of **Beard's Roman Women**. Protests against the practice of identifying the fictional Ronald Beard with the real Anthony Burgess. Presents a quiz of some 10 questions on literature which, he suggests, reviewers must be able to pass before they commit themselves to the trade of reviewing.

1469 "The Gospel According to Anthony Burgess." **New York Times**, Section II, 3 April 1977, pp. 1, 36.

[Editorial note describes controversy and withdrawal of support caused by Zeffirelli's statement that the film '**Jesus of Nazareth**' would depict Christ as a man rather than a divine miracle worker.] Sir Lew Grade announced that there would be this film. The Romans laid on a feast; Sir Lew was made a *cavaliere* of the Republic; and then there was a long silence as the author of the filmscript [Burgess] retired to his motor caravan to study the synoptic Gospels, Josephus, histories of the Roman Empire, manuals on the technique of crucifixion. Became very disatisfied with the accounts of Matthew, Mark and Luke (good propagandists but bad historians). Describes his characterization of Judas as an innocent tricked into betraying the Messiah. Also his attempts to give the twelve apostles recognizable human features and how, in the course of the writing, he was hounded by the theological experts of Radiotelevisone Italiana. Comments on his conception of Christ (more the Tiger than the gentle lamb) and on the injunction that we must change ourselves before we can change society. "Of the revolutionary nature of his program and its feasibility, given hard work and self-denial, I became more convinced than ever I had been when I was a good son of the Church."

1470 "Orwell's **1984**." **Times** (London), 20 April 1977, p. 12.

[For letter by William Alderson, see **Times** (London), 2 May 1977, p. 13.]

1471 "Tarot Tales." **Irish Press** (Dublin), 21 April 1977, p. 6.

Review of **The Castle of Crossed Destinies**, by Italo Calvino.

1472 "All About Yves." **New York Times Magazine**, 11 September 1977, pp. 118-21, 128-29, 132-33, 34, 38, 140.

About Yves Saint Laurent, the fashion designer.

1473 "In the Year of the Jubilee." **Times Literary Supplement**, no. 3909 (February 11, 1977) 147.

Review of **Majesty**, by Robert Lacey. "The one [anecdote] I liked best. . . relates to the royal automobile splashing a woman with mud in the Sandringham district. The woman yelled something. The Queen said: 'I quite agree with you, madam.' Prince Philip said: 'What did she say, darling?' The Queen said: 'Bastards.' . . . . Readers of the TLS, as opposed to **Country Life**, share few of her tastes and interests, but doggy horsey philistinism is a better guarantee of stability than a passion for Heidegger and John Cage." For letter by Zacharias P. Thundy, see TLS, 25 February 1977, p. 215.

1474 "Multi-plying the Many-minded." **Times Literary Supplement**, no. 3910 (February 18, 1977) 177.

Review of **The Consciousness of Joyce**, by Richard Ellmann. A long discussion of **Ulysses** in the light of Joyce's politics ("His work is sedulously condemned by certain sectors as reactionary, perhaps because he considered humanity not fundamentally changeable and thought the taste of a cheese sandwich more interesting than a Marxist tract"), some of the works in his 600 volume private library and his knowledge of European languages. Although this work reawakens a sleeping belief in the glory of making literature, he sincerely hopes that Ellmann will produce that long-delayed biography of Oscar Wilde.

1475 Review of **O America, When You and I Were Young**, by Luigi Barzini. **New York Times Book Review**, 3 April 1977, p. 9.

Barzini, the son of the great Barzini of Milan, first of the modern Italian journalists, is a charming, witty and erudite interpreter of Italians to the English-speaking world. The young Luigi's twin preoccupations were the English language, and the opposite sex, and the two subjects rarely interpenetrated. The orotundity of this book is at variance with the sharp cinematic memories of bar fights, necking and viewing gangster corpses in the line of duty. The prose is good, clean and idiomatic but, by suitable compression, its length could have been cut in half.

1476 "The Vocation of a Virtuoso." **Times Literary Supplement**, no. 3913 (April 8, 1977) 419.

Review of **Yehudi Menuhin: Unfinished Journey**, by Yehudi Menuhin. "Add to all this [musical "genius," loving-kindness and saintly character] a respect for the human frame which springs out of the physico-spiritual nexus of his primary vocation and has been nourished by contact with yoga, and you have a personality that puts to shame those of us who smoke, snarl, drink and cherish ill-health as a supposedly necessary ground for creativity." For letter by Yehudi Menuhin, see TLS, 22 April 1977, p. 488. Observes he has played the Berg concerto. To compare his style, as Burgess does, to that of a Scottish engineer, is singularly appropriate.

1477 "Celluloid Celebrants." **Times Literary Supplement**, no. 3921 (May 6, 1977) 546.

Review of **The Film Addict's Archive**, edited by Philip Oakes. "They always say film is a visual medium, but it is the things *said* we remember: this is bigger than both of us; God is a jealous God; this could be the beginning of a wonderful friendship; nobody's perfect. What is memorable is always a kind of literature."

1478 "Le mal francais: Is There a Reason for Being Cartesian?" **New York Times Magazine**, 29 May 1977, pp. 47-48, 52-53.

The English see many fine things in French culture that are absorbable. The Americans see France as something foreign, and France has had a minimal effect on the American way of life. The French vice is arrogance. They take an inordinate pride in their language and brutally correct those foreigners guilty of solecisms. They also take pride in being Cartesian, although few of them are sure of the meaning of the term. To some extent, the French are fine logicians and (witness Sartre, Camus, Claude Levi-Strauss) endowed with a great capacity for inventing philosophical systems. The French are good logicians in that they hate waste. Great cuisine and high *couture* begin with doing the best you can with the little you have. The French disease, as Alain Peyrefitte, the new Minister of Justice has been pointing out, is the gap between ideation and realization. Discloses the results of a French public opinion poll and observes that the Rabelaisean tradition (not the Cartesian) needs to be revived and fostered. Then gives an account of the illustrated adventures of Asterix the Gaul, a work which exemplifies the Rabelaisean tradition.

1479 "Lord Grade's Will." **Observer Review** (London), 29 May 1977, p. 28.

Review of **Will Shakespeare**, by John Mortimer. "Mr. Mortimer's novel about Shakespeare, a very difficult subject for fiction, foredraws critical incisors by calling itself 'an entertainment'." Confides that the idea of putting Shakespeares' life on the small screen was his own. The plan was to appeal to both a British and Italian audience. Hopes that the eventual telefilm made from Mortimer's sparkling piece of fiction will reflect Mortimer's contribution. Observes that directors have the power to cut when it pleases them. The book also reflects the exigencies imposed ("we never move far from the Rose-Theatre-Globe or from an adjoining tavern") by a limited budget. The book is plainly about the externals of Shakespeare's life; we are not permitted to look inside the fiddleshaped dome. "This [emphasis] is in order for a television series which it is hoped will hold its viewers; such viewers will want tossed chicken-bones, gadzookery, tits, fumbled plackets, but not too much of a player's lust either: this has to be good family viewing." Mr. Mortimer, QC, knows the law of Shakespeare's time, but he owes us more than 'an entertainment.'

1480 "What Literature Is About." **Irish Press** (Dublin), 2 June 1977, p. 6.

Review of **The Shrine and Other Other Stories**, by Mary Lavin. The title story "conveys what is most disturbing about Irish Catholicism — and the colonial variety it has set up in, for instance, the North of England; its inability to encompass good taste, a dour puritanism that denies life . . . . Mary Lavin is not a poet in the sense that she loves to indulge in floreate language — though she's not averse to a rare candenza [i.e. cadenza]. Her style is bare and direct, her dialogue artfully flat. But in her capacity to make much out of little, to compress an entire ethos into an apparently banal situation, she reminds us — far more than the erectors of post Flaubertain pyramids — what literature is about."

1481 "The Life in Orbit." **Times Literary Supplement**, 3 June 1977, p. 676.

Review of **The High Frontier; Human Colonies in Space**, by Gerard K. O'Neill.

1482 "Strands of Twisted Threads." **Irish Press** (Dublin), 9 June 1977, p. 11.

Review of **Yarns**, by John Jordan. "In 'Passion,' Mr. Jordan sums up in four pages the damnable sexual inhibitions which plague the Irish, even the very modern Irish, quite as much as the English . . . . Dympna and Bill have been married three weeks and are on holiday in Seville. (Don Juan's town, after all.) They have dinner and go to bed. Dympna is there first, 'her hair dull yellow against the pillow, and lying as she always did while she waited for him, like an effigy on a tomb.' Bill is shocked by the strength of his desire. 'Not even a husband has a right to feel like this.' So he drinks off a flask of cognac, thinking Dympna asleep. But Dympna is silently awake, praying for strength against temptation . . . ."

1483 "The Prince of Percussion." **Times Literary Supplement**, no. 3917 (June 10, 1977) 706.

Review of **Drum Roll**, by James Blades. "Jimmy is equally fascinating when he describes the contrivance of that memorable heart-beat which is to be heard in the battlements scene of Olivier's **Hamlet**. A stethophonic recording of a real heart was 'like someone consuming thick soup with a rhythmic intake,' so finally Vivien Leigh's fur coat was draped over a bass drum and Jimmy prodded with his finger tips." For letter by Ralph Leavis, see TLS, 17 June 1977, p. 733.

1484 "Growing Up an Only Child." **New York Times**, 15 June 1977, The Living Section, Section C, pp. 1, 11.

The **New York Times** cabled for a 750 word article ("My wife and I were asleep on the floor — we cannot afford a bed, not at French prices in our apartment when the bell rang viciously and awoke us"). Comments that he was a half-orphan a year after he was born, and a full orphan before the age of twenty-one. "The state of being parentless was to me less significant than being siblingless." Wishes he had had a sister ("We need the opposite sex in the bedroom next to ours, seen naked occasionally, growing to nubility, but as it were, defused") and remarks that, in the future, father and mother will be brother and sister to the only child. For letter by Mrs. F. St. Sauveur, see **New York Times**, 20 July 1977, Section C, p. 6.

1485 "Last of the Literary Dandies." **Observer** (London), 10 July 1977, p. 24.

1486 "Condemnations." **Irish Press** (Dublin), 21 July 1977, p. 6.

Review of **Proxopera**, by Benedict Kiely. This book about a peaceful citizen who is compelled to convey a gelignite bomb by the Brit-haters prompts him to reflect, moved as he is, on the whole damnable situation. "The techniques of modern terrorism do not allow for heroism in the victim. The gunmen know now that nobody minds dying, but that nobody can yet, if he or she is just, take on responsibility for somebody else's death. The time may be coming when one will have to see one's children and grandchildren killed before one's eyes — if the deaths of thousands are to be avoided and the responsibility will be made to be one's own . . . . When we reach the stage of open admission of killing because liking to kill, then we'll have arrived at the final honesty and horror. I seem to have adumbrated this already in the worst of my books." [The reference is probably to **A Clockwork Orange**.]

1487 "The Milesian Firbolg." **Times Literary Supplement**, no. 3933 (July 29, 1977) 909-910.

Review of **Tom Moore**, by Terence de Vere White. William Hazlitt thought little of Moore's melodies but then, he was not a musician. The near-banalities and tarnished elegances are deliberate: the meanings must not obtrude above the singable tunes. Moore "hits softly. Hazlitt wanted Moore to shout out words of Irish defiance in London drawing-rooms (and thus, as Hazlitt sometimes was, be thrown out), but Moore's way was one of delicate insinuation as far as the inflammatory libertarian themes were concerned."

1488 "Business as Usual." **Irish Press** (Dublin), 11 August 1977, p. 6.

Review of **The Danger Tree**, by Olivia Manning. "How bright this canvas is, how telling and memorable the banal words spoken, and the odd fitting characters who speak them. One has the impression of being in a living world full of people in a living time. 'In countries where a lot of mangoes are eaten,' says their host, Dobson, 'someone dies from mango poisoning every year.' Guy hates the tree and goes on eating the fruit. The radiance of the symbol will become clear enough to the reader, though not too clear. Olivia Manning is a very subtle writer."

1489 Review of **The Consul's File**, by Paul Theroux. **New York Times Book Review**, 21 August 1977, p. 1.

In this collection of short stories about Malaya, the American presence has replaced the British raj. Burgess predicted this development as far back as 1958 in his **The Long Day Wanes**. These stories about a Malayan Christmas, a maleficent tree (*orosylum indicum*) which almost kills a young American, the rape of a fat and graceless American girl may sound like fanciful shockers but Burgess, who has spent six years there "can only nod sagely and shiveringly at Theroux's terse narrations. His book is a rounded and many-sided. . . portrait of a typical Malayan town, with its jungle and paddy-fields . . . . We always had odd Frenchmen lurking about, taking notes. I remember meeting Jean Cocteau, who called Kuala Lumpur *Kouala l'impure*. He was right. The whole damned country is glamorous with impurity, and Paul Theroux has caught a great deal of it."

1490 "Twixt Proverb and Quote." **Times Literary Supplement**, no. 3937 (August 26, 1977) 1027.

Review of **A Dictionary of Catch Phrases British and American, From the Sixteenth Century to the Present Day**, by Eric Partridge. "Few objections are in order in such a work. 'Partridge is game,' as his best friend said on the Somme, and we should be thankful for so much rank tastiness." Corrects some errors, presents samples of catch phrases and observes that the demotic creativeness of the spoken language finds no counterpart in the English of the upper classes.

1491 "Anticipating Nothing." **Irish Press** (Dublin), 1 September 1977, p. 6.

Review of **Girl on a Bicycle**, by Leland Bardwell. "How terrible all the characters are, except Bernard, who loves her, but he also loves another woman who's having a baby and he has a wife somewhere. The horses are all right, they don't let anybody down, and they're neither Protestant nor Catholic.

How loathsome are the upper-class English and the lower-class Irish. How ghastly is wartime Dublin. *Anticipating nothing*; it sums up the whole situation.'' Grumbles that the printers fail to do justice to Ms. Bardwell's stylistic distinction.

1492 "That's What It's All About." **New Statesman**, v. 94, no. 2424 (September 2, 1977) 308.

Confesses he onced sinned and used parrot jargon ("That's what life's all about") when asked about the violence of **Clockwork**. He has also, corrupted by New York usage, used 'hopefully' as if it were *höffentlich*. This book of usage, which deals with words the average **Times** letter writer would regard as trouble spots (charismatic, clinical, gay, camp, ethnics) deals with them sensible and learnedly. "The pejorative kind of semantic change has always been commoner than the meliorative, human nature being what it is, and Mr. Howard shows how *student* is coming to mean irresponsible young layabout, just as *research* can signify the looking up of telephone numbers and the riffling through of stacks of old press cuttings." All the semantemes used by politicians (theology, metaphysical and academic in the mouth of Harold Wilson) are probably suspect. For a letter by W.D. Jones commenting on the etymology of the word "camp" see NS, v. 94, no. 2435 (November 18, 1977) 691.

1493 "The Big World of Dublin." **Irish Press** (Dublin), 15 September 1977, p. 6.

Review of **Farewell Companions**, by James Plunkett. "Plunkett's first and second novels [**Strumpet City** and the work under review] together form an ambitious panorama of changing unchanging Dublin. I think that anybody who wishes to understand the impact of great exterior events on ordinary people touched, as the Irish are, by that eternal on whose fabric history is but a transitory stain (God, I feel my own Irishry coming out here), has to read them. I think also that Plunkett's artistic career is just beginning. He may, if he has not already done so, have to go into exile and write about the big world called Notdublin. Of his fineness of ear and architectonic skill (this is a long novel), as well as his capacity for plumbing the human heart, I am in no doubt at all. But he must stop writing about Dublin."

1494 "Peking Drugs, Moscow Gold." **New York Times Book Review**, 25 September 1977, p. 9+

Review of **The Honourable Schoolboy**, by John Le Carré. The author has worked with the British Foreign Office, and his contribution to the fiction of espionage has its roots in the truth of how a spy system works. For this reason, his spies are grubbily realistic; his plot is devoid of fantastic schemes; and the locale is confined to Hong Kong where British influence still has some effect. "This is a very long book for its subject, and there is scene after scene — usually back in London where the Circus operates — in which the old fictional principle of Ockham's Razor (less is more) is relentlessly eschewed." The dialogues are commendably varied and real. On the other hand, they go on forever. The facetiousness, cliché-laden and often brutal, makes one's teeth ache. The technicalities are faultless, but the book is not a work of literature comparable to Conrad's **Under Western Eyes** or even Greene's **The Quiet American**.

1495 "Murray and His Monument." **Times Literary Supplement**, 30 September 1977, p. 1094-95.

Review of **Caught in the Web of Words**, by K.M. Elisabeth Murray. We know the scope of the work because we have the work. "The **OED** [Oxford English Dictionary, or Murray] though Murray did not live to edit all of it, and though, through its Supplements, it must be said to be always in the making, is as great a product of Victorian enterprise as the erections of Brunel or the Disraelian Empire." The record shows that the work brought Murray little profit. It brought him honorary doctorates and a worrying knighthood ("the tradesmen might put up their prices"), but it did not get him the recognition of the Oxford swells. Gives an account of some of the colorful characters who surrounded Murray and observes "There are naive people around who regard philologists as dull, forgetting that the rogue-god Mercury presides over language." For letter by Keith Walker, see TLS, 7 October 1977, p. 1149; 14 October 1977, p. 1200 (Frederick A. Pottle). Walker alleges that Burgess' arguments do not prove Dr Johnson a conservative in linguistic and lexicographical matters. Pottle comments on a point in the grammar of Robert Burns.

1496 "My Seven Wonders of the World." **Sunday Times Magazine** (London), 16 October 1977, p. 90-95.

His choices are limited by his temperament, physical endowment and myopia; they all share a common element of gross vulgarity. The Tiger Balm Gardens in Singapore has flowers and greenery "but the statues of strong men (healthy with Tiger Balm) are a fascinating horror." His second is a certain pet chameleon which, in the Sergeant's Mess went to heroic lengths to mimic the ingenious backgrounds. Tried on the name "James Joyce" it plainly got a little joy. His third wonder is the old British monetary system, now abandoned as un-Cartesian. Gilbert and Sullivan's **The Mikado** is in fourth place. The libretto is remarkable and intelligent even if it is notable for a certain misogyny and bloodthirstiness. The Petrarchan sonnet ranks fifth: it accommodates an incredible range of thought and feeling. Champagne, as well as Evelyn Waugh's cure for a champagne hangover, rank in the sixth place. The seventh is Fritz Lang's **Metropolis**. "The images of the recessive Future that I hold will always be those of Fritz Lang, despite the manifest cut-out quality of his skyscrapers and raised motorways. The leading lady, Brigitte Helm, plays both the Robot Siren and the Female Apostle to the Enslaved Workers, and changing fashions of acting and maquillage have not diminished her seductiveness in both roles."

1497 "Five Sonnets by Giuseppe Gioachino Belli, (1791-1863); Translated from the Roman Dialect by Anthony Burgess." **Malahat Review**, no. 44 (October 1977) 17-19.

Includes poems entitled "The Creation of the World," "The Earthly Paradise of the Beasts," "Pride Before a Fall," "Back to the Roots," and "Man."

1498 "Five Futures for Britain: Tucland." **New Society**, (November 17, 1977) 343-44.

[Burgess contributes one of five predictions about the future of Britain.] The British future can be predicted on the basis of the British present: a syndicalism that demands special rights and partial justice. Syndicalist tyranny always strikes at essentials. The country will be dominated by the unions [Tucland = the land of the Trades Union Congress], and it will be terribly dull. Television will prevail. Towns will be calculatedly utilitarian; there will be violence after dark. The old humanists, in revolt against trade unionism and state education, will live in catacombs; the police will keep them moving as tramps and dissidents. Trade unionists suppose that security is the main aim in life. Burgess believes that drama is, or was, the main end of man. It is possible that a war will come simply to dispel the tedium of television, sleep, more money. Discusses the war fought in his novel, **The Wanting Seed**.

1499 "The English Language." **Architectural Review**, v. 162, no. 969 (November 1977) 305-6.

Comments on certain aspects of English usage — the supplanting of "owing to" by "due to," the spreading use of "hopefully," the American use of "good" to serve as both adjective and adverb. Argues that language changes are inevitable: the uniformity of Orwellian Newspeak is a pipe-nightmare. Comments on vowel changes and the instability of short vowels (in *can* and *man*, *love* and *but*) as well as the influence of American English (and the American television market) on British diction and speech habits.

1500 "On the Glottal Frontier." **Times Literary Supplement**, no. 3948, November 25, 1977, p. 1378.

On pidgin languages and the possibility that Middle English is a kind of creole. "A creole is a sophisticated pidgin, with structures still simple but vocabulary larger, and it can serve as a mother tongue."

1501 "Homage to Barcelona." **New York Times Magazine**, 4 December 1977, pp. 44-45, 80, 84, 86, 88, 166, 167.

Account of a rail trip from Monaco to Barcelona. The train is late, but he is grateful not to fly and risk a final fiery dissolution. Comments on the banning of the Catalan language under Franco and observes that you need Latin to understand the tongues derived from the Roman legionaries. They arrive at the detested town of Avignon; he was once thoroughly robbed there. The Spanish border police revive the Franco years. Describes a good dinner; the wine is like bullfighter's blood. Then talks to the barman about Groucho Marx, admires the local graffiti, and observes the nudity in the bookstalls ("the new popular journalism is franker but ranker"). Describes Gaudi's masterpiece, the still unfinished church of the Sagrada Familia as well as the Casa Battilo. "The stark rectangular is anathema to Gaudi; hard stone must appear not merely soft but edible." Also describes Il Tibidabo and Montjuich. Provides brief summary of Catalanian politics and describes some of the early works of Picasso. Describes a meeting with Jorge Edwards, comments on his own **Christ the Tiger**, and praises the literary uses of regional dialects (you get away from abstractions). Then lunch with his Spanish publisher Paco Porrua, drinks with Alfonso Quinta Sadurni, Barcelona-born journalist, and discusses the King and the Church. Observes that it's time for Americans to discover Barcelona.

1502 "Writer' Writers." **New York Times Book Review**, 4 December 1977, p. 3.

[Burgess is asked to name the writer he most admires.] Since admiration is nothing without love and, given the death of Nabokov, he nominates J.B. Priestley. His last novel, **The Image Men**, is his best. Burgess has read it ten times. He admires "any writer who defies the etiolated standards of contemporary letters by producing much, reviving the old picaresque, and thundering away at the debasements of modern society. A Dickensian Christmas to him."

1503 "Joy to the Word." **New York Times Book Review**, 25 December 1977, pp. 1, 18.

Review of **The Joyful Christian**, by C.S. Lewis. Lewis became a very notable popular exegete of Holy Writ after his conversion to Christianity, but he is the cool Anglican to the core. He refuses, for example, to accept the doctrine of transubstantiation. "I have just come back from Naples, and I wondered there how Lewis's theology would go down with these passionate pagans who have no trouble in swallowing whole the Catholic sacramental system, along with sinning, stealing, knifing, reviling San Gennaro's statue for neglecting to bleed, seeing no real frontier between the quotidian and the eternal. Lewis, on the other hand, is the ideal persuader for the half-convinced, for the good man who would like to be a Christian but finds his intellect getting in the way."

1504 "You've Had Your Time; Being the Beginning of an Autobiography." **Malahat Review**, no. 44 (1977) 10-16.

Observes that he begins this chronicle on his 60th birthday, and that it serves as a substitute for suicide. Traces his family origins back to his great-grandfather. Tells some stories, humorous and hair-raising, about the exploits of his Uncle William or Billy, and talks about his unliterary father. His father "had no hobbies except on-the-course punting, watching cricket at Old Trafford, and drinking draught Bass in impressive quantities." Comments on the absence of distinguished men in the Wilson line. "I sometimes indulge the romantic dream that the family was impoverished by the Reformation, but I think soberly that, even if it had toed the Protestant line, it would economically, socially and culturally have been what it was." Calls himself a Lancashire Catholic member of the small shopkeeping class ("I have reacted powerfully against the shopkeeping element") with an unhealthy interest in free will and original sin. "Geoffrey Grigson, a Protestant middle-class poet, once called me 'coarse and unattractive,' meaning Lancashire Catholic." Briefly refers to his step-mother, and describes the reasons which led him to publish his books under the pseudonym Anthony Burgesss.

1505 "Foreword." In : **Anthony Burgess: A Bibliography**, by Paul Boytinck. [Norwood, Pa.] : Norwood Editions, 1977, pp. vii-ix.

This bibliography will provide information about the source of income of the man of letters. "At the moment it seems to me that men of letters will, in the final quarter of the century, gain sustenance from work that cannot properly be bibliographed. I am, I hope, coming to the end of what I call a televisual tetralogy, namely a foursome of television scrials about great men, possibly the greatest — Moses, Jesus Christ, Michelangelo, Shakespeare. Fascinating in the first flush of writing, these have gradually become a bore, chiefly because of the need to defer to other people's conceptions of the projects, and the final, screened, product will not be wholly mine . . . . So if the later phase of my bibliography seems to show that I am working less than before, this impression has to be contradicted by reference to advertisments in **Variety** or confirmation, by some means or other, of the fancied flash of a name among screen credits." Observes that reading the items helps him recall certain incidents of his life. One review, not specified, belongs to the night when his first wife died.

1506 "That Sweet Enemy." **Observer** (London), 19 February 1978, p. 12.

1507 "Good Books." **New York Times Book Review**, 12 March 1978, pp. 14, 15, 22.

Reviews of **Job Speaks; Interpreted From the Original Hebrew Book of Job**, by David Rosenberg; and **A Palpable God; Thirty Stories Translated From the Bible With an Essay on the Origins and Life of Narrative**, by Reynolds Price. Rosenberg is a considerable poet, and Price's essay on the art of narrative should now be required reading for creative writing courses.

1508 "Pass the Marie est malade, Please." **Times Literary Supplement**, 24 March 1978, p. 347.

Review of **Morris Dictionary of Word and Phrase Origins**, by William and Mary Morris. An etymological dictionary is fit for the study of a poet, not (*pace* Edwin Newman) a means to greater precision. The dictionary is devoid of scholarly apparatus (just *where* did Anthony Burgess use "dogmerd?") [in #1423] and, in its determination to make etymology fun, otherwise vague and occasionally inaccurate. Its true value lies in its useful coverage of American slang.

1509 "Saturday Review: Outlooks. Notes from the Blue Coast." **Saturday Review**, v. 5, no. 14 (April 15, 1978) 96.

Describes monied Monaco and his own hard-working place in this paradise. "There's an exquisite appropriateness in the fact that *monaco* is the Italian for 'monk.' I have to stick to my cell in my hairy robe and painfully get on with the manuscripts. The roulette wheel spins, unheard by me. Crepes suzette and peches Melba are consumed in the Hotel de Paris, their home of origin. I hammer the keys, unseduced. I never thought the onset of old age would be like this." Values the fact that you have to be nonpolitical in Monaco, the ease of exit from the place, but suggests that the writer lives in a perpetual hell.

1510 "Why Orwell's **1984** Revolution Has Already Taken Place." **Times** (London), 20 April 1977, p. 12.

"But the tyranny of the state as we see it now, and are likely to see it for centuries to come, is mainly fiscal . . . . We are oppressed not by fear of the thoughtpolice but by fiscal documents we don't understand and an apprehension that we may be breaking fiscal laws we don't even know exist." Observes that no cacotopian writer has yet written fiction based on the probable outcome of the present situation: England dominated by the trades unions; a drab worker's English rather than the subtleties of Orwell's doublethink; and presents some ideas for a novel on this topic. [Burgess was plainly thinking about his **1985**, first published in 1978.]

1511 "Enciclopedia Einaudi." **Times Literary Supplement**, 28 April 1978, p. 481.

Review of **Enciclopedia Einaudi**, v. 1 and 2. Turin: Einaudi. The new encyclopedias, first the **Encyclopaedia Britannica** and now this **Einaudi**, reduce the number of entries under individual headings — perhaps an editorial recognition that, such are the advances of knowledge, even an encyclopedia can no longer be encyclopedic. The entries in the **Einaudi** prove the work to be a compendium of ideas rather than facts. "The entries are essays of an essentially provisional kind, avoiding the listing of facts but not averse to speculation. The approach is sometimes lateral or medial, with no doorman wearing a museum uniform." It seems to be, as Jacques Nobecourt observed, an encyclopedia of doubt, not certitudes, relativity, not absolutes. It seems to mirror the present state of the Italian literary world.

1512 "Oh, Cuisine! A Touch of Israel in Rome." **Saturday Review**, v. 5, no. 15 (April 29, 1978) 45.

"Only European Communists are said to know the best European restaurants. Reactionaries like me eat at home or in snack bars or, at best, in such Paris hash joints as the Self Grill . . . ." Describes, in loving detail, a meal consumed in the ristorante Piperno.

1513 "The Freedom We Have Lost." **Time**, v. 111, no. 19 (May 8, 1978) 44, 49.

[**Time** essay on the killing of Aldo Moro by the Red Brigade.] "Since the assassination of the Kennedys, we seem to have no more shock to register about the killing of a public man." Observes that political leaders must be prepared to die as a price for their rise to greatness. The breakdown of order in the 20th century can be attributed to the realization that repression of the human atavistic impulse is not always a good thing. Argues that democracy is threatened by draconian police measures. Citizens must be prepared to accept an unwritten contract which balances the rational and atavistic in themselves. The essence of democracy is toleration of opposed political views. This central tenet must be inculcated in the family and promulgated by those in charge of the media of mass communication. "Unfortunately, tolerance seems to mean tolerance of the intolerable — like political kidnapping — but it is a price that for the moment has to be paid: we know the alternative."

1514 "Let's Have a Bloody Revolution." **Saturday Review**, v. 5, no. 16 (May 13, 1978) 48.

Account of a lecture tour in Italy. Considered, in Italy, *un poeta della violenza* on account of **Clockwork**, he first introduced himself as an unviolent, apolitical man who has written innumerable bland novellas about love. He also talked about the meaning of the term "British" ("it does not just mean horse-toothed lispers in the Royal Enclosure at Ascot; it also means rough-spoken, hardworking mixtures of Celt, Silurian, and North Teuton living on smoky slag heaps very far from Buckingham Palace"). In Bari, the very hotbed of the activist heresy, he talked about pornography and political didacticism and, in a country where it is impossible for writers to be apolitical, found himself roaring about decay and corruption and the immediacy of Joyce's message. Cites, as evidence of the activist heresy, the graffiti found on every square meter of Bari University walls.

1515 "Something Lyrical, Something Terrible." **Times Literary Supplement**, 26 May 1978, p. 576.

   Review of **Nonsense and Wonder; The Poems and Cartoons of Edward Lear**, by Thomas Byrom. "Those of us of the working class who had no nursery, and whose parents were too busy or illiterate to read Lear to us at bedtime, first met the limerick as a very brutal form and, when we became acquainted with Lear, naturally regarded his nonsense as a namby-pamby bowdlerization. It is a class matter." Comments on some of the Lear limericks, and observes that, compared to Lewis Carroll "Lear is the lesser nonsense-writer because one always feels uncomfortable in his presence: there is something going on that is creepy and unclean."

1516 "Notes from the Blue Coast: Is Italy a Burnt-Out Case?" **Saturday Review**, v. 5, no. 19 (June 24, 1978) 46

   [Reworking of ideas first published in #1513.] "But all that we're seeing now in Italy is an exaggerated projection of our own lack of faith in government, our translation of sexual permissiveness into the right to take bloody unilateral action on behalf of puerile notions of liberty, our unwillingness to see the triumph of the social contract as the result of centuries of struggle against arbitrary despotism. Despotism is so easy; democracy so difficult. Italians believe that democracy is more than difficult: it's impossible. Their governors will remain inefficient or corrupt so long as the governed expect them to be like that."

1517 Review of **The New Oxford Book of English Light Verse**, chosen by Kingsley Amis. **New York Times Book Review**, 25 June 1978, pp. 11, 45.

   W.H. Auden's "Oxford Book of Light Verse" included some harrowing verse which was considered light at the time because it was based on the life and language of ordinary people. In our time, light verse requires order, neatness, civility and high technical skill. The Victorians were masters at the art. Quotes some English and American light verse. Concludes that light verse may knock public figures, groups, races and whole nations, provided it is all done with rubber hammers. "Once earnestness steps in, the light goes out. That light is flickering badly in the 1970's, bemused as they are by earnestness, but the past, on the evidence of this fine collection, is all ablaze."

1518 "The Lord is My, etc.: Psalm 23." **Times Literary Supplement**, 7 July 1978, p. 760.

   Review of **Psalm Twenty-Three**, edited by K.H. Strange and R.G.E. Sandbach. "It is very Old Testament, with its sheep and eating fit to burst and getting drunk and a tribal god on your side and a sneer at your enemies and your hair dripping with oil. The Rev. William Wye Smith, whose head has been cheeptit wi' yle and whose cup is teemin' fu', has no right to say: 'David is aye unreelin' a pirn aboot Christ.' David is unreelin' a pirn about the God of David."

1519 "Notes from the Blue Coast: Germans and Other Absurdities." **Saturday Review**, v. 5, no. 21 (July 22, 1978) 58.

   On the inevitability of national stereotypes. Germans, greedy for food, fondly believe they are beloved from Tangiers to Denmark. An Englishman, defined as a *goddam ridicule*, will roar goddamns as he never would do at home. The Americans are poor tippers and inclined to anger at southern insouciance. The French react to criticism with arrogance, bureaucratism and pedantry. Suggests that the French and Americans should be kept rigorously apart from each other. The French tend to push an idea to the horrible Cartesian limit. "Once establish the notion of plastic-wrapped, near consumable ordures, and you end with Beaujolais in plastic bags . . . . Give the rationale behind short order cookery to a Frenchman, and. . . he will contrive seats of excruciating discomfort, glacial coffee, and *croque-monsieur* sandwiches made of discardable putty."

1520 Review of **Magdalene**, by Carolyn Slaughter. **Times Literary Supplement**, no. 3986 (August 25, 1978) 945.

   It takes great imaginative authority to attempt to supplant the myth of Mary Magdalene. He has created two Magdalenes of his own, in Zeffirelli's **Jesus of Nazareth** and in **L'Homme de Nazareth**, and found the great-hearted whore of legend a satisfactory counterpart to the raging six-foot Christ (Christ the Tiger) he envisaged. Ms. Slaughter's Christ, unnamed like the whore of Luke, no tiger, is described as a kind of dead lover in soft, anthoid, narcissistic prose. "If only the prose would occasionally accommodate a sonic brutality, a wisp of humour, a rasp of irony. If only Mary were not so joylessly concerned with the beauty of her hair and breasts and the swish of her skirt. Am I right in supposing that women novelists take more easily to narcissism than do men? And to masochism? Some nasty things happen in this novel, apart from that ultimate nastiness on Golgotha, and they are scored for muted strings."

1521 "Love and Sin in **1985**." **New York Times Book Review**, 13 August 1978, p. 3.

An excerpt from **1985**. Burgess' religion is a residual Christianity that oscillates between Augustine and Pelagius. Speculates if the ethics of the Gospels cannot be given a secular application, and wonders if a secular religion of loving oneself (difficult) and others cannot be introduced.

1522 "1948: An Old Man Interviewed." **New Society**, v. 44, no. 56 (October 5, 1978) 8-11.

[An extract of pp. 11-34 of Burgess' **1985**.] Includes reminiscences of grimy post-war British life, the effect of Winston Churchill's proposed anti-communist crusade on the troops, Sir Stafford Cripps and the nature of English socialism.

1523 "A Very European Story." **New York Times Book Review**, 7 October 1979, p. 14.

Review of **Candido; or, a Dream Dreamed in Sicily**, by Leonardo Sciascia. Translated by Adrienne Foulke. "There's madness enough in a Sicily where rigid Catholicism confronts equally rigid Communism, where the deadliest of the sins is generous, innocent simplicity . . . . Mr. Sciascia. . . is revealed here as a true Voltairean liberal, dubious about all modes of reform."

1524 "A Fish Among Feminists." **Times Literary Supplement**, 13 October 1978, p. 1141.

Review of **The Flounder and In the Egg and Other Poems**, by Günther Grass. "It is perhaps best to take this fantasy. . . as a celebration of life in all its gross particularity, with Grass still telling the German people to beware of the abstractions that have too often made them flounder in a nordic mist and to consult the needs of the stomach — *Butt* not gunners."

1525 "The People's English." **Times Literary Supplement**, 27 October 1978, p. 1255.

Review of **The Linguistic Atlas of England**, edited by Harold Orton, Stewart Sanderson and John Widdowson.

1526 "Under Sukarno's Shadow." **Times Literary Supplement**, 24 November 1978, p. 1359.

Review of **The Year of Living Dangerously**, by C.J. Koch. "The East is full of weird mixed personages, unsure of their racial and cultural allegiances, polyglot, half-sane brains crammed with a weird variety of information, their obsessions as intense and capricious as a blowtorch in a child's hand, frantically loyal and as frantically treacherous. In Billy Kwan Mr Koch has created one of the most memorable characters of recent fiction . . . ."

1527 Review of **Joyce's Voices**, by Hugh Kenner. **New York Times Book Review**, 10 December 1978, pp. 14, 51.

This book about Joyce is marked by a richness of detail and insight. Kenner rightly remarks that the mythic element in **Ulysses** is not important; that is, Joyce is not interested in evoking vague and ancient and irrelevant entities. **Ulysses** is an epic novel marked by the Muse and the me. "The Muse in **Ulysses** is a mad androgyne of incredible talents — work-mad, pastiche-mad, symbol-mad. The me has a humbler function, that of pushing along a narrative with a plain recit — or as plain as the Muse will allow." Kenner also has some useful things to say about the "Uncle Charles principle" of fiction: the willingness to allow the fictional narrative to be inflected by the presumed literary taste of the human subject busy on his fictional rounds. This principle is exemplified in the Eumaeus, Siren and Circe chapters of **Ulysses**.

1528 Anthony Burgess's Rome. [Videorecording] New York, N.Y.: Learning Corp. of America, 1978. 1 cassette. Duration: 51 min. Burgess takes the viewer on a grand tour of Rome.

1529 Anthony Burgess's Rome. [Motion picture] New York, N.Y.: Learning Corp. of America, 1978. 1 reel. 16 mm. Duration: 50 min. John McGreevy and Pat Ferns, producers; Christopher Chapman, director-writer-editor; Anthony Burgess, narrator.

1530 "Novel." **New Encyclopaedia Britannica**. 5th ed. Chicago: Encyclopaedia Britannica, 1978. Macropaedia, v. 13, pp. 276-99.

"The most arduous commission, not to say the most bizarre, that I have ever received was to write the article on "The Novel" for the most recent edition of **Encyclopaedia Britannica**. Arduous because of the need to be encyclopedic — that is to say, cover the entire field of long prose fiction (but what is **long**?) systematically yet comparatively briefly; bizarre because not only were the parameters imposed by Chicago (The Novel as Life Style; Pastoral Novel; Novel of Apprenticeship etc.) but also the word-lengths (Definition of Novel, 453; Chinese Novel, 316, or something like that). I was not quite a writer and not quite a machine. The work was not excessively well paid, but one got a complete set of the edition." [Quote from #1511.]

1531 "Mexican Thriller." **New York Times Book Review**, 7 January 1979, p. 11.

Review of **The Hydra Head**, by Carlos Fuentes. In most thrillers, as Conrad realized, there is an opposition of X and Y but not of good and evil. In this political novel about Mexican oil, "Perhaps the true distinction of the novel resides in its having forever dispensed with the possibilities of the spy thriller as a serious form . . . . But let everybody be quiet and the eye take in the machetes, the flame-colored bananas, the splash of hot sauce on the spectacles of a professor, and we're firmly set in the Mexico Dr. Fuentes has labored so hard to make us at least begin to understand."

1532 "Art of the Unconscious." **Saturday Review**, v. 6, no. 2 (January 20, 1979) 18.

Relates an elaborately detailed dream in which Ruskin is turned into an elephant. Observes that, despite the ease of interpreting the dream in sexual terms, to invest it with Oedipal or urinogenital significance is utterly nonsensical.

1533 "The Road of Excess." **Saturday Review**, v. 6, no. 3 (February 3, 1979) 38-40.

Current American best-selling fiction is marred by motiveless malignity and gratuitous violence. The trend was already there years ago when his American publishers lopped off the final chapter of his **A Clockwork Orange**. "There was, in Hemingway's creations, a residuum of boy-scout honor, stoicism, grace under pressure, but those are not to be found in the curious automata that stalk, ready with gun or phallus, round the surrealistic townscapes of the contemporary American novel." To justify the bizarre violence of William Burroughs or **The World According to Garp** by extravagent claims of the sickness of American society is mere foolishness and historical naiveté. Observes that one of his books about Jesus Christ was rejected because it said nothing shocking. Advises Americans to stop accepting the shameful knocking of America in *grand guignol* fiction. For himself, offered the choice between the latest novel by a brilliant young bisexual novelist from Manhattan, Kansas, and **Pride and Prejudice**, he will opt for the riveting Miss Austen every time.

1534 "The Grand Priests of Monte Carlo." **Saturday Review**, v. 6, no. 7 (March 31, 1979) 12.

An account of Monte Carlo social life during the lean winter months. The legend of exilic sybarites shamefully living it up in the land of bronzed taxdodgers dies hard. "The only exiles I see are men made chronically sad by some failed affair of the heart on a colder shore, working like mad at oceanography, the placing of buoys, or the dispensing of bar music in the minor hotels." One young American, currently selling T-shirts, is preparing to write the definitive life of Cotton Mather. He argues that Mather is the prototype of the single-minded go-getters in the corporations, the CIA and the Pentagon. The poems of Anne Bradstreet are going the rounds. Burgess is reading Jonathan Edwards' **Sinners in the Hands of an Angry God** to while away the hours during a touch of the flu. The seller of T-shirts, greatly daring, is proposing to replace the I LOVE YOU on his wares by a single scarlet A . . . .

1535 "Transatlantic Love Affair." **Saturday Review**, v. 6, no. 9 (April 28, 1979) 10.

The English and the Americans, to use the words of Paul Theroux, get on well together. It is true that Americans once considered Englishmen to have a monopoly on homosexuality, but the writhing of wild male bodies on California beaches is changing all that. American males and English females copulated like mad during the war and they've been the better for it. Given all that, it is clear that America and Britain must consider the idea of forming a political union, abolish the presidency, and install the conveniently present constitutional monarchy for which most Americans have a powerful nostalgia.

1536 "Ulysses, by James Joyce." **Observer Magazine** (London), 20 May 1979, p. 80.

1537 "Amateur Standing." **Saturday Review**, v. 6, no. 11 (May 26, 1979) 12.

Turning over some unanswered correspondence from literary agents whose contracts he has refused to sign, he discovers that he stands accused of "unprofessionalism." This charge prompts an argument against professionals and the practices of the professional man. "The great work of the world has always been done by amateurs. Jesus Christ was an amateur moralist and theologian. He did not belong to the sacerdotal profession, and the professionals of the Sanhedrin handed him over to the professionals of the Roman punitive arm. Michelangelo Buonarroti was trained as a painter, but left the trade early. He was trained also as a sculptor and did well in that job, but he is remembered no more for the David or Pieta than he is for the Sistine Chapel paintings, some fine architecture, innumerable superb sonnets, and some effective military installations. He was the supreme amateur, and so was Leonardo da Vinci. Nowadays the professional unions would restrict them to a single trade."

1538 "Prime Time for Hitler." **Saturday Review**, v. 6, no. 13 (June 23, 1979) 10.

Europeans have been duly horrified by **Holocaust**, but also somewhat bored by the lack of dramatic conflict. The series should have conveyed the incredible racist Nazi philosophy. It remains an example of ghastly Teutonic stupidity difficult to fight against. You can never get the better of stupidity. The popular appeal of the series lies partly in its sadism and the purely sartorial perfection of a well-fitting SS uniform. "Apart from a renewal of shame and horror, what can the TV series about the tribulations of the Jews, or blacks, effect? Usually a curiously abstracted anger that looks, bewildered, for a viable target. It's no good hating tyrants who don't exist any more, and it would be unfair to direct one's enmity at either liberal Germans or (in the case of blacks) breast-beating Americans." Seeing the series made him dream up a TV series about the suffering of English Catholics under the Reformation.

1539 "Let Them Eat Red." **Saturday Review**, v. 6, no. 15 (July 21, 1979) 12.

"In the north you eat white; in the south you eat red. So you may sum up the European cuisine." Describes a white meal consumed in Milan, discourses on the introduction of the pizza in the north, and devotes some time to the description of Chicken Marengo and its variations among the French *cuisiniers*. To draw a moral or metaphysical conclusion out of these ingredients is not easy, but "What came out of America's "good neighbor" policy toward South America in World War II? Carmen Miranda and the samba. What, in that same war, did the Allies and the Germans find they had in common? A liking for a song called "Lilli Marlene." If *poulet Marengo* was the only lasting outcome of a military career that slaughtered all the horses and most of the men of Europe, at least it is tasty. Has anything as valuable emerged from Vietnam?"

1540 "Funeral in Berlin." **Saturday Review**, v. 6, no. 18 (September 15, 1979) 10.

On a trip to East Berlin. "God must surely have needed more than an hour and a bit before deciding to burn up Sodom, but I, being only human, am limited in my tolerance. I would willingly have burned up the whole of East Germany after five minutes with the Cerberuses at Checkpoint Charlie." Notes the confiscation of his passport, the search for drugs, inflammatory literature, weapons and microcameras. The East German women, thank God, absorb the fashions of West Germany and undulate in homemade elegance. To get a drink is difficult and involves a stiffly formal routine. One's coat is lost in the process. Ennui threatens. Brecht can be seen in the West; prostitutes are not in sight. The only thing left to do is to return to Checkpoint Charlie where a general grilling ensues over the money spent in East Berlin. He gets the passport of one "Edouard Hecquet, bearded, unmarried, journalist by profession. I often wonder what has happened to its rightful owner. Is he cached in some oubliette weeping, trying to account still for some last unaccountable pfennigs?"

1541 "In Search of an African Pen." **Saturday Review**, v. 6, no. 22 (November 10, 1979) 40-44.

Brief survey of the literature about Africa. Mentions Joseph Conrad, his own **Devil of a State**, Saul Bellow, John Updike, Ernest Hemingway, Evelyn Waugh, Graham Greene, Doris Lessing, Nicholas Monsarrat, V.S. Naipaul, Ekwensi and Chinua Achebe. Concludes that "Africa does not exist, except as a part of the geopolitical world island, and hence the African novel will never exist either. We have to be content with Hemingwayesque evocations of a Kenyan moon over the safari campfire, or an exposition of the political wrongs of cities founded by Europeans. For the rest, it must be all regional fiction, and the people qualified to purvey it would not be interested in writing it even if they could write."

1542 "Creeping Towards Salvation." **Times Literary Supplement**, 23 November 1979, p. 11.

Review of **Shikasta**, by Doris Lessing. Argues that if space or science fiction is any good, it must be judged on the same terms as a work by Henry James or Jane Austen as an artful delineation of human character in credible situations. There is something disturbing about science fiction that deals with human problems from a cosmic viewpoint even while space probes are demonstrating that no life exists in the universe. "The virtue of Mrs. Lessing's novel lies in its rage and its hope and, of course, its humanity. The cosmic fancies become a mere decoration, not, as with true SF, the innutritious essence . . . . I have no doubt that the whole trilogy will be worthy of standing on the same shelf as **First and Last Men** and **Sirius** and **The Starmaker**. And this will not be because of its SF trappings."

1543 "That's not Poetry, That's Italian." **Saturday Review**, v. 6, no. 23 (November 24, 1979) 8.

He takes a brief vacation in Nice to escape the killing noise and heat of Monte Carlo. Then reads, in Italian, the poetry of Walter Savage Landor and briefly discusses poetic magic and the ease with which it can be lost in translation.

1544 "How to Be Your Very Own Best-Seller List." **New York Times**, 28 November 1979, p. 27.

[Excerpt of an article first published in the **Manchester Guardian Weekly**.] Observes it is possible to publish without publishers. In the days of Shakespeare and Dr. Johnson, there was none of the apparatus of editors, blurb-writer, publicists and sales managers. "Needless to say, the author got paid more than now: There weren't all those publishers' overheads." Publishers are mere intermediaries, but they wield the power. With publishers in the hands of the Seven Sisters [the seven major oil companies] a recent edition of Yeats's collected poems was destroyed; it did not sell 2,000 copies a year. "Whereas an author can make money from only one book at a time, a publisher can make money from hundreds. An author can afford bread and dripping and weak tea on a sale of four thousand copies, but a publisher can multiply all these minimal individual sales into a *caneton a la presse* and Mumm income. Publishers are made into knights and even barons; authors remain what they are." Soon, perhaps, publishing will be defined as a boy or girl with access to an electric typewriter, a Xerox machine, and a willingness to hawk uncommercial opuses in the streets.

1545 "The Santa Claus Story." **Times Literary Supplement**, no. 4005 (December 21, 1979) 149.

Long review of **Saint Nicholas of Myra, Bari, and Manhattan**, by Charles W. Jones.

1546 "Learn All About It and Throw It Away." (December 20-27, 1979) supplement ii-iv.

On paper-back best-sellers. It is possible to distinguish between transparent (T) and opaque (O) fiction. The T category can be further subdivided into T1, in which the author displays an individual voice and vision, and T2 in which the author sedulously keeps himself in the background but exploits a given subject matter (airports, hotels, banks, car factories). In exploitative fiction the characters must be simple and direct, the human relationships elementary, and the themes those of power or sex. In exploitative fiction the didactic and pornographic often conjoin. "A session of cunnilingus or, more probably, fellatio is followed or preceded by a mass of technical information. The reader who is ashamed of the thrill of raw eroticism has his guilt assuaged by having to go to a lecture on atomic physics or cybernetics." Includes fact-filled excerpts from various sociological novels: **The Prometheus Crisis**, by Thomas N. Scortia, **Condominium** by John P. MacDonald, **The Hermes Fall** by John Baxter. The reason we fight shy of great art, and embrace the second-rate sociological novel is that we want to be free; mediocre art grants us this freedom.

1547 "Experiencing the Riviera." **New York Times**, Travel Section, 17 February 1980, pp. 1, 28.

"Most of us go [to the Riviera] for sun, wine, garlic, pastis under striped umbrellas and naked girls broiling on the beach." Physicality is the essential thing. Warns that the Italian side has the monopoly on manners; the French, an ancient people devoid of illusions, are both arrogant and greedy. Comments on the principality of Monaco ("I have lived too long in Monte Carlo to have many delusions about its paradisal qualities. I work all day and am in bed by 9"), the Cannes film festival, Monaco motor rally ("speed and smoke and the growl of engines like rutting beasts"), and on some of the towns (Villefranche, Ventimiglia, Genoa, Albenga) to be found in the region between Cannes on the west and La Spezia on the east.

1548 "Engaging the Sensorium." **Times Literary Supplement**, 29 February 1980, p. 227.

Review of **Stravinsky: The Composer and His Works**, by Eric Walter White and **Conversations with Igor Stravinsky**, by Igor Stravinsky and Robert Craft. "Last summer, here in Monte Carlo (an appropriate place in which to discuss at least the earlier Stravinsky), we put on our evening clothes in great heat and climbed the hill to the Palais Princier to hear the final symphony concert of the season. The works played were Schumann's "Rhenish" Symphony and Brahms's First Piano Concerto. There was the thick brown sound, oppressive on a Mediterranean August evening, sour oboes mixing with horns like an Exeter stew. At supper afterwards Frank Sinatra, whose ear is not to be despised, said that we should have had the tempering of a little late Stravinsky. Air, light, space, wit, immense intelligence, brevity — the properties of Mediterranean art."

1549 "Wide Plastic Spaces." **Times Literary Supplement**, 30 May 1980, p. 601.

Review of **Imagining America**, by Peter Conrad. Begins with an account of the effect of Niagara Falls on famous visitors and observes that "plastic" is the only apt word to describe America ("Americans. . . acquiesce in the European view of their plasticity") and gives the response of Kipling, Wilde, Auden, Aldous Huxley and Isherwood to the American East and West Coasts. "Here is a bound and printed artifact about certain writers who made the journey west or east. They have nothing in common except that they all bought steamship tickets. And if their Americas have nothing in common either, well then, they never went to America."

1550 "Ameringlish Usage." **New York Times Book Review**, 20 July 1980, pp. 3, 17.

Review of **Paradigms Lost; Reflections on Literacy and Its Decline**, by John Simon. Simon's strictures, esthetic or linguistic, are usually unanswerable. Simon is a draconian elementary schoolmaster to errant journalists, mediapersons and elementary schoolmasters. "Mr. Simon always gives good logical reasons for the avoidance of solecisms. Because, like me, he considers Black English a tongue of deprivation and berates teachers who sentimentally drool over its alleged expressive virtues, he has been condemned as an elitist. Meat-and-potatoes frontiersmen condemn his prissiness, call him a spinster schoolmarm and promise to make his velvet-breeched posterior meet the mud. But Mr. Simon fights very courageously in a war he has no hope of winning." Given the presence of dialect it is difficult to lay down normative rules, but Simon is right to berate the slipshod expressions of Clive Barnes, Rex Reed and Barbara Walters.

1551 "Jong in Triumph." **Saturday Review**, v. 7, no. 12 (August 1980) 54-55.

Review of **Fanny: Being the True History of the Adventures of Fanny Hackabout-Jones**, by Erica Jong. She has written an authentic picaresque novel with a female protagonist. The style is literate, marked by verbal exactitude and the disposition of rhythm. "The pitch is that of **Moll Flanders**. . . and the revelations, when they come, go beyond anything the stationery licensors of Queen Anne or the Georges would have permitted. There is, of course, seduction, but there is also rape, maritime sodomy, obstetrical revelations, and well-researched attacks on such barbarities as swaddling-bands and filthy mid-wifery." The book is a glorification of life rather than a self-pitying jeremiad, and Erica Jong was the right hermaphrodite to write or endite it. He is delighted to belong to her sex.

1552 "Doctorow's 'Hit' is a Miss." **Saturday Review**, v. 7, no. 13 (September 1980) 66-67.

Review of **Loon Lake**, by E.L. Doctorow. "It is a difficult book and I don't think it is a successful one. But it is a very honorable attempt at expanding the resources of the genre . . . . This is a depressed and depressing story, not really much modified by learning Joe will triumph. Depression forbids over-much coherence." In a summing-up: "I am happy to learn that **Loon Lake** is already a popular book, in that it is a Book of the Month Club choice and eighty-odd thousand copies have already been printed. Happy because, whatever the faults of the work (nearly always the admirable faults of the overreacher), serious students of the novel must recognize here a bracing technical liberation, and such a recognition is being forced upon a readership probably happier with **Princess Daisy**." [For caustic references to this review, see #1777.]

1553 "A Seldom Civil Waugh." **Saturday Review**, v. 7, no. 14 (October 1980) 76-77.

Review of **The Letters of Evelyn Waugh**, edited by Mark Amory. Comments on the popular success, in U.S., of **Brideshead Revisited**. Waugh, of unimpeachable middle-class origin, was prepared to be called a snob. These letters show him agonizing over his faith ("His own heart was broken when the Johannine *aggiornamento* vulgarized the Church liturgy") and the faith of his titled friends. They are the letters of a man of great devoutness, caustic honesty and preternatural percipience. "His real nostalgia is less for a Catholic aristocracy than for the powerful mindlessness that used to be the strength of the British ruling class."

1554 "The Irish Art." **New Republic,** v. 183, no. 22 (November 19, 1980) 41.

[An adaptation of a preface to **Modern Irish Short Stories** ed. by Ben Forkner. See #968.] Argues that the Irish excel in the composition of short stories. Their sense of poetry enables them to establish atmosphere in a few words and then to concentrate on the Irish character. That character is idiosyncratic: its main component, which they share with Russians and Neapolitans, is a sense of logic which defies logic. "I spent two years recently as fiction critic for **The Irish Press** and was overwhelmed with volumes of short stories, mainly published in Dublin, which were rich in the age-old themes . . . . What is always most notable is the presence of a kind of grace — a moral elegance that frames all sorts of wretchedness."

1555 "The Genesis of **Earthly Powers.**" **Washington Post Book World,** 23 November 1980, pp. 1, 2, 13.

He writes for money (it pays the rent) and to satisfy a profound personal need to say something "deviously, laterally, wrapping the message in so many layers of paper art that, with luck, the reader may fail to get the message and take in only the art . . . . The novel is about the difficulty of deciding what is good and what is evil."

1556 A Conversation with Novelist Anthony Burgess. [Phonotape] New York, N.Y.: Encyclopedia Americana/CBS News Audio Resource Library, c1980. 1 cassette. Duration: 20 min. Recorded Dec. 2, 1980 in New York. Burgess talks about his career and his view of the role of the novelist. (Vital history cassettes; Dec. 80, no. 1)

1557 "Dubbing." In **The State of Language.** Ed. by Leonard Michaels and Christopher Ricks. Berkeley; London: University of California Press, 1980, pp. 297-303.

A discussion of the difficulties of dubbing. Gives an account of some humorous interludes and demonstrates how, with ingenuity and cunning, the dubbers succeed. Expresses his own preference for sub-titles.

1558 "Partridge in a Word Tree." In **Eric Partridge in His Own Words.** Ed. by David Crystal. New York: Macmillan, 1980, pp. 26-30.

[Biographical reminiscence in celebration of Eric Partridge.] Commissioned by Penguin books to do a dictionary of contemporary slang, Burgess consulted Partridge on the lexicographical agony. Partridge promptly invited him to cannibalize Partridge to the limit. The Partridge etymologies were often shaky, but he was right to maintain that some etymology is better than none at all. "Eric was brought up in a kind of dispossessed demotic tradition which prized the speech of the people as the repository of a dour philosophy of life. The downtrodden, who are the great creators of slang, hurl pithiness and colour at poverty and oppression." Regrets that Partridge did not pay more attention to the pronunciation of demotic speech. Those scholars who wince at his **Shakespeare's Bawdy** failed to recognize that the function of slang is mainly subversive. "Slang and literature alike tend to greater obscenity than decent people like to imagine. Eric celebrated indecency." It is a pity that he did not receive the public honours that were his due.

1559 "Foreword to a Bibliography." In Brewer, Jeutonne. **Anthony Burgess: A Bibliography.** Metuchen, N.J. ; London : Scarecrow Press, 1980, pp. v-vii.

His emotions on examining the bibliography are those of wonder and anger. He is filled with wonder at the industry and ingenuity of the bibliographer; he is moved to anger that one must write so much "in order to make a living, and not a very good living at that. I write these lines in Monaco, where the blue waters are totally obscured by the yachts that are anchored there. Not one of these yachts belongs to a man or woman who writes or has written. The nearest writer's yacht is at Cannes, and it belongs to Harold Robbins, the well-known carpetbagger, who, publicly proclaiming himself the greatest living writer, is probably not really a writer at all." Graham Greene, at 75, lives in a small apartment in Antibes and still worries about money. "My gratitude, then, to Professor Brewer, who has done a remarkable job . . . . If we define art as disinterested endeavour which meets little material reward, then this art of bibliography must be very great indeed. And, in the hands of Professor Brewer, it is.''

1560 "Exfoliations: Anthony Burgess on The Folio Society." **New York Times Book Review**, 18 January 1981, p. 23.

[An advertisement for this Book Club which has appeared in several different publications.]

1561 "Travels with Graham Greene." **Saturday Review**, v. 8, no. 1 (January 1981) 64-65.

Review of **Ways of Escape**, by Graham Greene. This book does not continue the autobiographical **A Sort of Life** on the ground that Greene's associates have their own right to privacy. Greene speculates that the writing of fiction is an act of therapy and wonders how the non-writing world copes. "It's a highly idiosyncratic constation. Most people do very nicely with games, liquor, sex, and work. And to see art as a bolthole or gloryhole makes it curiously dark and limited. Beethoven's Ninth? Michelangelo's *Pieta*? Modes of escape? Art surely tries to relate the madness and fear to an entity, a scheme of existence perhaps, which enables us to look them in the eye rather than escape from them.'' He has travelled much and used his travels in his fictions. A lover of the celluloid art, his devotion to film survived the libel suit following his harmless remarks concerning the "dimpled depravity" of Shirley Temple. He now puts on the toga of the stoic and tells us that he will probably end his days in Antibes. "Note that way of putting things — 'end my days' not 'savour my late seventies in the sun.' What I have seen of Greene in Antibes, a tall man of large vigor against a backdrop of other men's yachts, fond of food and good whisky, denies the melancholia of much of this book.'' There is not a dull page in the book and Greene, recently asked if he was disappointed at not getting the Nobel Prize, said no. "No," he said; he was awaiting a better prize than the Nobel. "What prize?" And Greene, with the satisfaction of an immortal, said: 'Death'.''

1562 "Burroughs's Bad Dreams." **Saturday Review**, v. 8, no. 3 (March 1981) 66.

Review of **Cities of the Red Night**, by William S. Burroughs. "Burroughs has undoubted literary gifts, but he has opted for a lack of intellectuality that makes his fantasies no more than loose collages in which the news is always the same — getting anally screwed with Bengal lights, attempting bizarre violence with an insufficient musculature, getting fixes . . . . Probably what Burroughs needs is a theology. Blake was a far greater fantasist and he demonstrated that no poet is big enough to create his own.''

1563 "Opening Hemingway's Mail." **Saturday Review**, v. 8, no. 4 (April 1981) pp. 64-65.

Review of **Ernest Hemingway: Selected Letters 1917-1961**. Ed. by Carlos Baker. Confesses he finds letter-writing the source of chagrin and even guilt. His heart goes out to the shade of Sir Thomas Beecham, who never opened a letter in his life unless it smelled of a check. Hemingway was apparently a prolific letter writer but "All that can be said in palliation of his cacoethes is old Hem, in writing to his buddies, did not try to write good." Quotes some of Hemingway's letters intended to cheer up ailing or bereaved recipients. Comments that the letters convey the undiluted Hemingway voice, telegraphese worked into an idiolect. Suggests that all authors make their characters sound like themselves. "The letters, since they essay no literary effects, are all the more a kind of literature — direct, pungent, highly idiosyncratic, and breathing speech more than lamp oil. The character who emerges is the one we already know — sweaty and in shorts and cussing readily — but there is no new and unexpected qualification (secret paedophilia or bookishness). The Hemingway of the letters is almost totally likable.''

1564 "Sleuthing Hammett." **Saturday Review**, v. 8, no. 7 (July 1981) 66-67.

Review of **Shadow Man: The Life of Dashiell Hammett**, by Richard Layman. Hammett, who died burdened with debt, along with symptoms of pulmonary cancer, emphysema, pneumonia, and diseases of the heart, liver, kidneys, spleen and prostate gland — tried to convert a popular genre into genuine art. He reached art the hard way — through a long apprenticeship to lowly craft. His style, lean and to the point, wears well. He had too hard a life to learn enthusiasm easily, but no writer who achieves even a moderate success in his lifetime and an unshakable status after it can easily be pitied. "We've been inoculated against overmuch compassion by the example of Dr. Johnson's great life of Richard Savage.''

1565 "Music for Professionals." **Quest** (Pasadena), v. 5, no. 6 (July/August 1981) 67-68.

Review of the **New Grove Dictionary of Music and Musicians**. Ed. by Stanley Sadie. These 20 vast volumes are excellently produced, crammed with scholarship, magnificently illustrated and a profound pleasure to handle. The old Grove was intended for the Victorian amateur ("To learn to blow brass intruments or sing oratorios was to find less harmful occupation than in the gin shop or whorehouse. To mount to heaven on wings of song was to close one's ears to the sirens of syndicalism"). The new Grove is a compendium for the musical intellectuals, for musicologists. If you look up the "Neapolitan sixth," or the plot of **Tristran and Isolde**, or the definition of a musical "wolf," the entries tend to confirm what you are already supposed to know. The musicologist contributors not only write well; they write out of a large endowment of literary knowledge; but even they cannot answer the question: What is music trying to do?

1565.1 "Pourquoi nous aimons cette famille d'usurpateurs." (Why We Love that Family of Usurpers) **Paris Match**, no. 1680 (August 7, 1981) 14-15.

His father, on his deathbed, made him swear to give his true allegiance to the the House of Stuart, not to the Hanoverian usurpers. Then discusses the charms of the monarchy. The crux of the matter is that unlike the damned politicians, the British monarchy has never inflicted harm on the people. Messrs. Mitterand and Reagan are politicians; hence dangerous; they want power. The Queen has moral authority which can guide her executives and her subjects alike. Witness her actions in preventing the publication, commissioned at great cost, of the wife of the Yorkshire Ripper. The current queen sets an example of incorruptibility against which the politicians must measure themselves. Describes the marriage of Prince Charles and Lady Diana (no skulking to the ceremony in an armored vehicle) and considers that his father, observing the ceremony from paradise or purgatory, will perhaps console himself with the thought that another Bonnie Prince Charlie will eventually mount to the throne.

1566 "A Great Russian on Great Russians." **Saturday Review**, v. 8, no. 1 (November 1981) 70-72.

Review of **Lectures on Russian Literature**, by Vladimir Nabokov. Nabokov who, in a previous volume dealt with English literature with a certain lack of humility, now considers Gogol, Turgenev, Dostoevsky, Tolstoy, Chekhov and Gorky. For Soviet fiction, with its official subservience to the State and masses, he had nothing but contempt. In the presence of the Russian masters, with their emphasis on the concrete (black curls on a white neck, the amorous velleities of frustrated love) he is humble and worshipful. Of Andrey Bely's **Petersburg**, which he considered one of the ten greatest novels of the century, he says nothing. The book is made so unremittingly out of the Russian language that it totally resists translation. It is a pity that he cannot resist niggling when he deals with Dostoevsky's **Crime and Punishment**. "But Nabokov. . . finds nothing of the true novelist about Dostoevsky. He describes his characters before embarking on dialogue, but never, in the manner of Tolstoy, retouches his portraits during the flow of speech. He should, Nabokov says, have been a playwright . . . . This volume. . . never once fails to instruct and stimulate. This is a great Russian talking of great Russians."

1567 "Anthony Burgess' Rome." IN **Cities; Created by John McGreevy**. New York: Clarkson N. Potter, 1981, pp. 222-245.

Burgess lives in Rome because he is a writer, and in Rome art is part of daily life. Rome is both a mother and a whore and, while it has many faults, it is never ungenerous. The city may seem all spires and steeples, "but the city is not built in the sky. It is built on dirt, earth, dung, copulation, death, humanity." There are two Romes: the fashionable Rome with its Via Veneto and the Trastevere district where people live and work. "I lived for a long time on the same busy square, and I would probably still be living there if the landlord had not thrown me out. I wrote a lot of books there. It is a noisy square [the Plaza Santa Cecilia], but I rather liked the noise; it was a sign that life was going on outside." Discusses Guiseppe Gioacchino Belli and his scurrilous poems, the Colosseum, the Theatre of Marcellus, the Ponte Milvio, St. Peter's Square and observes that the Romans are not a holy people. Then takes in the Vatican, the house where Keats died, the statues of Bernini, the memorial to the Unknown Soldier, the Borghese Gardens and quotes Belli. Rome will be here until the Day of Judgment.

1568 "Heinrich Böll's Cop Out." **Saturday Review**, v. 9, no. 1 (January 1982) 57-58.

Review of **The Safety Net**, by Heinrich Boll. This novel of the West German rich and powerful trying to protect themselves from death caused by a booby-trapped cigarette pack or a birthday cake, consists of a series of interior monologues. Böll fails to vary the tone and rhythm of these monologues to differentiate between the characters. To suggest, as the author does, that the solution to the problem of urban terrorism is to be found in socialism, will not do at all. "Böll's ancestral faith [Lutheranism] ought to tell him, as well as his readers, that there's no solution except learning to understand the terrible mixed-up nature of the human soul. His novel lacks the depth of a philosophical or theological matrix. The complication of its cast list is a substitute for complexity. This novel needed work. But probably a Nobel prize-winner is above that sort of thing."

1569 "A Talk with Graham Greene." **Saturday Review**, v. 9, no. 5 (May 1982) 44-47.

Describes a visit (the Burgess imagination drained, soul arid, bum left leg) to Greene who looks remarkably well in his middle seventies. They talk about the film adapations of Greene's novels, his preference for solid description and simplicity, some miscellaneous literary matters (Eliot, Conrad, Auden). Greene briefly discusses evil and Catholicism, some current writers (British and American) he admires and does not admire. Then, Burgess' leg giving him great difficulties, they trot off to lunch and discuss sausages, **Doctor Fischer** and, with some last minute raillery, part company.

1570 "Celebrating James Joyce." **Saturday Review**, v. 9, no. 6 (June 1982) 41-53.

In this year of the centenary, he has been talking about Joyce in three languages. Comments on the commemoration and execration of Joyce by Dubliners. Describes his early admiration for Joyce, the reception of Ulysses and relates something of its plot and method. Then discusses **Finnegans Wake** and explicates some of the book's passages. "His books are confessional, leaving out no sins but making no excuses. His eucharistic function is the conversion of quotidian bread into beauty, which Thomas Aquinas defined as the pleasing. He does not please Barbara Cartland [a popular novelist] nor Lord Longford, but he reminds us that life is a divine comedy and that literature is a jocose and serious business. He has left us in **Finnegans Wake** a little prayer that sums up his attitude to life. It is a very reasonable attitude: 'Loud, heap miseries upon us yet entwine our arts with laughters low'."

1571 "A Warning to 'Pitiful' America: TV is Debasing Your Lives." **TV Guide** v. 30, no. 38 (September 18, 1982) 12-13.

In American popular television, nobody reads, nobody thinks, nobody generates an idea other than a money-making or murderous one. Once asked to work on a script of a film based on the life of Shakespeare (never made) he was always asked to stress the motivation and make it simple. Yet complexity is found in all the world's best drama: **Hamlet** is fascinating because the prince perpetually puts off revenge. **Columbo** has a certain appeal (the detective combines a sharp deductive mind with an air of amiable, scruffy eccentricity), but the mindless simplicities of **Dallas** call out for censure because Americans may mistake simplistic characterizations for reality. "To regard intellectual excitement or human complexity as dangerous is in order for the Soviet Union, but hardly for the greatest democracy the world has ever seen."

About Burgess: Bibliography of Bibliography

1572 Boytinck, Paul. **Anthony Burgess; An Enumerative Bibliography with Selected Annotations**. [Norwood, Pa.]: Norwood Editions, 1973.

1573 David, Beverly R. "Anthony Burgess: A Checklist (1956-1971)." **Twentieth Century Literature, v. 19, no. 3 (July 1973) 181-188.**

1574 Holte, Carlton. "Additions to 'Anthony Burgess: A Checklist (1956-1971)'." **Twentieth Century Literature, v. 20, no. 1 (January 1974) 44-52.**

1575 Kennard, Jean E. "Anthony Burgess: Works — Criticism." In **Number and Nightmare; Forms of Fantasy in Contemporary Fiction**. Hamden, Conn.: Archon Books, 1975, pp. 230-32.

1576 Boytinck, Paul. **Anthony Burgess: A Bibliography. Works By and About Him Complete with Selected Annotations**. 2nd ed. With a Foreword by Anthony Burgess. [Norwood, Pa.]: Norwood Editions, 1977.

1577 Brewer, Jeutonne. **Anthony Burgess: A Bibliography**. With a Foreword by Anthony Burgess. Metuchen, N.J.: Scarecrow Press, 1980. (Scarecrow author bibliographies, no. 47)

1578 Coale, Samuel. "Criticism of Anthony Burgess: A Selected Checklist." **Modern Fiction Studies, v. 27, no. 3 (Autumn 1981) 533-36.**

Includes 26 critical articles and books, 9 interviews, and gives the citations of critical articles devoted to Burgess' fictional works. The arrangement of the latter section is chronological. The cut-off point is 1981 (i.e. includes all the articles found in this issue of **Modern Fiction Studies.)**

About Burgess: Dissertations

1579 Brown, Rexford Glenn. "Conflict and Confluence: the Art of Anthony Burgess."

Thesis — University of Iowa, 1971. **Dissertation Abstracts International,** v. 32, no. 7 (January 1972) 5220-5221A. Order no.: 72-8221.

1580 Stinson, John Jerome. "The Uses of the Grotesque and Other Modes of Distortion: Philosophy and Implication in the Novels of Iris Murdoch, William Golding, Anthony Burgess and J.P. Donleavy."

Thesis — New York University, 1971. **Dissertation Abstracts International**, v. 32, no. 1 (July 1971) 1533A. Order no.: 71-24, 76B.

1581 Cullinan, John Thomas. "Anthony Burgess' Novels: A Critical Introduction."

Thesis — Columbia University, 1972.

1582 Mablekos, Carole Marbes. "The Artist as Hero in the Novels of Joyce Cary, Lawrence Durrell, and Anthony Burgess."

Thesis — Purdue University, 1974. **Dissertation Abstracts International**, Section A, v. 36 (1975/76) 880A. Order no.: 74-20,590.

1583 Moran, Kathryn Lou. "Utopias, Subtopias, Dystopias in the Novels of Anthony Burgess."

Thesis-University of Notre Dame, 1974. **Dissertation Abstracts International**, Section A, v. 35, no. 4 (October 1974) 2286. Order no.: 74-20,590.

1584 Wagner, Kenyon Lewis. "Anthony Burgess's Mythopoeic Imagination: A Study of Selected Novels (1956-1968)."

Thesis — Texas Tech University, 1974. **Dissertation Abstracts International**, Section A, v. 35 (1974/75) no. 7926A. Order no.: 75-7437.

1585 Arnold, Voiza Olson. "Narrative Structure and the Readers' Theatre Staging of **Nothing Like the Sun**."

Thesis-University of Illinois at Urbana-Champaign, 1975. **Dissertation Abstracts International**, Section A, v. 36 (1975/76) 5634A. Order no.: 76-6680.

1586 Siciliano, Sam Joseph. "The Fictional Universe in Four Science Fiction Novels: Anthony Burgess' **A Clockwork Orange**, Ursula Le Guin's **The Word for World Is Forest**, Walter Miller's **A Canticle for Leibowitz**, and Roger Zelazny's **Creatures of Light and Darkness**."

Thesis-University of Iowa, 1975. **Dissertation Abstracts International**, Section A, v. 36 (1975/76) 8053A. Order no.: 76-13,443.

1587 Steffen, Nancy Lynn. "Burgess' World of Words."

Thesis-Brandeis University. **Dissertation Abstracts International**, v. 38, no. 5 (November 1977) 2781A. Order no.: 77,22,831.

1588 Holte, Carlton Thomas. "Taming the Rock: Myth, Model and Metaphor in the Novels of Anthony Burgess."

Thesis — University of California, Davis. **Dissertation Abstracts International**, v. 38, no. 10 (April 1978) 6143A. Order no.: 78-03615.

About Burgess: Books

1589 Dix, Carol M. **Anthony Burgess**. Ed. by Ian Scott-Kilvert. London: Longman, 1971. (Writers and their work, no. 222)

1590 Morris, Robert K. **The Consolations of Philosophy: An Essay on the Novels of Anthony Burgess**. Columbia: University of Missouri Press, 1971. (Literary frontiers edition)

1591 De Vitis, A.A. **Anthony Burgess**. New York: Twayne, 1972.

1592 Mathews, Richard. **Clockwork Universe of Anthony Burgess**. San Bernardino, Calif.: Borgo Press, 1978. (Milford series. Popular writers of today, v. 19)

1593 Aggeler, Geoffrey. **Anthony Burgess; The Artist as Novelist**. University, Ala.: University of Alabama Press, 1979.

1594 Coale, Samuel. **Anthony Burgess**. New York: Ungar, 1981. (Modern literature series)

About Burgess: Articles, Essays, Etc.

1595 Engelborghs, Maurits. "Romans van een Woordkunstenaar" (Novels by an Artist in Words). **Dietsche Warande en Belfort** (Antwerp), no. 1 [n.d.] 59-62.

1596 Hyman, Stanley Edgar. "Anthony Burgess' Clockwork Oranges." **New Leader**, January 7, 1963, pp. 22-23.

Describes Burgess as one of the newest and most talented of the younger British writers. Provides synopses of **The Right to an Answer, Devil of a State** and **A Clockwork Orange**. Finds that the language of the book (*nadsat*) is fascinating. Devotes about a page and a half to the rhyming slang, the gypsy talk and the Russian roots that make up *nadsat*. "Burgess has a superb ear, and he shows an interest in the texture of language rare among current novelists." Also briefly discusses **The Wanting Seed**. "Beneath Anthony Burgess' wild comedy there is a prophetic (sometimes cranky and shrill) voice warning and denouncing us, but beneath that, on the deepest level, there is love: for mankind, and for mankind's loveliest invention, the art of language." [Reprinted in #1601.]

1597 "Anthony Burgess; from Our Special Correspondent." **Times** (London), 16 January 1964, p. 136.

[Speaking of Writing, VIII.] Mr. Burgess, who has sometimes described himself as a comic novelist in the tradition of Rabelais, and who tends to shy at being pigeon-holed with Graham Greene and Evelyn Waugh, has given us a series of 10 robust, glittering, extravagantly inventive novels that defy all cut-and-dried classification. Burgess explains his current phenomenal rate of literary production, expresses his admiration of the Grub-Street tradition and comments that all writers should perhaps start to explore the resources of language along the lines of **Finnegans Wake**. The correspondent speculates that the sense of excitement found in the Burgess prose may be due to his detachment from England and the English.

1598 Mitchell, Julian. "Anthony Burgess." **London Magazine**, v. 3, no. 11 (February 1964) 48-54.

[One of the earliest and one of the best (non-academic) articles about Burgess. Quotes from a radio interview called 'New Comment.'] Praises the variety of Burgess' publications, and suggests that Burgess' reputation can rest on his *oeuvre* rather than a single book. "The typical Burgess protagonist is a teacher with a propensity for endless humiliation. Pelagian by instinct, he is harried by Augustinian doubts about his own behaviour, doubts which almost incapacitate him for effective action." Victor Crabbe of **The Malayan Trilogy** best exemplifies the type. "When drunk, which is quite often, his heroes swim in language, lingering ecstatically over puns and derivations and Joycean conceits." The novels are a curious and highly individual mixture of realism and farce — and language is the most important binding element. Burgess' strange way of seeing the world gives his novels their peculiar originality. Devotes a paragraph apiece to **One Hand Clapping, The Wanting Seed, The Right to an Answer** and **The Worm and the Ring**. Burgess' "motives are highly complex, literary, philosophical and critical; and he's prepared to use all the novelist's tricks to obtain the density and complexity he wants. ('Joyce,' he has said, 'is just the air one breathes.')" Comments on Burgess' ambiguous attitude towards art, and considers that the pagan element in Burgess' writing outweighs the Catholic influences.

1599 Nichols, Lewis. "In and Out of Books: Mr. Burgess." **New York Times Book Review**, 10 April 1964, p. 8.

[Burgess attends International Writers' Conference on first post-war visit to U.S.] Introduces Burgess to U.S. audience. A prodigious worker who has written 20 books. A medium tall man with turbulent hair, and a tendency to take the work seriously, but not himself. Will shortly publish **Tremor of Intent**. In taxi from airport to Manhattan his talk ranged from music to Tom Thumb, record reviewing, Peggy Lee. His listing of "wife" under recreations in **Who's Who** was a genial indulgence. He skipped the usual awed comment on the Manhattan skyline. Unusual man, this one.

1600 Horder, John. "Art That Pays." **Manchester Guardian**, 10 October 1964, p. 5.

[Interview.] Burgess talks about the **The Eve of Saint Venus**, his piano player of a father and his mother ("Beautiful Belle Burgess"), interest in music, teaching career and his first visit to Malaya ("enchanted with the country and angry with Somerset Maugham for writing all that stuff about planters' wives that I began writing my Malayan trilogy") and the rate of his literary production. "I write because

I've a childish inability to separate fantasy from reality. It's pathological, I suppose. I do write out of high spirits but the actual business can be a hell of a chore. My wife and I are not very in love with life — we both tend to be suicidal and manic-depressive . . . . I often go to see William Burroughs and the colony of English writers who live in Tangier, and they have very little to write about there.'' His recreations are playing the piano, composition of music and drink. [Many of the early biographical sketches are based on this interview.]

1601 Hyman, Stanley Edgar. "Anthony Burgess." In **On Contemporary Literature**. Edited by Richard Kostelanetz. New York: Avon Books, c1964, pp. 300-305.

[Reprint of #1596.]

1602 Wheldon, Huw. "Television and the Arts." **Listener**, v. 78, no. 1873 (February 18, 1965) 257-60.

Burgess' praise of television programs on pilots and ballerinas, while welcome, does not recognize and do justice to the elaborate planning, the blood and sweat, that goes into the actual work of production. "I have no wish to malign Mr. Burgess. I admire him as a novelist, and I recognize in him as a novelist and as a man a true generosity of spirit. I find it therefore all the more ironic and indeed disturbing that a man clearly so well disposed should exhibit misapprehensions which obscure the relevance and significance of a good deal that is done in television, and damage the chances of its being further developed." [For Burgess' reply, see #1096.]

1603 Kauffmann, Stanley. "Literature of the Early Sixties." **Wilson Library Bulletin**, v. 39, no. 9 (May 1965) 748-777.

[An essay on current English novels and novelists. For Burgess' **Honey for the Bears**, see pp. 763-64.] Burgess has a more interesting mind than Amis. His style never stoops to gags, but achieves its witty effects through pleasantly baroque artifice. Under the surface, there are streaks of darkness and horror as terrible as anything in Faulkner. Quotes a passage from the novel and describes Burgess as a considerable master of comic writing.

1604 Pritchard, William H. "The Novels of Anthony Burgess." **Massachusetts Review** (Summer 1966) 525-39.

Burgess has written 15 novels, and yet only one can be considered a slight or casual creation. Discusses five of the novels (**The Long Day Wanes, The Right to an Answer, A Clockwork Orange, The Wanting Seed**, and **Honey for the Bears**). Concentrates, in his critical asides, on the evidence of Burgess' ruthless literary sensibility. Poses the following questions: what are we to make of Burgess' fictional characters? what philosophical or other point do they convey and represent? are they too thin and insubstantial, or just right given the context? Concludes that Burgess has given us a group of novels distinguished by their abundant qualities of imaginative energy, creative invention, complicated wit and verbal delight.

1605 Isnard, Marcel. "Anthony Burgess." **Etudes Anglaises**, v. 19, no. 1 (January/March 1966) 45-54.

"When Burgess the philologist becomes Burgess the novelist. . . he enters into battle with words, constantly seeking to reveal semantic and phonetic riches."

1606 Walters, Raymond. "Say It with Paperbacks." **New York Times Book Review**, 4 December 1966, p. 60.

"Anthony Burgess is, of course, the enormously talented and versatile British writer whose article leads off this issue of the Book Review. A fair sampling of his fiction is offered in **Five Novels by Anthony Burgess**, a set that includes **A Clockwork Orange, Honey for the Bears, The Wanting Seed, The Right to an Answer** and **Nothing Like the Sun**." [Complete text of notice.]

1607 Derrick, Christopher. "This Our Exile: The Novels of Anthony Burgess." **Triumph**, v. 2, no. 2 (February 1967) 28-33.

Discusses the "Catholic" novelist and his works. Observes that the novel of assured belief has been supplanted by the novel of psychological stress. Burgess' novels are Catholic to a limited degree; there is no all-pervading smell of incense about his work. Yet his novels convey a sense of the limits of Liberalism, the willingness to believe in careful science and liberal reason. In his works, "One is constantly aware. . . of the whole verbal and conceptual system generated by the historical and institutional Church, particularly in England . . . ." Burgess' concern with original sin and the problem of evil gives his novels their Catholic content. Discusses, in this context, **The Worm and the Ring, The Wanting Seed, Tremor of Intent** and **A Clockwork Orange**. "As Chesterton pointed out, the doctrine of the Fall is the only *cheerful* view of the human condition. Ribald, sardonic and headlong in their manner, grim and even horrifying in their superficial content, the novels of Anthony Burgess illustrate the point . . . . Burgess reminds us that while Catholicism is intolerable — just as the Cross was intolerable for its Occupant — all alternatives are illusory and absurd. Sharp-toothed, the Hound of Heaven will get you in the end; but who can blame you for running?"

1608 Adler, Dick. "Inside Mr. Burgess." **Sunday Times** (London), 2 April 1967, pp. 47-50.

[Biographical sketch which conveys more useful information than many subsequent efforts.] Observes that Burgess is the most productive writer of quality working in England. His fecundity led critics to turn white. Cries of 'shame' and 'slow up!' punctuated their notices. Between November 1959 and August 1960 he had five novels ready for publication. He has still not moved into the upper financial stratum of writers like Graham Greene. Speculates if Burgess' integrity is the cause of his relatively poor sales, or the fact that Burgess (a lapsed Catholic who looks at Britain with the sour disdain of a jaded lover) belongs to no particular stream, main or otherwise. Describes the semi-detached house in Etchingham and the London house in Chiswick. Observes that you can dig Burgess' biography out of his books (**A Vision of Battlements, Inside Mr. Enderby, The Worm and the Ring**). In November 1959 he was invalided home with suspected brain tumor ("virtually on the first plane") with his wife Lynne as his nurse. Between November 1959 and August 1960, in order to leave an estate for his wife, he wrote **The Doctor is Sick, Inside Mr. Enderby, The Wanting Seed, One Hand Clapping** and rewrote **The Worm and the Ring**. Describes the events which led Burgess to review his own **Inside Mr. Enderby** for the **Yorkshire Post** and remarks that it raised a storm which took a year to die down. Gives an account of Burgess' writing habits.

1609 Cartey, Wilfred. "The Dawn, the Totem, the Drums." **Commonweal**, v. 86, no. 8 (May 12, 1967) 227-30.

[Discusses African literature. Cites Burgess' "The Writer's Purpose" in passing, but includes little of substance about Burgess or his work.]

1610 Hicks, Granville. "Fertile World of Anthony Burgess." **Saturday Review**, v. 50, no. 28 (July 15, 1967) 27, 29, 36.

Provides a biographical sketch of Burgess and appreciative summaries of **The Long Day Wanes, A Vision of Battlements, The Doctor is Sick, The Right to an Answer, The Wanting Seed, A Clockwork Orange** and **Nothing Like the Sun**. What holds Burgess' work together is a feeling about the modern world. "He dislikes the worship of technological progress, which seems to him to dominate both the United States and the Soviet Union. He distrusts power, especially when masked as benevolence, and consequently views with skepticism the Welfare State. He takes a kind of dialectical view of history . . . . As between the Pelagians and the Augustinians, to use his terms, he is committed to the latter, having no faith in the perfectibility of man." Burgess has a lively mind, a merciless gift for satire, stylistic originality of an extraordinary range, and a creative drive without parallel in our time, and Hicks looks forward to his new books with pleasure. [Written to mark the publication of 8 Burgess novels in the Ballantine ed.]

1611 "Books They Liked Best. . . and Books They Liked Least." **Washington Post Book World**, (December 3, 1967) 16-17.

Burgess liked: **Poems of Gerard Manley Hopkins, The Ambidextrous Universe** and **The Scope of Anthropology**. Disliked: **The Infirm Glory**. [A bare listing: no reasons given.]

1612 "Burgess, Anthony." In **Encyclopedia of World Literature in the 20th Century**, v. 4. Ed. by Frederick Ungar and Lina Mainiero. New York: Ungar, 1967, pp. 57-59.

1613 Wood, Michael. "A Dream of Clockwork Oranges." **New Society**, v. 11, no. 297 (June 6, 1968) 842-43.

Summarizes **The Wanting Seed, A Clockwork Orange, Honey for the Bears, Tremor of Intent** in terms of the dualism of good and evil in Burgess' work. "The attraction of a dualism is that it damns the neutrals, and Burgess, like Dante, hates neutrals above all things. Hence, I think, his sympathy for murderous young Alex . . . . Alex at least takes sides. He knows what evil is and he chooses it."

1614 Betts, Ernest. "Millions on a Musical About Shakespeare." **Times** (London), 24 August 1968, p. 18.

Burgess, well advanced with the writing of a musical film on Shakespeare, discusses the proposed musical comedy. He has visited William Conrad, the American producer and Joseph Mankiewicz, the director. Film to be on the same scale as "My Fair Lady" and "Camelot." Burgess answers the question how much Shakespeare we could see in a film of this magnitude ("quite a lot") and describes some of the problems (Elizabethan speech, the music a mixture of pop and Elizabethan). Film may be shot in York or Warwick rather than Stratford, no longer Shakespearian. [Due to the death of producer Conrad, this film was never made.]

1615 Davis, Earle. "Laugh Now — Think Later! The Genius of Anthony Burgess." **Kansas Magazine** (Manhattan, Kansas) 1968, pp. 7-12.

"I suggest that Burgess' accomplishment rests not only in his entertainment, but more importantly in what he has to say about the modern world . . . . Burgess has surely made decadence uproariously funny. He presents our society as a collection of fools, analyzing with devastating effect the psychoses of characters representative of almost every part of our world."

1616 Hicks, Jim. "Eclectic Author of His Own Five-Foot Shelf." **Life**, v. 65, no. 17 (October 25, 1968) 87-97.

[Part biographical sketch, part interview.] A prolific author, Burgess has also reviewed (legendary feat) some of his own books in the **Yorkshire Post** [see #448, 989]. Critics have concluded that he is an "artist of immense and finely developed talent. . . a professional, although his ration of income to words so far has been shockingly low." Describes the famous and contented year when Burgess wrote five novels to provide for his wife and future widow. Also talks about Malaya (teaching application made out while drunk and disaffected with derisory Banbury income), his love of music, some film scripts for **Enderby** and Shakespeare, and predicts that his future work will be more involuted and unsalable. Describes himself as a pubman who shuns the literary salon, and gives an account of his working habits. [Includes photographs of Burgess and his wife Liliana Macellari.]

1617 Dahlie, Hallvard. "Brian Moore: An Interview." **Tamarack Review**, no. 46 (Winter 1968) 7-29.

Moore observes that Bellow's craftsmanship is superior to that of English novelist Burgess. [See p. 23 for this remark. "We must do something about Moore," Burgess said to me, apropos of nothing, on first reading this sentiment.]

1618 Brooke-Rose, Christine. "Le roman experimental en Angleterre." **Les Langues Modernes**, v. 63, no. 2 (March-April 1969) pp. 158-68.

1619 Aggeler, Geoffrey. "Mr. Enderby and Mr. Burgess." **Malahat Review**, no. 10 (April 1969) 104-110.

Burgess has clearly established himself as one of the most gifted English or American novelists, and the majority of his novels are comic masterpieces. **Enderby Outside** is one of them. In his **Nothing Like the Sun**, Burgess observed that literature is an 'epiphenomenon of the action of the flesh.' Burgess is of course fully aware that this explanation explains little and, in **Enderby Outside**, the investigation is carried much further. Onanistic Enderby, visited by his muse, is invited to get all these old things out of his system, and to push on. The delectable girl offers herself to him, but Enderby, visualizing himself 'puffing in his slack whiteness,' is paralyzed by fear. The episode makes the point that great poetry cannot be expected from fearful little men who have opted to live without love. Burgess' point of view toward popular rock poets and the acid-inspired [i.e. LSD] chaos-obsessed disciples of William Burroughs suggests that he expects little in the way of significant verse from any of these practitioners. Observes that Burgess' forte is the short novel of 80,000 words, and five or six of his novels deserve to be ranked among the great comic novels in English.

1620 Sullivan, Walter. "Death Without Tears: Anthony Burgess and the Dissolution of the West." **Hollins Critic**, v. 6, no. 2 (April 1969) 1-11.

[Essay on Burgess' novels which pays particularly close attention to his fictional treatment of death.] Considers **A Clockwork Orange** (not as good as **1984** or chilling as **Brave New World** but quite good enough) and A **Vision of Battlements** ("not one of his strongest"). Discusses **The Long Day Wanes**, the casual stubbing out of Crabbe's life, and the sense of absurdity found in Burgess. "Man waxes and fades: acts, when they are performed at all, degenerate into meaninglessness. Nothing counts."

The same death without significance occurs in **The Right to an Answer**. "In Burgess' work, there is almost never actual sorrow, and this is right, because an absurd world cannot be tragic." Followed by an examination of **Enderby**. The death of Rawcliffe suggests that Burgess' fictional dead men are not corpses, but actors who tumble from cliffs with surprised looks on their faces. Death restores us all to a kind of dignity, and dignity is the one thing Burgess' essentially humourous characters are not allowed to have. Beneath all the surface motion of Burgess' heaving plots, the recurring theme is man's inability to act at all. The trouble with Enderby is that, while an outsider, no wild angel has appeared to him, demanding that he throw open the gates of all the ways of ecstasy and and glory. The trouble with **Nothing Like the Sun** is that it has a quality of artificiality; we cannot know what fires burned in Shakespeare's head and heart. Includes brief comments on **Tremor of Intent** and **The Wanting Seed**. "To revert once more to the paradox. . . the physical world is everything and it is nothing. It is what we have left and we use it violently. We gorge ourselves on the sensuous pleasures, we pursue danger, we laugh at death. But always Burgess is telling us, it does not matter. What is important is the vestigial sense of decency, the recollection of that country we yearn for but cannot return to, the modicum of virtue which in one way or another all of Burgess' heroes share. The beauty is in being alive, regardless of the limitations."

1621 Aggeler, Geoffrey. "The Comic Art of Anthony Burgess." **Arizona Quarterly**, v. 25, no. 3 (Autumn 1969) 234-51.

[Discussion of **The Long Day Wanes, A Clockwork Orange, The Wanting Seed, Nothing Like the Sun**, and **Tremor of Intent**.] These novels abundantly demonstrate Burgess' versatility, linguistic genius and devastating wit; they also reveal that curious blend of Catholicism and Manichaeism which is the basis of his terrible pessimism. The non-hero in many of Burgess' books (Enderby, Edwin Spindrift, Victor Crabbe) is modelled on Joyce's Leopold Bloom; he is, like Bloom, a sensitive, cultured, well-meaning but ineffectual cuckold. He suffers humiliations, including many and varied sexual humiliations; his only reward is an increase in knowledge which often deprives him of hope. Critics have quarreled with this representation of experience, but few of them deny Burgess' brilliance as a prose stylist.

1622 Lewis, Anthony. "I Love England, But I Will No Longer Live There." **New York Times Magazine**, November 3, 1968, pp. 38 +

[Long, memorable, wide-ranging interview.] The major theme is the oppression of the writer in kind but placid Welfare State Britain. "Britain does not like her writers very much. It humiliates them in its Honors List . . . . all poor Evelyn Waugh ever wanted was a knighthood. Of course, he never got it." Discusses his love for England, a suddenly improved digestion after defiant gourmandizing (pork, onions, Christmas pudding, claret), his arrival in Malaya, teaching days in Banbury, the loss of standards in schools, Arts Council subsidies for unproductive ideological drones, tax advantages of living in land of hated foe (France), Graham Greene and Minister of Culture Jennie Lee. Also comments on his love of music and early predilection for musical composition, start as a novelist, future writing plans, plutocratic Kingsley Amis, effect of Catholicism in moderating his hopes for Socialism, affinity for Orwell's politics, loveless childhood, inbred independence and hopes for the future. "The only things Britain will be noted for will be the sybaritic achievement of a totally responsible society."

1623 Page, Malcolm. "Anthony Burgess: The Artist as Performer." **West Coast Review**, v. 4, no. 3 (January 1970) 21-24.

Burgess, who visited Simon Fraser University on March 5, 1969, seemed to be an unhappy lapsed Catholic who covered his near despair for himself and society with mingled humor and cynicism. He is a man of restless imagination, full of provocative generalizations about contemporary writers, patient with television and newspaper interviewers, and he revealed himself as the veteran schoolteacher in a lecture to 350 university people. — AES, v. 14, no. 8 (April 1971) 517. No. 2447.

1624 Said, Marie. "Anthony Burgess Interviewed by Marie Said." **The Sunday Times of Malta**, 7 June 1970.

Preceded by biographical sketch. Observes that book criticism is a difficult art to practise in Malta; the books tend to be held up by the smuthounds. As a result, "There are certain periodicals which will never ask me to review books again. This is the fault of the Maltese State." He likes **A Clockwork Orange** very little; the book of his which he dislikes the least is **Enderby**. Prefers music composition to writing: it is comparatively mindless. He is working on a symphonic sketch called **Giggifogu** [Fireworks]. The backward state of Maltese culture is not attributable to its small size (consider Athens), or to British colonialism, but to the ruling oligarchy. Argues that it is not the function of the State to keep away the occasions of sin, and that the Maltese deserve to see the same progressive films, and to read honest books on the nature of man and society as Romans and Londoners. The failure of Maltese Catholicism is that "it tries to act for Caesar as well as God, despite Christ's insistence on the separateness of the two attributes. Indeed, it has tried to be Caesar. When a Church tries to build a theocratic state, embodying the individual will in the collective, then surely it's sinning in the direction of denying freedom of conscience." The Church in Malta has had too much secular power for so long that it will be reluctant to relinquish it — and young, intellectually curious Maltese will get out.

1625 Clemons, Walter. "Anthony Burgess: Pushing On." **New York Times Book Review**, November 29, 1970, p. 2

[Quick-moving interview-essay during Burgess' year at Princeton.] "He is 53, a big man of sturdy, ramshackle appearance, with a blunt disarming manner and awesome energy." Describes the sparsely furnished faculty apartment and Burgess' interest in music. "When I took up the novel I descried in it the same necessity you find in music to balance disparate elements." The common reaction to the quantity of his fiction ("People took to asking sneering questions: 'Have you written your monthly novel yet'?") leads to resigned annoyance. When the medical fraternity made a false diagnosis of a brain tumor he, along with his outspoken wife ("we weren't considered quite suitable") were bundled out of Malaya. Actually, he does not write a lot. His books, compared to American blockbusters, are short. He writes serious books "only to discover when the work is published that Burgess has done it again, another howlingly funny farce and all that. My God, I had to write **A Clockwork Orange** in a state of near drunkenness, in order to deal with material that upset me so much." His second marriage to the learned and lovely Liliana Macellari was unusually fortunate. [Comment by Clemons.] An ex-Roman Catholic ("I tried to get back in. . . and just at that moment the Pope came up with a new absurdity and I had to turn my back again") and exile from England ("ghastly taxes there") Burgess is a serious man who somehow makes people laugh.

1626 Friedman, Melvin J. **The Vision Obscured: Perceptions of Some Twentieth-Century Catholic Novelists**. New York: Fordham University Press, 1970.

For Burgess, see pp. 1, 6, 7-10.

1627 Hoffmann, Charles G. and A.C. Hoffmann. "Mr. Kell and Mr. Burgess: Inside and Outside Mr. Enderby." In **The Shaken Realist: Essays in Modern Literature in Honor of Frederick J. Hoffmann**. Ed. by Melvin J. Friedman and John B. Vickery. Baton Rouge: Lousiana State University Press, 1970, pp. 300-310.

In **One Hand Clapping**, Howard Shirley sets out to prove that money is a false god even on its own terms, but Janet Howard's Secondary Modern mind, full of endless and seemingly inconsequential information, compels Burgess to sacrifice complexity and subtlety of insight. Further, her transformation from conventional housewife to *femme fatale* is implausible. If **One Hand Clapping** fails to fuse the comic and the tragic, **Enderby** provides a book in which the search for self-identity is central to the entire work. The portrait of Enderby the poet (writing poetry on the toilet on tissue paper) is neither intended to shock nor to deprecate the creative process, "but to suggest in the Joycean sense that in the womb the word was made flesh." Enderby, unlike Howard Shirley, affirms the life of the mind. He can only regain his identity as a poet by assuming that of Rawcliffe, the Icarus to his Daedalus. "Reversing the Joycean motif that the son must displace the father, Burgess suggests that the Creator must become the Son (Logos) the word-man, defying society, rebellious, disobedient, aloof, but yet compassionate and undemanding."

1628 Schoenbaum, Samuel. "Burgess and Gibson." In his **Shakespeare's Lives**. Oxford: Clarendon Press, 1970, pp. 765-68.

[Synopsis of **Nothing Like the Sun** followed by a whiff or two of comment.] "An absurd gallimaufry of invention and (to put it mildly) dubious biographical theorizing, but Burgess has a redeeming gift of language . . . . Normal syntax dissolves; the effect is Elizabethan yet the spirit modern . . . . One may also discern in the sexual degradation of the protagonist a working out of the author's obsession rather than the fictionalizing of fact . . . . Through the alembic of his sullen craft [Burgess] transmutes the dross of his data into the impure gold, grotesquely shaped, of his fiction.''

1628.1 Solotaroff, Theodore. ''The Busy Hand of Burgess.'' In his **The Red Hot Vacuum and Other Pieces on the Writing of the Sixties**. New York: Atheneum, 1970, pp. 269-75.

Reprint of #324.

1629 Aggeler, Geoffrey. ''Between God and Notgod: Anthony Burgess' **Tremor of Intent**.'' **Malahat Review**, no. 17 (January 1971) 90-102.

Notes the standard features of the James Bond spy thrillers made popular and profitable by Ian Fleming. The discussion of the novel stresses the gullible Pelagian element in Roper that leads to a kind of willed naiveté in historical matters and the austerely Augustinian approach typical of Denis Hillier. ''Augustinians, such as Hillier, are more complex and more capable of intellectual growth because they are not inhibited by the simplistic formulae that Pelagians find convenient for explaining away subtle human problems.'' Also discusses the novel in terms of the neutrals (Theodorescu and Wriste), and Hillier's growing disatisfaction with the meaningless games of international espionage. Comments that Burgess has accomplished something rather amazing in combining the stock fleshly lusts of the thriller with very provocative eschatological statements and conjectures and concludes that ''In any case, whether or not Hillier's theology is sound, there can be little doubt that his story will be read and relished long after most of the contemporary spy thrillers have become literary curiosities of interest only to historians and idea-hungry dissertation writers.'' [Reprinted, with some changes and revisions, in his **Anthony Burgess: The Artist as Novelist**. University, Alabama: University of Alabama Press, 1979, pp. [185]-194. Annotation based on the book just cited.]

1630 Churchill, Thomas. ''An Interview with Anthony Burgess.'' **Malahat Review**, no. 17 (January 1971) 103-127.

[Burgess interviewed on the eve of his departure from Britain.] Burgess was living in a pretty tacky place, and not entirely by choice. He talks about his tax problems in England; the psychological satisfactions and paltry monetary rewards of journalism; his intention to write a regional novel set in Manchester on Rag Day. The comic element in his novels is never deliberate, but he is happy when readers laugh. Discusses (unwillingly) **A Clockwork Orange** (''a jeu de spleen'') and moves to **Enderby**. Yes, a poet is probably like that, total devotion to craft, needs only the smallest room in the house. ''But the idea is that the muse isn't quite Graves's White Goddesss; it is a *female* force, highly capricious. And may well be the inhibitor of normal sexual relations . . . .'' They move on to discuss masturbation, Philip Roth and an American friend who, trying to get Burgess laid after the death of his wife, paid a woman (''off-putting, rather charming in a way'') in the attempt to do it. An amusing interlude: Burgess quizzes his son on the whereabouts of some missing cigars. Then they discuss Evelyn Waugh, Anthony Powell, and Kingsley Amis and Braine (the latter two Tories now they are flush). Also his politics (''God knows what I am politically'') and Catholicism (''I will not allow Catholicism to go over to the converts and I will not allow the Protestants to attack it''). On to **The Wanting Seed**, Pelagianism and the oppression latent in socialism. On Sillitoe (''very much a double-think character and he makes me very angry. I don't think he's very intelligent, for one thing'') and his **Key to the Door** which totally misrepresented the case in Malaya. ''He never learned the bloody language even; he never *talked* with the Malays.'' On to **A Vision of Battlements** (''Very much myself, very much a self-portrait'') and his early struggles to get **Vision** and **The Worm and the Ring** published by Heinemann. Also his record as a failed composer, work on Shakespeare script (''a sort of musical'') and his visit to Hollywood after the death of his first wife. Finally, talks about his troubles in writing **Nothing Like the Sun** and the personality of Shakespeare, some American writers and his future writing plans.

1631 Evans, Robert O. ''**Nadsat**: The Argot and Its Implications in Anthony Burgess' **A Clockwork Orange**.'' **Journal of Modern Literature**. v. 1, no. 3 (March 1971) 406-10.

Devotes two pages (and fifty examples) to the demonstration that nadsat includes much borrowing from Russian. The purpose of this linguistic innovation, the fact that 3% of the diction is Russian, rather than Arabic or French, is to connote communist dictatorship, the society of **Darkness at Noon**, a society without moral values and devoid of hope. **We, Brave New World, Lord of the Flies** and **Darkness**

at Noon convey authenticity, a sense of verisimilitude. **A Clockwork Orange** fails on this score; Burgess suggests that brutality (as in the aversion therapy) can be used as a deterrent; he also suggests that the spectacle of brutality can itself brutalize. The medium is the message, and Burgess' novel depicts a nightmare which "breaks on the crux of verisimilitude. It fails to convince us because we do not believe in, as Mr. Branom called it, this kind of subliminal penetration. If that is so, it is certainly no moral fable of the importance of good and evil and human choice. It is a nightmare rather than a social satire." It is a tour-de-force but a "failure, on artistic grounds probably and surely on moral grounds."

1632 Weinkauf, Mary. "The God Figure in Dystopian Fiction." **Riverside Quarterly**, v. 4, no. 4 (March 1971) 266-71.

The god-surrogates are generally deliberate parodies of the Judeo-Christian God. They display in a parodic manner the qualities traditionally attributed to the Deity, but these qualities are largely illusory. Thus immortality, immutability, incorruptibility, omniscience, and infallibility are claimed for the god-figure, but they are usually only manipulations by the dictator-tyrant's spies or computers. Dystopian fiction today satisfies a real need as it dramatizes "the full horror of man's subservience to a politically created idol." The dystopian novels discussed are: **1984**, Eugene Zamiatin's **We**, Huxley's **Brave New World**, and **Ape and Essence**, L.P. Hartley's **Facial Justice**, C.L. Moore's **Doomsday Morning**, David Karp's **One**, **A Clockwork Orange**, **The Wanting Seed** and Waugh's **Love Among the Ruins**. AES, v. 15, no. 3 (November 1971) 147. No. 679.

1633 Riemer, George. "An Interview With Anthony Burgess." **National Elementary Principal**, v. 50, no. 6 (May 1971) 9-21.

On the education of the young. America is totally dishonest. It claims to want the Patrick Henry type and inculcates conformity instead. "Going through America, one is aware that its citizens are free; yet they behave as it is assumed people behave in Soviet Russia. Russian people assume they are not in a free country, but they behave as if they have a great deal of freedom. In the United States, it's the opposite way around." The failure of American television to educate children and adults is a scandal. Also comments on his own schooling, musical education, **A Clockwork Orange**, Lieutenant Calley, Charles Manson and American guilt, the ignorance of young American communards, praises the virtues of hard study, and questions the virtues of the American Constitution. Stresses the ability to read as the first educational aim and achievement. Calls for more eccentrics and enthusiasts in education and less cold, crop-haired specialists.

1634 Friedman, Melvin J. "Anthony Burgess and James Joyce: A Literary Confrontation." **Literary Criterion**, v. 9, no. 4 (Summer 1971) 71-83.

The chief value of Burgess's study of Joyce, **Re Joyce**, is its revelation of his debt to Joyce. The autobiographical bias of Burgess's criticism brings his own experience into a confrontation with Joyce's that illuminates the works of both. Burgess's devotion to Joyce is evident not only in **Re Joyce** but also in **A Shorter Finnegans Wake**. This sophisticated abridgement lays bare the linear movement of the novel which at first sight seems to be circular. The edition successfully projects the conflict between Shem and Shaun, a conflict especially relevant in the light of recent information about Joyce's relationship with his brother Stanislaus. Burgess has also underscored the importance of the novel's Victorian thought-pattern, particularly Joyce's adherence to Vico's **Scienza Nuova**. An important quality of Burgess, one that links him with Joyce, is his use of his wide reading, which is related to the Joycean fascination for language. Burgess's mocking view of Catholicism, his view of history, and the structure of his novels are some of the results of his confrontation with Joyce. AES, v. 17, no. 4 (December 1973) 250.

1635 Fernando, Lloyd. "Literary English in the South-East Asian Tradition." **Westerly**, no. 3 (September 1971) 7-13.

Survey article on literary English written in Malaya and Singapore. Devotes one paragraph to Burgess' Malayan trilogy, and notes that juxtaposition of races and cultures was, as Burgess himself has observed, the underground stimulus. [For Burgess, see p. 9.]

1636 Kateb, George. "Politics and Modernity: The Strategies of Desperation." **New Literary History**, v. 3, no. 1 (Autumn 1971) [93]-111.

[Pp. 91-98 constitute a discussion of the dilemmas and terrors prompted by the awesome growth in human power and its potential for abuse and alienation. Includes quotations from Rilke, Yeats, Frost, Heidegger, Hannah Arendt. The remaining pages are devoted to **The Wanting Seed**.] Examines the sentiments of Malthus on population growth and checks, and observes that Burgess departs from Malthus in having all the checks issue from governmental policy. Further, the government's policy to allocate scarcity, not abundance, is marked by fussy decency. Then examines the different governmental strategies, Pelphase, Interphase and Gusphase, and relates the first (liberal rationalism) and the last (Augustinian pessimism) to Burgess' Catholicism. "In short, power is powerless before the problem of scarcity induced by overpopulation. Scarcity is the one disease that is not a seeming cure; it may be the one disease without a cure; it is the parent of other diseases as it is the child of human powers. In Burgess's future world the diseased responses — the strategies of desperation — are each given the chance. All through the changes the intentions of the governors are steadily good. Their efforts, thanks to the reach of Burgess' talent, form a sequence of many of the major nightmares of this century's futurist imagination."

1637 Houston, Penelope. "Kubrick Country." **Saturday Review**, v. 44, no. 52 (December 25, 1971) 42

[Kubrick interviewed by the editor of **Sight and Sound**.] Kubrick talks about his first reading of **Orange** ("It seemed to me to be a unique and marvelous work of imagination and perhaps even genius"), his choice of Malcolm McDowell as Alex. Alex, like Richard III, should fill an audience with dislike and fear; instead, he disarms it with his candor, wit and intelligence. Argues that the subconscious finds release in Alex, and resents the fact that he is stifled and repressed by authority. Also discusses the stylized violence, the high-speed orgy, the sets and search for locations, the lenses used in the shooting, the total absence of post-synchronization, the camera work ("I did quite a few hand-held shots with the Arriflex merely wrapped in an Anorak"), his taste for surrealistic situations in fiction, the film on Napoleon, choice of subjects ("I'm very, very careful about this . . . . A great narrative is a kind of miracle.")

1638 Weiler, A.H. "**A Clockwork Orange** Wins Critics' Prize." **New York Times**, 29 December 1971, p. 22.

Gives best films, actors, scripts, etc., for the year 1971. "**A Clockwork Orange** won over **The Last Picture Show** on the second ballot by a vote of 31 to 24." [Circa 100w about **A Clockwork Orange**. Gives names of critics who voted.]

1639 "**A Clockwork Orange**." **Filmfacts**, v. 14, no. 24 (1971) 649-55.

Gives film credits, provides a synopsis and quotes those critics who liked the film (Vincent Carrol, "Murf," Judith Crist, Vincent Canby, Hollis Alpert,) and those who did not (Andrew Sarris, Stanley Kauffmann, Pauline Kael, Gary Arnold, Roger Ebert). Summarizes Burgess' reaction to the film, both his first impressions and afterthoughts. Also gives an account of the political/ideological debate between Fred M. Hechinger and the replies by Burgess, Kubrick and McDowell. Reprints, in full, the reviews of Paul D. Zimmerman [#161], Pauline Kael [#143] and Alan M. Kriegsman [#147]. An indispensable and convenient source for students of the film.

1640 Garrett, George. "**Nothing Like the Sun**." In **Survey of Contemporary Literature; Updated Reprints of 1500 Essay-Reviews from Masterplots Annuals, 1954-1969**. Vol. 5. Ed. by Frank N. Magill. New York: Salem Press, c1971, pp. 3323-3325.

This portrait of Shakespeare as a young man is a magnificent failure which, with all its flaws, is worth a baker's dozen of the more successful novels. Burgess' scholarship is sound (if somewhat dated). He provides a subtle demonstration of the growth of Shakespeare's art from hypothetical juvenilia to finished poems, and the novel includes images, vistas and incidents which will later appear, transformed and transmuted, in the plays. "Burgess knows his Shakespeare by heart, and the book offers fine hunting ground, good sport for scholars, amateur and professional." The language is lively, credible, genuinely remarkable. His faults include an overemphasis on the crudities of Elizabethan life; a failure to convey the *conventions* of the time; and a willingness to smuggle in various anachronistic Freudian, Marxian and Jungian notions under the guise of "relevance." "Politically and socially, Shakespeare emerges as the kind of pansy socialist Orwell ridiculed in *The Road to Wigan Pier*. There is plenty of sex of all kinds in the book, but the sexuality is extremely modern and self-conscious, as contemporary as the Profumo scandal. Religion, in an age when large numbers of people lived and died by and for faith, is not taken seriously at all.'' These are serious faults, but Burgess has chosen not to repeat himself in this truly bold and imaginative piece of work.

1641 LeClair, Thomas. "Essential Opposition: The Novels of Anthony Burgess." **Critique; Studies in Modern Fiction**, v. 12, no. 3 (1971) 77-94.

Burgess' fiction is characterized by an obsessive interest in the relation of opposites to one another. "Such preoccupation goes beyond the traditional concept of narrative conflict, for in Burgess' novels dialectic is itself a central theme as well as a method." Discusses, within this framework: **A Vision of Battlements, The Long Day Wanes, Time for a Tiger, Beds in the East, The Doctor is Sick, Devil of a State, The Right to an Answer, The Wanting Seed, A Clockwork Orange, Honey for the Bears, Tremor of Intent** and **Enderby**. "The explanation for this choice of technique may lie in literary influence (Burgess greatly admires Joyce, has obviously read Marx), in publishing history (his rate of production may necessitate writing to a *handy* opposition), or in aesthetic principle (he defines art as the 'representation of the Ultimate, under its aspect of unity, formal harmony, Brunoian reconciliation of opposites'). Whatever the explanation, Burgess' dialectic has not yet reached its completion, the total synthesis of value, character, and technique."

1642 Lodge, David. **The Novelist at the Crossroads and Other Essays on Fiction and Criticism**. Ithaca, N.Y.: Cornell University Press, 1971, pp. 19-21.

1643 Mablekos, Carole. "Enderby." In **Survey of Contemporary Literature; Updated Reprints of 1500 Essay-Reviews from Masterplots Annuals, 1954-1969**. Vol. 2. Ed. by Frank N. Magill. New York: Salem Press, c1971, pp. 1356-1362.

[Plot summary in the usual "Masterplots" tradition.]

1644 Tufte, Virginia. **Grammar as Style**. New York: Holt, Rinehart and Winston, 1971.

Burgess mentioned in passing on pp. 13, 79, 130, 190.

1645 Dix, Carol. "The Mugging Machine." **Manchester Guardian**, 1 January 1972, p. 8.

[Interview.] Burgess, on his occasional returns to England, now feels miserable. The British editions of his books are out of print. They discuss **A Clockwork Orange**, film version due to open January 13th. Burgess now lives in Malta, island populated by retired admirals and brigadiers ("that writer fellow with the wop wife") where the censorship is so bad they even go through the **Guardian** with felt pen and scissors. "He has worked non-stop, cheated death marvellously — has no intentions of stopping working now either. He never runs out of ideas for novels, he says, and is branching out into writing musicals." Confesses he would like to write a really witty musical. He has always had to see himself as only one step above the writer of pop-boilers, a writer by trade. Followed by a brief discussion of the Nadsat in **A Clockwork Orange**. "And in Alex, Burgess isn't just showing us how nasty little boys can be, and how relieved we should be that our civilised young sons aren't like that — it's the adults he holds in contempt."

1646 Weinraub, Bernard. "Kubrick Tells What Makes 'Clockwork Orange' Tick." **New York Times**, 4 January 1972, p. 26.

[Interview.] Kubrick received copy of **Clockwork** from Terry Southern. He was excited by the plot, ideas, characters, language. Alex should normally be an unsympathetic, perhaps an abhorrent character, but, like Richard III, he undermines moral disapproval of his evil ways. The power of the story derives from its glimpse into the depravity of man. "One of the most dangerous fallacies which has influenced a great deal of political and philosophical thinking is that man is basically good . . . ." Describes Kubrick's obsessive working habits, his views on the director's role, and his low opinion of reviewers. "No reviewer has ever illuminated any aspect of my work for me." 1,500w

1647 McGregor, Craig. "Nice Boy from the Bronx?" **New York Times**, Section II, 30 January 1972, pp. 1, 13.

[Part interview, part essay which denounces Kubrick and film.] **Clockwork** is macabre, simplistic, chillingly pessimistic. Kubrick defends its relevance and makes a case for the film as satire. His view of man is pessimistic, based on his own observation, and grounded in Christian theology. [McGregor interjects that this view is more heretical and Manichean than Christian.] The gratuitous violence of the film is defended on the ground that it's all in the book. Kubrick doubts that works of art change human character for good or bad. McGregor concludes that the film is a "Marvellously executed, sensationalist, confused and finally corrupt piece of pop trivia, signifying nothing." 2,500w

1648 "Anthony Burgess: the Author of **A Clockwork Orange** Now Switches His Attention to Napoleon's Stomach." **Publisher's Weekly**, v. 201 (January 31, 1972) 182-83.

[Interview.] On the differences between the English and American editions of **A Clockwork Orange**; the symbolic 21st chapter was lopped off by Americans on the grounds that "we're much tougher in America." On his novel **MF** and the failure of reviewers to read Levi-Strauss. Frank Kermode (a nascent Catholic) wrote the only perceptive review of the book [see #543]. Briefly comments on the novel and American novelists. "It's a pity that my books are used as texts — it smells of petrifaction." The perfection of Kubrick's **Orange** derives from its faithful adherence to the book. [For Kubrick's screenplay, see #112.] Pauline Kael's charge of coldness is incorrect; the book was intended as an "act of charity." Also outlines some ideas for the then unwritten **Napoleon Symphony**.

1649 Hechinger, Fred M. "A Liberal Fights Back." **New York Times**, Section II, 13 February 1972, p. 1, 33.

The film represents a trend which alert liberals should recognize as the voice of fascism. Movies reflect the American mood and in **R.P.M.** and **Easy Rider** liberals have been depicted as superannuated, well-intentioned and fuzzy-minded. McDowell has said: "People are basically bad. I always sensed that. . ." and that liberals cringe when confronted by **Clockwork** because it shows them the bloody realities. McDowell clearly echoes his master, Kubrick, who has written that man is an irrational, brutal, weak, silly and ignoble savage. If these pessimistic views prevail, the result will be the "repressive, illiberal, distrustful, violent institutions of fascism." [For Kubrick's and McDowell's reply, see #1651, 1652.]

1650 "Clockwork Marmalade." **Listener**, v. 87, no. 2238 (February 17, 1972) 197-199.

Feels himself involved in the controversy surrounding Kubrick's **A Clockwork Orange** ("technically brilliant, thoughtful, relevant, poetic, mind-opening"). The title derives from Cockney slang. "It was a traditional trope, and it asked to entitle a work which combined a concern with tradition and a bizarre technique." Recalls the concern with criminality in the late 50's and various influential theoreticians who proposed the use of aversion therapy to condition criminals into 'goodness.' The limited stock of free will is too precious to encroach on. The novel was intended to be a tract, or sermon, on the importance of the power of choice. Alex is evil, not merely misguided. Theologically, evil is not quantifiable, but it is possible to argue that the wish to diminish free will is the sin against the Holy Ghost. "What hurts me, as also Kubrick, is the allegation. . . that there is a gratuitous indulgence in violence which turns an intended homiletic work into a pornographic one." Observes that the work is an act of catharsis and charity; his own first wife was robbed and beaten by three G.I. deserters in 1942. The language of the book, *nadsat*, was deliberately adopted to turn the book into a brainwashing primer. "It looks as though I must go through life as the fountain and origin of a great film, and as a man who has to insist against all opposition, that he is the most unviolent creature alive. Just like Stanley Kubrick."

1651 Kubrick, Stanley. "Now Kubrick Fights Back." **New York Times**, Section II, 27 February 1972, pp. 1, 11.

[Reply to #1649.] The "Liberal Alert" so confidently set jangling by Hechinger's resonant lines of alarmed prose is baffling. He quotes not one line, refers to not one scene, analyses not one theme of the film, but simply lumps it in indiscrimately with a trend liberals should properly hate. The film, far from purveying the essence of fascism, worries against the new psychedelic fascism of the eye-popping, multimedia, quadrasonic, drug-oriented conditioning of human beings by other human beings. It is true that the film's view of mankind is less flattering (and less erroneous) than that propounded in Rousseau's **Emile**. Quotes Vincent Canby [see #127] Anthony Burgess [#1650] and John E. Fitzgerald [#135] on the moral content of the film. Also quotes extensively from Arthur Koestler and Robert Ardrey to present and defend his pessimistic views of man. 3,000w

1652 McDowell, Malcolm. "Malcolm McDowell Objects Too." **New York Times**, Section II, 27 February 1972, p. 11.

[Letter in reply to Hechinger's article.] He is an actor, not a journalist or philsopher. His views on social and political issues are likely to be guided by emotion rather than the steely logic [McDowell is probably ironic] of a Hechinger. His comment on the sentimentalism of liberals was despondent, not gleeful as Hechinger maintains. The complacency and cowardice of "intellectuals" makes them too timid to confront Kubrick's harsh allegory.

1653 Anon. "Notes on People." **New York Times**, 10 March 1972, p. 48.

[Brief news item.] Burgess will join staff of Tyrone Guthrie Theater, Minneapolis as writer and consultant. "Under a three year contract, Mr. Burgess will write plays and adapt others, and help in selecting works for the repertory."

1654 Brophy, Elizabeth. "**A Clockwork Orange**: English and Nadsat." **Notes on Contemporary Literature**, v. 2, no. 2 (March 1972) 4-5.

"But why a clockwork orange? Since oranges are naturally motionless, surely mechanical works are unnecessary and the symbol is poorly chosen." If we analyse the title as a compound of Russian and English, it can be read as Klok-vor-Or-ahngel which means "Ragthief or Angel." This reading of the title touches on the question of man's essential nature, plays on Hamlet's speech 'What a piece of work is man . . . .' In the same way, Enderby (End or be) recalls Hamlet's 'To be or not to be' monologue. This interpretation of the title is reinforced by the implied identity between Alex and F. Alexander. [Ingenious and learned, but see #1650.]

1655 Rice, Susan. "Stanley Klockwork's Cubrick Orange; a Viewer's Guide." **Media and Methods**, v. 8, no. 7 (March 1972) 39-43.

Comments on the meaning of the title and observes that nadsat has a peculiar fascination (and exerts a distancing effect) not found in the film. "Burgess is, at heart, more of a religio-humanistic pamphleteer than a visionary or prophet. His novel is less a futuristic tract than a kinky sermonette . . . . Burgess' double-mindedness — free choice must prevail/man's nature is perverse — results in a hero-less and ambivalent cautionary tale." Suggests that most of the critics deeply regretted their failure to pay attention to the style of **2001**. For this reason, they over-compensated by praising the style of **Clockwork**. Notes the differences between Burgess' novel and Kubrick's screenplay. Comments on some of the stills from the film and concludes that "whatever point Burgess' novel had is nullified by Kubrick's adolescent view of authority, by his relentless satirization of everything . . . . Ultimately, the single most significant value of **A Clockwork Orange** may be that of a cultural artifact rather than as a work of art. It will demonstrate to future generations that, in 1972, we could hail as a tour de force a film that neither elevated us, instructed us nor informed our vision."

1656 "Burgess, Anthony." **Current Biography**, v. 33 (May 1972) 11-13.

1657 Strick, Phillip. "Interview with Stanley Kubrick." **Sight and Sound**, v. 41, no. 2 (Spring 1972) 62-66.

1658 Dix, Carol. "Anthony Burgess." **Transatlantic Review**, v. 42/43 (Spring/Summer 1972) 183-191.

[Interview.] His **A Clockwork Orange** has never been popular in England. He went to Leningrad in 1961 to gather material for **Honey for the Bears**, found the Russians were having trouble with their teenagers, and then combined the dialects. Kubrick's film is a good adaptation. Doubts if the success of the film will bring him greater popular success in England. Observes that the expatriate writer (Maugham, Joyce, now Burgess) avoids parochialism and trendiness. Respects Kingsley Amis, but his great ideal is Joyce. His translation of **Finnegans Wake** into Italian with help of his wife Lilliana Macellari is meeting little encouragement from Italian publishers. **MF** was received with incomprehension in England; it was better understood in America. However, the book was an act of self-denial for him. He will probably not write another one like it. Also on his interest in music, the decision to become a full-time writer in 1959-60 at the age of 42, the reason for his pseudonyms, **Vision of Battlements**, **The Worm and the Ring**, **Earthly Powers** ("I find no trouble in writing a novel, just a danger in repeating attitudes and scenes"). Maltese censorship is extensive ("I want to go back though, to fight the bastards") and the Maltese Church is too powerful.

1659 Chew, Shirley. "Mr. Livedog's Day: The Novels of Anthony Burgess." **Encounter**, v. 38, no. 6 (June 1972) 57-64.

[Chiefly an essay on Burgess' work. Also reviews **MF**. SEE ALSO: #537.] Each of Burgess' novels is an attempt to rework, with extraordinary imagination, themes first introduced in **The Malayan Trilogy**. "The types of characters originally encountered in Malaya are often re-engaged and tried afresh under the pressures and lights of new circumstances. In this manner, Burgess establishes his conclusions about human nature, the relationship between power and character, beteen the artist, his art, and reality." Within this framework, discusses **Beds in the East, The Worm and the Ring, A Clockwork Orange, The Wanting Seed** and, more briefly, **Inside Mr. Enderby** and **Nothing Like the Sun**.

1660 Cullinan, John. "Anthony Burgess' **A Clockwork Orange**: Two Versions." **English Language Notes**, v. 9, no. 4 (June 1972) 287-92.

The truncated American edition transforms the book into a dark, witty parable in which Alex's extreme license is opposed to the state's extreme tyranny, and the reader shudders or delights in his Augustinian incorrigibility. The British Heinemann edition includes a final 21st chapter which presents us with an Alex who remarks that to be in a state of youth is to be a kind of clockwork orange, that the human propensity for violence is perversely childish. The same chapter, while perhaps open to the charge of sentimentality, presents a cyclical view of history in which Alex finds that he is powerless to prevent the violence of his (putative) future son. In the final chapter, Burgess is playing (*vide* Ludovico's technique) with Vico's notion of a cyclical recurrence "so central to **Finnegans Wake** which figures prominently in **The Wanting Seed** as well."

1661 Malko, George. "**Penthouse** Interview: Anthony Burgess." **Penthouse**, v. 3, no. 10 (June 1972) 82-84, 119.

[Highly relevant to **A Clockwork Orange**.] On charges that **A Clockwork Orange** has caused violence. Points out that the Old Testament (and even the Eucharist) have led the deranged to grotesquely violent acts. Discusses Moors murders and **Titus Andronicus**. "If everything is going to be safe there's going to be no art, and I want art; we all need art." Believes that, on the whole, Kubrick got the book right. Discloses that fear was his own first reaction on viewing film. The film will make Kubrick a millionaire, but he is not envious. "I feel a curious sense of elation, or power, that a thing of mine can make money, that it can work in this big world which people take so seriously." His literary output is declining as he is drawn into the world of showbiz. Discusses Borneo and his suspicion that he was invalided home for political reasons. Wrote five novels (and more miscellania) at Hove and later at a country house in Sussex. On Mods and Rockers and the discussion of behavior modification techniques by the learned which made him see red. On his publisher's insistence ("we're tougher than you are") that the 21st chapter be deleted from the American eds. The book and film, in his view, are complementary. On Napoleon as a bad lover, sufferer from hyper-acidity. Endorses a proposal to scrap all pornography laws. Comments on pornography and masturbation and the effect of pornography on him. Mentions his first wife's promiscuity ("My first wife would sleep with anybody and always justify it") and how, on occasion, it made him mad and irrational as any Sicilian. Accepts the notion of original sin. On guilt and My Lai, the mugging of his first wife by G.I. deserters, the close connection between the American campus and the art of letters, the excellence of the British police compared to American swag-bellied counterparts who sometimes seem to represent an alternative criminal body, Pakistanis in Britain, the American way of life. "The first thing in life is to earn a living for your wife and your family and yourself. To hell with the Shavian notion that the true artist lets his wife and children starve."

1662 Barr, C. "**Straw Dogs, A Clockwork Orange** and the Critics." **Screen**, v. 13, no. 2 (Summer 1972) 17-31.

[Extended examination of Peckinpah's **Straw Dogs** and **A Clockwork Orange**.] "In **Dirty Harry**, Siegel's point is the glorification of the man of brutal action. In **Straw Dogs**, Peckinpah's point is the horrible inevitability of human brutality, especially when an individual attempts to evade it. In **A Clockwork Orange** it is difficult to find Kubrick's point. Is he praising destructive activity over programmed passivity? Is he mocking all social-political institutions? Is he simply mocking? Everything! This lack of thematic focus is the major flaw of the film." However, it is clear that Kubrick believes that an erotically liberated culture (along the lines advocated by Marcuse) leads to destruction; that civilization is a veneer and, when it cracks, reveals the ape beneath the velvet; and that Alex, F. Alexander, and the Minister of the Interior, are all aspects (violence, sterile reason, political cunning) of the nightmare of western culture.

1663 Cullinan, John. "Anthony Burgess' 'The Muse: A Sort of SF Story'." **Studies in Short Fiction,** v. 9, no. 3 (Summer 1972) 213-20.

"The value of 'The Muse' stems from Burgess' success in dealing with two thorny epistemological problems in playfully grotesque terms. The story focusses on the disturbing question whether it is indeed futile to attempt to pin down Shakespeare the man and on Montaigne's even more fundamental query — 'What do I know?' — which Burgess answers in problematically Kantian terms. This is not to reduce 'The Muse' to an *exemplum*; it is more imaginative than discursive, and its epistemological bent is anything but didactic . . . . 'The Muse' essentially, and topically [i.e. typically?], mocks the whole Shakespeare industry; for, as Burgess himself has written, 'only the present is worth satirizing'."

1664 Hess, John L. "Prof. Burgess, Your Humble Narrator of Joyce." **New York Times,** 15 September 1972, p. 39.

An account of Burgess teaching his City College students in Mott Hall about **Ulysses.** Dressed in saffron shirt and light blue slacks, he growls that the heat is still unbearable. He reads with Irish passion, then provides cool English footnotes and warm commentaries. In a taxi after the lecture, he notes his progress on **Napoleon Symphony** and remarks on the buzzing of his electrical typewriter. Will teach two courses of undergraduate literature and one on creative writing each week.

1665 Handler, M.S. "Lillian Hellman Is Among Nine Named to City University Chairs." **New York Times,** 26 September, 1972, p. 38.

Notes appointment of Burgess as distinguished professor at City College. Annual salary: $36,250 (base pay: $31,250 + annual supplement of $5,000).

1666 Fitzpatrick, William P. "Anthony Burgess' Brave New World: The Ethos of Neutrality." **Studies in the Humanities,** v. 3, no. 1 (October 1972) 31-36.

Observes that Burgess may be compared to Dante. Both explore the fundamental ethical quandary which face their worlds. "Burgess writes of a world reminiscent of Hell's vestibule in which all is flux and insecurity, in which the coalescence rather than the collision of moral absolutes is the order of things." Argues that in **A Clockwork Orange** and **The Wanting Seed,** Burgess condemns the neutrals, the moral parasites, committed to nothing, who refuse to take sides in a world engaged in Manichean struggles and analyzes both novels with this point of view in mind.

1667 Anon. "University of Rochester Pays Tribute to Benefactor." **New York Times,** 11 November 1972, p. 67.

[Brief news item.] Death of Joseph C. Wilson, chairman of board, Xerox, and honorary chairman University board of trustees, prompts lectures by prominent authors, scientists. Burgess lectures on Joyce, **A Clockwork Orange.** Describes nadsat as his "technique for avoiding violent pornography."

1668 Anderson, Ken. "A Note on **A Clockwork Orange.**" **Notes on Contemporary Literature** (Carrollton, Ga.), v. 2 (November 1972) 5-7.

Observes that 'to orange' is a British colloquialism which means to suck dry, exhaust, deplete. Then considers the first recorded etymological use of 'orange' and observes that Alex's society is a kind of dried Orange, Pound's "an old bitch gone in the teeth." Quotes Burgess on the title. [See #1412.]

1669 "ATV in Six Million Pound European Co-Production Venture." **Times** (London), 19 December 1972, p. 5.

Sir Lew Grade, ATV chief executive officer, announces production of six-part life of Moses to be written by Anthony Burgess and Vittorio Bonicelli. Also announces some other productions.

1670 A Clockwork Orange (Phonotape). Pacifica Tape Library BC913. [1972?]

Interview with Milton Hoffman. Duration: 30 min., 10 sec.

1671 Connelly, Wayne C. "Optimism in Burgess' **A Clockwork Orange**." **Extrapolation: A Science-Fiction Newsletter**, v. 14, no. 1 (December 1972) 25-29.

The absence of the original 21st chapter in most American editions distorts the novel; it resembles a satire devoid of a moral center, a shriek of violence which remains horrifyingly neutral. Gives an account of the 21st chapter, complete with quotations, and remarks that, in its original form, the novel is a story of adolescence. Compares the narrative technique and style of this novel to **Huck Finn** and **The Catcher in the Rye.** Without the missing chapter, the story is that of Alex's Augustinian night; the last chapter of the original British edition successfully presents his Pelagian day.

1672 Enright, Dennis Joseph. "A Modern Disease: Anthony Burgess's Shakespeare." In his **Man Is an Onion**. London: Chatto and Windus, 1972, pp. 39-43.

In his novel, **Nothing Like the Sun**, Burgess follows G.B. Harrison in depicting the "dark lady" as Lucy Negro, the prostitute resoundingly known as the Abbess of Clerkenwell. This clever, tightly constructed book depicts a venereal Shakespeare filled with sexual loathing and misogyny. The portrait is one-sided. "Mr. Burgess's narrative might help to account for the rougher bits in the Sonnets, for Lear's remarks on the gentler sex, for Othello, Troilus, Leontes — but not for Hermione, Miranda, Imogen. . . [or] Cordelia . . . ." Burgess' Shakespeare follows in the luckless footsteps of Victor Crabbe and Mr. Spindrift — archetypal Burgess heroes who endure countless humiliations.

1673 Kagan, Norman. "A Clockwork Orange." In his **The Cinema of Stanley Kubrick**. New York: Holt, Rinehart and Winston, 1972, pp. 167-[187]

Provides details of Kubrick's efficient, obsessive preparation prior to filming. Gives a synopsis and observes that Kubrick has given three interpretations of the film: it is a social satire on psychological conditioning, a fairy tale of retribution and a presentation of a psychological myth. Also gives extracts from the critical opinions of Vincent Canby, Clayton Riley, Judith Crist, Jay Cocks, Paul Zimmerman, Pauline Kael and Robert Hughes. Comments on Kubrick's characteristic themes under the rubrics of "The Imaginary Worlds, Futility of Intelligence, Distrust of Emotion, Homicidal-Suicidal Pairings, Obsessed-Hero and Odyssey Toward Freedom and Knowledge."

1674 Aggeler, Geoffrey. "Incest and the Artist: Anthony Burgess's **MF** as Summation." **Modern Fiction Studies**, v. 18, no. 4 (Winter 1972-1973) 529-43.

In this novel, Burgess "has fused incest myths — Algonquin Indian and Greek — and given them new meaning as a devastating satiric indictment of contemporary Western cultural values that goes well beyond the criticisms levelled in the **Enderby** novels." Conveys plot summary, quotes Joseph Campbell on the single archetype behind the myths of Jonah, Oedipus, Hiawatha and Finn MacCool, gives an account of the Oedipus myth, Levi-Strauss's announcement of a remarkable similarity between the Amerindian myth and that of Oedipus, and remarks the existence of the 'riddle-incest nexus' in **Finnegans Wake** and Burgess' own consciousness. Confesses that he is a member of the professorial tribe who must fillet a separable meaning from the book, and suggests that it may be found in 1) its recoil from shoddy and chaotic artefacts produced by artistic charlatans, 2) repudiation of race consciousness, and 3) the 'incestuousness' of America which shows itself in xenophobia, isolationism and an unwillingness to take the United Nations seriously. [Reprinted, with some changes and revisions, in his **Anthony Burgess: The Artist as Novelist**. University, Alabama: University of Alabama Press, 1979, pp. [195]-207. Annotation based on the book just cited.]

1675 Anon. "Burgess to Write Script for 'Moses'." **New York Times**, Arts Section, 30 January 1973, p. 25.

[Very brief news item.] Burgess has agreed to write script for Italian British television production. Announces Moses would be based on "conflict between freedom and authority and the power that spoils and consumes."

1676 Fiore, Peter Amadeus. "Milton and Kubrick: Eden's Apple or a Clockwork Orange." **CEA Critic**, v. 35, no. 2 (January 1973) 14-17.

Alex is given over to fits of unbridled violence and sex; in the second part he becomes the victim of violence himself. The film raises the question: what is the essence of human nature? Kubrick describes man as an ignoble savage — brutal, weak, irrational and silly. McDowell, echoing Kubrick, asserts that people are basically bad and corrupt. Milton confronted this problem, the basic nature of man, in the 17th century. Taking his cue from Augustine's description of Adam and Eve before the Fall, he describes them as immortal, happy and sexually superlatively fulfilled. After the Fall, they lost the super-human component that prevailed in the Garden of Eden and reverted to common humanity. Augustine concluded that human nature was "vitiatum" (faulty, impaired, weakened, blemished), not "vitium" (inherently evil and corrupt). Both Augustine and Milton are more hopeful than Kubrick. "The clockwork orange is more fatal [to hope] than the apple of Eden."

1677 "2.5 m[illion pound] TV Series on Life of Shakespeare." **Times** (London), 6 February 1973, p. 1.

"ATV, the Midlands-based independent television Company, is to show a 2.5 million pound series on the life of Shakespeare, based on a book by Mr. Anthony Burgess." [The film based on Burgess' screenplay was never produced. See also #1382.]

1678 Cullinan, John. "Burgess' **The Wanting Seed**." **Explicator**, v. 31, no. 7 (March 1973) item 51 [ca. 2 pp.]

Michael Wood and Julian Mitchell have brought his attention to the fact that Burgess makes use of Paul Valery's poem **Le Cimetiere Marin** in the Epilogue, Chapter 4, of **The Wanting Seed**. Quotes the passage from the novel, stanzas 23 and 24 of the poem, and observes that Burgess can be as subtly allusive as his master, James Joyce.

1679 Cullinan, John. "The Art of Fiction XLVIII: Anthony Burgess." **Paris Review**, v. 14, no. 56 (Spring 1973) 119-63.

[Interview.] He is not worried by charges that he writes too much. "It has been a sin to be prolific only since the Bloomsbury group — particularly Forster — made it a point of good manners to produce. . . costively." Comments on the best time to work; he does most of his work in the afternoon. "The ideal reader of my novels is a lapsed Catholic and failed musician, short-sighted, color-blind, auditorily biased, who has read the books that I have read. He should also be about my age." Critics are not often helpful, but a bad review by a man he admires hurts terribly. His work as a professional reviewer forced him into alien territory, and paid the bills. Mentions his collaboration with Kubrick on a film version of Napoleon. Comments on the time it takes to finish a novel, with special reference to **Ulysses**. His **Joysprick** makes a phonetic analysis of Joyce's language in **Ulysses**. Observes that Molly Bloom is pure Nora Barnacle; Molly, the daughter of a major stationed in Gibraltor, would not talk or think like a Dublin fishwife. Argues that there is no qualitative difference between the novels written in his "terminal" year, 1959-1960, and the others. Demonstrates how it is possible to base prose fiction on musical forms. His Napoleon novel formally apes the **Eroica** symphony. Explains why the proposed film versions of **Enderby** and **Nothing Like the Sun** fell through. Talks about his planned novel on the 14th century and the Black Prince. Also about the Heinemann ed. of **A Clockwork Orange**. Kubrick discovered this version halfway through the film but considered the ending too milk-and-watery. Mentions other novels, **Parade's End** and **Way of All Flesh** which have appeared in different versions. Gives reasons for his contempt of the youth culture, why he likes to play jazz music. Also on James Joyce as an inimitable craftsman, F. Scott Fitzgerald, Hemingway, Defoe, Sterne, Evelyn Waugh, Graham Greene, and Francois Mauriac. His aversion to describing amorous details is due to the fact that he treasures physical love so highly. Observes that English Catholics take their religion seriously and confesses that he is a Manichee only in the widest sense that duality is the ultimate reality. Also on neutrals (Mr. Theodorescu) in his fiction, the necessity of an exotic, non-English milieu as a source for his fiction, Paris and Leningrad, the delights of "hot pot" and "lobscowse", politics ("To take socialism seriously, as opposed to minimal socialization — what American needs so desperately — is ridiculous"). Issues the pronunciamento that he is a Jacobite and wants the Stuart monarchy restored. If that ideal is not practicable, he will settle for a kind of anarchism. "All we can do is keep pricking our government all the time, disobeying all we dare (after all, we have livings to earn) asking why, maintaining a habit of distrust." On myth and structuralism in literature, the novel as the only big literary form left, and the mental strain, worry and self-doubt that afflict the professional novelist. [Reprinted in #1740.]

1680 Talbot, J. Milton. "Burgess on **Orange**: Not One of My Best." **Bucknellian**, v. 76, no. 15 (April 17, 1973) 1, 3.

[Burgess on the lecture tour of American colleges. This article, written by a student of Bucknell University, is probably typical of many published in the American collegiate press.] "The Forum was a sea of faces on Friday night, O my brothers, as all came to viddy and slooshy Anthony Burgess. And a very witty, oomny chelloveck he was, gavoreeting real horrorshow about this book that he had like written, called **A Clockwork Orange**." Includes brief biographical sketch. On American colleges: they are very good, but there are too many of them (academic factories, students insufficiently prepared). He is trying to keep out of the academic racket; writing and teaching are incompatible; they both require a tremendous amount of creative energy. Briefly talks about the **Napoleon Symphony** and the novelist's primary duty: to entertain ("I mean to give the reader joy, make him feel better, make him elated"). He is totally sick of talking about **Clockwork**. It is only one of his 28 books, and not the best by any means. He himself does not like it because it expresses an ethical purpose: that it is totally wrong to subordinate the human will entirely to this general will of the state or community.

1681 Dimeo, Steven. "The Ticking of an Orange." **Riverside Quarterly**, v. 5, no. 4 (April 1973) 318-21.

[Praise for Kubrick's film of **A Clockwork Orange**.] It is a brilliantly executed piece of professionalism which confirms Kubrick's controversial genius. Kubrick has adapted the novel with a fidelity uncommon in the film world. The question is: how successful has he been in making Burgess' vision his own? The answer is that Kubrick's satirical embellishments are sometimes trenchant; his visual devices are consistently successful; his command of the colour camera is always professional; and the props are eye-catching.

1682 Plank, Robert. "Sonnets in Celebration of the Film **A Clockwork Orange**." **Riverside Quarterly**, v. 5, no. 4 (April 1973) 322-23.

Three sonnets. Sample:

> This scene of double rape, quick as a flight
> Of nightmare birds, how did it get its shape?
> Kubrick has now revealed he found the trick
> While playing **Eine Kleine Nachtmusik**.
> His sound-effects are neat, and fast, and clear.
> But what's that rumble from below I hear?
> If you do not believe in ghosts, be brave:
> That's Mozart turning in his unmarked grave.

1683 Isaacs, Neil D. "Unstuck in Time: Clockwork Orange and Slaughter-House-Five." **Literature/Film Quarterly**, v. 1, no. 2 (April 1973) 122-31.

Kubrick's recreation of Alex's voice, which has a hyped musical quality, is even greater than Tony Richardson's success in that vein in **The Loneliness of the Long Distance Runner**. Kubrick has found masterful cinematic equivalents for that voice. The initial composition shot of the Korova milk bar is a triumph. Kubrick not only makes use of the novel's language, he also deploys the language of allusion and parody. Witness the transformation of F. Alexander into a Dr. Strangelove, the suggestion of the Jupitor room of **2001** in Alex's "suicide" room, and the evocation of the famous eating scene of **Tom Jones** when Alex chomps away in appalling self-satisfaction of his corrupt identity in company with the smirking Minister. That the people will sell their liberty for a quiet life is Burgess' explicit thematic lament, and he artfully wills us to choose the side of art and free will despite the possibly hideous consequences of that choice. Burgess' satire is Drydenesque, but Kubrick's satiric view is Hobbesian — a cold, hard look at the dialectical poles of free (violent) self and controlled order. [Written in an aphoristic style and difficult to summarize.]

1684 Anon. "Briefs on the Arts. Rubinstein Cited with Burgess." **New York Times**, 15 May 1973, p. 29.

[Very brief news item.] Burgess to receive Sixth Annual Award in Literature from National Arts Club.

1685 Plank, Robert. "The Place of Evil in Science Fiction." **Extrapolation**, v. 14, no. 2 (May 1973) 100-111.

On **A Clockwork Orange**.

1686 Anon. "Author Tries Hand at Book-Selling." **New York Times**, 2 June 1973, p. 18.

[Brief news item.] Burgess announces he will try to sell his translation of Rostand's **Cyrano de Bergerac** without the intermediacy of publisher Knopf. Will autograph copies of book at Rizzoli Screening Room.

1687 Weiler, A.H. "Whistle a Tune from Thomas Mann." **New York Times**, 3 June 1973, Section II, p. 11.

[Brief news item.] Burgess and Stephen Schwartz, composer of 'Pippin' and 'Godspell' to collaborate on a song and dance musical version of Thomas Mann's **The Transposed Head**.

1688 [Malamud, Phyllis.] "For Love or Money." **Newsweek**, v. 81, no. 23 (June 4, 1973) 62.

Announces that Burgess has managed not to make a lot of money from his protean off-campus career, and now acts as a hired literary gun at American colleges. He is appalled at the artlessness and wild indiscipline characteristic of the speech and writing of American students. Puts the blame on permissive teachers. Burgess was finally reduced to telling students what he thought of them. Quotes from #1423; the comments caused a stir. He is now considering, without much relish, an offer of a full-time job at Columbia.

1689 Platypus, Bill. "Bill Platypus's Paperbacks." **Spectator**, v. 230, no. 7566 (June 30, 1973) 819.

"In this context [the constant stream of pulp known as 'the modern novel'] Anthony Burgess has always just escaped sheer contemporaneity and in recognition of his pleasant but precarious achievement Penguin Books are issuing four of his earlier novels." The novels include **Inside Mr. Enderby, MF, The Wanting Seed, Honey for the Bears.** and **Urgent Copy.** [Complete text of notice.]

1690 Stinson, John J. "Anthony Burgess: Novelist on the Margin." **Journal of Popular Culture**, v. 7, no. 1 (Summer 1973) 136-51.

A traditionalist in moral values with a self-confessed anarchical bent, Burgess is in many ways a Modernist — an embittered disciple of the Old High Art whose death seems likely to be witnessed in our own day. His novels resemble a forcible and almost profane union of popular and elitist literature. "A sudden, shocking immersion of pedants or elitist artists into the steaming tank of mass taste and culture has come to be a kind of formula in Burgess's novels." His oeuvre is on the margin between serious fiction and entertainment. Considers some of the pop elements in **MF**. Traces Burgess' critical opinion of, and debt to, Charles Dickens. Many of Burgess' works fall in the category of the social picaresque. He also owes a debt to the novels of the Angry Young Men. Fierce rejection of social elitism, an element in the work of these authors, also shows itself in Burgess. One might argue that he is Modernistically elitist at core, but examination will not bear this out. Witness, for example, the amused condescension as Alex contemplates the liberal sociological ethic that equates cultural artifacts with goodness, social responsibility and taste. One may argue that Burgess has a satiric intention (witness his lambasting of the Crewsy Fixers in **Enderby**) but one must observe that the biggest laughs are at the expense of Enderby the poet (arrested "at an early post-infantile state of psychological development") rather than an idol of the rock culture. [I suspect Burgess would vigorously dispute this statement.] Discusses the elements of Pop Art (Andy Warhol, Tom Wesselmann) in connection with Burgess' **The Right to an Answer**. Notes, as final proof of Burgess' true pop credentials, that he is intent on rescuing Joyce from the professors, and making him accessible to the common people who love books.

1691 Morley, Sheridan. "Anthony Burgess Answers Back." **Times** (London), no. 58,853, 6 August 1973, p. 7c.

Burgess objects to the fact that he is now the target of official and public abuse. He feels this abuse should properly be directed at the film, or the film-maker rather than poor Burgess. "My book was about the ultimate absurdity of violence: somehow the film doesn't convey that — maybe it should have been even more violent to underline the point. Anyway we are now evidently in for a period of massive restraint and the sooner those bloody officials start telling us what we are going to be allowed to write and what we can't the better it will be. . . at least then we shall all know what we are supposed to be doing.'' These views will shortly be published in **Clockwork Testament**. Comments on his prolific production, including the famous year when he wrote five novels. Observes he is now busy on a television series called ''The Lawgiver'' and some musicals. One is based on the life of Shakespeare; the other on **Ulysses**. [For response by some lawyers, see #1692. It should perhaps be added that **Clockwork Testament** was at first intended to be a philosophical and polemical work. Burgess then decided that he was a novelist, not a thinker, and wrote a work of fiction instead.]

1692 Berlins, Marcel. ''Lawyers Reject Author's Attack.'' **Times** (London), 7 August 1973, p. 2.

[Response to #1691.] ''Immediate reaction in legal circles yesterday to Mr. Anthony Burgess's attack on judges who have condemned the film **A Clockwork Orange**, which was based on his book, is that his criticism is aimed at the wrong persons. Mr. Burgess said over the weekend that he was fed up with judges' vague attacks on his book and the film. 'These bloody judges and other people are just playing around on the fringes of a very difficult subject,' he said. 'Let us put the ball in their court and let them tell us what we may or may not write about.' Lawyers point out that it is for Parliament, not judges, to lay down the law. Judges merely interpret the law.'' Burgess was evidently reacting to Judge Desmond Bailey who described **Clockwork** as 'this dastardly film' because two juvenile hoodlums attributed their violent acts to the film.

1693 Severin-Lounsberry, Barbara. ''Holden and Alex: A Clockwork from the Rye?'' **Film Quarterly**, v. 22 (Summer 1973) 27-38.

In **A Clockwork Orange** (1962) Burgess seems to have adopted his protagonist, setting, narrative technique, diction, and even certain opinions from Salinger's **The Catcher in the Rye** (1951). The two books are nevertheless completely different: Salinger's is a psychological study with social implications, Burgess' a typically British novel, concerned to a much greater degree with society and with little in-depth psychological characterization. — AES, v. 19, no. 7 (March 1976) 459-60. No. 2181.

1694 Anon. ''Burgess, Originator of 'Clockwork,' Says 'Let Kubrick Defend Film','' **Variety**, v. 272 (August 1973) 2, 40.

Believes Kubrick's **A Clockwork Orange** is a remarkable work but protests that ''It is surely the duty of the maker of the film to speak out for his own work.'' As it is, Burgess is forced to defend both book and film, a tiresome assignment. Observes that he is ''the author of nearly 30 books and would like some of these to come under attack or at least read.'' Alleges he is misquoted by journalists. ''Most of the statements I'm alleged to have made have in fact been distortions of what I have really said. This can be blamed on the difficulties of telephonic communication . . . . But it can chiefly be blamed on the scrambling apparatus which resides in the brains of so many journalists.''

1695 Pritchard, Katherine. ''A Candid Interview with the Author of **A Clockwork Orange**.'' **Seventeen**, v. 32, no. 8 (August 1973) 236, 249-50.

There is no youth revolution: youth is not yet ready to rule, as proved by the agronomically ignorant communards in California. Study is hard slog, but it is, for all that, rewarding. The word 'relevance' has been debased; it refers to that which is relevant to individuals in particular political activities. These activists make the ''gross mistake of assuming that the whole of life can be defined in terms of political action. It cannot. Political action is a very small part of life.'' Fears that American education, particularly in the humanities, may be diluted and oversimplified. Also discusses the past, defines maturity (''When one can love another person, not for his or her body but for his or her mind, temperament, total personality''), discusses some American writers, comments on **A Clockwork Orange** (book and film), considers he loves the U.S. and comments on his own life as a student.

1696 Aggeler, Geoffrey. ''A Wagnerian Affirmation: **The Worm and the Ring**.'' **Western Humanities Review**, v. 27, no. 4 (Autumn 1973) [401]-10.

Quotes Burgess on the bitterness of his penurious life as a teacher in Banbury. The novel is a burlesque of Wagner's **Der Ring des Nibelungen**. Identifies some of the correspondences (Woolton = Wootan, Gardner = Fafner, Albert Rich = Alberich) as part of his running plot summary. It is a very bitter and pessimistic version of the **Ring**. ''Its bitterness extends beyond the arena of school politics. The wretchedness of Howarth's genteel poverty, the stupid tyranny of mindless Catholic orthodoxy, and the philistinism of the little English borough are all presented with angry force.'' The struggle between the liberal humanism of Woolton and the cynical autocracy of Gardner demonstrates Burgess' awareness of the inadequacies and dangers of both views as governing philosophies. Examines Howarth's Catholicism and quotes Burgess' disillusionment with post-Johanine Catholicism. Also considers the character of Lodge, the science teacher, and remarks that some of the minor female characters are equally well drawn. The novel ends with something like a Wagnerian affirmation of hope in the power of love, and suspects that Burgess' own point of view may be expressed in Howarth's reflections on the consolations of existence. [Reprinted, with some changes and revisions, in his **Anthony Burgess: The Artist as Novelist**. University, Alabama: University of Alabama Press, 1979, pp. 58-67. Annotation based on the book just cited.]

1697 Chalpin, Lila. "Anthony Burgess's Gallows Humor in Dystopia." **Texas Quarterly**, v. 16, no. 3 (Autumn 1973) 73-84.

Extended discussion and plot summary of **The Wanting Seed**. Pays particular attention to tracing the significance of the names given to Burgess' fictional characters. Concludes that "The major weakness of **The Wanting Seed** is that it is too much a *roman a thése*. This applies to most novels of dystopia. The characters are cartoons, cut off from deep experience and never hinting at the surprise 'round characters' always possess. Characters in satire tend to be straight-jacketed by tag names and archetypes. They suffer but never transcend or understand their suffering. They talk but never understand exactly what they're rebelling against."

1698 Evans, Robert O. "The *nouveau roman*, Russian Dystopias and Anthony Burgess." **Studies in the Literary Imagination**, v. 6, no. 2 (Fall 1973) 27-37.

A Clockwork Orange and **The Wanting Seed** are heavily larded with violence. The works suggest that Burgess borrowed a page from the French *nouveau roman* and "hung the works on fictive structures dependent on violence for their very shapes." To clarify the place of Burgess in contemporary literary history, it might be helpful to examine the anti-utopian convention. Burgess owes debts to Zamyatin and Orwell. The Russian revolution at first led to utopian, pro-revolutionary outbursts of poetic feeling: Sergey Esenin's "Inonia" and Mayakovsky's "The 150 Millions." Later poets, disillusioned with aspects of communism, objected to coercion and boredom in literature, to literature amazingly prim, smug and monotonous. Zamyatin epitomizes this protest by the Serapion Brethren as they came to be called. Unlike most dystopian novelists, who issue a warning to their readers (the horrors of collectivism, the dangers of a closed society) **A Clockwork Orange** is an expression of disgust about what has happened to people in our century. Similarly, **The Wanting Seed** grows more disgusting, or more disgusted, as it proceeds. "It is more an expression of vast loathing over what the author, a realist of no mean talent, makes us believe may be almost inevitable."

1699 Stinson, John J. "The Manichee World of Anthony Burgess." **Renascence**, v. 26 (Autumn 1973) 37-47.

The most insistent theme in Burgess' novels centers on the incongruous mixture of good and evil in a radically imperfect universe. Burgess terms his own view Manichean, the reference to the medieval heresy of radical dualism suggesting Burgess' repeated theme that to be strongly committed to either good or evil is both to know the other principle by opposition and to save oneself in the here-and-now and the hereafter. A proper understanding of this central theme allows one to understand the reason for the frequent appearance in Burgess' fiction of violence, the grotesque, black humor, and linguistic distortion. Two of his best known novels, **A Clockwork Orange** and **Nothing Like the Sun**, operate on strong polar principles but end in paradox since good and evil constantly interpenetrate. In both novels grotesque violence is a metaphor for incongruities both metaphysical and social but also a shock device whereby a harsh light is thrown on the darkness of man's heart and the darkness of the universe. But in an almost romantic vein, Burgess affirms the tragedy and triumph of man: Alex and WS are whole, estimable men who, not despite, but because of, strong animal natures find themselves irresistibly committed to a powerful response to life and all that it means to be totally human. (JJS) MLA Abstracts 1973.

1700 Kresh, Paul. "If Jane Austen Had Only Recorded **Pride and Prejudice**." **New York Times**, Section D, 25 November 1973, p. 36.

A review of two records (Caedmon TC 1417 and Spoken Arts SA 1120). The Caedmon record includes a reading from the first, second and fourth chapters of **A Clockwork Orange**. "He reads **A Clockwork Orange** with hair-raising energy and drive."

1701 Bunting, Charles T. "An Interview in New York with Anthony Burgess." **Studies in the Novel** (North Texas State University) v. 5, no. 4 (Winter 1973) 504-29.

Discusses "The Clockwork Condition" [later published as **Clockwork Testament**], the research which preceded the writing of **Napoleon Symphony** and the obscene outbursts of Napoleon the man, the difficulty of writing lyrics for **Cyrano!**, Shakespeare's musical interests, the identity of the "Dark Lady," his total distrust of A.L. Rowse, the Elizabethan English of **Nothing Like the Sun**, the dangerous nature of the American Constitution, the sort of novel he is trying to write, experimentation in the novel with an example out of the work of B.S. Johnson and reference to Sterne's **Tristram Shandy**, the limitations of some feminist novelists, the pleasures of living in or near Manchester and Lancaster, the similarities between the Sicilian and Northern English temperaments. Appraises Malta, Rome and New York as place in which to live and work and the deficiencies of American university students (informally dressed intellectual nullities), British tactics in dealing with Malayan guerillas. The dualism of **A Vision of Battlements** was suggested by the army and the Rock of Gibraltor. Also on some Catholic theological tenets or premises of which he approves, the danger of Skinner's **Beyond Freedom and Dignity**, the anticlericalism evident in his own novels, fornication as the cause of guilt in Graham Greene, the role of Frank Kermode as an excellent critic and nascent Catholic, his self-assessment as a good journalist but poor critic, the final chapter of **A Clockwork Orange** (English ed.), the achievement of James Joyce, old-fashioned fictional ways of Nabokov and Updike. Concludes with a brief account of his future writing plans and projects.

1702 McCracken, Samuel. "Novel into Film; Novelist into Critic: **A Clockwork Orange**. . . Again." **Antioch Review**, v. 32, no. 3 (1973) 427-36.

Argues that Alex is not deprived of free will. Alex can, after the aversion therapy, still choose between the thistle and the rose: suffer extreme nausea or eschew violence. Burgess' critical views are mistaken. Alex's free will is unimpaired; only his freedom of choice is circumscribed. "Neither the Treatment nor the prison diminish free will; this can be done only by a brain washing which makes the having of certain desires either impossible or compulsory, a process to which Alex is patently not subjected." Opposes social control by aversion therapy, but believes that "given the world of the novel, the State has pretty clearly opted for the best choice open to it." In the film, as opposed to the book, subtle (and not so subtle) shifts of emphasis combine to make Alex more likable and society more detestable. [Criticism based on the American ed.]

1703 Canby, Vincent. "Has Movie Violence Gone Too Far?" **Film 72/73; An Anthology by the National Society of Film Critics**. Edited by David Denby. New York: Bobbs-Merrill, 1973, pp. [121]-124.

We are in the middle of a new zap-plop-stab-splatter era of movie violence. Witness Polanski's **Macbeth** (a nicely decapitated Thane of Cawdor), **Harold and Maude** (realistic mock-suicides in a comedy), **Dirty Harry** (psychopathic splatterdom incarnate) and now **A Clockwork Orange**. The hero cheerily kicks the guts and genitals of a man whose wife he is about to rape. **Orange**, however, attempts to understand the meaning of violence and the social climate that tolerates it. Leonard Berkowitz discredited the notion of catharsis; the viewers of violent films showed symptoms of hostile behavior. **A Clockwork Orange** "is a horror show, but cool, so removed from reality that it would take someone who really cherished his perversion to get any vicarious pleasure from it. To isolate its violence is to ignore everything else that is at work in the movie. . ." including its soundtrack, photography, editing and the concern of the film, which is nothing less than the fate of mankind. [Reprinted from **New York Times**, 6 January 1972, p. ?]

1704 Reilly, Lemuel. "An Interview with Anthony Burgess." **Delaware Literary Review** (University of Delaware) v. 2 (1973) 48-55.

Each novel is a different artifact and requires a different technique. "I try to make every novel as different as I can, otherwise why bother?" Believes that Joyce would not have written an epic on the sea. Joyce had exhausted the possibilities of the waking day (**Ulysses**) and the sleeping night (**Finnegans Wake**). Observes that there is something weary about the language used in British novels. Americans are at least attempting to write "big" works of fiction in which they grapple with contemporary problems and the problems of language. He is complimented on his good ear for American usage in **MF** and responds that he has great difficulty with American speech because it's so close to English usage you can trip up if you are not careful. Remarks on the tremendous interest in myth today. Getting back to the world of myth will be the salvation of us all. Includes a very brief discussion of his novel **Napoleon Symphony** and observes that the writer can do what the hell he wants as long as the characters are strong enough.

1705 Kael, Pauline. "Stanley Strangelove." In her **Deeper Into Movies**. Boston; Toronto: Little Brown, 1973, pp. 373-78.

[Reprint of #143.]

1706 Carvalho, Alredo Leme Coelho de. "As Distopias de Anthony Burgess." **Revista de Letras da Faculdade de Filosofia, Ciencias, e Letras de Assis**, v. 15 (1973) 9-34.

[On **A Clockwork Orange** and **The Wanting Seed**.]

1707 Murdoch, Brian. "The Overpopulated Wasteland: Myth in Anthony Burgess' **The Wanting Seed**." **Revue des langues vivantes (Tidschrift voor levende Talen)**, v. 39, no. 3 (1973) 203-17.

Considers some of the criticisms leveled at Burgess' novel, quotes Northrop Frye on myth, and then discusses the myth of Parsifal in relation to Eliot's **The Wasteland** and, more extensively, to **The Wanting Seed**. Burgess has expanded the person of the Fisher King, maimed into infertility, to its limits: the whole population is sterile. Just as Parzifal hungers first after the grail, and then with a concern with his wife, so Tristram (Parzifal) engages on a quest for self where Beatrice-Joanna (Condwiramurs) represents the anima, the *Ewig-Weibliche*, the aspect of fecundity. Then considers the novel in some detail. "The purpose of this paper has not been the positivist source-seeing of the German critics in the nineteenth century; it is not *Quelleforschung*, and the value, indeed, of the mythological approach to literature does not lie, as Frye has indicated, in the establishing of whether or not a work is a recreation of the medieval Parzifal story, for example. While Burgess' novel may be an explicit or implicit reworking of the cyclic vegetation myth, the overall poetic form is more relevant: 'while the interpreter or commentator on a myth finds the profundity of the myth in its meaning as allegory, the poet, in recreating the myth, finds its profundity in its *archetypal framework*' [Frye] . . . . **The Wanting Seed** may have some stylistic infelicities; the comedy is on occasion somewhat heavy-handed. But this does not matter. The myth basis of the work informs it with enough of the high seriousness — in a literary and social sense — that it needs to establish it as perhaps the most important of Anthony Burgess' novels."

1708 "Burgess, Anthony." In **Celebrity Register**. Editor-in-chief: Earl Blackwell. New York: Simon & Schuster, 1973, p. 75.

[Brief biographical sketch chiefly based on the interview with Lewis. [See #1622.] Includes some errors and inaccuracies.]

1709 "Burgess, Anthony." **Current Biography Yearbook 1972**. New York: Wilson, 1973, pp. 54-57.

1710 Aggeler, Geoffrey. "Pelagius and Augustine in the Novels of Anthony Burgess." **English Studies**, v. 55, no. 1 (February 1974) 43-55.

Discusses **The Wanting Seed** and **A Clockwork Orange**. Both are novels of point-counter-point. Both are proleptic dystopias in which the Pelagian heresy is countered by the Augustinian insistence on original sin. Gives summaries of the Pelagian and Augustinian positions, and studies both novels in terms of the optimistic Pelagian point (man can find his way to salvation without divine grace) and the pessimistic Augustinian counterpoint (the fundamental wickedness of man prevents salvation without the free gift of God's grace).

1711 Krebs, Albin. "Notes on People." **New York Times**, April 11, 1974, p. 47.

Burgess protests the apparent confiscation of his house in Malta by the Maltese Government.

1712 Aggeler, Geoffrey. "A Prophetic Acrostic in Anthony Burgess' **Nothing Like the Sun**." **Notes and Queries**, N.S., v. 21 no. 4 (April 1974) 136.

The initial letters of each line in a sonnet written by the boy Shakespeare in this novel form an acrostic spelling 'Fatimah' forward and backward — the name of the dark lady from whom he later contracts syphilis, the disease that shapes his dramatic career. — AES, v. 18, no. 9 (May 1975) 582. No. 2883.

1713 Page, Eric. "Fears of Local Censorship Haunt the Book Trade." **New York Times**, 8 June 1974, p. 26.

Publishers and distributors panic in the wake of the Supreme Court ruling that permits states and communities to judge prurient works by applying the views of the "average persons, applying contemporary community standards" rather than a hypothetical national definition of obscenity. Other publishers fight back. Random House provides legal defense to Orem, Utah, bookseller served with a summons for selling copy of Burgess' **A Clockwork Orange** in Ballantine paperback ed. Perhaps the day of steamy paperback titillation is over? Title called **The Joy of Cooking** is out-selling book advertised as 'The Joys of Hooking.'

1714 "Zeffirelli to Direct a TV Life of Christ." **Times** (London), 31 July 1974, p. 18.

Announces that a six part television series on the life of Christ is planned by ATV/RAI. The work will be directed by Franco Zeffirelli. Anthony Burgess will write the script.

1715 Brown, Les. "NBC Buys an Anglo-Italian Series on the Life of Jesus." **New York Times**, 1 August 1974, p. 57.

NBC has bought RAI/ATV production of 'Jesus of Nazareth.' The production budget is in excess of $12 million. Franco Zeffirelli will be the director; Anthony Burgess, along with Suso Cecchi D'Amico, the two writers.

1716 Gilbert, Basil. "Kubrick's Marmalade: The Art of Violence." **Meanjin Quarterly**, v. 33, no. 2 (Winter 1974) 157-162.

Burgess wrote the book in reaction against the verdicts of reviewers, who saw him as a comic writer. Quotes judgments of some early reviewers who found the book hard to read. Pays tribute to Alex's learning; he is "familiar with such great operas as Friedrich Gitterfenster's **Das Bettzeug**; and, in a more modern vein, is enraptured by American Geoffrey Plautus's violin concerto played by Odysseus Choerilos with the Macon (Georgia) Philharmonic. [These immortal performances by great performers are, of course, Burgess' own inventions.] Alex is the perfect aristocrat of the hip generation." Quotes section in which ("gorgeousness and gorgeosity made flesh") Alex hears and praises a new violin concerto; the passage includes echoes of Yeats, Hopkins, Joyce and Shakespeare. Then gives account of how Kubrick came to make film. Examines the sets of the Korova milk bar, the **Time** essay which greeted film and, with sardonic irreverence, reports that pundits in law, causation and casuistry found the film the proximate cause of local Melbourne Australian mayhem among the rowdy young.

1717 [Jennings, C. Robert.] "Playboy Interview: Anthony Burgess. A Candid Conversation with the Visionary Author of **A Clockwork Orange**." **Playboy**, v. 21, no. 9 (September 1974) 69-86.

A Clockwork Orange was a "kind of personal testament made out of love and sorrow, as well as of ideas and theology." Describes the mugging of his first wife by GI deserters and explains how he sold the film rights of **Orange** for $3,000. Kubrick's Orange makes violence seem attractive. On his Catholicism and sense of good and evil, aversion therapy and the dangerous B.F. Skinner, his sad life at Princeton and the causal relation (if any) between violence in art and life. A very literary interview. Burgess gives his opinions on Tom Wolfe, Kurt Vonnegut, J.D. Salinger, Ken Kesey, J.R.R. Tolkien, Truman Capote, Norman Mailer, John Dos Passos, Sinclair Lewis, Hemingway, F. Scott Fitzgerald, Henry Miller, William Burroughs, Dylan Thomas, Brendan Behan. Also comments on his wife's discovery of Thomas' near impotence, masturbation and art, the cultural (not the sexual) *raison d'etre* of marriage, LSD, opium (he took some in the East in the Chinese manner), psychoanalysis, the dangerousness of the American myth, the defective American constitution, his preference for a parliamentary system in U.S., political leanings. Comments that artistic and violent impulses are allied (*vide* Hitler and Mussolini). Expresses regret at British entry into Common Market. Comments on Americanization of the West, space exploration, **1984**, the inevitability of cannibalism, Pope John XXIII and part of the plot of **Earthly Powers**, the afterlife, death and his preferred epitaph.

1718 Hamilton, Alex. "Roll Over Beethoven." **Australian** (Canberra) November 9, 1974, p. 16.

"He drew us armchairs to the fireplace, but the mantelpiece looked more likely, so he loaded it up with whisky and cigars and there we stood for hour upon hour, with the spoils and the smoke and the verbals between us like a pair of Toby Jugs on a gantry." On Burt Lancaster as Moses. "And very good in spite of that and everything. Quite pleased with him. Very modern thing, technically, flash forwards, jumpcut and that kind of. In on it, himself, he supposes, because he happens to be an English writer living in Rome. No great virtue. But makes for a lot of projects.'' On his film scripts for Michelangelo and Shakespeare (''the Americans come along simplifying to the limit''), **Nothing Like the Sun** and false notions of literary universality, **Napoleon Symphony**(writing it he's become a Buonapartista), Sir Lew Grade (''Frightening. Curious man, very ignorant, depth of it incredible, but gets things done'') and literary-musical correspondences between the Eroica and his shortish book on Boney. [A boozy interview recollected, one takes it, in breezy leisure.]

1719 Fitzpatrick, William P. ''Black Marketeers and Manichees: Anthony Burgess' Cold War Novels.'' **West Virginia University Philological Papers**, v. 21 (December 1974) 78-91.

In **Honey for the Bears** and **Tremor of Intent** Burgess explores the impact of his basically Manichaean world view as it influences human relationships from the personal to the international level. Redefining evil as that which is without true commitment, Burgess parades before the reader a reprise of solipsistic neutrals who form a microcosm of contemporary villainy. The plight of Burgess' heroes, Paul Hussey and Denis Hillier, is not merely to overcome the external wickedness that confronts them at every turn, but to conquer their inclination to accept neutrality instead of engagement. Both novels emphasize Burgess' position that morality is not the office of nations or races, but rather of individuals. — MLA Abstracts, 1974.

1720 Fulkerson, Richard P. ''Teaching **A Clockwork Orange**.'' **CEA Critic**, v. 37, no. 1 (November 1974) 8-10.

This novel, because it is brief, yet long enough for character and thematic development, is ideal for classroom use. The narrator-protagonist is an artist whose creative medium is violence. The theme of the novel — that freedom of choice is a prerequisite for moral behavior — is emphasized by the 12 repetitions of the question ''What's it going to be then, eh?'' AES, v. 20, no. 2 (October 1976) 109. No. 545.

1721 Fitzpatrick, William P. ''The Sworn Enemy of Pop: Burgess' Mr. Enderby.'' **Bulletin** (West Virginia Association of College English Teachers), v. 1, no. 1 (1974) 28-37.

[An elegant essay on **Enderby**.] Joyce's delight in his punny title **Chamber Music** has evidently inspired Burgess, and Enderby's ventosity, while hardly musical, is his body's counterpoint to his poetic effusions. The novel forms an extensive and animated critique of contemporary culture and of the failed artists who serve this swirl of pop phenomena. Enderby's quest pitilessly exposes the wasteland culture, but it wins for him the possibility of discovering through integrity and commitment an oasis where values and art can flourish. Includes comments on Enderby's poem (The Pet Beast), the significance of Rawcliffe, Enderby's sexual and amatory failures. Concludes that, though Enderby has failed, he is not a total failure like Rawcliffe. Enderby's withdrawal cannot produce major poetry, but the world of pop cannot produce poetry at all, except that which it steals from authentic voices, major and minor.

1722 Grigson, Geoffrey. ''On Collecting One's Reviews.'' In his **The Contrary View: Glimpses of Fudge and Gold**. Totowa, N.J.: Rowman and Littlefield, 1974, pp. 102-104.

[Reprint of #885.]

1723 Miles, Rosalind. ''Sexual Stereotypes and the Image of Woman.'' In her **The Fiction of Sex; Themes and Functions of Sex Differences in the Modern Novel**. New York: Barnes and Noble, 1974, pp. 41, 47-49, 187-88.

Fleetingly but passionately condemns Burgess' attitudes towards some women writers as shown by his **The Novel Now**. The gangland rape scene in **A Clockwork Orange** is quoted verbatim to prove the point that ''The novel brings out the latent violence and hostility to women which is implicit in the cult of bullhood.''

1724 Zaehner, Robert Charles. ''Rot in the Clockwork Orange.'' In his **Our Savage God; The Perverse Use of Eastern Thought**. New York: Sheed and Ward, 1974, pp. 19-73.

Brief running commentary [see pp.35-39] on the filmed version of **A Clockwork Orange** by the Spalding Professor of Comparative Religion at Oxford. Aleister Crowley and Charles Manson are discussed on the following pages of the same chapter.

1725 Edelhart, Mike. "More Fiction Writing Tips." **Writer's Digest**, August 1975, p. 13.

The writer of fiction should not begin with short stories. It does not permit psychological penetration, and it is no longer a marketable commodity. Confesses that a hotel vestibule in **MF** is derived from p. 167 of W.J. Wildinson's **Malay English Dictionary**. This kind of puzzle interests him and keeps him going.

1726 "Anthony Burgess." In **Modern British Literature**. New York: Ungar, 1975, pp. 74-80.

Includes excerpts from criticism published in periodicals. The novels discussed, or commented on, include **Nothing Like the Sun, Tremor of Intent, Enderby Outside, Enderby A Clockwork Orange** and **MF**.

1727 Fussell, Paul. "Theater of War." In his **The Great War and Modern Memory**. New York: Oxford University Press, 1975, pp. 222-28.

In **The Wanting Seed**, Tristram Fox takes an unwilling part in an E.S. [Extermination Session] which pits men against women. Selects passages from the novel which show the E.S. to be modelled on World War I. He concludes: "What does make **The Wanting Seed** an impressive work is its power of imagination and understanding. Assisted by extensive, indeed obsessed, reading in Great War memoirs and animated by a profound appreciation of the way the Great War established the prototype for modern insensate organized violence, Burgess has sensed both the alliance between war and theater and myth and cliché. Which is to say that he has located war as a major source of modern myth."

1728 Kennard, Jean. "Anthony Burgess: Double Vision." In **Number and Nightmare; Forms and Fantasy in Contemporary Fiction**. Hamden, Conn.: Archon Books, 1975, pp. 131-54.

A discussion of **A Clockwork Orange, The Wanting Seed, Tremor of Intent, Enderby** and **MF** which is guided by the following principle: "The basic method of each Burgess novel is to present the reader with two visions, sometimes two antithetical world views, sometimes two apparently opposed aspects of one personality, and to invite him to make a choice. The choice often proves to be a false one; the two visions are a double vision, a dualism, inseparable parts of the one reality."

1729 Scholes, Robert. **Structural Fabulation: An Essay on Fiction of the Future**. Notre Dame, Ind.: University of Notre Dame Press, 1975.

For Burgess, see pp. 23, 71, 79.

1730 Kennard, Jean. "MF: A Separable Meaning." **Riverside Quarterly**,v. 6 (1975) 200-06.

1731 Wagner, Geoffrey. "**A Clockwork Orange**." In his **The Novel and Cinema**. Rutherford, N.J.: Farleigh Dickinson Press, 1975, pp. 307-313.

Kubrick's film follows the book faithfully but drains it of ethos. Considers the ways in which violence in book (film) is muted by the words, or elegant visual compositions. Concludes that film has the greater power to shock: the eye always beats the ear. It is hard to find an ethos in Kubrick's film. In the book, Alex is a repulsive individual who has freely chosen evil. "It is the 'liberal's' attempt to institutionalize violence, to make it an effect rather than a cause (e.g. 'He's sick,' of some rapist), which Burgess surely sees as a modern distaster. However, his Alex is not clockwork. "Es irrt der Mensch, solang er strebt." A vital sinner is worthy of salvation; a socially-conditioned unit is not." Burgess has written a religious and mystical book on the nature of evil. Kubrick, in the concluding scenes of his film, has made a fairly banal statement about political opportunism.

1732 Anon. "All-Time Film Rental Champs." **Variety**, v. 281 (January 7, 1976) 20.

  A Clockwork Orange has earned $14,400,000 for the distributor in rental income. [This figure is not to be confused with total theatre grosses. See also: #1736, 1737.]

1733 Stinson, John J. "**Nothing Like the Sun**: The Faces in Bella Cohen's Mirror." **Journal of Modern Literature**, v. 5, no. 1 (February 1976) 131-47.

Burgess' novel about Shakespeare (WS), **Nothing Like the Sun**, is directly and pervasively influenced by James Joyce. In particular, the fictional life of Shakespeare follows the speculations of Stephen Dedalus as outlined in the Scylla and Charybdis episode of **Ulysses**. This observation is documented in some detail. Stinson then argues that **Nothing Like the Sun**, widely regarded as a *tour de force*, is itself a greater *tour de Force* than most critics have yet recognized. He finds, in the novel, words, phrases, or suggested lines of development which make it possible to arrive at startling equivalences (Burgess = Shakespeare; Burgess = Stephen; Stephen = WS; WS = Bloom; Anne = Molly). "Burgess' own art proceeds not from nature but from Stephen's 'art' and Joyce's art (and even beyond that to the Shakespeare books of Brandes, Lee and Harris that helped Joyce with Stephen's theory)" and this fact adds a whole intriguing layer of crisscrossing ironies to **Nothing Like the Sun**.

1734 Carson, Julie. "Pronominalization in **A Clockwork Orange**." **Papers on Language & Literature**, v. 12, no. 2 (Spring 1976) 200-205.

Alec [i.e. Alex] makes use of the pronoun 'you' when he is interacting with equals, or must give the cunning impression that his associates are equals. In positions of dominance, he reverts to the more formal 'thou.' Quotes from the novel to document this observation.

1735 Saunders, Trevor J. "Plato's Clockwork Orange." **Durham University Journal**, v. 68, no. 2 ; New Series, v. 37, no. 2 (June 1976) [113]-17.

Suggests that Plato would have made the filmed version of **A Clockwork Orange** compulsory viewing for his legislators. The hard-headed and ruthless pragmatism of the Minister of the Interior and the criminological passages in Plato's **Laws** share this one element: both are impatient with the assessment of moral responsibility and guilt which looks back to the offence. The difference is that the Minister has no interest in the criminal's desire to commit the crime (he only wants to avoid crime at any cost) while Plato's views are a startling anticipation of certain reformist theories of punishment. Plato recommends restitution of the victim; he also recommends unorthodox measures like talking to the criminal, or giving him gifts, and taking certain extenuating circumstances into account. What he would have learned from the film is that "radical, advanced penology will inevitably fail if it is out of step with the views and expectations of society at large." When the plain people are believers in retributive punishment, and the judges advocates of reformist penology, the result is the kind of tension evident in the film. The "cured" Alex is beset by his former victims; and any criminal so harrassed will soon revert to his old bad habits. "The merit of **A Clockwork Orange** is that it highlights a central difficulty of legislation, that of operating reformative penology as a sort of closed system. That is why I am suggesting that Plato might have been very willing to allow his legislators to view, in some suitable Platonic cave, a performance of **A Clockwork Orange**."

1736 Anon. "Clockwork Orange Pulls All Time High in Spain." **Boxoffice**, v. 109 (August 23, 1976) 10.

1737 Anon. "Clockwork Orange May be Spain's biggest Hit Ever." **Boxoffice**, v. 109 (September 13, 1976) E1.

1738 Robinson, Robert. "On Being a Lancashire Catholic." **Listener**, v. 96, no. 2477 (September 30, 1976) 397, 399.

[Interview.] On his self-exile, choice of Monaco as residence, status of man of letters on the continent, the events which led him to review his own **Inside Mr. Enderby** for the **Yorkshire Post**, and Stanley Kubrick's film version of the American ed. of **A Clockwork Orange**. "I have written other books, and **A Clockwork Orange** is very much a little *jeu d'esprit* written very rapidly to make a little money." This sound observation is followed by comments on his musical compositions, Lancashire Catholic background, the autobiographical elements in **Beard's Roman Women** and **Enderby**, the trade of book reviewing and a one paragraph exposition of his own fictional aims.

1739 Stinson, John J. "Waugh and Anthony Burgess: Some Notes Toward an Assessment of Influence and Affinities." **Evelyn Waugh Newsletter**, v. 10, no. 3 (Winter 1976) p. 11-12.

Explores some of the similarities and differences between Waugh and Burgess. **Devil of a State** is the novel most often mentioned; **A Vision of Battlements** is next. "There is a very general, but intriguing, overall correspondence of situation, tenor, mood, and theme between Burgess's **A Vision of Battlements**. . .and **Men at Arms**. The parallel becomes more intriguing when one notes that **Men at Arms** was published in 1952, and Burgess claims to have written **A Vision of Battlements** in 1949 although it was not published until 1965. But Burgess himself admits he has no proof of the date of actual composition, and there are some reasons for being skeptical that it was, in fact, as early as 1949."

1740 Cullinan, John. "Anthony Burgess." In **Writers at Work; The Paris Review Interviews**. Fourth series. Edited by George Plimpton. New York: Viking, c1976, pp. 327-358.

[Reprint of #1679.]

1741 "Burgess, Anthony." In **Contemporary Novelists**. 2d ed. Edited by James Vinson. London: St. James; New York: St. Martin's Press, 1976, pp. 204-208.

Includes chronology, brief bibliography, brief statement by Burgess on his work, and essay by Bernard Bergonzi. Bergonzi observes that **A Vision of Battlements** is prototypical Burgess in an undeveloped form: Ennis suffers many defeats, but fights back resiliently, and wins occasional tactical victories. Joyce and Evelyn Waugh, that master of cruel comedy, are the dominant influences. In **The Malayan Trilogy** we find the typically sad, comic, victimised hero and a highly episodic story line. The ideological component is not the liberal humanism of most English intellectuals, and Burgess remains deeply suspicious of most progressive social ideals and movements. In **A Clockwork Orange**, which works brilliantly as a metaphysical thriller, we again have an episodic plot. It rises, however, to a powerful climax. **The Right to an Answer**, one of Burgess' funniest books, is pervaded by a profound distaste for the contemporary English scene. **Clockwork**, along with **The Right to an Answer** and **The Wanting Seed**, are full of wit and inventiveness and convincing novels of ideas. The later novels combine the familiar combination of verbal brilliance and loose, episodic structure. In **Enderby**, as elsewhere, he has devised a convincing and interesting character, but can do nothing with him except thrust him into a rapid episodic narrative. **MF** and **Napoleon Symphony** demonstrate "Burgess' ceaseless ingenuity and inventiveness; but they provide few of the ordinary satisfactions of fiction. Burgess remains a uniquely clever and energetic novelist, but his recent development is not encouraging."

1742 Elsaesser, Thomas. "Screen Violence: Emotional Structure and Ideological Function in **A Clockwork Orange**." In **Approaches to Popular Culture**. Edited by C.W.E. Bigsby. Bowling Green, Ohio: Bowling Green University Popular Press, 1976, pp. 171-200.

[Long essay prompted, in part, by Barr's "**Straw Dogs, A Clockwork Orange** and the Critics." Marred by what Mencken, referring to Thorstein Veblen, once called "the learned gentleman's long, tortuous (and to me at least) intolerably flapdoodlish phrases."] Concrete economic interests manipulate consciousness, and the commercial cinema can probably be called the aesthetic exploitation of false consciousness. Followed by a discussion of film which postulates that the spectator is helplessly passive before the spectacle. This film raises the problem of violence and social control as one of its themes. One must not mistake the intelligence of its maker as a sign of his integrity. Examines the rape of the writer's wife, the killing of the cat-lady, Alex's identification with Christ, and the corporate violence against Alex which is calculated to spare the spectator nothing of Alex's emotional agonies or physical suffering. The best thing that can be said about the political stance of the film is that Kubrick and Burgess do not go out of their way to avoid confusion; the worst is that it is a demonstration of casuistry and Jesuitical logic which promotes an either/or dualism that paralyzes the intellect. "The real spectacle of violence — the job, the factory, the office, the family — is blanked out in the film, and into the blank is flashed the individual, anarchic physical violence of the hooligan, and the story-book nightmare violence of mad scientists and totalitarian politics. The panic fear of the physical assault on the one hand, and the equally panic fear of autocratic-technocratic state is mobilized to occult the emotional violence of the nuclear family, the economic violence of monopoly capitalism, the technological violence of production-line labour, the aesthetic violence of consumer terrorism."

1743 Irwin, William Robert. **The Game of the Impossible; A Rhetoric of Fantasy**. Urbana: University of Illinois Press, 1976.

For Burgess, see pp. x, 59, 80, 190, 192-94.

1744 Petix, Esther. "Linguistics, Mechanics, and Metaphysics: Anthony Burgess's **A Clockwork Orange** (1962)." In **Old Lines, New Forces; Essays on the Contemporary British Novel, 1960-1970**. Edited by Robert K. Morris. Rutherford, N.J.: Fairleigh Dickinson University Press, 1976, pp. 38-52.

Burgess' tremendous energy and soaring imagination have not been rewarded by an appropriate critical response, or an adequate income commensurate with the talents demonstrated by his thirty books. His fiction and mind are labyrinthine, and Burgess constructs his cosmogony to explain the ways of man to man: to see hope through failure; to set a course while adrift; to seek certainty in ambiguity. Argues that Nadsat soothes and unnerves the reader just as it softens the recorded atrocities. However, the language, for all its suggestion of the lonely wail of tomorrow wrenched from the desperate sighs of today, does not veil the deep and hard questions implicit in the work. Former cosmogonies were optimistic; the nihilists and existentialists of the present day confront us with notions of Sartre's nausea,

Heidegger's dread and Kierkegaard's *Angst*. Burgess has removed himself from these antipodean philosophies and propounded his own highly dualistic system in which man is asked to choose between the White, or Good God and the Black, or Evil God. Burgess presents his characters when they must confront the dualistic option. This pattern prevails in all his novels. In **A Clockwork Orange**, Burgess is not interested in charting the ultimate choices, but in pointing out that the choice must be free. Examines the imagery associated with Burgess' fictional dualism.

1745 Cole, William. "Trade-Winds." **Saturday Review**, v. 4, no. 18 (June 11, 1977) 43.

[Brief paragraph at end of article.] Time-Life Books gave a fine dinner to mark the publication of Burgess' **New York**. The guest of honor, Burgess, could not attend.

1746 Aggeler, Geoffrey. "Enderby Immolatus: Burgess' **The Clockwork Testament**." **Malahat Review**, no. 44 (October 1977) 22-46.

Extended commentary on the novel with special attention to the poetry of Hopkins and the attempts by B.F. Skinner to create the basis of a 'rational' society. Points to the origin of the name Sperr Lansing in Hopkins, identifies Professor Balaglas as B.F. Skinner and explains the appropriateness of the name. Comments on Enderby's experience at the University of Manhattan, on the theme of free will and human freedom (with quotations from Augustine and Luther), Enderby's identification with Elizabethan society rather than the paltry life of today, and speculates if the lady from Poughkeepsie is not a sort of anti-muse compared to the real thing in **Enderby Outside**. Remarks that the concluding scenes defy scholarly exegesis, and believes that **The Clockwork Testament**, while not a major achievement, "is a superb little satire, animated throughout by a fine rage and an unwearying wit." [Reprinted, with some changes and revisions, in his **Anthony Burgess: The Artist as Novelist**. University, Alabama: University of Alabama Press, 1979, pp. [94-109. Annotation based on the book just cited. The MR article includes four photographs of Burgess by William David Thomas.]

1747 Adams, Robert Martin. "Counterparts. Mod Romantics: Durrell and Burgess." In his **After-Joyce: Studies in Fiction after Ulysses**. New York: Oxford University Press, 1977, pp. 162-69.

[Brief commentary on **A Clockwork Orange** and **Tremor of Intent**. See pp. 166-69.] Burgess is another fringe-Joycean; his debt to Joyce is linguistic and musical. "Without its special dialect, **A Clockwork Orange** would be not only a sparse but a muddled book, with its bare bones in evident disarray." The dialect diverts attention to the surface of the novel: it serves to disguise Burgess' muddled attitude toward music (both an incitement to violence and contaminated by violence) and the unconvincing nature of the whole conditioning-experiment. "It is also a book, like those of Joyce, largely unconcerned with morality in any form. No doubt this was part of the reason for its popular success; it was an authentically cold book, at which a reader was entitled to shiver . . . . One can almost feel the pathetic, beseeching figure of Poetic Justice imploring the novelist for admittance to his book and being roughly shouldered away." In **Tremor of Intent** in the freakyspeak of characters like Hillier, Roper, Theodorescu, we have a dash of Joycean seasoning on a book of a pretty common order although the Joycean garnish is not used to contemptible effect.

1748 Beyer, Manfred. "Anthony Burgess: **Napoleon Symphony**." In **Englische Literatur der Gegenwart**. Hrsg. von Rainer Lengeler. Dusseldorf: August Bogel, 1977, pp. 313-[24].

Introduces Burgess to German readers, traces the correspondences between Beethoven's symphony and the novel, remarks on the historical accuracy of Burgess' novel, and considers some of the ways in which Burgess makes the presentation of this military butcher palatable to the reader.

1749 Hartveit, Lars. "Anthony Burgess, **A Clockwork Orange**. Impact and Form: The Limits of Persuasion." In his **The Art of Persuasion; A Study of Six Novels**. Bergen: Universitetsforlaget, 1977, pp. 117-31.

Considers some of the literary antecedents (Jonathan Wild, the Artful Dodger, Pinkie) of Alex and observes, following George Steiner, that culture (represented by Alex's love of classical music) is not a humanizing force. Describes the effect of classical music on ultraviolent Alex: it sharpens him up very nicely. Alex's description of his mayhem is characterized by a thoroughgoing aesthetic (not moral) approach. The same is true of his estimates of other characters, who are judged by their clothing and smell. In this context, the language of ordinary human affection when it enters the novel at all sounds utterly meaningless; and it is worth noting that the Treatment does not entail tenderness or any form of emotional therapy. The surface message of the novel (a man who cannot choose ceases to be a man) is not stated unambiguously: the characters who enunciate this point of view, both the clergyman and the writer, are presented in a satirical light. Examines nadsat, its rhythm, energy, playful reduplication, and observes that it takes away from the horror of the scene. "The reader has been brought up to the limits of persuasion. He moves in the course of the novel from his first intuitive response of repulsion and horror at acts of violence and inhumanity, through awareness of a world in which such features dominate, to a final recognition that pattern — the aesthetics of form — has replaced life, with its emphasis on ethical values."

1750 Neilson, Keith. **"Beard's Roman Women."** In **Magill's Literary Annual**, 1977: Essay-Reviews of 200 Outstanding Books Published in the United States during 1976."Englewood Cliffs, N.J.: Salem Press, c1977, pp. 81-85.

[Plot summary in the usual "Masterplots" tradition combined with occasional adverse comments.] Concludes that, ". . . in the end one does not know who is dead, alive, or resurrected. And one is not sure how much it really matters. Whether Burgess intends the final chapter to be a dreamlike reality or a realistic dream is probably unimportant: either way it is at least a serious artistic lapse and at the worst a deliberate copout. It is impossible to take the action of this last chapter seriously at any level, and that is a disservice to the rest of this potentially important novel. There are too many really fine things in the book simply to dismiss it: Burgess' wit, perception, a marvellous handling of the language, his deft, sympathetic characterization of his protagonist, his vivid, colorful rendering of Rome and environs, and the provocative notions he waves into his text. But the total is, alas, much less than the sum of the parts, because at the crucial moment Burgess leaves it to his narrative facility and his gagwriting skill to solve the problems created by his artistic vision."

1751 Schoenbaum, Samuel. "Early Employment and Marriage." In his **William Shakespeare: A Compact Documentary Life**. New York: Oxford University Press, 1977, pp. 84-85.

[Brief comment on Burgess' **Shakespeare**.] Discounts Burgess' speculation about the romantic entanglement between William Shakespeare and Anne Whateley. "There are no 'documented facts' about Anne Whateley, as Mr. Burgess is well aware, only one fact — the Register entry — and so we do not know whether she was 'chaste, not wanton and forward,' or 'sweet as May and shy as a fawn.' We cannot even say with reasonable assurance that she ever actually existed."

1752 Tilton, John Wightman. **"A Clockwork Orange**: Awareness is All." In his **Cosmic Satire in the Contemporary Novel**. Lewisburg, Pa.: Bucknell University Press, c1977, pp. 21-42.

The truncated Norton ed. is a lesser work than the original British (1962) ed. The American text leads to a false climax and a superficial principle: a man who cannot choose ceases to be a man. Contends that nadsat, far from distancing readers from the violence, seduces them into active participation. In this way, the novel makes the more complex point that evil and good are immanent in man. Both F. Alexander and the Prison Chaplain, champions of liberty and free choice respectively, are self-deluded about the truth of their vengeful and weak natures. Man, in fact, [freely?] oscillates between his good and evil urges. The State, by its repression, has intensified Alex's natural propensity to evil; by its conditioning, it has destroyed him as a man — not merely, as it claims, constructed a machine capable only of good. Chapter 21 of the Heinemann ed. establishes the truth that man is not either always good or evil, but a clockwork orange capable of both. "Recognition of this conception of man as a natural clockwork orange enables one to grasp the full, profoundly disturbing pessimism that gives the novel its terrifying power."

1753 Schoon, Margaret S. "Napoleon Symphony." In **Magill's Literary Annual, 1977: Essay-Reviews of 200 Outstanding Books Published in the United States during 1978**. Vol. 2. Englewood Cliffs, N.J.: Salem Press, c1977, pp. 525-28.

"In the presentation of this work, both its peculiar structure and its popular style, Burgess treads the thin line between the ridiculous and the sublime." The portrait of Napoleon shows us the cold-blooded, amoral conqueror as well as the family man beset by bickering at family dinners. The disasters of the wars are well presented from the foot soldier's point of view. "The work is not focused entirely on the horrors of war, however. Some of the turns of phrase are clever enough to evoke a chuckle and a few of the scenes are downright hilarious . . . . **Napoleon Symphony** is a high-class entertainment which takes its structural basis from the work of a great musician and its plot from the life of a great hero, and the two elements are deftly combined in the hands of a marvelously well-versed author."

1754 "Anthony Burgess, Elizabeth Morgan to Appear in Literary Programs." **Library of Congress Information Bulletin**, v. 37, no. 40 (October 6, 1978) 609-610.

[Preceded by brief biographical sketch.] Announces that Burgess is planning to deliver a lecture entitled "The Author Seduced, or The Engulfing Eye: Reflections on Literature and Film" on Tuesday, October 17, in the Coolidge Auditorium.

1755 Byrne, Kevin. "There Is No Place for Home." **Macleans**, v. 91, no. 26 (November 26, 1978) 62.

[Brief account of an interview.] Burgess disowns any purely literary comparison between **1984** and **1985**. His **1985** is a limpet, a squib, compared to Orwell's novel. Denies he has any political axe to grind. Prefers Monaco: it has a warmer climate and a Catholic community. He spoke up against the censorship in Malta and quickly became *persona non grata*. Moved out of Italy when he learned that his son was next on the terrorists' list of kidnapping victims.

1756 Rabinovitz, Rubin. "Mechanism vs. Organism: Anthony Burgess' **A Clockwork Orange**." **Modern Fiction Studies**, v. 24, no. 4 (Winter 1978/1979) 538-41.

Burgess explores free will, the meaning of violence and a cyclical theory of history. Shirley Chew and A.A. DeVitis agree that the 21st chapter of the original novel (deleted in the American ed.) was wisely omitted. However, the original version is not as sentimental as it appears on first sight; there is truth and even poetic justice in the idea that yesterday's reprobate will change diapers for his own neophyte reprobate. The omitted chapter makes clear that Burgess believes youth to be a time of clockwork violence. The fact that Alex accepts his son's future violence suggests a cyclical theory of history influenced less by Hegel than by Toynbee, Spengler, and the Eastern yin-yang principle. "Only a work of art, says Burgess, can achieve a synthesis of opposites which presents an immediate vision of unity. Obviously, **A Clockwork Orange** is meant to serve as an example of the sort of work that can truly reconcile opposing values."

1757 Rabinovitz, Rubin. "Ethical Values in Anthony Burgess' **Clockwork Orange**." **Studies in the Novel**, v. 11, no. 1 (Spring 1979) 43-50.

The libertarian-authoritarian (or Pelagian-Augustinian) opposition recurs in Burgess' fiction. It is found, for example, in **The Wanting Seed**; it is the subject of Enderby's unfinished poem in **The Clockwork Testament**. In the opening pages of **A Clockwork Orange**, permissive Pelagians are clearly in control. With the spread of anarchic conditions, a subdued Augustinianism takes its place. On the basis of the available novelistic evidence it is imprecise to assume that Burgess consistently favors either an Augustinian or Pelagian point of view. In **Clockwork**, the vicious qualities of little Alex are juxtaposed to the Pelagian virtues of F. Alexander. "The relativism resulting from this evenhanded treatment of contrasting values, however, sometimes leaves Burgess open to a charge of moral ambiguity." Hillier, in **Tremor of Intent**, denounces neutrals who ignore or disengage themselves from the Pelagian-Augustinian cyclical system; in his view, the neutrals are morally inferior to the evil-doers. Alex is the evil-doer incarnate. The scientists who destroy his freedom of choice are the neutrals. It is perhaps the superiority of evil-doers to neutrals that explains Alex's redemption in the original version of **A Clockwork Orange**. Burgess' moral point of view still seems ambiguous and Rabinovitz examines Burgess' interest in Manichaeism, the yin-yang principle, and his attitude towards the state, to answer the charge of ambiguity. Concludes that Burgess the man is unambiguous; Burgess the writer is artful in his capacity to play the roles of both the depraved Alex and the virtuous F. Alexander.

1758 Kauffmann, Jean-Paul. "Beyond **A Clockwork Orange**: Anthony Burgess' Productive Life in Monaco." **Atlas World Press Review**, v. 26, no. 5 (May 1979) 58.

[Excerpted from the socialist **Le matin** of Paris.] Observes that Burgess' first wife was tortured and raped [she was beaten and robbed but not raped], that Burgess fled Rome for fear of terrorists. Describes Burgess' appearance, the Monaco apartment and relates part of the talk (about cooking and the French national character). "Quite naturally, we turn to the film of **A Clockwork Orange** which he had seen again in Nantes a few weeks ago. He doesn't agree totally with the slant that Kubrick gave it. 'In my book there was a linguistic curtain between the violence and the reader that wasn't in the film.' He also questions Kubrick's ending, and the meaning of Alex's recovery.''

1759 Aggeler, Geoffrey. ''Pelagius and Augustine: **A Clockwork Orange.**'' In his **Anthony Burgess; The Artist as Novelist.** University, Ala.: University of Alabama Press, 1979, pp. 169-184.

[An informed running commentary on the novel.] Burgess wrote the novel in response to proposed treatment of criminals by certain behaviorists, and what he read and saw of the ''stilyagi'' in Leningrad and ''teddy boys'' in London. Comments on the Russian component of nadsat. Also considers the significance of the name Alex and the sense in which the hoodlum, although the snarling possessor of many words, is incapable of handling abstractions (hence wordless). In the novel, a lax Pelagian government is succeeded by an Augustinian regime which advocates behavior modification techniques and the suppression of political opposition. F. Alexander's position in the novel is not that of Burgess; the former is a confirmed, self-deluded Pelagian, while Burgess is not blinded to concrete human realities by political or philosophical beliefs. Includes an account of the Heinemann (1962) ed. and concludes that ''The message of the chapter that was omitted is that, if there is hope, it is in the capacity of individuals to grow and learn by suffering and error.''

1760 ''Burgess, Anthony.'' In **Novels and Novelists; A Guide to the World of Fiction.** Ed. by Martin Seymour-Smith. New York: St. Martin's Press, 1979, p. 108.

[Brief survey of Burgess' work coupled with brief but forceful appraisals.] Burgess has never done better than in his trilogy about Malaya. ''He has used literally every device to achieve his fictional ends, but has not yet quite discovered what these ends are: he rejects the notion of the meaninglessness of life. . . but as he looks about him he sees nothing but nihilism and rot. He is a major writer, always worth reading, who may still produce the great novel everyone expects from him.''

1761 Meyers, Walter E. ''1985.'' In **Magill's Literary Annual, 1979: Essay-Reviews of 200 Outstanding Books Published in the United States during 1978.** Vol. 2. Englewood Cliffs, N.J.: Salem Press, c1979, pp. 484-89.

[A summary of Burgess' argument in the essay section and plot summary in the usual ''Masterplots'' tradition. Includes two paragraphs of comment.] The novel stands on the knife-edge between conservatism and hysteria. The closed shop is a fact of life in many states. Still, there has been a decline in union membership. A note of shrillness defeats Burgess' purpose. To say that the Second Vatican Council abolished Christianity is extreme, and **1984** is the greater of the two books.

1762 Hanson, Stephen L. ''Ernest Hemingway and His World.'' In **Magill's Literary Annual, 1979: Essay-Reviews of 200 Outstanding Books Published in the United States during 1978.** Vol. 1. Englewood Cliffs, N.J.: Salem Press, c1979, pp. 196-99.

Some critics have treated Hemingway with disdain. Others, determined to explore the relationship between the author's mind and craft, rely on archetypal myths or Freudian approaches. In his balanced portrait, Burgess notes the faults of the man and the virtues of the writer. Burgess' ''strength as a critic and, indeed, the strength of the book is the conveyance of a sense of balance and of perspective. The Hemingway style was a new and original contribution to world literature, he concludes, emphasizing that the Hemingway code of courage, the Hemingway hero and his stoical holding on against odds, have exerted an influence beyond literature. Ultimately the insufficiences of the man, as delineated by Burgess, maimed the creative work.''

1763 Sheldon, Leslie. ''Newspeak and Nadsat: The Disintegration of Language in **1984** and **A Clockwork Orange.**'' **Studies in Contemporary Satire**, v. 6 (1979) 7-13.

Orwell's Newspeak and Burgess' Nadsat provide touchstones for profound spiritual impoverishment. Demonstrates that Alex loves violence for its own sake and observes that it is ''Burgess's terrible utopian vision that evil is more central to humanity than good. Evil is the last bastion of individuality.'' While Nadsat is more organic and varied than Newspeak, Burgess clearly makes the point that men have become so degraded they have nothing to communicate. The educated speakers of Burgess' novel (Branom, Brodsky, F. Alexander) either utter inanities or express a view of life which is actually little more elevated than Alex's ultra-lust for ultraviolence. "It is with actual relief that the reader of Burgess's novel realizes that Alex begins to 'recover' after his savage conditioning. It is a final knife-twist that through satirical exposure the reader has come to cherish the half-humanity of a sadistic murderer."

1764 Shorter, Eric. "Regions." In **Drama; The Quarterly Theatre Review** (London), no. 135 (January 1980) 51.

[Review of dramatized version of **The Eve of Saint Venus**.] This performance at the Wolsey Theater, Ipswich, directed by Antony Tuckey, includes too many characters from lounge hall stock. "Endearing nanny, gormless parlour maid, comic vicar, vague baronet, pompous Labour MP, intimidating lady journalist and so on." The comedy suggests that marriage should not be entered lightly or automatically and that some experience, mystical or otherwise, is needed to prepare the partners. With more pace, editing and less trivial characterisation, it would not seem so pretentious, "and the derivation of its theme from Burton's **Anatomy of Melancholy** mightn't sound so imposing."

1765 Mentzer, Thomas L. "The Ethics of Behavior Modification: **A Clockwork Orange** Revisited." **Essays in Arts and Sciences**, v. 9, no. 1 (May 1980) 93-105.

Presents a resume of **A Clockwork Orange**. Discusses Skinner's theories. Then gives instances of people successfully changed by behavior modification (a depressed 49-year old woman, a peddler of appliance contracts, a 5-year old boy with feminine behavior, a schizophrenic mental patient). Observes that behavior modification at these levels is efficacious. Lists some abuses of behavior of modification but is, on the whole, a partisan of the treatment. "Burgess did not have the benefit of these findings when he wrote **A Clockwork Orange**. If he had, the novel might have been quite different, had it been written at all. Alex would have become a reformed person, rather than merely being shackled by the chains of conditioning." Then proceeds to list the ethical guidelines which will, if put into effect, successfully prevent abuses of behavior modification. [Mentzer does not describe the treatment that would transform an ingratiating sadist into a harmless citizen.]

1766 Palumbo, Ronald J. "Names and Games in **Tremor of Intent**." **English Language Notes**, v. 18 (September 1980) 48-51.

The word play in the novel is intended to underscore the disparity between atemporal religious values and the mundane and petty realities of the modern political state. Comments on Michael Drayton's **Polyolbion**, British martyrs with the surname "Roper," the names given to the hero (Dennis Hillier and Sebastian Jagger), Theodorescue and Miss Devi and observes that the coded message ZZWM DDHGEM EH IJNZ OJNMU E XWI OVU ODVP yields the typically British apology DEAR HILLER IM MORE SORRY THAN I CAN SAY THAT. "The apology is for sending Hillier to be assassinated by another of their technicians; the comic touch is that, despite his fifteen years of service, the agency has misspelled his name."

1767 Linklater, Andro. "Musical Voices." **Listener**, v. 104, no. 2684 (October 23, 1980) 555.

[Review of one of Burgess' lectures in the "Thoughts on Music and Literature" series given at the University of Kent.] When Burgess hunts after the meaning of sound, he follows it through hedge and thicket although you may sometimes unworthily suspect that the fox he catches is not the one he originally pursued. Burgess evidently denied that human values are to be found in music. "'There is,' he asserted 'no morality in music' and, uttered in that harshly inflected voice with the throaty timbre of a tenor bullfrog, you hardly dared doubt the assertion. Only with his concluding words, 'Music means nothing. Music is structure, nothing more,' did you wonder whether such a scabbed and mangy brush really belonged to the animal which had given us such a good run." Comments on Burgess' lecture style.

1768 "Fascinating Rhythms." **Listener**, v. 104, no. 2681 (October 2, 1980) 435.

[Review of a lecture entitled "Under the Bam." This lecture is the first of four lectures delivered at the University of York under the general title "Thoughts on Music and Literature."] Burgess commented on the song sung by Edward the Bastard in **King Lear**, on T.S. Eliot's **The Wasteland, Sweeney Agonistes**. He also argued that the music of jazz is the music of speech rhythms.

1769 Darling, Lynn. "The Haunted Exile of Novelist Anthony Burgess." **Washington Post**, Style Section, 26 December 1980, pp. D1, D9.

[Burgess interviewed during a promotional tour to plug **Earthly Powers**.] Discusses American talk shows, the fame of **A Clockwork Orange** (the fact provokes a shuddering groan), the subversive function of literature, Norman Mailer and Truman Capote, reason for his departure from Italy, application to Channel Islands, Malaysia (an ugly squat little Tamil lusted after his wife, but was foiled), reputed brain tumor, death of his first wife LLewela [here called Lynn] after assault by three G.I. deserters, invitation to visit Hollywood issued by William Conrad ("death is crap"), absence of love among promiscuous female American college students, his lack of belief in divorce, unwillingness to show emotion, Pope John XXIII and the changes in the Church ("a whole area of my heart was cauterized"), his pleasure in good literature, good painting and good architecture, his exclusion from the British literary establishment, and his future writing and travelling plans. Wants only a quiet life, a measure of peace and a peaceful death.

1770 Dudar, Helen. "Burgess: A Nomad Pens a Big Book." **Los Angeles Times** Calendar [CAL], 28 December 1980, p. 55.

[Burgess interviewed on the run in Monaco.] "He says it seemed time to try a big book [**Earthly Powers**]. And it has not escaped his notice that publishing gives special care to the kind of big books that excite big advances." He views Pope John XXIII with heavy disapproval. "'I think he was a bad man. I think he was dangerous.' Burgess is a lapsed Catholic, and the church he does not worship in is pre-aggiornamento- . . . . The narrator of his saga is a Maughamesque homosexual writer . . . . 'What will happen now,' he predicted, 'is they'll say I'm a homosexual. No man less homosexual ever lived, which is a damned nuisance'." Includes brief comments on Burgess' life in Malta and Rome. Expresses his dislike of the French and his willingness to review books sent his way.

1771 Koenig, Rhoda. "The Unearthly Powers of Anthony Burgess." **Saturday Review**, v. 7 (December 1980) 34-37.

[Interview occasioned by publication of **Earthly Powers**.] Describes the Monaco apartment. The talk ranges over English food, Karl Marx, Groucho Marx, **A Clockwork Orange**, Somerset Maugham as the model for Kenneth Toomey, Burgess 'cousin' George, the Archbishop of Manchester as the model, along with Pope John XXIII, of Campanati. Discusses the historical license in the book, prohibition ("prohibition was a *sin*"), scraps of Burgess autobiography in the book, his interest in music and future writing plans.

1772 Guetti, James. "Voiced Narrative: **A Clockwork Orange**." In his **Word-Music; The Aesthetic Aspect of Narrative Fiction**. New Brunswick, N.J.: Rutgers University Press, 1980, pp. 54-76.

[Abstract, sometimes awkward and difficult, but rewarding.] "For describing both of these aspects of voiced narrative — its music and the feeling that the experience of its images does not depend upon ordinarily communicated meaning — Anthony Burgess' **A Clockwork Orange** is for me the best possible example." Nadsat produces an effect of extraordinary energy. Reproduces extracts of nadsat and comments on the effects produced. Doubts that the effects of the novel derive from a translation into a more standard and normal terminology, the tendency of the professional literary critic intent on instant intelligibility. Comments on the alleged violent episodes in the book and the distancing effects conveyed by the diction. The violence in both book and film is not *perceived* as violence; it is accepted as a form of joy or gaiety. William Burroughs' remark ("The fact that it is also a very funny book may pass unnoticed") is quite apt. The work conveys the happiness of farce or burlesque, and it is as close to the pleasures of music as a work of fiction can achieve.

1773 Coyle, Wallace. "**A Clockwork Orange**." In his **Stanley Kubrick; A Guide to References and Resources**. Boston: G.K. Hall, 1980, pp. 52-55.

A valuable bibliography of Kubrick's work. Includes coverage of **A Clockwork Orange**, which proved very useful in compiling this bibliography.

1774 Duffy, Charles F. "From Espionage to Eschatology: Anthony Burgess's **Tremor of Intent**." **Renascence**, v. 32 (1980) 79-88.

Tremor parodies the James Bond novels of Ian Fleming as well as the cold war novels of John Le Carré. Demonstrates the mythic parallels to Homer's **Odysseus** (Wriste = Polyphemus; Miss Devi = Circe;

Theodorescu = Poseidon) and examines the references to bread in the novel to demonstrate that Burgess is working towards the theme of transubstantiation. "At his best [Burgess] can be the stern moral prophet in a Greeneland more terrifying than Graham's, and yet can by his Joycean exuberance outstrip Chesterton's optimistic incarnationalism. **Tremor of Intent** is one of Burgess's finest achievements in moral prophecy and sheer delight in language, and it may well be the most profound work in the history of the spy novel."

1775 Johnstone, J.K. "Burgess, Anthony." In **Encyclopedia Americana**(International Edition.) Danbury, Conn.: Americana Corp., c1980, v. 4, p. 786.

Brief biographical sketch. The list of Burgess' books ends with **Inside Mr. Enderby**, first published in 1963.

1776 Steinberg, Cobbett S. "Top 200 Moneymaking Films of All Time." In his **Film Facts**. New York: Facts on File, 1980, p. 7.

Lists **A Clockwork Orange** in 133d position. The film has earned the distributor $15,400,000 in rental income. [This total is based on the January 3, 1977 listing found in **Variety**; it should not be confused with total theater grosses.]

1777 Griffin, Bryan F. "Whoring After the New Thing; E.L. Doctorow and the Anxiety of Critical Reception." **The American Spectator**, v. 14, no. 1 (January 1981) 7-14.

Long attack on Doctorow's **Loon Lake** and the reviewers who have praised his work. See pp. 7, 10 for caustic notice of Burgess' review.

1778 Mitgang, Herbert. "Busy Burgess." **New York Times Book Review**, 18 January 1981, p. 39.

[An account of a press meeting at which Burgess talked about **Earthly Powers**.] His 43d book was longer in the making than his other books: nearly 10 years. This long gestation cannot be blamed on Princess Grace of Monaco. He sees a fair amount of the Princess, but she attends to her Palace and he to his books. Felt the time had come to do something big. Wrote steadily for about 18 months, turning out about a thousand words a day. Announces that he is planning to write more big books. Observes he can work on one novel in the morning and another in the afternoon.

1779 Shames, Laurence. "Malcolm McDowell Thinks Before He Acts." **Esquire**, v. 95, no. 4 (April 1981) 42-49.

[Interview. Includes passing comments on **Clockwork**.] "**Clockwork** was the apotheosis of the smirk, the vehicle through which McDowell's leer became a cultural emblem, a demonic mask behind which lurked the nastiest impulses of us all. As 'ultra-violent' Alex the droog, McDowell became a virtuoso of the id. 'I was born to play that part,' he says now, with a strange blend of pride and compunction. The ambivalence is understandable. The character he created on the screen raped with zest and pillaged with relish. He was Seventies self-indulgence taken to the limit . . . . 'They've taught me a lesson, those nasty bastards [the roles he has played] . . . a lesson in acting and a lesson in human nature; if you can get it across that your character loves life, really *gobbles* it, then an audience will forgive you anything — rape, rolling old drunks, vileness of any sort'."

1780 "A Clockwork Orange." In **Magill's Survey of Cinema**. English Language Films. 2d series. Edited by Frank N. Magill. Englewood Cliffs, N.J.: Salem Press, c1981, pp. 475-79.

Includes credits and lists principal characters. Provides list of Kubrick's works. The remainder consists of plot summary of the film. [Includes one inaccuracy. Burgess' wife was assaulted in 1943; she was *not* raped. She died in March 1968 of cirrhosis of the liver; the physical and psychological complications of the initial assault afflicted her until her death.]

1781 Aggeler, Geoffrey. "Faust in the Labyrinth: Burgess' **Earthly Powers**." **Modern Fiction Studies**, v. 27, no. 3 (Autumn 1981) 517-31.

Includes comments on the Faustian theme in Mann's **Doctor Faustus** and Malcolm Lowry's **Under the Volcano**. Finds the origin of the title in Hobbes's **Leviathan** and quotes from Maugham's **Don Fernando** to define the psychology of the homosexual. Then on to the etymology of the word "catamite," traces down the origin of some groans induced by fellated bliss ("*Solitam. . . Minotauro. . . pro caris corpus*") to Catullus. Suggests that Burgess' reference to fragments of Catullus is his way of introducing the Pelagian versus Augustian theme that becomes the central concern of the novel. Discusses Toomey's Augustinianism and Don Carlo's Pelagianism. Believes that Burgess' attack on Pope John XXIII ("the most beloved pontiff of modern times") is wrong-headed, and concentrates the remainder of his essay on the Faustian drama of Carlo Campanati. In the novel "Burgess is clearly in command of his material . . . . I tend to agree with those who call it his 'masterpiece,' though it is certainly not without flaws. Parts of it are, as I have said, wearisome, and the language is occasionally pendant. The flaws are, however, minor and unavoidable in a work so large and ambitious. Overall it is a magnificent performance, what we have been waiting for from Burgess."

1782 Bly, James I. "Sonata Form in **Tremor of Intent**." **Modern Fiction Studies**, v. 27, no. 3 (Autumn 1981) 489-504.

"One of the more complex musical forms and the one used as the base pattern for **Tremor of Intent** is sonata-form. The four major divisions of this form, which correspond to the four parts of the novel, are the exposition, the development, the recapitulation, and the coda. Each of these major sections has internal compositional principles that govern such elements as the introduction of thematic subjects, fragmentation of motifs, and transformations in the re-presentation of subjects. An analysis of the novel shows that Burgess utilizes not only the broad structural divisions but also adapts the internal principles of development to his work." Makes extensive use of diagrams to demonstrate the existence of thematic relationships.

1783 Coale, Samuel. "An Interview with Anthony Burgess." **Modern Fiction Studies**, v. 27, no. 3 (Autumn 1981) 429-51.

Talks about his parents, step-mother and their huge pub ("The Golden Eagle"), the reason for his interest in Christopher Marlowe, his teaching days in Banbury and Malaya, reason for his unpopularity among the expatriate community in Brunei, his life in the 'terminal' year and the declining health of his first wife, his affair with Liliana Macellari ("the liason [liaison] was not a regular one. It was very very clandestine"). Discusses religion and his sense of exclusion from the Protestant majority, the loss of faith at Xaverian College, his horror at reading Joyce's **Portrait** ("I was so horrified [by the sermon on hell] that I was scared back into the Church"), the personal effect of the ceremony and aesthetics of the Church, the difference between aesthetic good and ethical good, Manichaeism. Also on modernism in literature, postmodernism ("a ridiculous phrase"), and his approach to diction and structure in fiction ("one should go through a great deal of trouble to be cunningly clumsy"), Ezra Pound, T.S. Eliot and Hopkins. There is a page on the subject of free will. Followed by his opinions of **A Clockwork Orange** and the character of Enderby ("I could have spent my life with this damn character"), **The Wanting Seed**, **Earthly Powers** and homosexuality, his personal vision, the Grimm fairy tales and **Tristram Shandy**.

1784 Coale, Samuel. "The Ludic Loves of Anthony Burgess." **Modern Fiction Studies**, v. 27, no. 3 (Autumn 1981) 453-63.

An essay on Burgess' novels (with particular reference to **MF, Napoleon Symphony, Enderby**) which argues (quoting Burgess all the while to drive home the point) that the role of the poet (novelist) is to impose order on chaos. "Burgess' plots have a tendency to twitch and gyrate, absurd episodes tumbling one upon the other, with one harried soul at the center of the black comedy, struggling for some way out, some accommodation with meaning and personal reconciliation." Burgess' description of Saul Bellow's maturer work may best describe his own: ". . . the delineation of a complex dissatisfied personality, a heaving centre with a periphery glittering with near-hallucinatory detail. Man seeking self-definition is plot enough."

1785 Lucas, Timothy R. "The Old Shelley Game: Prometheus & Predestination in Burgess' Works." **Modern Fiction Studies**, v. 27, no. 3 (Autumn 1981) 465-78.

Considers the extent to which Burgess' later themes are prefigured in earlier books. Then, in a discussion of **MF**, notes the existence of **MF**'s foreshadowing techniques and, in an extended discussion, finds the evidence of Burgess' use of **Prometheus Unbound** in **MF**. "Like Mary Shelley's Frankenstein, Miles Faber is a modern Prometheus. The resemblance, however, is more figurative (that is to say 'comic') than actual (that is to say 'mythic'). The fact that Faber is black. . . shows us, on this comic and figurative level, how chained Faber has been preconceptually to a prejudicial Caucasian crag."

1786 Ray, Philip E. "Alex Before and After: A New Approach to Burgess' **A Clockwork Orange**." **Modern Fiction Studies**, v. 27, no. 3 (Autumn 1981) 479-87.

"The specific thesis that this essay will argue for is twofold: that Burgess has the owner of HOME represent the person Alex will become, his future self, and the boy who does not yet exist represent the person he has already been, his past self, in order to express the view that human growth is inevitable; and that the tripartite structure of the novel directly mirrors this chronological sequence of Alex's identities."

1787 Stinson, John J. "Better to Be Hot or Cold: **1985** and the Dynamic of the Manichaean Duoverse." **Modern Fiction Studies**, v. 27, no. 3 (Autumn 1981) 505-16.

Burgess' reputation is not yet secured. Critics have made the old charges: writes too fast; a prodigally gifted hack who writes for money; lacks respect for his readers; needs discipline; ideas half-baked. Summarizes some of the charges made against **1985**, and then looks for the evidence of Manichaeism in this novel, complete with quotations from Dante and references to Conrad's **Heart of Darkness**. "The paradox of evil leading to good, or even of evil being a kind of good in itself, that appears in Conrad, Eliot, and Greene, Burgess uses heavily and integrally in his work, giving brief bowing acknowledgments of sorts at least to Eliot and Greene." **1985** advances the condemnation of moral neutrality found elsewhere in Burgess' fiction since it represents the antithesis of all that Burgess stands for, which can be expressed in the words of the savage in Huxley's **Brave New World**: "I want God, I want poetry, I want real danger, I want freedom, I want goodness. I want sin." In **1985** Burgess condemns the apathy, torpor, indifference and moral neutrality found in present-day England, and he excoriates the neutrals' furious pursuit of the empty banner.

1788 Bockris, Victor. **With William Burroughs; A Report from the Bunker**. New York: Seaver Books, 1981, p. 74.

One paragraph mention of pub-crawl by Burroughs and Burgess. Asked if he saw many writers in London, Burgess reportedly replied: "No, they're all a bunch of swine."

1789 Gooden, Philip. "Burgess, Anthony." In **Makers of Modern Culture**. New York: Facts on File, 1981, pp. 81-82.

Brief biographical sketch and critical appraisal. The list of works cited ends with **1985** (published 1978).

1790 "Burgess Talks Caveman." **Horizon**, v. 24, no. 12 (December 1981) 12.

J.H. Rosny's novel **Quest for Fire** is untainted by dialogue and screenwriter Gerard Brach decided that an audience would be hard to hold with two hours of rustling twigs. So Burgess was asked to create a primitive language. He did so by creating a language based on Indo-European roots. Observes that the language of primitive man involved a complicated grammar.

1791 Simon, John. "Laughing Violence." In **Reverse Angle; A Decade of American Films**. New York: Potter, c1982, pp. 53-56.

The success of Burgess' respected novel depends on words, and particularly on certain curious macaronic puns [gives examples] to express the author's overwhelming, but cheerfully expressed, pessimism. Kubrick, autodidact and self-styled intellectual, misses three main points. First, the relentless but laughing pessimism. His ending, in which Alex gambols in the snow with a serenely smiling blonde, is a huge cop-out. Second, the music on the soundtrack includes Beethoven along with a mixed bag of minor music; and an Alex who relishes songs by Freed and Brown fails to convey the grand ironic point of the failure of culture to civilize us. Third, the tragicomic vandalism practiced on all language (witness Alex's 'two terrific and very enormous mountains,' his 'how to comport yourself publicwise') is slurred over or omitted as unsuitable to the medium of film. McDowell is excellent; the choice of Magee is less felicitous. "He even overdirects the basically excessive Magee to the point where the actor's eyes erupt like missiles from a launching pad, and his face turns into every shade of a Technicolor sunset. The minor characters tend to be similarly overdone or travestied. There are, to be sure, a few lively moments in the film, including a well-handled scene or two, and some of the futuristic gadgets are fun; but no one ever questioned Kubrick's talent as a gadgeteer."

Index

This index is primarily an author/title index. Subject entries, when they appear, are chiefly confined to names in literature and music. Items marked with an asterisk (*) are especially noteworthy.

Brophy, Elizabeth, 1654
"Brotherhood, The," 1251
"Brothers Grimm and Their Famous Law for Linguists," 1358
Brown, Clarence, *as subject*, 1142
Brown, Francis, *as subject*, 1378
Brown, Ivor, *as subject*, 1147, 1345
Brown, Les, 1715
Brown, Rexford Glenn, 1579
Browne, Joseph, 880
Browning, Elizabeth Barrett, *as subject*, 1407
Browning, Robert, *as subject*, 986, 1407
Brownlow, Kevin, *as subject*, 984
Broyard, Anatole, 182
Brudnoy, David, 360
Brumm, Walter, *as subject*, 91, 167
Buckley, Charles Burton, *as subject*, 1206
Bucknell University, 1680
Budnik, Dan, *as subject*, 614
BUGIARDA, 1107
Buitenhuis, Peter, 659, 935
Bunting, Charles T., 1701
Bunuel, Luis, 1446
"Buoyant Bawdiness: TREMOR OF INTENT Proves Anew the Artistry of Anthony Burgess,"
    860
Burchfield, R.W., *as subject*, 1456
Burdick, Eugene, *as subject*, 1067
"Burgess and Bellow," 664
"Burgess and Gibson," 1628
BURGESS, Anthony:
        Appointed distinguished professor of English at City College, 1665; Attends International Writers' Conference, 1599; Chiswick house described, 1608; Compared to Dante, 1666; Compared to Kingsley Amis, 1603; Compared to Saul Bellow, 1617; Concern with original sin, 1607; Considered as a 'Catholic' novelist, 1607; Etchingham house described, 1608; Fictional treatment of death, 1620; Income, 1076, 1402, 1345, 1616; Interviews: *see* Interviews; Joins Tyrone Guthrie Theater as writer and consultant, 1653; Musical on life of Shakespeare, 1614; On "Holocaust," 1538; On **1985** and **1984**, 1755; On A CLOCKWORK ORANGE (film), 1412 — SEE ALSO: Interviews; On A CLOCKWORK ORANGE, 1024, 1109 — SEE ALSO: Interviews; On a graduation ceremony at Fordham, 1437; On adoption of the pseudonym 'Anthony Burgess,' 1504; On African literature, 1541; On American and English 'English,' 1195; On American constitution, 1701; On American elementary education, 1633; On American novelists, 1140; On American television, 1339, 1406; On army days in Gibraltar, 1258; On art students, 1000; On Arts Council, 1219; On Australia, 1400; On avant-garde writing, 1151; On Barcelona, 1501; On BEARD'S ROMAN WOMEN, 41.5; On Beatles (Pop Group), 1013, 1031; On Beethoven, 1384; On being a Lapsed Catholic, 1258.1; On being an only child, 1484; On Black Studies, 1371; On Blackspeak, 1433; On books he would like to see published, 1253; On British socialist government, 1199, 1247, 1318; On Catholics and Catholicism, 1091, 1115, 1208, 1214, 1225, 1265, 1278, 1307, 1390, 1455, 1503, 1504, 1538, 1553, 1569; On censorship, 1366; On Christianity, 1041; On Christmas in Malaya, 1357; On Christmas, 1022; On Christopher Marlowe, 1031; On CLOCKWORK TESTAMENT, 1422, 1433; On color blindness, 1226; On Common Market, 1231; On cook books, 1354; On courtesy in daily life, 1239; On CYRANO, 1421, 1433, 1435, 1436; On decimal coinage,

On TIME FOR A TIGER, 1010, 1389; On translators and translating, 1396; On TREMOR OF INTENT, 1109; On TRISTRAM SHANDY, 1134; On VISION OF BATTLEMENTS, 1630; On visit to Hollywood, 1630; On Winston Churchill, 1406; On women in the year 1969, 1373; On World Soccer Championship (1974), 1441; On writers and political commitment, 1301; On writing short stories, 977; Reviewed his own INSIDE MR. ENDERBY for YORKSHIRE POST, 448, 989, 1608, 1616; Ruthless literary sensibility, 1604; Typical Burgess hero, 1598; Vacation trip to Leningrad, 985; View of neutrals and neutralism, 1613; View of technological progress and power, 1610; Wrote 5 novels in one year, 1608, 1616.

CAVALIER OF THE ROSE, 970
CAVIAR FOR BREAKFAST, 1270
Cayton, Robert F., 936
"Celebrating James Joyce," 1570
CELEBRITY REGISTER, 1708
Celine, Louis-Ferdinand, *as subject*, 1150
CELLO SYMPHONY,
"Celluloid Celebrants," 1477
CENTAUR, THE, 1149
Centre national d'art et de culture Georges Pompidou, 1465
Chabrier, Hortense, 166
Chabrier, Hortense, *as subject*, 90, 508, 576
Chalpin, Lila, 1697
Champagne, 1496
Chapman, Christopher, *as subject*, 1529
Chapman, Robert, 455
Chaucer, Geoffrey, *as subject*, 1404
Checkpoint Charlie, 1538
"Chekhov for Ireland," 1080
Chekhov, Anton, *as subject*, 1121
Cherisey, Gloria de, *as subject*, 25
Cheshire, David, 536
Chesterton, Gilbert Keith, 956
Chew, Shirley, 537, 1659
"Child of the Century," 294
Chipchase, Paul, 591
"Choosing to Die," 1461
"Christ the Tiger," 1501
Christie, Agatha, *as subject*, 1322
CHRISTMAS RECIPE, 965
CHRISTOPHER MARLOWE, 1091
Churchill, Thomas, 1630
Ciglic, M., 128
"Cineast as Moralizer," 145
CINEMA OF STANLEY KUBRICK, 1673
CITIES OF THE RED NIGHT, 1562
City College, 1664, 1665
CITY OF SCARLET AND GOLD, 987
Clark, Jeff, 284
Classe, A., *as subject*, 1462
Claudel, Paul, *as subject*, 1106
Cleary, Jon, *as subject*, 988
Clemons, Walter, 1625
Cleworth, Joan, *as subject*, 1432
"Clockwork Hero Meets His End," 198
"Clockwork Kumquat," 723
"Clockwork Marmalade," 1412, 1650
CLOCKWORK ORANGE.
        (Book by Burgess), 75-85; articles, etc.: 1596, 1604, 1607, 1613, 1621, 1631,
        1632, 1650, 1654, 1659, 1660, 1661*, 1666, 1668, 1670, 1671, 1680, 1685, 1690,
        1693 1698, 1699, 1700, 1701, 1702, 1706, 1710, 1713, 1716*, 1717*, 1720, 1724,

"Mugging Machine," 1645
"Mulligan Stew; Irving Wallace Rewrites ULYSSES," 1405
"Multilingual," 1077
MULTIPLE MODERN GODS AND OTHER STORIES, 1085
"Multiplying the Many-minded," 1474
Muntz, Hope, *as subject*, 1256
"Murder Most Fair — by Agatha the Good," 1322
"Murdoch's Eighth," 391
Murdoch, Brian, 1707
Murdoch, Iris, 391, 1060
"Murf," *as subject*, 1639
Murhpy, Robert, *as subject*, 1114
"Murray and His Monument," 1495
Murray, Isobel, 56
Murray, John, 57, 189, 394, 548, 602, 721
Murray, K.M. Elisabeth, *as subject*, 1495
Murray, Patrick, *as subject*, 1277
"Muse: A Sort of SF Story," 980; article, 1663
"Music at the Millennium," 1453
"Music for a Great City," 1051
"Music for Professionals," 1565
"Music from A CLOCKWORK ORANGE," 117
MUSIC FROM THE SOUNDTRACK: STANLEY KUBRICK'S A CLOCKWORK ORANGE, 116
"Music Week," 755
"Musical 'Cyrano,'" 218
"Musical Cyrano Comes a Cropper," 224
"Musical Voices," 1767
"Musings from Morocco," 329
"My Country, 'tis of Thee," 1324
"My Dear Students; A Letter," 1423
"My Friend, the Pope," 287
MY LIFE AND LOVES, 1070
MY LIFE AND TIMES, 1411
"My Seven Wonders of the World," 1496
"Mysteries," 1107

Nabokov, Vladimir, *as subject*, 1096, 1123, 1204, 1266, 1502, 1566
Nadsat, 1596, 1631, 1654 — SEE ALSO: CLOCKWORK ORANGE
"Nadsat: The Argot and Its Implications in Anthony Burgess' A CLOCKWORK ORANGE," 1631
Naipaul, V.S., *as subject*, 1541
Nairn, Tom, 640
NAKED APE, 1366
NAKED CAME THE STRANGER, 1387
NAKED LUNCH, 1072
"Naked Mr. Gibbon," 1216
"Names and Games in TREMOR OF INTENT," 1766
NAPOLEON SYMPHONY, 572-575; articles, etc.: 1748, 1753, 1784; reviews, 578-613;
  translations, 576-577
NARANJA MECANICA, 95-96
"Narrative Structure and the Reader's Theatre Staging of NOTHING LIKE THE SUN," 1585
NARRENSCHIFF, 1029
Nash, Manning, 549
NATURAL, THE 989
NATURE AND HUMAN NATURE, 1221